Microsoft® Office 2007

FUNDAMENTALS

Laura Story
Dawna Walls

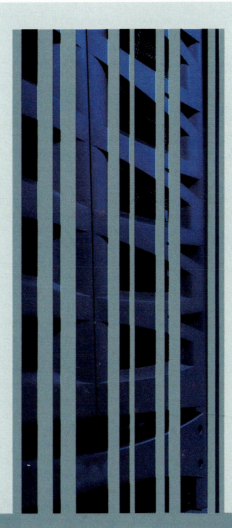

COURSE TECHNOLOGY
CENGAGE Learning™

Australia • Brazil • Japan • Korea • Mexico • Singapore • Spain • United Kingdom • United States

Microsoft® Office 2007 Fundamentals
Laura Story and Dawna Walls

Executive Editor: Donna Gridley

Product Manager: Allison O'Meara

Development Editors: Amanda Brodkin,
Kim T. M. Crowley

Associate Product Manager: Amanda Lyons

Editorial Assistant: Kimberly Klasner

Content Project Manager: Catherine G. DiMassa

Marketing Manager: Valerie Lauer

Director of Manufacturing: Denise Powers

Text Designer: Shawn Girsberger

Manuscript Quality Assurance Lead: Jeff Schwartz

Manuscript Quality Assurance Reviewers:
John Freitas, Serge Palladino, Danielle Shaw,
Susan Whalen

Copy Editor: Mark Goodin

Proofreader: Vicki Zimmer

Indexer: Rich Carlson

Art Director: Kun-Tee Chang

Cover Designer: Robert Pehlke

Cover Image: Gettyimages

Compositor: GEX, Inc.

© 2010 Course Technology/Cengage Learning

ALL RIGHTS RESERVED. No part of this work covered by the copyright herein may be reproduced, transmitted, stored or used in any form or by any means graphic, electronic, or mechanical, including but not limited to photocopying, recording, scanning, digitizing, taping, Web distribution, information networks, or information storage and retrieval systems, except as permitted under Section 107 or 108 of the 1976 United States Copyright Act, without the prior written permission of the publisher.

For product information and technology assistance, contact us at
Cengage Learning Customer & Sales Support, 1-800-354-9706

For permission to use material from this text or product, submit all requests online at **www.cengage.com/permissions**
Further permissions questions can be emailed to
permissionrequest@cengage.com

ISBN-13: 978-0-324-78311-7
ISBN-10: 0-324-78311-6

Course Technology
20 Channel Center Street
Boston, Massachusetts 02210
USA

Cengage Learning is a leading provider of customized learning solutions with office locations around the globe, including Singapore, the United Kingdom, Australia, Mexico, Brazil, and Japan. Locate your local office at:
international.cengage.com/region

Cengage Learning products are represented in Canada by Nelson Education, Ltd.

To learn more about Course Technology, visit **www.cengage.com/coursetechnology**

To learn more about Cengage Learning, visit **www.cengage.com**.

Any fictional data related to persons or companies or URLs used throughout this book is intended for instructional purposes only. At the time this book was printed, any such data was fictional and not belonging to any real persons or companies.

Printed in the United States of America
1 2 3 4 5 6 7 12 11 10 09

ABOUT THIS BOOK

Microsoft Office 2007 Fundamentals introduces students to the programs included in the Microsoft Office 2007 suite of software. By following the lessons presented in this text, students will quickly and efficiently learn to use Word, Excel, PowerPoint, Access, and Publisher to create professional-looking documents, spreadsheets, presentations, databases, and publications. *Microsoft Office 2007 Fundamentals* presents the basic features and commands for each of these programs in an easy-to-follow, hands-on approach.

It is very important that students watch their screen carefully as they work through the exercises in this book. If a student clicks the mouse or presses keys without understanding what is happening, they will miss a great deal. It is also important to work through each lesson within a unit in the order presented. Each lesson builds on what was learned in previous lessons, so it is vital to complete lessons thoroughly and in order. Instructors may choose to work through the units in a different order; for example, it does not matter whether the instructor approaches the Access unit before completing the Word unit.

Every effort is made throughout this book to use Microsoft terminology when working with the programs. The first few times a student uses a tool within a program, the student might need to refer to this book or the Help system to refresh their memory about the steps involved.

Some keyboards do not have the full range of keys; however, students should be able to access a needed keystroke with alternate combination keys, which are described in the lessons.

Instructors can assign as many or as few of the projects at the end of the lesson as they like. The projects concentrate on the main concepts covered in the lesson and provide valuable opportunities to apply or extend the skills learned in the lesson.

About the Authors

Laura Story and Dawna Walls, both graduates of Texas Tech University, have co-authored three books together for Course Technology and have collaborated on dozens of other writing and editing projects during the past two decades, including software textbooks, user's guides, tutorials, i-manuals, site documentation, training material, and supplements. With similar backgrounds in technical writing, Web development, computer education, and the IT industry, they bring a breadth of experience and expertise to the teaching process.

Start-up Checklist

Microsoft Office Professional 2007 System Requirements

Hardware

- 500 megahertz (MHz) processor or higher
- 256 megabyte (MB) RAM or higher
- 2 gigabyte (GB) hard disk; a portion of this disk space will be freed after installation if the original download package is removed from the hard drive
- CD-ROM or DVD drive
- 1024 × 768 or higher resolution monitor

Software

- Microsoft Windows XP with Service Pack (SP) 2, Windows Server 2003 with SP1, or later operating system such as Microsoft Windows Vista

Micrososoft Windows Vista Home Basic Recommended System Requirements

- 1 GHz 32-bit (×86) or 64-bit (×64) processor
- 512 MB of system memory
- 20 GB hard drive with at least 15 GB of available space
- Support for DirectX9 graphics and 32 MB of graphics memory
- DVD-ROM drive
- Audio Output
- Internet access (fees may apply)

Features of This Book

Microsoft Office 2007 Fundamentals covers the primary features and commands of each program in self-contained units. Units can comprise multiple lessons. Units with multiple lessons include unit review sections that present a summary of exercise and practice activities and serve as an additional learning tool. Within each lesson, the program's various features and tools are first presented in a conceptual discussion, as well as the skills required to understand these features. Appendices on Microsoft Outlook and the Vista operating system extend students' understanding of the Office suite.

Microsoft Office 2007 Fundamentals emphasizes learning by doing through the hands-on application of concepts. Each conceptual discussion is followed by a Step-by-Step exercise that allows students to apply the concepts just covered. Commands and buttons students should click during the exercises, and text the students should type, are all shown in boldface text. Figures showing students what their screen should look like at certain points in the Step-by-Step help them stay on track.

The figures in this book show the Office program windows as they appear at a screen resolution of 1024 × 768; modifying screen settings might cause the buttons, Ribbons, and other Office features to look slightly different on students' screens. Regardless of any visual discrepancy, students will be able to follow the steps and complete the exercises by referring to the figures in each lesson. Each lesson has been through Course Technology's rigorous quality assurance testing program to ensure the validity of the steps and data files provided with the book.

Many lessons require students to use data files. Data files are posted on www.cengage.com/coursetechnology on the title information page (which you may find by searching by title or ISBN), and on the Review Pack and Instructor Resource CD.

Students can expand their mastery of the text content by referring to text in the Extra for Experts boxes, which provides advanced information related to conceptual information. Warning boxes address potential issues students might encounter and offer solutions to those problem scenarios. Key vocabulary terms appear in boldface and italic type in the text where they are defined. Key vocabulary terms are also compiled in a glossary at the end of the text for easy reference.

Each lesson concludes with a lesson summary, a vocabulary list of terms defined in the lesson, multiple-choice exercises, fill-in-the-blank exercises, individual projects, teamwork or Web projects, and Critical Thinking activities, all of which are designed to help students practice the skills covered in the lesson. The instructor might assign a combination of these exercises.

To complete all Lessons, this book will require approximately 24 hours of classroom contact time. Hours required for end-of-lesson activities and reviews vary depending on the number and type of activities selected.

INSIDE FUNDAMENTALS

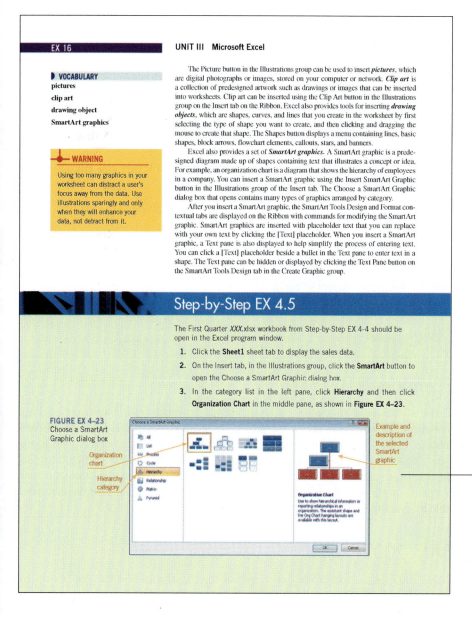

Step-by-Step Exercises offer "hands-on practice" of the material just learned. Each exercise uses a data file or requires you to create a file from scratch.

Lesson opener elements include the **Objectives** and **Suggested Completion Time**.

End of Lesson elements include the **Summary**, **Vocabulary Review**, **Review Questions**, **Lesson Projects**, and **Critical Thinking Activities**.

Instructor Resources Disk

ISBN-13: 978-0-324-78327-8
ISBN-10: 0-324-78327-2

The Instructor Resources disk contains the following teaching resources:

The Data and Solution files for this course
ExamView® tests for each lesson; ExamView is a powerful testing software package that allows instructors to create and administer printed, computer (LAN-based), and Internet exams
Instructor's Manual that includes lecture notes for each lesson and references to the end-of-lesson activities and Unit Review projects
Answer Keys that include solutions to the lesson and unit review questions
Copies of the figures that appear in the student text
Suggested Syllabus with block, two quarter, and 18-week schedule
Annotated Solutions and Grading Rubrics
PowerPoint presentations for each lesson
Spanish glossary

ExamView®

This textbook is accompanied by ExamView, a powerful testing software package that allows instructors to create and administer printed, computer (LAN-based), and Internet exams. ExamView includes hundreds of questions that correspond to the topics covered in this text, enabling students to generate detailed study guides that include page references for further review. The computer-based and Internet testing components allow students to take exams at their computers, and save the instructor time by grading each exam automatically.

SAM 2007

SAM 2007 helps bridge the gap between the classroom and the real world by allowing students to train and test on important computer skills in an active, hands-on environment.

SAM 2007's easy-to-use system includes powerful interactive exams, training or projects on critical applications such as Word, Excel, Access, PowerPoint, Outlook, Windows, the Internet, and much more. SAM simulates the application environment, allowing students to demonstrate their knowledge and think through the skills by performing real-world tasks.

SAM 2007 includes built-in page references so students can print helpful study guides that match the textbooks used in class. Powerful administrative options allow instructors to schedule exams and assignments, secure tests, and run reports with almost limitless flexibility.

ACKNOWLEDGMENTS

Many thanks to Donna Gridley for this opportunity; to Kim Crowley and Amanda Brodkin for the vital role they played in shaping this book with their editorial expertise; to the reviewers for their helpful feedback; to Allison O'Meara for her skillful management of this project; and to Cathie DiMassa and the GEX team for their excellent production work.

Laura Story: To my kids, Zephyr and Mesa, who plan to have their names in much bigger lights someday—thanks for putting up with my divided attention and computer domination during this project, and most of all for keeping me laughing. And to M—ongoing thanks for sharing the journey…and for waiting patiently to pop the cork when deadlines took precedence.

Dawna Walls: Thanks, John, for your love, support, advice, and patience throughout this project. Thanks also for taking up the slack for me in so many ways and for bringing home takeout on a regular basis. Luke and Leah, thank you for tolerating my schedule, reminding me about what is important, and letting me get coffee when I needed it.

Reviewers:
Angela Bachert
Deanna Amenta
Donna Parker
Jerusalen Howard
Kelly Sofran
Kimberly D. Wathington
Paula McGuigan
Sarah Kane
Susan Brooks

Bring Your Course Back To the BASICS

***Developed with the needs of new learners in mind, the* BASICS** series is ideal for lower-level courses covering basic computer concepts, Microsoft Office, programming, and more. Introductory in nature, these texts are comprehensive enough to cover the most important features of each application.

Computer Concepts BASICS

Hard Spiral:
ISBN-13: 978-1-4239-0461-8
ISBN-10: 1-4239-0461-3

Softcover:
ISBN-10: 1-4239-0462-1
ISBN-13: 978-1-4239-0462-5

This revised fourth edition puts computer literacy information at your fingertips by teaching Microsoft Office 2007 skills, Web page creation techniques, computer ethics, and more. Whether used for an introductory course or in conjunction with software tutorial instruction, this text proves to be the best solution for computer education.

CONTENTS

Preface   iii

UNIT I   GETTING STARTED

LESSON 1
Working with Microsoft Office 2007   GS 3

Introduction to Microsoft Office 2007	GS 4
Starting an Office Program	GS 4
Identifying the Parts of an Office Window	GS 5
Accessing Contextual Tools	GS 11
Customizing Office Programs	GS 13
Getting Help with Office	GS 17
Closing an Office Program	GS 20
Summary	GS 20
Unit Review	GS 24

UNIT II   MICROSOFT WORD

LESSON 1
Understanding Word Fundamentals   WD 3

Introduction	WD 4
Examining the Word Program Window	WD 4
Starting Word and Opening an Existing Document	WD 4
Navigating the Word Document	WD 6
Selecting Text	WD 9
Entering Text	WD 13
Saving a Document	WD 14
Changing Document Views	WD 16
Changing Page Formatting	WD 18
Previewing and Printing a Document	WD 22
Closing a Document	WD 24
Summary	WD 25

LESSON 2
Editing and Formatting Text   WD 29

Introduction	WD 30
Creating a New Document	WD 30
Formatting Text	WD 32
Setting Tabs	WD 38
Formatting Paragraphs	WD 40
Editing Test: Deleting, Moving and Copying	WD 48
Using Undo, Redo, and Repeat	WD 50
Finding and Replacing Text	WD 52
Proofing a Document	WD 53
Summary	WD 59

LESSON 3
Formatting Documents   WD 65

Introduction	WD 66
Creating New Documents Using Templates	WD 66
Changing Document Themes	WD 69
Applying Quick Styles	WD 72
Working with Lists	WD 73
Adding Page Backgrounds	WD 76
Creating Columns	WD 80
Adding Headers and Footers	WD 82
Inserting and Breaking Pages	WD 88
Summary	WD 94

LESSON 4
Working with Graphic Objects   WD 99

Introduction	WD 99
Inserting and Modifying Illustrations	WD 99

CONTENTS

Inserting and Modifying Objects	WD 113
Creating and Modifying Tables	WD 120
Summary	WD 124
Unit Review	WD 129

UNIT III — MICROSOFT EXCEL

LESSON 1
Understanding Excel Fundamentals — EX 3

Introduction	EX 4
Examining the Excel Program Window	EX 4
Starting Excel and Opening an Existing Workbook	EX 5
Navigating in a Worksheet	EX 7
Saving Workbooks	EX 10
Selecting Cells	EX 11
Entering Data	EX 13
Editing Cell Contents	EX 16
Using Undo and Redo	EX 18
Managing Worksheets	EX 19
Changing Workbook Views	EX 21
Printing Workbooks	EX 25
Closing a Workbook	EX 30
Summary	EX 31

LESSON 2
Formatting and Editing Worksheets — EX 35

Introduction	EX 36
Creating a New Workbook	EX 36
Formatting Cells	EX 37
Applying Themes and Styles	EX 47
Using Conditional Formatting	EX 51
Working with Rows and Columns	EX 53
Finding and Replacing Data	EX 56
Copying and Moving Worksheet Data	EX 59
Checking Spelling	EX 61
Summary	EX 63

LESSON 3
Using Formulas and Functions — EX 67

Introduction	EX 68
Entering Formulas	EX 68
Understanding Cell References and Copying Formulas	EX 71
Using Functions	EX 75
Reviewing and Editing Formulas	EX 79
Summary	EX 82

LESSON 4
Working with Charts and Graphics — EX 87

Introduction	EX 88
Understanding Charts	EX 88
Creating Charts	EX 89
Modifying Charts	EX 92
Inserting and Modifying Illustrations	EX 101
Summary	EX 105
Unit Review	EX 109

UNIT IV — MICROSOFT POWERPOINT

LESSON 1
Understanding PowerPoint Fundamentals — PPT 3

Introduction	PPT 4
Examining the PowerPoint Program Window	PPT 4
Starting PowerPoint and Opening an Existing Presentation	PPT 5
Understand Slides	PPT 6
Navigating a PowerPoint Presentation	PPT 7
Viewing a Presentation	PPT 8
Modify Slides	PPT 12
Saving a Presentation	PPT 18
Previewing and Printing Presentations	PPT 20
Closing a Presentation	PPT 23
Summary	PPT 24

CONTENTS

LESSON 2
Formatting and Modifying Presentations — PPT 29

Introduction	PPT 30
Creating a New Blank Presentation	PPT 30
Creating a New Presentation with a Template	PPT 31
Formatting Text	PPT 34
Formatting Paragraphs	PPT 37
Checking Spelling	PPT 41
Finding and Replacing Text	PPT 42
Applying Themes	PPT 44
Customizing Slide Masters	PPT 46
Summary	PPT 49

LESSON 3
Enhancing the Presentation — PPT 55

Introduction	PPT 56
Inserting and Modifying Illustrations	PPT 56
Creating and Modifying Tables	PPT 70
Inserting a Text Box	PPT 72
Inserting Headers and Footers	PPT 73
Inserting Special Effects	PPT 74
Summary	PPT 78
Unit Review	PPT 83

UNIT V — MICROSOFT ACCESS

LESSON 1
Understanding Access Fundamentals — AC 3

Introduction	AC 4
Understanding Database Concepts	AC 4
Planning and Designing a Database	AC 6
Exploring the Access Program Window	AC 6
Starting Access and Creating a New Database	AC 7
Creating a Table in Datasheet View	AC 9
Opening an Existing Database	AC 14
Opening Tables and Navigating Records	AC 16
Modifying Field Properties	AC 20
Summary	AC 23

LESSON 2
Creating Queries, Forms, and Reports — AC 27

Introduction	AC 28
Creating Queries	AC 28
Creating and Using Forms	AC 31
Modifying the Form's Design	AC 36
Creating Reports	AC 40
Modifying and Printing Reports	AC 44
Sorting and Filtering Records	AC 47
Summary	AC 50
Unit Review	AC 55

UNIT VI — MICROSOFT PUBLISHER

LESSON 1
Understanding Publisher Fundamentals — PB 1

Introduction	PB 2
Examining the Publisher Program Window	PB 2
Starting Publisher and Opening a Template	PB 3
Navigating the Publication	PB 6
Entering and Formatting Text	PB 6
Saving a Publication	PB 11
Formatting the Publication and Changing the Template	PB 12
Inserting Graphics	PB 14
Previewing and Printing a Publication	PB 21
Closing a Publication	PB 24
Summary	PB 24

UNIT VII MICROSOFT INTEGRATION

LESSON 1
Understanding Integration Fundamentals INT 1

Introduction INT 2
Methods for Sharing Information Between Office Programs INT 2
Linking and Embedding INT 2
Creating a PowerPoint Presentation from a Word Outline INT 8
Creating a Mail Merge Document INT 10
Importing and Exporting Data INT 13
Summary INT 19

APPENDIX A: UNDERSTANDING WINDOWS VISTA FUNDAMENTALS VIS 1

APPENDIX B: UNDERSTANDING OUTLOOK FUNDAMENTALS OL 1

GLOSSARY 1

INDEX 9

Estimated Time for Unit: 1.5 hours

UNIT 1

GETTING STARTED

LESSON 1 **1.5 HRS.**
Working with Microsoft Office 2007

LESSON 1

Estimated Time: 1.5 hours

Working With Microsoft Office 2007

■ OBJECTIVES

Upon completion of this lesson, you should be able to:

- Describe Microsoft Office 2007 and its programs.
- Start an Office program.
- Identify the parts of an Office window.
- Access contexual tools.
- Customize Office programs.
- Get help with Office.
- Close an Office program.

■ DATA FILES

You do not need data files to complete this lesson.

■ VOCABULARY

badge
contextual tabs
dialog box launcher
gallery
groups
integrate
interface
KeyTip
launch
Live Preview
Microsoft Office 2007
Mini toolbar
Office
Office Button
Quick Access Toolbar
Ribbon
ScreenTip
suite
tabs
…

GS 3

UNIT I Getting Started

Introduction to Microsoft Office 2007

Microsoft Office 2007, or ***Office***, is a group of computer programs that provide different tools for completing certain tasks. For example, you can create documents, analyze data, organize information, and prepare presentations. Even though the Office programs help you to accomplish different tasks, they all work alike using the same basic ***interface***. This means the programs have a similar appearance; they share common elements and commands; and many tasks are performed the same way in each program. Once you learn how to work with one program, you know the fundamentals of the other programs as well.

Office comes in different suites. Each ***suite*** combines some or all of the Office programs into one package. The Office programs on your computer will vary depending on which Office suite is installed, but at a minimum you will have Word 2007 and Excel 2007. **Table GS 1–1** describes all the Office programs. You can also visit the Microsoft Office Web site at *http://office.microsoft.com/products* to learn more about the various Office suites available or to get more information about individual Office programs.

Each Office program is also designed to work well together, or ***integrate***, with the other programs in the suite by easily sharing or transferring information. You will learn more about how to integrate Office programs later in this book.

In this lesson, you will learn some basic skills for using Office programs. Because Word is probably the most widely used Office program, this lesson uses Word to demonstrate these skills, but you can use the same procedures for other programs.

> **VOCABULARY**
> **Microsoft Office 2007**
> **Office**
> **interface**
> **suite**
> **integrate**
> **launch**

TABLE GS 1–1 Office 2007 programs

PROGRAM	DESCRIPTION
Word	Word-processing program used to create documents such as letters, research papers, memos, and reports
Excel	Spreadsheet program used to enter, calculate, analyze, and visually represent numerical data
PowerPoint	Presentation program used to create a collection of slides containing text, pictures, charts, and other visual items for slide shows, meetings, or Web pages
Access	Database program used to compile, track, report, and manage related information
Publisher	Publication program used to create and edit publications such as newsletters, brochures, flyers, or business cards
Outlook	A personal information manager used to send and receive e-mail, set up a calendar, manage tasks, and record contacts

Starting an Office Program

To begin using an Office program, you first need to start or ***launch*** it. You can do this by clicking the Start button on the Windows taskbar, and then clicking the program name (or folder and then program name) on the All Programs menu, or by double-clicking a program icon on the desktop. Once the program is started, you can begin using it to create a new document or file, or you can open an existing file. Once you

> **EXTRA FOR EXPERTS**
>
> To create a desktop shortcut to an Office program, right-click the name of the program, point to Send To, and then click Desktop (create shortcut) to place a program icon on the desktop. Then you can double-click the program icon on the desktop to open the program.

LESSON 1 Working with Microsoft Office 2007

begin using the Office program frequently, it will be listed on the left side of the Start menu, and you can also click the program name from that list to open the program.

Throughout this book, it is assumed that your computer is turned on and the Windows Vista desktop is displayed on your computer screen. You can learn more about working in the Windows Vista operating system in Appendix A.

Step-by-Step GS 1.1

1. Click the **Start** button on the Windows taskbar. The Start menu opens.
2. Click **All Programs**. A list of programs and program folders opens in the left pane of the Start menu. This list will vary depending on the programs that are installed on your computer.
3. Click the **Microsoft Office** program folder (scroll if necessary). A list of Microsoft Office programs opens, as shown in **Figure GS 1–1**.

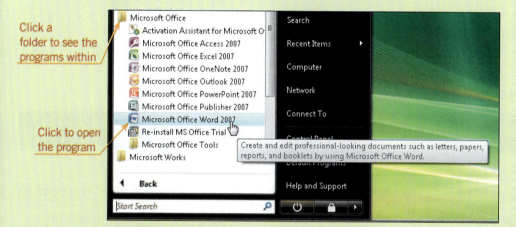

FIGURE GS 1–1
All Programs pane

4. Click **Microsoft Office Word 2007**. Microsoft Office Word 2007 starts and its program window opens on the desktop with a new, blank document displayed.

Identifying the Parts of an Office Window

When you start Word, you will see a program window similar to the one in **Figure GS 1–2**. Many parts of this window are the same for other programs in the Office 2007 suite. Use this figure and **Table GS 1–2** to become familiar with these common elements.

UNIT I Getting Started

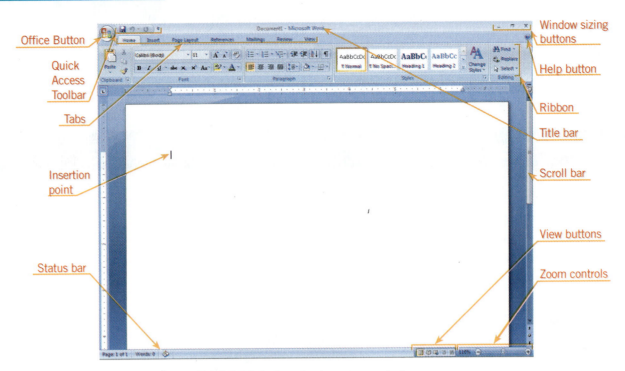

FIGURE GS 1-2 Word program window

TABLE GS 1-2 Common window elements for Office 2007 programs

ELEMENT	DESCRIPTION
Ribbon	Collection of commands organized by tabs and groups
Office Button	Contains common Office 2007 commands, such as New, Open, Save, Save As, and Print
Quick Access Toolbar	Keeps icons for frequently used commands, such as Save, Undo, and Redo, in a convenient location
Title bar	Shows name of active program and file
Help button	Provides assistance with a program
Insertion point	Blinking vertical bar indicating where the next character you type will appear
Scroll bar	Used to adjust view in the document window to view another part of the document
Status bar	Displays information about current position and settings
View buttons	Changes the way a document, worksheet, or presentation is displayed on the screen
Zoom controls	Magnifies or decreases the content currently displayed on the screen

Ribbon

Using the Ribbon

The *Ribbon*, shown in **Figure GS 1-3**, is an element of the program window that displays and organizes the commands and tools of the program for easy access.

LESSON 1 Working with Microsoft Office 2007

FIGURE GS 1–3 The Ribbon

Commands on the Ribbon are organized into categories, called *tabs*, and each one relates to a particular type of activity in that program. You can click a tab to activate it and display related commands. On a tab, commands are organized logically into *groups*. For example, the Home tab includes the Font group of commands, with options for selecting types, size, and applying font styles. The tabs on the Ribbon can also change depending on the task you are working on. The Table Tools tabs in Word are displayed only when a table is selected, for instance. These are called *contextual tabs*.

Some groups have a *dialog box launcher* in the lower-right corner—a small arrow that you click to open a dialog box or task pane with more options for executing a command. Dialog boxes appear on top of the program window, and task panes appear to the side.

To choose a command, you click a button on the Ribbon. If a button has an arrow, you can click the arrow to open a menu and choose from a list of options.

Some tabs on the Ribbon include galleries. A *gallery* is a set of options that shows you a sample end result, which simplifies the process of making choices. If a gallery has more options than those shown on the Ribbon, you can click the More button to see the full gallery. When using galleries, you can take advantage of *Live Preview*, a feature that applies the editing or formatting change to your document as you point to a gallery option. This allows you to experiment with the end result before actually making a selection.

> **VOCABULARY**
> tabs
> groups
> contextual tabs
> dialog box launcher
> gallery
> Live Preview

> **EXTRA FOR EXPERTS**
> To increase available window space, you can collapse the Ribbon by double-clicking the name of the active tab. To restore the Ribbon, double-click a tab again.

Step-by-Step GS 1.2

A new, blank document from Step-by-Step GS 1.1 should be open in the Word program window.

1. Click the **Insert** tab and notice the commands available.
2. Click each tab on the Ribbon and notice how the commands are organized in groups.
3. Click the **Home** tab to display the commands available on this tab.
4. In the Clipboard group, click the **Clipboard dialog box launcher** to open the Clipboard task pane.
5. In the Font group, click the **Font dialog box launcher** to open the Font dialog box. Your screen should look similar to **Figure GS 1–4**.

FIGURE GS 1-4
Dialog box and task pane

Task pane

Dialog box

6. Click the **Cancel** button to close the Font dialog box.
7. Click the **Close** button on the Clipboard task pane to close it.
8. Click the **Paste** button list arrow to display the menu shown in **Figure GS 1-5**.

FIGURE GS 1-5
Button with menu

Click arrow to open menu

9. Click a blank area of the document window to close the menu, and then type your **first name** and **last name**.
10. On the Home tab, in the Styles group, click the **More** button to display the Styles gallery.
11. Point to the **Intense Quote** style and notice how Live Preview displays what that change would look like in your document, as shown in **Figure GS 1-6**.

LESSON 1 Working with Microsoft Office 2007

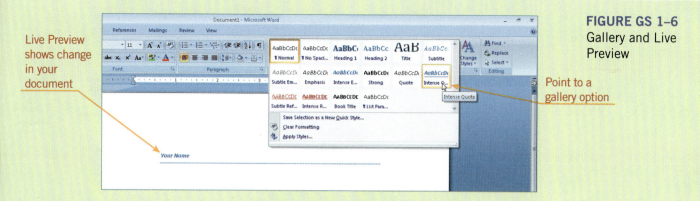

FIGURE GS 1-6
Gallery and Live Preview

12. Click the **Title** style in the gallery to change your name to that style.
13. Leave the document open for use in the next Step-by-Step.

Using the Office Button

The Office Button is located in the upper-left corner of the program window, and you can click it to access file-related commands, such as those used to open, save, print, and close documents. When you point to a command that includes an arrow, a list of related tasks is displayed on the right.

Customizing the Quick Access Toolbar

The Quick Access Toolbar is located next to the Office Button on the title bar and contains regularly used tools, making them easy to find. The Save, Undo, and Redo commands are available by default, but you can add others by clicking the Customize Quick Access Toolbar button to display a menu listing common commands that you can select to add. You can also click More Commands to see additional ones.

The Quick Access Toolbar can be positioned in two places in the program window—in its default location on the title bar, or just below the Ribbon. You can move the Quick Access Toolbar so that it is located below the Ribbon by clicking the Show Below the Ribbon command located on the Customize Quick Access Toolbar menu. To move it back to its default position, click Show Above the Ribbon on the menu.

> **EXTRA FOR EXPERTS**
>
> You can add a command to the Quick Access Toolbar directly from the Ribbon. Right-click the command on the Ribbon that you want to add, and then click Add to Quick Access Toolbar on the shortcut menu.

Step-by-Step GS 1.3

The document from Step-by-Step GS 1.2 should be open in the Word program window.

1. Click the **Office Button** 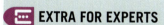 on the Ribbon to open the Office Button menu.
2. Point to **Print** to display the list of related commands, as shown in **Figure GS 1–7**.

FIGURE GS 1–7
Office Button menu

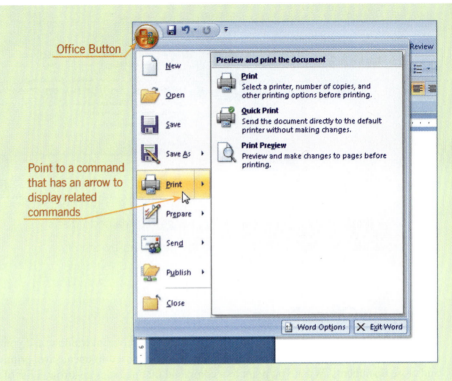

3. Point to each command with an arrow on the menu to see the related commands that are available.
4. Click a blank area of the document window to close the menu.
5. Click the **Customize Quick Access Toolbar** button  on the Quick Access Toolbar to display the menu shown in **Figure GS 1–8**.

FIGURE GS 1–8
Quick Access Toolbar and menu

6. Click **Show Below the Ribbon** to move the Quick Access Toolbar below the Ribbon, as shown in **Figure GS 1–9**.

LESSON 1 Working with Microsoft Office 2007

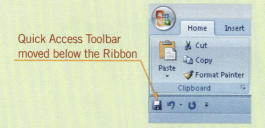

FIGURE GS 1–9
Quick Access Toolbar positioned below the Ribbon

7. Click the **Customize Quick Access Toolbar** button again, and click **Show Above the Ribbon** to move the Quick Access Toolbar back to its original location.

8. Leave the document open for use in the next Step-by-Step.

Accessing Contextual Tools

Some tools in Office are visible all the time, and others are displayed only when you need them. Just as contextual tabs on the Ribbon become available when you are working with certain items, there are also contextual tools that are displayed only when needed. These contextual tools provide shortcuts to help you access commands more quickly when you are working with selected items.

Using the Mini Toolbar and Shortcut Menus

The **Mini toolbar** is a small toolbar of common formatting commands that becomes available when you select text. The Mini toolbar opens above the selected text and is transparent, becoming active only after you point to a command on it. When you move the mouse pointer away from the selected text, the Mini toolbar closes. You cannot customize the Mini toolbar.

The active Mini toolbar also opens at the top of the shortcut menu that opens when you right-click selected text or a selected object, as shown in **Figure GS 1–10**. Shortcut menus provide a quick way to access relevant commands. You close the Mini toolbar and shortcut menu by either pressing the Esc key or clicking elsewhere in the document.

> **VOCABULARY**
> **Mini toolbar**

UNIT I Getting Started

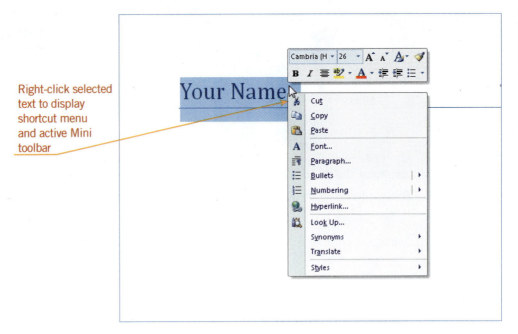

Right-click selected text to display shortcut menu and active Mini toolbar

FIGURE GS 1–10 Mini toolbar and shortcut menu

Using KeyTips

If you prefer using the keyboard instead of the mouse, you can access all the options on the Ribbon using KeyTips. A *KeyTip* is a small label with a letter or number, called a *badge*, that appears on each button, menu, or command on the Ribbon when you press the Alt key, as shown in **Figure GS 1–11**. You can execute a command by pressing the KeyTip or a sequence of KeyTips. The KeyTips disappear when you are finished, or you can press the Alt key again to remove the KeyTips without executing a command.

▶ **VOCABULARY**
KeyTip
badge

KeyTip

FIGURE GS 1–11 KeyTips

Step-by-Step GS 1.4

The document from Step-by-Step GS 1.3 should be open in the Word program window.

1. Select **Your Name** in the document. The transparent Mini toolbar opens, as shown in **Figure GS 1–12**.

FIGURE GS 1–12
Mini toolbar

Mini toolbar is transparent when text is first selected

2. Point to any button on the Mini toolbar to activate the toolbar.
3. Move the mouse pointer away from the Mini toolbar until it closes.
4. Right-click **Your Name** to display the shortcut menu and active Mini toolbar.
5. Click **Cut** on the shortcut menu to remove your name. The Mini toolbar and shortcut menu also close.
6. Press **Alt** to display the KeyTips on the Ribbon.
7. Press the **W** key, which is the KeyTip for the View tab. The View tab becomes the active tab and each command displays a KeyTip, as shown in **Figure GS 1–13**.

FIGURE GS 1–13
KeyTips on View tab

8. Press the **J** key to zoom your document to 100% of its normal size, if it is not already. Notice that the KeyTips disappear after you have executed a command.
9. Leave the document open for use in the next Step-by-Step.

Customizing Office Programs

The default Office program settings are not always ideal for everyone. It is easy to customize various aspects of the Office programs to suit the way you work.

Changing Program Options

You can customize program settings in any Office program. For example, in Word, you can click the Office Button and then click the Word Options button at the bottom of the menu to open the Word Options dialog box. In this dialog box, you can customize settings for various tools of the program. You customize program settings in the other Office programs following a similar procedure.

UNIT I Getting Started

Using Zoom Controls

You can control the size of your document on the screen using the Zoom controls, shown in **Figure GS 1–14**, located on the right side of the status bar. To zoom out and see more of your document, click the Zoom Out button. To zoom in and see a closer view of your document, click the Zoom In button. Or you can move the Zoom slider to the percentage zoom setting you want. To access more zoom options, click the Zoom level button to open the Zoom dialog box.

> **EXTRA FOR EXPERTS**
>
> In the programs that have Zoom controls, you can also access zoom settings in the Zoom group on the View tab of the Ribbon.

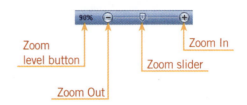

FIGURE GS 1–14   Zoom controls

Resizing Program Windows

There are three sizing buttons on the right side of the title bar that you can use to adjust the size of the program window—the Minimize button, the Restore Down/Maximize button, and the Close button. See **Figure GS 1–15**. Click the Minimize button to reduce the window to a program button on the Windows taskbar. When you want to redisplay the program window, click the program button on the taskbar. If you want to make the program window smaller so you can see some of the desktop, click the Restore Down button. The Restore Down button changes to the Maximize button, which you can then click to make the window full size again. To close the open document and the program, click the Close button.

> **EXTRA FOR EXPERTS**
>
> When you right-click the Windows taskbar, a shortcut menu opens with options to cascade all open program windows, show windows stacked, show windows side by side, or show the desktop by minimizing all windows at once.

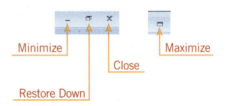

FIGURE GS 1–15   Windows resizing buttons

You can also manually resize the program window by pointing to a corner or border of a minimized window until the mouse pointer changes to a two-headed arrow. Then you can click and drag the border or corner to resize the window as desired.

Step-by-Step GS 1.5

The document from Step-by-Step GS 1.4 should be open in the Word program window.

1. Click the **Office Button** to open the Office Button menu.
2. Click the **Word Options** button in the lower-right corner of the menu. The Word Options dialog box opens, as shown in **Figure GS 1–16**.

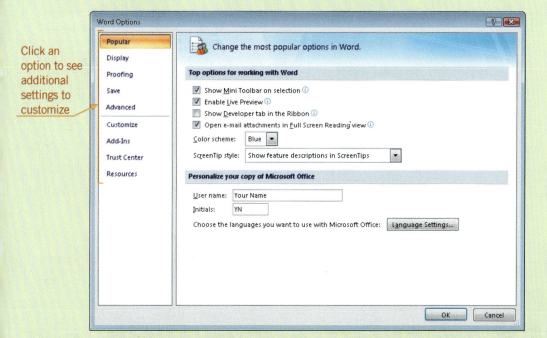

FIGURE GS 1–16
Popular page of Word Options dialog box

Click an option to see additional settings to customize

3. Click each of the options in the left pane to view the related settings in the right pane that you can customize, and then click the **Cancel** button to close the Word Options dialog box.
4. Click the **Zoom Out** button on the status bar to zoom your document to 90%.
5. Click the **Zoom In** button twice to zoom your document to 110%.
6. Drag the **Zoom** slider to the left until your document zooms to approximately 75%.
7. Click the **Zoom level** button 75% to display the Zoom dialog box. See **Figure GS 1–17**.

FIGURE GS 1–17
Zoom dialog box

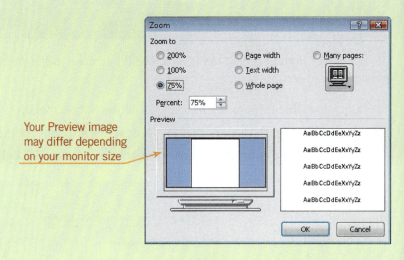

Your Preview image may differ depending on your monitor size

8. In the Zoom to section, click the **100%** option button, and then click the **OK** button to close the Zoom dialog box.
9. Click the **Minimize** button — on the title bar to reduce the window to a button on the taskbar.
10. Click the **Word** program button on the taskbar to display the Word program window again.
11. Click the **Restore Down** button . The window is resized.
12. Position the mouse pointer on the lower-right corner until it changes to a two-headed arrow, as shown in **Figure GS 1–18**, and then click and drag down to the right to make the window bigger.

FIGURE GS 1–18
Resized window

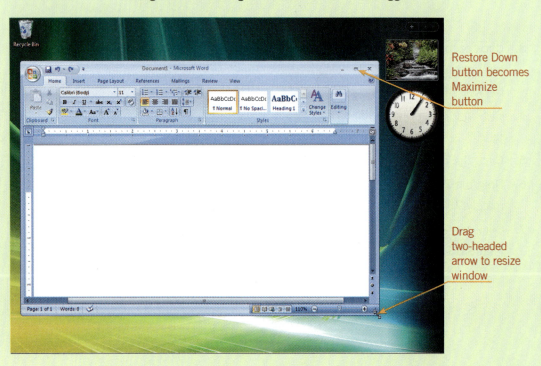

Restore Down button becomes Maximize button

Drag two-headed arrow to resize window

13. Click the **Maximize** button to change the window back to full size.
14. Leave the document open for use in the next Step-by-Step.

LESSON 1   Working with Microsoft Office 2007

Getting Help with Office

You will learn many skills in this book, but if you need more information on how to use the tools in Office to accomplish a task, there are several ways to get help using the Office Help system.

Using the Help Window

You can get help by clicking the Microsoft Office Help button on the right side of the Ribbon, or you can press F1 to open a Help window. **Figure GS 1–19** shows the Word Help window. You can use the Help window to browse topics or search for a specific word or phrase. You can also view a complete table of contents for the Help system by clicking the Show Table of Contents button in the Help window. When working with Help, you can choose to display the Help window on top of the open program window, or you can choose to reduce the Help window to a button on the Windows taskbar. You select these options for displaying the Help window by clicking the Keep On Top and Not On Top buttons.

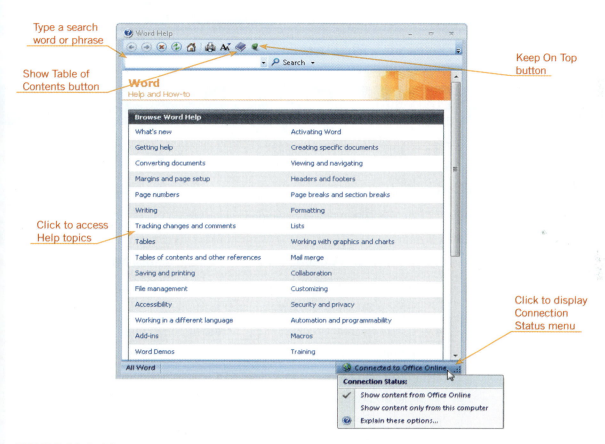

FIGURE GS 1–19   Word Help window

At the bottom of the Help window, there is the Connected to Office Online button that you can click to display the Connection Status menu. You can use this menu to choose whether you want to access online or offline content in the Help window.

UNIT I Getting Started

Using ScreenTips

Another way to get more information is to rest the mouse pointer on a button to display a box with descriptive text, called a *ScreenTip*. As shown in **Figure GS 1–20**, a ScreenTip includes the button name, a keyboard shortcut if there is one, and a description of the button's function. If a Help icon is displayed, you can press F1 to open a Help window with more information about that topic.

> **VOCABULARY**
> ScreenTip

> **EXTRA FOR EXPERTS**
> Keyboard shortcuts can be used to navigate through a document or work more efficiently by pressing certain keys or key combinations. You can use the Help system to learn more about the keyboard shortcuts available in each program.

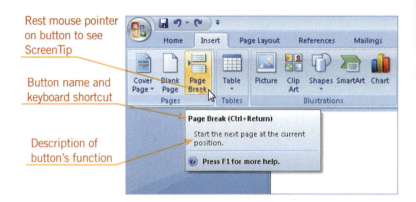

FIGURE GS 1–20   ScreenTip

Step-by-Step GS 1.6

The document from Step-by-Step GS 1.5 should be open in the Word program window.

1. Click the **Microsoft Office Word Help** button on the right side of the Ribbon. The Word Help window opens with a list of links to various Help topics.
2. In the Browse Word Help section, click the **Getting help** link.
3. In the list of topics that are displayed, click the **Find the content you need in the Help window** link, and read the first section of information.
4. In the Search text box, type **ScreenTip**, and then click the **Search** button.
5. In the list of topics that is displayed, click the **Show or hide ScreenTips** link, and read the first section of information.
6. Click the **Show Table of Contents** button. Your Help window should look similar to **Figure GS 1–21**.

LESSON 1 Working with Microsoft Office 2007   GS 19

FIGURE GS 1–21
Word Help window displaying table of contents

7. Click the **Connected to Office Online** button in the bottom right of the Word Help window to display the Connection Status menu, click **Explain these options**, and then read the first section of information that is displayed in the Word Help window.

8. Point to each button on the Word Help toolbar to display the button's ScreenTip, and then click the **Hide Table of Contents** button.

9. Click the **Keep On Top** button and then click your Word document. The Help window is reduced to a button on the taskbar.

10. Click the **Word Help** button on the taskbar to display the Help window again.

11. Click the **Not On Top** button and then click the Word document. Notice that the Help window stays on top of the document.

12. Click the **Close** button on the Help window's title bar to close the Word Help window and return to the document.

13. On the Home tab, in the Paragraph group, point to each button to display the ScreenTip and read the descriptive text.

14. Leave the document open for use in the next Step-by-Step.

UNIT I Getting Started

Closing an Office Program

When you have only one document open in a program, you can click the Close button on the title bar to close the document and exit the program at the same time. If any changes to your work have not been saved, a message box will appear asking if you want to save the document before closing.

Step-by-Step GS 1.7

The document from Step-by-Step GS 1.6 should be open in the Word program window.

1. Click the **Close** button 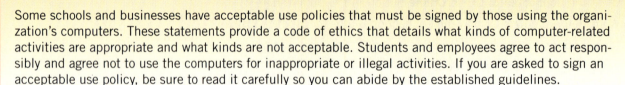 on the Word title bar.
2. When a message box opens asking if you want to save the changes to the document, click the **No** button. The Word program window closes, and you return to the desktop.

ETHICS IN TECHNOLOGY

Some schools and businesses have acceptable use policies that must be signed by those using the organization's computers. These statements provide a code of ethics that details what kinds of computer-related activities are appropriate and what kinds are not acceptable. Students and employees agree to act responsibly and agree not to use the computers for inappropriate or illegal activities. If you are asked to sign an acceptable use policy, be sure to read it carefully so you can abide by the established guidelines.

SUMMARY

In this lesson, you learned:

- About Microsoft Office 2007 and its programs.
- How to start an Office program using the Start menu.
- The parts of an Office program window, including the Ribbon, Office Button, Quick Access Toolbar, title bar, Help button, insertion point, scroll bar, and status bar.
- To access contextual tools, including the Mini toolbar, shortcut menus, and KeyTips.
- Ways to customize various aspects of Office programs to suit your work style, such as changing program options, using Zoom controls, and resizing the program windows.
- To get help with Office using the Help window and ScreenTips.
- How to close an Office program.

LESSON 1 Working with Microsoft Office 2007

VOCABULARY REVIEW

Define the following terms:

badge	KeyTip	Office Button
contextual tabs	launch	Quick Access Toolbar
dialog box launcher	Live Preview	Ribbon
gallery	Microsoft Office 2007	ScreenTip
groups	Mini toolbar	suite
integrate	Office	tabs
interface		

REVIEW QUESTIONS

MULTIPLE CHOICE

Select the best response for the following statements.

1. To begin using an Office program, you first need to open or _____ it.
   A. integrate
   B. customize
   C. launch
   D. resize

2. If a gallery has more options than those shown on the Ribbon, you can click the _____ button to see the full gallery.
   A. Help
   B. All
   C. More
   D. Options

3. To open a list of installed programs from the Start menu, click _____.
   A. All Programs
   B. Open Programs
   C. List Programs
   D. Show Programs

4. The _____ displays information about current position and settings.
   A. title bar
   B. scroll bar
   C. taskbar
   D. status bar

5. If a button on the Ribbon has an arrow, you can click the arrow to open a _____.
   A. dialog box
   B. menu
   C. task pane
   D. toolbar

6. You can use the _____ to open, save, print, and close your documents and perform other file-related tasks.
   A. Office Button
   B. Ribbon
   C. Start button
   D. Quick Launch Toolbar

7. Which of the following commands is *not* available by default on the Quick Access Toolbar?
   A. Save
   B. Print
   C. Undo
   D. Redo

8. To display KeyTips on the Ribbon, press the _____ key.
   A. Shift
   B. Ctrl
   C. Alt
   D. F1

9. When you click the Restore Down button on the title bar, it changes to the _____ button.
   A. Restore Back
   B. Close
   C. Minimize
   D. Maximize
10. To display a ScreenTip, _____ a button.
    A. click
    B. right-click
    C. point to
    D. double-click

FILL IN THE BLANK

Complete the following sentences by writing the correct word or words in the blanks provided.

1. The Office programs on your computer will vary depending on which Office _____ is installed.
2. The _____ button is a common Office program element that provides assistance with a program.
3. _____ on the Ribbon will only appear when the commands on it are needed for the task you are doing.
4. _____ is a feature that applies the editing or formatting change to your document as you point to a gallery option.
5. The _____ toolbar is displayed above the selected text or object and is transparent, becoming active only after you point to a command on it.
6. A(n) _____ is displayed when you right-click selected text.
7. You can customize Word settings by clicking the _____ and then clicking the Word Options button at the bottom of the menu.
8. You can control the size of your document in the document window using the _____ controls on the right of the status bar.
9. You can use the _____ menu to choose whether you want to access online or offline content in the Help window.
10. When you have only one document open in a program, you can click the Close button on the _____ to close the document and exit the program at the same time.

PROJECTS

PROJECT GS 1–1

1. Use the Start menu to open Word 2007.
2. Click the Page Layout tab on the Ribbon.
3. In the Page Setup group, click the dialog box launcher to open the Page Setup dialog box.
4. Close the Page Setup dialog box.
5. Display KeyTips and use them to open the Office Button menu, and then open the Word Options dialog box.
6. Display the Advanced options.
7. Close the Word Options dialog box.
8. Right-click the blank document to display the Mini toolbar and shortcut menu.
9. Press Esc to close the Mini toolbar and shortcut menu.
10. Minimize the program window to a button on the taskbar.
11. Click the Word program button on the taskbar to restore the window.
12. Close Word.

PROJECT GS 1–2

1. Open Microsoft Office Word 2007.
2. In the first line of the blank document, type **Getting Started Lesson.**
3. Click the Page Layout tab on the Ribbon, and then click the Themes button to display the Themes gallery.
4. Point to the different gallery options to see the document themes change using Live Preview, and click one you like.
5. Use the Zoom slider to zoom the document to 110%.
6. Click the Zoom Out button to zoom the document to 90%.
7. Click the Zoom level button to display the Zoom dialog box.
8. Zoom the document to 100%, and click the OK button to close the Zoom dialog box.
9. Click the Restore Down button to make the window smaller.
10. Click and drag to resize the window and make it half its current size.
11. Maximize the window to make it full size again.
12. Leave Word and the document open for use in Project GS 1–3.

LESSON 1 Working with Microsoft Office 2007

PROJECT GS 1-3

The document from Project GS 1-2 should be open in the Word program window.

1. Open the Word Help window.
2. Display the Connection Status menu, and click Show content from Office Online, if it is not already selected.
3. In the Browse Word Help section, click the Training link.
4. In the Topics section, click the Keyboard shortcuts in the 2007 Office system link.
5. Read the course overview.
6. Close the browser window.
7. In the Word Help window, click the Keep On Top button.
8. Display the Help table of contents.
9. Close the Word Help window.
10. Leave Word and the document open for use in Project GS 1-4.

ON YOUR OWN

Complete the lessons and practice sessions in the *Keyboard shortcuts in the 2007 Office system* online training course that you accessed in Step 4.

PROJECT GS 1-4

The document from Project GS 1-3 should be open in the Word program window.

1. Move the Quick Access Toolbar below the Ribbon.
2. Display the Word Help window.
3. Search for the demo titled *Place your favorite commands on the Quick Access Toolbar* and watch it.
4. In the Word Help window, click the Not On Top button.
5. Hide the Table of Contents.
6. Close the Word Help window.
7. Move the Quick Access Toolbar above the Ribbon.
8. Close the document without saving changes, and then close Word.

ON YOUR OWN

Open each program included in your Office suite. Explore all the Ribbon tabs and see what commands are available. Open the program options and view the various settings available for customizing the program.

■ CRITICAL THINKING

ACTIVITY GS 1-1

When using Office programs, it will be helpful if you can troubleshoot any problems you may encounter. If you were working with Word and couldn't see all the text on the Ribbon, or the icons on the Ribbon were displayed in a different order, what could be the cause? How would you solve this issue? Use the Help system to find out.

ACTIVITY GS 1-2

In this lesson, you learned how to open an Office program. If you want to save time, you can configure your system so that a specific Microsoft Office program opens whenever you turn on your computer. Use the Help system to find out how to start a specific program whenever Microsoft Windows starts.

Estimated Time for Unit: 9 hours

UNIT II

MICROSOFT WORD

LESSON 1   **1.5 HRS.**
Understanding Word Fundamentals

LESSON 2   **2 HRS.**
Editing and Formatting Text

LESSON 3   **2 HRS.**
Enhancing Documents

LESSON 4   **2 HRS.**
Working with Graphic Objects

Estimated Time: 1.5 hours

LESSON 1

Understanding Word Fundamentals

■ OBJECTIVES

Upon completion of this lesson, you should be able to:

- Open an existing Word document.
- Navigate a document.
- Select text.
- Enter text.
- Save a document.
- Change document views and page formatting.
- Preview and print a document.
- Close a document.

■ VOCABULARY

collate
document
drag
I-beam
insertion point
landscape
margins
portrait
select
word-processing software
word wrap

■ DATA FILES

To complete this lesson, you will need these data files:

Step WD 1-1.docx
Project WD 1-1.docx
Project WD 1-2.docx
Project WD 1-3.docx
Project WD 1-4.docx

WD 3

VOCABULARY
word-processing software
document

Introduction

Microsoft Word 2007 is the word-processing program included in the Microsoft Office 2007 suite of software. **Word-processing software** lets you insert and manipulate text and graphics to create all kinds of professional-looking documents. A **document** is written information that can be printed on paper or distributed electronically. Examples of documents include lists, letters, reports, flyers, brochures, and any other types of written information. As in other Office programs, the various writing and editing tools in Word are organized on the Ribbon tabs. Word includes predefined styles, formats, and effects to help you create documents that are attractive, well-organized, and make an impact. Before you start creating documents, you need to learn basic skills such as opening, saving, and printing documents. In this lesson, you will learn techniques for performing fundamental skills using Word.

Examining the Word Program Window

A Word file is called a document. When you start Word, a blank document opens, as shown in **Figure WD 1–1**. Use this figure to become familiar with the parts of the Word program window. The default file name of a new document is *Document1*, and it is displayed at the top of the screen in the title bar. You can begin typing text in the document at the insertion point.

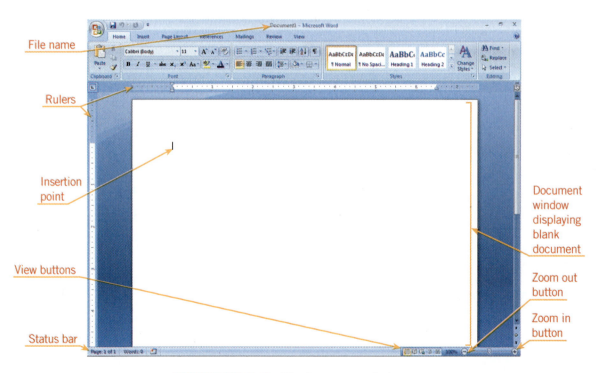

FIGURE WD 1–1 Word program window

Starting Word and Opening an Existing Document

To begin using Word, you first need to open it. You can do this by clicking the Start button on the Windows taskbar, and then clicking the program name on the All Programs menu, or by double-clicking a Word program icon on the desktop. Once Word is started, you can begin using it to create a new document or open an existing document.

LESSON 1 Understanding Word Fundamentals

To open an existing document, you can search for and then open Word files using the Open dialog box, as shown in **Figure WD 1–2**. Word provides three methods for displaying the Open dialog box. The most common method is through the Open command found on the Office Button menu. You can also add an Open command to your Quick Access Toolbar, or use the Ctrl+O keyboard shortcut.

You can use the Open dialog box to find and open existing files on your hard drive, CD, or other removable media; on a network drive to which you are connected; on your organization's intranet; or on the Internet.

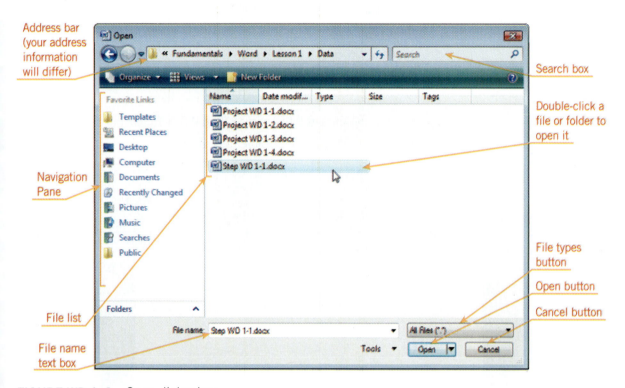

FIGURE WD 1–2 Open dialog box

The following are parts of the Open dialog box:

- The Navigation Pane displays favorite links to folders that contain documents. You can view a folder's contents or open the folder from the Navigation Pane.
- The Address bar at the top of the dialog box shows the folder path.
- The File type button lists other file types you can choose to open.
- The Open button provides options for opening files, including opening the original file, opening a read-only version (when you want to open a file but keep the original file intact), or opening a copy of the original. If you open a copy or read-only version and edit or change the file, you cannot save changes to the original file. You can, however, use the Save As command to save your revisions with a new filename.
- The Search box allows you to find a file by name, file type, or location.
- The Cancel button closes the dialog box without opening a file.

EXTRA FOR EXPERTS

By default, the names of the most recent files you opened in Word will be listed in the Recent Documents list on the Office Button menu. You can click a file in the list to open it. You can customize the number of files displayed in the list using the Advanced section of the Word Options dialog box.

UNIT II Microsoft Word

Step-by-Step WD 1.1

1. Click the **Start** button on the Windows taskbar. The Start menu opens.
2. Click **All Programs**. A list of programs and program folders opens.
3. Click the **Microsoft Office** program folder. A list of Office programs opens.
4. Click **Microsoft Office Word 2007**. Word starts and its program window opens on the desktop with a new, blank document displayed.
5. Click the **Office** button on the Ribbon and then click **Open** to display the Open dialog box.
6. If necessary, navigate to the folder containing the data files for this lesson. Double-click the file named **Step WD 1-1.docx** in the File list. The document opens, as shown in **Figure WD 1–3**.

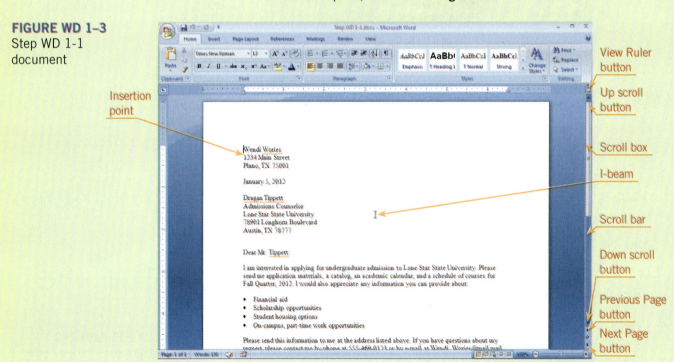

FIGURE WD 1–3
Step WD 1-1 document

7. Leave the document open for use in the next Step-by-Step.

Navigating the Word Document

One of the most useful aspects of word-processing software is the freedom it gives you to move around the page, which you do by moving the insertion point from place to place within the document. The **insertion point** is the blinking vertical bar that signals where any text you type will appear.

You can move the insertion point several ways: with the mouse; with the arrow, Home, PgUp, PgDn, End, and Tab keys; and with the Go To command.

▶ **VOCABULARY**
insertion point

LESSON 1 Understanding Word Fundamentals

Using the Mouse

The mouse pointer looks like an **I-beam** (the letter *I*) when you slide it over text. The easiest way to move the insertion point in existing text is to position the I-beam pointer where you want to work, and then click. When you move the mouse pointer beyond the text area in the left margin, it becomes a selection arrow pointer that you can click to select lines, paragraphs, or the entire document. When you click in the right margin, the insertion point moves to the text closest to where you clicked.

If you want to move to a position not displayed in the document window, use the scroll bars or the mouse wheel to change the document's visible area. To move up or down the document quickly, you can *drag*, or press and hold the mouse button on the scroll box and move the scroll box up or down the scroll bar. To enter text in a new area, you must place the insertion point where you want to make a change. **Table WD 1–1** contains directions for using the scroll bars.

▶ **VOCABULARY**
I-beam

drag

TABLE WD 1–1   Using scroll bars

DO THIS	TO
Click the up or down scroll button	Scroll up or down one line
Click above or below the scroll box in the vertical bar	Scroll up or down one screen
Drag the scroll box	Move to a new location
Click the left or right scroll button	Scroll left or right
Click Previous Page or Next Page button	Move to the previous or next page
Right-click the scroll bar	Select a scroll location from the shortcut menu

Your mouse might have a scroll wheel that is located between the left and right mouse buttons. You can roll the wheel with your finger to scroll up and down, and, depending on the type of mouse, horizontally as well.

Using the Keyboard Shortcuts

Table WD 1–2 contains some of the keys and key combinations you can use to move the insertion point.

TABLE WD 1–2 Using keystrokes to navigate

PRESS KEY(S)	TO MOVE
Left arrow ←	One character to the left
Right arrow →	One character to the right
Up arrow ↑	One line up
Down arrow ↓	One line down
End	To the end of a line
Home	To the beginning of a line
Page Up	Up one screen
Page Down	Down one screen
Ctrl+End	To the end of the document
Ctrl+Home	To the beginning of the document

Using the Go To Command

The Go To command lets you move the insertion point to various locations in your document. You could use Go To to jump to a specific page, section, line, comment, or other element within a document. To use Go To, you open the Find and Replace dialog box, which is accessed using the Go To command on the Find menu in the Editing group (located on the Home tab of the Ribbon). You can also click the page number on the status bar to display the Go To tab.

> **EXTRA FOR EXPERTS**
>
> You can also use the Bookmark button on the Insert tab to move around a document. For example, you can place a bookmark at a position in your document that you often return to for editing. Whenever you want to locate that position, simply use either the Bookmark or Go To command.

Step-by-Step WD 1.2

The document from Step-by-Step WD 1.1 should be open in the Word program window.

1. Point to the down scroll button , and click and hold the mouse button until you scroll to the end of the document. Click to the right of the last word of the document.

2. Press **Home** to move the insertion point to the beginning of the line.

3. Press **Ctrl+Home**. The insertion point moves to the beginning of the document.

4. On the Home tab, in the Editing group, click the **Find** button arrow and then click the **Go To** tab. The Find and Replace dialog box opens with the Go To tab selected, as shown in **Figure WD 1–4**.

LESSON 1   Understanding Word Fundamentals

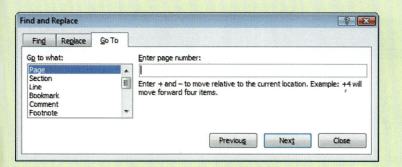

FIGURE WD 1–4
Go To tab in the Find and Replace dialog box

5. In the Go to what list box, click **Line**.

6. Type **20** in the Enter line number text box, and then click the **Go To** button. The insertion point moves to line 20. Click the **Close** button to close the Find and Replace dialog box.

7. Press **Ctrl+End**. The insertion point moves to the end of the document.

8. Drag the scroll box to the top of the scroll bar.

9. Click anywhere in the right margin. The insertion point moves to the text closest to where you clicked.

10. Click to the left of the *J* in *January* to move the insertion point.

11. Leave the document open for use in the next Step-by-Step.

Selecting Text

Before you can format text or move or delete text or graphics, you must *select*, or highlight, the text or object you want to change. You can select text with the mouse or the keyboard. When you select text and then start typing, the selected text is deleted and replaced with the first character you type.

You can cancel a selection by pressing an arrow key or clicking in white space outside the selection.

▶ **VOCABULARY**
select

Selecting with the Mouse

You are probably already familiar with selecting text with the mouse by dragging across the text. When the mouse pointer is moved to the left margin, it changes to a selection arrow pointer that you can click or drag to select various amounts of text. Triple-clicking in the left margin selects an entire document. **Table WD 1–3** describes some additional techniques for selecting text.

TABLE WD 1-3 Selecting with the mouse

DO THIS	TO SELECT
Drag across the text you want to select or Place the insertion point at the beginning of the selection, then press and hold the Shift key and click at the end of the selection	Any item or amount of text
Double-click the word	Word
Click the left margin to the left of the line	Line of text
Drag in the left margin to the left of the lines	Multiple lines of text
Press and hold the Ctrl key, and then click anywhere in the sentence	Sentence
Double-click the left margin of the paragraph, or triple-click the paragraph	Paragraph
Triple-click the left margin	Entire document
Press and hold the Alt key, and then drag vertically over the text	Vertical block of text
Select the first item, press and hold the Ctrl key, and select additional items	Multiple items that aren't side by side

Step-by-Step WD 1.3

The document from Step-by-Step WD 1.2 should be open in the Word program window.

1. Click to the left of the *J* in *January* and then drag across the date **January 5, 2012** to select it, as shown in **Figure WD 1-5**.

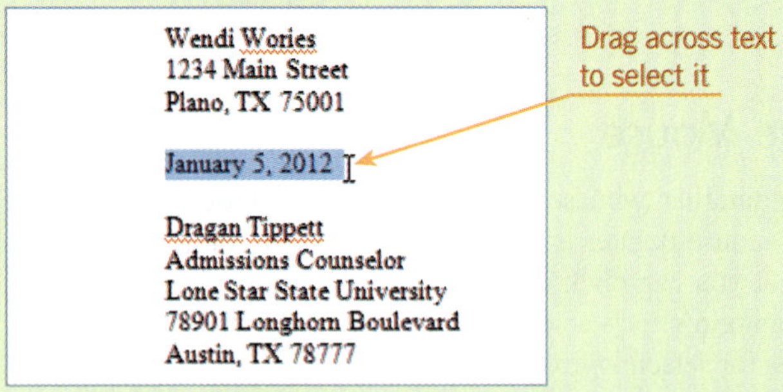

FIGURE WD 1-5
Dragging to select text

Wendi Wories
1234 Main Street
Plano, TX 75001

January 5, 2012

Dragan Tippett
Admissions Counselor
Lone Star State University
78901 Longhorn Boulevard
Austin, TX 78777

Drag across text to select it

2. Click a blank area on the right side of the document window to cancel the selection.
3. Point to an area in the margin to the left of the date, and ensure that the pointer changes to a right-pointing arrow, then click to select the date again.

LESSON 1   Understanding Word Fundamentals

4. Click a blank area on the right side of the document window to cancel the selection.

5. Double-click the margin to the left of the paragraph to select the first three-line paragraph.

6. Triple-click somewhere in the paragraph below the bulleted list to select the entire paragraph, as shown in **Figure WD 1–6**. You might have to try triple-clicking a few times before you are successful.

Triple-click within a paragraph to select it

FIGURE WD 1–6
Selecting a paragraph

7. Double-click the word **January** in the date line. Press and hold **Ctrl**, and double-click the year **2012** in the date to select multiple items that are not adjacent.

8. Click a blank area on the right side of the document window to cancel the selections.

9. Leave the document open for use in the next Step-by-Step.

UNIT II Microsoft Word

> **EXTRA FOR EXPERTS**
>
> You can select all the text in a document with the same formatting by selecting a portion of the text, clicking the Home tab on the Ribbon, clicking the Select button in the Editing group, and then clicking Select Text with Similar Formatting.

Selecting with the Keyboard

Table WD 1–4 describes the keystrokes you use to select text and graphics with the keyboard.

TABLE WD 1–4 Keyboard commands

PRESS KEYS	TO SELECT
Shift+right arrow →	One character to the right
Shift+left arrow ←	One character to the left
Ctrl+Shift+right arrow →	To the end of a word
Ctrl+Shift+left arrow ←	To the beginning of a word
Shift+End	To the end of a line
Shift+Home	To the beginning of a line
Ctrl+Shift+down arrow ↓	To the end of a paragraph
Ctrl+Shift+End	To the end of a document
Ctrl+Shift+Home	To the beginning of a document
Ctrl+A	The entire document

Step-by-Step WD 1.4

The document from Step-by-Step WD 1.3 should be open in the Word program window.

1. Click at the beginning of the document.
2. Press **Shift+End**. The line is selected.
3. Press the **down arrow** key to cancel the selection. Position the insertion point at the end of the second line.
4. Press and hold **Shift** and press the **left arrow** key to select the **t** in *Street*.
5. Continue pressing and holding **Shift** while pressing the **left arrow** key until the word **Street** is selected, as shown in **Figure WD 1–7**.

FIGURE WD 1–7
Selecting one character at a time

Wendi Wories
1234 Main Street
Plano, TX 75001

January 5, 2012

Dragan Tippett
Admissions Counselor

LESSON 1   Understanding Word Fundamentals   WD 13

6. Press and hold **Ctrl** and press the **A** key to select the entire document.
7. Press the **up arrow** key to cancel the selection.
8. Leave the document open for use in the next Step-by-Step.

Entering Text

To add new text, position the insertion point where you want to insert text and then type the text. Word enters text at the insertion point—to the left of anything that may be there already.

When you see a wavy red or green line underneath text, it means that Word has detected a possible spelling or grammatical error. Ignore the wavy lines for now; you will learn how to check the underlined text in Lesson 2.

When you enter text, Word uses a feature called *word wrap* to automatically continue text to the next line within a paragraph. When you finish a paragraph, press Enter to create the first line of a new paragraph.

> **VOCABULARY**
> word wrap

Step-by-Step WD 1.5

The document from Step-by-Step WD 1.4 should be open in the Word program window.

1. Click at the beginning of the line that begins *I am interested*.
2. Type **I am a senior at Cougar Hill High School.** Press the **spacebar** to create a space between sentences, as shown in **Figure WD 1–8**. Notice that the text at the end of the line wrapped to the next line.

FIGURE WD 1–8
Entering new text

Insertion point now follows new sentence and space

Wendi Wories
1234 Main Street
Plano, TX 75001

January 5, 2012

Dragan Tippett
Admissions Counselor
Lone Star State University
78901 Longhorn Boulevard
Austin, TX 78777

Dear Mr. Tippett:

I am a senior at Cougar Hill High School. I am interested in applying for undergraduate admission to Lone Star State University. Please send me application materials, a catalog, an academic calendar, and a schedule of courses for Fall Quarter, 2012. I would also appreciate any information you can provide about:

- Financial aid
- Scholarship opportunities
- Student housing options
- On-campus, part-time work opportunities

Please send this information to me at the address listed above. If you have questions about my request, please contact me by phone at 555-469-0123 or by e-mail at Wendi_Wories@mail.mail.

3. Select the word **work** in the fourth bulleted list item.
4. Type **employment**. Notice that the word *work* was deleted after you typed the *e* in *employment*.
5. Leave the document open for use in the next Step-by-Step.

Saving a Document

The first time you save a document, the options for saving include the Save command on the Office Button menu, the Save As command on the Office Button menu, or the Save button on the Quick Access Toolbar. Each of these methods displays the Save As dialog box (see **Figure WD 1–9**).

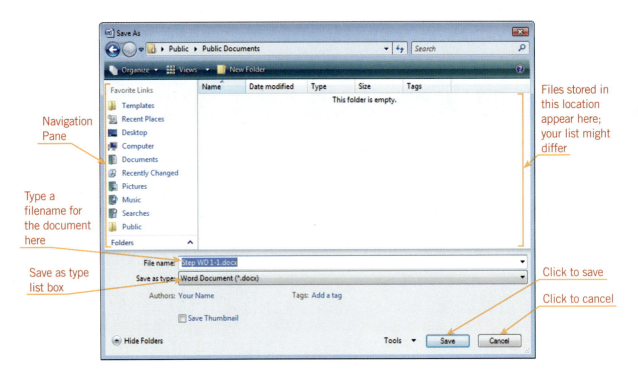

FIGURE WD 1–9   Save As dialog box

EXTRA FOR EXPERTS

Word 2007 files have a .docx extension and cannot be opened with previous versions of Word. If you need to share files with someone using an earlier version, you can use the Word 97-2003 Document command on the Save As submenu, which is located on the Office Button menu, to save files with the .doc extension.

After you save a file for the first time, the Save command saves your file with the previously specified name in the location you specified. The Save As command opens the Save As dialog box, in which you can make a copy of the file with a new name, location, or file type. The Save as type list box lets you save a document in another format or as a template. You might need to change the file format or program and version if you share files with others who use different software. You will learn more about templates later in this book. To save a document in a specific location, you use the Navigation Pane to navigate to the folder in which you want to save the document.

Once you have saved the file, you can use the Save button on the Quick Access Toolbar or the Save command on the Office Button menu to update it.

LESSON 1 Understanding Word Fundamentals

WD 15

Word's AutoRecover feature automatically saves your document at regular intervals so that you can recover at least some of your work in case of a power outage or other unexpected shutdown. You can turn this feature on or off and change the setting to save more or less often by opening the Word Options dialog box from the Office Button menu. On the Save page, specify a number in the Save AutoRecover information every *x* minutes box. However, you should not rely on this automatic saving feature. Remember to save your work often.

Step-by-Step WD 1.6

The document from Step-by-Step WD 1.5 should be open in the Word program window.

1. Click the **Office** button and then click **Save As** to open the Save As dialog box.
2. Navigate to the location where you will save your files.
3. Click the **File name** text box. Type **Admissions Letter XXX** (replace *XXX* with your initials) in the box. See **Figure WD 1–10**.

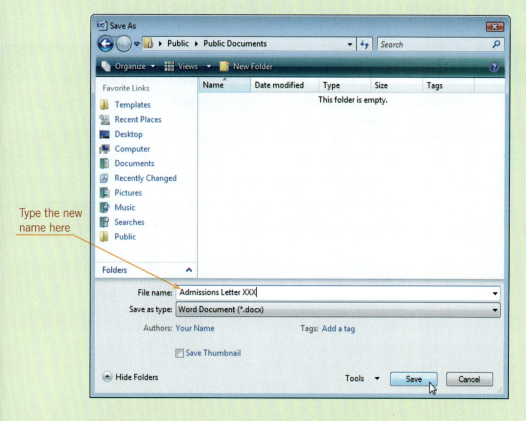

FIGURE WD 1–10
Save As dialog box

Type the new name here

4. Click the **Save** button to save a copy of the document with the new name in the specified location.
5. Leave the document open for use in the next Step-by-Step.

Changing Document Views

You might find it useful to preview how your document would look as a printout, as a Web page, or in an outline. Word provides five different views using the buttons in the Document Views group on the View tab on the Ribbon. You can also use the View buttons on the right side of the status bar to switch easily from view to view. The five Document Views are:

- Print Layout, which displays the page as it will print, including headers, footers, footnotes, and graphics. It is the most common view.
- Full Screen Reading view, which maximizes the space available for reading documents on the screen.
- Web Layout, which shows you how your document would look as a Web page.
- Outline, which displays the structure of your document in classic outline format.
- Draft view, which displays the document for editing purposes. Elements such as headers and footers are not shown.

You can display a ruler to help you position text and graphics on your pages. For the ruler to be visible, a check mark must appear next to the Ruler command in the Show/Hide group, which appears on the View tab of the Ribbon. Or, you can click the View Ruler button, found at the top of the vertical scroll bar.

> **EXTRA FOR EXPERTS**
>
> When you open a Word document attached to an e-mail message, it is opened in Full Screen Reading view by default. However, you can turn off this feature using the Don't Open Attachments in Full Screen command in the View Options menu that is displayed in Full Screen Reading view.

Step-by-Step WD 1.7

The Admissions Letter *XXX*.docx document from Step-by-Step 1.6 should be open in the Word program window.

1. Click the **View** tab on the Ribbon. In the Document Views group, notice that the document is displayed in Print Layout view.
2. In the Show/Hide group, notice the Ruler check box. If necessary, click the **Ruler** check box to display the Ruler. See **Figure WD 1–11**.

FIGURE WD 1–11
View tab

Ruler check box

Document Views group

LESSON 1   Understanding Word Fundamentals

3. In the Document Views group, click the **Web Layout** button to display the letter as it would appear as a Web page in a browser.

4. Click the **Outline** button. Notice the commands available on the Outlining tab.

5. In the Close group, click the **Close Outline View** button. Your document should once again be in Print Layout View.

6. Click the **View** tab. In the Document Views group, click the **Draft** button.

7. In the Document Views group, click the **Full Screen Reading** button to open the document in the Full Screen reading window. Notice the commands available on the toolbar, as shown in **Figure WD 1–12**.

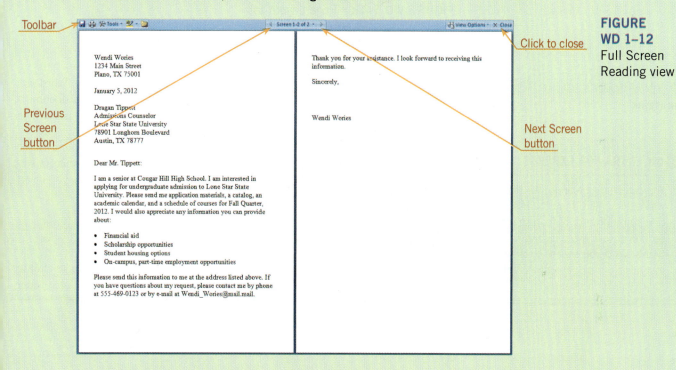

FIGURE WD 1-12 Full Screen Reading view

8. Click the **Close** button or press **Esc** to return to Print Layout view.

9. Leave the document open for use in the next Step-by-Step.

Changing Page Formatting

One of the first things you do when working with a new document is to format the page. Formatting the page involves setting margins, establishing the size of the paper you will be using for printouts, and determining whether your document will be horizontally or vertically oriented.

You can use the Page Setup group of commands on the Page Layout tab, shown in **Figure WD 1–13**, to change how you set up a document's pages. Open the Page Setup dialog box for access to more options.

FIGURE WD 1–13   Page Layout tab

Setting Margins

Margins are the white space that borders the text on the edges of a page. Word sets default margins for new documents, but you can change them to fit your document requirements. Most printers cannot print all the way to the edge of the paper, and therefore, printers have rules for minimum margin settings.

You set margins using the Margins button in the Page Setup group, found on the Page Layout tab on the Ribbon. Word provides commands for common margin settings, as shown in **Figure WD 1–14**. The Custom Margins command lets you insert custom measurements for the top, bottom, left, and right margins.

Choosing Paper Size

You can use the Size button and menu, also found in the Page Setup group, to choose from a list of common paper sizes. **Figure WD 1–15** shows the list of available paper sizes. The More Paper Sizes command lets you create a custom paper size.

> **VOCABULARY**
> **margins**

> **EXTRA FOR EXPERTS**
> You can change margins for the whole document, from the insertion point forward, or for a selected section of text. Word inserts a section break if you choose to change margins from the insertion point forward or for a selection.

LESSON 1 Understanding Word Fundamentals

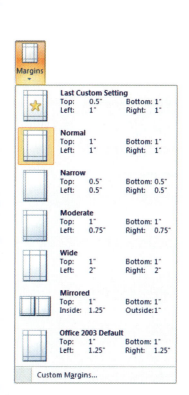

FIGURE WD 1-14
Margins menu

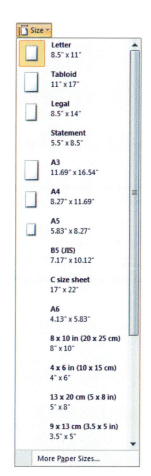

FIGURE WD 1-15
Paper Size menu

EXTRA FOR EXPERTS

You can change paper size and orientation for the whole document or for part of the document. If you change the paper size or orientation from the insertion point forward, Word inserts a section break before the insertion point. If you change the paper size or orientation for selected text, Word inserts a section break before and after the selected text.

Changing Orientation

While most documents are set up in a vertical orientation, called *portrait*, sometimes you might need to use a horizontal setup, called *landscape*, shown in **Figure WD 1-16**. Word's default page orientation is portrait, but you can change to landscape using the Orientation button found in the Page Setup group.

VOCABULARY
portrait
landscape

UNIT II Microsoft Word

FIGURE WD 1–16 Portrait and landscape orientation

LESSON 1 Understanding Word Fundamentals

Step-by-Step WD 1.8

The Admissions Letter *XXX*.docx from Step-by-Step WD 1.7 should be open in the Word program window.

1. Click the **Page Layout** tab on the Ribbon. In the Page Setup group, click the **Margins** button to open the Margins menu.
2. Click **Wide** to apply left and right margins that are 2 inches wide.
3. Click the **Margins** button again and then click **Custom Margins**. The Page Setup dialog box opens, as shown in **Figure WD 1–17**.

FIGURE WD 1–17
Page Setup dialog box

4. Type **1.5** in the Top text box and then click the **OK** button.
5. Click the **Size** button in the Page Setup group on the Page Layout tab.
6. Click **Legal** to change the page height to 14 inches. Scroll down the document and notice the new, longer page.
7. Click the **Size** button and then click **Letter** to return to the original page size setting.
8. Click the **Orientation** button in the Page Setup group and click **Landscape**. Scroll down and notice that the new layout caused the letter to go to two pages.

9. Click the **Orientation** button and click **Portrait** to return to the original page orientation.
10. Save the document and leave it open for use in the next Step-by-Step.

Previewing and Printing a Document

You will need to print most of the documents that you create. Whether you are working with a letter, a fax, or other type of document, you will likely send it to another user, distribute printouts in a meeting, post a flyer, or have some other need for a printed version. You can save time and paper by using the Print Preview tool to correct mistakes and change formatting before you use the Print command.

Previewing Printouts

You can preview entire pages of a document before printing using the Print Preview option on the Print menu on the Office Button menu. You can zoom in and out to see different magnifications of a document and even edit the document in this view. Word displays the current page when you click the Print Preview command. If you have not changed the default setting, you should see a one-page display like the one in **Figure WD 1–18**. The pointer changes from an arrow to a magnifying glass. You can zoom in on an area of a document by clicking the area you want to magnify. To return to the original magnification, click again. To edit a document while in Print Preview mode, you clear the Magnifier check box in the Preview group to change the pointer back to its normal mode.

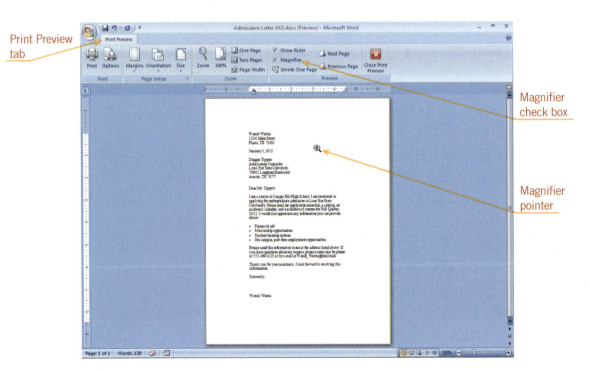

FIGURE WD 1–18   Print Preview

LESSON 1   Understanding Word Fundamentals

WD 23

You can perform other preview tasks using the tools on the Print Preview tab. The key Print Preview tools include:

- The Print button prints the document with default settings.
- Buttons in the Page Setup group let you make changes to the margins, orientation, or page size.
- The Zoom button displays the Zoom dialog box where you can select a change magnification.
- The 100% button allows you to view the page at 100 percent of the normal size.
- The Show Ruler check box allows you to display the ruler when you want to change the page layout.
- The Magnifier zooms in on an area of a document. Notice that the Magnifier option is automatically selected (the check box has a checkmark).
- The Shrink One Page button is used to make a document with a short paragraph on a page by itself fit on the previous page.
- The Close Print Preview button returns to the previous view.

Printing Documents

You use the Print command on the Office Button menu to open the Print dialog box, shown in **Figure WD 1–19**. The settings in the Print dialog box will differ according to the printer you are using, but some options are common to all printers, including:

- The Printer area, where you select a printer from the list of available printers
- The Page range area, where you indicate whether to print all pages, the current page, or specified pages of a document
- The Copies area, where you indicate the quantity of copies to print and whether to *collate* the pages, which prints them in order
- The Options button, which displays a dialog box that lets you make other decisions about how your document will be printed
- The Properties button, which lets you change the paper type, size and orientation, and other options for your printer

▶ **VOCABULARY**
collate

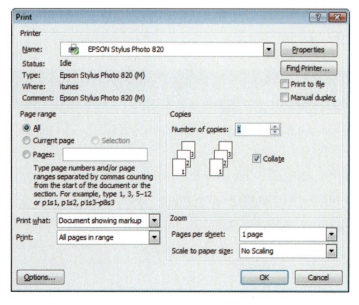

FIGURE WD 1–19   Print dialog box

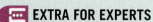 **EXTRA FOR EXPERTS**

You can use the Quick Print command on the Print submenu of the Office Button menu to print to the default printer without opening the Print dialog box.

Step-by-Step WD 1.9

The Admissions Letter *XXX*.docx from Step-by-Step WD 1.8 should be open in the Word program window.

1. Click the **Office** button. Point to **Print** and then click **Print Preview** on the menu.
2. Point to the upper-left area of the page, and click the Magnifier pointer.
3. On the Print Preview tab in the Preview group, click the **Magnifier** check box to change to edit mode.
4. Click the beginning of the document and press **Enter** two times.
5. Click the **Magnifier** check box to leave edit mode.
6. Click the Magnifier pointer on the letter to zoom back to the original display.
7. In the Preview group, click the **Close Print Preview** button to return to Print Layout view.
8. Click the **Office Button** and then click **Print**. Notice the options you have available in the Print dialog box. Click the **OK** button. If you have been instructed not to print, click the Cancel button in the Print dialog box.
9. Save the document and leave it open for use in the next Step-by-Step.

Closing a Document

When you are finished with a document, you can remove it from your screen using the Close command. To close a document without closing Word, choose the Close command on the Office Button menu. When you have only one document open, you can click the Close button on the title bar to close the document and exit the program at the same time. The software prompts you to save your work if you made any changes since you last saved.

Step-by-Step WD 1.10

The document from Step-by-Step WD 1.9 should be open in the Word program window.

1. Click the **Office** button and then click **Close**. The document closes and the Word program window remains open.
2. Click the **Close button** on the title bar to close Word.

LESSON 1   Understanding Word Fundamentals   WD 25

TECHNOLOGY CAREERS

Computer support technicians, or help-desk personnel, provide assistance and advice to computer users. Help technicians must be able to communicate effectively to interpret the user's problem. They must also be knowledgeable about the hardware, software (such as Microsoft Word), or system they are providing support for so they can help to solve the problem. Help technicians receive constant training and certification to stay current with the latest technology developments.

SUMMARY

In this lesson, you learned:

- To open an existing document using the Open dialog box.
- Ways to move the insertion point in the Word document using the mouse, keyboard shortcuts, and the Go To command.
- To select text using the mouse and the keyboard.
- That when you enter text, Word automatically wraps it to the next line.
- How to save a document using the Save As dialog box.
- The five different ways to view a document.
- Ways to change margins, paper size, and orientation.
- To preview a document using Print Preview and print a document using the Print dialog box.
- To close a file.

VOCABULARY REVIEW

Define the following terms:

collate	I-beam	portrait
document	insertion point	select
drag	landscape	word-processing software
	margins	word wrap

REVIEW QUESTIONS

MULTIPLE CHOICE

Select the best response for the following statements.

1. To open a file as read-only means _____.

   A. to open the original file
   B. to open a file but keep the original intact
   C. to open a copy of the original file
   D. to open a file in Full Screen Reading view

2. If you click the mouse one time when the pointer is in the left margin, you select the _____.

   A. line
   B. word
   C. paragraph
   D. entire document

3. The Find and Replace dialog box contains the _____ command.
   - A. Orientation
   - B. Go To
   - C. Print
   - D. Print Preview

4. The mouse pointer looks like a(n) _____ when you move it over text.
   - A. arrow pointer
   - B. insertion point
   - C. I-beam
   - D. scroll bar

5. When you enter text, Word uses a feature called _____ to automatically wrap text to the next line.
   - A. navigation
   - B. mirrored margins
   - C. multi-selection
   - D. word wrap

6. After you save a file for the first time, the _____ command saves your file to the previously specified name and location.
   - A. Save As
   - B. Open
   - C. Save
   - D. File

7. _____ is a time- and paper-saving tool because it allows you to correct mistakes and change formatting before printing.
   - A. Word wrap
   - B. Full Screen Reading view
   - C. Landscape Orientation
   - D. Print Preview

8. Legal is a common _____.
   - A. orientation
   - B. page size
   - C. margin setting
   - D. print option

9. _____ view maximizes the space available for reading documents on the screen.
   - A. Web Layout
   - B. Outline
   - C. Full Screen Reading
   - D. Print Layout

10. In the Print dialog box, the Page range area has options for _____.
    - A. printing either all pages, the current page, or specified pages of a document
    - B. selecting a printer
    - C. changing paper type, size, and orientation
    - D. specifying the number of copies to print

FILL IN THE BLANK

Complete the following sentences by writing the correct word or words in the blanks provided.

1. You can cancel a selection by pressing a(n) _____ key.
2. A _____ _____ _____ lets you insert and manipulate text and graphics to create all kinds of professional-looking documents.
3. You can hold _____ and press _____ to move to the beginning of a document.
4. You can _____-click a word to select it.
5. You can click a paragraph _____ times to select it.
6. When you select text and then start typing, the selected text is _____ and replaced with the first character you type.
7. _____ are the white space separating the text on a page from the edges of the paper.
8. Vertical orientation is called _____.
9. In Print Preview, the _____ is used to zoom in on an area of a document.
10. Click the _____ button to close a document.

LESSON 1 Understanding Word Fundamentals

■ PROJECTS

PROJECT WD 1–1

1. Open the file **Project WD 1-1.docx** from the folder containing the data files for this lesson.
2. Use the Save As command on the Office Button menu to save the document with the filename **Lone Star Fax *XXX*.docx** (replace *XXX* with your initials).
3. Click to the right of the Comments section of the fax and type the following text:

    Thank you for your application. However, I need some additional information. Please fill out the attached form and return it to me as soon as possible.

4. Press **Ctrl+Home** to move the insertion point to the beginning of the document.
5. Type **Lone Star State University** and press **Enter**.
6. Save, print, and close the document.

PROJECT WD 1–2

1. Open the file **Project WD 1-2.docx** from the folder containing the data files for this lesson.
2. Save the document with the filename **Graduation Postcard *XXX*.docx** (replace *XXX* with your initials).
3. Change the Page Orientation to landscape.
4. Use the Size menu to change the page size to 4 × 6 in (10 × 15 cm).
5. Change the Margins to Narrow.
6. Click below the last line of text and type **RSVP to (469) 555-0155**.
7. Save the document.
8. Use Print Preview to view the document.
9. Print the document. (If you do not have 4 × 6 paper in your printer, most printers will let you print on letter-size paper. You can trim it later if you wish.)
10. Close Print Preview and close the document.

ON YOUR OWN

Open **Graduation Postcard *XXX*.docx** and change the look of this document by setting custom margins and a custom page size of your choice. Save and close the document.

PROJECT WD 1–3

1. Open the file **Project WD 1-3.docx** from the folder containing the data files for this lesson.
2. Save the document with the filename **Computer Care *XXX*.docx** (replace *XXX* with your initials).
3. Use the Go To command to move the insertion point to page 3.
4. Select the word newspaper on the first line of page 3 and type **Internet**.
5. Drag the scroll box to the top of the scroll bar and click at the beginning of the document.
6. Use Print Preview to view the document.
7. View two pages of the document on the screen.
8. Close Print Preview.
9. View the document using Full Screen Reading view.
10. Use the Next Screen and Previous Screen buttons to scroll through the pages.
11. Close Full Screen Reading view.
12. Save and close the document.

ON YOUR OWN

Open **Computer Care *XXX*.docx,** change the margins to Mirrored, and experiment with the gutter measurement in the Page Setup dialog box. Use Print Preview to view the results. Save and close the document.

PROJECT WD 1–4

1. Open the file **Project WD 1-4.docx** from the folder containing the data files for this lesson.

2. Save the document with the filename **Florida Admissions XXX.docx** (replace *XXX* with your initials).

3. Select *January 5* and type **February 23**.

4. In the letter address, select *Dragan Tippett* and type **Marc Zimprich.**

5. Select *Lone Star State University* and the two address lines below it and type the following:

   Florida Park University

   09876 Palm Tree Road

   Orlando, FL 32868

6. In the greeting line, select *Tippett* and type **Zimprich**.

7. In the first paragraph, select *Lone Star State University* and type **Florida Park University**.

8. Change the margins to Normal.

9. View the document using Print Preview.

10. Turn off the magnifier and add four blank lines at the beginning to center the letter on the page.

11. Close Print Preview.

12. Save, print, and close the document.

ON YOUR OWN

Open **Florida Admissions XXX.docx**, delete the four blank lines at the beginning of the document and use the Vertical alignment option on the Layout tab of the Page Setup dialog box to center the letter attractively on the page. Save and close the document.

WEB PROJECT

PROJECT WD 1–5

1. Open the file **Florida Admissions XXX.docx** from the folder containing the data files for this lesson.

2. Save the document with the filename **Florida Address XXX.docx** (replace *XXX* with your initials).

3. Assume you are planning on attending college in Florida. Search the Web for the names of three colleges in the greater Miami area.

4. In the document, replace the existing address information with the address of one of the colleges you looked up on the Web.

5. Save, print, and close the document.

 CRITICAL THINKING

ACTIVITY WD 1–1

You will inevitably encounter a situation in which you change your mind about printing a document—after you have sent it to the printer. How do you cancel printing? Use Help to find out. Try it by printing one of the document from this lesson and then canceling it.

ACTIVITY WD 1–2

A power outage, low battery level, or other problem can cause your Word document to shut down before you have a chance to save it. What happens to the document you are working on if Word suddenly closes or the power goes out? Use Help to learn about document recovery and the AutoRecover command. Locate and evaluate your AutoRecover settings.

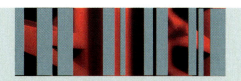

Estimated Time: 2 hours

LESSON 2

Editing and Formatting Text

■ OBJECTIVES

Upon completion of this lesson, you should be able to:

- Create a new document.
- Format text.
- Set tabs.
- Format paragraphs.
- Delete, move, and copy text.
- Use Undo, Redo, and Repeat.
- Find and replace text.
- Proof a document.

■ DATA FILES

To complete this lesson, you will need these data files:

Step WD 2-2.docx
Step WD 2-7.docx
Step WD 2-8.docx
Step WD 2-10.docx
Project WD 2-1.docx
Project WD 2-2.docx
Project WD 2-3.docx
Project WD 2-4.docx
Project WD 2-5.docx

■ VOCABULARY

characters
Clipboard
copy
cut
drag-and-drop
first line indent
font
hanging indent
indents
leaders
negative indent
paragraph
paste
point size
...

WD 29

UNIT II Microsoft Word

Introduction

After you have created a document, you will likely need to fine-tune it using Word tools for formatting and editing. Formatting refers to how your documents look, whereas editing refers to revising, changing, and correcting the wording of your documents. The word *formatting* is also used to describe the visual text characteristics. The ongoing processes of formatting and editing add interest, clarity, and emphasis to the documents you create. You can easily format and edit text as you write, or format and edit after you have organized your thoughts within the document. Formatting and editing can occur in either order, and most people find that they go back and forth interchangeably between the two tasks.

Creating a New Document

You can create a new blank document using the Blank document button in the New Document dialog box, shown in **Figure WD 2–1**. To display the dialog box, choose the New command on the Office Button menu.

Step-by-Step WD 2.1

1. Start Word, if necessary.
2. Click the **Office** button on the Ribbon and then click **New**. The New Document dialog box opens with the Blank document button selected, as shown in **Figure WD 2–1**.

FIGURE WD 2–1
New Document dialog box

Blank document button

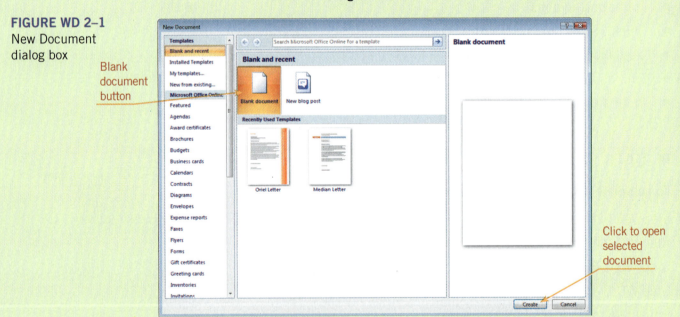

Click to open selected document

3. Click the **Create** button. A new, blank document opens, as shown in **Figure WD 2–2**.

LESSON 2   Editing and Formatting Text

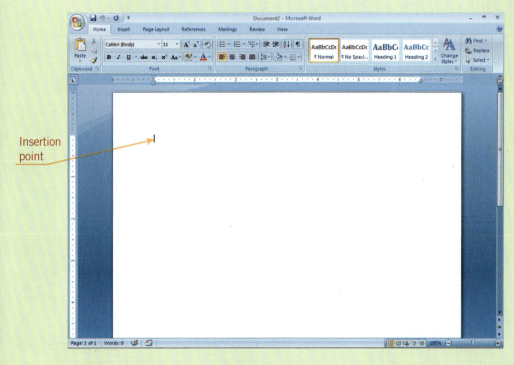

FIGURE WD 2-2
New blank document

Insertion point

4. Type **June 11, 2012** and press **Enter** twice to move the insertion point down two lines.

5. Type **Dear Professor Reynolds,** and then press **Enter**.

6. Type **I am enjoying your course on South American cultures and would like to learn more about the Yanomamo tribe. Can you recommend some books or research papers? Thank you.** and then press **Enter** twice.

7. Type **Sincerely,** and then press **Enter**. Type **Chris Estabrook** to sign the note.

8. Your document should look similar to **Figure WD 2-3**. Save the document as **Reynolds Note XXX.docx** (replace *XXX* with your initials) and close the document.

FIGURE WD 2–3
Reynolds Note *XXX*.docx file

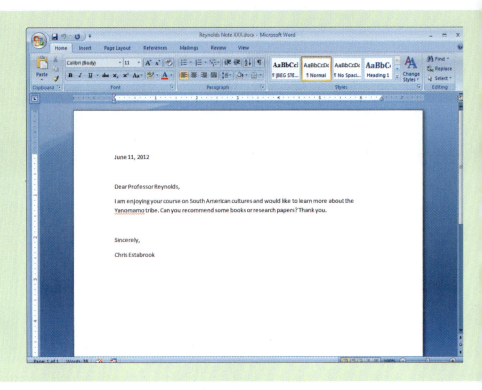

Formatting Text

▶ **VOCABULARY**
character

Characters are individual letters, numbers, symbols, punctuation marks, and spaces. You can apply one or more formats to a single character or multiple characters. The character formats you can apply are font and font size; font style such as italic and bold; and font effects such as underline, color, and change case. The Font group is on the Home tab of the Ribbon, shown in **Figure WD 2–4**, and contains buttons for formatting text. Later in this lesson you will learn to copy formats using the Format Painter button in the Clipboard group.

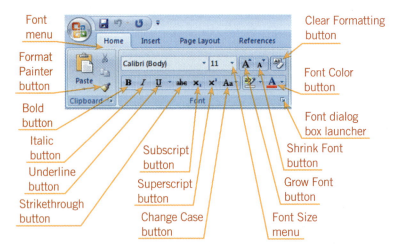

FIGURE WD 2–4 Font group on the Home tab

LESSON 2 Editing and Formatting Text

You can make several changes at once and see a preview of your choices in the Font dialog box, which you can display using the dialog box launcher.

Changing Fonts and Font Sizes

The *font* is the design of a set of letters and numbers. Each set has a name. Below are some examples.

Times New Roman   Arial   **Impact**

The Font menu displays each font's design and is divided into three sections to make it easier for you to choose the appropriate font: Theme Fonts, Recently Used Fonts, and All Fonts. You can also access the Font menu on the Mini toolbar. By default, Word uses the Calibri 11 point font. You change to a different font by selecting text and choosing one of the fonts listed on the Font menu or in the Font dialog box. You can also choose to begin typing text with a new font by selecting the font at the insertion point.

Font sizes are measured in points. *Point size* refers to a measurement for the height of characters. A point is equal to approximately 1/72 inch. A 10-point font is approximately 10/72 inch high. The examples below show what different point sizes look like in the Times font.

8 Point 12 Point 24 Point 36 Point

To change the font size for existing text, you first select the text and then choose a new size on the Font Size menu or in the Size list in the Font dialog box. You can change the size of text you are about to enter by choosing a new size at the insertion-point location.

The Grow Font button increases font size one increment on the Font Size menu, which may be one point, two points, or eight points in the larger sizes, and the Shrink Font button decreases the size one increment.

Applying Font Styles and Effects

Font styles are variations in the shape or weight of a font's characters. Bold, italic, and underline are common font styles that you can access easily in the Font group.

The Effects area of the Font dialog box contains 11 different formatting effects, from Strikethrough to Hidden. You can apply more than one effect at a time. The strikethrough, subscript, superscript, and change case buttons are also available in the Font group.

Use the Change Case button to change the case, or capitalization, of text quickly. The Change Case menu has five options:

- Sentence case—capitalizes the first word in each sentence.
- lowercase—changes all characters to lowercase.
- UPPERCASE—changes all characters to capitals.
- Capitalize Each Word—capitalizes the first character of each word.
- tOGGLE cASE—changes each character to the opposite of how it was originally typed.

To change the color of text, you apply one of the color choices available through the Font Color button arrow.

> **VOCABULARY**
> font
> point size

> **EXTRA FOR EXPERTS**
> You can format text using shortcut keys: Ctrl+B to apply bold, Ctrl+I to apply italic, and Ctrl+U to underline text.

> **EXTRA FOR EXPERTS**
> The Underline button menu in the Font group contains eight line styles and the Underline Color command. The More Underlines command displays the Font dialog box, which contains 17 different ways to underline text. When you choose the Words only underline option, Word underlines only words and not the spaces between words.

Step-by-Step WD 2.2

1. Start Word and open **Step WD 2-2.docx** from the folder containing the data files for this lesson.

2. Save the document as **Zare Resume XXX.docx** (replace *XXX* with your initials).

3. On the Home tab, in the Editing group, click the **Select** button and click **Select All** to select all the text in the document.

4. On the Home tab, in the Font group, click the **Font button arrow** and click **Baskerville Old Face**, as shown in **Figure WD 2–5**. All of the document text changes from the default font, Calibri, to the new font. If your computer does not have Baskerville Old Face available, click another font of your choice.

FIGURE WD 2–5
Font button and menu

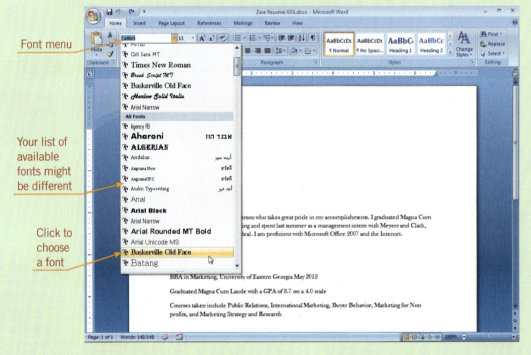

5. With the text still selected, click the **Font Size button arrow** and click **12** to increase the point size of the text.

6. In the Font group, click the **Shrink Font** button one time to change the point size back to 11.

7. Select **Mandy Zare.** In the Font group, click the **Underline** button to underline the selected text.

8. Make sure Mandy Zare is still selected. In the Font group, click the **Bold** button to change the selected text to bold.

LESSON 2   Editing and Formatting Text

9. Make sure Mandy Zare is still selected. In the Font group, click the **Change Case** button Aa▾ and click **UPPERCASE**, as shown in **Figure WD 2–6**.

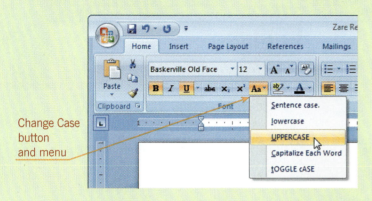

FIGURE WD 2–6
Change Case button and menu

10. Click the **Change Case** button again and click **Capitalize Each Word** to change the capitalization style.
11. Make sure Mandy Zare is still selected. In the Font group, click the **dialog box launcher** to open the Font dialog box.
12. In the Font menu, click **Arial Rounded MT Bold** or another font of your choice. In the Size menu, click **14**. In the Underline style menu, click **(none)**. In the Effects section, click the **Small caps** check box. See **Figure WD 2–7**. Click the **OK** button to close the dialog box.

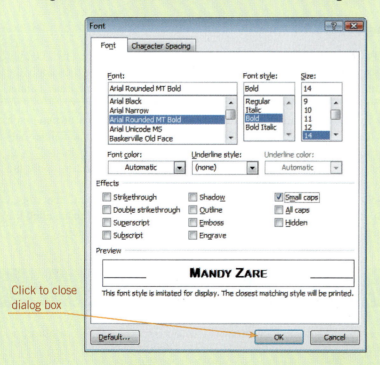

FIGURE WD 2–7
Font dialog box

13. Make sure Mandy Zare is still selected. In the Font group, click the **Font Color** button arrow and click **Blue** from the Standard Colors section of the gallery, as shown in **Figure WD 2–8**.

FIGURE WD 2–8
Font Color gallery

14. Save the document and leave it open for use in the next Step-by-Step.

Clearing Formatting

To remove formatting from selected text, you perform the same steps you took to apply the formatting, which effectively reverses the formatting. For example, if you want to remove bold formatting that you added to a word, you would click the Bold button again to remove the bold formatting from selected text. Or, use the Clear Formatting button to remove all formatting from selected text. Reversing a font change does not work in the same way; if you want to restore a font you had previously used, you must select the text and use the Font button arrow to change the font back to the original type.

Using the Format Painter

The Format Painter button can save you time and provide consistency by allowing you to copy text that contains multiple formatting characteristics and then apply the same formatting to other parts of the document. When you click the Format Painter button, your mouse pointer changes to an I-beam with a paintbrush.

To copy formatting of a section of text, you first select the text or paragraph that contains the formatting you want to copy and then click the Format Painter button. The mouse pointer will change to an I-beam with a paintbrush "loaded" with the copied format. Next you can select the text to which you want to apply the formatting.

Double-clicking the Format Painter button allows you to "paint" the copied formatting to more than one selection. When you finish painting formats, click the Format Painter button or press the Esc key to turn off the Format Painter.

Step-by-Step WD 2.3

The Zare Resume *XXX*.docx document from Step-by-Step WD 2.2 should be open in the Word program window.

1. Select the word **Summary** in the document.
2. On the Home tab, in the Font group, click the **Bold** button **B**, the **Italic** button *I*, and the **Underline** button U to modify the selected text.

LESSON 2 Editing and Formatting Text   WD 37

3. With Summary still selected, click the **Clear Formatting** button to change the text back to the default style of Calibri, 11 point.

4. In the Font group, click the **Bold** button to apply bold formatting.

5. In the Font group, click the **Grow Font** button twice to increase the size to 14 point.

6. Make sure Summary is still selected. On the Home tab, in the Clipboard group, click the **Format Painter** button. The pointer changes to an I-beam with a paintbrush beside it.

7. Drag across **Education**, as shown in **Figure WD 2–9.** When the entire word is selected, release the mouse button to apply the new formatting.

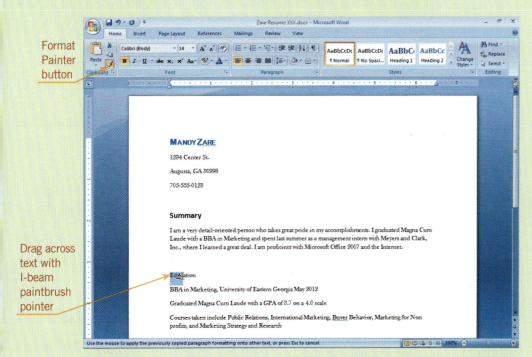

FIGURE WD 2–9
Format Painter

8. Make sure Education is still selected. In the Clipboard group, double-click the **Format Painter** button. The pointer changes to an I-beam with a paintbrush beside it.

9. Select **Experience** to apply the new formatting.

10. Select **Activities**. The new formatting is applied.

11. Click the **Format Painter** button again to turn it off.

12. Save and leave the document open for use in the next Step-by-Step.

Setting Tabs

Tabs are used to align or position text in a document. Word has default tab stops set at one-half-inch intervals from the left margin. If no other tabs are set, pressing the Tab key moves the insertion point to each default tab stop. However, you may need to set your own tab stops to align text at different locations. Word offers five types of tab stops, as described in **Table WD 2–1**.

TABLE WD 2–1 Tab stops

TAB	DESCRIPTION
L	The left tab aligns text flush left at the tab stop.
⌐	The right tab aligns text flush right at the tab stop.
⊥	The center tab centers text at the tab stop.
⊥.	The decimal tab aligns characters on the decimal point at the tab stop.
|	The bar tab displays a vertical line at the tab stop.

Setting Tabs Using the Ruler

The Tab Selector button, which is located below the Ribbon in the left portion of the horizontal ruler, is used to pick the type of tab you want to set. Clicking the Tab Selector changes the type of tab. When you click on the ruler, a tab stop is inserted. To remove a tab stop, drag it off the ruler. To move a tab stop, drag it to another location on the ruler. When setting tab stops in existing text, be sure to select the paragraph or paragraphs in which you want to set or change tab stops.

Setting Tabs Using the Tabs Dialog Box

The Tabs dialog box contains options for setting precise tabs, changing tab alignment, and choosing *leaders*, which are dotted, dashed, or solid lines used to fill the empty space before a tab stop. You access the Tabs dialog box through the Tabs button in the Paragraph dialog box or by double-clicking a tab on the ruler.

> **EXTRA FOR EXPERTS**
>
> You can clear all the tabs by clicking the **Clear All** button in the Tabs dialog box.

▶ **VOCABULARY**
leaders

Step-by-Step WD 2.4

The Zare Resume *XXX*.docx document from Step-by-Step WD 2.3 should be open in the Word program window.

1. Click the **View Ruler** button at the top of the vertical scroll bar, if necessary, to display the ruler.
2. Click to the left of *Mandy Zare*.
3. Press **Tab**. Notice that the text moves over to the default one-half inch tab stop.

Introducing *The new and revolutionary* Jacuzzi® Hydrotherapy Shower.

AGING = PAIN

For many, arthritis and spinal disc degeneration are the most common source of pain, along with hips, knees, shoulders and the neck. In designing the Jacuzzi Hydrotherapy Shower, we worked with expert physicians to maximize its pain relieving therapy by utilizing the correct level of water pressure to provide gentle yet effective hydrotherapy.

JACUZZI® SHOWER = RELIEF

Four Jacuzzi® ShowerPro™ Jets focus on the neck, back, hips, knees and may help ease the pain and discomfort of:

- Arthritis
- Circulation Issues
- Aches and pains
- Neuropathy
- Sciatica
- Inflammation

The Jacuzzi® Hydrotherapy Shower provides a lifetime of comfort and relief... safely and affordably.

As we age, the occasional aches and pains of everyday life become less and less occasional. Most of us are bothered by sore muscles, creaky joints and general fatigue as we go through the day- and it's made worse by everything from exertion and stress to arthritis and a number of other ailments. Sure, there are pills and creams that claim to provide comfort, but there is only one 100% natural way to feel better... hydrotherapy. Now, the world leader in hydrotherapy has invented the only shower that features Jacuzzi® Jets. It's called the Jacuzzi® Hydrotherapy Shower, and it can truly change your life.

For over 50 years, the Jacuzzi® Design Engineers have worked to bring the powerful benefits of soothing hydrotherapy into millions of homes. Now, they've created a system that can fit in the space of your existing bathtub or shower and give you a lifetime of enjoyment, comfort and pain-relief. They've thought of everything. From the high-gloss acrylic surface, slip-resistant flooring, a hand-held shower wand, a comfortable and adjustable seat, to strategically-placed grab bars and lots of storage, this shower has it all.

Why wait to experience the Jacuzzi® Hydrotherapy Shower? Call now... it's the first step in getting relief from those aches and pains.

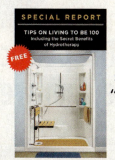

Call toll free now to get your FREE special report "Tips on Living to be 100"

Mention promotional code *101236*.

1-844-743-7519

© 2015 Aging In The Home Remodelers

What Are You Raking For?

Cyclone Rake — Make Fall Cleanup Easy

Learn More — REQUEST A FREE INFORMATION KIT

Call: **1-800-605-3644**
or Visit: **CycloneRake.com**

Use Promo Code **BB1015** when you call, or enter it on our website for a special offer on any Cyclone Rake purchased by 12/30/2015.

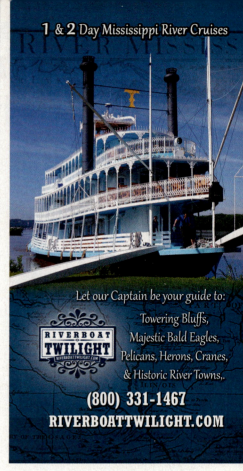

1 & 2 Day Mississippi River Cruises

Let our Captain be your guide to:
Towering Bluffs,
Majestic Bald Eagles,
Pelicans, Herons, Cranes,
& Historic River Towns.

RIVERBOAT TWILIGHT

(800) 331-1467
RIVERBOATTWILIGHT.COM

NEW

MADE IN USA

"I love these planters. They are perfect for every season and any plant. Everything looks better in nature."

"Surreal Planters are unbelievably realistic."

MANUFACTURER'S LIFETIME Warranty

"The perfect planters! They're beautiful, durable, lightweight and horticulturally superior!"

- Built from the molds of real logs with authentic bark texture!
- Individually hand painted with UV-resistant (fade-free) paint
- Made of high density, space-age polyurethane that's waterproof and tough
- Keep plants cool in hot temps, warm in cold temps and retain water better

See the entire line of Surreal Planters at
surrealplanters.com

Surreal — "So Real" Performance Planters

NATURE INNOVATIONS | 2800 BLACKSMITH LN | KERRVILLE, TX 78028

LESSON 2 Editing and Formatting Text

4. Press **Backspace**. The text returns to the left margin.
5. Notice that a Left Tab is displayed in the Tab selector. Click the ruler at approximately 4.25", as shown in **Figure WD 2–10**. A left tab is inserted.

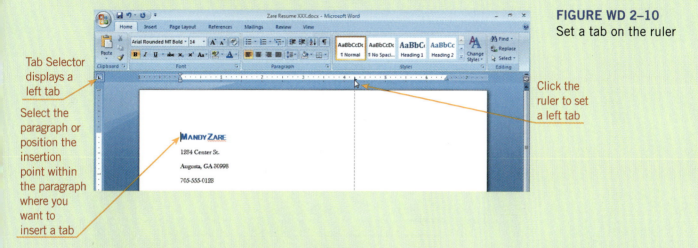

FIGURE WD 2–10
Set a tab on the ruler

Tab Selector displays a left tab

Select the paragraph or position the insertion point within the paragraph where you want to insert a tab

Click the ruler to set a left tab

6. Press **Tab**. The text moves to the tab stop.
7. In the Education section, select the line that begins *BBA in Marketing*.
8. Press and hold **Ctrl**, and select the first line in the Experience section, which begins *Internship with Meyers and Clark*.
9. On the Home tab, in the Paragraph group, click the **dialog box launcher** to open the Paragraph dialog box.
10. Click the **Tabs** button to open the Tabs dialog box.
11. Type **6.25** in the Tab stop position box. In the Alignment section, click the **Right** option button, and in the Leader section, click the **2** option button, as shown in **Figure WD 2–11**. Click the **OK** button to close the Tabs dialog box.

FIGURE WD 2–11
Tabs dialog box

12. In the first line of the Education section, click to the left of the date, *May 2012*, and press **Tab**. The date moves to the right tab stop and leaders are inserted.

13. In the Experience section, click to the left of the date, *Summer 2012*, and press **Tab**. The text moves to the right tab stop and leaders are inserted, as shown in **Figure WD 2–12**.

FIGURE WD 2–12
Setting tabs

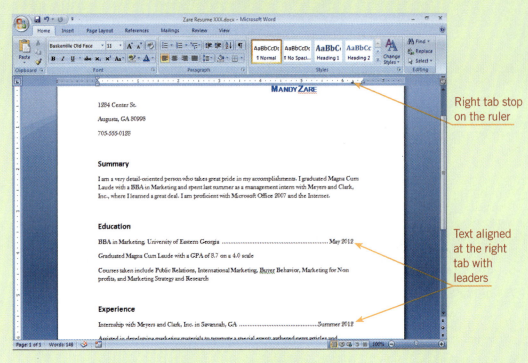

14. Save the document and leave it open for use in the next Step-by-Step.

Formatting Paragraphs

The alignment, spacing, and indentation of text in a document depend on the formatting you apply to paragraphs. Word refers to any amount of text or other items followed by a paragraph mark as a ***paragraph***.

To apply paragraph formatting, position your insertion point anywhere in a paragraph. Word will apply the paragraph formats you select to the entire paragraph. You cannot apply paragraph formatting to only a selection of the paragraph.

The Paragraph group on the Home tab, shown in **Figure WD 2–13**, contains buttons for changing paragraph formatting. You can access additional commands in the Paragraph dialog box, which you can display by clicking the dialog box launcher.

▶ **VOCABULARY**

paragraph

LESSON 2   Editing and Formatting Text

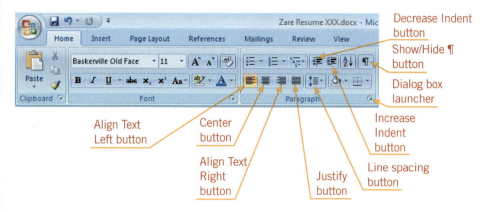

FIGURE WD 2-13   Paragraph group on the Home tab

Using Show/Hide ¶

It can be difficult to tell how many spaces, paragraph marks, tabs, and other nonprinting symbols exist within a document, especially if your document contains various font styles and sizes. These characters affect the appearance of your document, and it is often helpful to have the nonprinting symbols displayed when editing text. The Show/Hide ¶ button in the Paragraph group on the Home tab of the Ribbon displays or hides paragraph marks, spaces, tabs, and other nonprinting symbols. See **Figure WD 2–14**.

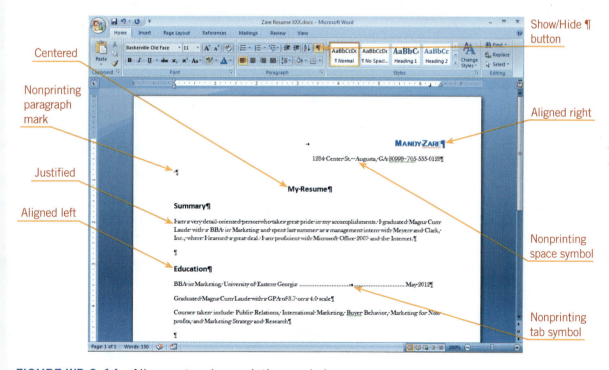

FIGURE WD 2-14   Alignment and nonprinting symbols

Aligning Text

You can left-align, center, right-align, or justify text in Word, as shown in **Figure WD 2–14**. The easiest way to align text is to use the alignment buttons in the Paragraph group on the Home tab. **Table WD 2–2** describes alignment options.

TABLE WD 2-2 Alignment options

OPTION	BUTTON	SHORTCUT KEYS	DESCRIPTION
Align Text Left		Ctrl+L	Lines up text flush with the left margin and leaves a ragged right edge.
Align Text Right		Ctrl+R	Lines up text at the right margin and leaves a ragged left edge.
Center		Ctrl+E	Centers the text between the margins.
Justify		Ctrl+J	Aligns text flush with the left margin and flush with the right margin.

Step-by-Step WD 2.5

The Zare Resume XXX.docx document from Step-by-Step WD 2.4 should be open in the Word program window.

1. On the Home tab, in the Paragraph group, click the **Show/Hide ¶** button ¶ to display the nonprinting symbols.
2. Select the paragraph mark after *Center St*.
3. Press **Delete** to delete the paragraph mark and move up the line below.
4. Press the **Spacebar** twice to add extra spaces.
5. Select the paragraph mark after the zip code *30998* and press **Delete**. The paragraph mark is deleted and the line below moves up.
6. Press the **Spacebar** twice to add extra spaces.
7. Select **Mandy Zare** and the address and telephone lines. On the Home tab, in the Paragraph group, click the **Align Text Right** button to align text at the right margin.
8. Click before the *Summary* heading. Type **My Resume** and press the **Enter** key.
9. Select **My Resume**. On the Home tab, in the Paragraph group, click the **Center** button to center the paragraph.
10. Select the paragraph under the Summary heading. In the Paragraph group, click the **Justify** button to justify the paragraph.
11. Select the paragraph under the Education heading that begins *Courses taken include* and click the **Justify** button to justify the paragraph.
12. Select the paragraph under the Experience heading that begins *Assisted in developing* and click the **Justify** button to justify the paragraph.

LESSON 2 Editing and Formatting Text   WD 43

13. On the Home tab, in the Paragraph group, click the **Show/Hide ¶** button to hide the nonprinting symbols.
14. Save the document and leave it open for use in the next Step-by-Step.

Setting Line Spacing

Line spacing determines the vertical distance between lines of text in a paragraph. The space allocated for single spacing is just a little taller than the point size used for the largest font size on the line. When you choose double spacing, the line is approximately twice the point size of the characters. If a line contains a large character, graphic, or formula, Word increases the spacing for that line.

The Line spacing button on the Home tab in the Paragraph group lets you choose a common line spacing option, such as 1.0 (single spacing) or 2.0 (double-spacing). You can also display the Paragraph dialog box, which contains options for creating custom line spacing.

You can add space before (above) or after (below) a paragraph without pressing the Enter key by entering measurements in the Before and After boxes in the Spacing section of the Paragraph dialog box or in the Paragraph group on the Page Layout tab of the Ribbon. If you choose the Remove Space Before Paragraph option on the Line spacing menu, all space will be removed. Likewise, the Remove Space After Paragraph command removes space following the paragraph. When the paragraphs do not have preceding or following line spaces, these commands change to Add Space Before Paragraph and Add Space After Paragraph. These commands add 12 pts of spacing before or after a paragraph.

> **EXTRA FOR EXPERTS**
>
> If you choose **At least**, **Exactly**, or **Multiple** in the Spacing section of the Paragraph dialog box, you enter a value for the line size and Word no longer adjusts for font sizes used on the line.

Step-by-Step WD 2.6

The Zare Resume *XXX*.docx document from Step-by-Step WD 2.5 should be open in the Word program window.

1. Select **Mandy Zare** and the address and telephone number below it.
2. On the Home tab, in the Paragraph group, click the **Line spacing** button  and click **2.0**. The line spacing is increased to 2.0 or double spacing. See **Figure WD 2–15**.

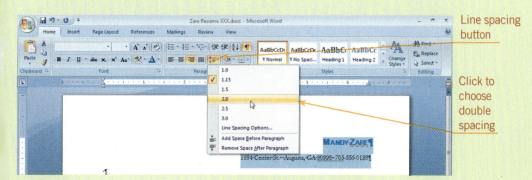

FIGURE WD 2–15
Line spacing button and menu

3. In the Paragraph group, click the **Line spacing** button and click **1.0**. The line spacing is decreased to 1.0, or single spacing.

4. In the Paragraph group, click the **Line spacing** button and click **Remove Space After Paragraph** to change the spacing.

5. In the Paragraph group, click the **Line spacing** button and click **Add Space Before Paragraph** to change the spacing.

6. Select **My Resume**.

7. On the Home tab, in the Paragraph group, click the **dialog box launcher** to open the Paragraph dialog box.

8. On the Indents and Spacing tab, in the Spacing area, click the **up arrow** on the Before menu three times or until it reads 18 pt, and then click the **Line spacing** menu button and click **Double**, as shown in **Figure WD 2–16**.

FIGURE WD 2–16
Paragraph dialog box

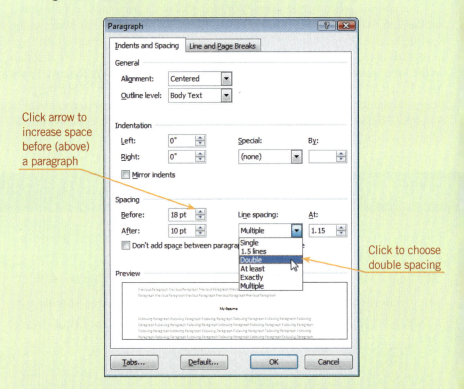

9. Click the **OK** button to accept the settings. Spacing is added above the paragraph and line spacing is changed to double.

10. Save and close the document.

LESSON 2 Editing and Formatting Text

Setting Indents

Indents are the spaces between text and the margin. You can indent text on the left, right, or on both sides. When you indent only the first line of a paragraph, it is called a *first line indent*. A *negative indent*, also called an outdent, extends into the left margin. A *hanging indent* occurs when you indent all the lines from the left except the first one.

Figure WD 2–17 shows several ways you can use indentation to set paragraphs off from other text in your documents.

> **VOCABULARY**
> indents
> first line indent
> negative indent
> hanging indent

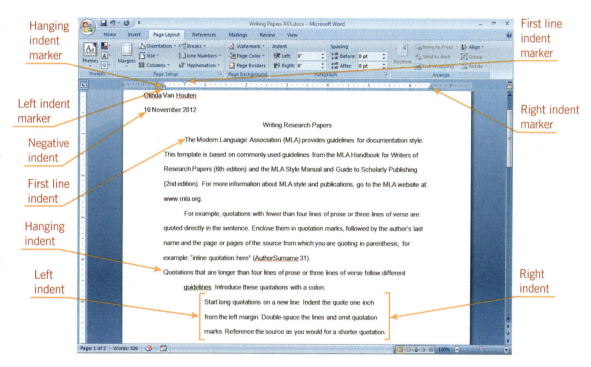

FIGURE WD 2–17 Indents

Do not use the Tab key or the Spacebar to create indents. Also, do not attempt to control indentation by pressing the Enter key at the end of each line. These methods make editing a Word document or converting a document to another file format very difficult. Instead, set precise measurements for paragraph indents in the Paragraph dialog box, as shown in **Figure WD 2–18**.

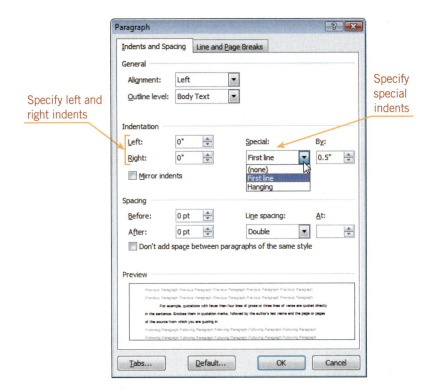

FIGURE WD 2–18 Paragraph dialog box

You can also specify left and right indents in the Paragraph group on the Page Layout tab of the Ribbon. In addition, you can control paragraph indents by dragging the indent markers on the horizontal ruler. The ruler contains three left indent markers and one right indent marker. The First Line indent marker controls the indentation of the first line of a paragraph. The Hanging indent marker indents all lines except the first one.

The Left indent marker box beneath the Hanging indent marker indents the entire paragraph from the left. The Right indent marker indents a selected paragraph from the right. To use these markers, make sure the insertion point is in the paragraph you want to indent and then simply drag the appropriate marker to the desired position on the ruler.

Use the Increase Indent and Decrease Indent buttons in the Paragraph group to set and remove indents quickly. Each time you use one of these buttons, you increase or decrease the indent by one-half inch.

Step-by-Step WD 2.7

1. Open **Step WD 2-7.docx** from the folder containing the data files for this lesson. Save the document as **Writing Papers XXX.docx** (replace *XXX* with your initials).

2. Select the name and date on the first two lines of the document.

3. Click and drag the **Left Indent marker** one-half inch to the left to create a negative indent, as shown in **Figure WD 2–19**.

LESSON 2 Editing and Formatting Text

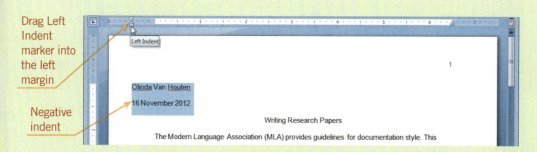

FIGURE WD 2–19
Negative Indent

Drag Left Indent marker into the left margin

Negative indent

4. Click in the paragraph that begins *The Modern Language*. Click and drag the **First Line Indent** marker to the right one-half inch, as shown in **Figure WD 2–20**.

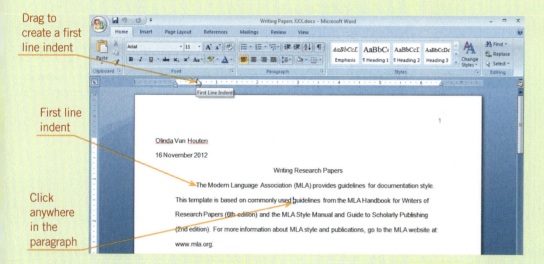

FIGURE WD 2–20
First line indent

Drag to create a first line indent

First line indent

Click anywhere in the paragraph

5. Triple-click the first paragraph to select it.
6. On the Home tab, in the Clipboard group, click the **Format Painter** button.
7. Drag across the second and third paragraphs with the paintbrush pointer to apply the same formatting.
8. Click the fourth paragraph, which begins with *Start long quotations*. Click the **Increase Indent** button to indent the paragraph one-half inch.
9. On the Page Layout tab, in the Paragraph group, click the **Indent Right** up arrow five times, or until the text box reads 0.5", as shown in **Figure WD 2–21**. The paragraph is indented one-half inch from the right margin.

Indent Left

Indent Right

Click to increase the right indent

FIGURE WD 2–21
Left and right indents

10. Scroll to the second page of the document and select the five lines below the *Works Cited* title.
11. On the Page Layout tab, in the Paragraph group, click the **dialog box launcher** to open the Paragraph dialog box.
12. In the Indentation area, click the **Special** menu arrow and then click **Hanging**. The 0.5" measurement automatically appears in the By box.
13. Click the **OK** button to close the Paragraph dialog box. Now the five lines are formatted for hanging indents if they wrap to another line.
14. Save and close the document.

Editing Text: Deleting, Moving, and Copying

During the writing process, you will often find that you need to remove, rearrange, and revise text. The Cut, Paste, and Copy commands in the Clipboard group on the Home tab of the Ribbon, shown in **Figure WD 2-22**, can help.

FIGURE WD 2–22 Clipboard group

VOCABULARY
Clipboard
cut
paste
copy

Deleting Text

Deleting text is just about as common as typing text, and the easiest way to delete text you just typed is to use the Backspace and Delete keys on the keyboard. The Backspace key removes characters to the left of the insertion point, whereas the Delete key removes characters to the right of the insertion point. You can also delete selected text by pressing either the Delete or Backspace keys.

Cutting, Copying, and Pasting Text

The Clipboard is a convenient way to move or copy text not only within a document but also to other Word documents, Office files, and other files such as PDF documents and e-mail messages. The **Clipboard** is an area of memory that temporarily stores a cut or copied selection. The cut or copied selection remains in the Clipboard until you cut or copy another selection from Word or another program or until you shut down the computer.

To move a selection, you *cut* or remove the selection from one position and *paste* the selection into another position. When you *copy* a selection, you duplicate the selection so you can paste the selection into another position without deleting it from its original location.

EXTRA FOR EXPERTS

When you display the Office Clipboard task pane using the dialog box launcher in the Clipboard group, you can collect up to 24 items and then paste the items one at a time or all at once. You can also switch back and forth between Office programs; for example, you could copy an item in Word, copy another in Excel, and then open PowerPoint and paste them both. The items in the Clipboard remain there until you quit all Office programs.

LESSON 2 Editing and Formatting Text

WD 49

You can use the Cut, Copy, and Paste buttons in the Clipboard group or use the commands on the shortcut menu to move or copy data from one location to another. Use the Paste Special command on the Paste button menu to paste links or embed Clipboard contents in the format you specify. The Paste Hyperlink command on the Paste menu is used to insert the contents of the Clipboard as a hyperlink and is only available if the cut or copied selection is from a program that supports linking.

Using Drag-and-Drop Editing

You can use the ***drag-and-drop*** feature to move or copy a selection to a new location on your screen. To move text, you select and drag text with the mouse and then release the mouse button to "drop" the text in its new location.

To copy text, you select, drag, and drop text while holding the Ctrl key. When you copy a selection, you will see a plus sign (+) with the pointer. When you move or copy a selection using the drag-and-drop method, the selection is not stored in the Clipboard.

> **VOCABULARY**
> drag-and-drop

Step-by-Step WD 2.8

1. Open **Step WD 2-8.docx** from the folder containing the data files for this lesson. Save the document as **Zare Resume Edit *XXX*.docx** (replace *XXX* with your initials).

2. In the Summary section, click after the *y* in *very*.

3. Press **Backspace** until the word is deleted and there is one blank space between words.

4. In the last paragraph of the Education section, select **Public Relations** (include the comma and the blank space in the selection).

5. On the Home tab, in the Clipboard group, click the **Cut** button. The words are removed from the screen, leaving the insertion point at the beginning of the word *International*.

6. Click before the letter *a* in *and Marketing Strategy* at the end of the line and then click the **Paste** button to insert the text you cut in Step 5.

7. In the Education section, click before the *G* in *Graduated* and press **Delete** until the word *Graduated* and the space after it is deleted, as shown in **Figure WD 2–23**.

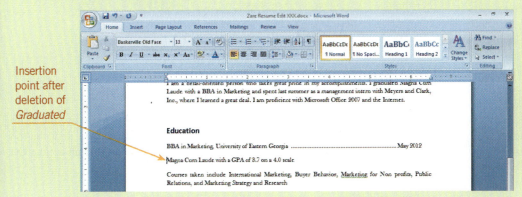

FIGURE WD 2–23
Zare Resume Edit

Insertion point after deletion of *Graduated*

8. In the Education section, select the words **Strategy and Research** on the last line and click the **Copy** button.

9. Click after the *s* in *Public Relations* (before the comma) and then click the **Paste** button to paste a copy of the words in a new location.

10. In the last line of the Experience section, select the word **Microsoft** and drag the dotted line insertion point to precede the word *Word*, as shown in **Figure WD 2–24**, and release the mouse button to "drop" the word in its new location. Adjust spacing between words if necessary.

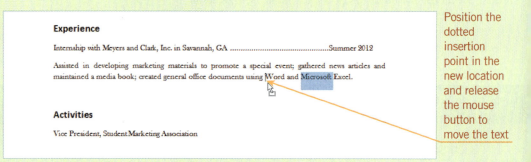

FIGURE WD 2–24 Drag-and-drop editing

Position the dotted insertion point in the new location and release the mouse button to move the text

11. Save the document and leave it open for use in the next Step-by-Step.

Using Undo, Redo, and Repeat

Sometimes you will need to reverse, or undo, your most recent action. The Undo button on the Quick Access Toolbar, shown in **Figure WD 2–25**, undoes the last action; clicking the Undo button a second time undoes the prior action, and so on. If you click the Undo button arrow, you see a list of actions you can undo. Not all actions can be undone. The Undo ScreenTip changes to reflect the last action that can be undone. For example, if you just pasted text, the screen tip would say Undo Paste, because Paste was the last action you performed, and you can undo it with one click of the Undo button. Some actions cannot be undone; if you cannot undo an action, such as saving a file, the command changes to Can't Undo.

> **WARNING**
>
> Get into the habit of undoing (reversing) a mistake immediately after you make it, because the Undo menu can be confusing to use. For example, if you undo the third item on the menu, the first two items are undone as well. You might not remember what those actions were, or you might not notice the effect within your document when the actions are undone.

Quick Access Toolbar
Undo button
Repeat button

FIGURE WD 2–25 Quick Access Toolbar

If you perform an undo action but then decide against the undo, use the Redo button on the Quick Access toolbar to reverse an Undo action. The Redo button arrow displays a list of actions you can redo. When you cannot redo an action, the button is dimmed.

LESSON 2 Editing and Formatting Text   WD 51

The Repeat command on the Quick Access toolbar repeats your last action. If you cannot repeat the action, the command changes to Can't Repeat. If your last action was an undo, the Repeat command changes to Redo.

Step-by-Step WD 2.9

The Zare Resume Edit *XXX*.docx document from Step-by-Step WD 2.8 should be open in the Word program window.

1. In the Education section, select **Buyer Behavior**.
2. On the Home tab, in the Clipboard group, click the **Cut** button. The selected words are removed from the screen.
3. Click the **Undo** button arrow on the Quick Access Toolbar. Click **Cut** at the top of the list, as shown in **Figure WD 2–26**. (Your list might look different.) The words *Buyer Behavior* reappear in their previous location.

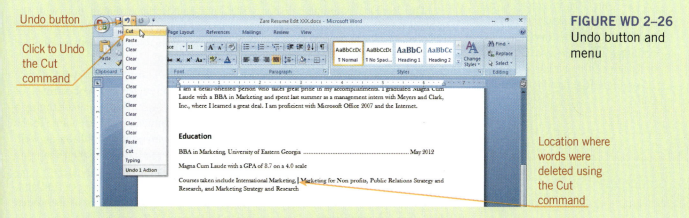

FIGURE WD 2–26
Undo button and menu

4. Click the **Redo** button on the Quick Access Toolbar to remove the words from the document.
5. Click the **Undo** button on the Quick Access Toolbar to return the words to the document.
6. Click after *Public Relations Strategy and Research* (before the comma), press the **Spacebar**, and then type **Topics**.
7. Click the **Repeat** button. The inserted text is repeated.
8. Click the **Undo** button. The repeated word is removed from the screen.
9. Save and close the document.

Finding and Replacing Text

The Find and Replace commands are two separate commands that are often used together to find and replace text, formats, and other items. The Find and Replace commands are located in the Editing group on the Home tab, as shown in **Figure WD 2–27**.

FIGURE WD 2–27 Editing group on the Home tab

>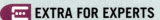
> **EXTRA FOR EXPERTS**
>
> You can search for all occurrences of a word and highlight them on the screen using the Reading Highlight button. Choose Highlight All to turn on the feature and choose Clear Highlighting to turn it off.

You can use the Find command alone to search for a specific word or phrase in a document. In the Find tab of the Find and Replace dialog box, you can type a word or phrase in the Find what box and click Find Next to search for each occurrence.

The Replace command displays the Find and Replace dialog box with the Replace tab active. Type the text you want to find in the Find what box and the text you want to replace it with in the Replace with box. Use the Find Next and Replace buttons to make just one replacement at a time.

You can use the Replace All button to replace all occurrences of a word at once without confirming each one. But be sure you want to replace every occurrence of the word. For instance, you can run into trouble using Replace All when changing a person's name, such as Jackson to Johnson. If a company name or city name in the document contains the name Jackson, Replace All changes it to Johnson as well. Since Word also replaces partial words, you can also run into trouble when changing the word *and* to *or* because it would change the word *sand* to *sor*.

Use the More button to display the expanded dialog box to refine your find-and-replace operations by matching case, finding only specific formats, and using special characters. You can limit the Replace search by selecting all or part of a document, or by selecting Up or Down in the Search menu.

Step-by-Step WD 2.10

1. Open **Step WD 2-10.docx** from the folder containing the data files for this lesson and save it as **Research Letter XXX.docx** (replace *XXX* with your initials).

2. On the Home tab, in the Editing group, click the **Find** button.

3. Type **Trey Research Company** in the Find what box and click **Find Next**. The first occurrence of *Trey Research Company* is selected in the document.

4. Click the **Replace** tab on the Find and Replace dialog box. Type **Trey-Davis Research Corporation** in the Replace with box, as shown in **Figure WD 2–28**.

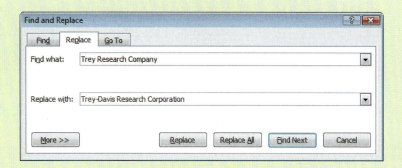

FIGURE WD 2–28
Find and Replace dialog box

5. Click the **Replace All** button to replace all occurrences of *Trey Research Company*.
6. A message box is displayed telling you that three replacements were made. Click the **OK** button to close the message box. Leave the Find and Replace dialog box open.
7. Click a blank area on the letter to remove the selection. Press **Ctrl+Home** to position the insertion point at the beginning of the document with nothing selected.
8. Type **Jackson** in the Find what box and press **Tab** to move to the Replace with box. Type **Johnson** and click the **Find Next** button. Notice that clicking the Find Next button only selects the name Jackson; it does not perform a replacement operation yet, even though you have entered a replacement term in the Replace with box.
9. The first occurrence of Rudra Jackson's last name is highlighted. Click the **Replace** button to replace it with Johnson.
10. The name of Rudra Jackson's company is highlighted. Click the **Find Next** button to leave the company name unchanged.
11. The second occurrence of Rudra Jackson's last name is highlighted. Click the **Replace** button to change the name.
12. Click the **Find Next** button to skip the company name and then click the **Find Next** button again to skip Jackson Hole.
13. Click the **OK** button to close the dialog box telling you the search is finished. Click the **Close** button to close the Find and Replace dialog box.
14. Save the document and leave it open for use in the next Step-by-Step.

Proofing a Document

One of the last steps in creating a document is refining the text and checking for mistakes. The Proofing group on the Review tab of the Ribbon, shown in **Figure WD 2–29**, contains commands to help you look up words in a dictionary or thesaurus, check spelling and grammar, and count the words in the document.

FIGURE WD 2–29 Proofing group on the Review tab

Checking Spelling and Grammar

Word automatically checks spelling and grammar as you type by comparing a document's language to Word's built-in dictionary and grammar rules. Word flags words that might be misspelled with a wavy red underline. If Word detects a grammatical construction that does not conform to rules of grammar, it adds a wavy green underline to the language in question. You can right-click a word that has a red or green wavy line and see a shortcut menu with suggestions for corrections. If you don't want to use one of the suggested corrections, you can change the text manually.

You can also check all spelling and grammar in a document with a single action using the Spelling & Grammar button in the Proofing group on the Review tab. This approach is useful when you have finished editing a document, but you want to check it one more time to make sure you didn't miss any mistakes or introduce errors while editing. When a possible error is detected, Word displays the Spelling and Grammar dialog box to show you the error and suggest a correction. Use the Change button in the Spelling and Grammar dialog box to correct an error, or use the Change All button to correct all instances of the same error.

When you use the Spelling & Grammar button, Word checks the entire document from the insertion point forward and then works from the beginning of the document to the insertion point. To check only a portion of a document, select the area before starting the check.

The spell checker will flag many proper nouns and other words as being incorrect. Ignore the word or phrase, or ignore all occurrences of the word or phrase, using the Ignore Once or Ignore All buttons as you spell check documents.

Remember, the Spelling and Grammar feature does not eliminate the need to proofread a document. If a word you misspelled is another English word (for example, you typed *there* instead of *their*), the spelling feature will not detect the error. Likewise, the grammar feature is not foolproof. Although it finds many common errors, the Spelling and Grammar feature does not always understand the context of the text and may suggest inappropriate corrections. Be sure to look at suggestions carefully before you decide to accept them.

> **EXTRA FOR EXPERTS**
>
> Word defaults to checking documents in the English language, but you can use the editing and proofing tools to check text in other languages, which you might want to do if you are writing a paper for a foreign language class. Use the Set Language command in the Proofing group on the Review tab to choose a language.

> **EXTRA FOR EXPERTS**
>
> Word's main dictionary contains most common words, including country names, names of many U.S. cities, some company names, and many proper names. However, you probably use words that are not in Word's main dictionary. You can add those words to a custom dictionary so Word does not flag them each time you type them.

Step-by-Step WD 2.11

The Research Letter *XXX*.docx document from Step-by-Step WD 2.10 should be open in the Word program window.

1. If necessary, click at the beginning of the document.

2. On the Review tab, in the Proofing group, click the **Spelling & Grammar** button to open the Spelling and Grammar dialog box.

3. Click the **Ignore Once** button to ignore the suggestions for changing the name, as shown in **Figure WD 2–30**.

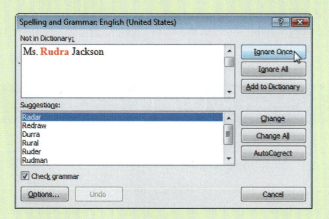

FIGURE WD 2–30
Spelling and Grammar dialog box

4. Click the **Delete** button to remove the second occurrence of *for*.
5. Click the **Change** button to accept the suggestion to capitalize the *t* in *This*.
6. Click in the Fragment box, delete the period after *company*, and click the **Change** button, as shown in **Figure WD 2–31**, to remove the period and combine two incomplete sentences into one.

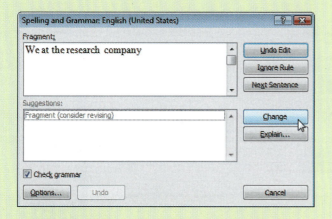

FIGURE WD 2–31
Spelling and Grammar dialog box

7. Click the **Change** button to accept the correct spelling of *vendors*.
8. Click **center** in the Suggestions list and click **Change** to accept the correct spelling.
9. To respond to the prompt that the spelling and grammar check is complete, click the **OK** button.
10. Save the document and leave it open for use in the next Step-by-Step.

Looking up a Word in the Dictionary

If you need to look up the definition of a word, you can do so using the Research command in the Proofing group on the Review tab. The Reference Books list contains a list of references that are searchable with Word's Research tool. Another way to look up a word's definition is to right-click a word and choose Look Up from the shortcut menu.

Step-by-Step WD 2.12

The Research Letter *XXX*.docx document from Step-by-Step WD 2.11 should be open in the Word program window.

1. In the first paragraph, second sentence, right-click the word **provider** and click **Look Up** on the shortcut menu. The Research pane opens displaying results, as shown in **Figure WD 2–32**.

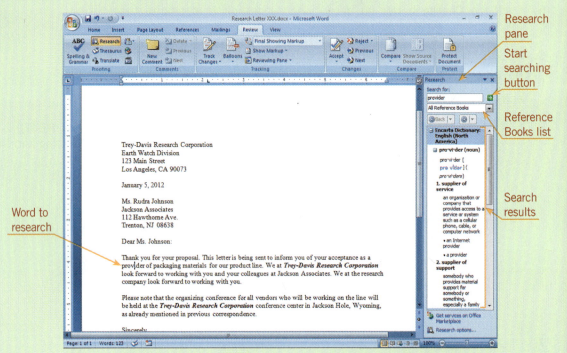

FIGURE WD 2–32
Research pane

2. Save the document and leave it open for use in the next Step-by-Step.

Using the Thesaurus

Make your documents even more interesting and effective using the Thesaurus to replace a word or phrase with a synonym, an antonym, or a related word. The Thesaurus button in the Proofing group opens the Research task pane with a list of suggested replacement terms. View more results by selecting a new reference book or search site.

Step-by-Step WD 2.13

The Research Letter *XXX*.docx document from Step-by-Step WD 2.12 should be open in the Word program window.

1. In the first paragraph, second sentence, right-click the word **inform** to open the shortcut menu.
2. Point to **Synonyms** on the shortcut menu and then click **notify** on the submenu to replace *inform* with *notify*, as shown in **Figure WD 2–33**.

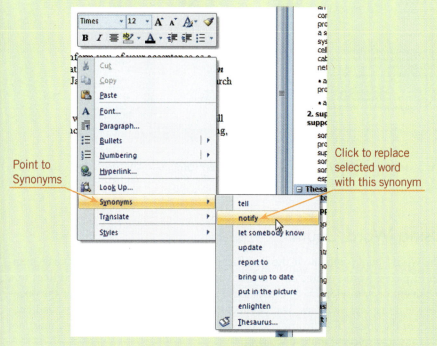

FIGURE WD 2–33
Shortcut menu

3. In the second paragraph, first sentence, press and hold **ALT** while clicking **conference**. The word *conference* is looked up in the Research pane.
4. Scroll to the bottom of the Research pane and click the **plus sign** next to Thesaurus to display the list of synonyms for *conference*.
5. Click the arrow to the right of *meeting* to open a shortcut menu, and then click the **Insert** command from the menu, as shown in **Figure WD 2–34**. The word *meeting* replaces the word *conference* in the document.

FIGURE WD 2–34
Thesaurus

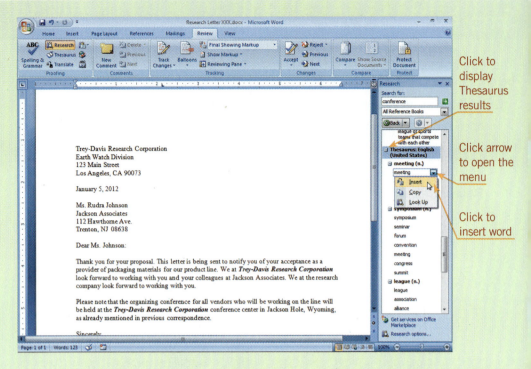

6. Save the document and leave it open for use in the next Step-by-Step.

Using Word Count

The Word Count command in the Proofing group on the Review tab counts the number of pages, words, characters (with or without spaces), paragraphs, and lines in a document or in a selection. When you use this command, Word analyzes the document and displays statistics. You can include text in textboxes, footnotes, and endnotes in the count. To perform a word count for the entire document, you must not have any text selected in the document.

Step-by-Step WD 2.14

The Research Letter *XXX*.docx document from Step-by-Step WD 2.13 should be open in the Word program window.

1. Be sure nothing is selected in the document. On the Review tab, in the Proofing group, click the **Word Count** button. The Word Count dialog box opens with the results, as shown in **Figure WD 2–35**.

LESSON 2   Editing and Formatting Text

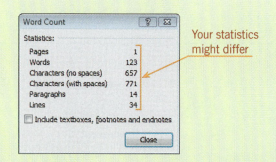

FIGURE WD 2–35
Word Count dialog box

2. Click the **Close** button to close the dialog box.
3. Save and close the document.
4. Close Word.

TECHNOLOGY CAREERS

With the rapid expansion of computer technology, there comes an increased demand for people who can write clear and concise hardware and software documentation. Technical writers are specially trained for this purpose. The information they communicate must be accurate and understandable. In the computer industry, technical writers may use Microsoft Word to write software instructions, reference manuals, or installation guides.

SUMMARY

In this lesson, you learned:

- That you create a new document using the New Document dialog box.
- Formatting text changes fonts, font sizes, font styles, and font effects.
- Clearing formatting removes all new formats.
- The Format Painter copies formatting characteristics and applies it to selected text.
- How to set tabs using the ruler and the Tabs dialog box.

- How to format paragraphs by aligning text and setting line spacing and indents.
- How to move, delete, cut, copy, and paste text and use drag-and-drop editing.
- That editing tasks typically involve undo, redo, and repeat commands.
- How to use Find and Replace to find and replace text, formats, and other items.
- That documents are corrected and improved using the Spelling & Grammar checker, looking up words in the Dictionary, finding synonyms with the Thesaurus, and using Word Count.

VOCABULARY REVIEW

Define the following terms:

characters	first line indent	negative indent
Clipboard	font	paragraph
copy	hanging indent	paste
cut	indents	point size
drag-and-drop	leaders	

REVIEW QUESTIONS

MULTIPLE CHOICE

Select the best response for the following statements.

1. _____ measures the height of characters.
   - A. Point size
   - B. Font
   - C. Toggle case
   - D. Drag-and-drop

2. You can use the _____ button to change the capitalization of text quickly.
   - A. Underline
   - B. Bold
   - C. Change Case
   - D. Grow Font

3. The mouse pointer looks like a(n) _____ when you use the Format Painter.
   - A. arrow pointer
   - B. insertion point
   - C. rectangle
   - D. I-beam with a paintbrush

4. The _____ button duplicates a selection so you can paste it into another position.
   - A. Format Painter
   - B. Paste
   - C. Cut
   - D. Copy

5. _____ can be added in the Tabs dialog box.
   - A. Indents
   - B. Leaders
   - C. Line Spacing
   - D. Justification

6. _____ is the alignment option that aligns text flush with the left and right margins.
   - A. Align Text Left
   - B. Align Text Right
   - C. Justify
   - D. Center

7. A _____ indent occurs when you indent all the lines from the left except the first one.
   - A. negative
   - B. first line
   - C. right
   - D. hanging

8. Use the _____ button when you want to reverse an Undo action.
   - A. Redo
   - B. Undo
   - C. Repeat
   - D. Change Case

9. The _____ button replaces all occurrences of a selection at once without confirming each one.
   - A. Format Painter
   - B. Replace All
   - C. Replace
   - D. Find

LESSON 2 Editing and Formatting Text

10. The _____ command analyzes a document and displays statistics on the number of pages, words, characters, paragraphs, and lines in a document.
    A. Thesaurus
    B. Research
    C. Spelling & Grammar
    D. Word Count

FILL IN THE BLANK

Complete the following sentences by writing the correct word or words in the blanks provided.

1. _____ are letters, numbers, symbols, punctuation marks, and spaces.
2. A(n) _____ is the design of a set of letters and numbers.
3. When you use the Cut or the Copy button, a copy of the cut or copied text is placed in the _____.
4. Use the _____ button to display nonprinting marks when editing.
5. Any amount of text followed by a paragraph mark is considered to be a(n) _____.
6. _____ are the spaces between the text and the margin.
7. When you delete something by mistake, immediately click the _____ button.
8. An easy way to find every occurrence of a word in a document is to use the _____ command.
9. Word automatically checks _____ and _____ as you type.
10. You can use the _____ to replace a word with a synonym, an antonym, or a related word.

■ PROJECTS

PROJECT WD 2-1

1. Open the file **Project WD 2-1.docx** from the folder containing your data files and save it as **Spelling&Grammar *XXX*.docx** (replace *XXX* with your initials).
2. Run the Spelling and Grammar checker to correct the mistakes.
3. Save and close the document.

ON YOUR OWN

The Spelling & Grammar checker missed at least one mistake. Can you find it? Open the **Spelling&Grammar *XXX*.docx** file, correct the error, then save and close the document.

PROJECT WD 2-2

1. Open the file **Project WD 2-2.docx** from the folder containing your data files and save it as **ABC Computers *XXX*.docx** (replace *XXX* with your initials).
2. Change all the text to Calibri 12 point.
3. Center *ABC Computers* and its address.
4. Apply bold to ABC Computers and its address and change the point size to 14.
5. Change the font color of *ABC Computers* to Orange.
6. Create half-inch first-line indents on the three paragraphs that make up the body of the letter.
7. In the first paragraph, look up a synonym for the word *operation* and insert it.
8. Save and close the document.

ON YOUR OWN

Open the **ABC Computers *XXX*.docx** file and change the letterhead for *ABC Computers* by applying different fonts, sizes, styles, effects, alignment, and/or spacing. Save and close the document.

PROJECT WD 2-3

1. Open **Project WD 2-3.docx** from the folder containing your data files and save it as **Appointment Policy XXX.docx** (replace the *XXX* with your initials).
2. Right-align the heading *Yasinski Family Practice*. Change the line spacing to double with 18 point spacing before the paragraph and 10 point after the paragraph.
3. Left-align the date, *September 2012*.
4. Center the *Appointment Policy* title.
5. Justify the paragraph that begins *To remain on schedule*. Change the line spacing of the paragraph to 2.0, and remove the space after the paragraph.
6. Select the four-line address and telephone number. Insert a left tab at tab stop position 3.8" and move the text to the tab stop.
7. Save and close the document.

ON YOUR OWN

Open the **Appointment Policy XXX.docx** file and use the Thesaurus to replace two words with synonyms. Save and close the document.

PROJECT WD 2-4

1. Open the file **Project WD 2-4.docx** from the folder containing your data files and save it as **Travel Destinations XXX.docx** (replace *XXX* with your initials).
2. Show nonprinting symbols.
3. Select the list of cities and center it.
4. Select *Austria* (be sure to select the paragraph mark, too) and move it above Turkey.
5. Select *United Kingdom* and move it above *China*.
6. Select *Italy* and move it above *United States*.
7. Delete *Mexico*.
8. Undo the deletion.
9. Change the line spacing of the list to 1.5, and remove the space after the paragraphs.
10. Hide nonprinting symbols.
11. Save and close the document.

PROJECT WD 2-5

1. Open the file **Project WD 2-5.docx** from the folder containing your data files and save it as **Computers XXX.docx** (replace the *XXX* with your initials).
2. Center the title, change it to 18 point, and change the case to uppercase.
3. Select the heading *Prepare for Power Surges*, and change the format to bold, 14 point Arial.
4. With the heading still selected, add 12 point spacing before the paragraph and 6 pt after the paragraph.
5. Use the Format Painter to apply the format to the remaining six headings.
6. Justify, double-space, and add a one half-inch first-line indent to all the paragraphs of text (not the headings or the title).
7. Use Word Count.
8. Use Find and Replace to find the word *Computer* and replace all occurrences with **PC**.
9. Save and close the document.

ON YOUR OWN

Open the **Computers XXX.docx** file. Use the More options in the Find and Replace dialog box to find all occurrences of PC that have bold formatting and replace them with the word **Computer** with bold formatting. Save and close the document.

WEB PROJECT

PROJECT WD 2-6

Search the Web for a digital camera (or other item) to purchase. Decide on the particular camera you would like to purchase; then comparison shop at two other sites. Copy relevant data from the Web sites such as price, shipping costs, availability, and service, and paste it into a new blank document. Create a neatly organized report that compares the data from each site. Decide which site you would purchase from and why. Name and save the document. Be prepared to share your information and decision with the class.

LESSON 2 Editing and Formatting Text

◼ CRITICAL THINKING

ACTIVITY WD 2-1

Open the Zare Resume document and save it with a new name. Use this document to create your own resume, applying what you've learned about editing and formatting text. Be creative, and be prepared to share your resume with the class, noting the changes or additions you made to the original document.

ACTIVITY WD 2-2

Play "Stump the Spelling & Grammar Checker" by writing one or two sentences containing at least three mistakes that Word's spelling and grammar checker cannot detect. Compare sentences with classmates. Are you surprised at the results? Explore the settings available for adding functionality to the Spelling & Grammar checker. Is there a setting that you can change that will allow Word to detect one or more of the mistakes in your sentences? If so, is this an option you should turn on? Why or why not?

ACTIVITY WD 2-3

What are wildcards? Use Word Help to find out what they are and how to use them when searching Word documents. Be prepared to give two examples of how to use wildcards to find certain words in a document.

Estimated Time: 2 hours

LESSON 3

Formatting Documents

■ OBJECTIVES

Upon completion of this lesson, you should be able to:

- Use templates to create new documents.
- Change document themes.
- Apply Quick Styles.
- Work with lists.
- Add page backgrounds.
- Create columns.
- Use built-in headers or footers.
- Insert and break pages.

■ DATA FILES

To complete this lesson, you will need these data files:

Step WD 3-3.docx
Project WD 3-2.docx
Project WD 3-3.docx
Project WD 3-4.docx

■ VOCABULARY

borders
bullets
columns
cover page
footer
header
list
orphan
page break
sort
style
template
themes
watermark
widow
...

UNIT II   Microsoft Word

Introduction

You learned in the previous lesson that formatting text makes it more attractive and easier to read. Formatting an entire document has the same result. Adding formatting elements such as styles, themes, columns, headers, footers, and page numbers enhances the appearance of a document and helps guide the reader through the document.

Creating New Documents Using Templates

One method of quickly and attractively formatting documents is to use templates. A *template* is a master copy, or model, for a certain type of document. Word includes templates for many common types of documents, including memos, letters, fax cover sheets, and reports.

Templates contain settings for margins, page size and orientation, and text and/or graphics that are standard for a particular type of document. For instance, instead of having to create a layout each time you want to type a memo, you can use one of the memo templates included in Word.

As you learned in the previous lesson, when you create a new blank document using the Blank document button in the New Document dialog box, the blank document that opens is actually a copy of the Normal template that happens to appear blank. This Normal template contains settings for margins, page size and orientation, and text styles and serves as a starting point for creating a new document. It is possible to change the settings in the Normal document template, named Normal.dotm, but any changes made to the template are applied to all future blank documents.

Word has templates for creating various kinds of documents, such as brochures, flyers, and greeting cards. Some templates come already installed with Word, and you can access them by clicking the Installed Templates category in the Templates section of the New Document dialog box, shown in **Figure WD 3–1**. Many more templates are available online, which you can access by clicking a category in the Microsoft Office Online section of the New Document dialog box. You can also use the Search box to look for a template by keywords. When you have selected the template you want, you can click the Create button (if it is an installed template) or the Download button (if it is an online template) to open the template.

> **VOCABULARY**
> **template**

> **EXTRA FOR EXPERTS**
>
> You can bypass the New Document dialog box and open a new blank document using the New command on the Quick Access Toolbar. If the New command is not visible on your Quick Access Toolbar, you can add it by clicking the Customize Quick Access Toolbar button and clicking New on the menu.

> **WARNING**
>
> To use a template from Microsoft Office Online, you must download it. The first time you download a template, Microsoft will verify that the software you are using is authentic. You cannot download templates without genuine Microsoft Office software.

LESSON 3 Formatting Documents

WD 67

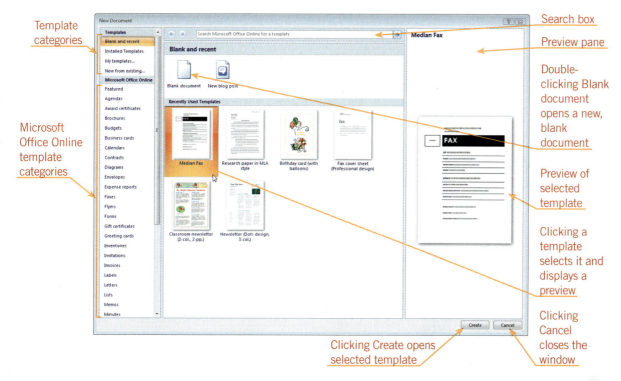

FIGURE WD 3-1 New Document dialog box

To display the New Document dialog box, use the New command on the Office Button menu. When you open a template from the New Document dialog box, you are actually opening a copy of the template, so the original template is not altered. Add your own text in a template by clicking the placeholder text, such as *[Type your text here]*, which tells you where to insert your text, and then begin to type. Name and save a new document using the Save or Save As command.

> **EXTRA FOR EXPERTS**
>
> Word templates are saved as the Word Template type with the extension .dotx. If you want to save a document as a template, click the Office button on the Ribbon, point to Save As, and click Word Template from the submenu.

Step-by-Step WD 3.1

1. Start Word.

2. Click the **Office Button** and then click **New**. The New Document dialog box opens.

3. Click **Installed Templates** to display the installed templates in the center pane.

4. In the Installed Templates section, scroll down and click **Oriel Letter**. Notice the preview in the right pane.

5. Confirm that the Oriel Letter button is selected, then click the **Create** button. The template opens on your screen.

6. Click the **[Pick the date]** placeholder and click the down arrow that is displayed. Click the **Today** button on the calendar, as shown in **Figure WD 3-2**.

FIGURE WD 3-2
Class Confirmation *XXX*.docx document

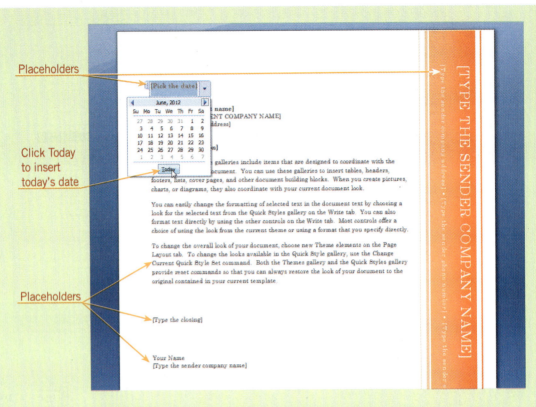

7. Click the [**Type the recipient name**] placeholder and type **Ridge Nixon** to overwrite the placeholder.

8. Click the placeholders in the document (some might require double-clicking to select all the text in the placeholder) and type the text below:

   [Type the recipient company name]: **Nixon Sullivan**

   [Type the recipient address]: **54321 Sun Cliff Drive**

   Colorado Springs, CO 80956

   [Type the salutation]: **Dear Mr. Nixon:**

9. Click the body of the letter to display the placeholder [Type the body of the letter]:

   Thank you for enrolling in our class. All classes begin at 9 a.m. and end at 4 p.m. We look forward to seeing you in the Word Fundamentals class on January 25.

   [Type the closing]: **Sincerely,**

   Your Name (Your name might already appear here if you have personalized your copy of Microsoft Office with a user name.): Type your first and last name.

LESSON 3 Formatting Documents

WD 69

[Type the sender company name]: **Super Computer Services, Inc.** (Notice that the company name is automatically inserted in the Type the sender company name placeholder in the orange sidebar.)

10. Click the placeholders in the orange sidebar (don't worry about the placeholders being turned sideways, you can type as usual) and replace with the following text:

    [Type the sender company address]: **10001 Nations Drive, Colorado Springs, CO 80955**

    [Type the sender phone number]: **970-555-1000**

    [Type the sender e-mail address]: **supercomputerservices@mail.mail**

11. Save the file as **Class Confirmation XXX.docx** (replace XXX with your initials) and leave it open for use in the next Step-by-Step.

Changing Document Themes

Modern word-processing software such as Word provides so many different fonts, sizes, colors, font styles, and effects that it can be difficult to figure out which formatting options you should use together to create a professional-looking document. Unless you have an eye for design, choosing one font for headings and a coordinating font for text can be tricky. To make these decisions easier, Word includes built-in *themes*, which are sets of formatting choices that include colors, fonts, and effects that were predesigned to work well together. The themes are available in other Office programs as well, so you can apply the same theme to an Excel spreadsheet, a Word report, and a PowerPoint presentation, resulting in a professionally coordinated package of files.

Each document you create is associated with one of Word's document themes. Even a new blank document is based on a theme. When you change the theme, you change the entire document's color scheme, fonts, and effects to the new design theme. Word provides several different built-in themes, or you can customize a theme using the buttons in the Themes group on the Page Layout tab on the Ribbon. See **Figure WD 3–3**.

▶ **VOCABULARY**
themes

FIGURE WD 3–3 Themes group on the Page Layout tab

The Themes button displays a gallery of built-in theme choices and several menu commands. You can use the Theme Colors button to change the pre-established colors for a theme. The Theme Fonts button applies a new set of fonts, and the Theme Effects button lets you choose new line and fill effects.

UNIT II Microsoft Word

If you change the theme of a document and decide you liked the original look better, you can use the Reset to Theme from Template command on the Themes button menu to revert to the document's original theme. To see more choices, use the More Themes on Microsoft Office Online command, or use the Browse for Themes command to locate a document that contains a theme you want to apply to the current document. After you have customized a theme, you can use the Save Current Theme command to name and save it to the Document Themes folder.

Step-by-Step WD 3.2

The Class Confirmation *XXX*.docx document from Step-by-Step WD 3.1 should be open in the Word program window.

1. On the Page Layout tab in the Themes group click the **Themes** button and point to **Opulent**. Notice that the Live Preview allows you to see the document as it would look with the theme applied, as shown in **Figure WD 3–4**.

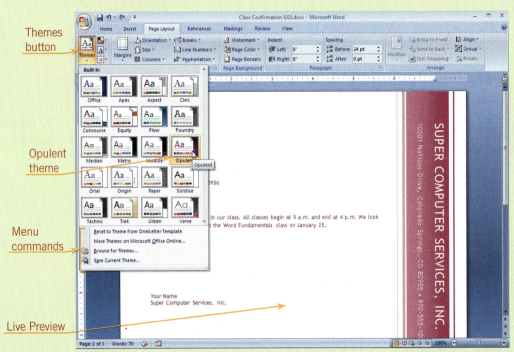

FIGURE WD 3–4
Themes button and gallery

2. Click **Concourse**. The new theme is applied.

3. In the Themes group, click the **Theme Colors** button and click **Urban**, as shown in **Figure WD 3–5**. The new color is applied.

LESSON 3   Formatting Documents

WD 71

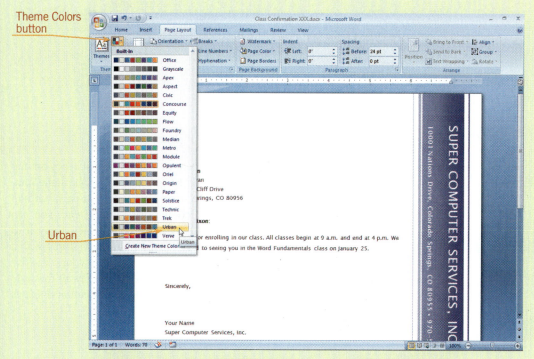

FIGURE WD 3–5
Theme Colors button and menu

4. In the Themes group, click the **Theme Fonts** button, scroll down and click **Paper**, as shown in **Figure WD 3–6**. The new fonts are applied. Notice how the applied theme changes have altered the appearance of the document.

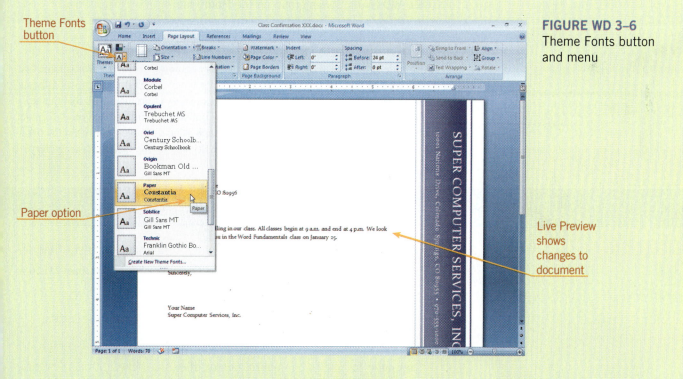

FIGURE WD 3–6
Theme Fonts button and menu

5. In the Themes group, click the **Themes** button and click **Reset to Theme from Oriel Letter Template**. The original theme is applied.

6. Save and close the document.

> **VOCABULARY**
> style

> **EXTRA FOR EXPERTS**
>
> For ease of maintaining consistent formatting in documents, base new documents on a template, format all text with styles, and change formatting by updating styles. By using the Heading styles, you can incorporate advanced features such as tables of contents and indexes.

Applying Quick Styles

When you are formatting documents, it is important to maintain consistency among page elements. For example, each heading should be formatted with the same font, font style, size, and color. However, it could take some time to format each heading by manually applying the font, style, size, and color separately. Instead, you can save all those formatting specifications into a style, name it, and then apply it to each heading at once. A *style* is a set of character or paragraph formats stored with a name. Word provides predefined styles you can use, or you can create your own. The Quick Styles gallery in the Styles group on the Home tab displays a few of the style buttons that are available, as shown in **Figure WD 3–7**. The More button displays the entire gallery.

FIGURE WD 3–7 Styles group on the Home tab

To apply a style, select the text that you want to change and click a style.

The styles available in the Quick Styles gallery coordinate with the Word theme that has been applied to a document. Remember, even a new blank document has a theme applied, so the styles available in the Quick Styles gallery coordinate with that theme.

You can format a paragraph with any font, font size, alignment, and other formats you want to create a new style using that paragraph as an example. Just select the paragraph and click Save Selection as a New Quick Style from the Quick Styles gallery.

Step-by-Step WD 3.3

1. Open **Step WD 3-3.docx** from the folder containing the data files for this lesson and save the document as **Caring for Your Computer XXX.docx** (replace *XXX* with your initials).

2. Scroll down and select the first heading, *Prepare for Power Surges*.

3. On the Home tab, in the Styles group, click the **Heading 1** button. (If you need to display the entire gallery, click the More button.) The new style is applied.

4. Select the heading *Keep Your Computer Clean*.

5. Press and hold **CTRL** while selecting the remaining five headings.

LESSON 3   Formatting Documents   WD 73

6. In the Styles group, click the **Heading 1** button to apply the style to all of the selected headings at once.

7. Select the title, *CARING FOR YOUR COMPUTER*.

8. In the Styles group, click the **More** button on the Quick Styles gallery to display the entire gallery.

9. Click the **Title** button, as shown in **Figure WD 3–8**. The new style is applied.

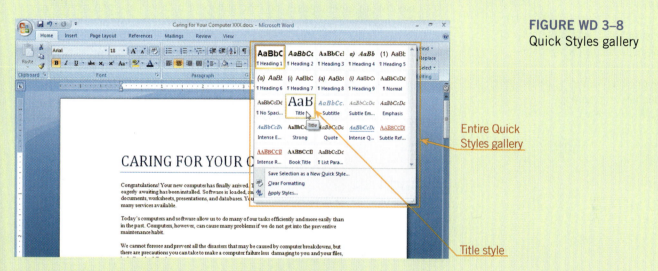

FIGURE WD 3–8
Quick Styles gallery

10. Save the file and leave it open for use in the next Step-by-Step.

Working with Lists

A *list* is a series of related words, numbers, or phrases. As you go about your day, you probably make lists of things to do, grocery items to pick up, or assignments that are due. You can create lists with bullets or numbers and sort them using the buttons in the Paragraph group of the Home tab on the Ribbon, shown in **Figure WD 3–9**.

▶ **VOCABULARY**
list

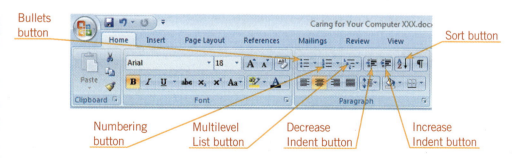

FIGURE WD 3–9   Paragraph group on the Home tab

VOCABULARY

bullets

sort

EXTRA FOR EXPERTS

You should number a list when the items need to be in order, such as instructions, or if the number of items in the list is significant. Use bullets for a list if the items in the list do not require a specific order, such as a grocery list.

Adding Bullets and Numbering to Lists

Bullets and numbers help organize items arranged in a list. **Bullets** are symbols that mark the beginning of each entry in a list. The Bullets button adds the default bullet style, a small circle, to a list, and the Numbering button adds the default numbering style, the number and a period, to a list. When using bulleted and numbered lists, each list item begins on its own line of the document. If you want to change the bullet or number style, you can choose from the available styles or define a new style.

The Bullets and Numbering buttons can be used two ways. You can select an existing list and then click the Bullets button or the Numbering button to add bullets or numbers, or you can click the Bullets or Numbering button before you create a list to have Word automatically add the bullets or numbers as you type. When you use this method, press Enter and click the button again to turn off bullets or numbers when you are finished typing the list.

Word automatically renumbers a numbered list when you insert, move, copy, or delete items. A new bullet is added on a blank line when you press Enter at the end of a bulleted item.

The Multilevel list button is used to create an outline. You can use the Increase Indent and Decrease Indent buttons to promote or demote items to different outline levels.

Sorting Lists

When you want to organize data in ascending or descending order, you can use the Sort button on the Home tab in the Paragraph group to open the Sort Text dialog box. When you *sort* text, Word rearranges selected text, numbers, or dates alphabetically, numerically, or chronologically.

When you choose ascending order, text is sorted from A to Z, numbers are sorted from 1 to 9, and dates are sorted from earliest to latest. Descending order sorts text from Z to A, numbers from 9 to 1, and dates from latest to earliest.

The Sort Text dialog box, as shown in **Figure WD 3–10**, allows you to sort by up to three levels and choose other sort options.

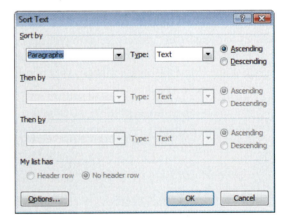

FIGURE WD 3–10 Sort Text dialog box

LESSON 3   Formatting Documents

WD 75

Step-by-Step WD 3.4

The Caring for Your Computer *XXX*.docx document from Step-by-Step WD 3.3 should be open in the Word program window.

1. In the first section of the document, select the four-line list that begins with Prepare for Power Surges.

2. On the Home tab, in the Paragraph group, click the **Numbering** button arrow and click the **numbers with parentheses** format from the Numbering Library, as shown in **Figure WD 3–11**. The format is applied.

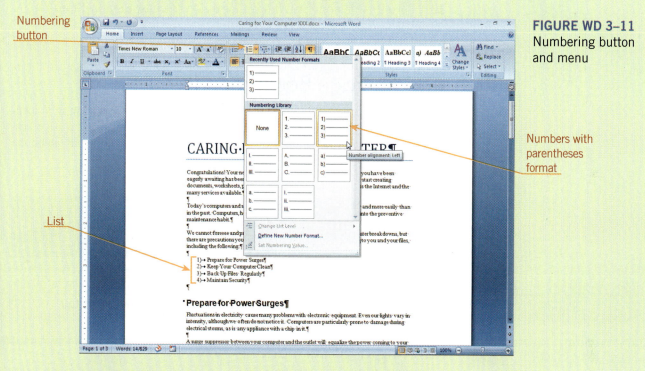

FIGURE WD 3–11 Numbering button and menu

3. Click at the end of the line *Keep Your Computer Clean* and press **Enter**. The number 3) is inserted and the remaining items are renumbered.

4. Type **Avoid Static Electricity** to add a new list item.

5. Select the entire list and click the **Numbering** button to remove the numbering.

6. With the list still selected, click the **Bullets** button. The default bullet format is applied.

7. With the list still selected, click the **Bullets** button arrow and click the **square bullet** format from the Bullet Library. The format is applied.

8. Click at the end of the list item *Maintain Security* and press **Enter**. A new bullet is inserted.

9. Type **Continue Learning**.

10. Select the entire list. On the Home tab, in the Paragraph group, click the **Sort** button to display the Sort dialog box.

11. Click **OK** to sort the list in ascending order using the default settings in the dialog box.

12. On the Quick Access Toolbar, click the **Undo** button to remove the sort, because this list needs to be in the same order as the headings in the document.

13. Save the file and leave it open for use in the next Step-by-Step.

Adding Page Backgrounds

You can add interest, emphasize text, or include important information in a document by inserting a watermark, changing the page color, or inserting a page border using the buttons in the Page Background group on the Page Layout tab on the Ribbon, shown in **Figure WD 3–12**.

FIGURE WD 3–12 Page Background group on the Page Layout tab

Inserting a Watermark

> **VOCABULARY**
> **watermark**

A *watermark* is text or a graphic that appears behind text in a document. A watermark can display a company logo or text, such as the word *Draft* or *Confidential*, in the background of each printed page, as shown in **Figure WD 3–13**. Word provides built-in watermarks, or you can create a custom watermark.

LESSON 3 Formatting Documents

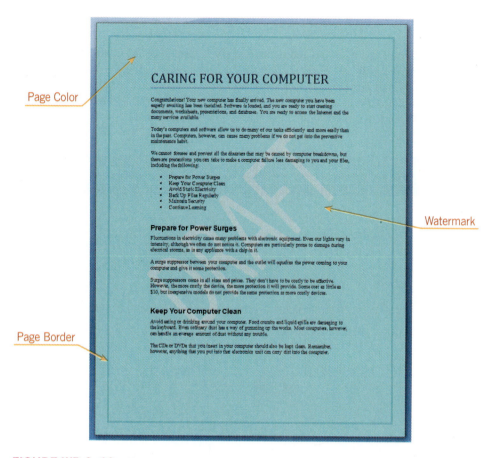

FIGURE WD 3-13 Document with watermark

Changing the Page Color

While adding colors to pages can look attractive on the computer screen, you should use color sparingly if you intend to print a document, because it can make the text difficult to read and it requires a lot of printer ink. Consider using light colors or shades of color for best results. Use the Page Color button to add a background color to a Web page or a document that you know will be viewed only on the computer.

To help you further customize page backgrounds, the Page Color menu offers Theme Colors, Standard Colors, or No Color options. The More Colors command allows you to create a custom color, and the Fill Effects command lets you add a gradient, texture, pattern, or picture after selecting a background color.

UNIT II   Microsoft Word

Adding a Page Border

Documents such as flyers and invitations often have decorative borders that outline the page. You can add *borders*, or lines that frame the page, using the Page Borders button, which displays the Borders and Shading dialog box. Borders can be solid, dashed, dotted, or multiple lines, or small repeated artwork pictures or designs. You can add borders to the whole document or to sections of a document.

> **VOCABULARY**
> borders

Step-by-Step WD 3.5

The Caring for Your Computer *XXX*.docx document from Step-by-Step WD 3.4 should be open in the Word program window.

1. On the Page Layout tab, in the Page Background group, click the **Watermark** button. The gallery is displayed.

2. Scroll down to the Disclaimers section and click the **DRAFT 1** option, as shown in **Figure WD 3–14**. The word *DRAFT* now appears behind the existing text.

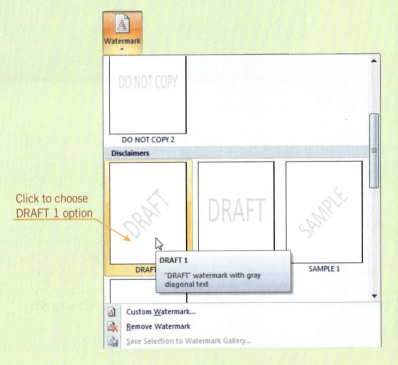

FIGURE WD 3–14
Watermark button and menu

3. In the Page Background group, click the **Page Color** button.

4. In the Theme Colors section, click the **Aqua, Accent 5, Lighter 80%** button, as shown in **Figure WD 3–15**, to apply a light aqua background to the document.

LESSON 3   Formatting Documents

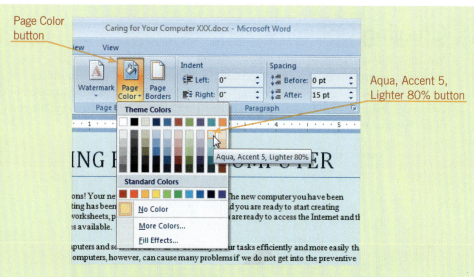

FIGURE WD 3–15
Page Color menu

5. In the Page Background group, click the **Page Borders** button. The Borders and Shading dialog box opens.

6. In the Setting area, click **Box**, and in the Style area, scroll down and click the **double line** style.

7. In the Color section, click the button arrow to display the color menu. In the Theme Colors section, click **Aqua, Accent 5** on the top row. In the Width area, click **1 ½ pt**. Your dialog box should look similar to the one shown in **Figure WD 3–16**.

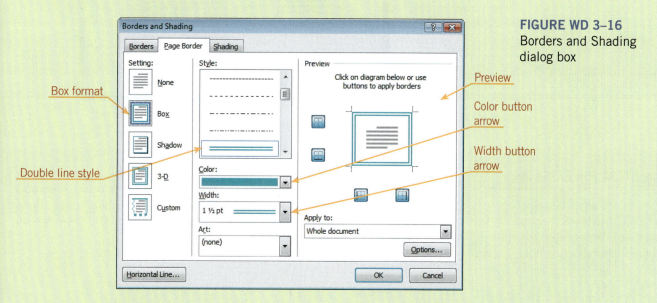

FIGURE WD 3–16
Borders and Shading dialog box

8. Click the **OK** button. The border is applied.

9. Click the **Page Color** button again and click **No Color** on the menu to remove the page color.

10. Save the document and leave it open for use in the next Step-by-Step.

VOCABULARY
columns

Creating Columns

You often see newspapers, newsletters, and brochures formatted into two or more *columns*, or vertical sections, in which text flows from the bottom of one column to the top of the next, as shown in **Figure WD 3–17**. Usually, text that is formatted in columns is easier to read because your eye doesn't have to travel as far to get the end of the line and then return to the beginning of the next line.

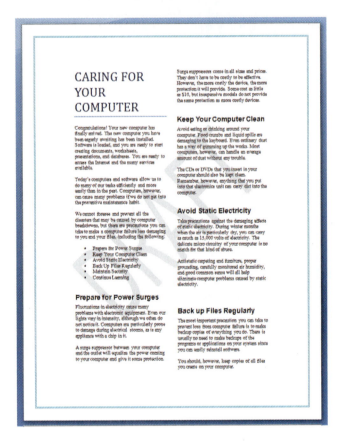

FIGURE WD 3–17 Two-column layout

The Columns button in the Page Setup group on the Page Layout tab on the Ribbon lets you format all or part of a document in columns of equal or unequal width. The More Columns command opens the Columns dialog box, which allows you to create custom column formats by choosing the number of columns you want and specifying the width of individual columns.

> **EXTRA FOR EXPERTS**
>
> You can add a line between columns by inserting a checkmark in the Line between check box in the Columns dialog box.

Step-by-Step WD 3.6

The Caring for Your Computer *XXX*.docx document from Step-by-Step WD 3.5 should be open in the Word program window.

1. Click at the top of the page to make sure no text is selected.
2. On the Page Layout tab on the Ribbon, in the Page Setup group, click the **Columns** button.
3. Click **Three** on the menu, as shown in **Figure WD 3–18**. The text, including the title, is formatted into three columns.

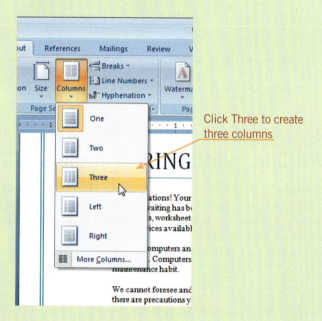

FIGURE WD 3–18
Columns button and menu

4. In the Page Setup group, click the **Columns** button again, and then click **More Columns**. The Columns dialog box opens.
5. In the Presets area, click **Two**. In the Width and spacing area, click the **up arrow** in the Width box until 2.6" is displayed, as shown in **Figure WD 3–19**. The Spacing measurement automatically adjusts to .3".

FIGURE WD 3–19
Columns dialog box

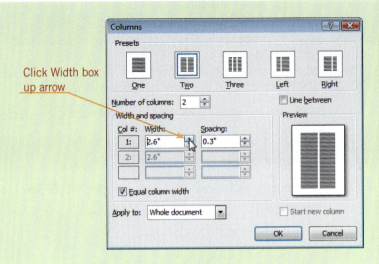

6. Click the **OK** button. The text is formatted into two columns.
7. Save the file and leave it open for use in the next Step-by-Step.

Adding Headers and Footers

▶ **VOCABULARY**
header
footer

A *header* is text or graphics that appears in the top margin of each page in a document. A *footer* refers to text that appears in the bottom margin of each page in a document. You can use headers and footers to include useful information that you would not include as document text, such as document titles and page numbers, as shown in **Figure WD 3–20**. Headers and footers can also include dates, times, logos, and other information.

LESSON 3   Formatting Documents

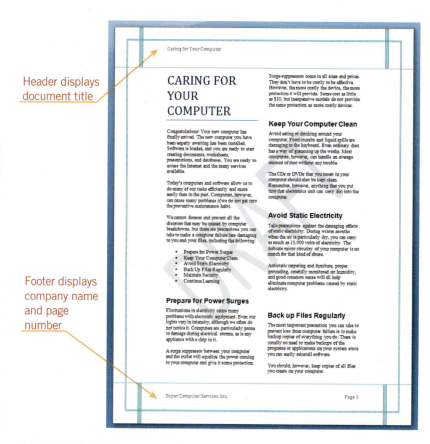

FIGURE WD 3–20   Document with header and footer

To create a header or footer, you use the Header, Footer, and Page Number buttons, located in the Header & Footer group on the Insert tab on the Ribbon. See **Figure WD 3–21**. These buttons provide a gallery of predesigned, built-in headers, footers, and page number formats that you can use for your documents. They also provide Blank styles you can use to create your own headers and footers.

FIGURE WD 3–21   Header & Footer group on the Insert tab

Inserting Headers and Footers

When you insert a header or footer, it is placed on each page of the document, and Word displays the Header & Footer Tools Design contextual tab with more options for formatting and displaying the header or footer. You can opt not to print a header or footer on the first page of a document, and you can specify a different header or footer for odd and even pages.

UNIT II Microsoft Word

The header and footer areas are set off from the body of the document with a nonprinting dashed line. Text and graphics in the document are visible, but dimmed. You can type and format text in the header or footer area the same way you do in the document.

You can double-click a header or footer to edit it, or choose the Edit Header or Edit Footer command on the menus. The Header and Footer menus also contain options for editing and removing headers and footers.

Step-by-Step WD 3.7

The Caring for Your Computer *XXX*.docx document from Step-by-Step WD 3.6 should be open in the Word program window.

1. On the Insert tab on the Ribbon, in the Header & Footer group, click the **Header** button. Scroll down and click the **Pinstripes** header, as shown in **Figure WD 3–22**.

FIGURE WD 3–22
Header button and menu

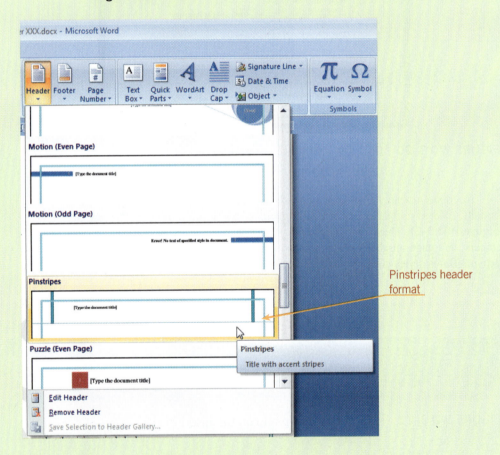

LESSON 3 Formatting Documents

WD 85

2. The header is inserted and the Header & Footer Tools Design contextual tab is displayed on the Ribbon, as shown in **Figure WD 3–23**. Select the **[Type the document title]** placeholder, if necessary.

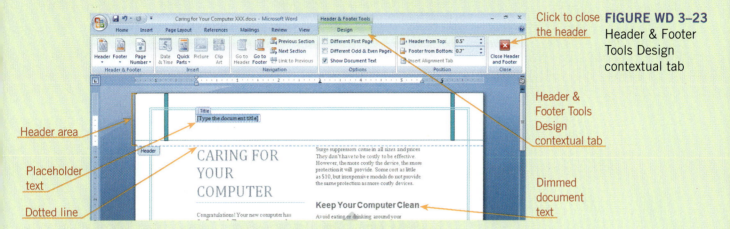

FIGURE WD 3–23 Header & Footer Tools Design contextual tab

3. Type **Caring for Your Computer** as the document name.

4. On the Header & Footer Tools Design contextual tab, in the Header & Footer group, click the **Close Header and Footer** button. The header area is closed, along with the Header & Footer Tools tab.

5. On the **Insert** tab on the Ribbon, in the Header & Footer group, click the **Footer** button. Scroll down and click the **Pinstripes** footer, as shown in **Figure WD 3–24**. The footer is inserted and the Header & Footer Tools Design contextual tab is displayed on the Ribbon.

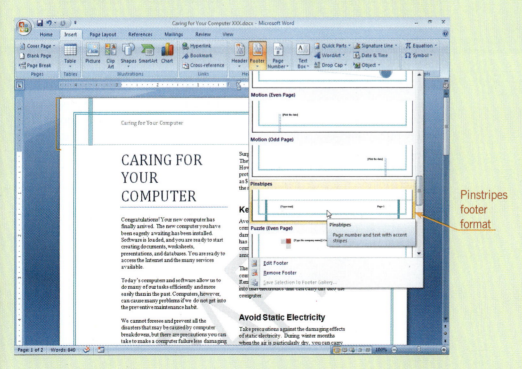

FIGURE WD 3–24 Footer button and menu

6. Click the [Type text] placeholder and type **Super Computer Services, Inc.**, as shown in **Figure WD 3–25**.

FIGURE WD 3–25
Footer

7. Press **Tab**. On the Header & Footer Tools Design contextual tab, in the Insert group, click the **Date & Time** button to display the Date and Time dialog box. Click the **OK** button to accept the default time format and insert the current date.

8. On the Header & Footer group, click the **Footer** button and then click **Remove Footer**. The footer is removed.

9. On the Header & Footer Tools Design contextual tab, in the Close group, click the **Close Header and Footer** button.

10. Save the file and leave it open for use in the next Step-by-Step.

Inserting Page Numbers

There may be times when you want to display only a page number in a header or footer. The Page Number button in the Header & Footer group inserts a page number with no additional content. From the Page Number menu, you can choose from a variety of built-in formats for inserting page numbers at the top or bottom of the page, in the margin, or at the current position of the insertion point. You can also change the format of a page number or remove the page number.

After you insert a page number, the Header & Footer Tools Design contextual tab is displayed on the Ribbon and allows you to choose additional options for page numbers. You can specify a position and opt to not display the number on the first page of a document.

Step-by-Step WD 3.8

The Caring for Your Computer *XXX*.docx document from Step-by-Step WD 3.7 should be open in the Word program window.

1. On the Insert tab, in the Header & Footer group, click the **Page Number** button and point to **Bottom of Page**. A submenu is displayed.

2. Scroll down to the With Shapes section and click **Outline Circle 2,** as shown in **Figure WD 3–26**. A new footer with a page number is inserted and the Header & Footer Tools Design contextual tab is displayed on the Ribbon.

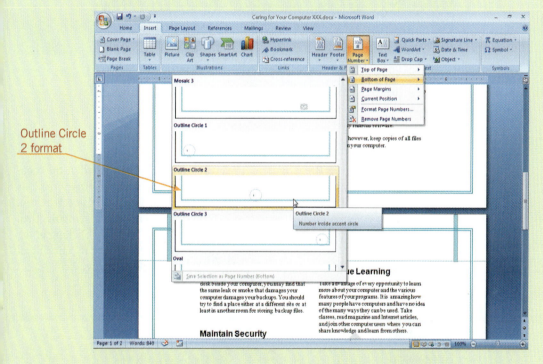

FIGURE WD 3–26
Page Number button and menu

3. In the Header & Footer group on the Header & Footer Tools Design contextual tab, click the **Page Number** button and click **Format Page Numbers**. The Page Number Format dialog box opens.

4. In the Number format area, click the **Number format** button arrow and click the **-1-, -2-, -3-,...** format. Click the **OK** button to apply the new numbering format.

5. On the Header & Footer Tools Design contextual tab, in the Close group, click the **Close Header and Footer** button.

6. Save the document and leave it open for use in the next Step-by-Step.

VOCABULARY

page break
widow
orphan

Inserting and Breaking Pages

A *page break* ends a page and starts a new one. At the end of a page, Word inserts automatic page breaks and starts a new page. As you reformat or edit, Word adjusts these page breaks. There may be times when you need to insert a manual page break in a different location. Word will always break the page at a manual page break. If you need to insert a blank page for a graphic or block of text you intend to insert, you can use a page break to do so. When you create reports or other documents that need cover sheets, you can insert a cover page at the beginning of the document. The Cover Page, Blank Page, and Page Break buttons in the Pages group on the Insert tab on the Ribbon let you add or break pages. These buttons are shown in **Figure WD 3–27**.

FIGURE WD 3–27   Pages group on the Insert tab

Inserting a Page Break

When you use the Page Break button, a manual page break is inserted at the location of the insertion point. Word inserts a dotted line with the words *Page Break*, as shown in **Figure WD 3–28**, that you can see when you use the Show/Hide ¶ button. If you need to delete a manual page break, display the nonprinting symbols, then select and delete the page break. You can also delete a page break by clicking at the left (the beginning) of the page break and pressing the Delete key, or by clicking at the end (at the right) of the page break and pressing the Backspace key.

FIGURE WD 3–28   Manual page break

You cannot delete an automatic page break, but you can change the way Word inserts them using the Line and Page Breaks tab in the Paragraph dialog box, which you can display using the dialog box launcher in the Paragraph group on the Home tab on the Ribbon. Widow/Orphan control is toggled on by default, so Word does not allow single lines or words to be displayed at the top (*widow*) or bottom (*orphan*) of an otherwise empty page. You can use the Keep with next option to specify that selected paragraphs don't continue over page breaks, but instead are kept together on a page. The Keep lines together option specifies that lines in a paragraph be

LESSON 3 Formatting Documents

kept together on a page, and the Page break before option specifies that a certain paragraph will always be at the top of a page.

Word provides other types of page breaks to help you format complex documents. Tools for column breaks and text wrapping breaks can be found on the Breaks button and menu in the Page Setup group on the Page Layout tab.

Inserting a Section Break

Section breaks are used to control a document's layout. A section can be as small as a single paragraph or as long as an entire document. When you break a document into sections, you can format each section differently. A Continuous section break starts a new section on the current page and a Next Page section break starts a new section on the next page. You can also specify that the new section start on an odd or even page. Use the Breaks button and menu in the Page Setup group of the Page Layout tab to insert a section break, as shown in **Figure WD 3–29.**

FIGURE WD 3–29 Page Setup group on the Page Layout tab

After you insert a section break, the words Section Break and the kind of break (for example, Next Page) appear on the dotted line, similar to a page break. To remove a section break, select it or click to the left of it and press the Delete key.

Inserting a Blank Page

When you need to insert a blank page anywhere in a document, place the insertion point where you want to add the page and click the Blank Page button. Word will insert a page break and display a new page. You can delete the added page by displaying nonprinting symbols and deleting the page break.

Step-by-Step WD 3.9

The Caring For Your Computer *XXX*.docx document from Step-by-Step WD 3.8 should be open in the Word program window.

1. On the Home tab, in the Paragraph group, click the **Show/Hide ¶** button ¶, if necessary, to display the nonprinting symbols.

2. At the bottom of the second column on page 1, click the beginning of the last paragraph, which begins *You should, however.*

3. On the Insert tab, in the Pages group, click the **Page Break** button. A page break is inserted, and the paragraph moves to the next page, as shown in **Figure WD 3–30**.

FIGURE WD 3–30
Page break inserted

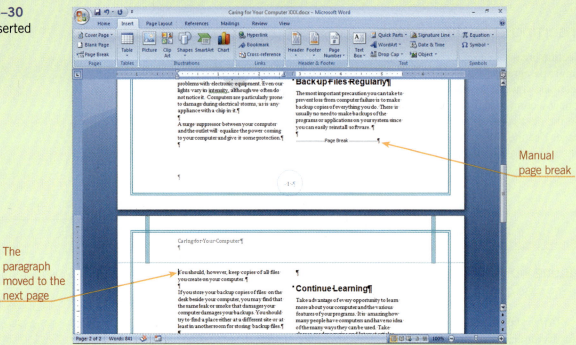

4. In the Pages group, click the **Blank Page** button. A new blank page is inserted.

5. Scroll up if necessary, and select the paragraph mark and the page break on the blank page, as shown in **Figure WD 3–31**.

FIGURE WD 3–31
Select the page break

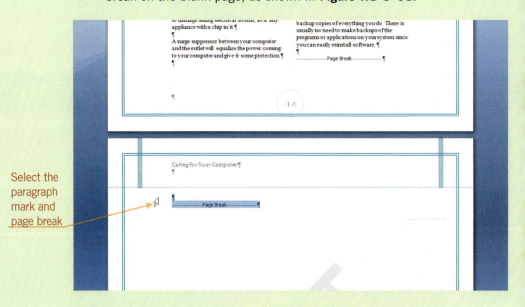

6. Press **Delete**. The page break and the blank page are removed.

LESSON 3 Formatting Documents

7. On page 2, select the last two paragraphs in the first column, beginning with *You can use a screen saver*.

8. On the Page Layout tab, in the Paragraph group, click the **dialog box launcher**. The Paragraph dialog box opens.

9. Click the **Line and Page Breaks** tab. In the Pagination area, click the **Keep with next** check box, as shown in **Figure WD 3–32**.

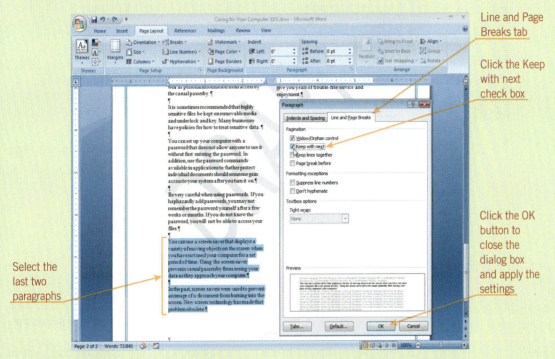

FIGURE WD 3–32 Use the Keep with next option

10. Click the **OK** button. The paragraphs are moved to the top of the next column, keeping them with the next paragraph and making the columns more even.

11. Click to the left of the title at the top of the document to make sure no text is selected.

12. In the Page Layout tab, in the Page Setup group, click the **Columns** button, and click **One** to change the format from two columns to one.

13. Click at the end of the title, and press **Enter** to add a blank line.

14. In the first paragraph, click before the *C* in *Congratulations!*. In the Page Setup group, click the **Breaks** button and then click **Continuous**, as shown in **Figure WD 3–33**, to insert a continuous section break.

FIGURE WD 3-33
Breaks button and menu

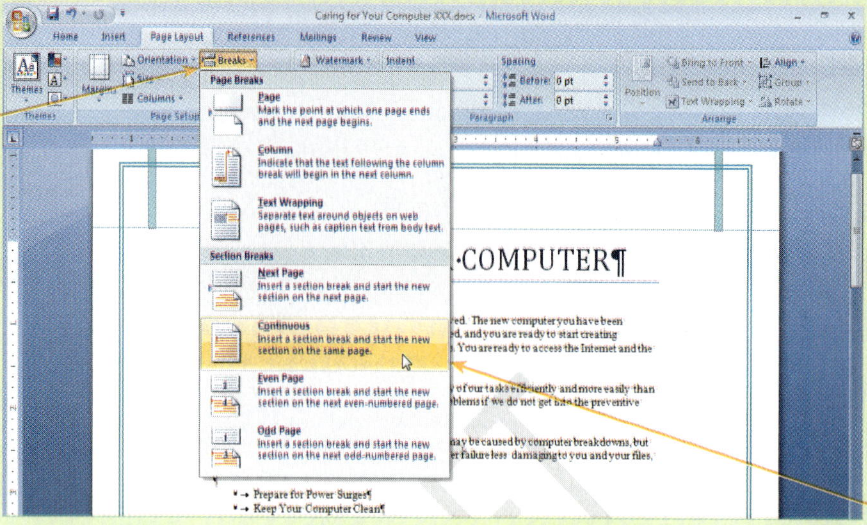

Breaks button

Click the Continuous command to insert a continuous section break

15. Click in the first paragraph, which begins *Congratulations!* In the Page Setup group, click the **Columns** button and click **Two** to change the format in the section to a two-column layout.

16. Save the document and leave it open for use in the next Step-by-Step.

Adding a Cover Page

▶ **VOCABULARY**
cover page

A *cover page* is the first page of a document that provides introductory information about the document, such as the title, author, and date. The Cover Page button provides a gallery of built-in cover pages you can use in your documents.

A cover page is always inserted at the beginning of a document, no matter where the insertion point is located when you click the Cover Page button. The Remove Current Cover Page command removes a cover page.

You can replace the placeholder text in a cover page with your own text, as you do when using a template or a header or footer. Sometimes, however, you may want to delete a placeholder, which contains a small program called a content control that provides instructional text for the user and then disappears when new text is inserted.

Step-by-Step WD 3.10

The **Caring For Your Computer *XXX*.docx** document from Step-by-Step WD 3.9 should be open in the Word program window.

1. On the Insert tab on the Ribbon, in the Pages group, click the **Cover Page** button and scroll down to click the **Pinstripes** option, as shown in **Figure WD 3–34**. A cover page is inserted at the beginning of the document.

LESSON 3   Formatting Documents

FIGURE WD 3-34
Cover Page button and menu

2. Right-click the **[Type the document subtitle]** placeholder to display the shortcut menu and then click **Remove Content Control**, as shown in **Figure WD 3–35**, to delete the placeholder.

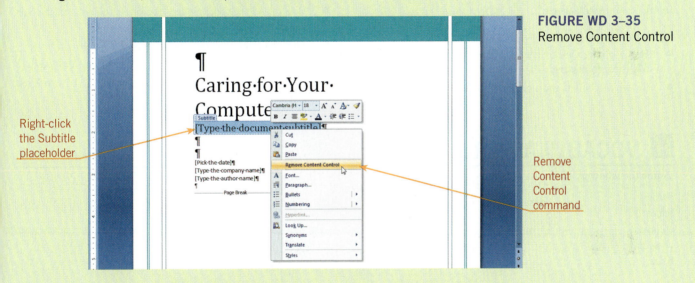

FIGURE WD 3-35
Remove Content Control

3. Click the remaining placeholders and replace them with the following:

   [Pick the date]: **Today's date**

   [Type the company name]: **Super Computer Services, Inc.**

   [Type the author name]: Your *first* and *last name*

4. Right-click **Super Computer Services, Inc.** and click **Remove Content Control** to remove the content control without removing the text.

5. Right-click your name and click **Remove Content Control** to remove the content control without removing the text.

6. Click the **Home** tab on the Ribbon. In the Paragraph group, click the **Show/Hide ¶** button ¶ to hide nonprinting characters.

7. Save and close the document and then close Word.

ETHICS IN TECHNOLOGY

Software Piracy

The unauthorized use of copyrighted software is considered software piracy. The software industry estimates that it loses billions of dollars each year when people copy, distribute, or use software in an illegal manner. The penalties for using or distributing a pirated copy of Microsoft Word could include large fines or even imprisonment.

SUMMARY

In this lesson, you learned:

- How to create new documents using templates.
- That applying Quick Styles is a convenient way to maintain consistent formatting.
- How to add bullets and numbering to lists.
- How to add page backgrounds such as watermarks, page color, and page borders.
- That you can format documents in even or uneven columns.
- Ways to format documents using built-in headers or footers.
- How to insert blank pages and cover pages and how to insert and delete page breaks.

VOCABULARY REVIEW

Define the following terms:

borders	header	style
bullets	list	template
columns	orphan	themes
cover page	page break	watermark
footer	sort	widow

REVIEW QUESTIONS

MULTIPLE CHOICE

Select the best response for the following statements.

1. You can replace the text in a template by clicking the _____ text and typing.

   A. italicized   C. Theme
   B. placeholder   D. preview

2. _____ are sets of formatting choices that include colors, fonts, and effects that were selected to work well together.

   A. Themes   C. Watermarks
   B. Templates   D. Placeholders

LESSON 3 Formatting Documents

WD 95

3. The _____ button displays the entire Quick Styles Gallery.
   - A. Styles
   - B. Home
   - C. More
   - D. Heading 1

4. _____ are symbols that mark the beginning of each entry in a list.
   - A. Numbers
   - B. Watermarks
   - C. Placeholders
   - D. Bullets

5. A _____ is text or a graphic that appears behind text in a document.
   - A. page border
   - B. bullet
   - C. watermark
   - D. placeholder

6. You can use the _____ button to add gradient, texture, pattern, or a picture to the background of a page.
   - A. Page Color
   - B. Page Border
   - C. Header
   - D. Cover Page

7. Newspapers, newsletters, and brochures are often formatted into two or more _____.
   - A. watermarks
   - B. placeholders
   - C. columns
   - D. nonprinting symbols

8. A _____ is text or graphics that is displayed in the top margin of each page in a document.
   - A. footer
   - B. header
   - C. placeholder
   - D. page border

9. You can see a manual page break if you click the _____ button.
   - A. Cover Page
   - B. Columns
   - C. Page Number
   - D. Show/Hide ¶

10. A _____ provides introductory information about a document, such as the title, author, and date.
    - A. page break
    - B. cover page
    - C. blank page
    - D. placeholder

FILL IN THE BLANK

Complete the following sentences by writing the correct word or words in the blanks provided.

1. A(n) _____ is a master copy for a certain type of document.
2. The Theme _____ button lets you choose new line and fill effects.
3. A(n) _____ is a set of character or paragraph formats stored with a name.
4. Word _____ a numbered list when you insert, move, copy, or delete items.
5. The Multilevel list button is used to create a(n) _____.
6. The _____ _____ button displays the Borders and Shading dialog box.
7. Text formatted in _____ is easier to read.
8. A(n) _____ is text or graphics that is displayed in the bottom margin of each page in a document.
9. A (n) _____ _____ ends a page and starts a new one.
10. A (n) _____ page is always inserted at the beginning of a document, no matter where the insertion point is located.

PROJECTS

PROJECT WD 3-1

1. Create a new document using the Median Resume template from the Installed Templates category of the New Document dialog box. Save the document as **Verhoff Resume XXX.docx** (replace *XXX* with your initials).

2. Replace the placeholders with the following information:

   [Your Name]: **Karin Verhoff**

   [Select the Date]: **Today's date**

   [Type your address]: **5555 Shady Oak Dr., Ashland, OR 97590**

   [Type your phone number]: **541-555-1023**

   [Type your e-mail address] : **karinverhoff@mail.mail**

   [Type your website address]: **karinverhoff.com**

   [Type your objectives]: **I am an accomplished accountant, but I would love to leave my office job to pursue a career in the outdoor industry as an adventure guide for a tourism company.**

   [Type the school name]: **Florida Park University**

   [Type the completion date]: **2000**

   [Type list of degrees, awards and accomplishments]: **B.S. in Accounting and Finance**

   [Type the job title]: **Staff Property Accountant**

   [Type the company name]: **Vande Associates**

   [Start date]: **September 2000**

   [End date]: **Present**

   [Type list of job responsibilities]: **Prepared monthly, quarterly and annual financial statements**

   Provided balance sheet account analysis

   Analyzed escrow and reconciliation of all escrow accounts

   [Type list of skills]: **Wilderness First Aid**

   Mountain Biking

   Rock Climbing

   Fly Fishing

3. Adjust spacing, if necessary, so that the resume fits on one page.

4. Save and close the document.

ON YOUR OWN

Open the **Verhoff Resume XXX.docx** file and change the document theme and experiment with the styles to change the look of the resume. Save and close the document.

PROJECT WD 3-2

1. Open the file **Project WD 3-2.docx** from the folder containing the data files for this lesson and save it as **Reappointment Letter XXX.docx** (replace *XXX* with your initials).

2. Add the Confidential 1 watermark to the page background.

3. Insert the Stacks footer with the following company information:

   Lone Star State University / 78901 Longhorn Boulevard / Austin, TX 78777

4. Insert the Stacks header with the following document title information:

   Office of the President

5. Apply the Strong style to FY 2012 and FY 2013

6. Apply the Strong style to the entire TOTAL line.

7. Change the document theme to Paper.

8. Save and close the document.

LESSON 3   Formatting Documents

ON YOUR OWN

Open the **Reappointment Letter** *XXX*.**docx** file and add a background color with a fill effect, such as a gradient, texture, pattern, or picture. Save and close the document.

PROJECT WD 3–3

1. Open the file **Project WD 3-3.docx** from the folder containing the data files for this lesson and save it as **MLA Guidelines** *XXX*.**docx** (replace *XXX* with your initials).
2. Change the numbered list to the default bullet style.
3. Sort the list in ascending order.
4. Apply the Title style to the *Writing Research Papers* title and to the *Works Cited* heading.
5. Change the theme to Metro.
6. Click to the left of the *Works Cited* heading and insert a continuous page section break.
7. In the section at the top of the page, insert the Right uneven column style.
8. Remove the header.
9. Insert a box style, dotted line (the second format in the list), ½ pt page border using Green Accent 1.
10. Save and close the document.

ON YOUR OWN

Open the **MLA Guidelines** *XXX*.**docx** file and change the font, size, alignment, color, and/or font style of the *Writing Research Papers* heading. Save the new format as a Quick Style with a new name, add it to the Quick Style gallery, and apply it to the *Works Cited* heading. Save and close the document.

ON YOUR OWN

Open the **MLA Guidelines** *XXX*.**docx** file, delete the section break, and insert a page break instead. Change the format to three columns. Save and close the document.

PROJECT WD 3–4

1. Open the file **Project WD 3-4.docx** from the folder containing the data files for this lesson and save it as **Pizza Menu** *XXX*.**docx** (replace *XXX* with your initials).
2. Change the theme to Verve.
3. Change the Theme Colors to Opulent.
4. Change the style of the quote at the bottom of the document to Intense Quote.
5. Insert the Tiles cover page.
6. Delete the subtitle and author's name placeholders and then replace the remaining placeholders with the following text:

   Home: **Purple Street Pizza**

   [Type the document title]: **Menu**

   [Year]: **Current Year**

   [Type company address]: **7765 Purple Street, New Orleans, LA 70198**
7. Insert a page color using **Lavender Background 2**.
8. Save and close the document.

ON YOUR OWN

Open the **Pizza Menu** *XXX*.**docx** file and insert a custom text watermark. You choose the text, font, size, color, and layout. Save and close the document.

WEB PROJECT

PROJECT WD 3–5

Explore the templates available in the Microsoft Office Online section of the New Document dialog box. This dialog box will acquire templates from the Microsoft Web site, so you must be connected to the Internet and have permission to download a document. Choose a favorite template to download and modify to your specifications.

 ## TEAMWORK PROJECT

PROJECT WD 3–6

In small groups, invent a business with a name, address, and slogan. Create a letterhead, business card, and fax cover sheet using one of Word's document themes. Assign each person in the team one of the documents to create. Utilize templates and styles. Work together to make sure the documents coordinate. Elect a team leader to present the documents to the class.

 ## CRITICAL THINKING

ACTIVITY WD 3–1

Create a new document using the Median Report template from the Installed Templates category of the New Document dialog box and save it with a new name. View the picture in the document. Think about the various reasons for including such an image in a document. How you would feel to visit a place like the scene included in the template? Perhaps you have been somewhere like it in the past, you are planning to go somewhere similar in the future, or you would not be interested in being in such a place at all. Create a report as if you have been there and are reporting your experience to the class. Write your observations and experiences in a one-page report. Replace the placeholders with new text. Be sure to use Quick Styles to format headings and other text elements. Include a quote. Be prepared to share your report with the class.

ACTIVITY WD 3–2

Type a list of careers that interest you. Use the Define New Bullet command to create your own bulleted list style. Copy the list and paste it below the first list. Now arrange the items in the copied list, ranking them in order of interest to you. Create your own numbered list style using the Define New Number Format command.

ACTIVITY WD 3–3

Use Word Help to locate and view the demo: *Headers and footers made simple*.

ACTIVITY WD 3–4

Open the Class Confirmation *XXX*.docx file from the folder containing the data files for this lesson. Center the letter vertically on the page and adjust any spacing or other issues to format the letter attractively on the page.

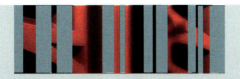

Estimated Time: 2 hours

LESSON 4

Working with Graphic Objects

■ OBJECTIVES

Upon completion of this lesson, you should be able to:
- Insert and modify illustrations.
- Insert and modify objects.
- Create and modify tables.

■ DATA FILES

To complete this lesson, you will need these data files:

Step WD 4-1.docx
Step WD 4-9.docx
Project WD 4–1.docx
Project WD 4–2.docx

■ VOCABULARY

building block
cell
chart
clip art
drawing objects
drop cap
floating picture
inline object
pictures
Quick Parts
selection handles
SmartArt graphic
table
text box
WordArt
...

Introduction

Graphics are visual components that add impact to documents and help explain the meaning of the text. Pictures, shapes, clip art, SmartArt, charts, WordArt, text boxes, and drop caps are all types of graphics that you can add to and customize in your Word documents. Tables provide another way to illustrate, explain, or supplement text. In this lesson, you will learn to insert and modify these graphic elements. Use buttons on the Insert tab on the Ribbon, shown in **Figure WD 4–1**, to insert various types of graphic objects.

UNIT II Microsoft Word

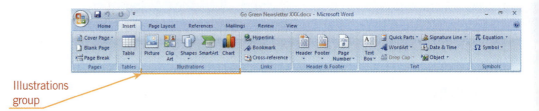

Illustrations group

FIGURE WD 4–1 Illustrations group on the Insert tab

Inserting and Modifying Illustrations

Pictures, shapes, clip art, SmartArt, and charts are types of illustrations you can add to your Word documents. The Insert tab on the Ribbon provides a range of options for working with these various types of graphics. When you click a button in the Illustrations group, you will be able to choose the graphic you want to insert using a dialog box, task pane, or menu, depending on the type of illustration. After you insert an illustration, you have many options for modifying it, most of which are the same for each type of illustration.

Inserting and Modifying Pictures

The Picture button in the Illustrations group on the Insert tab can be used to insert ***pictures***, or digital photographs or images, that are stored on your computer or network. You can insert pictures of various formats, including .tif, .gif, and .jpeg.

The Picture button opens the Insert Picture dialog box, which you can use to navigate to and insert a picture file from your computer or network. When a picture is inserted at the insertion point, it is an ***inline object*** that moves with the text around it. Text does not wrap around inline objects. You can change a picture's configuration to a ***floating picture*** that can be positioned so that text can wrap around and flow in front of or behind a picture.

Before you can modify or size a picture, clip art, or shape you must select it. To select a graphic, such as a picture or drawing, within a document and display the selection handles, click the graphic once. The small circles and squares at the sides and corners of the graphic are called ***selection handles.*** You drag these handles to change the graphic's size. When you want to resize a graphic proportionally, that is, to maintain the original height:width ratio, you must display the sizing pointer and drag a corner handle. Some types of graphics require that you hold the Shift key while dragging a corner handle when sizing proportionally. If you want to distort a graphic horizontally or vertically, drag a middle handle.

You can click the green rotate circle at the top of a graphic to rotate it on its central axis left or right to any position.

When a graphic is selected, you can copy, paste, and delete it the same as you would text using the Cut, Copy, and Paste commands. A copy of a graphic is the same size and contains the same formatting as the original graphic. When you paste a copy of a graphic, the new copy might appear on top of or next to the original. Simply drag it to the desired position.

After you insert a picture and any time the picture is selected, the Picture Tools Format contextual tab is displayed on the Ribbon. This tab contains commands for adjusting the picture, modifying the picture style, arranging the picture on the page, and resizing the picture precisely.

▶ **VOCABULARY**
pictures
inline object
floating picture
selection handles

EXTRA FOR EXPERTS

Hold the Shift key when using rectangular or oval drawing shapes or tools to draw squares or circles. To create a straight line, hold the Shift key while using line tools.

EXTRA FOR EXPERTS

Large files can take longer to download and some may be rejected by e-mail servers. Including pictures in documents increases file size, but you can use the Compress Pictures button to decrease a picture's file size by reducing the resolution, or the number of pixels in a picture.

LESSON 4   Working with Graphic Objects

WD 101

Step-by-Step WD 4.1

1. Start Word.

2. Open **Step WD 4-1.docx** from the folder containing the data files for this lesson and save the document as **Go Green Newsletter XXX.docx** (replace *XXX* with your initials).

3. On the Insert tab, in the Illustrations group, click the **Insert Picture from File** button to open the Insert Picture dialog box.

4. Navigate to the **Sample Pictures** folder and double-click to open it.

5. Click **Forest Flowers** (or another picture of your choice) to select the image and then click the **Insert** button. The picture is inserted on the page as an inline graphic, as shown in **Figure WD 4–2**, and the words are moved down the page.

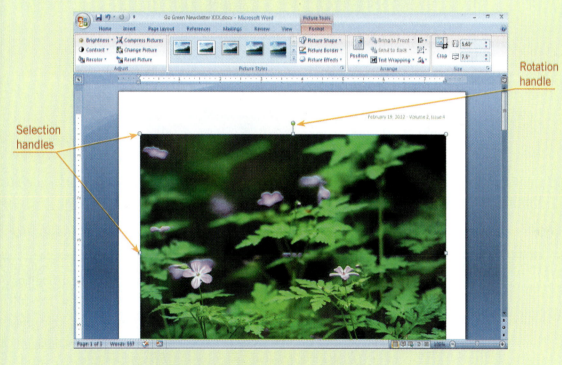

FIGURE WD 4–2
Inserted inline image displays selection and rotation handles

6. On the Picture Tools Format contextual tab, in the Arrange group, click the **Text Wrapping** button and click **Behind Text** to change the picture to a floating picture and position it behind the text.

7. Display the ruler, if necessary.

8. In the Size group, click the **Crop** button to display the cropping handles at the sides and corners of the picture.

9. Click the bottom center cropping handle (scroll down, if necessary) and drag it up until you reach approximately the 2.75" mark on the vertical ruler, then release the mouse button to remove the bottom portion of the picture, as shown in **Figure WD 4–3**.

FIGURE WD 4–3
Cropped picture

10. In the Picture Styles group, click the **More** button 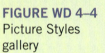 to open the Picture Styles gallery.

11. Click the **Center Shadow Rectangle** option, as shown in **Figure WD 4–4**, to apply a shadow around the picture.

FIGURE WD 4–4
Picture Styles gallery

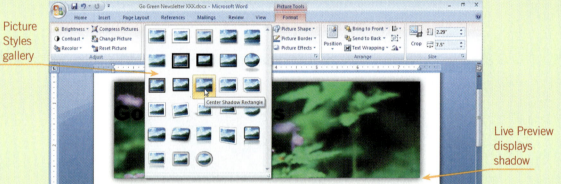

12. In the Adjust group, click the **Compress Pictures** button to display the Compress Pictures dialog box.

13. Click the **Options** button to display the Compression Settings dialog box and click the **OK** button to accept the default settings. Click the **OK** button to close the Compress Pictures dialog box. (You won't notice the change on your screen, but Word changes the resolution of the image.)

14. Save the document and leave it open for use in the next Step-by-Step.

Inserting and Modifying Shapes

Word provides a set of common shapes that you can add to documents with one click and drag of the mouse. The Shapes button on the Insert tab on the Ribbon displays a menu containing lines, basic shapes, block arrows, flowchart elements, callouts, stars, and banners that you can insert anywhere in your document.

LESSON 4   Working with Graphic Objects

After inserting a shape, you can delete it using the Delete key while the shape is selected, or use the Undo button immediately after creating the shape.

Shapes, curves, and lines are considered *drawing objects*, which are created with Word and become part of your document, rather than being a separate file. After you insert a shape into a document, the Drawing Tools Format contextual is displayed on the Ribbon with commands for modifying drawing objects. If you want to create a drawing using more than one shape or line, you can insert a drawing canvas on which to create your drawing. The canvas serves as a frame for your drawing and a boundary between your drawing and the rest of your document. The New Drawing Canvas command is located at the bottom of the Shapes menu.

> **VOCABULARY**
> drawing objects

> **EXTRA FOR EXPERTS**
> You might want to combine shapes to create a drawing object. You can select more than one object at a time by holding the Shift key while you click each of the objects. Use the Group command to combine them into one object.

Step-by-Step WD 4.2

The Go Green Newsletter *XXX*.docx document from Step-by-Step WD 4.1 should be open in the Word program window.

1. On the Insert menu, in the Illustrations group, click the **Shapes** button to display the gallery.
2. In the Basic Shapes category, click the **Rectangle**, as shown in **Figure WD 4–5**. The mouse pointer changes to a crosshair.

FIGURE WD 4–5
Shapes button and menu

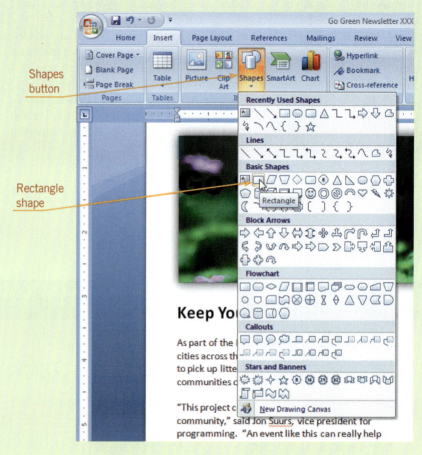

3. Click the crosshair above the upper-left corner of the *G* in *Go* drag down and to the right diagonally across the words to create an outline similar to the one in **Figure WD 4–6**. After you release the mouse button, a white rectangle shape appears, covering the text.

FIGURE WD 4–6
Drawing a shape

4. On the Drawing Tools Format tab, in the Shape Styles group, click the **More** button to display the Shape Styles gallery.

5. Click the green **Linear Up Gradient – Accent 3** option (fourth from the left on the fifth row).

6. In the Shadow Effects group, click the **Shadow Effects** button to display the menu.

7. In the Drop Shadow category, click the **Shadow Style 5** option on the second row to apply this subtle shadow style.

8. In the Arrange group, click the **Text Wrapping** button and click **Behind Text** to move the rectangle behind the text. Your screen should look similar to **Figure WD 4–7**.

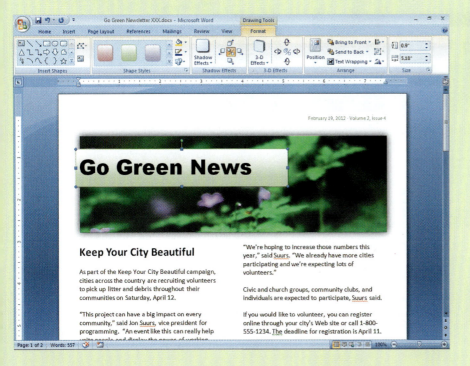

FIGURE WD 4–7
Go Green Newsletter

9. Save the document and leave it open for use in the next Step-by-Step.

Inserting and Modifying Clip Art

Clip art is artwork such as drawings or images that can be used in documents. The Clip Art button in the Illustrations group displays the Clip Art task pane, shown in **Figure WD 4–8**, which you can use to search for and insert clip art located on your computer, network, or on the Internet. The task pane contains a Search for text box where you can enter a keyword to find related clip art. The Search in menu lets you choose which collections to search, and the Results should be menu lets you choose the type of media file you are searching for, including clip art, pictures, sounds, and movies.

> **VOCABULARY**
> clip art

> **WARNING**
>
> You can use the images, sounds, and movies Microsoft provides with Word or for free on its Web site in any advertising, promotional and marketing materials, or product or service created with Word, provided the material, product, or service is for noncommercial purposes. You may not sell any promotional and marketing materials or any products or services containing the images.

UNIT II Microsoft Word

FIGURE WD 4–8 Clip Art task pane

Point to a graphic in the Clip Art task pane and an arrow appears that displays a menu with the Insert command as well as other commands for copying, moving, and previewing clip art file properties. You can also insert clip art by clicking the image in the task pane. Contextual tabs let you modify clip art.

Step-by-Step WD 4.3

The Go Green Newsletter *XXX*.docx document from Step-by-Step WD 4.2 should be open in the Word program window.

1. Click to the left of the *G* in *Go Green News*.
2. On the Insert tab, in the Illustrations group, click the **Clip Art** button to display the Clip Art task pane.
3. In the Search for box, type **sprouts**. If necessary, click the **Search in** box arrow, and click the **Everywhere** check box to insert a checkmark. Click the **Go** button to start the search.
4. In the Clip Art task pane, point to the picture of the sprout shown in **Figure WD 4–8**, in the results pane. (The sprout clip art might appear in a different location in your Clip Art task pane.)
5. Click the button arrow on the right side of the image to display a menu.
6. Click **Insert** to insert the clip art at the location of the insertion point.

LESSON 4 Working with Graphic Objects

WD 107

7. Point to the lower-right corner handle. The pointer changes to a double-headed arrow. Click the **double-headed arrow** on the corner handle and drag it toward the center of the clip art to resize the image to be approximately 3/4-inch square, as shown in **Figure WD 4–9**.

FIGURE WD 4–9
Resized clip art

8. On the Picture Tools Format tab, in the Adjust group, click the **Recolor** button.
9. In the Dark Variations category, click the green **Accent color 3 Dark** option (fourth from the left) to change the color of the clip art.
10. Click the **Undo** button on the Quick Access Toolbar.
11. Click the **Close** button on the Clip Art task pane to close it.
12. Save the document and leave it open for use in the next Step-by-Step.

Inserting and Modifying SmartArt

Sometimes the best way to convey information is to use a chart or diagram. For example, an organization chart clearly shows the hierarchy of who reports to whom, while a flow chart depicts a course of actions. A ***SmartArt graphic*** is a predesigned diagram made up of shapes containing text that illustrates a concept or idea. The organization chart shown in **Figure WD 4–10** is an example of one type of SmartArt graphic you can create easily in Word. Other types of SmartArt graphics include lists, processes, cycles, hierarchies, relationships, matrixes, and pyramids.

▶ **VOCABULARY**
SmartArt graphic

UNIT II Microsoft Word

FIGURE WD 4–10 Organization chart SmartArt graphic

You insert a diagram using the Insert SmartArt Graphic button in the Illustrations group of the Insert tab on the Ribbon. SmartArt graphics are inserted with placeholder text, much like the placeholders used in templates. You can replace the placeholder text with your own text.

After you insert a SmartArt graphic, the SmartArt Tools Design and Format contextual tabs are displayed on the Ribbon and provide access to a range of tools for customizing the graphic.

When you insert a SmartArt graphic, a Text pane is also displayed to help simplify the process of entering text. You can click a [Text] placeholder beside a bullet in the Text pane to enter text in a shape. The Text pane can be hidden or displayed by clicking the Text Pane button on the SmartArt Tools Design tab in the Create Graphic group.

Step-by-Step WD 4.4

The Go Green Newsletter *XXX*.docx document from Step-by-Step WD 4.3 should be open in the Word program window.

1. Scroll to page 2 and click a blank line at the top of the right column.
2. On the Insert tab, in the Illustrations group, click the **Insert SmartArt Graphic** button to open the Choose a SmartArt Graphic dialog box.
3. Click the **Cycle** category and click the **Block Cycle** option, as shown in **Figure WD 4–11**, and then click the **OK** button to insert the graphic into the document. Notice the Text pane is also displayed.

LESSON 4 Working with Graphic Objects

WD 109

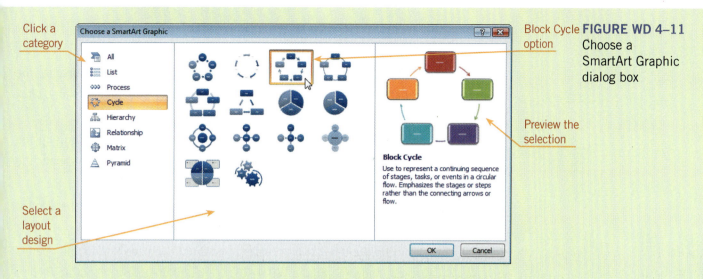

FIGURE WD 4–11 Choose a SmartArt Graphic dialog box

4. Click the top shape within the block cycle graphic to select it, if necessary, and press **Delete** to remove it.

5. Press **Delete** again to delete a second shape.

6. On the top shape, click the **[Text]** placeholder and type **Reduce**. Notice that the text automatically adjusts to fit in the shape.

7. Click the right shape placeholder and type **Reuse**.

8. In the Text pane, click the **[Text]** placeholder and type **Recycle** beside the third bullet.

9. On the SmartArt Tools Design tab, in the Layouts group, click the **More** button to display the Layouts gallery and click the **Multidirectional Cycle** layout, as shown in **Figure WD 4–12**.

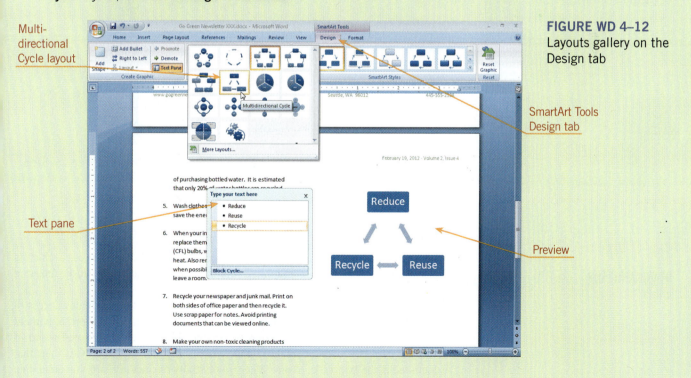

FIGURE WD 4–12 Layouts gallery on the Design tab

10. In the Create Graphic group, click the **Text Pane** button to hide the Text Pane.

11. In the SmartArt Styles group, click the **More** button to display the SmartArt Styles gallery. In the Best Match for Document category, click the **Moderate Effect** option, the fourth choice on the first row.

12. In the SmartArt Styles group, click the **Change Colors** button. In the green Accent 3 category, click the **Colored Fill - Accent 3** option, the second choice in the row.

13. Select the **Reuse** shape on the SmartArt graphic. In the Create Graphic group, click the **Right to Left** button to switch the layout.

14. Point to the lower-center resize handle until you see the double-headed arrow, shown in **Figure WD 4–13**. Click and drag down about an inch to increase the size of the graphic.

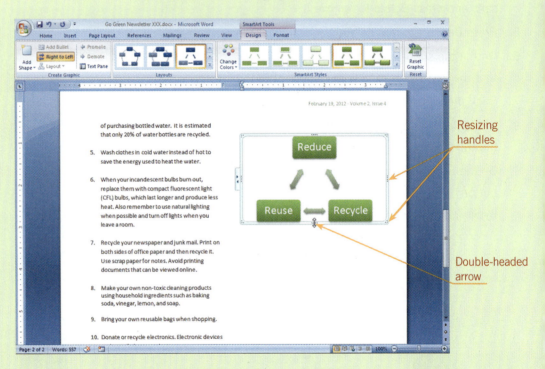

FIGURE WD 4–13
Resize a SmartArt graphic

15. Save the document and leave it open for use in the next Step-by-Step.

Inserting and Modifying Charts

When you need to illustrate or compare data, such as budget figures, a chart is the way to go. A ***chart*** is a graphical representation of data that can be inserted into Word.

The Chart button in the Illustrations group on the Insert tab provides access to different types of charts, such as bar, line, or pie. Using a chart in a Word document differs slightly from using other types of graphics because charts are composed of numerical data. The data that makes up the chart is stored in an Excel worksheet that is included in the Word file. (*Note:* When you initially create the chart, you enter data

▶ **VOCABULARY**
chart

LESSON 4   Working with Graphic Objects

in the Excel worksheet; however, you do not need to be familiar with Excel to create a chart.)

As with other types of graphics, after you insert a chart within a document, Word displays the Chart Tools Design, Layout, and Format contextual tabs for customizing the chart.

Step-by-Step WD 4.5

The Go Green Newsletter *XXX*.docx document from Step-by-Step WD 4.4 should be open in the Word program window.

1. On page 1, click to the left of the *K* in *Keep Your City Beautiful*.
2. On the Insert tab, in the Illustrations group, click the **Insert Chart** button to display the Insert Chart dialog box.
3. Click the **Pie** category, as shown in **Figure WD 4–14**, and click the **OK** button to accept the default Pie chart type. An Excel spreadsheet opens with sample data that you will replace.

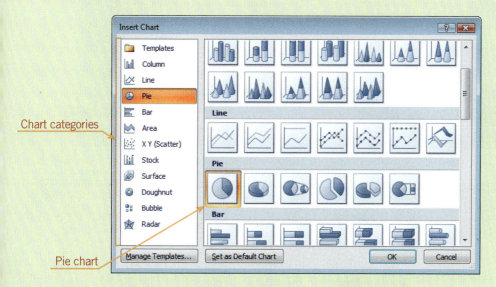

FIGURE WD 4–14
Insert Chart dialog box

4. Click in cell B1, which contains the word *Sales*, and type **Where does our trash go?**
5. Click cell A2 and type **Incinerator**. Press **Tab** to move to cell B2. Type **13%** and press **Tab** to move to the next active cell.
6. In cell A3, type **Recycling Center**. Press **Tab** to move to cell B3. Type **30%** and press **Tab**.
7. In cell A4, type **Landfill**. Press **Tab** to move to cell B4. Type **55%** and press **Tab**.
8. In cell A5, type **Other**. Press **Tab** to move to cell B5. Type **2%**.

9. Click the **Close** button ✕ of the Excel window to close the spreadsheet and view the chart in the document.

10. If necessary, click the chart to select it. On the contextual Chart Tools Format tab, in the Arrange group, click the **Position** button and click the **Position in Bottom Left with Square Text Wrapping** option, as shown in **Figure WD 4–15**. The chart is now positioned in the lower-left corner of the first page.

FIGURE WD 4–15
Position button and menu

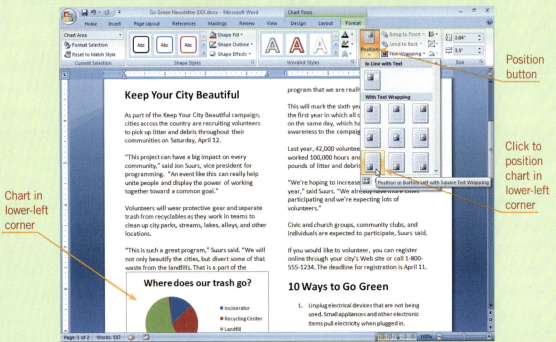

11. Scroll down, if necessary, and select the chart. On the contextual Chart Tools Layout tab, in the Labels group, click the **Data Labels** button and click the **Inside End** option. Data labels are added to each piece of the pie chart.

12. On the contextual Chart Tools Design tab, in the Chart Styles group, click the **More** button ⩔ to display the Chart Styles gallery. Click **Style 37**, as shown in **Figure WD 4–16**.

LESSON 4 Working with Graphic Objects

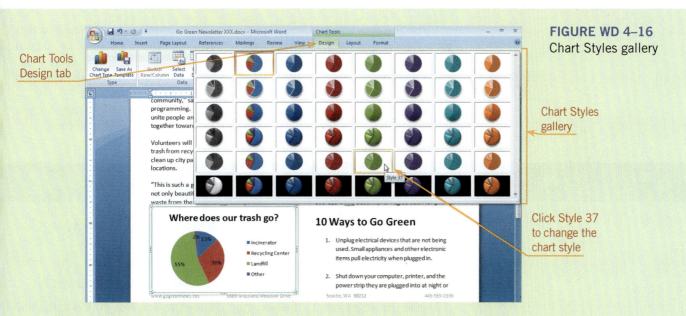

FIGURE WD 4–16
Chart Styles gallery

13. In the Type group, click the **Change Chart Type** button to display the Change Chart Type dialog box. Click the **Column** category and the **Stacked Column** type (second option from left on the top row) and click the **OK** button to replace the pie chart with a stacked column chart.

14. Click the **Undo** button on the Quick Access Toolbar to revert back to the pie chart.

15. Save the document and leave it open for use in the next Step-by-Step.

Inserting and Modifying Objects

You just learned to insert graphic objects that are made up mainly of pictures, drawings, and shapes to add interest to documents. In addition to these eye-catching images, you can also use objects that are largely made up of text as graphic elements in documents. Text boxes, WordArt, Drop Caps, and Quick Parts are examples of such objects you can insert using the buttons in the Text group of the Insert tab on the Ribbon, shown in **Figure WD 4–17**.

FIGURE WD 4–17 Text group on the Insert tab

Inserting a Text Box

A *text box* is a container that allows you to position text and/or graphics. Text boxes can be especially useful for adding enlarged quotations (called pull quotes) to documents, but also for keeping paragraphs and graphics together and for making text flow around other text or graphics.

▶ **VOCABULARY**
text box

UNIT II   Microsoft Word

The Text Box button is located in the Text group on the Insert tab. The Text Box gallery contains predesigned text boxes you can insert into documents, or you can draw a new blank text box. Text boxes can be moved and resized; options are available for modifying borders, fills, and effects. You can apply custom formatting to text within a text box the same way you would any text.

The Text Box Tools Format contextual tab is displayed on the Ribbon when you insert a text box. This tab contains tools for modifying and moving text boxes.

Step-by-Step WD 4.6

The Go Green Newsletter *XXX*.docx document from Step-by-Step WD 4.5 should be open in the Word program window.

1. Position the insertion point before the *K* in *Keep Your City Beautiful*.
2. On the Insert tab, in the Text group, click the **Text Box** button to display the Text Box gallery.
3. Scroll down and click the **Stacks Quote**.
4. Click the placeholder text and type **"An event like this can really help unite people and display the power of working together toward a common goal."**
5. Select the text you just typed. On the Home tab, in the Font group, click the **Font** button arrow and click **Cambria** to change the font.
6. Select the text box and position the pointer over a dotted line until you see the four-headed move pointer, then drag it to the top of the second column.
7. Select the text box. On the Text Box Tools Format tab, in the Arrange group, click the **Text Wrapping** button and click **Top and Bottom** so that text will not wrap around the sides of the text box if it is resized smaller. Your screen should look similar to **Figure WD 4–18**.

LESSON 4 Working with Graphic Objects

FIGURE WD 4–18
Text Box

8. Save the document and leave it open for use in the next Step-by-Step.

Inserting and Modifying WordArt

WordArt is a drawing tool that turns words into a graphics image. You can use the WordArt feature to create interesting text effects to enhance documents. WordArt lets you fit text into a variety of shapes, use unusual alignments, and add three-dimensional effects. The bright colors and unusual alignments can be fun to combine, but you must make sure the graphic you create is appropriate for the document. For example a rainbow-colored curvy design would not be appropriate for a report in an attorney's office, but it might be suitable for a child care center newsletter. The WordArt button is located in the Text group on the Insert tab.

You edit a WordArt drawing object the same way you edit other Word graphics. You can resize the WordArt graphic, change its style, add borders, and reposition it. When a WordArt object is selected, the WordArt Tools Format contextual tab is displayed.

> **VOCABULARY**
> **WordArt**

Step-by-Step WD 4.7

The Go Green Newsletter *XXX*.docx document from Step-by-Step WD 4.6 should be open in the Word program window.

1. Scroll to page 2 and select the heading *Did You Know?*.
2. On the Insert tab on the Ribbon, in the Text group, click the **WordArt** button and click **WordArt style 9**, as shown in **Figure WD 4–19**. The Edit WordArt Text dialog box opens.

FIGURE WD 4–19
WordArt button and gallery

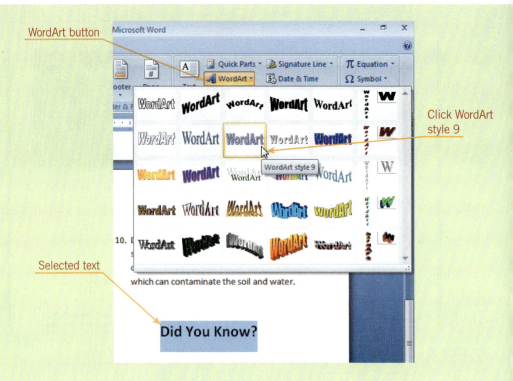

3. Click the **OK** button to insert the WordArt.
4. On the contextual WordArt Tools Format tab, in the WordArt Styles group, click the **More** button to display the WordArt Styles gallery.
5. Click **WordArt style 15**.
6. In the Text group, click the **Edit Text** button to display the Edit WordArt Text dialog box.
7. Click the **Font** button arrow, scroll through the menu of fonts, and then click **Cambria**.
8. Click the **Size** button and then click **24**.
9. Click the **Bold** button and then click the **OK** button to close the dialog box.
10. In the Text group, click the **Spacing** button and click the **Tight** option.
11. In the WordArt Styles group, click the **Shape Fill** button arrow, and click **Olive Green, Accent 3, Darker 50%** to change the color slightly to match the other colors in the document, as shown in **Figure WD 4–20**.

LESSON 4 Working with Graphic Objects WD 117

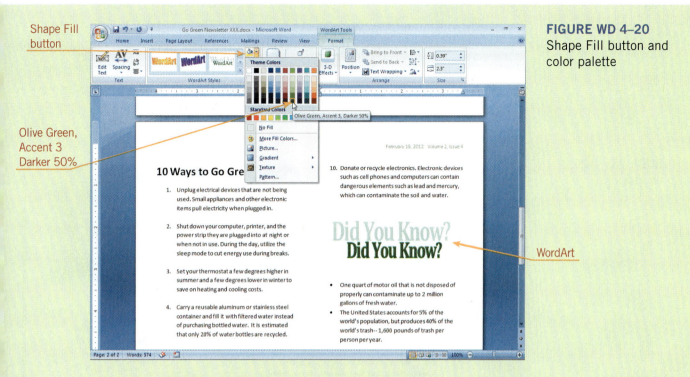

FIGURE WD 4–20
Shape Fill button and color palette

12. Save the document and leave it open for use in the next Step-by-Step.

Inserting a Drop Cap

A ***drop cap*** is a large initial capital letter or a large first word used to add interest to text, such as at the beginning of a document. The Drop Cap button in the Text group on the Insert tab displays a menu with options for inserting a drop cap within a paragraph or in the margin. The Drop Cap Options command lets you specify additional options.

▶ **VOCABULARY**
drop cap

Step-by-Step WD 4.8

The Go Green Newsletter *XXX*.docx document from Step-by-Step WD 4.7 should be open in the Word program window.

1. Select the *A* in *As* in the first paragraph of text on page 1.
2. On the Insert tab, in the Text group, click the **Drop Cap** button and then click the **Dropped** option.
3. Using the tools on the Home tab on the Ribbon, change the font color to **Olive Green, Accent 3, Darker 50%** and apply bold to the drop cap.

4. Your drop cap should look similar to **Figure WD 4–21**. Take a moment to review the page. If a few lines of text from the *Keep Your City Beautiful* article have moved to the next page, adjust the placement of the chart if necessary, and reduce the size of the text box and/or move it slightly higher in the column so that all the text for that article fits on one page.

FIGURE WD 4–21
Drop cap

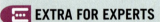
Drop cap

5. Save the document and leave it open for use in the next Step-by-Step.

Creating and Inserting Quick Parts

In the previous activities, you have inserted predesigned document parts, such as headers, text boxes, and cover pages called ***building blocks***. These reusable parts are accessible in galleries and are stored in the Building Blocks Organizer. A ***Quick Part*** is a type of building block made up of an image and/or text that you can create, save, and reuse, such as a company logo or address.

The Quick Parts button is located in the Text group of the Insert tab. The Quick Parts menu contains the Building Blocks Organizer command that opens the Building Blocks Organizer where you can insert, delete, edit, and preview building blocks. The Save Selection to Quick Parts Gallery command saves a selected item, such as a company letterhead, to the Building Blocks Organizer. Once you save a selection as a building block, it becomes available in the Quick Parts gallery.

▶ **VOCABULARY**
building blocks
Quick Part

▣ **EXTRA FOR EXPERTS**

To insert a Quick Part, you can type the name you saved it with and press F3.

LESSON 4   Working with Graphic Objects

WD 119

Step-by-Step WD 4.9

The Go Green Newsletter *XXX*.docx document from Step-by-Step WD 4.8 should be open in the Word program window.

1. In the document title, click after the *s* in *Go Green News*.
2. Drag to the left to select *Go Green News* and the sprout clip art. (Make sure you select only the sprout clip art and the text, because these will become your Quick Part.)
3. On the Insert tab on the Ribbon, in the Text group, click the **Quick Parts** button and click **Save Selection to Quick Part Gallery**, as shown in **Figure WD 4-22**. The Create New Building Block dialog box opens.

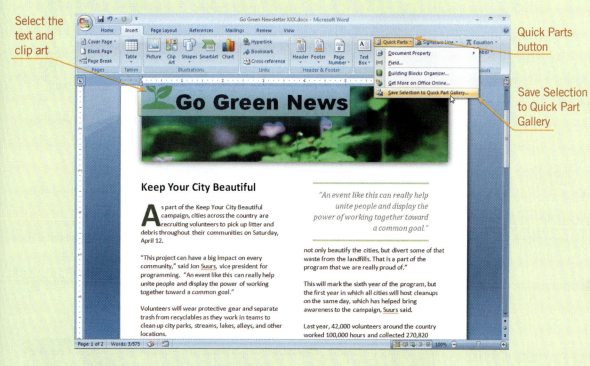

FIGURE WD 4-22 Quick Parts button and menu

4. Notice that Word has inserted a name for this building block and that it will be stored in the Quick Parts gallery. Click the **OK** button to save it to the Building Blocks Organizer.
5. Save the document and close it using the Close command on the Office Button menu.
6. Open **Step WD 4-9.docx** from the folder containing the data files for this lesson and save it as **Go Green Sales Letter *XXX*.docx** (replace the *XXX* with your initials).

7. On the Insert tab, in the Text group, click the **Quick Parts** button and click the **Go Green News** quick part from the menu, as shown in **Figure WD 4–23**, to insert it into the document.

FIGURE WD 4–23 Quick Parts gallery

8. Save the document and leave it open for use in the next Step-by-Step.

Creating and Modifying Tables

A *table* is a grid of horizontal rows and vertical columns of numbers, text, or graphics, as shown in **Figure WD 4–24**. It is often easier to align text using tables than using tabs. A *cell* is the intersection of a row and a column. You move from cell to cell from left to right and then down to the next row by pressing Tab. You can move out of a table when you reach the last cell by pressing the down arrow key or by clicking outside of the table.

▶ **VOCABULARY**
table
cell

2012 Sales				
	Qtr1	Qtr2	Qtr3	Qtr4
Collins, J.	$38,456	$56,934	$34,457	$36,421
Jenkins, S.	$31,213	$29,456	$37,432	$32,534
Wong, Y.	$25,421	$32,365	$44,343	$33,893
Haig, H.	$32,238	$28,452	$26,476	$46,222

FIGURE WD 4–24 Table

Word offers several ways to create a table using the Table button in the Tables group on the Insert tab. You can use the Insert Table grid, the Insert Table dialog box, the Draw Table command, or the Quick Tables command.

▶ **EXTRA FOR EXPERTS**

Quick Tables are predesigned tables, such as calendars, that you can insert in your documents. Word comes with several built-in table formats that are stored in the Quick Tables gallery on the Table button menu, and you can add your own table to the gallery using the Save Selection to Quick Tables Gallery command.

LESSON 4 Working with Graphic Objects

Creating a Table

To insert a new blank table, you use the Table button menu in the Tables group of the Insert tab to specify the number of columns and rows. To modify the table design with an added row, you can press Tab in the last cell to create a new row and move the insertion point into it.

> **EXTRA FOR EXPERTS**
>
> You can drag across the grid on the Insert Table menu to create a table with up to 10 columns and 8 rows.

Step-by-Step WD 4.10

The Go Green Sales Letter *XXX*.docx document from Step-by-Step WD 4.9 should be open in the Word program window.

1. Click the second blank line below the second paragraph that begins *We recently conducted*.
2. On the Insert tab, in the Tables group, click the **Table** button to display the Insert Table menu.
3. Click the **Insert Table** command on the menu to open the Insert Table dialog box.
4. In the Number of columns box, type **2** and press **Tab**.
5. In the Number of rows box, type **12**, as shown in **Figure WD 4–25**.

FIGURE WD 4–25
Insert Table dialog box

6. Click the **OK** button to insert the blank table.
7. Type the following data in the table as shown, pressing **Tab** to move to the next cell and to the next row.

Reader Survey Responses	
Characteristic	Percentage
Recycle regularly	94%
Purchase "green" products often	44%

Reader Survey Responses	
Are concerned about the environment	86%
Have an income above $60,000	57%
Have a college degree	66%
Are under the age of 40	38%
Are above the age of 40	62%
Are female	65%
Are male	35%

8. Save the document and leave it open for use in the next Step-by-Step.

Modifying a Table

You can apply different fonts, font styles, and font sizes to table text the same way you apply them to other text in a document. To apply a style or other formatting to a table, you first need to select the table by clicking the Table Move handle outside the upper-left corner of the table.

When you insert a table, the contextual Table Tools Design and Layout tabs are displayed with options for modifying a table.

> **EXTRA FOR EXPERTS**
>
> When you want to insert more than one row or column, select the number of rows before choosing the Insert Above or Insert Below command from the Table Tools Layout tab. Word inserts that many rows or columns.

> **EXTRA FOR EXPERTS**
>
> You can use the Convert Text to Table command on the Table button menu to convert text separated by paragraph marks, commas, tabs, or other characters to cells in a table. You can also reverse the process to convert a table to paragraphs or tabbed text.

Step-by-Step WD 4.11

The Go Green Sales Letter *XXX*.docx document from Step-by-Step WD 4.10 should be open in the Word program window.

1. If necessary, click the table to display the Table Move Handle in the upper-left corner of the table.

LESSON 4 Working with Graphic Objects   WD 123

2. Click the **Table Move Handle** to select the entire table.
3. On the contextual Table Tools Design tab, in the Table Styles group, click the **More** button to display the Table Styles gallery.
4. Scroll the gallery if necessary, and point to the **Medium Grid 1 - Accent 3** style, shown in **Figure WD 4–26**, then click to apply the style.

FIGURE WD 4–26
Table Styles gallery

5. On the contextual **Table Tools Design** tab, in the Table Style Options group, click the **First Column check box** to remove the checkmark indicating that special formatting should be applied to the first column.
6. Click to the left of the first row to select it. On the contextual Table Tools Layout tab, in the Merge group, click the **Merge Cells** button to combine the two cells into one.
7. In the Alignment group, click the **Align Center** button to center the title.
8. Click to the left of the blank second row to select it. In the Rows & Columns group, click the **Delete** button arrow and click **Delete Rows** from the menu to delete the row.
9. Select the row that contains *Have a college degree*. In the Rows & Columns group, click the **Insert Below** button to insert a new row.
10. In the blank row, type **Vote regularly**. Press **Tab** and type **71%**.
11. In the Cell Size group, click the **AutoFit** button and then click **AutoFit Contents** to resize the columns to fit the contents.

12. In the Table group, click the **Properties** button to display the Table Properties dialog box.
13. In the Alignment area, click **Center** and then click the **OK** button to center the table horizontally.
14. Save and close the document, and then close Word. If you get a warning message about saving the building blocks file, click **Yes**.

ETHICS IN TECHNOLOGY

Copyrighted Images

There are many colorful graphics and beautiful pictures displayed on the Web. But as you surf the Internet, remember that copyright laws apply online also. You cannot just download an image from a Web page and use it in your Word documents or other files without permission. Some images are freely available, but always check an image's copyright before taking it for your own purposes.

SUMMARY

In this lesson, you learned:

- To insert and modify pictures, shapes, clip art, SmartArt, and charts to add visual impact to documents.
- That text objects such as text boxes, WordArt, drop caps, and Quick Parts can be used to add interest to documents.
- Text can be efficiently aligned and presented in rows and columns using tables.

■ VOCABULARY REVIEW

Define the following terms:

building block	drop cap	selection handles
cell	floating picture	SmartArt graphic
chart	inline object	table
clip art	pictures	text box
drawing objects	Quick Parts	WordArt

■ REVIEW QUESTIONS

MULTIPLE CHOICE

Select the best response for the following statements.

1. The green circle at the top of a graphic is used to _____ a graphic.

   A. insert
   B. crop
   C. resize
   D. rotate

LESSON 4 Working with Graphic Objects

WD 125

2. Small circles and squares at the sides and corners of a graphic are called _____.
   - A. SmartArt
   - B. pictures
   - C. selection handles
   - D. rotate circles

3. Text cannot wrap around _____ objects.
   - A. floating
   - B. drawing
   - C. graphic
   - D. inline

4. Enter a _____ to search for related clip art in the Clip Art task pane.
   - A. keyword
   - B. formula
   - C. picture
   - D. placeholder

5. An organization chart is an example of a _____.
   - A. table
   - B. WordArt graphic
   - C. picture
   - D. SmartArt graphic

6. The data that makes up a chart is stored in a(n) _____.
   - A. table
   - B. Excel worksheet
   - C. Quick Part
   - D. Word document

7. A _____ is a container that allows you to position text and/or graphics.
   - A. chart
   - B. placeholder
   - C. table
   - D. text box

8. A _____ is a large initial capital letter or a large first word used to add interest to text.
   - A. chart
   - B. WordArt style
   - C. drop cap
   - D. Quick Part

9. Predesigned document parts, such as headers and cover pages, are called _____.
   - A. text boxes
   - B. building blocks
   - C. drop caps
   - D. placeholders

10. The _____ command combines cells so you can center a heading over an entire table.
    - A. Merge Cells
    - B. Properties
    - C. Insert Table
    - D. Group

FILL IN THE BLANK

Complete the following sentences by writing the correct word or words in the blanks provided.

1. _____ are digital photographs or images.
2. Shapes, curves, and lines are considered _____ objects.
3. You can search for pictures, sounds, and movies in the _____ _____ task pane.
4. SmartArt graphics are inserted with _____ that you can replace with your own text.
5. A(n) _____ is used to illustrate or compare data.
6. A pull quote is an example of a(n) _____ _____.
7. _____ turns words into a graphics image.
8. A(n) _____ _____ is a type of building block that you can create, save, and reuse.

9. A(n) _____ is the intersection of a row and a column.

10. You can add a new row to a table by pressing _____ in the last cell.

■ PROJECTS

PROJECT WD 4–1

1. Open the **Project WD 4–1.docx** document from the folder containing the data files for this lesson and save it as **Earth Day Award** *XXX*.**docx** (replace *XXX* with your initials).

2. Insert the Autumn Leaves photo (or another picture of your choice) from the Sample Pictures folder. Position and crop it as shown in **Figure WD 4–27**.

3. Compress the picture for improved print resolution.

4. Insert the 24-Point star shape as shown. Fill it with Center Gradient –Accent 3 style and apply the Shadow Style 5.

5. Position the insertion point before the *E* in *Earth Day* at the bottom of the page. Search for and insert the Earth clip art as an inline graphic at the bottom of the page. Resize it and recolor it to the blue Accent color 1 Light.

6. Select the clip art and the Earth Day 2012 text and save it to the Quick Parts gallery.

7. Insert a line approximately 4 inches long above *Committee Chair*.

8. Save and close the document.

FIGURE WD 4–27   Earth Day Award *XXX*.docx

PROJECT WD 4–2

1. Open the **Project WD 4–2.docx** document from the folder containing the data files for this lesson and save it as **Sales Memo** *XXX*.**docx** (replace *XXX* with your initials).

2. Merge the cells in the first row and center the title.

3. Insert a blank row above the second row.

4. Add the following data in the new row:

| Qtr1 | Qtr2 | Qtr3 | Qtr4 |

5. Select the table and apply the blue Medium Shading 2-Accent 1 table style.

6. Insert the Contrast Sidebar from the Text Box gallery. In the placeholder, type **Connerton Manufacturing**. **Specializing in eco-friendly business solutions**.

7. Insert the Earth Day 2012 Quick Part (or type Earth Day 2012) at the bottom of the page and type **Award Winner** after it.

8. Save and close the document.

LESSON 4 Working with Graphic Objects

ON YOUR OWN

Open the **Sales Memo *XXX*.docx** document and sort the rows using the first column. Save and close the document.

ON YOUR OWN

Open the **Sales Memo *XXX*.docx** document and add a total row and insert formulas to sum up each column. Save and close the document.

ON YOUR OWN

Delete the Earth Day 2012 and Go Green News Quick Parts from the Building Blocks Organizer.

PROJECT WD 4–3

1. Create a new blank document and save it as **Profits *XXX*.docx** (replace *XXX* with your initials).
2. Create a Line with Markers chart using the following data:

	Product 1	Product 2	Product 3
Northeast	23,456	53,547	59,034
Midwest	41,703	29,048	46,900
Pacific	63,345	99,331	33,987
Atlantic	53,806	107,853	52,357

3. Change the chart to a Clustered Column chart.
4. Add data labels using the Outside End option.
5. Add a chart title above the chart named *Profits*.
6. Format the chart using Style 27 from the Chart Styles gallery.
7. Save and close the document.

ON YOUR OWN

Open the **Profits *XXX*.docx** file and edit the Product 1 data for the Northeast to 41,987. Save and close the document.

PROJECT WD 4–4

1. Create a new blank document and save it as **Organization Chart *XXX*.docx** (replace *XXX* with your initials).
2. Create the document shown in **Figure WD 4–28**. (*Hint*: Select the President shape and use the Add Shape button to add an assistant. Select the SmartArt graphic and apply the Intense Effect Smart Art style and change the color of the graphic to Colored Fill - Accent 2.)
3. Save and close the document.

FIGURE WD 4–28   Organization Chart *XXX*.docx

ON YOUR OWN

Open the **Organization Chart *XXX*.docx** file and create WordArt using the Organization Chart title. Save and close the document.

WEB PROJECT

PROJECT WD 4–5

Create a logo for the Sandy Beach resort using one or more pieces of clip art, WordArt, pictures, SmartArt, or shapes. Use the *Clip art on Office Online* link at the bottom of the Clip Art task pane to search for free images on the Microsoft Web site that you can use in your logo. Browse the site for additional hints and tips on how to use clip art effectively.

 ## TEAMWORK PROJECT

PROJECT WD 4–6

With a partner, create a two-page newsletter on the topic of your choice, such as your favorite sport, a place you would like to visit, or your favorite hobby. Work together to plan and write the articles and format the document. Include appropriate graphic objects, such as drop caps, text boxes, and clip art.

 ## CRITICAL THINKING

ACTIVITY WD 4–1

Search for the demo in Word Help titled Spice up your text with SmartArt graphics and watch it. How can this feature add emphasis to text and data? What types of SmartArt graphics work best for different kinds of data?

ACTIVITY WD 4–2

Search the Clip Art task pane for an advertising character to promote a favorite product. Insert the clip art and create an advertisement using the picture. Crop, resize, rotate, and adjust contrast, brightness, or coloration to change the graphic. Use shapes and other objects such as WordArt to display the character's name and/or slogan. Be prepared to share your advertisement with the class.

ACTIVITY WD 4–3

Did you know that text boxes can be linked? Use Word Help to learn how to link text boxes. Create a text box and type a paragraph of text in the text box. Insert a second text box, add some text, and link it to the first. Experiment with the size of the text boxes so that your text fits within both text boxes. How many text boxes can be linked? Can text boxes be linked across pages? How could text box linking be helpful in a document?

UNIT II REVIEW

Word

REVIEW QUESTIONS

MULTIPLE CHOICE

Select the best response for the following statements.

1. A(n) _____ is written information that can be printed on paper or distributed electronically.
   - A. margin
   - B. document
   - C. insertion point
   - D. I-beam

2. Which feature automatically saves your document at regular intervals so that you can recover at least some of your work in case of a power outage or other unexpected shutdown?
   - A. Quick Access Toolbar
   - B. Print Preview
   - C. AutoRecover
   - D. word wrap

3. When you click the _____ button, the software prompts you to save your work if you made any changes since you last saved.
   - A. Margins
   - B. Save
   - C. Help
   - D. Close

4. The _____ button allows you to copy multiple text formatting characteristics and then apply the same formatting to other parts of the document.
   - A. Paste
   - B. Copy
   - C. Redo
   - D. Format Painter

5. _____ is the vertical distance between lines of text in a paragraph.
   - A. Line spacing
   - B. Indentation
   - C. Alignment
   - D. Point size

6. A _____ is a series of related words, numbers, or phrases.
   - A. theme
   - B. list
   - C. style
   - D. bullet

WD 129

7. When you break a document into _____, you can control a document's layout by formatting each differently.
   A. paragraphs C. sections
   B. lists   D. styles

8. _____ are vertical sections in which text flows from the bottom of one section to the top of the next.
   A. Pages   C. Lists
   B. Columns D. Styles

9. A(n) _____ object moves with the text around it.
   A. recolored C. inline
   B. cropped   D. floating

10. _____ lets you fit text into a variety of shapes, use unusual alignments, and add three-dimensional effects.
    A. WordArt   C. A table
    B. Clip art D. A drop cap

FILL IN THE BLANK

Complete the following sentences by writing the correct word or words in the blanks provided.

1. The _____ _____ is the blinking vertical bar that signals where any text you type will appear.
2. Before you can format text or move or delete text or graphics, you must _____, or highlight, the text or object you want to change.
3. Click the _____ button to access the New command.
4. Word flags words that might be misspelled with a wavy _____ underline.
5. _____ contain settings for margins, page size and orientation, and text and/or graphics that are standard for a particular type of document.
6. When you _____ text, Word rearranges selected text, numbers, or dates alphabetically, numerically, or chronologically.
7. A(n) _____ is text or graphics that appears in the top margin of each page in a document.
8. _____ are digital photographs or images.
9. A(n) _____ _____ is a large initial capital letter or a large first word used to add interest to text.
10. A(n) _____ is an arrangement of rows and columns of numbers, text, or graphics.

■ PROJECTS

PROJECT WD 1

1. Open a new blank document and save it as **Postcard *XXX*.docx** (replace XXX with your initials).
2. Change the paper size to A5.
3. Set the orientation to landscape.
4. Change the margins to Narrow.
5. Change the page layout to two even columns.
6. Type the word **move** in the Search for box of the Clip Art task pane and insert the black-and-white picture of the multiple chess pieces.
7. Press Enter to position the insertion point at the top of the second column, and type the following text:

   We Moved! (Press Enter three times.)

   Visit us at our new location:

   Games, Gifts & Gadgets Galore

UNIT II REVIEW Word

WD 131

1900 Newberry Street
Providence, RI 02987
401-555-3456

8. Center all the text and change the point size to 12.
9. Select *Games, Gifts & Gadgets Galore* and apply bold.
10. Select the bold line and the three lines below it. Change the line spacing to 1.0 with no space after the paragraph.
11. Select *We Moved!* and create WordArt using WordArt style 4 with Impact font, size 54 point.
12. Change the Theme fonts to Module.
13. Save and close the document.

ON YOUR OWN

Open the **Postcard** *XXX***.docx** file. Add a page border and recolor the picture. Save and close the document.

PROJECT WD 2

1. Open the file **Project WD 2.docx** from the folder containing the data files for this lesson and save it as **Thank You** *XXX***.docx** (replace *XXX* with your initials).
2. Change the page size to 13 x 20 cm (5 x 8 in).
3. Create custom margins of .75 inches on top, bottom, left, and right.
4. Change the text to Gil Sans MT, 12 point.
5. Select the *W* at the beginning of the first paragraph and insert a drop cap.
6. Select the three sentences after the colon beginning with *Add flavors*, and create a bulleted list using square bullets.
7. Use the Thesaurus to change the word *want* in the second sentence to the synonym **would like**.
8. Select all the text and justify it.
9. Show nonprinting characters.
10. Select the words *Thank You* and insert WordArt using WordArt style 13 using Gil Sans MT bold, 40 point.
11. Change the fill of the WordArt to Blue, Accent 1, Darker 50%. Add a Gradient, using the Dark Variation, From Center option.
12. Select the WordArt and rotate it 180 degrees so it is upside down. (*Hint*: Use the Rotate button in the Arrange group on the WordArt Tools Format contextual tab.) When you print this document on both sides and fold it in the middle, the words Thank You will be on the front and the other text inside.
13. Save the document and leave it open for use in the next project.

PROJECT WD 3

The document Thank You *XXX*.docx from Project 2 should be open in the Word program window.

1. Save the document as **Thank You 2** *XXX***.docx** (replace *XXX* with your initials).
2. Press Enter to insert a blank line below the upside down WordArt.
3. Open the ClipArt task pane and search for clip art with the keyword **coffee**.
4. Insert the picture of the coffee cup with the blue background.
5. Resize the picture to approximately 1½" square.
6. Flip the picture vertically.
7. Hide nonprinting characters.
8. Draw a text box at the bottom of the first page, as shown in **Figure WD 1**, and type and format the text shown.

UNIT II REVIEW   Word

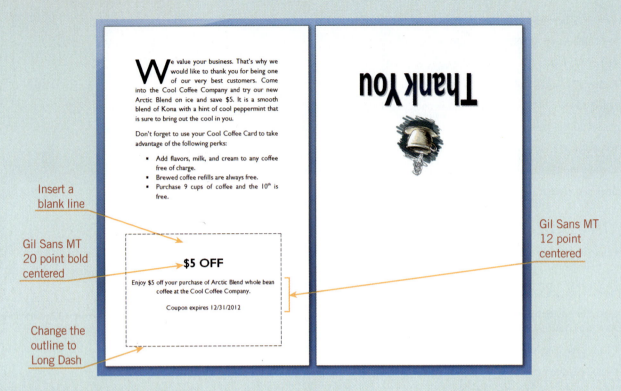

FIGURE WD 1   Thank You 2 *XXX*.docx

9. Save and close the document.

ON YOUR OWN

Open the **Thank You 2 *XXX*.docx** file. Change the color of the drop cap and add a color fill to the text box. Save and close the document.

PROJECT WD 4

1. Open the file **Project WD 4.docx** from the folder containing you data files for this lesson and save it as **Proposal Letter *XXX*.docx** (replace *XXX* with your initials).
2. Select *ABC Computers* and apply the Title style from the Quick Styles gallery.
3. Select the two-line address and apply the Subtitle style.
4. Select the remaining text in the letter and apply the Normal style.
5. Click the blank line after the paragraph that begins *Please look over the following table.* Insert a table with four columns and seven rows.
6. Enter text in the table as shown.

Hardware/ Software Solutions			
Item	Description	Availability	Price
Color printer	ColorJet Pro	2-day delivery	$450.00
Computer	ComQuest 2	In stock	$2599.99
Scanner	ScanMaster PE	2-day delivery	$529.99
Software	FileMaster 7	In stock	$899.00

UNIT II REVIEW Word

7. Select the numbers in the Price column and insert a decimal tab to align the numbers at the decimal point.
8. Merge the cells in the first row and center the title horizontally and vertically.
9. Apply the Medium Shading 2 - Accent 1 table style, in the fifth row in the gallery, to the entire table.
10. Deselect the First Column table style option.
11. Save the document and leave it open for use in the next project.

PROJECT WD 5

The Proposal Letter *XXX*.docx document from Project 4 should be open in the Word program window.

1. Save the document as **Proposal Letter 2 *XXX*.docx** (replace *XXX* with your initials).
2. Insert a blank row below the first row.
3. Change the document's theme to Foundry.
4. Check the spelling and grammar. Ignore the company and personal names and correct the misspelled words and grammar mistakes.
5. Use Find and Replace to change all occurrences of *Chung* to **Baldwin**.
6. Insert a diagonal confidential watermark.
7. Insert the Alphabet footer and replace the placeholder text with the company telephone number, **214-555-1234**.
8. Delete the word *Page* and the page number in the footer.
9. Create a Quick Part using the ABC Computers title at the top of the page.
10. Insert the Conservative cover page.
11. Delete the Company content control (and the words Thompson Steele), and insert the ABC Computers quick part.
12. Type **Equipment Proposal** as the document's title and delete the subtitle and abstract content controls.
13. Type **Cathan Baldwin** as the author of the document, and insert the current date as indicated.
14. Save and close the document and exit Word.

ON YOUR OWN

Open the **Proposal Letter *XXX*.docx** file. Sort the table in ascending order by the Price column. Save and close the document.

WEB PROJECT

Visit a job search Web site and conduct a search for jobs that require the use of Microsoft Word. What job titles require experience with Word? What level of experience is required? What are the other job requirements? What are the salary ranges? Choose a job that you would be interested in and read the entire job description. Choose a letter template and write a letter of application for the job. Explain the reasons why you believe you are qualified for the job as well as why you believe the job is right for you.

TEAMWORK PROJECT

With a partner, research the history of your school. Find out when it was established, who or what it was named after, how many students attend, and other relevant information. Create a brochure detailing this information that will be given to new students. Collaborate on the planning, writing, and design. With your instructor's permission, access the Microsoft Office Online brochure templates in the New Document dialog box for ideas. If you wish, you may download and use one of the templates, but be sure to choose one that was provided by Microsoft. When your project is complete, present it to the class.

CRITICAL THINKING

ACTIVITY WD 1

Create a one-page flyer announcing an upcoming school event. Assume the flyer will be posted in approved areas around the school. Use appropriate wording and graphics to convey the necessary information.

ACTIVITY WD 2

Create a table that displays your schedule of classes. Include columns for the class name, room number, time, day, instructor, and any other relevant information. Apply your choice of formatting and table styles.

PORTFOLIO CHECKLIST

Lesson 1

_____ Florida Admissions *XXX*.docx

_____ Graduation Postcard *XXX*.docx

_____ Lone Star Fax *XXX*.docx

Lesson 2

_____ Appointment Policy *XXX*.docx

_____ Spelling&Grammar *XXX*.docx

_____ Zare Resume Edit *XXX*.docx

Lesson 3

_____ Caring for Your Computer *XXX*.docx

_____ Verhoff Resume *XXX*.docx

Lesson 4

_____ Go Green Newsletter *XXX*.docx

_____ Sales Memo *XXX*.docx

Unit Review

_____ Postcard *XXX*.docx

UNIT III

MICROSOFT EXCEL 2007

Estimated Time for Unit: 7 hours

LESSON 1   **1.5 HRS.**
Understanding Excel Fundamentals

LESSON 2   **2 HRS.**
Formatting and Editing Worksheets

LESSON 3   **2 HRS.**
Using Formulas and Functions

LESSON 4   **1.5 HRS.**
Working with Charts and Graphics

LESSON 1

Understanding Excel Fundamentals

Estimated Time: 1.5 hours

■ OBJECTIVES

Upon completion of this lesson, you should be able to:
- Open an existing workbook.
- Navigate in a worksheet.
- Save a workbook.
- Select cells and enter data.
- Edit cell contents.
- Manipulate worksheets in the workbook.
- Change workbook views.
- Preview and print worksheets.
- Add headers and footers.
- Close a workbook.

■ DATA FILES

To complete this lesson, you will need these data files:

Step EX 1-1.xlsx
Project EX 1-1.xlsx
Project EX 1-3.xlsx
Project EX 1-4.xlsx
Project EX 1-5.xlsx
Activity EX 1-1.xlsx

■ VOCABULARY

active cell
cell
cell reference
column
footer
formula bar
freeze panes
header
Name box
range
row
select
sheet
sheet tab
spreadsheet software
workbook
workbook window
worksheet
...

EX 3

UNIT III   Microsoft Excel

VOCABULARY
spreadsheet software
workbook
worksheet
sheet
sheet tab
workbook window
columns

Introduction

Microsoft Excel 2007 is the spreadsheet program included in the Microsoft Office 2007 suite of software. ***Spreadsheet software*** is used to calculate, analyze, and visually represent numerical data. You can perform a variety of tasks, from creating budgets to tracking inventory to totaling sales figures.

As in other Office programs, the various tools for entering and editing data in Excel are organized on the Ribbon tabs. Excel includes predefined formulas, functions, and charts that allow you to quickly and accurately perform calculations—from the most basic to complex. With Excel you can create worksheets that are attractive, well organized, and that help you manage data effectively. Before you discover Excel's power to calculate and represent data quickly and easily, you need to learn basic skills such as opening, saving, and printing. In this lesson, you will learn techniques for performing fundamental skills using Excel.

Examining the Excel Program Window

An Excel file is called a ***workbook***. Each workbook contains a collection of related worksheets. A ***worksheet*** (also commonly called a spreadsheet or just a ***sheet***) is the grid with columns and rows where you enter and summarize data.

When you start Excel, a blank workbook opens, as shown in **Figure EX 1–1**. Use this figure to become familiar with the parts of the Excel program window.

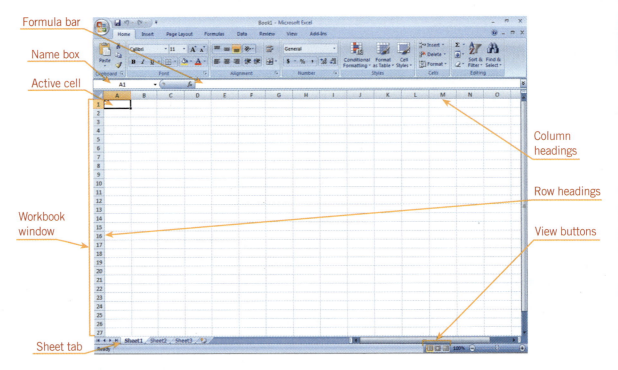

FIGURE EX 1–1   Excel program window

EXTRA FOR EXPERTS
You can access the Popular options in the Excel Options dialog box to change the number of sheets that are included by default in a new workbook.

By default, a new workbook contains three worksheets. The name of each sheet is displayed on a ***sheet tab*** at the bottom of the program window. In **Figure EX 1–1**, Sheet1 is the active sheet, as it is the one displayed in the ***workbook window***. You can add as many sheets as you need to a workbook, as much as 255 worksheets.

Columns in the worksheet are displayed vertically and are labeled with column headings from left to right beginning with A through Z, then AA through AZ, and

LESSON 1 Understanding Excel Fundamentals

so on. ***Rows*** are displayed horizontally and have numbered row headings running consecutively down the left side of the worksheet.

The rectangle where a column and row intersect is called a ***cell***. Each cell is identified by a ***cell reference***—the column letter heading followed by the row number heading, such as B5. The cell that is selected is called the ***active cell***, which means it is ready for data entry. Clicking a cell makes it active, as indicated by a thick black border around it. The column letter and row number headings of the active cell are also shaded for easy identification.

The ***Name box*** below the Ribbon displays the cell reference of the active cell. The ***formula bar*** next to the Name box displays the value or formula of the active cell.

> **VOCABULARY**
> rows
> cell
> cell reference
> active cell
> Name box
> formula bar

Starting Excel and Opening an Existing Workbook

To begin using Excel, you first need to start the program. You can do this by clicking the Start button on the Windows taskbar, and then clicking the program name on the All Programs menu, or by double-clicking an Excel program icon on the desktop. Once Excel starts, you can begin using it to create a new workbook or open an existing workbook.

To open an existing workbook, you can search for and then open the workbook file using the Open dialog box. See **Figure EX 1-2**. Excel provides three methods for displaying the Open dialog box. The most common method is through the Open command found on the Office Button menu. You can also add an Open command to your Quick Access Toolbar or use the keyboard shortcut Ctrl+O.

> **EXTRA FOR EXPERTS**
>
> By default, the names of the most recent files you opened in Excel will be listed in the Recent Documents list on the Office Button menu. You can click a file in the list to open it. You can customize the number of files displayed in the list using the Advanced section of the Excel Options dialog box.

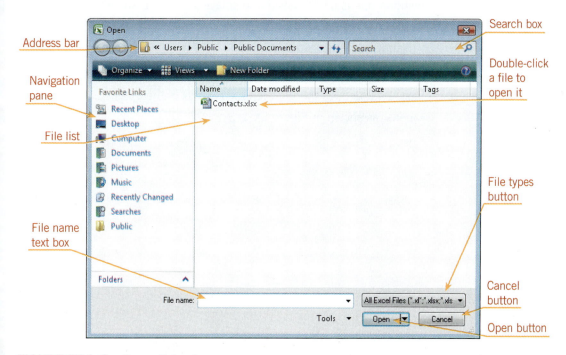

FIGURE EX 1-2 Open dialog box

You can use the Open dialog box to find and open existing files on your hard drive, CD, or other removable media; on a network drive to which you are connected; on your organization's intranet; or on the Internet. Double-clicking a file in the File list will open the file.

UNIT III Microsoft Excel

The following are parts of the Open dialog box:

- The Navigation Pane displays favorite links to folders that contain workbooks. You can view a folder's contents or open the folder from the Navigation Pane.
- The Address bar at the top of the dialog box shows the folder path.
- The Search box allows you to find a file by name, file type, or location.
- The File type button lists other file types you can choose to open.
- The Open button provides options for opening files, including opening the original file, opening a read-only version (when you want to open a file but keep the original file intact), or opening a copy of the original. If you open a copy or read-only version and edit or change the file, you cannot save changes to the original file. You can, however, use the Save As command to save your revisions with a new filename.
- The Cancel button closes the dialog box without opening a file.

Step-by-Step EX 1.1

1. Click the **Start** button on the Windows taskbar. The Start menu opens.
2. Click **All Programs**. A list of programs and program folders opens.
3. Click the **Microsoft Office** program folder. A list of Microsoft Office programs opens.
4. Click **Microsoft Office Excel 2007**. Excel 2007 starts and its program window opens on the desktop displaying a new, blank workbook.
5. Click the **Office** button on the Ribbon, and then click **Open** to display the Open dialog box.
6. If necessary, navigate to the folder containing the data files for this lesson. Double-click the file **Step EX 1-1.xlsx** in the File list. The workbook opens, as shown in **Figure EX 1–3**.

LESSON 1 Understanding Excel Fundamentals

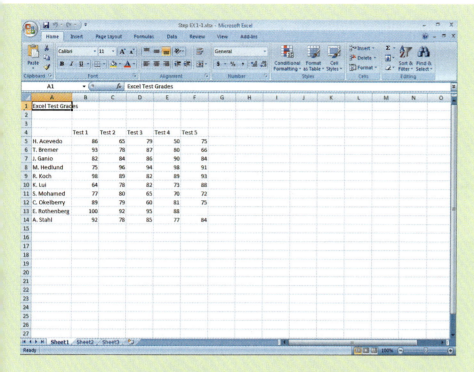

FIGURE EX 1–3
Step EX 1-1.xlsx workbook

7. Leave the workbook open for use in the next Step-by-Step.

Navigating in a Worksheet

A worksheet can, and often does, contain more data than what can be displayed within the workbook window. You can use the scroll bars, scroll boxes, and scroll arrows to move through a worksheet. When you drag the vertical scroll box, a ScreenTip displays the number of the topmost row that is visible in the workbook window. When you drag the horizontal scroll box, the ScreenTip displays the letter of the leftmost column that is visible in the workbook window, as shown in **Figure EX 1–4**.

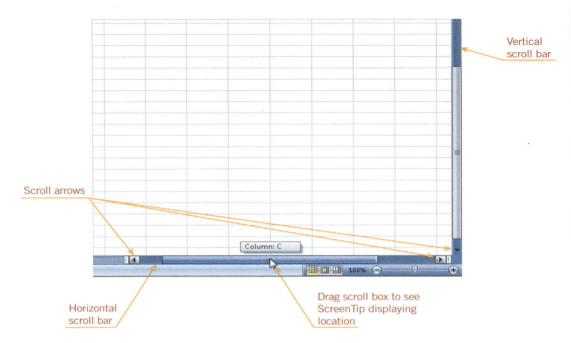

FIGURE EX 1–4 ScreenTip on horizontal scroll box

Clicking the scroll arrows on the vertical scroll bar moves the worksheet up or down one row. Clicking the scroll arrows on the horizontal scroll bar moves the worksheet left or right one column. You can also navigate using the keyboard and the Go To command.

Using the Keyboard

Table EX 1–1 contains some of the keys and key combinations you can use to move around a worksheet. When you use these keystrokes, you change the active cell.

TABLE EX 1–1 Using keystrokes to navigate the worksheet

PRESS KEY(S)	TO MOVE
Left arrow ←	One cell to the left
Right arrow →	One cell to the right
Up arrow ↑	One cell up
Down arrow ↓	One cell down
Page Up	Up one screen
Page Down	Down one screen
Home	To the first cell of a row
Ctrl+Home	To cell A1 at the beginning of the worksheet
Ctrl+End	To last cell of the worksheet containing data or formatting

LESSON 1   Understanding Excel Fundamentals

Using the Go To Command

You can use the Go To dialog box to navigate to a particular location in the worksheet. The Go To dialog box is opened by clicking the Go To command on the Find & Select menu in the Editing group on the Home tab. When you enter the cell name or range name in the Reference text box and click OK, the active cell moves to that specific location. This command is especially helpful when you want to move to a part of the worksheet that is not visible in the workbook window.

> **EXTRA FOR EXPERTS**
>
> You can also navigate to cells that meet certain conditions or contain specific data. Click the Special button in the Go To dialog box to display the Go To Special dialog box and then select an option, such as Comments, Blanks, or Last cell.

Step-by-Step EX 1.2

The Step EX 1-1.xlsx workbook from Step-by-Step EX 1.1 should be open in the Excel program window.

1. Press **Ctrl+Home** to move to cell A1 in the worksheet, if necessary.
2. Press the **right arrow** → key to move one cell to the right, to cell B1.
3. Press the **down arrow** ↓ key to move down one cell, to cell B2.
4. Click and drag the **scroll box** on the horizontal scroll bar as far right as possible and notice the ScreenTip displaying the letter of the leftmost column that is visible on the screen, column C.
5. In the Editing group on the Home tab on the Ribbon, click the **Find & Select** button, and then click **Go To** on the menu to display the Go To dialog box.
6. In the Reference text box, type **A7**, as shown in **Figure EX 1–5**, and then click the **OK** button to close the dialog box and move to cell A7.

FIGURE EX 1–5
Go To dialog box

7. Press **Ctrl+End** to move to the last cell of the worksheet containing data or formatting, cell F14.
8. Press **Home** to move to the first cell of the row, cell A14.
9. Click cell **D7** to move to that cell.
10. Click the **down scroll arrow** on the vertical scroll bar to move the worksheet down one row, so row 2 becomes the top row displayed in the workbook window.

11. Press **Page Down** to move down one page, to cell D34. Because it is not a long worksheet, no data is visible in the worksheet grid.
12. Press **Ctrl+Home** to move to cell A1.
13. Leave the workbook open for use in the next Step-by-Step.

Saving Workbooks

The first time you save a workbook, the options for saving include clicking the Save command on the Office Button menu, clicking the Save As command on the Office Button menu, or clicking the Save button on the Quick Access Toolbar. Each of these methods displays the Save As dialog box shown in **Figure EX 1–6**.

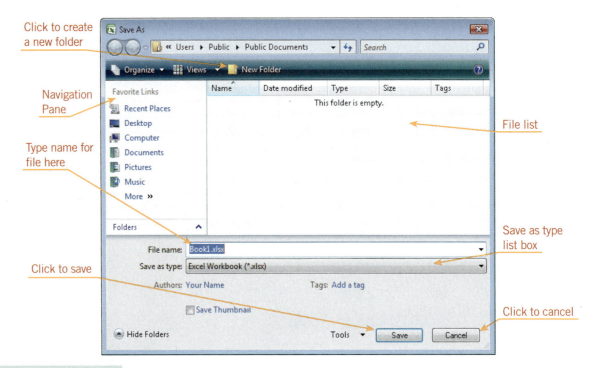

FIGURE EX 1–6 Save As dialog box

EXTRA FOR EXPERTS

Excel 2007 uses a new file format based on Extensible Markup Language (XML), which provides benefits such as more compact files, improved file recovery, better privacy, and improved data integration. Excel files saved in the new format have an .xlsx file extension and cannot be opened with previous versions of Excel. If you need to share files with someone using an earlier version, you can use the Excel 97-2003 Workbook option in the Save As section of the Office Button menu, which saves files with the previous .xls extension.

After you save a file the first time, you can use the Save button on the Quick Access Toolbar or the Save command on the Office Button menu to update it as you make changes to it. The Save As command opens the Save As dialog box, in which you can make a copy of the file with a new name, location, or file type. The Save As type list box provides options for saving a workbook in another format or as a template. You might need to change the file format or program and version if you share files with others who use different software. To save a worksheet in a specific location, you use the Navigation Pane of the Save As dialog box to navigate to the folder in which you want to save the workbook.

Excel's AutoRecover feature automatically saves your workbook at regular intervals so that you can recover at least some of your work in case of a power outage or other unexpected shut down. However, you should still save your work often and not rely on this automatic saving feature. You can change how frequently to save AutoRecover information or disable the AutoRecover feature by opening the Save page in the Excel Options dialog box from the Office Button menu.

LESSON 1   Understanding Excel Fundamentals   EX 11

Step-by-Step EX 1.3

The Step EX 1-1.xlsx workbook from Step-by-Step EX 1.2 should be open in the Excel program window.

1. Click the **Office Button** and then click **Save As** to open the Save As dialog box.
2. Navigate to the location where you will save your files.
3. Click the **File name** text box and type **Test Grades *XXX*.xlsx** (replace *XXX* with your initials).
4. Click the **Save** button to save a copy of the workbook with the new name in the specified location.
5. Leave the workbook open for use in the next Step-by-Step.

Selecting Cells

Before you can enter data or use Excel commands, you must *select*, or highlight, a cell or range. You can select a single cell by clicking it. A *range* is a group of cells. It can be a column, a row, or a group of cells forming a rectangle. A range is identified by the name of the cell in the upper-left corner of the range and the cell in the lower-right corner of the range, separated by a colon (:). For example, a range that includes all the cells between cells A1 and D5 is identified as A1:D5.

Excel identifies a selected range by using a different background color for the cells included in the range (except for the first cell, which does not change color), as shown in **Figure EX 1–7**. The row number and column letter of any cells in the range are also shaded a different color. You can deselect a cell or range by pressing an arrow key or clicking any cell in the worksheet.

▶ **VOCABULARY**
select
range

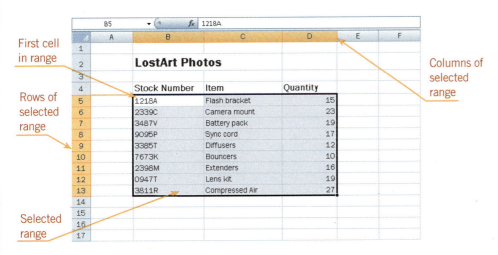

FIGURE EX 1–7   Selected range

UNIT III Microsoft Excel

You can select ranges or cells that are nonadjacent, meaning not side by side, by pressing the Ctrl key while you click. You can select a column and a row at the same time using the same method. **Table EX 1–2** shows how to select cells using the mouse. You can also select cells using the keyboard by pressing and holding the Shift key and using the arrow keys to extend the selection. Another way to select a range is to type the range reference (for example, A1:C5) in the Name box and then press the Enter key.

TABLE EX 1–2   Selecting cells using the mouse

TO SELECT	DO THIS
A single cell	Click the cell.
A range of cells	Click the first cell in the range (in the upper-left corner) and drag to the last cell in the range (in the lower-right corner). Or click the first cell in the range and then hold the Shift key and click the last cell in the range.
Nonadjacent cells or ranges	Press and hold the Ctrl key as you click or drag to select additional cells or ranges.
An entire row	Click the row heading.
An entire column	Click the column heading.
All cells on the worksheet	Click the Select All button in the upper-left corner of the workbook window.

Step-by-Step EX 1.4

The Test Grades *XXX*.xlsx workbook from Step-by-Step EX 1.3 should be open in the Excel program window.

1. Click cell **C8** to select it, as shown in **Figure EX 1–8**.

FIGURE EX 1–8
Selected cell

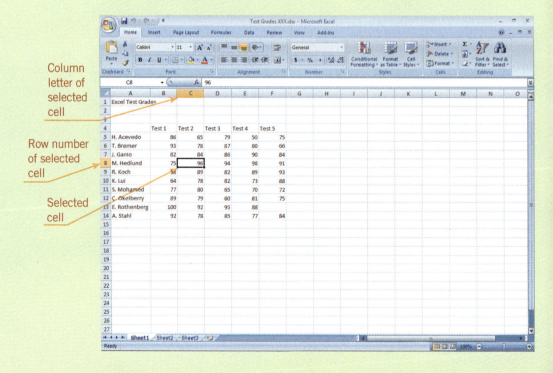

LESSON 1 Understanding Excel Fundamentals

2. Click cell **B5** and drag to cell **F14** to select the range B5:F14. Notice the selected range is shaded, except the first cell which does not change color.

3. Click the **row heading 10** to select the entire row. Notice the whole row is shaded, including the row number.

4. Press **Ctrl** and then click the **column heading E** to select the entire column while row 10 is still selected. Your screen should look similar to **Figure EX 1–9**.

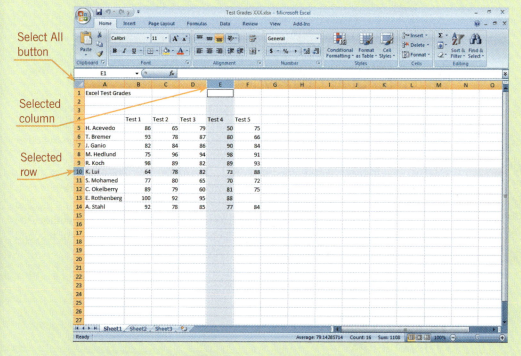

FIGURE EX 1–9
Selected column and row

5. Click the **Name** box, type **A5:A14**, and then press **Enter** to select that range.

6. Click the **Select All** button to select the entire worksheet.

7. Click cell **A1** to select it. Notice all the other cells on the worksheet are deselected.

8. Leave the workbook open for use in the next Step-by-Step.

Entering Data

You can enter data in Excel by typing numbers or text in the active cell and pressing the Enter key or clicking the Enter button on the formula bar. The cell below then becomes the active cell. Entering data and then pressing the Tab key selects the cell to the right, making it the active cell. You can also press an arrow key after typing data to enter it, and then move to the cell above or below or to the right or left.

As you enter data in a cell, the data is displayed in the active cell and in the formula bar, as shown in **Figure EX 1–10**. As you begin entering data, the message in the status bar changes from *Ready* to *Enter*. You can click the Cancel button on the formula bar or press the Esc key to cancel the entry you started to type.

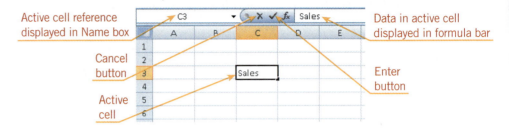

FIGURE EX 1–10 Formula bar

Understanding Data Types

Data in a cell can be text, such as letters, symbols, and other numeric characters, or numeric, such as values, dates, and times. Generally speaking, numeric data can be used in calculations, whereas text cannot. Excel automatically determines whether data is text or numeric as you enter it.

By default, text is left-aligned in a cell and numbers are right-aligned, as shown in **Figure EX 1–11**. If you want to enter a number (such as a postal code) as text, you can type an apostrophe before the number to signal that it is not to be used in calculations. Otherwise, a postal code such as 07458 would be displayed without the leading zero and would be right-aligned. If a cell contains a combination of text and numbers, the contents are left-aligned.

> **WARNING**
>
> The alignment of data in a cell is not an accurate indicator of the data type. For example, do not assume data in a cell is numeric just because it is right-aligned. Cell alignment can be changed without affecting the data type.

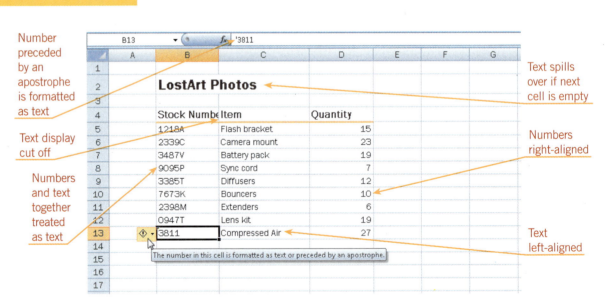

FIGURE EX 1–11 Data types

Text entries are often used as labels or headings that identify the numeric data you enter in a worksheet. If you enter text in a cell that is longer than the cell can display, it may spill over into empty cells to the right. The entire entry is still stored in the one cell, even though some of it is visible in adjacent cells. If the cell to the

LESSON 1   Understanding Excel Fundamentals

EX 15

right already contains data, the text displayed in the cell in which it was entered is truncated, or cut off. The entire entry is still stored in the cell even though you cannot see all of it.

Step-by-Step EX 1.5

The Test Grades *XXX*.xlsx workbook from Step-by-Step EX 1.4 should be open in the Excel program window.

1. In cell F13, type **87**. Notice that the number is displayed in the cell and in the formula bar and the *Ready* message on the left of the status bar changes to *Enter*, as shown in **Figure EX 1–12**.

Formula bar displays cell contents

Ready message changes to Enter when you type data

FIGURE EX 1–12
Entering data

	A	B	C	D	E	F	G	H
1	Excel Test Grades							
2								
3								
4		Test 1	Test 2	Test 3	Test 4	Test 5		
5	H. Acevedo	86	65	79	50	75		
6	T. Bremer	93	78	87	80	66		
7	J. Ganio	82	84	86	90	84		
8	M. Hedlund	75	96	94	98	91		
9	R. Koch	98	89	82	89	93		
10	K. Lui	64	78	82	73	88		
11	S. Mohamed	77	80	65	70	72		
12	C. Okelberry	89	79	60	81	75		
13	E. Rothenberg	100	92	95	88	87		
14	A. Stahl	92	78	85	77	84		

2. Press **Esc** to cancel the entry.
3. In cell F13, type **89** and then press **Enter** to enter the number. Notice the number is right-aligned in the cell.
4. In cell A2, type **Winter Term** and press the **right arrow** → key to enter the text and move the active cell to the right. Notice the text is left-aligned in the cell.
5. In cell A4, type **Name**.
6. Click the **Cancel** button ✗ on the formula bar to cancel the entry.

7. In cell A4, type **Student** and then click the **Enter** button on the formula bar to enter the text. Your screen should look similar to **Figure EX 1–13**.

FIGURE EX 1–13
Data entered in worksheet

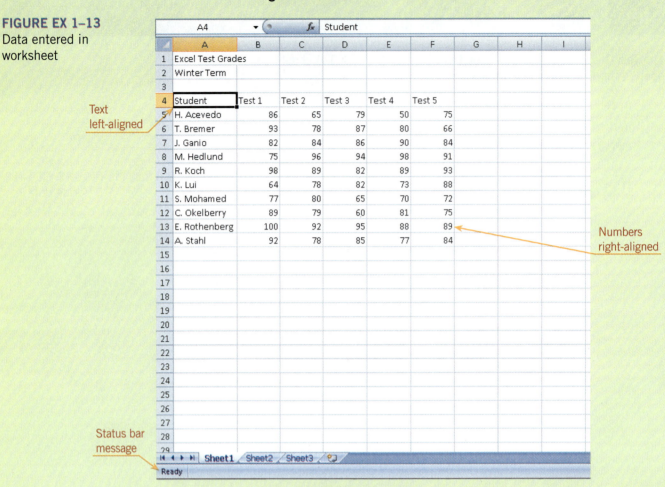

8. Click the **Save** button on the Quick Access Toolbar to save the changes to the workbook.
9. Leave the workbook open for use in the next Step-by-Step.

Editing Cell Contents

When you need to make changes to the data in your worksheet, you can overwrite the existing contents using the same methods you use to enter data in a blank cell. When you select a cell, type new data, and press the Enter key, the new data replaces the original cell contents.

You can also edit or delete data directly in the cell by selecting the cell and pressing F2 or double-clicking the cell. Or, you can select the cell and click in the formula bar. In the cell or the formula bar, you can click and drag to select the data or position the insertion point using arrow keys. Then you can use the Backspace or Delete keys to remove data, or type new data.

LESSON 1 Understanding Excel Fundamentals

If you want to remove all the data from a cell, you can clear it by right-clicking a cell and clicking the Clear Contents command or by using the Clear button located in the Editing group of the Home tab on the Ribbon. When you click the Clear button, a menu is displayed with options to clear the cell's formats, the cell's contents, or to clear the cell's comments. You can also choose to clear the cell of all contents, comments, and formatting at once.

Step-by-Step EX 1.6

The Test Grades *XXX*.xlsx workbook from Step-by-Step EX 1.5 should be open in the Excel program window.

1. Click cell **E5** to select it, type **65**, and then press **Enter** to replace the cell contents.

2. Double-click cell **A14** to activate it and then double-click the name **Stahl** to select it, as shown in **Figure EX 1–14**.

FIGURE EX 1–14 Editing contents in a cell

3. Type **Teal** to edit the cell contents and then press **Enter**.

4. Click cell **A4** to select it and then click at the end of the word *Student* in the formula bar to position the insertion point.

5. Press the **Spacebar** to insert a space and then type **Student Name** in the formula bar, as shown in **Figure EX 1–15**.

FIGURE EX 1–15 Editing contents in the formula bar

6. Click the **Enter** button on the formula bar to enter the changes in the cell.

7. Select the range **A5:F5**.

8. On the Home tab on the Ribbon, in the Editing group, click the **Clear** button, and then click **Clear All** on the menu to clear the contents and formatting from the cells in that range.

9. Save the workbook and leave it open for use in the next Step-by-Step.

UNIT III Microsoft Excel

Using Undo and Redo

You will often find it necessary to reverse, or undo, your most recent action. The Undo button on the Quick Access toolbar, shown in **Figure EX 1–16**, undoes the last action; clicking the Undo button a second time undoes the prior action, and so on. If you click the Undo button arrow, you see a list of actions you can undo. Not all actions can be undone. The Undo ScreenTip changes to reflect the last action that can be undone. For example, if you just entered the value of 65 in cell E5, the screen tip would read *Undo Typing '65' in E5*, because this was the last action you performed, and you can undo it with one click of the Undo button. Some actions cannot be undone; if you cannot undo an action, such as saving a file, then the button is dimmed and the ScreenTip reads *Can't Undo*.

> **WARNING**
>
> Get into the habit of undoing (reversing) a mistake immediately after you make it, because the Undo menu can be confusing to use. For example, if you undo the third item on the menu, the first two items are undone as well. You might not remember what those actions were, or you might not notice the effect within your worksheet when they are undone.

FIGURE EX 1–16   Undo and Redo buttons

If you perform and undo an action but then decide against the undo, you can use the Redo button on the Quick Access toolbar to reverse an Undo action. The Redo button arrow displays a list of actions you can redo. When you cannot redo an action, the button is dimmed and the ScreenTip reads Can't Redo.

Step-by-Step EX 1.7

The Test Grades*XXX*.xlsx workbook from Step-by-Step EX 1.6 should be open in the Excel program window.

1. In cell G4, enter **Test 6**.
2. In cell G6, enter **76**.
3. Click the **Undo** button arrow 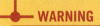 on the Quick Access Toolbar. Click the second item from the top of the menu, **Typing 'Test 6' in G4**, as shown in **Figure EX 1–17**. The last two actions are undone in the worksheet.

FIGURE EX 1–17
Undo button menu

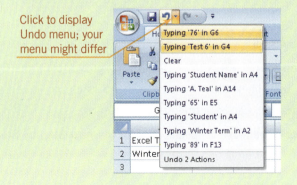

4. In cell G4, enter **Quiz 1**.

LESSON 1 Understanding Excel Fundamentals

EX 19

5. Click the **Undo** button on the Quick Access Toolbar to undo the action.
6. Click the **Redo** button on the Quick Access Toolbar to redo the action.
7. Save the workbook and leave it open for use in the next Step-by-Step.

Managing Worksheets

You can customize a workbook by renaming, inserting, or deleting the worksheets as needed. You can move from worksheet to worksheet by clicking a sheet tab to make a different worksheet active.

Renaming a Worksheet

By default, the worksheets contained in a new workbook are labeled Sheet1, Sheet2, and Sheet3. You can rename them with descriptive names to better identify the data they contain. When you double-click the sheet tab, the sheet name is selected and you can type a new name, as shown in **Figure EX 1–18**. You can also right-click a sheet tab and then click Rename on the shortcut menu.

> **EXTRA FOR EXPERTS**
>
> Another way to help identify a worksheet is to change the tab color by right-clicking a sheet tab, clicking Tab Color on the shortcut menu, and then clicking a color in the palette.

FIGURE EX 1–18 Rename a worksheet

Inserting a Worksheet

When you want to add another worksheet to your workbook, you can do so quickly by clicking the Insert Worksheet button to the right of the sheet tabs. You can also insert a worksheet by clicking the Insert button arrow in the Cells group on the Home tab on the Ribbon, and then clicking Insert Sheet or by right-clicking a sheet tab and then clicking Insert on the shortcut menu to display the Insert dialog box, as shown in **Figure EX 1–19**.

UNIT III   Microsoft Excel

FIGURE EX 1–19   Insert dialog box

> **WARNING**
>
> If there is any data in the worksheet you are deleting, a message box will open asking you to confirm you want to delete the sheet. Deleting a sheet will permanently delete the data it contains. You cannot undo this command, so be sure you want to take this action.

Deleting a Worksheet

If you don't need a worksheet, you can delete it from the workbook by right-clicking the sheet tab to display the shortcut menu and then clicking Delete. Or on the Home tab on the Ribbon, in the Cells group, click the Delete button arrow and then click Delete Sheet.

Moving or Copying Worksheets within a Workbook

If you need to order worksheets in a more logical way within a workbook, it is easy to rearrange them by clicking a sheet tab and dragging it to a new position. A page icon is displayed beneath the mouse pointer and a black arrow helps you choose the position as you drag. You can copy a worksheet by pressing and holding the Ctrl key while you drag. The page icon will display a plus sign when you are copying a worksheet.

You can also open the Move or Copy dialog box, shown in **Figure EX 1–20**, by right-clicking a sheet tab and clicking Move or Copy on the shortcut menu. You can select where to position the worksheet in the Before sheet list box and select the Create a copy check box if you want to copy the worksheet.

> **EXTRA FOR EXPERTS**
>
> You can move or copy worksheets to another workbook by right-clicking the sheet tab, clicking Move or Copy, to open the Move or Copy dialog box, and then selecting a different workbook from the To book list box.

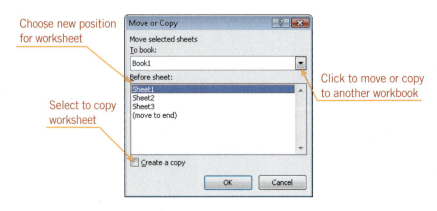

FIGURE EX 1–20   Move or Copy dialog box

LESSON 1   Understanding Excel Fundamentals   EX 21

Step-by-Step EX 1.8

The Test Grades *XXX*.xlsx workbook from Step-by-Step EX 1.7 should be open in the Excel program window.

1. Right-click the **Sheet1** sheet tab and click **Rename** on the shortcut menu to select the name.
2. Type **Winter** and press **Enter** to rename the worksheet.
3. Double-click the **Sheet2** sheet tab to select the name.
4. Type **Fall** and press **Enter** to rename the worksheet.
5. Click the **Fall** sheet tab and drag it to the left. When the black arrow is positioned before the *Winter* sheet tab, as shown in **Figure EX 1–21**, release the mouse button to move the worksheet.

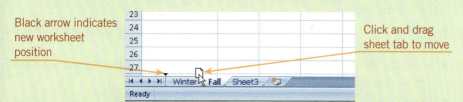

FIGURE EX 1–21
Move a worksheet

6. Click the **Insert Worksheet** button to the right of the Sheet3 sheet tab to insert a new worksheet named *Sheet1*.
7. Right-click the **Sheet1** sheet tab and click **Insert** on the shortcut menu to display the Insert dialog box.
8. Click the **OK** button to insert a new worksheet named *Sheet2*.
9. On the Home tab on the Ribbon, in the Cells group, click the **Insert** button arrow, and then click **Insert Sheet** to insert a new worksheet named *Sheet4*.
10. Click the **Sheet3** sheet tab, press and hold **Shift**, and then click the **Sheet1** tab to select four sheet tabs—*Sheet3*, *Sheet4*, *Sheet2*, and *Sheet1*.
11. On the Home tab, in the Cells group, click the **Delete** button arrow and then click **Delete Sheet** to delete all four selected sheet tabs so only the *Fall* and *Winter* worksheets remain in the workbook.
12. Save the workbook and leave it open for use in the next Step-by-Step.

Changing Workbook Views

You might find it useful to preview how your worksheet would look as a printout, see where the pages would break when the worksheet is printed, create a custom view, or view more data on the screen. Excel provides five different views using the buttons in the Workbook Views group on the View tab on the Ribbon, as shown in

UNIT III Microsoft Excel

Figure EX 1–22. You can also switch easily between the first three of these views by using the View buttons located on the right side of the status bar.

FIGURE EX 1–22   Workbook views

The five workbook views are:

- Normal, which is the view most commonly used.
- Page Layout, which displays the worksheet as it will print so you can make any necessary changes.
- Page Break Preview, which you can use to view and adjust page breaks before printing a worksheet.
- Custom Views, which you can use to create, apply, or delete a view you have created, that has specific display or print settings.
- Full Screen, which maximizes the space available for viewing data on the screen by hiding the Ribbon, the formula bar, and the status bar.

Freezing and Unfreezing Panes

The Freeze Panes command located on the View tab on the Ribbon, in the Window group, as shown in **Figure EX 1–23**, is useful when you want to keep some parts of a large worksheet visible while you scroll to another. When you *freeze panes*, you lock specified rows or columns into place.

▶ **VOCABULARY**
freeze panes

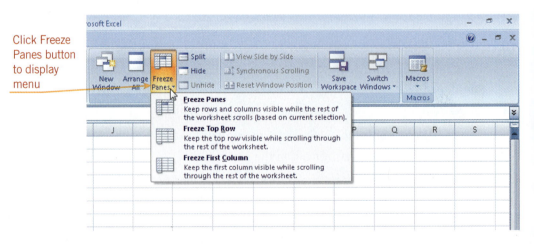

FIGURE EX 1–23   Freeze Panes menu

LESSON 1 Understanding Excel Fundamentals

You can use the Freeze Panes options to freeze the top row, the first column, or an area that you select. You select an area to freeze in one of the following ways:

- To freeze a row or rows, select the row below the row(s) you want to freeze.
- To freeze a column or columns, select the column to the right of the columns(s) you want to freeze.
- To freeze both, select the cell below and to the right of the row(s) and column(s) you want to freeze.

You can freeze panes only at the top and left of the worksheet, not in the middle. A solid line on the worksheet indicates that the area above and/or to the left is frozen. When you want to unfreeze panes, click the Freeze Panes command in the Window group on the View tab on the Ribbon, and then click Unfreeze Panes.

> **EXTRA FOR EXPERTS**
>
> The commands on the View tab in the Window group offer more ways that you can change how worksheets and workbooks are displayed on the screen. For example, you can split a worksheet into multiple panes, open a new window, tile all open program windows, or hide the current window.

Step-by-Step EX 1.9

The Test Grades *XXX*.xlsx workbook from Step-by-Step EX 1.8 should be open in the Excel program window.

1. Click the **View** tab on the Ribbon. In the Workbook Views group, notice that the Normal View button is selected, as this is the default view.

2. On the View tab, in the Workbook Views group, click the **Page Layout** button to display the worksheet as it would appear when printed.

3. On the View tab, in the Workbook Views group, click the **Page Break Preview** button to preview where pages will break when the worksheet is printed, as shown in **Figure EX 1–24**. If a Welcome to Page Break Preview dialog box opens, click the **OK** button to close it.

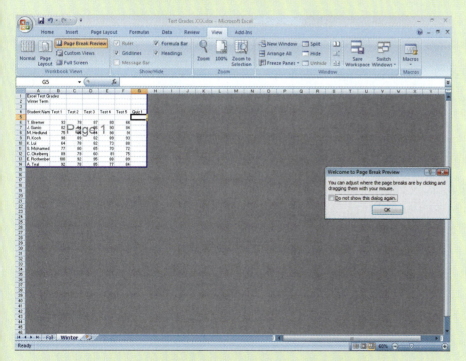

FIGURE EX 1–24
Page Break Preview

4. On the View tab, in the Workbook Views group, click the **Custom Views** button to display the Custom Views dialog box.

5. In the Custom Views dialog box, click the **Add** button to display the Add View dialog box, as shown in **Figure EX 1–25**.

FIGURE EX 1–25
Add View dialog box

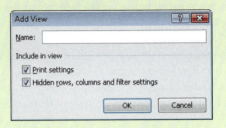

6. Click the **Cancel** button to close the Add View dialog box without creating a custom view.

7. On the View tab, in the Workbook Views group, click the **Full Screen** button to display the worksheet in full screen mode.

8. Press **Esc** to return to the previous view.

9. On the View tab, in the Workbook Views group, click the **Normal View** button to display the worksheet in Normal view.

10. Click cell **B5** to select the cell below and to the right of where you want to freeze panes.

11. On the View tab on the Ribbon, in the Window group, click the **Freeze Panes** button and then click **Freeze Panes** to freeze the panes, as indicated by the solid line (see Figure EX 1–26).

FIGURE EX 1–26
Freeze panes

12. Scroll down and to the right to see that the panes are frozen.

13. Save the workbook and leave it open for use in the next Step-by-Step.

Printing Workbooks

Often you will want to print the worksheets that you create to distribute or keep. You can add headers and footers so you can include useful information on a printed worksheet, such as the file name or date. If you only want to print part of a worksheet, you can set the print area. You can save time and paper by using the Print Preview feature to correct mistakes and change formatting before printing.

Adding Headers and Footers

A *header* is text that appears in the top margin of a worksheet when printed, and a *footer* refers to text that appears in the bottom margin of a worksheet when printed. You can use headers and footers to include useful information that you would not include in the worksheet grid, such as page numbers, titles, the date, or a logo. To create a header or footer, you click the Header & Footer button, located in the Text group on the Insert tab on the Ribbon. The Header & Footer Tools contextual tab opens on the Ribbon, and a header placeholder appears at the top of the worksheet, and a footer placeholder appears at the bottom of the worksheet.

The header and footer placeholders are divided into three sections—a left section, a middle section, and a right section. You can either type the text you want to appear in each section, or you can click an element on the Header & Footer Elements tab of the Header and Footer Tools Design contextual tab on the Ribbon, which is shown in **Figure EX 1–27**. For example, if you wanted to include the current date in the right section of a worksheet's header, you would click the right section of the header placeholder, and then click the Current Date button in the Header & Footer Elements group. The code *&[Date]* is displayed, and when you click outside the right section of the header placeholder, the actual date is displayed in the header. When you work with headers and footers, you are in Page Layout view. If you return to Normal view, the headers and footers close, and the Header & Footer Tools contextual tab is removed from the Ribbon.

> **VOCABULARY**
> header
> footer

> **WARNING**
> The Freeze Panes command is not compatible with Page Layout view. To work with headers and footers in Page Layout view, the panes must be unfrozen.

FIGURE EX 1–27 Header & Footer Tools Design tab

Setting the Print Area

Unless you specify otherwise, Excel will print all the data on the active worksheet. If you only want to print part of the worksheet, you can set the print area by selecting the range(s) you want to include and then click the Print Area button in the Page Setup group of the Page Layout tab on the Ribbon. The menu that is displayed contains options for setting the print area and clearing the print area. The defined print area will be saved with the worksheet, so you need to clear it if you want to print the entire worksheet or workbook again.

Step-by-Step EX 1.10

The Test Grades *XXX*.xlsx workbook from Step-by-Step EX 1.9 should be open in the Excel program window.

1. Click the **Insert** tab on the Ribbon, then click the **Header & Footer** button in the Text group. When a message is displayed, click **OK** to unfreeze panes.

2. On the Header & Footer Tools Design tab, in the Header & Footer Elements group, click the **Current Date** button to add a placeholder for the current date to the middle section of the header placeholder, as shown in **Figure EX 1–28**.

FIGURE EX 1–28
Worksheet header

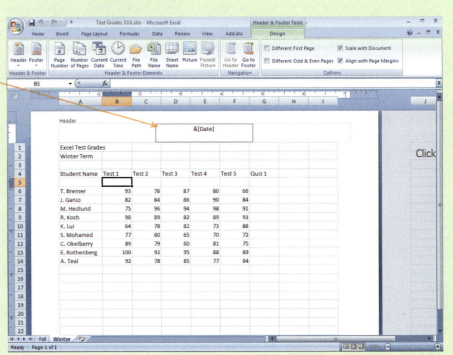

3. Click the right section of the header. Notice that the placeholder you inserted in the middle section now displays the current date.

4. On the Header & Footer Tools Design tab, in the Navigation group, click the **Go to Footer** button to switch to the footer placeholder.

5. Click the left section of the footer placeholder and type **your first and last name**, as shown in **Figure EX 1–29**.

LESSON 1 Understanding Excel Fundamentals

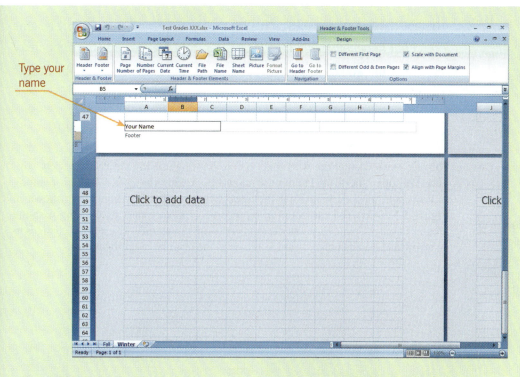

FIGURE EX 1–29
Worksheet footer

6. Click any blank cell in the worksheet to close the Header & Footer Tools Design tab.

7. On the View tab on the Ribbon, in the Workbook Views group, click the **Normal View** button.

8. Scroll up, if necessary, and select the range **A4:F14** in preparation for setting the print area.

9. On the Page Layout tab on the Ribbon, in the Page Setup group, click the **Print Area** button and then click **Set Print Area** to define the range you want to print. The print area is outlined with a dotted border, as shown in **Figure EX 1–30**.

FIGURE EX 1–30
Print area

10. On the Page Layout tab on the Ribbon, in the Page Setup group, click the **Print Area** button and then click **Clear Print Area** to clear the print area.
11. Save the workbook and leave it open for use in the next Step-by-Step.

Previewing a Worksheet

You can preview an entire worksheet before printing it using the Print Preview window. You open the Print Preview window by clicking the Office Button, pointing to Print, and then clicking Print Preview. The Print Preview window is shown in **Figure EX 1–31**. You can zoom in on an area of a worksheet by clicking with the pointer (a magnifying glass) on the area you want to magnify. The pointer changes to an arrow and you can click again to return to the original magnification.

> **EXTRA FOR EXPERTS**
>
> If you do not want the worksheet gridlines to print, or be displayed in the workbook window, you can click the Gridlines check box on the View tab on the Ribbon in the Show/Hide group to remove the check mark.

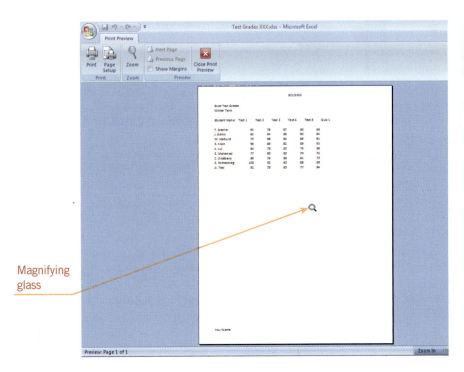

FIGURE EX 1–31   Print Preview

In the Print Preview window, you can click the following:

- Print button to display the Print dialog box in which you can select a printer, determine the number of copies to print, and specify what part of the workbook you want to print
- Page Setup button to display the Page tab of the Page Setup dialog box group so you can make changes to the orientation, scaling, paper size, or print quality
- Zoom button to display the worksheet at a larger magnification
- Next Page button to display the next page of the worksheet
- Previous Page button to display the previous page of the worksheet

LESSON 1 Understanding Excel Fundamentals

- Show Margins check box to display the worksheet margins; click again to hide the margins
- Close Print Preview button to return to the workbook window

Printing Worksheets

You use the Print command on the Office Button menu to access the Print dialog box. See **Figure EX 1–32**.

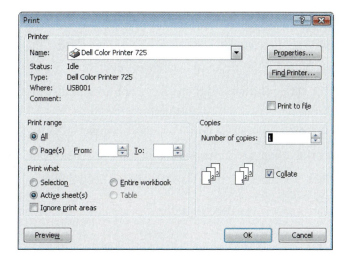

FIGURE EX 1–32 Print dialog box

The settings in the Print dialog box will differ according to the printer you are using, but some options are common to all printers, including:

- The Printer section, where you select a printer from the list of available printers
- The Properties button, which lets you change the print quality; paper type, size, and orientation; and other options for your printer
- The Print range section, where you specify whether to print all pages or specified pages of a worksheet
- The Copies section, where you indicate quantity of copies to print and whether to collate the pages, which prints them in order
- The Print what section, where you can choose to print a selection, the active sheet(s), the entire workbook, just a table, or choose to ignore the print areas
- The Preview button, which displays the worksheet in Print Preview

> **EXTRA FOR EXPERTS**
>
> You can point to Print on the Office Button menu and then use the Quick Print command to print to the default printer without making changes.

Step-by-Step EX 1.11

The Test Grades *XXX*.xlsx workbook from Step-by-Step EX 1.10 should be open in the Excel program window.

1. Click the **Office Button**. Point to **Print** and then click **Print Preview** on the menu to open the Print Preview window.

2. Point to the upper-left corner of the workbook displayed in the Print Preview window, and click the magnifying glass pointer to zoom in on the worksheet.

3. Click the worksheet again to return to the original magnification.

4. On the Print Preview tab, in the Print group, click the **Page Setup** button to display the Page Setup dialog box.

5. Click the **Cancel** button to close the Page Setup dialog box without making changes.

6. On the Print Preview tab, in the Preview group, click the **Close Print Preview** button to return to the workbook window.

7. Click the **Office Button** and then click **Print** to open the Print dialog box. Notice the options you have available in the Print dialog box and then click the **OK** button to print the worksheet. If you have been instructed to not print, click the Cancel button in the Print dialog box.

8. Leave the workbook open for use in the next Step-by-Step.

Closing a Workbook

When you are finished working with a workbook, you can close it using the Close command. To close a workbook without closing Excel, you select the Close command on the Office Button menu. When you only have one workbook open, you can click the Close button on the title bar to close the workbook and exit the program at the same time. If you have made changes to the workbook since you last saved it, a message box will open, giving you the option to save your work before closing the workbook.

Step-by-Step EX 1.12

The Test Grades *XXX*.xlsx workbook from Step-by-Step EX 1.11 should be open in the Excel program window.

1. Click the **Close** button X on the title bar. The Excel program window closes, and you return to the desktop.

LESSON 1   Understanding Excel Fundamentals   EX 31

SUMMARY

In this lesson, you learned:

- How to open an existing workbook.
- Methods of navigating in a worksheet using the mouse, keyboard, and Go To command.
- How to save a workbook.
- The processes for selecting cells, entering data, and editing data.
- To use the Undo and Redo commands to undo or reverse previous actions.
- Ways to manage worksheets by renaming, inserting, deleting, moving, or copying worksheets.
- How to change worksheet views.
- How to add headers and footers.
- Ways to preview and print a worksheet.
- To close a workbook.

VOCABULARY REVIEW

Define the following terms:

active cell	freeze panes	sheet
cell	header	sheet tab
cell reference	name box	spreadsheet software
column	range	workbook
footer	row	workbook window
formula bar	select	worksheet

REVIEW QUESTIONS

MULTIPLE CHOICE

Select the best response for the following statements.

1. The _____ below the Ribbon displays the cell reference of the active cell.
   - A. formula bar
   - B. Navigation Pane
   - C. Name box
   - D. Address bar

2. To move to the first cell of a row, press the _____ key(s).
   - A. Page Up
   - B. Home
   - C. Ctrl+Home
   - D. Ctrl+End

3. The Go To dialog box is opened by clicking the Go To command on the Find & Select menu in the Editing group on the _____ tab on the Ribbon.
   - A. Home
   - B. Insert
   - C. Page Layout
   - D. View

4. To select nonadjacent cells or ranges, hold the _____ key as you click or drag to select additional cells or ranges.
   - A. Shift
   - B. Ctrl
   - C. Alt
   - D. Enter

5. By default, numbers are _____ in a cell.
   A. left-aligned   C. centered
   B. right-aligned   D. justified

6. If you want to remove all the data from a cell, you can clear it using the _____ command on the Home tab on the Ribbon, in the Editing group.
   A. Delete   C. Replace
   B. Remove   D. Clear

7. To add another worksheet to your workbook, you can click the Insert Worksheet button to the right of the _____.
   A. Office Button   C. Quick Access Toolbar
   B. sheet tabs   D. View buttons

8. If you don't need a worksheet, you can delete it by _____ on the sheet tab to display the shortcut menu and then clicking Delete.
   A. clicking   C. right-clicking
   B. double-clicking   D. none of the above

9. Which workbook view is the most commonly used?
   A. Normal   C. Page Break Preview
   B. Page Layout   D. Full Screen

10. When you are finished with a file, you can remove it from your screen using the _____ command.
    A. Remove   C. Exit
    B. Clear   D. Close

FILL IN THE BLANK

Complete the following sentences by writing the correct word or words in the blanks provided.

1. A(n) _____ contains a collection of related worksheets.
2. The rectangle where a column and row intersect is called a(n) _____.
3. The _____ command lets you make a copy of the file with a new name, location, or file type.
4. Excel's _____ feature automatically saves your workbook at regular intervals so that you can recover at least some of your work in case of a power outage or other unexpected shut down.
5. The _____ tab on the Ribbon has many options to help you create a header or footer.
6. Use the _____ button on the Quick Access toolbar when you want to reverse an Undo action.
7. You can copy a worksheet by holding down the _____ key while you drag the sheet tab.
8. The _____ workbook view displays the worksheet as it will be printed so you can make any necessary changes.
9. The _____ command on the View tab on the Ribbon, in the Window group, is useful for large worksheets when you want to keep some parts of the worksheet visible while you scroll to another part of the worksheet.
10. You can preview an entire worksheet before printing using the _____ option on the Print menu in the Office Button menu.

PROJECTS

PROJECT EX 1–1

1. Open the file **Project EX 1-1.xlsx** from the folder containing the data files for this lesson.
2. Use the Save As command on the Office Button menu to save the workbook with the filename **LostArt** *XXX***.xlsx** (replace *XXX* with your initials).
3. Rename the Sheet1 tab, **Items to Reorder**.
4. Create a header with the filename in the center section.
5. Switch to Normal view and freeze column A.
6. Scroll to the right to see that the first column is frozen.
7. In cell A15, enter **9085D**.
8. In cell B15, enter **Camera bag**.
9. In cell C15, enter **4**.
10. Edit cell A3 to display **Stock #**.
11. Edit cell B12 so the letter **"A"** in *Air* is lowercase.
12. Undo the change you made in Step 11, then redo the action.
13. Save the workbook, and leave it open for use in Project EX 1–2.

PROJECT EX 1–2

The LostArt XXX.xlsx workbook from Project EX 1–1 should be open in the Excel program window.

1. Save the workbook as **LostArt2** *XXX***.xlsx** (replace *XXX* with your initials).
2. Navigate to the last cell in the worksheet containing data or formatting and change the contents of that cell to 5.
3. Create a copy of the *Items to Reorder* worksheet.
4. Rename the new worksheet, **Items on Backorder**.
5. Select the range C4:C15 on the Items on Backorder worksheet.
6. Clear all contents and formatting from the selected range.
7. Edit cell C3 to display **Backordered**.
8. Edit cells C7 and C13 to display an **"X"**.
9. Unfreeze column A and freeze the rows above row 4.
10. Scroll down to see that the pane is frozen.
11. Move the *Items on Backorder* worksheet so it is the first worksheet in the workbook.
12. Select the Sheet2 and Sheet3 sheet tabs and delete the worksheets.
13. Save and close the workbook.

PROJECT EX 1–3

1. Open the file **Project EX 1-3.xlsx** from the folder containing the data files for this lesson.
2. Save the workbook with the filename **Term Schedule** *XXX***.xlsx** (replace *XXX* with your initials).
3. In cell A1, replace *School Name* with the name of your school.
4. In cell A2, replace *Term* with *Spring*.
5. View the worksheet in Full Screen view.
6. Return to Normal view.
7. Create a header with your name in the center section.
8. Create a footer with the current date in the center section.
9. Return to Normal view.
10. Freeze the rows above row 5 and to the left of column B. Scroll down and to the right to see that the panes are frozen.
11. Use Print Preview to preview your worksheet.
12. In the Print Preview window, zoom in and then close Print Preview.
13. Select the range B4:F10 and set the print area.
14. Save, print, and close the workbook.

ON YOUR OWN

Open the **Term Schedule** *XXX***.xlsx** workbook, and customize the header and footer by adding other elements from the Header & Footer Elements group on the Header & Footer Tools Design tab on the Ribbon. Experiment with placing elements in the left and right sections of the header or footer. Save and close the workbook.

PROJECT EX 1–4

1. Open the file **Project EX 1-4.xlsx** from the folder containing the data files for this lesson.
2. Save the workbook with the filename **Chess Club** *XXX***.xlsx** (replace *XXX* with your initials).
3. In cell A4, type your first and last name.
4. In cell B4, type today's date.
5. In cells C4:H4, enter your contact information in the appropriate columns.
6. Use the skills you have learned in this lesson to enter data for at least six more members in the appropriate cells. Use your classmates' names and contact information, or create some fictitious data.

7. Use the Go To command to move to cell I4 and enter Elected president for next year.
8. Rename the worksheet **Member Info**.
9. Insert a new worksheet and name it **Tournament Dates**.
10. Switch to the Member Info sheet and use Page Break Preview to see where the pages will break when the worksheet is printed.
11. Switch to Page Layout view.
12. Return to Normal view.
13. Select the range A3:C10 and set the print area.
14. Save, print, and close the workbook.

ON YOUR OWN

Open the **Chess Club** *XXX*.xlsx workbook, and then create a custom view for the worksheet that includes the print settings, and name the custom view **Custom** *XXX*.xlsx (replace *XXX* with your initials). Save and close the workbook.

WEB PROJECT

PROJECT EX 1–5

1. Open the file **Project EX 1-5.xlsx** from the folder containing the data files for this lesson.
2. Save the workbook with the filename **Hotels** *XXX*.xlsx (replace *XXX* with your initials).
3. Rename the first worksheet **Dallas**.
4. Assume you are going on a trip to Dallas. Search the Web for information on hotels in that city. In the range B4:C8, list the names of five hotels where you would like to stay and the price per night.
5. Delete Sheet2 and Sheet3.
6. Save and close the workbook.

ON YOUR OWN

Open the **Hotels** *XXX*.xlsx workbook, then copy the *Dallas* worksheet, and rename it **Chicago** (or another city where you would like to stay). Search for five hotels and the price per night in that city and record them in the new worksheet, replacing and editing data as needed. Save and close the workbook.

TEAMWORK PROJECT
PROJECT EX 1–6

Open a workbook that you used in this lesson. Have a partner call out cell references to move to or ranges to select (for example, "move to cell Z155" or "select range D10:H25"). See how quickly you can navigate to the cells or select ranges. Use different methods and see which one you prefer. For an extra challenge, try navigating to cells that meet certain conditions or contain specific data using the Go To Special dialog box (for example, blank cells).

 CRITICAL THINKING

ACTIVITY EX 1–1

Open the file **Activity EX 1-1.xlsx** from the folder containing the data files for this lesson, then perform the following tasks, using Excel Help if necessary:

- Save the workbook as an Excel 97-2003 Workbook with the filename **All About Me** *XXX*.xls.
- Add data about yourself in cells C3:C8.
- Continue the list, adding at least five more facts about yourself.
- Create a header and insert a picture of yourself (or another picture that you like) and resize as needed.
- Hide the gridlines on the worksheet.
- Rename Sheet1 with your name and change the color of the sheet tab.
- Save, print, and close the workbook.

ACTIVITY EX 1–2

Search for the demo in Excel Help titled *Freeze or unfreeze rows and columns* and watch it. What is the purpose of freezing rows and columns? Open a workbook you used in this lesson and practice freezing and unfreezing panes, including the options to freeze only the top row or the first column. When panes are frozen, try viewing the worksheet in Page Layout view. What happens? Close the workbook without saving the changes.

Estimated Time:
2 hours

LESSON 2

Formatting and Editing Worksheets

■ OBJECTIVES

Upon completion of this lesson, you should be able to:
- Create a new workbook.
- Format cells.
- Apply themes and styles and use conditional formatting.
- Adjust column widths and row heights.
- Insert and delete rows and columns.
- Find and replace data.
- Copy and move worksheet data.
- Check spelling.

■ DATA FILES

To complete this lesson, you will need these data files:
- Step EX 2-4.xlsx
- Step EX 2-9.xlsx
- Project EX 2-1.xlsx
- Project EX 2-3.xlsx
- Project EX 2-6.xlsx

■ VOCABULARY

conditional formatting
cell style
Clipboard
copy
cut
drag-and-drop
fill
font
font style
paste
point size
theme
...

UNIT III Microsoft Excel

Introduction

Now that you know the fundamentals of working with Excel, you will learn more about how to use Excel's editing and formatting features to enhance the appearance of a worksheet. In this lesson, you will learn how to create a new workbook; how to format a workbook; and how to organize data to get the information you need.

Creating a New Workbook

As you already learned, a new blank workbook is displayed in the program window when you open Excel. You can also create a new workbook at any time by clicking the New command on the Office Button menu. This opens the New Workbook dialog box, as shown in **Figure EX 2–1**. When you click the Create button with the Blank Workbook icon selected, a new blank workbook is created.

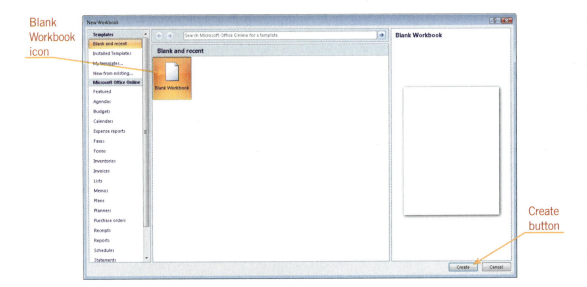

FIGURE EX 2–1 New Workbook dialog box

> **EXTRA FOR EXPERTS**
>
> When you do not want to create a workbook from scratch, you can choose one of the many templates available. Excel templates are pre-designed workbooks—such as billing statements, monthly budgets, or sales reports—that can save you time. You can access installed and online templates from the New Workbook dialog box.

When creating a new workbook, spend some time planning it first. Think about what you want the worksheet to accomplish, what information needs to be included, and possible ways to organize the data. You can even sketch out a design with the basic format of the rows and columns. It will always be possible to make adjustments to the worksheet later, but it is helpful to have a well-designed starting point.

LESSON 2   Formatting and Editing Worksheets

EX 37

Step-by-Step EX 2.1

1. Start Excel.
2. Click the **Office Button** and then click **New** to open the New Workbook dialog box.
3. Select the **Blank Workbook** icon in the center pane, if necessary, then click the **Create** button to open a new blank workbook.
4. Click cell **B2**, type **ZPM Courier Service**, and then press **Enter**.
5. Click cell **F1**, type **Weekly Time Sheet**, and then press **Enter**.
6. Save the workbook as **Time Sheet XXX.xlsx** (replace XXX with your initials).
7. Continue creating the worksheet by entering the data for rows 4 through 17 of the worksheet, as shown in **Figure EX 2–2**.

	A	B	C	D	E	F	G	H	I	J	K
1						Weekly Time Sheet					
2		ZPM Courier Service									
3											
4		4001 East Millerton Road									
5		Suite 400									
6		Portland, OR 97214									
7											
8		Week ending:									
9											
10		Day	Client	Billable	Other	Total					
11		Monday									
12		Tuesday									
13		Wednesday									
14		Thursday									
15		Friday									
16		Saturday									
17		Sunday									
18											
19											
20											
21											

Enter data in these rows

FIGURE EX 2–2
Creating a worksheet

8. Save the workbook and leave it open for the next Step-by-Step.

Formatting Cells

There are numerous ways that you can format cells. You can format the contents of the cell by specifying a number format, setting the alignment of the text or numbers in the cell, and selecting a font and font style and color. You can also format the cell itself by choosing to show the borders of the cell and setting the border style, and by adding a background color or pattern, referred to as a *fill*. The most common cell formatting options are located on the Home tab on the Ribbon in the Font, Alignment, and Number groups. You can also click the dialog box launcher in these groups to open the Format Cells dialog box, shown in **Figure EX 2–3**, and click the tabs in the dialog box to access additional cell formatting options. Once you have applied a cell format to a cell, it is easy to copy the formatting to other cells using the Format Painter button, located in the Clipboard group on the Home tab.

▶ **VOCABULARY**
fill

UNIT III Microsoft Excel

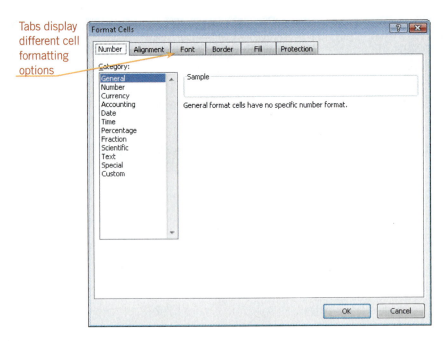

FIGURE EX 2-3 Format Cells dialog box

Setting Font Formats

> **VOCABULARY**
> font
> point size

A *font* is the design of a set of letters and numbers. Each set has a name. The Font group on the Home tab on the Ribbon, shown in **Figure EX 2-4**, includes options for selecting fonts, font size, font style, underline, and font color. You can also click the dialog box launcher in the Font group to open the Font tab of the Format Cells dialog box to access additional font options such as special font effects.

FIGURE EX 2-4 Font group on the Home tab

> **EXTRA FOR EXPERTS**
>
> You can change the default Excel font and font size for new workbooks by opening the Excel Options dialog box from the Office Button menu, and selecting a new default font from the Use this font list box on the Popular page of the dialog box.

The default font used in all Excel workbooks is Calibri. You can select a different font by selecting a cell or range of cells and choosing one of the fonts listed on the Font menu in the Font group on the Home tab. The Font menu displays each font's design and is divided into two sections: Theme Fonts and All Fonts. You can also select a font from the Font list box on the Font tab of the Format Cells dialog box, and preview the selected font in the Preview box.

Font sizes are measured in points. *Point size* refers to a measurement for the height of characters. A point is equal to approximately 1/72 inch. A 10-point font is approximately 10/72 inch high. You can change the font size by selecting the cell or range of cells and then selecting a size from the Font Size menu or in the Size list box on the Font tab of the Format Cells dialog box.

LESSON 2 Formatting and Editing Worksheets

You can use the Increase Font Size button to increase the font size or the Decrease Font Size button to decrease the font size. These buttons are located on the Home tab, in the Font group. You can also select a specific font size from the Size list box on the Font tab of the Format Cells dialog box.

Font styles are changes in the shape or weight of a font's characters, such as **bold** and *italic*. You can change the font style by clicking the Bold and Italic buttons in the Font group on the Home tab, or by selecting a font style from the Font style list box on the Font tab of the Format Cells dialog box. The Underline button in the Font group on the Home tab has a menu with two options. More underline options are available on the Font tab of the Format Cells dialog box.

You can select the font color by clicking the Font Color button in the Font group on the Home tab on the Ribbon. If you click the Font Color button, the most recently used font color is applied to the selected cell. If you click the Font Color button arrow, a menu is displayed with theme colors and standard colors, as shown in **Figure EX 2–5**. Or, you can click More Colors on the menu to select a custom color. The Font tab of the Format Cells dialog box also includes more font color choices.

> **VOCABULARY**
> font style

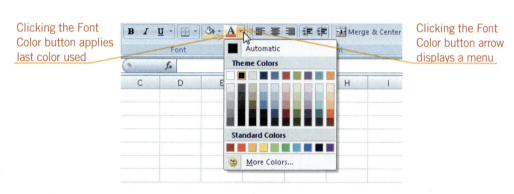

Clicking the Font Color button applies last color used

Clicking the Font Color button arrow displays a menu

FIGURE EX 2–5 Font Color menu

Step-by-Step EX 2.2

The Time Sheet *XXX*.xlsx workbook from Step-by-Step EX 2.1 should be open in the Excel program window.

1. Select cell **B2**. On the Home tab on the Ribbon, in the Font group, click the **Font** arrow `Calibri` to display the Font menu.

2. In the Theme Fonts section of the Font menu, click **Cambria**, as shown in **Figure EX 2–6**, to change the font to the theme font for headings.

FIGURE EX 2-6
Font menu

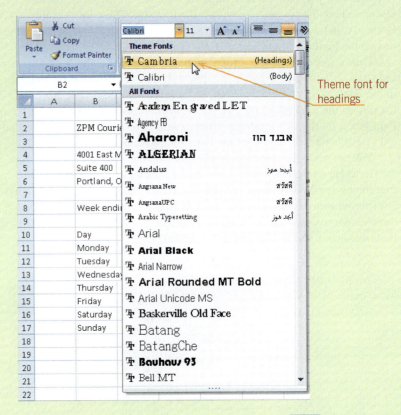

3. With cell B2 still selected, click the **Font Size** arrow on the Home tab in the Font group to display the Font Size menu and then click **20** to change the font size of the text. Notice that the row height automatically adjusts to accommodate the larger font size.

4. With cell B2 still selected, click the **Decrease Font Size** button on the Home tab in the Font group to change the font size of the text to 18.

5. With cell B2 still selected, click the **Bold** button on the Home tab in the Font group to bold the text.

6. With cell B2 still selected, click the **Underline** button arrow on the Home tab in the Font group to display the Underline menu and then click **Double Underline**.

7. With cell B2 still selected, click the **Font Color** arrow on the Home tab in the Font group to display the Font Color menu and then click the **Red, Accent 2** theme color (first row, sixth from left).

8. Save the workbook and leave it open for use in the next Step-by-Step.

LESSON 2 Formatting and Editing Worksheets

Using the Format Painter

Once you have applied formatting to cells, you can use the Format Painter button in the Clipboard group on the Home tab to add the same formatting to other cells. This is useful because you can copy multiple formatting characteristics at once, such as font, font size, effects, and color.

To copy formatting of a cell, you first select the cell that contains the formatting you want to apply to other cells, and then click the Format Painter button. Your mouse pointer changes to a plus sign with a paintbrush. Then, you select the cells to which you want to apply the formatting.

If you want to add the formatting to more than one cell, you can double-click the Format Painter button so that it stays active. When you finish painting formats, click the Format Painter button again or press the Esc key to turn off Format Painter.

Adding and Removing Cell Borders

Borders can be applied to any side of a cell using predefined styles or by creating custom borders. If you click the Borders button in the Font group of the Home tab, the most recently used border style is applied. You can apply a different predefined style by clicking the Borders button arrow and selecting an option on the menu. The Border menu is divided into two sections: Borders, with preset border styles, and Draw Borders, with options for drawing your own border. Clicking More Borders opens the Border tab of the Format Cells dialog box, where you can create a custom border by choosing a line style and color.

Changing Fill Color

You can change a cell's background color using the Fill Color button in the Font group on the Home tab. If you click the Fill Color button, the most recently used color is applied. If you click the Fill Color button arrow, a menu of colors is displayed. You can choose theme colors, standard colors, no fill color, or click More Colors to select a custom color. The Fill tab of the Format Cells dialog box also includes options for filling a cell with patterns or gradients.

Step-by-Step EX 2.3

The Time Sheet *XXX*.xlsx workbook from Step-by-Step EX 2.2 should be open in the Excel program window.

1. Select cell **B2**. On the Home tab, in the Clipboard group, click the **Format Painter** button to activate it. Notice the rotating border around cell B2, indicating this cell's formatting is ready to be copied.

2. Click cell **F1** to apply the same formats as cell B2.

3. Select cells **B4:D6**. On the Home tab, in the Font group, click the **Borders** button arrow to display the Borders menu, as shown in **Figure EX 2–7**.

FIGURE EX 2–7
Borders menu

4. Click **Thick Box Border** to apply that border style to the selected range.
5. With cells B4:D6 still selected, click the **Fill Color** button arrow in the Font group on the Home tab to display the Fill Color menu.
6. Click the **Red, Accent 2, Lighter 80%** option, as shown in **Figure EX 2–8**. Click a blank area of the worksheet to view the newly applied cell formatting.

FIGURE EX 2–8
Fill Color menu

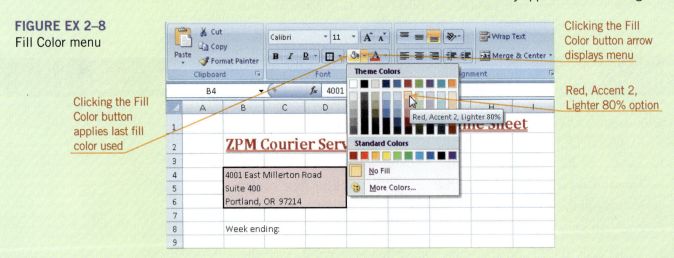

7. Save and close the workbook.

LESSON 2 Formatting and Editing Worksheets

Changing Cell Alignment

Using the buttons in the Alignment group on the Home tab, shown in **Figure EX 2–9**, you can left-align, center, or right-align cell contents. You can also align the contents to the top, middle, or bottom of a cell. The Orientation button allows you to rotate text. Using the Decrease Indent and Increase Indent buttons, you can change the margin between the border and the cell contents.

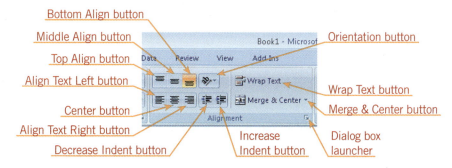

FIGURE EX 2–9 Alignment group on the Home tab

You can use the Wrap Text command to display text in a cell on multiple lines so it is all visible. To align text over several columns or rows, you can use the Merge & Center button to join selected cells together into one larger cell, which is useful for creating labels. Once cells are merged, the content from the upper-left cell in the range is preserved, and the upper-left cell becomes the cell reference for the merged cells. More options for positioning data within a cell are located on the Alignment tab of the Format Cells dialog box.

Clearing Cell Formats

Sometimes you might want to remove all the formatting from a cell or range of cells. On the Home tab, in the Editing group, you can click the Clear button and select Clear Formats to remove all of the formatting that has been applied to the cell or range that you have selected. The contents will not be affected.

Step-by-Step EX 2.4

1. Open **Step EX 2-4.xlsx** from the folder containing the data files for this lesson.
2. Save the workbook as **Time Sheet2 *XXX*.xlsx** (replace *XXX* with your initials).
3. Select cells **A2:I2**. On the Home tab, in the Alignment group, click the **Merge & Center** button arrow to display the Merge & Center menu, shown in **Figure EX 2–10**.

FIGURE EX 2–10
Merge & Center menu

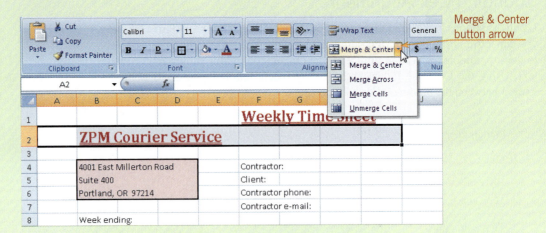

4. Click **Merge & Center** to join the cells in the range together and center the contents. Notice that the row height reverts back to its original size.

5. Select cells **F4:G4**. On the Home tab, in the Alignment group, click the **Merge & Center** button to join the cells together and center the contents.

6. With cells **F4:G4** still selected, click the **Align Text Right** button in the Alignment group on the Home tab to right-align the cell contents.

7. With cells **F4:G4** still selected, click the **Increase Indent** button in the Alignment group on the Home tab to increase the space between the cell border and the cell contents.

8. With cells **F4:G4** still selected, click the **Format Painter** button in the Clipboard group of the Home tab to activate it, and then select the range **F5:G7** to copy the cell formats from F4:G4.

9. Select cells **D10:F10**. On the Home tab, in the Alignment group, click the **Wrap Text** button to make the text in each cell visible by displaying it over two lines.

10. Select cell **H10**. On the Home tab, in the Alignment group, click the **Middle Align** button to center the text between the top and bottom of the cell.

11. With cell **H10** still selected, click the **Center** button in the Alignment group on the Home tab to center the text in the cell.

12. Select cell **F1**. On the Home tab, in the Editing group, click the **Clear** button arrow to display the Clear menu.

13. Click **Clear Formats** to clear all the formatting from the cell. Your workbook window should look similar to **Figure EX 2–11**.

LESSON 2 Formatting and Editing Worksheets

EX 45

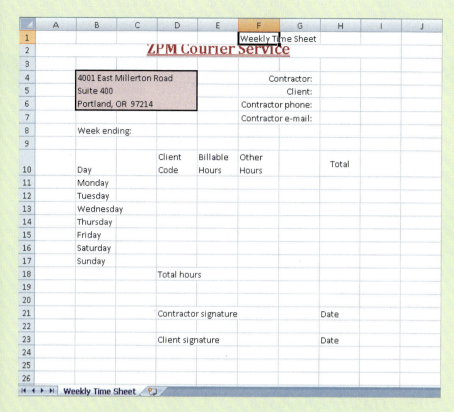

FIGURE EX 2-11
Time Sheet2 *XXX*.xlsx worksheet

14. Save the workbook and leave it open for use in the next Step-by-Step.

Applying Number Formats

When you enter a number in a cell, Excel automatically applies the General format, which basically displays numbers the way you type them. If you enter a number preceded by a dollar sign, Excel automatically formats the cell for currency. If you type a percentage sign following a number, Excel formats the cell for percentage. You can enter dates or times in a variety of formats that Excel will recognize, although they will be displayed in the default date or time format.

To change a number format for a selected cell, you can use the buttons found on the Home tab, in the Number group, as shown in **Figure EX 2-12**.

> **WARNING**
>
> If a number is too long to fit in a cell because of the cell formatting, Excel displays pound signs (###). Later in this lesson, you will learn how to widen a column to display all the data in the column.

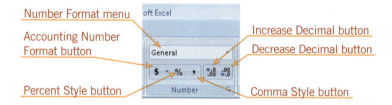

FIGURE EX 2-12 Number group on the Home tab

Clicking the Number Format list arrow in the Number group opens a menu of number format options you can choose from. The Accounting Number Format button provides currency options. You can also use the Percent Style, Comma Style, Increase Decimal, and Decrease Decimal buttons to quickly apply other common changes to the number format. You can click the dialog box launcher in the Number group on the Home tab to open the Number tab of the Format Cells dialog box.

Step-by-Step EX 2.5

The Time Sheet2 *XXX*.xlsx workbook from Step-by-Step EX 2.4 should be open in the Excel program window.

1. In cells **D11:F15**, enter the numbers shown in **Figure EX 2–13**. Notice that the Number Format list box in the Number group on the Home tab displays *General* for each of these numbers.

FIGURE EX 2–13
Entering numbers in General format

	A	B	C	D	E	F	G
9							
10		Day		Client Code	Billable Hours	Other Hours	
11		Monday		1544	6	1	
12		Tuesday		2103	4	2	
13		Wednesday		1544	6	0	
14		Thursday		1544	3	2	
15		Friday		1170	7	0	
16		Saturday					
17		Sunday					

Numbers to enter

2. In cell **D19**, enter **Hourly rate**.
3. In cell **F19**, enter **75**.
4. Select cell **F19**, if necessary. On the Home tab, in the Number group, click the **Number Format** arrow to display the Number Format menu, as shown in **Figure EX 2–14**.

FIGURE EX 2–14
Number Format menu

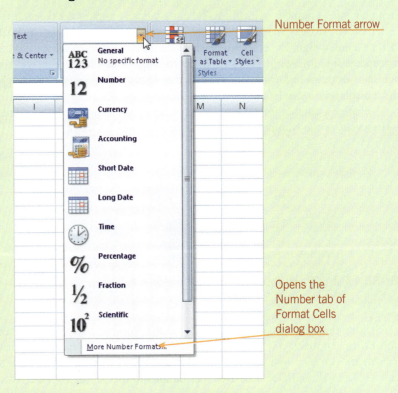

Number Format arrow

Opens the Number tab of Format Cells dialog box

LESSON 2 Formatting and Editing Worksheets   EX 47

5. On the Number Format menu, click **Currency** to change the number format of the cell.

6. With cell **F19** still selected, click the **Decrease Decimal** button in the Number group on the Home tab to show one fewer decimal place. Click the **Decrease Decimal** button again to remove the decimal place from the number.

7. In cell **I21**, type **July 22**, and then press **Enter**. Notice how Excel automatically changes the format to the default date format when you enter the contents.

8. Select cell **I21**. On the Home tab, in the Number group, click the **Number Format** arrow to display the Number Format menu and click **Short Date** to format the cell with a short date format.

9. Save the workbook and leave it open for use in the next Step-by-Step.

Applying Themes and Styles

If you want to quickly change the look of individual cells or an entire workbook, you can use predefined formatting options that Excel provides, such as themes and styles. Using themes and styles allows you to apply multiple formats at one time and helps keep formatting in the workbook consistent. Excel provides a variety of built-in themes and styles for you to choose from or you can create your own custom ones. Some of the options are displayed in galleries, so you can use Live Preview to see what the formatting changes would look like before applying them to your workbook.

Applying Themes

A *theme* is a set of predesigned formatting elements—including colors, fonts, and effects—that can be applied to an entire workbook. You can use the commands in the Themes group on the Page Layout tab on the Ribbon, as shown in **Figure EX 2–15**, to apply themes to a workbook. Clicking the Themes button displays a gallery of options, organized alphabetically, so you can choose a theme and change the color, font, and effects at the same time. If you want to only change one element, you can click the Theme Colors, Theme Fonts, or Theme Effects button.

▶ **VOCABULARY**
theme

FIGURE EX 2–15 Themes group on the Page Layout tab

UNIT III Microsoft Excel

On the Themes menu, you can click More Themes on Microsoft Office Online to find additional theme choices, or use the Browse for Themes command to locate a workbook that contains a theme you want to apply to the current workbook. After you have customized a theme, you can use the Save Current Theme command to name and save it to the Document Themes folder.

Working with Table Styles

You can select a range of related data in a worksheet and format it as an Excel table using table styles. Excel automatically converts the data to a table and places sort and filter arrows on the column headers to help you manage and analyze the table data. You can also specify formats for the individual table elements, such as the header row containing titles for the columns, and a totals row that uses predefined formulas to total the values in the table.

When you select a range of cells and then click the Format as Table button in the Styles group on the Home tab, a gallery of Light, Medium, and Dark table style options opens, as shown in **Figure EX 2–16**. Notice that many of these styles include alternating bands of color, which makes text in a table easier to read. Once you click a table style, the Format As Table dialog box opens, in which you can verify or adjust the range of data for the table and specify whether it includes headers.

FIGURE EX 2–16 Table Styles gallery

When the data is formatted as a table, a contextual Table Tools Design tab is displayed on the Ribbon providing advanced tools designed for sorting the table

LESSON 2 Formatting and Editing Worksheets

data, filtering the table data, and transferring the data to another file for interpretation. If you do not want to work with the data in a table, you can convert the table to a regular range and still keep the table formatting by right-clicking the table, pointing to Table, and clicking Convert to Range.

Applying Cell Styles

A defined combination of formatting characteristics—such as number, alignment, font, border, and fill—is called a *cell style*. Cell styles can save time because you can apply multiple formatting characteristics in one step. They also help you format a worksheet consistently because you can apply the same cell style to common elements, such as headings, and know that they will be formatted the same way. Excel has a variety of built-in styles that can be accessed by clicking the Cell Styles button in the Styles group on the Home tab to display a gallery of cell styles. The cell styles available are determined by which theme has been applied to the workbook. If you switch themes, the available cell styles change to match.

> **VOCABULARY**
> cell style

Step-by-Step EX 2.6

The Time Sheet2 *XXX*.xlsx workbook from Step-by-Step EX 2.5 should be open in the Excel program window.

1. On the Page Layout tab on the Ribbon, in the Themes group, click the **Themes** button to display the Themes gallery.

2. In the Themes gallery, point to the **Foundry** theme, as shown in **Figure EX 2–17**, to see what the applied theme would look like using Live Preview.

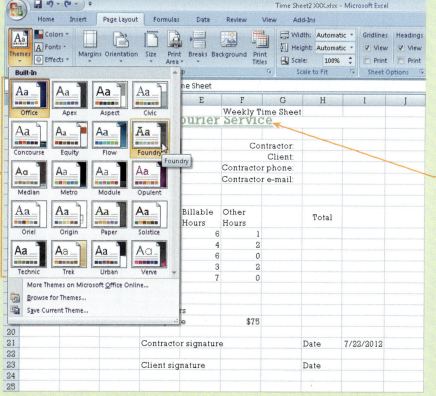

FIGURE EX 2–17
Applying a theme

Themes gallery

Foundry option applied using Live Preview

3. Click the **Foundry** theme. Notice that some of the cell formats you previously applied are changed to match the new theme.
4. Select cells **B10:H17**.
5. On the Home tab, in the Styles group, click the **Format as Table** button to display a gallery of options.
6. Click the **Table Style Light 9** option (second row, second option from the left) to display the Format As Table dialog box, as shown in **Figure EX 2–18**.

FIGURE EX 2–18
Format As Table dialog box

7. In the Format As Table dialog box, click the **My table has headers** check box to select this option, and click **OK** to close the dialog box and format the range as a table, with filter arrows on the column headers. Notice that the Table Tools Design contextual tab is displayed on the Ribbon.
8. Right-click the table, point to **Table** on the shortcut menu, and select **Convert to Range**. When a message box opens, click **Yes** to convert the table to a normal range and remove the filter arrows from the headings.
9. Select the **A2:I2** merged cell.
10. Click the **Cell Styles** button 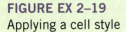 in the Styles group on the Home tab on the Ribbon to display a gallery of options.
11. Point to the **Title** option to see what the applied cell style would look like using Live Preview, as shown in **Figure EX 2–19**.

FIGURE EX 2–19
Applying a cell style

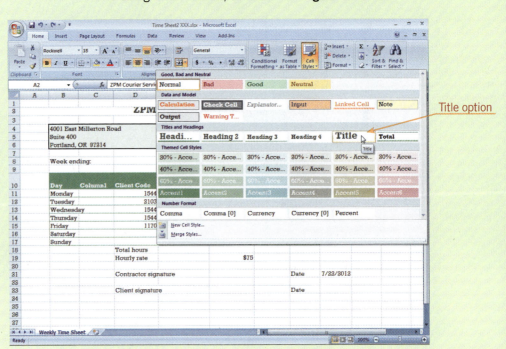

LESSON 2 Formatting and Editing Worksheets

EX 51

12. Click the **Title** option to apply that cell style. Notice the row height does not allow for the text to be displayed fully. You will learn how to correct this later in this lesson.

13. Select cell **B8**. On the Home tab, in the Styles group, click the **Cell Styles** button, and then click **Heading 4** in the gallery of options to apply that cell style.

14. Save the workbook and leave it open for use in the next Step-by-Step.

Using Conditional Formatting

You can also use formatting techniques to analyze data by visually identifying key data or trends in data. *Conditional formatting* is a feature of Excel that enables you to apply specific formatting to cells that meet specific conditions. This can be useful if, for example, you want sales figures above or below a certain figure to stand out. When you click the Conditional Formatting button on the Home tab in the Styles group, a menu is displayed with built-in options. For example, you could choose to highlight all the cells containing duplicate values or to highlight the top 10 items in a range.

Table EX 2–1 lists the specific conditional formats that you can apply.

> **VOCABULARY**
> conditional formatting
>
> **EXTRA FOR EXPERTS**
> You can create your own conditional formatting rule by clicking New Rule on the Conditional Formatting menu to open the New Formatting Rule dialog box. Clicking Manage Rules on the Conditional Formatting menu will open the Conditional Formatting Rules Manager where you can create, edit, delete, and view all the formatting rules in the workbook.

TABLE EX 2–1 Conditional formats

FORMAT	DESCRIPTION	OPTION EXAMPLE
Highlight Cells Rules	Formats cells containing text, numbers, or date/time values based on criteria that you specify	Greater Than
Top/Bottom Rules	Formats the top or bottom values in a range based on criteria you provide	Bottom 10%
Data Bars	Compares values in cells relative to other cells; data bar length represents the value in the cell	Blue Data Bar
Color Scales	Visually compares data using shades of two or three colors that represent higher or lower values	Green–Yellow–Red Color Scale
Icon Sets	Classifies data into three to five categories where an icon represents a range of values	3 Arrows (Colored)

Step-by-Step EX 2.7

The Time Sheet2 *XXX*.xlsx workbook from Step-by-Step EX 2.6 should be open in the Excel program window.

1. Select cells **E11:E15**.
2. On the Home tab, in the Styles group, click the **Conditional Formatting** button to display the Conditional Formatting menu.
3. On the Conditional Formatting menu, click **Data Bars**, and then point to **Green Data Bar** on the submenu to see what the data would look like with the conditional formatting applied, as shown in **Figure EX 2–20**.

FIGURE EX 2–20
Applying conditional formatting

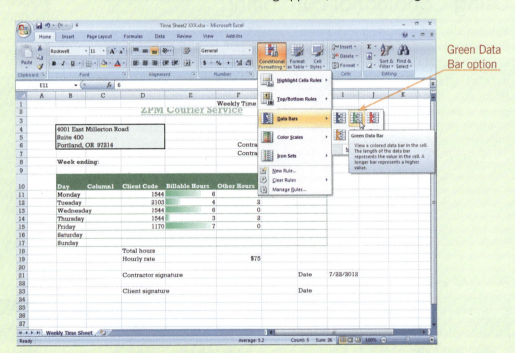

4. Click **Green Data Bar** to apply colored data bars that represent the values in the cells.
5. Select cells **F11:F15**.
6. On the Home tab, in the Styles group, click the **Conditional Formatting** button, point to **Highlight Cells Rules**, and then click **Equal To** to display the Equal To dialog box, shown in **Figure EX 2–21**.

FIGURE EX 2–21
Equal To dialog box

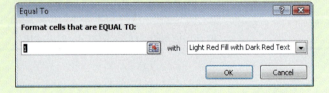

LESSON 2   Formatting and Editing Worksheets

7. In the Format cells that are EQUAL TO box, type **0** (the number zero) and then click **OK** to close the dialog box, and apply a light red fill with dark red text to all numbers in the selected range that are equal to zero.

8. Save the workbook and leave it open for use in the next Step-by-Step.

Working with Rows and Columns

You can alter the structure of a worksheet by making changes to the rows and columns. When you create a new workbook, columns are set to a default width of 8.43 characters and rows are set to a default height of 12.75 points. These default sizes may not accommodate the data in your worksheet. For example, some cell contents might get truncated, or cut off, because the column width is too narrow. Or the font size may be taller than the default row height when you merge and center cells. To correct these types of problems, you can adjust the size of the columns and rows in the worksheet. You can change these settings for all columns and rows in a worksheet by clicking the Select All button before making adjustments, or you can just select the individual column(s) or row(s) that you want to adjust.

You can also insert and delete rows in a worksheet. Other cells, rows, or columns shift to make a place for the insertion. The commands for working with rows and columns are located in the Cells group on the Home tab, as shown in **Figure EX 2–22**.

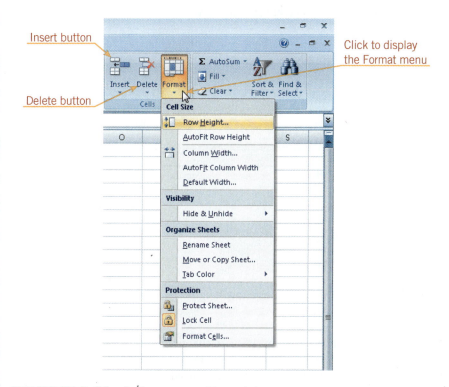

FIGURE EX 2–22   Cells group on Home tab

UNIT III   Microsoft Excel

Adjusting Column Width

An easy way to adjust column width is using the mouse to drag the right border of the column heading to the width you want. A ScreenTip is displayed showing the new width as you drag. If you double-click the right border of the column heading, the column automatically resizes to fit the data currently in the column. You can also resize a column to fit its widest entry by clicking the Format button in the Cells group on the Home tab, and then clicking AutoFit Column Width.

If you want to specify an exact width, you can click the Format button in the Cells group on the Home tab and then click Column Width on the menu, or right-click a column letter and click Column Width on the shortcut menu to display the Column Width dialog box, as shown in **Figure EX 2–23**, and enter a new width.

FIGURE EX 2–23   Column Width dialog box

Adjusting Row Height

You will not typically need to use the Row Height commands, because Excel changes the row height automatically to accommodate the data and font size. But when necessary, you can adjust row height using the same methods as for adjusting column width.

Using the mouse, you can click the row heading border and drag up or down to a new height, as shown in **Figure EX 2–24**.

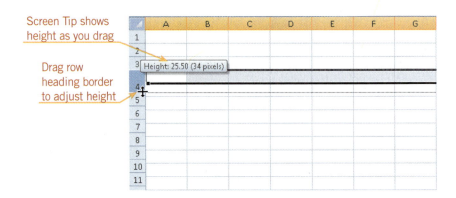

FIGURE EX 2–24   Drag to change row height

By clicking the Format button in the Cells group on the Home tab, you can display the menu to access the Row Height command, which opens the Row Height dialog box, or use the AutoFit Row Height command that changes the row height to automatically adjust to fit the contents.

Inserting a Row or Column

When you click the Insert button arrow in the Cells group on the Home tab, a menu opens with options of inserting a row or a column. If you click Insert Sheet Rows, a new row will be inserted above the current selection. If you click Insert Sheet Columns, a new column will be inserted to the left of the current selection. The same number of columns or rows that you have selected will be inserted, so to insert multiple columns or rows at a time, you would select the same number that you want to insert before clicking the command.

If you click the Insert Cells command, the Insert dialog box opens, where you can also insert cells, as well as an entire row or an entire column. See **Figure EX 2–25**.

FIGURE EX 2–25   Insert dialog box

Deleting a Row or Column

When you delete rows or columns, the rows beneath the deleted row and the columns to the right of the deleted column automatically shift up or left to fill in the space. Clicking the Delete button arrow in the Cells group on the Home tab will display a menu with the option to delete rows or columns. If you click the Delete Cells command, the Delete dialog box opens, in which you can also delete cells, as well as an entire row or an entire column.

Step-by-Step EX 2.8

The Time Sheet2 *XXX*.xlsx workbook from Step-by-Step EX 2.7 should be open in the Excel program window.

1. Select cell **B13**.
2. On the Home tab, in the Cells group, click the **Format** button and then click **AutoFit Column Width**. The column widens to accommodate the data in the cell.
3. Click the **column A header** to select column A.
4. Drag the **right column A heading border** to the left until the ScreenTip reads *Width: 3.50 (33 pixels)*, as shown in **Figure EX 2–26**.

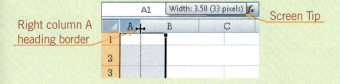

FIGURE EX 2–26
Dragging to adjust column width

5. Click the **row 2 header** to select row 2.
6. On the Home tab, in the Cells group, click the **Format** button and then click **Row Height** to display the Row Height dialog box.
7. In the Row height text box, type **25** and then click **OK** to close the dialog box and increase the height of the row.
8. Select cell **A1**.
9. On the Home tab, in the Cells group, click the **Delete** button arrow and then click **Delete Sheet Rows** to delete row 1 and shift the other cells up.
10. Select cell **A17**.
11. On the Home tab, in the Cells group, click the **Insert** button arrow and then click **Insert Sheet Rows** to insert a row above the selected cell.
12. Select **column C**, and then click the **Delete** button in the Cells group on the Home tab to delete the column and shift the other cells left. Note that even though column C displays data that spills over from column B, it does not contain any data that will be deleted.
13. Delete **column F**. Note that even though column F contains data from cells that you merged and centered, no data is deleted when you delete this column. Your worksheet should look similar to **Figure EX 2–27**.

FIGURE EX 2–27
Formatted worksheet

14. Save and close the workbook.

Finding and Replacing Data

The Find and Replace commands are two separate commands that are often used together to find and replace data, formats, formulas, and other items. The Find command is useful for locating specific data or moving to a particular location in the worksheet. The Replace command is useful for changing data or formatting in a worksheet. You can click the Find & Select button in the Editing group on the Home tab to access the Find and Replace commands.

LESSON 2 Formatting and Editing Worksheets

When you click the Find command, the Find tab of the Find and Replace dialog box opens, as shown in **Figure EX 2–28.** In this dialog box, you can type data in the Find what list box and click the Find Next button to search for each occurrence. The Options button shows or hides additional Find options, such as searching for a specific format. If you click the Find All button, each occurrence is listed in the Find and Replace dialog box and you can move to a specific occurrence by clicking it to make the cell active.

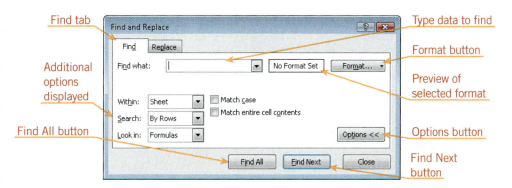

FIGURE EX 2–28 Find tab of the Find and Replace dialog box with options displayed

The Replace command displays the Find and Replace dialog box with the Replace tab active, as shown in **Figure EX 2–29.** Type the data you want to find in the Find what list box and the data you want to replace it with in the Replace with list box. The Options button shows or hides additional options. Use the Find Next and Replace buttons to make just one replacement at a time.

You can use the Replace All button to replace all occurrences of data at once without confirming each instance. Each occurrence of the replaced data will be displayed in a list at the bottom of the Find and Replace dialog box, and you can move to a specific occurrence by clicking it to make the cell active.

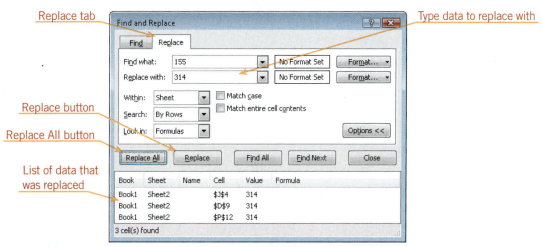

FIGURE EX 2–29 Replace tab of the Find and Replace dialog box with Options displayed

UNIT III   Microsoft Excel

Step-by-Step EX 2.9

1. Open **Step EX 2-9.xlsx** from the folder containing the data files for this lesson.
2. Save the workbook as **Team Stats XXX.xlsx** (replace XXX with your initials).
3. On the Home tab on the Ribbon, in the Editing group, click the **Find & Select** button to display the menu, and then click **Find** to display the Find tab of the Find and Replace dialog box.
4. In the Find what list box, type **2B** and then click the **Find Next** button to move to the first occurrence of the text 2B in the worksheet, cell F3.
5. Click the **Find All** button to display all occurrences of the text in a list at the bottom of the Find and Replace dialog box.
6. Click the **Replace** tab in the Find and Replace dialog box to make the Replace tab active.
7. In the Replace with list box, type **Doubles**. Your workbook window should look similar to **Figure EX 2–30**.

FIGURE EX 2–30
Replacing data

8. Click the **Replace** button to replace the first occurrence of 2B with Doubles.
9. Click the **Options** button to see all the options available when finding and replacing data.
10. Click the **Close** button to close the Find and Replace dialog box.
11. Save the workbook and leave it open for use in the next Step-by-Step.

LESSON 2 Formatting and Editing Worksheets

EX 59

Copying and Moving Worksheet Data

Excel offers different ways to move or copy data. You can use the *Clipboard*—an area of memory that temporarily stores up to 24 cut or copied selections—or you can use the drag-and-drop method.

Cutting, Copying, and Pasting to the Clipboard

The Clipboard is a convenient way to move or copy text not only within a worksheet but also to other Excel workbooks, Office files, and other files such as PDF documents and e-mail messages. The cut or copied selections remain on the Clipboard until you delete them or exit all Office programs.

To move a selection, you *cut* or remove the contents (data and formatting) from a cell or range and *paste* it into another cell or range. When you *copy* a selection, you duplicate the contents so you can paste it into another cell or range without deleting it from its original location. You need only select the top left cell of the paste area because Excel will set the paste area to match the same size and range as the cells you are pasting.

After selecting the cell or range you want to move or copy (indicated by a rotating border around the cells), you can use the Cut, Copy, and Paste buttons in the Clipboard group on the Home tab, as shown in **Figure EX 2–31**. Clicking the dialog box launcher opens the Clipboard task pane so you can view, paste, or delete items.

> **VOCABULARY**
> Clipboard
> cut
> paste
> copy
> drag-and-drop

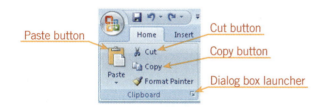

FIGURE EX 2–31 Clipboard group of Home tab

The Paste button menu offers a variety of ways to paste copied data, such as pasting only formulas, pasting only values, or pasting all contents except the borders. When you use the Paste Special command, additional options are available in the Paste Special dialog box. When you paste data in a cell or range, Excel replaces any existing data.

You can also right-click a selection and use the commands on the shortcut menu to move or copy data from one location to another.

> **EXTRA FOR EXPERTS**
>
> There are many useful keyboard commands in Excel. As you work, you may decide you prefer them to the Ribbon or mouse method of performing a task. For example, you can quickly copy contents by pressing Ctrl+C, cut contents by pressing Ctrl+X, or paste contents by pressing Ctrl+V.

Using the Drag-and-Drop Method

You can use the *drag-and-drop* method to move or copy a selection to a new location in your worksheet. If you position the mouse pointer on the border of a selected cell or range, it will change to a cross with an arrow. Then you can press and hold the mouse button while dragging the cell or range to its new position. You release the mouse button to drop the selection in its new location.

To copy a selection, you would hold the Ctrl key while you drag and drop the selection. When you copy a selection, you will see a plus sign (+) with the pointer.

When you move or copy a selection using the drag-and-drop method, the selection is not stored on the Clipboard.

> **WARNING**
>
> If you use the drag-and-drop method to place a selection in a location that already contains data, Excel will display a message asking if you want to replace the contents of the destination cells.

Step-by-Step EX 2.10

The Team Stats *XXX*.xlsx workbook from Step-by-Step EX 2.9 should be open in the Excel program window.

1. On the Home tab, in the Clipboard group, click the **dialog box launcher** to open the Clipboard task pane.

2. Select cell **B4**. On the Home tab, in the Clipboard group, click the **Copy** button to display a rotating border around the cell.

3. Select cell **B11**. On the Home tab, in the Clipboard group, click the **Paste** button to paste the copied data into the cell.

4. Click the **Paste Options** icon arrow that is displayed at the bottom right of the cell to open a menu of pasting options, as shown in **Figure EX 2–32**.

FIGURE EX 2–32 Paste options

5. Click **Match Destination Formatting** to make the cell fill color match the table style, and press **Esc** to remove the rotating border from the copied cell.

6. Select cell **B5**.

7. Click the **list arrow** next to *P* in the Clipboard task pane to display a menu, and click **Paste**, as shown in **Figure EX 2–33**, to paste the data again.

FIGURE EX 2–33 Clipboard task pane

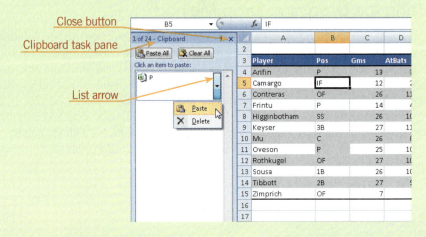

LESSON 2 Formatting and Editing Worksheets

8. Click the **Paste Options** icon arrow, and then click **Match Destination Formatting** on the menu.
9. Click the **Close** button in the Clipboard task pane to close the Clipboard task pane.
10. Select cell **G8** and point to the bottom border until the pointer changes to a cross with an arrow.
11. Press and hold **Ctrl** to display a small plus sign, and then click and drag to cell **G11**, as shown in **Figure EX 2–34**. Notice the ScreenTip displaying the new location.

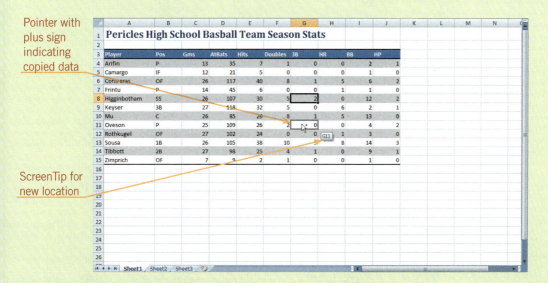

FIGURE EX 2–34
Drag-and-drop copied data

12. Release the mouse button and Ctrl to paste the copied data.
13. Use the **Format Painter button** to copy the formatting from cell G9 to cell G11.
14. Save the workbook and leave it open for use in the next Step-by-Step.

Checking Spelling

When you are finished creating a workbook, it is a good idea to check it for any spelling mistakes. Clicking the Spelling button in the Proofing group on the Review tab on the Ribbon opens the Spelling dialog box where you can correct any errors. In this dialog box, the Not in the Dictionary text box displays the possible misspelling and the Suggestions list box offers possible fixes for the word. You can select a suggestion or type your own correction and then use the Change button to correct an error, or use the Change All button to correct all instances of the same error. The spell checker will flag many proper nouns as being incorrect. You can choose to ignore a specific instance of a word or you can choose to have Excel ignore all occurrences of the word. If it is a mistake that you make frequently, you can set Excel to automatically correct the word any time you misspell it.

> **WARNING**
>
> Using the Spelling feature does not eliminate the need to proofread a worksheet. If a word you misspelled is another English word (for example, you typed *form* instead of *from*), the spelling feature will not detect the error.

Step-by-Step EX 2.11

The Team Stats *XXX*.xlsx workbook from Step-by-Step EX 2.10 should be open in the Excel program window.

1. Select cell **A1**.
2. Click the **Review** tab on the Ribbon. In the Proofing group, click the **Spelling** button to display the Spelling dialog box, as shown in **Figure EX 2–35**.

FIGURE EX 2–35
Spelling dialog box

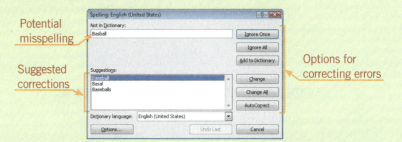

3. In the Spelling dialog box, click the **Change** button to change *Basball* to Excel's suggested spelling and move to the next possible spelling error.
4. In the Not in Dictionary text box, edit *Gms* to read *Games* and then click the **Change** button to accept this correction and move to the next possible spelling error.
5. Click the **Ignore Once** button to ignore *AtBats*.
6. Click the **Close** button to close the Spelling dialog box.
7. Click the **OK** button to close the message that the spelling check is complete.
8. Save and close the workbook and then close Excel.

NET BUSINESS

Excel has numerous templates that can help you get started creating workbooks for a small business—including agendas, budgets, calendars, expense reports, invoices, and memos. You can apply the same theme to all your documents or create your own customized theme that reflects the style of your business. Then if you save each type of worksheet as a template, you will have a set of professional-looking forms and documents that all coordinate. You can upload them to your company intranet, so they can be easily accessed and used as many times as needed.

LESSON 2   Formatting and Editing Worksheets

EX 63

SUMMARY

In this lesson, you learned:

- How to create new workbooks.
- Various ways to format cells.
- How to apply themes and styles.
- Conditional formatting can help highlight and interpret data.
- The processes for adjusting column widths and row heights.
- Methods of inserting and deleting rows and columns.
- How to find, replace, copy, and move worksheet data.
- It is a good idea to check spelling.

VOCABULARY REVIEW

Define the following terms:

conditional formatting	cut	font style
cell style	drag-and-drop	paste
Clipboard	fill	point size
copy	font	theme

REVIEW QUESTIONS

MULTIPLE CHOICE

1. Many of the most common cell formatting options are located on the _____ tab on the Ribbon.
   - A. Home
   - B. Insert
   - C. Page Layout
   - D. Review

2. Font _____ are changes in the shape or weight of a font's characters.
   - A. sizes
   - B. effects
   - C. styles
   - D. colors

3. Which button can be used to change the margin between the border and the text in a cell?
   - A. Orientation
   - B. Increase Indent
   - C. Text Wrap
   - D. Merge & Center

4. The cell styles available are determined by which _____ has been applied to the workbook.
   - A. conditional formatting
   - B. table style
   - C. number format
   - D. theme

5. When you create a new workbook, columns are set to a default width of _____ characters.
   - A. 8
   - B. 8.43
   - C. 12
   - D. 12.75

6. Excel changes the _____ automatically to accommodate the data and font size.
   - A. row height
   - B. column width
   - C. cell style
   - D. cell alignment

7. When you insert a new column, it is inserted _____.
   A. to the right of the current selection
   B. to the left of the current selection
   C. at the beginning of the worksheet
   D. at the end of the worksheet

8. If you wanted to highlight the top 10 items in a range, which feature would you most likely use?
   A. cell styles
   B. table style
   C. conditional formatting
   D. Format Painter

9. To copy a selection, hold the _____ key while you drag and drop the selection.
   A. Shift
   B. Alt
   C. Enter
   D. Ctrl

10. In the Spelling dialog box, you can click the _____ button to correct all instances of the same error.
    A. AutoCorrect
    B. Change
    C. Change All
    D. Ignore All

FILL IN THE BLANK

Complete the following sentences by writing the correct word or words in the blanks provided.

1. A(n) _____ is a master copy of a certain type of worksheet that has predesigned layout, style, and formatting.
2. Once you have applied formatting to cells, you can use the _____ button to add the same formatting to other cells.
3. You can use the _____ command to display text in a cell on multiple lines so it is all visible.
4. When you enter a number in a cell, Excel automatically applies the _____ format.
5. A(n) _____ is a set of predesigned formatting elements—including colors, fonts, and effects—that can be applied to an entire workbook.
6. When data is formatted as a table, a contextual _____ tab is displayed on the Ribbon.
7. _____ is a feature of Excel that enables you to apply specific formatting to cells that meet specific conditions.
8. The _____ command is useful for locating specific data or moving to a particular location in the worksheet.
9. The _____ is an area of memory that temporarily stores up to 24 cut or copied selections.
10. When you _____ a selection, you duplicate the contents so you can paste it into another cell or range without deleting it from its original location.

PROJECTS

PROJECT EX 2-1

1. Open the **Project EX 2-1.xlsx** workbook from the folder containing the data files for this lesson.
2. Save the workbook as **Bus Parts *XXX*.xlsx** (replace *XXX* with your initials).
3. Select cell A1. Change the font to **Cambria**, the font size to 18, the font style to bold, and the font color to Blue, Accent 1.
4. Select cell A2. Change the font to Cambria, the font size to 12, the font style to italic, and the font color to Blue, Accent 1.
5. Change the width of columns A, C, and D to 11.00 (82 pixels).
6. Change the width of column B to 36.00 (257 pixels).
7. Select cell A4. Center and bold the text.

LESSON 2 Formatting and Editing Worksheets

8. Use the Format Painter to copy the formatting from cell A4 to cells B4:D4.
9. Select cells C5:D12. Change the number format to currency.
10. Merge and center A1:D1.
11. Merge and center A2:D2.
12. Save the workbook and leave it open for use in the next project.

PROJECT EX 2–2

The Bus Parts *XXX*.xlsx workbook from Project EX 2-1 should be open in the Excel program window.

1. Save the workbook as **Bus Parts2 *XXX*.xlsx** (replace XXX with your initials).
2. Select cells A1:D2 and add a Thick Box Border.
3. With cells A1:D2 still selected, fill the cells with a Blue, Accent 1, Lighter 60% color.
4. Select cell A4 and change the text to Item Number.
5. With cell A4 still selected, wrap the text.
6. Select cells B4:D4 and middle-align the text in the cells.
7. Select A4:D4 and add a bottom double border.
8. Delete row 3.
9. Check the spelling of the worksheet and change each error to the first suggested option.
10. Save and close the workbook.

PROJECT EX 2–3

1. Open the **Project EX 2-3.xlsx** workbook from the folder containing the data files for this lesson.
2. Save the workbook as **Employee List *XXX*.xlsx** (replace *XXX* with your initials).
3. Change the theme to Urban.

4. Select cell A1 and change the cell style to Title.
5. Select cells A2:C2 and change the cell style to Heading 2.
6. Insert a row above row 3.
7. Select cells A3:C3 and clear the formatting.
8. Select cells A4:G4. Center the text, bold the text, and change the cell style to 20%-Accent1.
9. Delete column D.
10. Insert a column before column A, and change the width to 2.00 (25 pixels).
11. Use AutoFit to change the width of column E.
12. Save the workbook and leave it open for use in the next project.

PROJECT EX 2–4

The Employee List *XXX*.xlsx workbook from Project EX 2-3 should be open in the Excel program window.

1. Save the workbook as **Employee List2 *XXX*.xlsx** (replace *XXX* with your initials).
2. Select cells B6:B26. Center the data and change the number format to Number with zero (0) decimal places.
3. Select cells G6:G26 and change the number format to Currency with zero (0) decimal places.
4. Delete row 5.
5. In column G, highlight the top 10 items with Light Red Fill with Dark Red Text.
6. Select cell A1. Search for Edwards and replace the second occurrence with Evans.
7. Select cell E7. Copy and paste the text to cell E19.
8. Select cells B4:G25 and format as a table with Table Style Medium 2. (Note: Your table has headers.)
9. Convert the table to a normal range.
10. Save and close the workbook.

ON YOUR OWN

Open the **Employee List2 *XXX*.xlsx** file. Reformat the range B4:G25 as a table. Explore the options on the Table Tools Design tab in the Table Style Options group and experiment with changing them. For example, remove the header row; add a total row; emphasize the first column or the last column; or change from banded rows to banded columns. Save and close the workbook.

ON YOUR OWN

Open the **Employee List2 *XXX*.xlsx** file. In column G, clear the conditional formatting and then apply different conditional formatting options. For example, highlight cells between two values; highlight values in the bottom 10%; or use color scales, data bars, or icon sets to represent values in the cells. Save and close the workbook.

WEB PROJECT

PROJECT EX 2–5

When you want to reinforce what you have already learned or learn more about a new skill, Microsoft has online training available that can be a great resource. Search Excel Help for the online training session titled *Get to know Excel 2007: Create your first workbook*. Complete the lessons and practice sessions.

 TEAMWORK PROJECT

PROJECT EX 2–6

Open the workbook **Project EX 2-6.xlsx** from the folder containing the data files for this lesson and save it as **Open Water XXX.xlsx**. With a partner, use the skills you have learned in this lesson to format the worksheet attractively. When you are finished, compare your results with others in your class and discuss which commands you used and why. Vote on the worksheet of the team whose formatting you like the best.

 CRITICAL THINKING

ACTIVITY EX 2–1

Think of a worksheet you would like to create. Perhaps you want a personal budget, an expense report, a schedule, or a receipt. Spend some time deciding what type of information it will contain and how it will be designed, then sketch a rough draft on paper. After planning your worksheet, use Excel to create it. Compare it to your original design. Did you need to make any adjustments? Now search through the Excel templates for the same type you created (e.g., agenda, planner, time sheet) and download it. Compare the template to yours. How is it similar or different? Are there any changes you want to make to your worksheet based on the template?

ACTIVITY EX 2–2

Search for the demo in Excel Help titled *Data takes shape with conditional formatting* and watch it. What are the benefits of conditional formatting? How can conditional formatting help you answer specific questions about your data? What is the difference between color scales, data bars, and icon sets—and when would you format cells using each one?

LESSON 3

Using Formulas and Functions

Estimated Time: 2 hours

■ OBJECTIVES

Upon completion of this lesson, you should be able to:
- Enter formulas in a worksheet.
- Understand cell references.
- Copy formulas.
- Use functions.
- Review and edit formulas.

■ DATA FILES

To complete this lesson, you will need these data files:

Step EX 3-1.xlsx
Project EX 3-1.xlsx
Project EX 3-3.xlsx
Activity EX 3-3.xlsx

■ VOCABULARY

absolute reference
argument
arithmetic operator
Auto Fill
comparison operator
constant
error value
fill handle
formula
function
mixed reference
operator
order of operations
relative reference
syntax
...

UNIT III Microsoft Excel

Introduction

The real power of a spreadsheet program such as Excel is its ability to perform simple and complex calculations on worksheet data. In this lesson, you will learn how to enter formulas to perform calculations. You will also be introduced to Excel's functions—those predefined formulas that allow you to construct complex mathematical, statistical, financial, and other formulas. The commands for working with formulas and functions are located on the Formulas tab on the Ribbon.

Entering Formulas

A *formula* is a set of instructions used to perform calculations on values in a worksheet. Formulas can set up a relationship between two or more cells. You might, for instance, want Excel to total the numbers in a range of cells. An Excel formula must begin with the equal sign (=), and is followed by the set of instructions for completing a calculation.

A formula's instructions contain operators and the values you want calculated. An *operator* is a sign or symbol that indicates what calculation is to be performed. The most commonly used operators are *arithmetic operators* used for addition, subtraction, multiplication, division, and exponentiation.

For example, the formula =3+2 entered in a cell will return a resulting value of 5 in the cell in which the formula is entered. In this case, the values are *constants*, which are numbers entered directly into a formula that do not change. More commonly, formulas in Excel use cell references to identify the cells containing the values you want to use in the formula. If cell C1 contained the value of 3 and cell D1 contained the value of 2, you could use the formula =C1+D1 to return a value of 5. The benefit to using cell references in a formula is that the results will automatically be updated if the values in those cells change.

You can also use a combination of constants and cell references in a formula. For example, in the formula =C9+5, the equal sign (=) indicates that it is a formula, C9 is a cell reference, the plus sign (+) is an operator, and the number 5 is a constant. Excel calculates the formula's result by adding five to the value in cell C9. If the value in C9 changed, the formula result would also be updated.

Table EX 3–1 lists the arithmetic operators and examples of how they are used in formulas.

> **VOCABULARY**
> formula
> operator
> arithmetic operator
> constant

> **EXTRA FOR EXPERTS**
> When entering a formula, you can minimize typing errors by using the Formula AutoComplete feature. When you enter an equal sign (=) and then begin typing, a drop-down list of functions, arguments, and names beginning with those letters are displayed. Click to select from the list and enter it into the formula.

TABLE EX 3–1 Arithmetic operators

OPERATOR	OPERATION	EXAMPLE	DESCRIPTION
+ (plus sign)	Addition	A7+D9	Adds the values in cells A7 and D9
– (minus sign)	Subtraction	A7–D9	Subtracts the value in D9 from the value in A7
* (asterisk)	Multiplication	A7*D9	Multiplies the value in A7 by the value in D9
/ (forward slash)	Division	A7/D9	Divides the value in A7 by the value in D9
% (percent sign)	Percent	A7*25%	Calculates 25% of the value in A7
^ (caret)	Exponentiation	A7^4	Raises the value in A7 to the fourth power

LESSON 3   Using Formulas and Functions

One way to enter a formula in a cell is to type it. For example, if you want to add the values in cells B5 through B8 and enter the result in cell B9, you can enter the formula =B5+B6+B7+B8 in cell B9 and press the Enter key. The result is displayed in the cell, but the formula is what is actually contained in the cell. You can see the formula in the formula bar when the cell is active, as shown in **Figure EX 3–1**.

	A	B	C	D	E	F	G	H
1	Sweet Time Tea Company							
2	Sales Projections							
3								
4	Region	Jan-Feb	Mar-Apr	May-Jun	Jul-Aug	Sep-Oct	Nov-Dec	
5	East	$35,000	$38,000	$41,000	$44,000	$47,000	$50,000	
6	West	$36,000	$39,000	$42,000	$45,000	$48,000	$51,000	
7	North	$40,000	$43,000	$46,000	$49,000	$52,000	$55,000	
8	South	$30,000	$33,000	$36,000	$39,000	$42,000	$45,000	
9		$141,000						

Formula bar: B9   fx =B5+B6+B7+B8

Formula displayed in formula bar
Result of formula displayed in cell

FIGURE EX 3–1   Entering formulas

You get the same result by using the mouse to activate cell B9, typing =, clicking cell B5, typing +, clicking B6, typing +, clicking B7, typing +, clicking B8, and pressing the Enter key. This method of pointing and clicking to enter cell references eliminates the need to look up cell references and avoids potential typing errors.

If you see a problem in your results after you enter a formula, you can view the formula by selecting the cell and reviewing the formula in the formula bar. Often it is the cell references that contain an error. Excel uses a simple color-coding method to identify the cell references used in the formula. Excel displays each cell reference in the formula and the border of the corresponding cell in the worksheet with a distinct color, as shown in **Figure EX 3–2**.

	A	B	C	D	E	F	G	H
1	Sweet Time Tea Company							
2	Sales Projections							
3								
4	Region	Jan-Feb	Mar-Apr	May-Jun	Jul-Aug	Sep-Oct	Nov-Dec	
5	East	$35,000	$38,000	$41,000	$44,000	$47,000	$50,000	
6	West	$36,000	$39,000	$42,000	$45,000	$48,000	$51,000	
7	North	$40,000	$43,000	$46,000	$49,000	$52,000	$55,000	
8	South	$30,000	$33,000	$36,000	$39,000	$42,000	$45,000	
9		=B5+B6+B7+B8						

Formula bar: SUM   fx =B5+B6+B7+B8

Cell reference color matches corresponding cell border color

FIGURE EX 3–2   Color-coded cells

UNIT III Microsoft Excel

> **VOCABULARY**
> order of operations
> comparison operator

Some formulas will contain more than one arithmetic operator. Excel follows the *order of operations*, a specific sequence used to calculate the value of a formula. When you use operators, Excel performs calculations in the normal algebraic precedence. That means the calculations are executed from left to right in the following order:

1. Exponentiation (^)
2. Multiplication (*) or division (/)
3. Addition (+) or subtraction (-)

If you want to change the order of operations, you use parentheses to group expressions in your formula. The expression inside the parentheses gets calculated first. The example below shows how the order of operations can affect the resulting value of a formula.

3 + 7 * 2 = 17
Multiplication calculation is done first, then addition: 7 x 2 = 14 + 3 = 17
(3 + 7) * 2 = 20
Parentheses calculation is done first: 3 + 7 = 10 x 2 = 20

Using *comparison operators*, shown in **Table EX 3-2**, you can compare two values to obtain a logical value, either TRUE or FALSE.

TABLE EX 3–2 Comparison operators

OPERATOR	MEANING	EXAMPLE	DESCRIPTION
=	Equal to	A7=D9	Displays the value TRUE if the values in cell A7 and D9 are equal; displays the value FALSE if the two values are not equal
>	Greater than	A7>D9	Displays the value TRUE if the value in cell A7 is greater than the value in cell D9; displays the value FALSE if the value in cell A7 is less than or equal to the value in cell D9
<	Less than	A7<D9	Displays the value TRUE if the value in cell A7 is less than the value in cell D9; displays the value FALSE if the value in cell A7 is greater than or equal to the value in cell D9
>=	Greater than or equal to	A7>=D9	Displays the value TRUE if the value in cell A7 is greater than or equal to the value in cell D9; displays the value FALSE if the value in cell A7 is less than the value in cell D9
<=	Less than or equal to	A7<=D9	Displays the value TRUE if the value in cell A7 is less than or equal to the value in cell D9; displays the value FALSE if the value in cell A7 is greater than the value in cell D9
<>	Not equal to	A7<>D9	Displays the value TRUE if the value in cell A7 is not equal to the value in cell D9; displays the value FALSE if the value in cell A7 is equal to the value in cell D9

LESSON 3   Using Formulas and Functions

EX 71

Step-by-Step EX 3.1

1. Start Excel.
2. Open **Step EX 3-1.xlsx** from the folder containing the data files for this lesson.
3. Save the workbook as **Trip Budget XXX.xlsx** (replace *XXX* with your initials).
4. In cell **B12**, type **= B8+B9+B10+B11**. Your worksheet window should look similar to **Figure EX 3–3**.

FIGURE EX 3–3
Typing a formula

5. Click the **Enter** button ✓ on the formula bar to enter the formula. Notice the formula is displayed in the formula bar and the resulting value $2,110 is displayed in cell B12.
6. In cell **C12**, type **=**, click cell **C8**, type **+**, click cell **C9**, type **+**, click cell **C10**, type **+**, and then click cell **C11**.
7. Press **Enter** to enter the formula in cell C12 and display the resulting value, $2,058.
8. Save the workbook and leave it open for use in the next Step-by-Step.

Understanding Cell References and Copying Formulas

Excel uses relative, absolute, and mixed cell references. These are especially important to understand when you are copying formulas. You can copy formulas the same way you copy data, using the Cut, Copy, and Paste commands. Or, you can use the Auto Fill command.

Copying formulas is not as straightforward as copying formatting or text entries. When you copy, or move, a formula to another location in the worksheet, it can change depending on what type of cell references it contains.

UNIT III Microsoft Excel

VOCABULARY
relative reference
absolute reference
mixed reference

A *relative reference* means the reference to a cell changes in relation to the location of the formula. For example, if you enter the formula =B9+B10 in cell B11, you are indicating Excel needs to add the contents in cells B9 and B10, the two cells immediately above cell B11. If you copy that same formula to C11, Excel adjusts the formula to add the values in the two cells immediately above cell C11 (cells C9 and C10). This saves you the time of typing a new formula each time. **Figure EX 3–4** shows a formula with relative references that has been copied.

Formula with relative references → (B11: =B9+B10, C11: =C9+C10 with values B9=190, B10=145, C9=200, C10=225) ← *Cell references change when formula is copied*

FIGURE EX 3–4 Using relative cell references in a formula

An *absolute reference* is a permanent reference to a cell and does not change in relation to the location of the formula. You create an absolute reference by typing a dollar sign before the column letter and before the row number ($B$9). If you copy a formula with absolute references ($B$9+$B$10) from one cell to another cell, it stays exactly the same, as shown in **Figure EX 3–5**. Absolute references can be useful when you want to reference the same cell repeatedly in different formulas or use the same formula in a different location in the workbook.

Formula with absolute references → (B11: =$B$9+$B$10, D12: =$B$9+$B$10 with values B9=190, B10=145, C9=200, C10=225) ← *Cell references do not change when formula is copied*

FIGURE EX 3–5 Using absolute cell references in a formula

EXTRA FOR EXPERTS

An easy way to switch a cell reference in an existing formula without having to retype the formula is to use the F4 key. Select the cell that contains the formula, select the cell reference that you want to change in the formula bar, and then press F4 to cycle through the cell reference types.

Sometimes you may only want part of the formula to change when it is copied and part of it to stay the same. A *mixed reference* contains both relative and absolute cell references. For example, the cell reference $B9 has an absolute column and a relative row; B$10 has a relative column and an absolute row. When you copy a formula with a mixed cell reference, the relative reference changes based on the new location, but the absolute reference does not. **Figure EX 3–6** shows a formula with relative column references and absolute row references and how it changes when copied.

LESSON 3 Using Formulas and Functions

EX 73

Formula with mixed references →

	A	B	C	D
8				
9		190	200	
10		145	225	
11		=B$9+B$10		
12				
13			=C$9+C$10	
14				
15				
16				
17				
18				

Relative column references change when formula is copied; absolute row references do not

FIGURE EX 3–6 Using mixed cell references in a formula

> **VOCABULARY**
> Auto Fill
> fill handle

Auto Fill is a feature that you can use to automatically fill in worksheet data in any direction. You can use it to copy data or formatting. You can also use it to quickly copy a formula down a column or across a row by dragging the fill handle of the cell containing the formula. The ***fill handle*** is a little black square in the lower-right corner of the selected cell. When you point to the fill handle, the pointer turns to a black cross that you can click and drag over adjacent cells as far as you want to copy the formula. When you release the mouse button, the range is filled with the results of the copied formulas.

When you finish using the fill handle, the Auto Fill Options button is displayed next to the fill handle, and you can click it to display a menu if you want to choose to fill only the formatting or to fill without formatting.

> **EXTRA FOR EXPERTS**
>
> The fill handle can also be used to fill in a series. For example, you can click a cell containing the word *June* and then drag the fill handle to automatically fill in the previous or following months in adjacent cells.

Step-by-Step EX 3.2

The Trip Budget *XXX*.xlsx workbook from Step-by-Step EX 3.1 should be open in the Excel program window.

1. Select cell **D8**, type **=B8-C8**, and then press **Enter** to enter a formula with relative references, and display the value $50 in the cell.

2. Select cell **D8** and point to the fill handle to change the pointer to ✚.

3. Click and drag the **fill handle** to cell **D11**, as shown in **Figure EX 3–7**. When you release the mouse button, the formula in cell D8 is copied and the cells are filled with formula results.

FIGURE EX 3–7
Copying a formula using Auto Fill

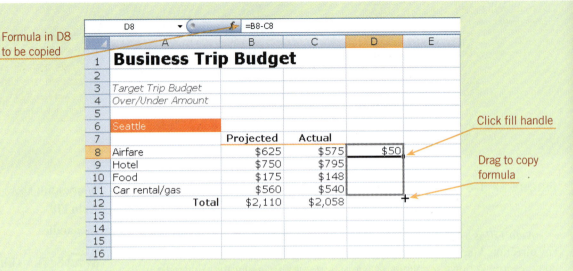

4. In cell **D7**, type **Difference** and press **Enter**.
5. Select cell **C7** and then click and drag the fill handle to cell **D7**. When you release the mouse button, the data is copied and the Auto Fill Options button is displayed.
6. Click the **Auto Fill Options** button and click **Fill Formatting Only**, as shown in **Figure EX 3–8**, to copy the formatting, but not the data.

FIGURE EX 3–8
Copying formatting using Auto Fill

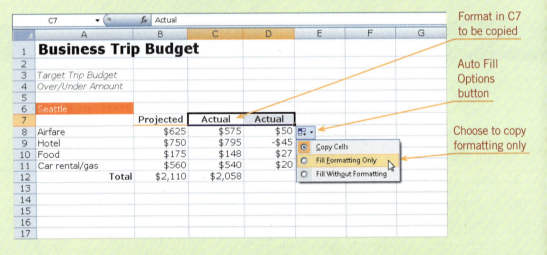

7. Click a blank cell in the worksheet and notice that the formatting in cell D7 is now the same as the formatting in cell C7.
8. In cell **B3**, type **=$B$12*110%** and press **Enter** to enter a formula with absolute references, and display the value of $2,321 in the cell.
9. In cell **B4**, type **=$B$3-C12** and press **Enter** to enter a formula with mixed references, and display the value of $263 in the cell.
10. Save the workbook and leave it open for use in the next Step-by-Step.

LESSON 3 Using Formulas and Functions

Using Functions

Excel provides the user with built-in formulas, called *functions*, that enable you to perform complex calculations easily. Instead of entering all the cell references and operators as you have done in previous exercises, you can use a function in a formula to tell Excel to perform a calculation. For example, the SUM function totals the values in a range of cells, which is easier than typing each cell reference separately.

A function must follow a set of established rules, called *syntax*, that specifies how the function must be entered. The standard syntax for Excel functions is:

=Function name (argument1, argument2…)

Most functions require an argument. An *argument*, which follows the function name and is enclosed in parentheses, refers to the text, numbers, or cell references on which the function is to be performed. For example, in the function =SUM(B8:B11), the range B8:B11 is the argument. If you use more than one argument in a function, separate them with a comma.

Hundreds of functions are available in Excel, and they are organized into categories based upon their general purpose, such as Financial, Date and Time, and Statistical. **Table 3–3** lists examples of some functions from the various categories.

> **VOCABULARY**
> **function**
> **syntax**
> **argument**

TABLE EX 3–3 Examples of functions

FUNCTION	CATEGORY	RETURNS	EXAMPLE
PMT	Financial	The equal payments needed to repay a loan at a fixed interest rate for a specific number of periods	=PMT(.01,24,20000) calculates the monthly payments needed to repay a $20,000 loan at 1% monthly interest for 24 months
OR	Logical	TRUE if any of the arguments are true; FALSE if none of the arguments are true	=OR(A8<100) returns TRUE if the value in A8 is less than 100 and FALSE if the value in A8 is greater than or equal to 100
LOWER	Text	All letters in the cell as lowercase	=LOWER(A15) converts all the letters in A15 to lowercase
DATE	Date & Time	The number that represents the date	=DATE(2012,6,12) returns 6/12/2012
SQRT	Math & Trig	The square root of the number in the argument	=SQRT(A6) calculates the square root of the value in A6
COUNT	Statistical	The number of cells in a range that contain numbers	=COUNT(A2:A7) counts all the cells in the range that contain numbers

You can use the AutoSum command on the Home tab in the Editing group, or on the Formulas tab in the Function Library group to quickly total a range of cells without manually typing the formula. You usually do not need to even select a range because if you select a cell to the right or below a range of numbers, Excel automatically includes that range in the formula when you click the AutoSum button, as shown in **Figure EX 3–9**.

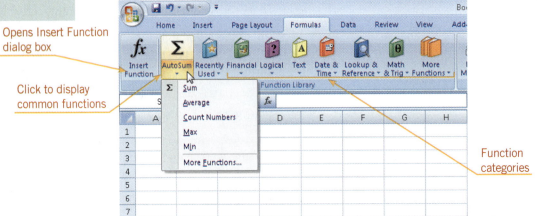

FIGURE EX 3–9 Using AutoSum

EXTRA FOR EXPERTS

When you select a range, the results of three common statistical functions—Average, Count, and Sum—for the selected cells are displayed in the status bar at the bottom of the program window. You can change which summary calculations are displayed by right-clicking the status bar to open the Customize Status Bar menu and clicking to select or deselect options.

When you click the AutoSum button arrow in the Function Library group on the Formulas tab on the Ribbon, a menu of the most common statistical functions is displayed, as shown in **Figure EX 3–10**. The Average function returns the average of a set of values; the Count Numbers function counts the number of cells in a range that contain numbers; the Max function returns the largest value in a set of values; and the Min function returns the smallest value in a set of values. You can also use the commands in the Function Library group on the Formulas tab to choose other functions from other categories.

FIGURE EX 3–10 Function Library group on Formulas tab

Another way to choose a function is to click the Insert Function button in the Function Library group on the Formulas tab to open the Insert Function dialog box, shown in **Figure EX 3–11**.

LESSON 3 Using Formulas and Functions

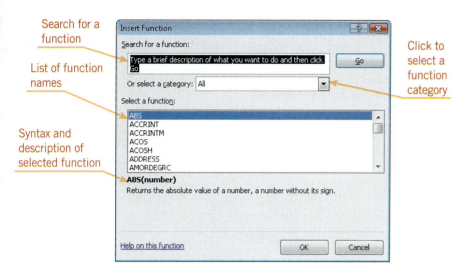

FIGURE EX 3–11 Insert Function dialog box

Once you select a function in the Insert Function dialog box or on the Ribbon, Excel opens the Function Arguments dialog box, shown in **Figure EX 3–12**. The Function Arguments dialog box displays the name of the function, each of its arguments, the current result of a function, and the current result of the entire formula. The Function Arguments dialog box makes it easy to enter arguments for functions. You can either type the arguments into this dialog box, or click the Collapse button to hide the Function Arguments dialog box temporarily, and click the cells to be used as cell references in the argument. When you finish selecting cells for the argument, click the Expand button to redisplay the dialog box. If no arguments are required, the Function Arguments dialog box will display a message and you can simply click OK to close the dialog box and enter the function.

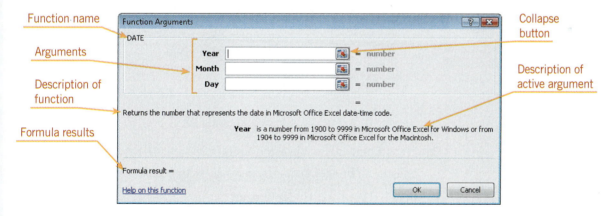

FIGURE EX 3–12 Function Arguments dialog box

Step-by-Step EX 3.3

The Trip Budget *XXX*.xlsx workbook from Step-by-Step EX 3.2 should be open in the Excel program window.

1. Select cell **D12**. Click the **Formulas** tab on the Ribbon, and then click the **AutoSum** button in the Function Library group to enter the SUM function in cell D12. Notice that Excel automatically selects the range D8:D11.

2. Press **Enter** to enter the formula.

3. In cell C15, enter **Average difference**.

4. Select cell **E15**. Click the **AutoSum** button arrow on the Formulas tab in the Function Library group to display a menu.

5. On the menu, click **Average** to enter the AVERAGE function in cell E15. Notice the blinking insertion point appears between the argument parentheses. With the blinking insertion point between the parentheses, type **D8:D11**. Your worksheet should look similar to **Figure EX 3–13**.

FIGURE EX 3–13 Insert AVERAGE function

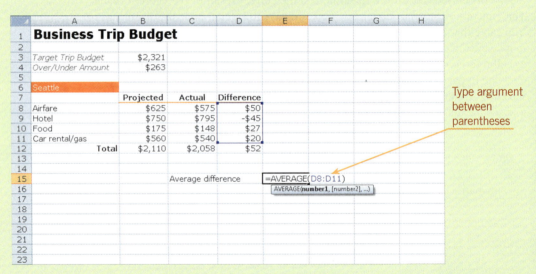

6. Press **Enter** to calculate the average difference between the projected and actual budget amounts and display the value of $13 in cell E15.

7. In cell C16, enter **Under budget?**.

8. Click cell **E16**. On the Formulas tab, in the Function Library group, click the **Logical** button to display a menu.

9. On the menu, click **OR** to display the Function Arguments dialog box.

10. In the Function Arguments dialog box, click the **Collapse** button in the Logical1 box to collapse the dialog box.

11. Click cell **B4** to add an argument to the function in cell E16, as shown in **Figure EX 3–14**, and then click the **Expand** button to expand the

LESSON 3 Using Formulas and Functions

Function Arguments dialog box. Notice the cell reference B4 is displayed in the Logical1 text box in the Function Arguments dialog box.

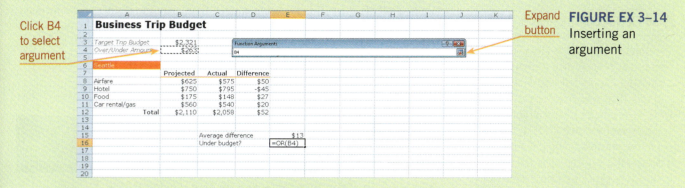

FIGURE EX 3-14 Inserting an argument

12. In the Logical1 text box, after B4, type **>0**. This argument indicates to Excel that if the value in cell B4 is greater than 0, then the value TRUE should be displayed in cell E16.

13. Click **OK** to enter the formula and display TRUE in cell E16, since the current value in B4 is greater than zero.

14. Save the workbook and leave it open for use in the next Step-by-Step.

Reviewing and Editing Formulas

You can choose to display the formulas in a worksheet instead of the resulting values. This can be helpful if you want to print a copy of your worksheet showing all the formulas for documentation, or if you want to review the formulas for accuracy. To display the formulas, click the Show Formulas button in the Formula Auditing group on the Formulas tab. Or you can quickly switch between displaying values and formulas by using the keyboard shortcut Ctrl+~.

Sometimes you may need to check the formulas in your worksheet for accuracy. The commands in the Formula Auditing group on the Formulas tab can help you check for errors and troubleshoot your formulas. When you click the Error Checking button, Excel checks for common errors in your worksheet and displays the Error Checking dialog box with options for resolving the error, as shown in **Figure EX 3-15**.

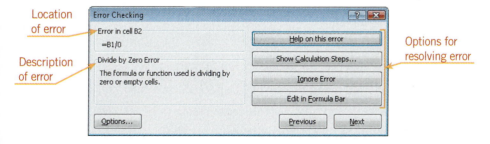

FIGURE EX 3-15 Error Checking dialog box

VOCABULARY
error value

EXTRA FOR EXPERTS

A circular reference is a type of error that occurs when a formula refers to its own cell reference. In this case, a warning box is displayed to identify the problem and prompt you to correct it. If the formula containing the error is complex, you can click OK in this warning box to open a Help window with information on how to locate and correct the circular reference.

Excel indicates when a formula you have entered results in an error by displaying an *error value*. For example when the cell containing a formula result displays *#DIV/0!*, Excel is indicating a number in the formula is divided by zero, or the formula references a cell that contains no value. If a cell contains a series of number symbols, ######, the cell is not wide enough to display the results of the formula. In this case, you can display the value by widening the column. A cell with an error also displays a triangle in the upper-left corner. When you click the cell, an icon is displayed and you can point to it to display a ScreenTip describing the type of error.

Table EX 3–4 lists common error values and what they indicate.

TABLE EX 3–4 Error values

ERROR VALUE	DESCRIPTION OF ERROR
#DIV/0!	Formula contains a number divided by zero
#NA	A value in the formula is not available in the worksheet
#NAME?	Formula contains incorrect text; this often occurs when a function name is misspelled
#NUM!	Invalid use of a number in the formula, or when text is used in a formula or function's argument when a number is required
#REF!	Formula or function uses a cell reference that is no longer valid, which can occur if a cell or range of cells was deleted from the worksheet
#VALUE!	Incorrect argument type used in the function or formula
#####	Cell is not wide enough to display formula results

If you want to change or edit a formula, you can activate the cell containing the formula, type your changes in the formula bar, and then press the Enter key. You can also double-click the cell containing the formula or activate the cell and then press the F2 key, which highlights each cell or range of cells with a different color so you can easily edit the formula in the cell.

Step-by-Step EX 3.4

The Trip Budget *XXX*.xlsx workbook from Step-by-Step EX 3.3 should be open in the Excel program window.

1. Double-click cell **B3** to display the formula in the cell.
2. In the formula bar, delete 110, type **105**, and then press **Enter** to edit the formula and calculate the new results. The new value of $2,216 appears in cell B3. Notice the value in cell B4 also changes (to $158).
3. Click the **Formulas** tab on the Ribbon, and then click the **Show Formulas** button in the Formula Auditing group. The formulas are displayed in the worksheet, as shown in **Figure EX 3–16**.

LESSON 3   Using Formulas and Functions

EX 81

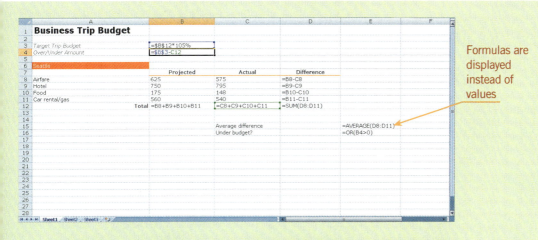

FIGURE EX 3-16
Displaying formulas

4. On the Formulas tab, in the Formula Auditing group, click the **Show Formulas** button again to display the values.

5. Delete rows 3 and 4. Notice that cell E14 now contains the error value #REF! and a green triangle appears in the upper-left corner of the cell, because the formula in this cell references one of the cells you just deleted.

6. Click cell **E14** and point to the icon to the left of the cell to read the ScreenTip that explains the type of error, as shown in **Figure EX 3-17**.

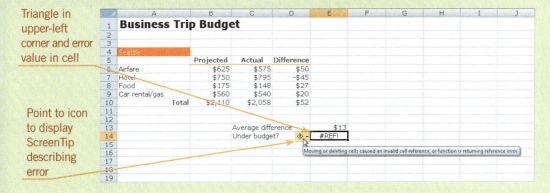

FIGURE EX 3-17
Cell with an error

7. Double-click cell **E14** to display the formula in the cell.

8. In the formula in cell E14, delete #REF! and click **D10** to correct the formula, as shown in **Figure EX 3-18**.

FIGURE EX 3-18
Correcting a formula

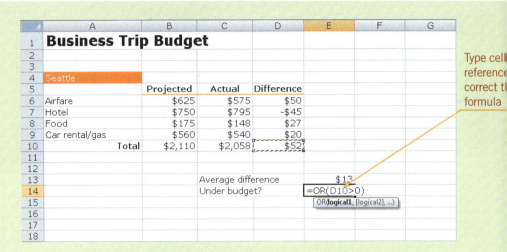

9. Press **Enter** to edit the formula and resolve the error. The value TRUE appears in cell E14.

10. Save and close the workbook and then close Excel.

SUMMARY

In this lesson, you learned:

- Ways to enter a formula.
- The different types of cell references.
- How to copy a formula.
- Various ways to review and edit formulas.
- Functions are easy-to-use, predefined formulas that can be used in worksheets to perform various calculations.

VOCABULARY REVIEW

Define the following terms:

absolute reference	constant	mixed reference
argument	error value	operator
arithmetic operator	fill handle	order of operations
Auto Fill	formula	relative reference
comparison operator	function	syntax

REVIEW QUESTIONS

MULTIPLE CHOICE

Select the best response for the following statements.

1. All formulas must begin with _____.

    A. parentheses ( )   C. a caret (^)

    B. the equal sign (=)   D. the greater than sign (>)

LESSON 3   Using Formulas and Functions   EX 83

2. Each cell reference in the formula is coded with a different _____.
   A. font   C. border
   B. point size   D. color

3. A forward slash (/) is an example of a(n) _____.
   A. arithmetic operator   C. argument
   B. cell reference   D. order of operations

4. What is the result of the following formula: =C6+D6*3, where cell C6 contains the value of 4 and cell D6 contains the value of 5?
   A. 17   C. 23
   B. 19   D. 27

5. Which of the following is a relative reference?
   A. B4   C. B$4
   B. $B4   D. $B$4

6. Which is *not* an option on the Auto Fill Options menu?
   A. Copy Cells   C. Fill Formatting Only
   B. Clear Cells   D. Fill Without Formatting

7. To edit a formula, double-click the cell containing the formula or select the cell and press the _____ key.
   A. Ctrl   C. F2
   B. Alt   D. F4

8. Excel indicates when a formula you have entered results in an error by displaying a(n) _____ in the cell.
   A. ScreenTip   C. fill handle
   B. error value   D. nothing

9. A(n) _____ refers to the values or cell references on which a function is to be performed.
   A. operator   C. constant
   B. mixed reference   D. argument

10. A function must follow a set of established rules, called _____, which specifies how the function must be entered.
    A. syntax   C. relative reference
    B. order of operations   D. calculation

FILL IN THE BLANK

Complete the following sentences by writing the correct word or words in the blanks provided.

1. The commands for working with formulas and functions are located on the _____ tab on the Ribbon.

2. A(n) _____ is a set of instructions used to perform calculations on values in a worksheet.

3. Numbers entered directly into a formula that do not change are called _____.

4. A(n) _____ is a sign or symbol that indicates what calculation is to be performed.

5. A(n) _____ reference is a permanent reference to a cell and does not change in relation to the location of the formula.

6. _____ is a feature that you can use to automatically fill in worksheet data in any direction.

7. The _____ is a little black square in the lower-right corner of the selected cell used for copying formulas or cell formatting.

8. A(n) _____ is a built-in formula.

9. To enter cell references as an argument, click the Collapse button to hide the _____ dialog box temporarily so it is not in your way.

10. A cell with an error has a(n) _____ _____ in the upper-left corner.

PROJECTS

PROJECT EX 3-1

1. Open the **Project EX 3-1.xlsx** workbook from the folder containing the data files for this lesson.
2. Save the workbook as **Open Water XXX.xlsx** (replace XXX with your initials).
3. In cell A23, enter **Total** and apply bold formatting.
4. Click cell B23. Use the AutoSum command to get a total for the range B5:B22.
5. Copy the formula in B23 to C23:M23.
6. In cell N4, enter **Total**.
7. Copy the formatting only from cell M4 to cell N4.
8. Click cell N5. Use the AutoSum command to get a total for the range B5:M5.
9. Copy the formula in N5 to N6:N23.
10. Widen column N so the value in N23 is displayed instead of ######.
11. Save the workbook and leave it open for use in the next project.

PROJECT EX 3-2

The workbook Open Water XXX.xlsx from Project EX 3-1 should be open in the Excel program window.

1. Save the workbook as **Open Water2 XXX.xlsx** (replace XXX with your initials).
2. In cell A25, enter **Highest Sales**.
3. In cell B25, enter a function to determine the highest amount of sales in the range B5:B22. (*Hint*: Use the Max function on the AutoSum menu.)
4. Copy the function in cell B25 to cells C25 through M25.
5. In cell A26, enter **Lowest Sales**.
6. In cell B26, enter a function to determine the lowest amount of sales in the range B5:B22. (*Hint*: Use the Min function on the AutoSum menu.)
7. Copy the function in cell B26 to cells C26 through M26.
8. In cell A27, enter **Average Sales**.
9. In cell B27, enter a function to determine the average amount of sales in the range B5:B22. (*Hint*: Use the AVERAGE function).
10. Copy the function in cell B27 to cells C27 through M27.
11. Format the data in the range B25:M27 for Currency with zero decimals, if it is not already.
12. Save and close the workbook.

ON YOUR OWN

Open the **Open Water2 XXX.xlsx** workbook, and create a formula that determines which employee had the highest total sales for the year. Save and close the workbook.

PROJECT EX 3-3

1. Open the **Project EX 3-3.xlsx** workbook from the folder containing the data files for this lesson.
2. Save the workbook as **Tea Invoice XXX.xlsx** (replace XXX with your initials).
3. In cell E10, enter **Total**.
4. In cell E11, enter a formula to multiply the value in cell C11 by the value in cell D11.
5. Copy the formula in cell E11 to cells E12 through E15.
6. In E11:E15, change the number format to currency with two decimal places.
7. In cell E18, use the AutoSum command to get a total for the range E11:E17.
8. In cell E19, create a formula that calculates a 7% sales tax on the value in cell E18. (*Hint*: Use the formula =7%*E18.)
9. In cell E20, enter **7.95**.
10. In cell E21, enter a formula with absolute references that totals cells E18:E20.
11. Save the workbook and leave it open for use in the next project.

PROJECT EX 3-4

The workbook Tea Invoice XXX.xlsx from Project EX 3-3 should be open in the Excel program window.

1. Save the workbook as **Tea Invoice2 XXX.xlsx** (replace XXX with your initials).
2. In cell E19, edit the formula from a 7% sales tax to 6% sales tax.
3. Display the formulas in the worksheet.
4. Check the worksheet for errors.

LESSON 3 Using Formulas and Functions

5. Display the values in the worksheet.
6. In cell B23, enter **Qualifies for discount?**
7. In cell C23, create a formula using the OR function with E21>300 as the argument. (*Hint*: Use the Function Arguments dialog box.)
8. Save and close the workbook.

ON YOUR OWN

Open the **Tea Invoice2** *XXX*.**xlsx** file, and then in cell A8, create a function that inserts the current date and time. (*Hint*: Use the NOW function.) Save and close the workbook.

WEB PROJECT

PROJECT EX 3-5

Visit Web sites of companies that sell cell phone plans. Create a worksheet containing information about at least three different options—including the price of the cell phone, cost of the cell plan per month, how many minutes are included, cost of features such as text messaging, and any additional charges. Use a formula to determine the best plan for your budget. Use functions to determine the highest price plan, the lowest price plan, and the average price of the plans.

TEAMWORK PROJECT

PROJECT EX 3-6

With a partner, open the Insert Function dialog box. Browse through all the various categories and familiarize yourselves with the various functions available in each one. Click a function to see the description displayed below it. Choose one that you want to know more about and click Help on this function link to get more information. Learn as much as possible about it. Present your findings to the class and include a worksheet you have created that demonstrates the use of the function.

CRITICAL THINKING

ACTIVITY EX 3-1

In Excel, you can create a defined name that you assign to a cell or range of cells and then use the defined name as a reference in formulas. Use Excel Help to learn the different ways you can define a name for a range, how to use defined names in a formula, and how to use the Name Manager to create, edit, delete, or find names in a workbook. Open an existing workbook and then create at least one defined name for a range of cells and use the defined name in a formula.

ACTIVITY EX 3-2

Search for the demo in Excel Help titled *Create formulas with Formula AutoComplete* and watch it. How can this feature help you avoid syntax or typing mistakes? How does defining names for ranges of cells make it easier to create formulas?

ACTIVITY EX 3-3

You can also use the fill handle to fill a series, which can be useful. Use Excel Help to find out how this Auto Fill feature works. Then open the file **Activity EX 3-3.xlsx** from the folder containing the data files for this lesson and save it as **Auto Fill** *XXX*.**xlsx** (replace *XXX* with your initials). Using the existing data, create a vertical Auto Fill series for each of the items listed below:

- A series of months from March through August
- A series of days from Monday through Friday
- A series of times from 2:00 through 9:00
- A series of labels from Employee1 through Employee5
- A series of years from 2012 through 2020 (*Hint*: You have to select two entries before filling the rest.)

Save and close the workbook and then close Excel.

LESSON 4

Working with Charts and Graphics

Estimated Time: 1.5 hours

■ OBJECTIVES

Upon completion of this lesson, you should be able to:

- Describe the elements of a chart.
- Create a chart.
- Modify a chart.
- Insert and modify illustrations.

■ DATA FILES

To complete this lesson, you will need these data files:

Step EX 4-1.xlsx
Project EX 4-1.xlsx
Project EX 4-4.xlsx
Activity EX 4-1.xlsx

■ VOCABULARY

chart
chart area
chart sheet
clip art
data marker
data series
data source
drawing object
embedded chart
gridlines
horizontal axis
legend
pictures
plot area
SmartArt graphic
title
vertical axis
WordArt
...

Introduction

Charts and graphics add visual impact to worksheets and help convey the meaning of the worksheet data. Excel includes chart tools that can help make data clearer, more visually interesting, and easier to read and understand. Charts allow users to see at a glance patterns or relationships in the worksheet data, for example, whether sales are rising or falling. Excel also includes graphics, or illustration, tools that let you add visual interest to your workbooks. You can add and manipulate pictures, clip art, shapes, and SmartArt. In this lesson, you will learn to insert and modify charts and graphic elements. You will use buttons in the Illustrations and Charts groups on the Insert tab, shown in **Figure EX 4–1**, to insert various types of charts and illustrations.

FIGURE EX 4–1   Insert tab on the Ribbon

Understanding Charts

> **VOCABULARY**
> chart

When you need to illustrate or compare data, it is helpful to use a chart. A ***chart*** is a graphical representation of worksheet data. There are a variety of different chart types you can use to represent your data, depending on what you want to convey to your audience. **Table EX 4–1** shows some of the types of charts available in Excel. Buttons for the most common chart types are located in the Charts group on the Insert tab on the Ribbon.

TABLE EX 4–1   Common chart types

TYPE	BUTTON	USEFUL FOR
Column		Displaying changes in data over time; comparing data
Line		Displaying continuous data over time; showing trends
Pie		Plotting data from one row or column; showing values as a percentage of a whole
Bar		Comparing individual items
Area		Showing changes over time
Scatter		Plotting many data points; comparing data without representing time lapse

Charts are made up of different parts, or elements. Depending on the type of chart, not every element will be included. Some elements are displayed by default, and others can be displayed if needed. If you do not want a chart element displayed,

LESSON 4 Working with Charts and Graphics

you can hide it. Use **Figure EX 4–2** and **Table EX 4–2** to become familiar with some of the basic elements of a chart.

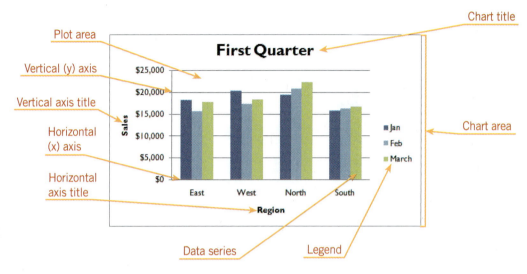

FIGURE EX 4–2 Elements of a chart

TABLE EX 4–2 Chart elements

ELEMENT	DESCRIPTION
Chart area	The complete chart and all its elements, which includes the plot area, titles, axes, legend, and any other objects
Plot area	The area in the chart where the values from the data series are displayed graphically; this includes the axes and data series
Axes (vertical and horizontal)	The lines on a chart that are used to measure and represent data series values. The horizontal axis (x) is used for showing categories, and the vertical axis (y) is used for plotting values.
Data marker	A dot, a bar, or a symbol used to represent one number from the worksheet; related data markers in a chart constitute a data series
Data series	A series of related values from the worksheet graphically represented by a distinct data marker in the plot area
Legend	A list that identifies the patterns or colors of the data series or categories in a chart
Title	Descriptive name that identifies a chart or axis
Gridlines	Lines extending from the vertical or horizontal axes across the plot are of a chart

Creating Charts

The first step in creating a chart is to select the *data source*, which is the range of cells that contain the data you want to display in the chart. You can use column and row labels as axes titles or data marker labels in the chart by including them in your range selection.

▶ **VOCABULARY**
data source

EXTRA FOR EXPERTS

If you frequently create the same type of chart, you can set it as the default chart type to be used when creating a new chart by clicking the Set as Default Chart button in the Insert Chart dialog box.

Next, you need to decide what type of chart you want to use. When you click a button in the Charts group on the Insert tab, the subtypes available for that type of chart are displayed. You can point to a subtype to display a ScreenTip with its description and then click to insert the type of chart you want. When you click the Charts dialog box launcher, the Insert Chart dialog box opens, as shown in **Figure EX 4–3**, where you can also choose from categories of different types of charts.

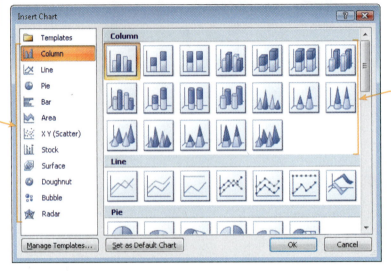

FIGURE EX 4–3 Insert Chart dialog box

After the chart is created, the Chart Tools Design, Layout, and Format contextual tabs are displayed on the Ribbon so that you can modify the chart. These tabs are displayed on the Ribbon only when a chart or one of its elements is selected. When you select a chart, the corresponding data on the worksheet is color-coded so you can easily identify it.

When you create a chart, Excel links the chart to its related data on the worksheet. If the worksheet data is changed, Excel automatically updates the chart.

Step-by-Step EX 4.1

1. Start Excel.
2. Open the **Step EX 4-1.xlsx** workbook from the folder containing the data files for this lesson.
3. Save the workbook as **First Quarter XXX.xlsx** (replace XXX with your initials).
4. Select range **A4:D8**.
5. On the Insert tab on the Ribbon, in the Charts group, click the **Bar** button and point to the **Clustered Bar** subtype in the 2-D Bar section, as shown in **Figure EX 4–4**.

LESSON 4 Working with Charts and Graphics

EX 91

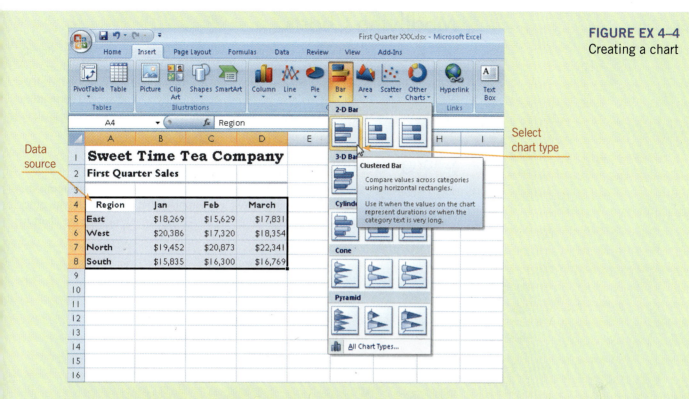

FIGURE EX 4–4
Creating a chart

6. Click the **Clustered Bar** chart type to create a chart in the worksheet. Your worksheet window should look similar to **Figure EX 4–5**. Notice the color-coded data in the worksheet and the Chart Tools contextual tabs.

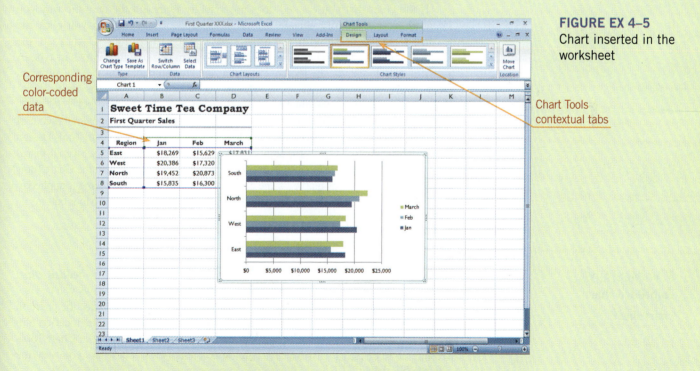

FIGURE EX 4–5
Chart inserted in the worksheet

7. Edit the contents of cell **B4** to read **January**. Notice when you enter the new text, the legend on the chart is automatically updated.
8. Edit the contents of cell **C4** to read **February**.
9. Save the workbook and leave it open for use in the next Step-by-Step.

Modifying Charts

Once you have created a chart, you may want to make changes to it. You may decide you want to change the design of your chart—for example, use a different chart type to depict the worksheet data. Sometimes the design of the chart is ideal, but the chart elements need adjusting. You also can enhance charts by adding special formatting options such as shapes or WordArt to chart elements.

Changing Chart Design

The Design tab, shown in **Figure EX 4–6**, includes commands for changing the chart type, saving the formatting and layout as a template that can be used with other charts, applying a quick layout, changing the chart's style, and moving the chart to another worksheet.

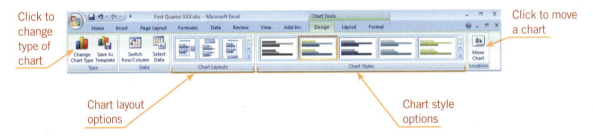

FIGURE EX 4–6 Chart Tools Design tab

If the chart that you created does not visually represent the data the way you intended, you can easily change it to another type of chart. When you click the Change Chart Type button in the Type group on the Chart Tools Design tab, the Change Chart Type dialog box opens allowing you to select a different chart type.

It is easy to change the look of your chart by choosing a layout that has different chart elements or by applying a style to change the formatting. Excel has a variety of pre-defined options to help you quickly customize your chart. The layouts and styles available depend on the type of chart you are working with. To change the overall layout of the chart, you can choose a layout in the Chart Layouts group on the Chart Tools Design tab or click the More button for additional layouts. You can change the overall visual look of the chart by choosing a style option in the Chart Styles group on the Chart Tools Design tab. The colors available for the chart styles depend on which theme is applied to the workbook. To see the full gallery of style options, you can click the More button.

Moving and Sizing Charts

By default, a newly created chart is placed in the worksheet as an ***embedded chart*** that is a graphic object and is saved as part of the worksheet. This allows you to view or print the chart along with its source data. You can also choose to place the chart on a ***chart sheet***, which is a separate sheet in the workbook. To change the location of a chart, you can click the Move Chart button in the Location group of the Chart Tools Design tab to display the Move Chart dialog box and then select where you want the chart to be placed.

▶ **VOCABULARY**
embedded chart
chart sheet

LESSON 4 Working with Charts and Graphics

To move a selected chart within the worksheet, you can click its border and drag it to a new location. You can resize the chart by selecting it and then dragging one of the dotted sizing handles, as shown in **Figure EX 4–7**. To resize a chart proportionally, press and hold the Shift key while dragging a corner handle.

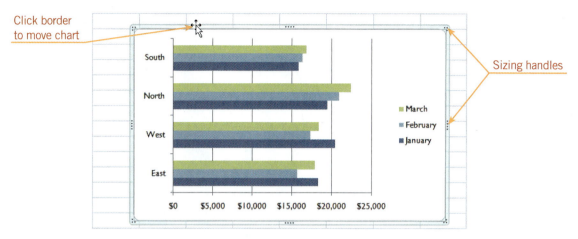

FIGURE EX 4–7 Moving or resizing a chart

Step-by-Step EX 4.2

The First Quarter *XXX*.xlsx workbook from Step-by-Step EX 4.1 should be open in the Excel program window.

1. Click the **chart area** to select the chart. Confirm the entire chart is selected by making sure *Chart Area* displays in the Chart Elements list box located in the Current Selection group on the Chart Tools Format tab or the Layout tab.

2. On the Chart Tools Design tab, in the Type group, click the **Change Chart Type** button to open the Change Chart Type dialog box.

3. Click **Column** in the list of chart categories in the left pane. The Clustered Column subtype is selected by default in the right pane. Click **OK** to close the dialog box and change the chart type.

4. On the Chart Tools Design tab, in the Chart Layouts group, click the **More** button to display the menu.

5. Click **Layout 8**, as shown in **Figure EX 4–8**, to change the chart layout.

FIGURE EX 4–8
Changing the chart layout

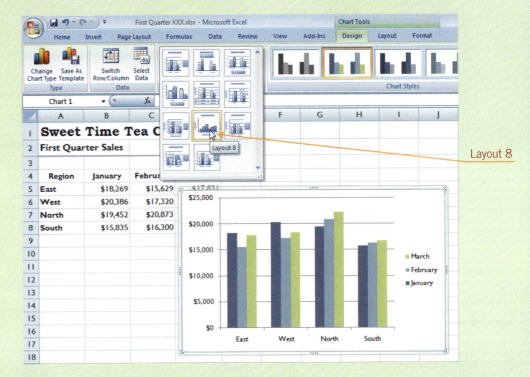

6. On the Chart Tools Design tab, in the Chart Styles group, click the **More** button to display the gallery.

7. Click **Style 12**, as shown in **Figure EX 4–9**, to change the chart style.

FIGURE EX 4–9
Changing the chart style

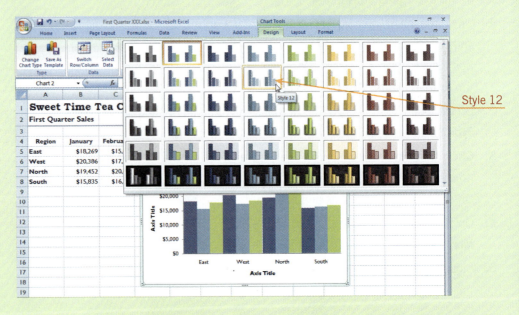

8. Click the **upper-right resizing handle** on the chart. The pointer changes to a double-headed arrow. Press and hold **Shift**, while dragging the sizing handle up and to the right, to approximate the chart size shown in **Figure EX 4–10**.

LESSON 4   Working with Charts and Graphics   EX 95

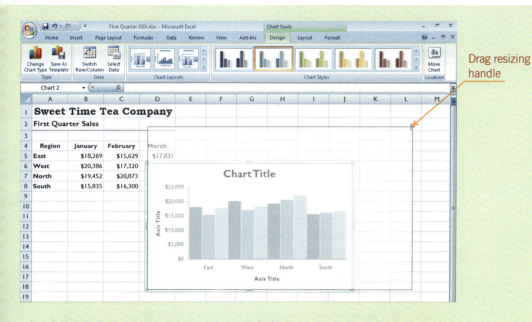

FIGURE EX 4–10
Resizing the chart

9. Release both the mouse button and Shift to enlarge the chart.
10. On the Chart Tools Design tab, in the Location group, click the **Move Chart** button to open the Move Chart dialog box.
11. Click the **New sheet** option button and type **1st Q Sales Chart** in the New sheet text box, as shown in **Figure EX 4–11**, and then click the **OK** button to move the chart to a new worksheet named 1st Q Sales Chart in the workbook.

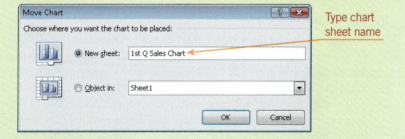

FIGURE EX 4–11
Move Chart dialog box

12. Click the **Sheet1** tab to confirm that the chart has been moved from that worksheet.
13. Save the workbook and leave it open for use in the next Step-by-Step.

Modifying Chart Elements

The Chart Tools Layout tab, shown in **Figure EX 4–12**, includes buttons you can use to insert pictures, shapes, and text boxes into the chart; display, hide, and specify the location of chart elements; format the axes and plot area; or change the titles and labels that appear in the chart.

UNIT III Microsoft Excel

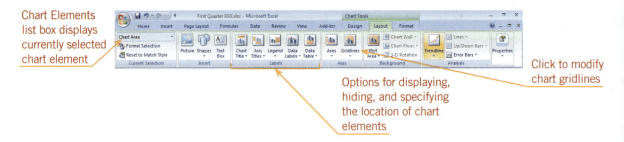

FIGURE EX 4–12 Chart Tools Layout tab

To modify a specific element of a chart, you must first select it by positioning the pointer on a chart element until a ScreenTip appears, as shown in **Figure EX 4–13**, identifying the element, and then clicking. A selection box surrounds the selected chart element. The currently selected chart element is displayed in the Chart Elements list box in the Current Selection group of the Chart Tools Format tab, and the Chart Tools Layout tab changes based on which chart element is currently selected. You can also click the Chart Elements list arrow in the Current Selection group and select a different chart element on the menu to activate it for modifying.

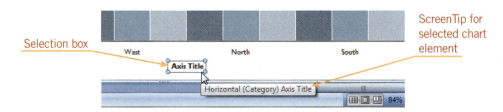

FIGURE EX 4–13 Selecting a chart element

You can change the text in a chart title or chart element label by selecting it, typing new text, and pressing the Enter key. To display, hide, or change the location of a chart element, you can click a button in the Labels, Axes, or Background groups and then select whether to display the element and where.

To make any chart with axes easier to read, you can choose to display gridlines. You can display horizontal or vertical gridlines across the plot area of the chart by clicking the Gridlines button in the Axes group on the Chart Tools Layout tab.

Step-by-Step EX 4.3

The First Quarter *XXX*.xlsx workbook from Step-by-Step EX 4.2 should be open in the Excel program window.

1. Click the **1st Q Sales Chart** sheet to display the worksheet with the chart.
2. On the Chart Tools Layout tab, in the Labels group, click the **Axis Titles** button to display a menu.
3. Point to **Primary Vertical Axis Title** and then click **None**, as shown in **Figure EX 4–14**, to hide the vertical axis title.

LESSON 4   Working with Charts and Graphics

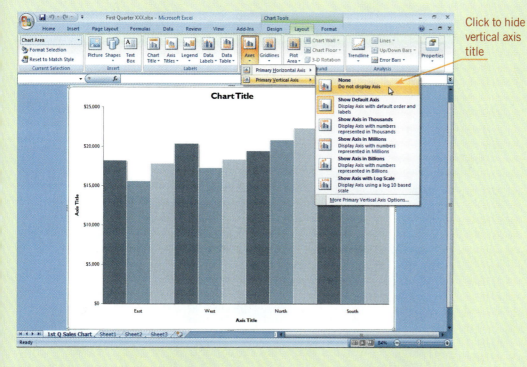

FIGURE EX 4-14
Hiding a chart element

4. On the Chart Tools Layout tab, in the Labels group, click the **Legend** button, and then click **Show Legend at Top** to display the legend beneath the title.

5. On the Chart Tools Layout tab, in the Current Selection group, click the **Chart Elements** list arrow, and then click **Chart Title**, as shown in **Figure EX 4-15**, to select the chart title.

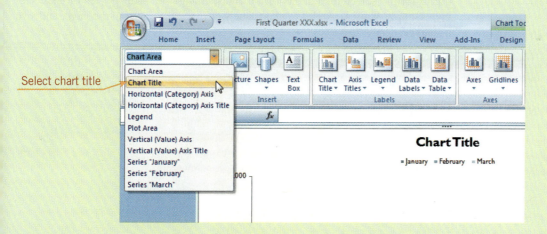

FIGURE EX 4-15
Chart Elements menu

6. Type **Sales** and notice the text is displayed in the formula bar. Press **Enter** to change the chart title to *Sales*.

7. Click the horizontal axis title **Axis Title** at the bottom of the chart to select it. Notice that the Chart Elements list box changes to display *Horizontal (Category) Axis Title*.

8. Type **Month** and press **Enter** to change the horizontal axis title to *Month*.

9. On the Chart Tools Layout tab, in the Axes group, click the **Chart Gridlines** button, point to **Primary Vertical Gridlines**, and then click **Major Gridlines** to display vertical gridlines between the months. Your workbook window should look similar to **Figure EX 4–16**.

FIGURE EX 4–16
1st Q Sales Chart worksheet

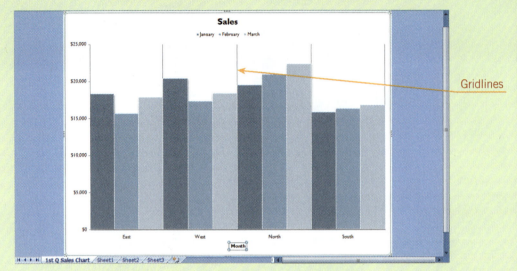

10. Save the workbook and leave it open for use in the next Step-by-Step.

Formatting Chart Elements

The Chart Tools Format tab, shown in **Figure EX 4–17**, includes commands you can use to format selected elements of the chart, change the shape styles of chart elements, apply WordArt styles to chart labels, arrange the chart on the page, and size a chart precisely.

FIGURE EX 4–17 Chart Tools Format tab

You can also click the Format Selection button in the Current Selection group on the Chart Tools Format tab to open the Format dialog box and access additional formatting options. The options available will depend on which chart element you have selected. For example, if you selected an axis, the options for formatting an axis would be displayed, as shown in **Figure EX 4–18**.

LESSON 4 Working with Charts and Graphics

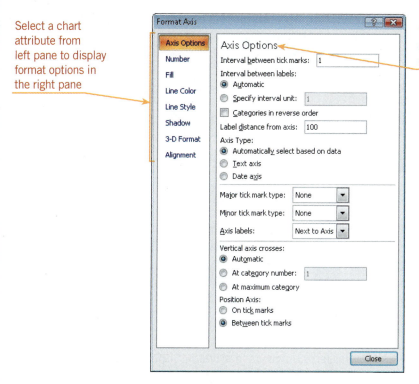

Select a chart attribute from left pane to display format options in the right pane

Title in right pane will change depending on chart element selected in left pane

FIGURE EX 4–18 Format dialog box

WordArt is a drawing tool that turns words into a graphics image. You can use the WordArt feature to create interesting text effects to enhance charts. WordArt lets you fit text into a variety of shapes, use unusual alignments, and add three-dimensional effects.

> **VOCABULARY**
> **WordArt**

Step-by-Step EX 4.4

The First Quarter *XXX*.xlsx workbook from Step-by-Step EX 4.3 should be open in the Excel program window.

1. Select the chart title, **Sales**.

2. On the Chart Tools Format tab, in the Shape Styles group, click the **More** button ⏷ to display a gallery of options.

3. Click the **Light 1 Outline, Colored Fill – Accent 2** option, as shown in **Figure EX 4–19**.

FIGURE EX 4-19
Shape Styles gallery

4. Select the far-left column in the chart (**Series "January" Point "East"** data bar), shown in **Figure EX 4–20**. Notice that the entire East data series in the chart is selected.

5. On the Chart Tools Format tab, in the Shape Styles group, click the **Shape Fill** arrow, point to **Gradient**, and click the **Linear Diagonal** option in the Dark Variations section, as shown in **Figure EX 4–20**, to fill the data series with a gradient.

FIGURE EX 4-20
Shape Fill menu

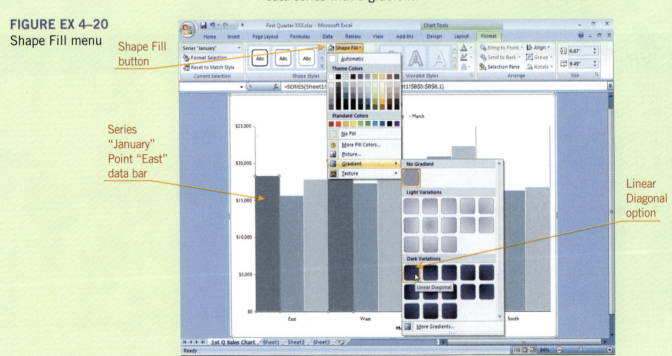

6. At the bottom of the chart, click **Month**, the Horizontal (Category) Axis Title.

LESSON 4 Working with Charts and Graphics

EX 101

7. On the Chart Tools Format tab, in the WordArt Styles group, click the **More** button to open the WordArt styles gallery, and click the **Gradient Fill – Accent 1** option, as shown in **Figure EX 4–21**, to apply a WordArt style to the axis title.

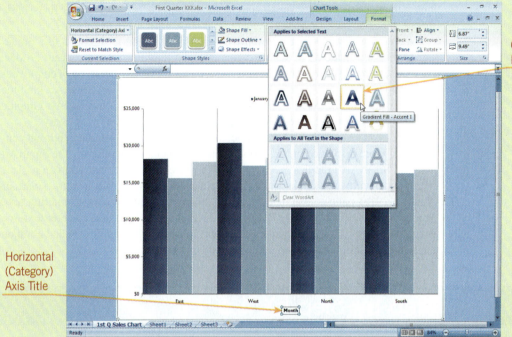

FIGURE EX 4–21
WordArt Style gallery

8. On the Chart Tools Format tab, in the Size group, click the **Shape Height** arrow until the number in the box is 6.5", and click the **Shape Width** arrow until the number in the boxes is 9.5" to change the size of the chart.

9. Save the workbook and leave it open for use in the next Step-by-Step.

Inserting and Modifying Illustrations

Like charts, other types of illustrations such as pictures, clip art, shapes, and SmartArt are also commonly referred to as graphics, which you can use to add visual impact to worksheets. The commands to insert illustrations are located on the Insert tab on the Ribbon, in the Illustrations group, as shown in **Figure EX 4–22**.

FIGURE EX 4–22   Illustrations group on the Insert tab

UNIT III Microsoft Excel

> **VOCABULARY**
> pictures
> clip art
> drawing object
> SmartArt graphics

> **WARNING**
> Using too many graphics in your worksheet can distract a user's focus away from the data. Use illustrations sparingly and only when they will enhance your data, not detract from it.

The Picture button in the Illustrations group can be used to insert *pictures*, which are digital photographs or images, stored on your computer or network. *Clip art* is a collection of predesigned artwork such as drawings or images that can be inserted into worksheets. Clip art can be inserted using the Clip Art button in the Illustrations group on the Insert tab on the Ribbon. Excel also provides tools for inserting *drawing objects*, which are shapes, curves, and lines that you create in the worksheet by first selecting the type of shape you want to create, and then clicking and dragging the mouse to create that shape. The Shapes button displays a menu containing lines, basic shapes, block arrows, flowchart elements, callouts, stars, and banners.

Excel also provides a set of *SmartArt graphics*. A SmartArt graphic is a predesigned diagram made up of shapes containing text that illustrates a concept or idea. For example, an organization chart is a diagram that shows the hierarchy of employees in a company. You can insert a SmartArt graphic using the Insert SmartArt Graphic button in the Illustrations group of the Insert tab. The Choose a SmartArt Graphic dialog box that opens contains many types of graphics arranged by category.

After you insert a SmartArt graphic, the SmartArt Tools Design and Format contextual tabs are displayed on the Ribbon with commands for modifying the SmartArt graphic. SmartArt graphics are inserted with placeholder text that you can replace with your own text by clicking the [Text] placeholder. When you insert a SmartArt graphic, a Text pane is also displayed to help simplify the process of entering text. You can click a [Text] placeholder beside a bullet in the Text pane to enter text in a shape. The Text pane can be hidden or displayed by clicking the Text Pane button on the SmartArt Tools Design tab in the Create Graphic group.

Step-by-Step EX 4.5

The First Quarter *XXX*.xlsx workbook from Step-by-Step EX 4-4 should be open in the Excel program window.

1. Click the **Sheet1** tab to display the sales data.
2. On the Insert tab, in the Illustrations group, click the **SmartArt** button to open the Choose a SmartArt Graphic dialog box.
3. In the category list in the left pane, click **Hierarchy** and then click **Organization Chart** in the middle pane, as shown in **Figure EX 4–23**.

FIGURE EX 4–23
Choose a SmartArt Graphic dialog box

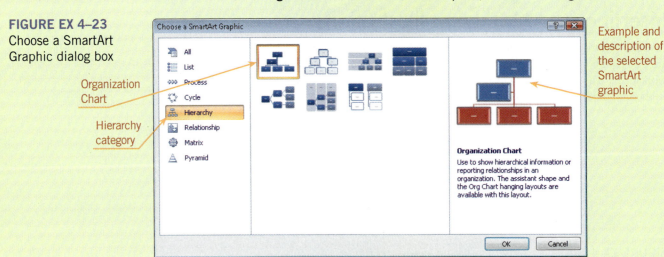

Organization Chart

Hierarchy category

Example and description of the selected SmartArt graphic

LESSON 4 Working with Charts and Graphics

EX 103

4. Click the **OK** button to close the dialog box and insert the SmartArt graphic in the worksheet. The Text pane opens next to the SmartArt graphic organization chart. (*Note*: If the Text pane does not open, click the Text Pane button on the SmartArt Tools Design tab in the Create Graphic group to display it.)

5. Click the **[Text]** placeholder in the rectangle at the top of the SmartArt graphic and type **Regional Sales Directors**. Notice that the placeholder text is replaced as you type, and the first bullet in the Text pane now reads *Regional Sales Directors*.

6. Select the second level shape on the SmartArt graphic, as shown in **Figure EX 4–24**, and press **Delete** to remove the box.

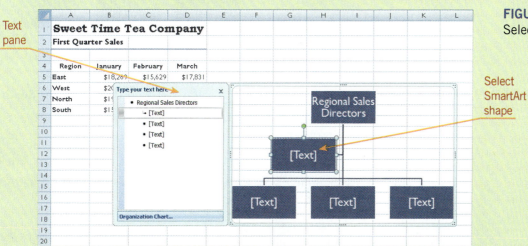

FIGURE EX 4–24
Selecting a SmartArt shape

7. Click the **[Text]** placeholder in the left rectangle shape of the SmartArt graphic and type **Karen Friske, East**.

8. Click the **[Text]** placeholder in the middle shape of the SmartArt graphic and type **Marin Bezio, West**.

9. Click the **[Text]** placeholder in the right shape of the SmartArt graphic and type **Tai Yee, North**.

10. With the **Tai Yee, North** shape still selected, click the **SmartArt Tools Design** tab on the Ribbon, if necessary. In the Create Graphic group, click the **Add Shape** arrow and then click **Add Shape After**, as shown in **Figure EX 4–25**, to insert a new shape.

FIGURE EX 4–25
Add Shape menu

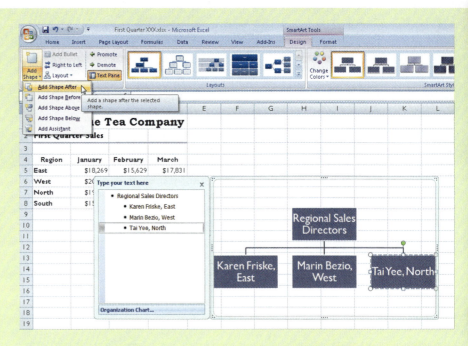

11. Click the last bullet in the Text pane and type **Darin Lockert, South**. Notice that the text is also inserted on the new shape you created.

12. On the SmartArt Tools Design tab, in the SmartArt Styles group, click the **More** button to display a gallery of styles and then click **Brick Scene**, as shown in **Figure EX 4–26**, to change the style of the SmartArt graphic.

FIGURE EX 4–26
SmartArt Styles gallery

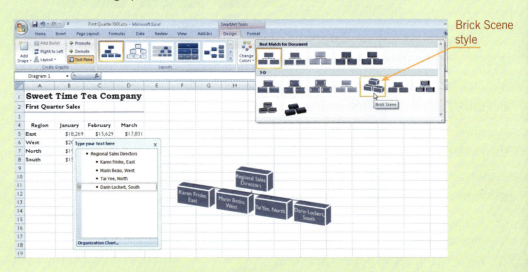

13. Click a blank cell in the workbook to deselect the SmartArt graphic.
14. Save the workbook, close it, and exit Excel.

LESSON 4   Working with Charts and Graphics   EX 105

SUMMARY

In this lesson, you learned:

- About the elements of a chart.
- How to create a chart.
- Ways to modify a chart.
- How to insert and modify illustrations.

VOCABULARY REVIEW

Define the following terms:

chart	data source	pictures
chart area	drawing object	plot area
chart sheet	embedded chart	SmartArt graphic
clip art	gridlines	title
data marker	horizontal axis	vertical axis
data series	legend	WordArt

REVIEW QUESTIONS

MULTIPLE CHOICE

Select the best response for the following statements.

1. A(n) _____ is a dot, a bar, or a symbol used to represent one number from the worksheet.
   - A. axis
   - B. data marker
   - C. data series
   - D. legend

2. A _____ chart shows values as a percentage of a whole.
   - A. column
   - B. line
   - C. pie
   - D. bar

3. The _____ is the range of cells that contain the data for the chart.
   - A. plot area
   - B. chart area
   - C. data source
   - D. data series

4. The Chart Tools _____ tab contains commands used to change the chart type, chart layout, chart style, or move the chart.
   - A. Design
   - B. Layout
   - C. Format
   - D. Data

5. To work with a specific element of a chart, you must first _____.
   - A. display the Chart Tools Design tab
   - B. move the chart element to a separate chart sheet
   - C. resize the chart proportionally
   - D. select the chart element

6. When you click the Charts dialog box launcher on the Insert tab, the _____ dialog box opens.
   - A. Insert Chart
   - B. Format Chart
   - C. Chart Tools
   - D. Change Chart Type

7. When a chart is selected, the corresponding data on a worksheet is _____.
   A. hidden
   B. displayed on a separate sheet
   C. color-coded
   D. a drawing object

8. Commands to add pictures, clip art, shapes, and SmartArt to your worksheet are located on the _____ tab on the Ribbon.
   A. Home
   B. Insert
   C. Design
   D. Format

9. _____ is a collection of predesigned artwork that can be inserted into worksheets.
   A. A picture
   B. A shape
   C. Clip art
   D. SmartArt

10. Which type of illustration would you use to quickly insert an organization chart in your worksheet?
    A. picture
    B. clip art
    C. shapes
    D. SmartArt

FILL IN THE BLANK

Complete the following sentences by writing the correct word or words in the blanks provided.

1. A(n) _____ is a graphical representation of worksheet data.

2. The _____ identifies the colors or patterns assigned to the various data series in the plotted area of a chart.

3. Buttons for the most common chart types are located in the Charts group on the _____ tab.

4. A(n) _____ chart is useful for plotting many data points and comparing data without considering the lapse of time.

5. By default, a newly created chart is placed on the worksheet as a(n) _____ chart that is a graphic object and is saved as part of the worksheet.

6. To resize a chart proportionally, hold the _____ key while dragging a corner handle.

7. _____ is a drawing tool that turns words into a graphics image.

8. You can use the _____ dialog box to change the location of a chart.

9. Clicking the _____ button in the Illustrations group on the Insert tab displays a menu containing lines, basic shapes, block arrows, flowchart elements, callouts, stars, and banners.

10. A _____ is a diagram that illustrates text.

PROJECTS

PROJECT EX 4–1

1. Open the **Project EX 4-1.xlsx** workbook from the folder containing the data files for this lesson.
2. Save the workbook as **Sales Projections XXX.xlsx** (replace XXX with your initials).
3. Select the range A4:G8 and use it to create a 2-D Clustered Bar chart.
4. In cell B7, change the value to $42,000.
5. Select the chart and change the chart type to Clustered Column.
6. Change the chart layout to Layout 9.
7. Change the chart style to Style 7.
8. Use the sizing handles to enlarge the chart to approximately twice its current size.
9. Move the chart to a separate chart sheet in the workbook and name the chart sheet Sales Projections Chart.
10. Save the workbook and leave it open for use in the next project.

LESSON 4 Working with Charts and Graphics

PROJECT EX 4–2

The Sales Projections *XXX*.xlsx workbook from Project EX 4-1 should be open in the Excel program window.

1. Save the workbook as **Sales Projections2 *XXX*.xlsx** (replace *XXX* with your initials).
2. Hide the vertical (value) axis title.
3. Change the horizontal (category) axis title to read *Months*.
4. Move the legend to the left side of the chart.
5. Add a title above the chart that reads *Yearly Sales Projections*.
6. Change the gridlines to display horizontal gridlines for major and minor units.
7. Use the Chart Elements list in the Current Selection group on the Chart Tools Layout tab to select the chart area and then change the shape style to Colored Fill – Accent 5.
8. Change the shape fill of the East data series to Brown, Accent 6.
9. Change the format of the title to the WordArt style Gradient Fill – Accent 6, Inner Shadow.
10. Save and close the workbook.

ON YOUR OWN

Open the **Sales Projections2 *XXX*.xlsx** workbook and change the shape fill, shape outline, and shape effects of the East, West, North, and South data series to achieve a consistent look of your choice. Save and close the workbook.

PROJECT EX 4–3

1. Open a new blank workbook.
2. Save the workbook as **Tea Types *XXX*.xlsx** (replace *XXX* with your initials).
3. Insert a Hierarchy List SmartArt graphic.
4. Replace the first [Text] bullet placeholder on the left with **Black**.
5. Replace the second [Text] bullet placeholder underneath it with **Irish Breakfast**.
6. Replace the third [Text] bullet placeholder underneath it with **Earl Grey**.
7. Add another shape after Earl Grey with **Darjeeling** as the text.
8. Continue adding to the SmartArt graphic until it looks like **Figure EX 4–27**.
9. Change the SmartArt style to Subtle Effect.
10. Save and close the workbook.

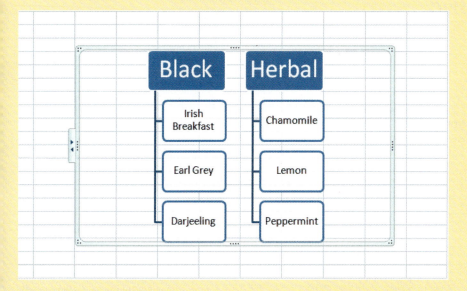

FIGURE EX 4–27
Tea Types *XXX*.xlsx workbook

ON YOUR OWN

Open the **Tea Types *XXX*.xlsx** workbook and add a Green category to the SmartArt graphic, with Gunpowder, Citron, and Sencha as the tea types. Save and close the workbook.

PROJECT EX 4–4

1. Open the **Project EX 4-4.xlsx** workbook from the folder containing the data files for this lesson.
2. Save the workbook as **Blood Pressure XXX.xlsx** (replace *XXX* with your initials).
3. Select the range B3:D17 and use it to create a Line chart.
4. Change the chart layout to Layout 4.
5. Add a horizontal axis title that reads **Day.**
6. Change the legend to show at the top.
7. Add horizontal gridlines for major units.
8. Change the shape style of the chart area to Subtle Effect – Accent 1.
9. Save and close the workbook, and exit Excel.

ON YOUR OWN

Open the **Blood Pressure XXX.xlsx** workbook. Move the chart to a separate chart sheet and change the layout, format, and style to best visually represent the data. Compare your chart with a classmate. Save and close the workbook.

WEB PROJECT

PROJECT EX 4–5

In the Clip Art task pane, click Clip art on Office Online. Explore the featured collections and browse through the clip art categories. Find at least one clip art illustration that you might want to use in a workbook and download it.

TEAMWORK PROJECT

PROJECT EX 4–6

With a partner, learn more about the other types of Excel charts that are not listed in Table EX 4–2 from the lesson. What are bubble charts used for? How can you present data in a combination chart? What kind of data can be plotted in a doughnut chart? What types of values do radar charts compare? When is a surface chart useful? Choose one of these types and create a chart. Make a brief presentation to the class about your chart type.

CRITICAL THINKING

ACTIVITY EX 4–1

Open **Activity EX 4-1.xlsx** from the folder containing the data files for this lesson. Save the workbook as **Kayak Sales XXX.xlsx** (replace *XXX* with your initials). Use the data in cells A4:L5 to create a line chart. Use the skills you have learned in this lesson to make the chart look as similar as possible to the one shown in **Figure EX 4–28**. Save and close the workbook.

FIGURE EX 4–28 Kayak Sales *XXX*.xlsx workbook

ACTIVITY EX 4–2

Search for the demo in Excel Help titled *Spice up your text with SmartArt graphics* and watch it. Create a worksheet, and use the List category to create a SmartArt graphic listing at least three each of your favorite breakfast, lunch, and dinner foods. Modify it using the commands on the SmartArt Tools Design and Format tabs. Save the workbook as **Favorite Foods XXX.xlsx** (replace *XXX* with your initials).

ACTIVITY EX 4–3

Create a worksheet that has a column for your daily activities and a column for the number of hours you spend doing each activity. Create a chart that best represents the data, and format it attractively. Insert at least one illustration. Save the workbook as **Time Chart XXX.xlsx** (replace *XXX* with your initials).

UNIT III REVIEW

Excel

REVIEW QUESTIONS

MULTIPLE CHOICE

Select the best response for the following statements.

1. _____ are displayed horizontally and are numbered consecutively down the left side of the worksheet.
   A. Columns
   B. Rows
   C. Cells
   D. Sheets

2. As you enter data in a cell, the data is displayed in the active cell and in the _____.
   A. Name box
   B. sheet tab
   C. formula bar
   D. status bar

3. Which workbook view displays the worksheet as it will print so you can make any necessary changes?
   A. Normal
   B. Page Layout
   C. Page Break Preview
   D. Full Screen

4. Once you have applied formatting to cells, you can use the _____ button to add the same formatting to other cells.
   A. Format Painter
   B. Format Cells
   C. Clipboard
   D. Conditional Formatting

5. Which of the following is not affected when you apply a theme to a workbook?
   A. colors
   B. fonts
   C. effects
   D. number formats

6. A(n) _____ is a set of instructions used to perform calculations on values in a worksheet.
   A. operator
   B. constant
   C. formula
   D. syntax

EX 109

7. A(n) _____ reference means the reference to a cell changes in relation to the location of the formula.
   A. absolute
   B. relative
   C. mixed
   D. cell

8. When you click the _____ button arrow in the Function Library group on the Formulas tab of the Ribbon, a menu of the most common statistical functions is displayed.
   A. AutoSum
   B. Auto Fill
   C. Insert Function
   D. Function Arguments

9. A _____ chart displays continuous data over time and shows trends.
   A. column
   B. line
   C. pie
   D. bar

10. Which command would you use to insert a predesigned diagram made up of shapes containing text that illustrates a concept or idea?
    A. Picture
    B. Clip Art
    C. Shapes
    D. SmartArt

FILL IN THE BLANK

Complete the following sentences by writing the correct word or words in the blanks provided.

1. A(n) _____ is the grid with columns and rows where you enter and summarize data.

2. A group of selected cells is called a(n) _____.

3. The _____ tab on the Ribbon includes the Font group that includes options for selecting fonts, font size, font style, underline, and font color.

4. To align text over several columns or rows, you can use the _____ button to join selected cells together into one larger cell.

5. You can adjust the size of all the columns and rows in the worksheet by clicking the _____ button before making changes.

6. An Excel formula must begin with a(n) _____.

7. B$10 is an example of a(n) _____ reference.

8. The range of cells that contains the data for the chart is called the _____.

9. The Chart Tools _____ tab contains commands you can use to insert pictures, shapes, and text boxes into the chart; display, hide, and specify the location of chart elements; format the axes and background; add lines or bars for analysis; or change the chart name.

10. You can change the location of a chart by placing it on a(n) _____, which is a separate sheet in the workbook.

PROJECTS

PROJECT EX 1

1. Start Excel.

2. Open the file **Project EX 1.xlsx** from the folder containing the data files for this review and save it as **Baseball XXX.xlsx** (replace XXX with your initials).

3. Insert a row after row 1.

4. In cell A2, enter the text **Baseball Team Season Stats**.

5. Apply the table style Table Style Medium 1 to the range A4:J16.

6. Convert the table to a normal range so that the filter arrows are not displayed at the top of each column.

7. Clear the contents in cells J5:J16.

UNIT III Microsoft Excel

8. Replace the text in cell J4 with **Batting Average** and widen column J to fully display the text.
9. In cell J5, create a formula that divides the hits in cell E5 by the number of at bats in D5.
10. Apply a Number format displaying three decimal places to the contents of cell J5.
11. Copy the formula in J5 to cells J6:J16.
12. Save the workbook, and leave it open for use in the next project.

PROJECT EX 2

The Baseball *XXX*.xlsx workbook from Project EX 1 should be open in the Excel program window.

1. Save the workbook as **Baseball2 *XXX*.xlsx** (replace *XXX* with your initials).
2. Change the theme to Apex.
3. Rename the worksheet **Season Stats**.
4. Delete the Sheet2 and Sheet3 worksheets from the workbook.
5. In cell A1, change the cell style to Title.
6. In cell A2, change the cell style to Heading 4.
7. In cells J5:J16, use the Highlight Cells Rules conditional formatting to format cells that are greater than .300 with Light Red Fill with Dark Red Text.
8. Change the width of column J to 9.
9. Apply Wrap Text to the text in cell J4.
10. Center the text in cells B4:J4.
11. Search for the word **Mu** and replace it with **Mew**.
12. Save and close the workbook.

ON YOUR OWN

Open the **Annual Sales2 *XXX*.xlsx** workbook and use functions to determine how many players are on the team, which player played the fewest games, which player had the most hits, the total number of home runs hit, and the team batting average. Save and close the workbook.

ON YOUR OWN

Open the **Baseball2 *XXX*.xlsx** workbook and insert a SmartArt graphic below the data using the Equation option in the Relationship category to illustrate the concept that "Effort + Teamwork = Success". Use the SmartArt Tools Design and Format tabs to format the graphic attractively. Save and close the workbook.

PROJECT EX 3

1. Open the file **Project EX 3.xlsx** from the folder containing the data files for this review and save it as **Annual Sales *XXX*.xlsx** (replace *XXX* with your initials).
2. In cell A1, change the font to Cambria, 18 point.
3. In cell A2, change the font to Cambria, 14 point.
4. Merge and center the contents of cells A1:E1.
5. Merge and center the contents of cells A2:E2.
6. Apply a Bottom Double Border to the range A2:E2.
7. In cell A4, apply bold formatting to the text and change the font color to Dark Blue, Text 2.
8. Copy the formatting from cell A4 to cells B4:E4.

9. Change the height of row 4 to 20.
10. Middle align and center the text in cells A4:E4.
11. Apply the Currency format displaying zero decimals to the contents of cells B5:E22.
12. Save the workbook, and leave it open for use in the next project.

PROJECT EX 4

The Annual Sales *XXX*.xlsx workbook from Project EX 3 should be open in the Excel program window.

1. Save the workbook as **Annual Sales2 *XXX*.xlsx** (replace *XXX* with your initials).
2. Copy the text in cell A4 to cell A23.
3. Replace the text in A23 with the text **Total**.
4. In cell B23, sum the values in cells B5:B22.
5. Copy the formula from cell B23 to cells C23:E23.
6. Use the data in the range B23:E23 to create a Clustered Column chart.
7. Change the chart type to a Pie chart.
8. Change the chart layout to Layout 4.
9. Change the chart style to Style 11.
10. Move the chart so that all of the worksheet data is visible. Resize the chart if necessary.
11. Save and close the workbook.

ON YOUR OWN

Open the **Annual Sales2 *XXX*.xlsx** workbook. Move the chart to a separate sheet in the workbook. Add a chart title, legend, and data labels. Apply shape styles and WordArt styles to enhance the chart. Save and close the workbook.

PROJECT EX 5

1. Create a new, blank workbook.
2. Save the workbook as **Mileage Log *XXX*.xlsx** (replace *XXX* with your initials).
3. Enter the text in the worksheet, as shown in Figure EX–1.

	A	B	C	D	E	F	G	H	I
1	Mileage Log								
2									
3	Employee Name		Rate Per Mile						
4	Vehicle Description		Total Mileage						
5	Authorized By		Total Reimbursement						
6									
7	Date	Starting Location	Destination	Trip Purpose	Odometer Start	Odometer End	Mileage	Reimbursement	
8									
9									
10									
11									
12									

FIGURE EX–1 Mileage Log *XXX*.xlsx worksheet

4. In cell A8, type today's date and format it as a Short Date.
5. In cell B8, enter the text **Preston Oaks**.
6. In cell C8, enter the text **Buckley Center**.
7. In cell D8, enter the text **Client meeting**.
8. In cell E8, enter the value **23,745**.
9. In cell F8, enter the value **23,792**.
10. In cell D3, enter the value **.79** and apply the Currency format displaying two decimals.

UNIT III Microsoft Excel

11. In cell G8, create a formula that subtracts the value in cell E8 from the value in cell F8.
12. In cell H8, create a formula that multiplies the value in G8 by the value in D3. Use an absolute reference for the value in D3.
13. Copy the formatting from cell D3 to cell H8.
14. Save and close the workbook.

ON YOUR OWN

Open the **Mileage Log *XXX*.xlsx** workbook, and enter your name in cell B3 and a car description in cell B4. Make at least three more entries. Create a formula in D4 to get the total mileage and create a formula in D5 to get the total reimbursement. Save and close the workbook.

ON YOUR OWN

Open the **Mileage Log *XXX*.xlsx** workbook and use the skills that you have learned in this unit to format the worksheet attractively. Preview and then print the worksheet. Save and close the workbook.

PROJECT EX 6

1. Open the file **Project EX 6.xlsx** from the folder containing the data files for this review, and save it as **Salary List *XXX*.xlsx** (replace *XXX* with your initials).
2. Copy the contents of cell G5 to cells G6:G25.
3. In cell H5, correct the formula to add the salary in cell F5 to the benefits in cell G5.
4. Copy the formula in cell H5 to cells H6:H25.
5. Replace all occurrences of *Resources* with *Services*.
6. Insert a header in the center section displaying the current date.
7. Insert a footer in the left section displaying the file name.
8. View the worksheet in Full Screen view.
9. Return to Page Layout view and then switch to Normal view.
10. Change the page layout to landscape orientation.
11. Spell check the worksheet and change *Employe* to *Employee* and change *Deprtment* to *Department*.
12. Freeze panes before column D and above row 5.
13. Switch to Page Break Preview and then back to Normal view.
14. Save and close the workbook.

ON YOUR OWN

Open the **Salary List *XXX*.xlsx** workbook and apply a theme. Use functions to find the lowest, highest, and average total salary. Save and close the workbook.

WEB PROJECT

Search Excel Help for the demo titled *Create charts in Excel 2007* and watch it. Visit a weather Web site and create a new worksheet that records the high and low temperatures in your city for the past week. Create a chart to visually represent your data, using the chart type that best conveys the information to your audience.

TEAMWORK PROJECT

With a partner, choose a tab on the Ribbon and review each command that you learned about and how it is used. Choose at least one command on that tab that you did not learn about in this unit and use Excel Help to research its purpose. Present your findings to the class and demonstrate how that command would be used in a workbook.

CRITICAL THINKING

ACTIVITY EX 1

Create a personal budget worksheet that summarizes your monthly income and expenses. Spend time planning before you begin, by making a list of the type of information you will need to include, any formulas you will use for calculations, and make a sketch of how you will structure the rows and columns in the worksheet. Include columns for projected and actual amounts, as well as one for the difference between them. Use at least three formulas or functions in the worksheet. Format the worksheet attractively.

ACTIVITY EX 2

You work for a local organization that helps provide relief for victims of disaster. Use Excel to create a charitable receipt that can be given to those who donate money or other items to help prevent, prepare for, and respond to emergencies in your area. Insert at least one illustration on the worksheet. Preview and print the receipt.

PORTFOLIO CHECKLIST

_____	Lesson 1	LostArt2 *XXX*.xlxs
_____		Test Grades *XXX*.xlsx
_____	Lesson 2	Team Stats *XXX*.xlsx
_____		Time Sheet2 *XXX*.xlsx
_____	Lesson 3	Open Water2 *XXX*.xlsx
_____		Trip Budget *XXX*.xlsx
_____	Lesson 4	First Quarter *XXX*.xlsx
_____		Sales Projections2 *XXX*.xlsx
_____	Unit Review	Annual Sales2 *XXX*.xlsx
_____		Baseball2 *XXX*.xlsx

Estimated Time for Unit: 5 hours

UNIT IV

MICROSOFT POWERPOINT

LESSON 1   1 HR.
Understanding PowerPoint Fundamentals

LESSON 2   1.5 HRS.
Formatting and Modifying Presentations

LESSON 3   2.5 HRS.
Enhancing the Presentation

LESSON 1

Understanding PowerPoint Fundamentals

Estimated Time: 1 hour

■ OBJECTIVES

Upon completion of this lesson, you should be able to:

- Examine the PowerPoint program window.
- Start PowerPoint and open an existing presentation.
- Understand slides.
- Navigate a PowerPoint presentation.
- View a presentation.
- Modify slides.
- Save a presentation.
- Preview and print a presentation.
- Close a presentation.

■ DATA FILES

To complete this lesson, you will need these data files:

Step PPT 1-1.pptx
Project PPT 1-1.pptx
Project PPT 1-2.pptx
Project PPT 1-4.pptx

■ VOCABULARY

bullets
collate
drag-and-drop
I-beam
insertion point
layout
masters
Notes pane
Outline tab
placeholders
presentation
presentation software
slide
Slide pane
Slides tab
thumbnails
…

UNIT IV Microsoft PowerPoint

Introduction

Microsoft PowerPoint 2007 is the presentation program included in the Microsoft Office 2007 suite of software. **Presentation software** lets you prepare a series of slides that are referred to collectively as a presentation. Examples of presentations include employee orientations, sales projections, and business plans.

As in other Office programs, the various tools in PowerPoint are organized on the Ribbon tabs. PowerPoint offers a variety of preformatted designs and backgrounds for slides and graphics that can help you create professional presentations.

Examining the PowerPoint Program Window

A PowerPoint file is called a presentation. A **presentation** is a collection of slides that communicates ideas, facts, suggestions, or other information to an audience. Presentations can be viewed on a computer screen, shown to an audience using projection equipment, distributed as printouts, or published to the Internet for viewing in a browser.

When you start PowerPoint, a blank presentation opens, as shown in **Figure PPT 1–1**. Use this figure to become familiar with the parts of the PowerPoint program window.

> **VOCABULARY**
> presentation software
> presentation
> Slides tab
> thumbnails
> Outline tab
> Slide pane
> Notes pane

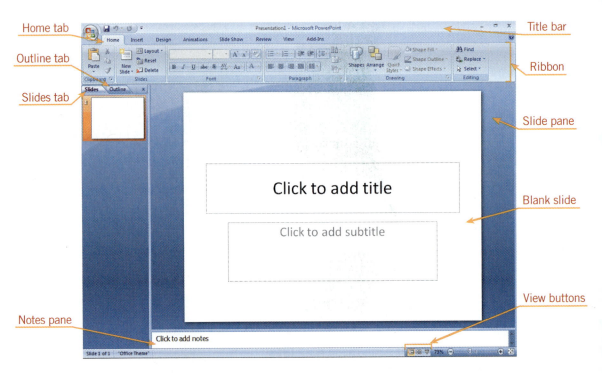

FIGURE PPT 1–1 PowerPoint program window

The default file name of a new presentation is *Presentation1,* and it is displayed at the top of the screen in the title bar. The screen in Normal view is divided into three sections. The Slides tab and Outline tab share the left pane. The **Slides tab** displays **thumbnails**, or miniature pictures, of the slides in the presentation. The **Outline tab** displays the text of each slide in outline form. The **Slide pane** displays the selected slide from the Slide tab or Outline tab. You can insert and edit text and graphics in the Slide pane. The **Notes pane** provides an area for you to type speaker notes for the presentation. The three main view buttons—Normal, Slide Sorter, and Slide Show—are located on the status bar.

LESSON 1 Understanding PowerPoint Fundamentals

Starting PowerPoint and Opening an Existing Presentation

To begin using PowerPoint, you first need to open it. You can do this by clicking the Start button on the Windows taskbar, and then clicking the All Programs menu, clicking the Microsoft Office folder and then clicking the program name, or by double-clicking a PowerPoint program icon on the desktop. Once PowerPoint is started, you can begin using it to create a new presentation or open an existing presentation.

To open an existing presentation, you can search for and then open PowerPoint files using the Open dialog box, as shown in **Figure PPT 1-2**. PowerPoint provides three methods for displaying the Open dialog box. The most common method is through the Open command found on the Office Button menu. You can also add an Open command to your Quick Access Toolbar or use the Ctrl+O keyboard shortcut.

You can use the Open dialog box to find and open existing files on your hard drive, CD, or other removable media; on a network drive to which you are connected; on your organization's intranet; or on the Internet.

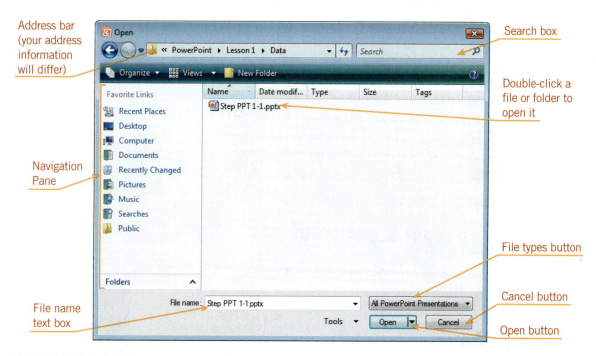

FIGURE PPT 1-2 Open dialog box

The following are parts of the Open dialog box:

- The Navigation Pane displays favorite links to folders that contain documents. You can view a folder's contents or open the folder from the Navigation Pane.
- The Address bar at the top of the dialog box shows the folder path.
- The File type button lists other file types you can choose to open.
- The Open button provides options for opening files, including opening the original file, opening a read-only version (when you want to open a file but keep the original file intact), or opening a copy of the original. If you open a copy or read-only version and edit or change the file, you cannot save changes to the original file. You can, however, use the Save As command to save your revisions with a new filename.

> **EXTRA FOR EXPERTS**
>
> By default, the names of the most recent files you opened in PowerPoint will be listed in the Recent Documents list on the Office Button menu. You can click a file in the list to open it. You can customize the number of files displayed in the list using the Advanced section of the PowerPoint Options dialog box.

UNIT IV   Microsoft PowerPoint

- The Search box allows you to find a file by name, file type, or location.
- The Cancel button closes the dialog box without opening a file.

Step-by-Step PPT 1.1

1. Click the **Start** button on the Windows taskbar. The Start menu opens.
2. Click **All Programs**. A list of programs and program folders opens.
3. Click the **Microsoft Office** program folder. A list of Office programs opens.
4. Click **Microsoft Office PowerPoint 2007**. PowerPoint starts and its program window opens with a new, blank presentation displayed.
5. Click the **Office** button on the Ribbon, and then click **Open** to display the Open dialog box.
6. If necessary, navigate to the folder containing the data files for this lesson. Double-click the file named **Step PPT 1-1.pptx** in the File list. The presentation opens as shown in **Figure PPT 1–3**.

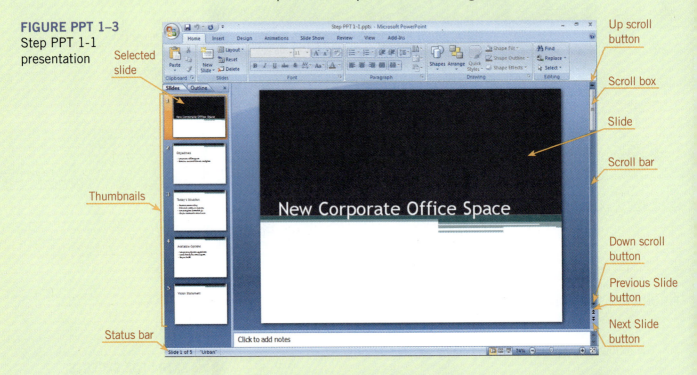

FIGURE PPT 1–3 Step PPT 1-1 presentation

7. Leave the presentation open for use in the next Step-by-Step.

Understanding Slides

> **VOCABULARY**
> slide

A *slide* is a single image composed of text, graphics, or other content. A presentation is usually made up of many different slides. After a slide is displayed as part of a presentation, it is removed from the screen and the next slide in the presentation

LESSON 1   Understanding PowerPoint Fundamentals

appears. Slides contain various kinds of content, including text, bullets, pictures, clip art, and charts, in an assortment of combinations and layouts. A slide's *layout* controls how text and other objects are arranged on a slide. For instance, a layout might display a title at the top, text in a column on the left, and a picture with a caption on the right. PowerPoint contains many built-in design themes that you can choose from to apply a set of coordinated fonts, colors, and backgrounds to slides. You will learn more about these in Lesson 2.

▶ **VOCABULARY**
layout

Navigating a PowerPoint Presentation

There are many different ways to move around within a presentation. In Normal view, shown in **Figure PPT 1–3**, you can click a thumbnail in the Slides tab to select it and display it in the Slide pane. In all but Slide Show view, you can move from slide to slide by:

- Clicking the Next Slide and Previous Slide buttons on the vertical bar.
- Clicking the up or down scroll buttons on the vertical scroll bar.
- Dragging the scroll box until you see the number and title of the slide you want displayed on a ScreenTip.
- Pressing the Page Up or Page Down key.
- Pressing the Up arrow or Down arrow key.

As you move through a presentation, the status bar shows the number of the displayed slide and the total number of slides in the presentation.

In Slide Show view, you can click each slide to move through the slides. You also can use the Page Down and Page Up keys to move through the slides, and the Esc key to exit a slide show.

Step-by-Step PPT 1.2

The Step PPT 1-1.pptx presentation from Step-by-Step PPT 1.1 should be open in the PowerPoint program window.

1. With slide 1 displayed, click the **Next Slide** button ⤓ on the vertical scroll bar.

2. Drag the scroll box until you see *Slide: 4 of 5 Available Options* on a ScreenTip next to the scroll bar, as shown in **Figure PPT 1–4**, and then release the mouse button.

FIGURE PPT 1–4
Navigate using ScreenTips

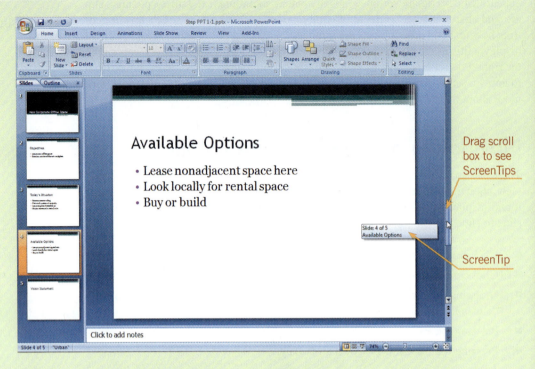

3. Press **Page Up** twice to move to slide 2.
4. Click the **Scroll up** button to move up to slide 1.
5. Drag the scroll box to the bottom of the vertical scroll bar.
6. Click the **slide 1** thumbnail in the left pane to display slide 1.
7. Leave the presentation open for use in the next Step-by-Step.

Viewing a Presentation

PowerPoint has seven views for working with a presentation—four views for preparing and delivering the presentation, and three views for editing masters. To change the view, use the buttons in the Presentation Views group on the View tab on the Ribbon, as shown in **Figure PPT 1–5**.

FIGURE PPT 1–5 Presentation Views group on the View tab

LESSON 1 Understanding PowerPoint Fundamentals

Preparing and Delivering a Presentation with Views

The views for preparing a presentation are Normal, Slide Sorter, and Notes Page. Slide Show view is used to deliver a presentation to a group or audience.

Normal view displays the screen in three sections—Outline and Slides tabs in the left pane, Slide pane, and Notes pane—so you can work on all parts of your presentation in one place. **Figure PPT 1–6** shows Normal view displaying the Outline tab where you can see your entire presentation, enter text and rearrange bullet points and paragraphs, and modify the slide sequence. To adjust the size of the panes, click and drag the pane borders.

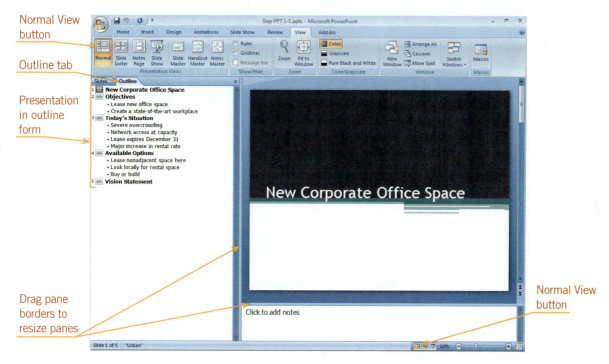

FIGURE PPT 1–6 Outline tab in Normal view

Use Slide Sorter view to display thumbnail versions of all slides in a presentation, as shown in **Figure PPT 1–7**. You can easily reorder slides, add transitions, and set timings using this view.

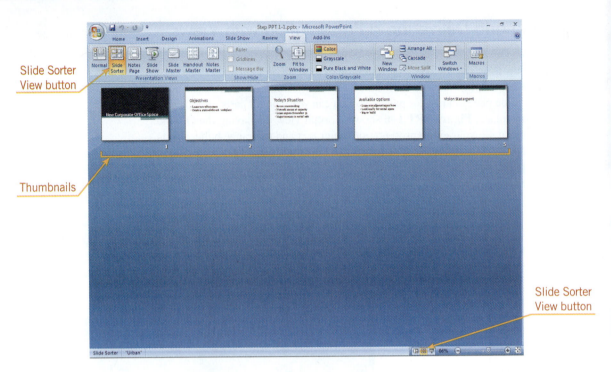

FIGURE PPT 1–7   Slide Sorter view

Notes Page view, shown in **Figure PPT 1–8**, allows you to enter and edit notes on a full screen instead of just in the tiny Notes pane at the bottom of the Normal view. Notes are comments or other information that you can prepare ahead of time and then share with the audience as you deliver a presentation. The audience cannot see notes in a slide show; you print them for your own use during the presentation.

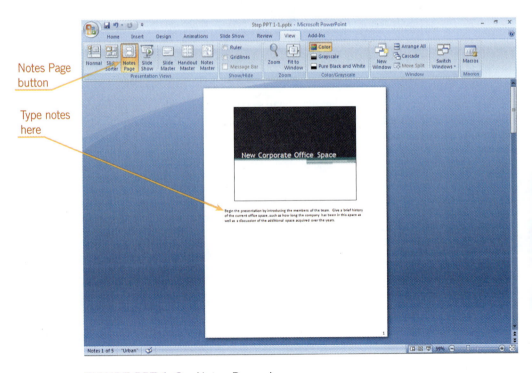

FIGURE PPT 1–8   Notes Page view

LESSON 1   Understanding PowerPoint Fundamentals

PPT 11

Slide Show view is used to deliver a presentation to an audience. When you run the presentation, or slide show, each slide fills the entire screen and as you advance through the slides, you can see the transitions, animations, and effects that you have added. When you are finished viewing the presentation, you can press the Esc key to return to the previous view.

> **EXTRA FOR EXPERTS**
>
> You can use the keyboard shortcut F5 to switch to Slide Show view.

Editing Masters with Views

The master views are Slide Master, Handout Master, and Notes Master. These views display *masters*, which are like blueprints that control the layout and design of the slides, handouts, and notes. When you make a change to a master, the change affects every slide in the presentation. For example, in Slide Master view, shown in **Figure PPT 1–9**, you could change the bullet styles that are used on each slide in the presentation. The Slide Master view displays thumbnails of the layout masters in the left pane and the selected master on the right. The contextual Slide Master tab is displayed on the Ribbon with additional commands. The Notes Master and Handout Master views also display an additional tab on the Ribbon. You will learn more about masters in Lesson 2.

> **VOCABULARY**
> masters

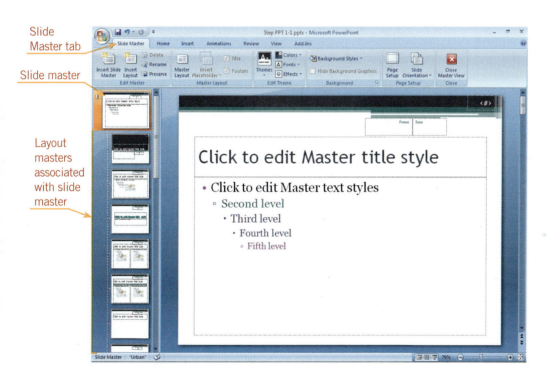

FIGURE PPT 1–9   Slide Master view

Step-by-Step PPT 1.3

The Step PPT 1-1.pptx presentation from Step-by-Step PPT 1.2 should be open in the PowerPoint program window.

1. Click the **Outline** tab to display the presentation in outline form. The outline for the entire presentation is displayed, as well as the slide with which you are currently working.

2. Hover your mouse pointer over the view buttons on the status bar until you see the ScreenTip identifying each of the view buttons: Normal, Slide Sorter, and Slide Show.

3. Click the **Slide Sorter** button to change the view. You see a thumbnail of each of the slides.

4. Click the **Slide Show** button. The slide now appears as it would if you were running the slide show. Click your mouse button to advance through the presentation, and then press **Esc** to return to Slide Sorter view when the slide show is over.

5. On the View tab on the Ribbon, in the Presentation Views group, click the **Notes Page** button. Notice the large area below the slide that contains notes related to the slide.

6. On the View tab, in the Presentation Views group, click the **Notes Master** button to open Notes Master view. Here you can change the text styles of notes or add headers and footers that would appear on each notes page when printed.

7. In the Close group, click the **Close Master View** button.

8. On the View tab, in the Presentation Views group, click the **Slide Master** button to display Slide Master view.

9. On the Slide Master tab, in the Close group, click the **Close Master View** button.

10. On the View tab, in the Presentation Views group, click the **Normal** button to display Normal view.

11. Leave the presentation open for use in the next Step-by-Step.

Modify Slides

As you create and edit a presentation, you may find that you need to make changes to the slides that make up the presentation. These changes might require adding or deleting slides, changing a slide's layout, and entering and editing text.

Selecting Slides

You can select a single slide in Slide Sorter view or in Normal view by clicking it. In later lessons, you will learn to add slide backgrounds or transitions to multiple slides. To make changes to more than one slide at a time, you can select a group of slides by clicking the first slide in the group you want to select, holding the Ctrl key, and clicking each of the slides you want.

When you need to deselect a slide or a group of selected slides, click in the blank space outside the selection.

LESSON 1   Understanding PowerPoint Fundamentals

Inserting and Deleting Slides

You can add and delete slides as well as change the layout of slides using the buttons in the Slides group on the Home tab, shown in **Figure PPT 1–10**.

Slides group

FIGURE PPT 1–10   Slides group on the Home tab

You can add an unlimited number of new slides to a presentation using the New Slide button arrow. The New Slide button arrow displays a gallery of built-in layouts for the new slide, including options for a title slide, slides showing title and content sections, and other styles of slides that reflect the design theme of your presentation. In addition to the layout gallery, the New Slide button arrow includes Duplicate Selected Slides, Slides from Outline, and Reuse Slides commands.

You can select a thumbnail on the Slides tab in Normal view and the new slide will be inserted after the selected slide. Or, you can click in the left pane between thumbnails to display a long, blinking insertion point indicating the location where the new slide will be inserted. To remove one or more selected slides from a presentation, use the Delete button in the Slides group, or select a slide and press Delete.

> **EXTRA FOR EXPERTS**
>
> You can insert an exact copy of an existing slide using the Duplicate Selected Slides command. Just select the slide you want to duplicate and choose the Duplicate Selected Slides command from the New Slide menu.

Changing Slide Layout

The Layout button contains the same layout options as the New Slide command. You can change the layout of the current slide (rearranging the placeholders) to a new layout at any time and the text on the slide will adjust to the new layout. The Reset button changes the slide's layout and formatting back to the default settings.

Step-by-Step PPT 1.4

The Step PPT 1-1.pptx presentation from Step-by-Step PPT 1.3 should be open in the PowerPoint program window.

1. Click the **slide 5** thumbnail to select it.
2. On the Home tab, in the Slides group, click the **New Slide** button arrow and then click the **Two Content** layout as shown in **Figure PPT 1–11**. PowerPoint inserts the slide as slide 6.

FIGURE PPT 1-11
New slide gallery

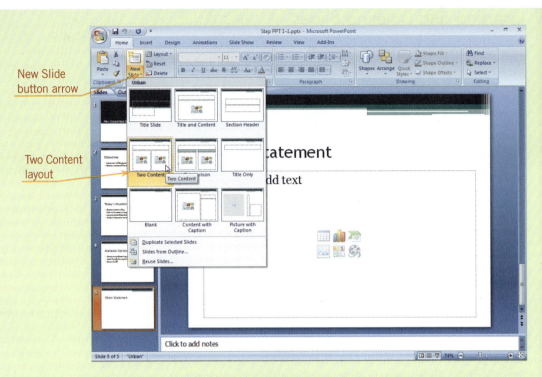

3. On the Home tab, in the Slides group, click the **New Slide** button arrow and then click **Title and Content**. The new slide is added as slide 7.

4. In the left pane, click **slide 4** to select it.

5. On the Home tab, in the Slides group, click the **Layout** button and click **Two Content**. Notice that the text on the slide adjusted to the new layout.

6. Click the **Layout** button again and click **Title and Content**. The text adjusts to the new layout.

7. In the left pane, click **slide 6** to select it.

8. On the Home tab, in the Slides group, click the **Delete** button to remove the slide from the presentation.

9. On the View tab, in the Presentation Views group, click the **Slide Sorter** button, click **slide 1**, hold the **Ctrl** key, click **slide 3** and **slide 5**, and release the **Ctrl** key. Notice that all three slides are surrounded by selection borders, as shown in **Figure PPT 1–12**.

LESSON 1   Understanding PowerPoint Fundamentals

PPT 15

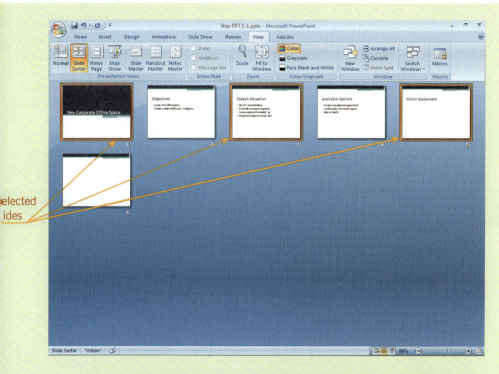

FIGURE PPT 1–12
Selected nonadjacent slides

10. Click in the blank space in Slide Sorter view to deselect the slides.
11. On the View tab, in the Presentation Views group, click the **Normal** button.
12. Leave the presentation open for use in the next Step-by-Step.

Entering Text on a Slide

When PowerPoint displays a new slide in a presentation, the new slide contains *placeholders*, which are specific areas on the slide, indicated by dotted rectangles, where you insert text or other content, such as bulleted lists or graphics. You can move, resize, and rotate a placeholder to customize its position on the slide.

To enter text in a placeholder, click the *I-beam* (which is the shape of the mouse pointer in a text area) anywhere on the placeholder to select it. A blinking cursor, called an *insertion point*, indicates where your entry will appear. Type the text, and then click a blank space on the slide outside the placeholder to deselect.

Many of PowerPoint's slide layouts contain bulleted lists. *Bullets* are small symbols that mark the beginning of a list item. When you begin typing, PowerPoint automatically inserts the bullet for the first list item and wraps text for you. Use the Tab key to indent to a second level in the bulleted list. PowerPoint automatically indents the subordinate bulleted item and may give the entry a different bullet symbol. Use the Increase List Level and Decrease List Level buttons in the Paragraph group of the Home tab to move up to a higher level or down to a lower level.

You can also add text to a slide by typing text in the Outline tab. As you type, the text is entered on the slide. Entering text in the Outline tab is useful for organizing and developing your presentation.

After you enter text in a placeholder, you can easily edit, insert, delete, or copy text from one slide to another. Editing text in a presentation is the same as editing text in Word or other Microsoft Office programs. When you want to insert text in a placeholder that already contains text, you can click the I-beam to position the insertion

> **VOCABULARY**
> **placeholders**
> **I-beam**
> **insertion point**
> **bullets**

point and type the additional text. New text appears to the left of the insertion point. To delete text in a placeholder, position the insertion point and press Backspace to delete characters to the left of the insertion point. Press Delete to delete characters to the right of the insertion point. When deleting more than a few characters, select the text to be deleted and press Delete.

You might need to delete a placeholder to make room for text in another placeholder, or to remove content from a slide. Delete a placeholder by selecting it and pressing the Delete key. To reverse, or undo, an action, use the Undo button on the Quick Access Toolbar. If you perform an undo action but then decide against the undo, use the Redo button on the Quick Access Toolbar to reverse the undo action.

Step-by-Step PPT 1.5

The Step PPT 1-1.pptx presentation from Step-by-Step PPT 1.4 should be open in the PowerPoint program window.

1. Slide 6 should be displayed in the Slide pane.
2. Click the **Click to add title** placeholder and type **Recommendation** as shown in **Figure PPT 1–13**.

FIGURE PPT 1–13
Enter text in placeholders

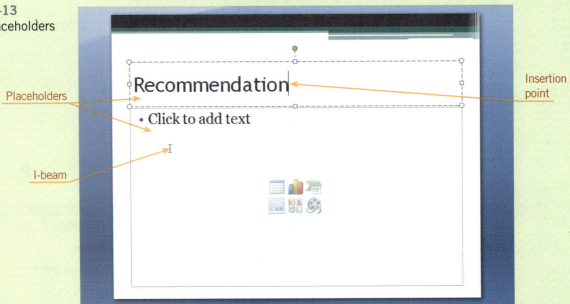

3. Click the **Click to add text** placeholder and type **Appoint a Relocation Committee**.
4. Press **Enter** and then press **Tab** to indent to a second level in the bulleted list. Notice the bullet is a different color and style.
5. Type **Determine workplace requirements** and press **Enter** to enter the first subbullet.
6. Type **Visit sites available for sale or rent** and press **Enter** to enter the second subbullet.

LESSON 1   Understanding PowerPoint Fundamentals

7. Click the **Decrease List Level** button to return to the first bullet level.
8. Click the **Outline** tab to practice entering text in the outline.
9. In the slide 6 section of the outline, click the blank line under *Visit sites available for sale or rent*.
10. Type **Make recommendations by 9/25** and press **Enter**. Notice that the text is also entered on the slide as you type.
11. Type **Management decision by 10/17**.
12. Click the **Slides** tab.
13. Leave the presentation open for use in the next Step-by-Step.

Copying and Moving Data

You probably have experience moving or copying text in Word or other Office programs using the Cut, Copy, and Paste commands. These commands, located in the Clipboard group on the Home tab in PowerPoint, work the same way to move and copy text within a slide or between slides in a presentation.

You can use the *drag-and-drop* feature to move or copy a selection to a new location on the same slide in the presentation. To move text or graphics, you select and drag with the mouse and then release the mouse button to "drop" the item in its new location. You also can use the drag-and-drop feature to rearrange slides in Slide Sorter view. When dragging and dropping slides in Slide Sorter view, the insertion point is much longer.

To copy text, you select, drag, and drop text while holding the Ctrl key. When you copy a selection, you will see a plus sign (+) with the pointer. When you move or copy a selection using the drag-and-drop method, the selection is not stored in the Clipboard.

▶ **VOCABULARY**
drag-and-drop

Step-by-Step PPT 1.6

The Step PPT 1-1.pptx presentation from Step-by-Step PPT 1.5 should be open in the PowerPoint program window.

1. On slide 2, select the second bulleted list item **Create a state-of-the-art workplace**.
2. On the Home tab, in the Clipboard group, click the **Copy** button.
3. Display slide 5. Click the **Click to add text** placeholder.
4. On the Home tab, in the Clipboard group, click the **Paste** button to insert the copied text.
5. Click the **Slide Sorter View** button to switch to Slide Sorter view.

6. Click **slide 5** and drag the move pointer to the left until you see the long insertion bar located on the right of slide 1, as shown in **Figure PPT 1–14**.

FIGURE PPT 1–14
Drag and drop to rearrange slides

Long insertion point

Move pointer

Selected slide

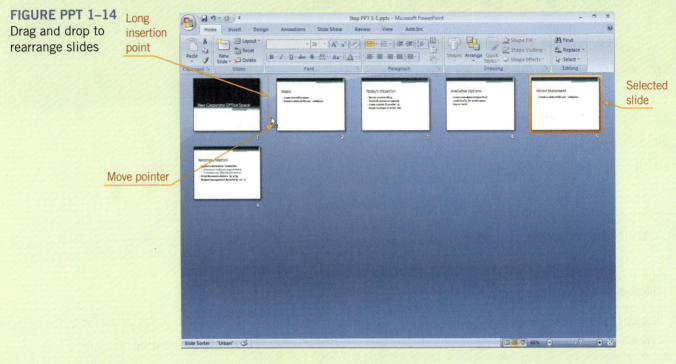

7. Release the mouse button to drop the slide into its new location.
8. With slide 2 selected, press **Delete** to remove the slide from the presentation.
9. Click the **Normal View** button to switch to Normal view.
10. Leave the presentation open for use in the next Step-by-Step.

Saving a Presentation

The first time you save a presentation, the options for saving include the Save button on the Office Button menu, the Save As button on the Office Button menu, or the Save button on the Quick Access Toolbar. Each of these methods displays the Save As dialog box, as shown in **Figure PPT 1–15**.

LESSON 1 Understanding PowerPoint Fundamentals

PPT 19

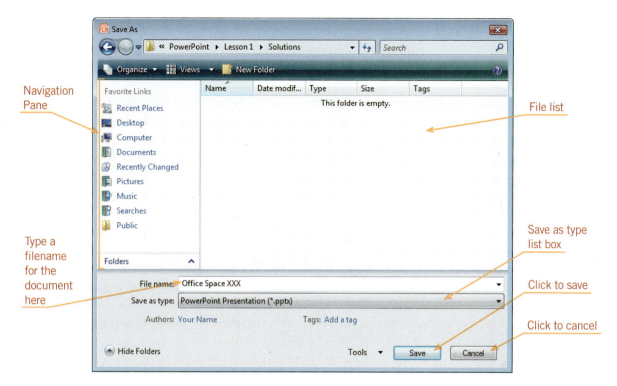

FIGURE PPT 1–15 Save As dialog box

After you save a file the first time, the Save command saves your file with the previously specified name in the location you specified. The Save As command lets you make a copy of the file with a new name, location, or file type. The Save as type menu lets you save a presentation in another format or as a template. You will learn more about PowerPoint templates later in this book. You might need to change the file format or program and version if you share files with others who use different software. To save a presentation in a specific location, you use the Navigation Pane to navigate to the folder in which you want to save the presentation. Once you have saved the file, you can use the Save button on the Quick Access Toolbar or the Save command on the Office Button menu to save your changes.

PowerPoint's AutoRecover feature automatically saves your presentation at regular intervals so that you can recover at least some of your work in case of a power outage or other unexpected shutdown. You can turn this feature on or off and change the setting to save more or less often by opening the PowerPoint Options dialog box from the Office Button menu. On the Save page, specify a number in the Save AutoRecover information every *x* minutes box. However, you should not rely on this automatic saving feature. Remember to save your work often.

> **EXTRA FOR EXPERTS**
>
> Microsoft PowerPoint 2007 files have a .pptx extension and cannot be opened with previous versions of PowerPoint. If you need to share files with someone using an earlier version, you can use the PowerPoint 97-2003 Presentation option in the Save As section of the Office Button menu, which saves files with the .ppt extension.

Step-by-Step PPT 1.7

The Step PPT 1-1.pptx presentation from Step-by-Step PPT 1.6 should be open in the PowerPoint program window.

1. Click the **Office Button** and then click **Save As** to open the Save As dialog box.

2. Navigate to the location where you will save your files.

3. If necessary, select **Step PPT 1-1.pptx** in the File name text box. Type **Office Space *XXX*.pptx** (replace *XXX* with your initials) in the box to rename the file.

4. In the Save as type list, make sure PowerPoint Presentation (*.pptx) is displayed.

5. Click **Save** to save a copy of the presentation with the new name in the specified location.

6. Leave the presentation open for use in the next Step-by-Step.

Previewing and Printing Presentations

Presentations are usually delivered on a computer or projection screen, but there are times when you may need to distribute a printout of the presentation, for example as a handout to accompany a speech or lecture. You can save time and paper by using Print Preview to review your choices.

Previewing Printouts

You can preview entire pages of a presentation before printing by using the Print Preview option on the Print submenu on the Office Button menu. PowerPoint displays the current slide and the Ribbon changes to the Print Preview tab when you click the Print Preview command. If you have not changed the default settings, your screen should look similar to the one in **Figure PPT 1–16**. In Print Preview, the pointer changes from an arrow to a magnifying glass, which lets you zoom in on an area of a slide by clicking the area you want to magnify. To return to the original magnification, click again. The tools on the Print Preview tab include the following:

- The Print button displays the Print dialog box where you can set printing options.
- The Options button and menu allows you to edit the headers and footers, select color or grayscale printing, scale to fit the paper, add frames to slides, print comments and markup, print hidden slides, or change printing order.
- The Page Setup group contains commands for choosing what to print and changing the orientation.
- The Zoom button displays the Zoom dialog box where you can select a different magnification.
- The Fit to Window button zooms the slide to fit within the window.
- In the Preview group, you can use the Next Page and Previous Page buttons to display slides.
- Use the Close Print Preview button to return to the previous view.

LESSON 1   Understanding PowerPoint Fundamentals

PPT 21

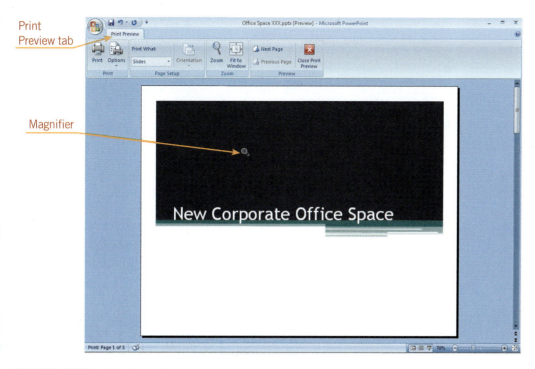

FIGURE PPT 1–16   Print Preview

Printing a Presentation

Both the Print command on the Office Button menu and the Print button in the Print group of the Print Preview tab display the Print dialog box, as shown in **Figure PPT 1–17**.

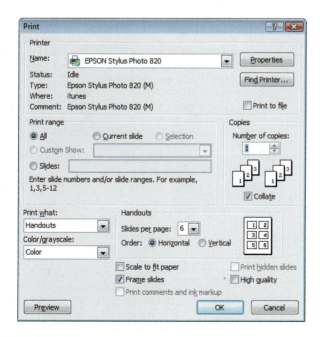

FIGURE PPT 1–17   Print dialog box

> **EXTRA FOR EXPERTS**
>
> You can use the Quick Print command on the Print submenu of the Office Button menu to print to the default printer without opening the Print dialog box.

UNIT IV   Microsoft PowerPoint

The settings in the Print dialog box will differ according to the printer you are using, but some options are common to all printers, including the following:

- The Printer area, where you select a printer from the list of available printers
- The Print range area, where you specify whether to print all slides, the current slide, or specified slides of a presentation
- The Copies area, where you indicate quantity of copies to print and whether to *collate* the pages, which prints them in order
- The Print what area, where you can choose to print slides, handouts, notes pages, or outline view as well as indicate whether to print in color or grayscale. If you choose to print handouts, the Handouts section becomes active, and you can indicate the number of slides to print per page (printing four, six, or nine slides per page instead of one or two saves paper) and whether to print them in order horizontally or vertically.
- At the bottom of the Print what area, you can specify to scale slides to fit the paper, add a frame around slides, print comments, print hidden slides, and select high-quality printouts.

VOCABULARY
collate

Step-by-Step PPT 1.8

The Office Space *XXX*.pptx presentation from Step-by-Step PPT 1.7 should be open in the PowerPoint program window.

1. Click the **Office Button**. Point to **Print** and then click **Print Preview** on the menu.

2. Point to the upper-left area of the page, and then click the **Magnifier** pointer to zoom in.

3. On the Print Preview tab in the Page Setup group, click the **Print What** list box arrow and click **Handouts (3 Slides Per Page)**. The screen displays three slides per page with lines for notes, as shown in **Figure PPT 1–18**.

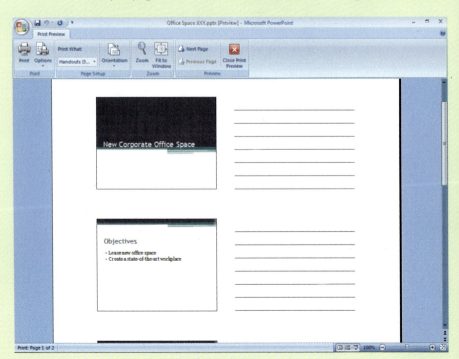

FIGURE PPT 1–18
Handouts (3 Slides Per Page)

LESSON 1 Understanding PowerPoint Fundamentals

4. In the Zoom group, click the **Fit to Window** button to see the entire page.
5. In the Page Setup group, click the **Print What** list box arrow and click **Handouts (6 Slides Per Page)**. The screen displays the handout as it will look when printed.
6. In the Print group, click the **Print** button to display the Print dialog box. Notice that the options you selected are displayed in the Print what and Handouts areas.
7. Click the **OK** button to print the handout. If you have been instructed not to print, click the **Cancel** button in the Print dialog box.
8. In the Preview group, click the **Close Print Preview** button.
9. Save the presentation and leave it open for use in the next Step-by-Step.

Closing a Presentation

When you are finished with a presentation, you can remove it from your screen using the Close command. To close a presentation without closing PowerPoint, choose the Close command on the Office Button menu. When you only have one presentation open, you can click the Close button on the title bar to close the presentation and exit the PowerPoint program at the same time. The software prompts you to save your work if you made any changes since you last saved.

Step-by-Step PPT 1.9

The Office Space *XXX*.pptx presentation from Step-by-Step PPT 1.8 should be open in the PowerPoint program window.

1. In Normal view, display slide 5.
2. In the last bulleted item, change the date from 10/17 to 10/7.
3. Click the **Close** button ✕ on the program title bar. The Microsoft Office PowerPoint message box is displayed, as shown in **Figure PPT 1-19**.

FIGURE PPT 1-19
Microsoft Office PowerPoint message box

4. Click **Yes** to save and close the presentation and exit PowerPoint.

TECHNOLOGY CAREERS

Corporate trainers may provide job-specific training courses in-house for large companies or they may work as contractors to provide more general professional development training to many different companies. They may present to large audiences or work one-on-one with clients. Video conferencing and online discussion boards may be utilized to promote participation and collaboration. Corporate trainers often use presentation software such as PowerPoint to deliver dynamic slide shows as part of a training course.

SUMMARY

In this lesson, you learned:

- A presentation is a way of communicating ideas, facts, suggestions, or other information to an audience. PowerPoint is a software program that helps you create presentations.
- How to start PowerPoint and open an existing presentation.
- That to move around a presentation, you can click buttons on the vertical or horizontal scroll bars, drag the scroll box, press the Page Up or Page Down key, or press the Up arrow or Down arrow.
- Normal, Slide Sorter, Notes Page, Slide Show, Slide Master, Handout Master, and Notes Master views are the seven PowerPoint views.
- How to insert, delete, and change slide layout.
- How to enter text on a slide, click the placeholder, and then begin typing.
- How to use the Save As command to save a presentation for the first time.
- How to preview presentations before printing slides, handouts, or notes.
- When you close a presentation, PowerPoint prompts you to save your work if you made any changes since you last saved.

VOCABULARY REVIEW

Define the following terms:

bullets
collate
drag-and-drop
I-beam
insertion point
layout

masters
Notes pane
Outline tab
placeholders
presentation
presentation software

slide
Slide pane
Slides tab
thumbnails

REVIEW QUESTIONS

MULTIPLE CHOICE

Select the best response for the following statements.

1. The _____ provides an area for you to type speaker notes for the presentation.

    A. Notes pane   C. Slides tab
    B. Slide pane   D. Outline tab

LESSON 1 Understanding PowerPoint Fundamentals

2. PowerPoint's _____ feature automatically saves your presentation at regular intervals so that you can recover at least some of your work in case of a power outage or other unexpected shutdown.
   A. Save
   B. AutoRecover
   C. Placeholder
   D. Clipboard

3. _____ are small symbols that mark the beginning of a list item.
   A. Placeholders
   B. I-beams
   C. Slides
   D. Bullets

4. If you perform an undo action but then decide against the undo, use the _____ button to reverse an Undo action.
   A. Undo
   B. Redo
   C. Repeat
   D. Delete

5. _____ are rectangles with dotted lines around them for inserting text or other content.
   A. Slides
   B. Clipboards
   C. Layouts
   D. Placeholders

6. _____ view can be used to rearrange the order of slides.
   A. Normal
   B. Slide Show
   C. Slide Sorter
   D. Notes Page

7. _____ view allows you to make global changes to slides, handouts, or notes that affect the entire presentation.
   A. Normal
   B. Slide Show
   C. Slide Sorter
   D. Master

8. Press the _____ key to exit a slide show.
   A. Delete
   B. Esc
   C. Ctrl
   D. Enter

9. The _____ feature is used to move or copy a selection to a new location.
   A. drag-and-drop
   B. Undo
   C. Redo
   D. layout

10. In the Print dialog box, the Print range area has options for _____.
    A. printing either all slides, the current slide, or specified slides of a presentation
    B. selecting a printer
    C. changing paper type, size, and orientation
    D. specifying the number of copies to print

FILL IN THE BLANK

Complete the following sentences by writing the correct word or words in the blanks provided.

1. A(n) _____ is a way of communicating ideas, facts, suggestions, or other information to an audience.
2. A(n) _____ is a single image composed of text, graphics, or other content.
3. _____ controls how text and other objects are arranged on a slide.
4. The Slide and Outline tabs are located on the left side of the screen in _____ view.
5. _____ are like blueprints that control the layout and design of the slides, handouts, and notes.
6. You can use the _____ dialog box to find and open existing files on your hard drive, CD, or other removable media.

7. _____ is the shape the mouse pointer takes in a text area.

8. To _____ a placeholder, click the blank space outside the placeholder.

9. Press _____ to start a new bulleted item.

10. When you _____ a presentation, the software prompts you to save your work if you made any changes since you last saved.

■ PROJECTS

PROJECT PPT 1-1

1. Start PowerPoint and open the presentation **Project PPT 1-1.pptx** from the folder containing the data files for this lesson and save it as **Tracking Graduates XXX.pptx** (replace *XXX* with your initials).

2. Switch to Slide Show view and advance through the entire presentation.

3. Display slide 1 in Normal view.

4. Change the presenter's name to your name.

5. Display slide 2.

6. Insert a new slide with the Title Only layout.

7. Type **When does tracking begin?** in the title placeholder.

8. Change the layout of the slide to Title and Content.

9. Type **One year after graduation** in the content placeholder.

10. Switch to Slide Sorter view.

11. Move slide 4 to the slide 2 position.

12. Delete slide 2.

13. Save and close the presentation.

PROJECT PPT 1-2

1. Open the presentation **Project PPT 1-2.pptx** from the folder containing the data files for this lesson.

2. Save the presentation with the filename **Health Challenge XXX.pptx** (replace *XXX* with your initials).

3. On slide 1, replace *presenter name* with your name.

4. On slide 2, type **Improve company image** as the fourth bulleted item in the list.

5. Change the layout of slide 3 to Title and Content.

6. Delete slide 4.

7. On slide 6, in the second bulleted item, delete the words *in what areas*.

8. In the fourth bulleted item, delete the word *yet* and type **need**.

9. Indent the second and third bulleted items to a second level.

10. Display slide 1.

11. Switch to Slide Show view and advance through the entire presentation.

12. Save the presentation and leave it open for use in the next project.

PROJECT PPT 1-3

The **Health Challenge XXX.pptx** presentation from Project PPT 1-2 should be open in the PowerPoint program window.

1. Save the presentation as **Health Challenge 2 XXX.pptx** (replace *XXX* with your initials).

2. Select slide 4 and view in Notes Page view.

3. Type the following speaker note in the placeholder:

   Discuss the brands and types of equipment that will be available, such as the exercise bikes and treadmills. Remember to ask if there are any questions.

4. Switch to Normal view. On the Outline tab, insert the following new first-level bulleted item as the first item on slide 6:

   Health Challenge committee has been created

5. Preview the presentation in Print Preview and print handouts 6 per page.

6. Save and close the presentation.

ON YOUR OWN

Open **Health Challenge 2 XXX.pptx** Print the one page that contains notes. Close the presentation without saving changes.

PROJECT PPT 1–4

1. Open the presentation **Office Space XXX.pptx** from the folder containing the data files for this lesson.
2. Display slide 4.
3. Copy the three bulleted items on the slide.
4. Close the file without saving changes.
5. Open the presentation **Project PPT 1-4.pptx** from the folder containing the data files for this lesson.
6. Save the presentation as **Office Space Progress XXX.pptx** (replace *XXX* with your initials).
7. On slide 2, paste the copied text stored on the Clipboard into the content placeholder.
8. Switch to Slide Sorter view and move slide 6 to the slide 5 position.
9. Move slide 7 to the slide 6 position.
10. Switch to Slide Show view and advance through the entire presentation.
11. Save and close the presentation.

ON YOUR OWN

Open **Office Space Progress XXX.pptx**. Add speaker notes to two of the slides and change two slide layouts. Save and close the presentation.

WEB PROJECT

PROJECT PPT 1–5

Search the Microsoft Web site (www.microsoft.com) for information about Microsoft PowerPoint 2007. Create a presentation consisting of four or five slides that gives basic details about the software, such as features, system requirements, and price. Be prepared to show your presentation to the class.

 TEAMWORK PROJECT

PROJECT PPT 1–6

With a partner, plan a presentation that encourages students to take some kind of action. For example, you may want them to participate in a new recycling program, attend an event, or participate in a fund-raising activity. Use the Outline tab in Normal view to create the presentation using at least five slides.

 # CRITICAL THINKING

ACTIVITY PPT 1–1

Use PowerPoint Help to find and read the article titled, "Tips for creating and delivering an effective presentation." Which three of the tips do you think are most important and why? Start PowerPoint and use the default *Presentation1* file to create a simple four-slide presentation detailing the three tips that you thought were most important. Use the default title slide and insert three new slides for the tips. Save the presentation with a meaningful name. Be prepared to share your presentation with the class.

ACTIVITY PPT 1–2

Use PowerPoint Help to learn about reusing slides from another presentation. The Reuse Slides command is located in the New Slide menu. Experiment with the process. Try reusing slide 4 from the Office Space *XXX*.pptx file as slide 2 in the Office Space Progress *XXX*.pptx file. When you are finished, close each file without saving changes. What are the pros and cons of reusing slides?

ACTIVITY PPT 1–3

Create a five-slide presentation that describes a recent scientific discovery, a favorite person from history, or a recent election. Be prepared to share your presentation with the class.

Estimated Time: 1.5 hours

LESSON 2

Formatting and Modifying Presentations

■ OBJECTIVES

Upon completion of this lesson, you should be able to:

- Create a new blank presentation.
- Use templates to create new presentations.
- Format text and paragraphs.
- Check spelling.
- Find and replace text.
- Apply themes.
- Customize slide masters.

■ VOCABULARY

alignment
characters
font
font styles
Format Painter
layout masters
point size
slide master
template
themes
...

■ DATA FILES

To complete this lesson, you will need these data files:

Step PPT 2-5.pptx
Project PPT 2-3.pptx
Project PPT 2-4.pptx

PPT 29

UNIT IV Microsoft PowerPoint

Introduction

Now that you are familiar with PowerPoint basics, you are ready to use PowerPoint's tools to create presentations. In this lesson, you will learn to create a new blank presentation and create a presentation from a template. Like other Microsoft Office programs, PowerPoint lets you format text and paragraphs and use tools such as the spelling checker and the Find and Replace feature. In addition, you will learn how to tailor your presentation by applying themes and customizing slide masters.

> **EXTRA FOR EXPERTS**
>
> You can bypass the New Presentation dialog box and open a new blank presentation using the New command on the Quick Access Toolbar. If the New command is not visible on your Quick Access Toolbar, you can add it by clicking the Customize Quick Access Toolbar button and clicking New on the menu.

Creating a New Blank Presentation

A blank presentation is a clean canvas. It contains one title slide with two areas for content, or placeholders. Creating a presentation involves choosing the slide layouts that you want and applying fonts, colors, and formats. You might prefer a plain white background to showcase the data or photos in your presentation, or perhaps a colorful look would better suit your needs. Try to present your information efficiently by minimizing the number of slides in your presentation and limiting the amount of text on each slide. You can create a new blank presentation using the Blank Presentation button in the New Presentation dialog box, shown in **Figure PPT 2–1**. To display the dialog box, choose the New command on the Office Button menu.

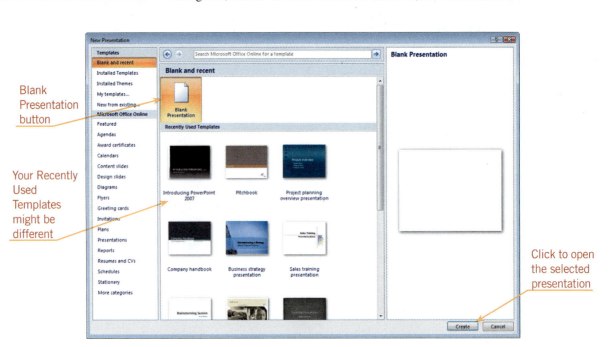

FIGURE PPT 2–1 New Presentation dialog box

LESSON 2 Formatting and Modifying Presentations PPT 31

Step-by-Step PPT 2.1

1. Start PowerPoint.
2. Click the **Office** button on the Ribbon and then click **New**. The New Presentation dialog box opens with the Blank Presentation button selected.
3. Click the **Create** button to open a new, blank presentation, as shown in **Figure PPT 2–2**.

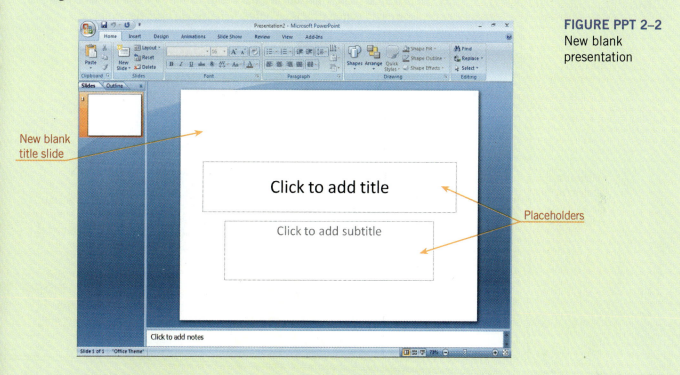

FIGURE PPT 2–2
New blank presentation

4. Click the **Click to add title** placeholder and type **My Favorite Movies**.
5. Click the **Click to add subtitle** placeholder and type your name.
6. Save the presentation as **Favorite Movies XXX.pptx** (replace *XXX* with your initials) and close it.

Creating a New Presentation with a Template

One method of creating a well-organized and attractive presentation quickly is to use a template. A ***template*** is a sample presentation that provides a pattern or model that you can follow to create your own presentation. PowerPoint includes templates for many common types of presentations, including employee orientations, financial performance reports, company handbooks, photo albums, and business plans.

A presentation template contains a group of slides with a common theme and background style, but the added advantage of using a template is that it offers suggestions for content that is standard for a particular type of presentation, giving

▶ **VOCABULARY**
template

WARNING

To use a template from Microsoft Office Online, you must download it. The first time you download a template, Microsoft will verify that the software you are using is authentic. You cannot download templates without genuine Microsoft Office software.

you an outline of topics to help you get started. For instance, instead of having to create an employee orientation presentation from scratch, a template contains slides with content or suggestions for content that is typical in such a presentation, such as company background, benefits, policies, work hours, and required paperwork. You can then replace the suggested content on each slide with your own.

PowerPoint includes many templates that come already installed, and you can access them by clicking the Installed Templates category in the Templates section of the New Presentation dialog box, shown in **Figure PPT 2–3**. Many more templates are available online; you can access these by clicking the presentations category in the Microsoft Office Online section of the New Presentation dialog box. You can also use the Search box to look for a template by keywords. When you have selected the template you want, you can click the Create button (if it is an installed template) or the Download button (if it is an online template) to open the template.

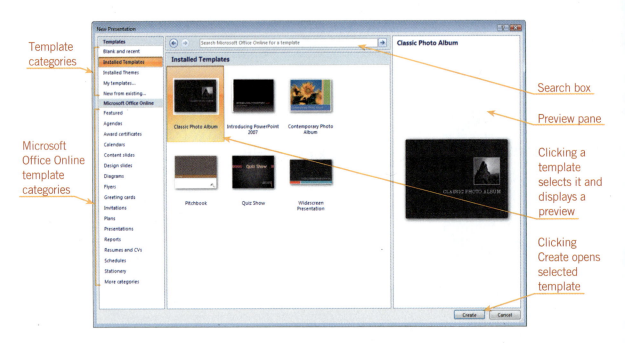

FIGURE PPT 2–3 Installed Templates in the New Presentation dialog box

EXTRA FOR EXPERTS

PowerPoint templates are saved as the PowerPoint Template type with the extension .pptx. If you want to save a presentation as a template, click the Office button on the Ribbon, point to Save As, and click Other Formats and choose PowerPoint Template from the Save as type list.

To display the New Presentation dialog box, use the New command on the Office Button menu. When you open a template from the New Presentation dialog box, you are actually opening a copy of the template, so the original template is not altered. Add your own text to a template by clicking a placeholder and then typing to replace the current content with your own. Name and save a new presentation using the Save or Save As command.

LESSON 2   **Formatting and Modifying Presentations**

PPT 33

Step-by-Step PPT 2.2

1. Click the **Office** button and then click **New**. The New Presentation dialog box opens.
2. Click **Installed Templates** in the left pane to display the installed templates in the center pane.
3. In the Installed Templates section, click **Classic Photo Album**, if necessary, to select it. Notice the preview in the right pane.
4. Confirm that the Classic Photo Album button is selected, then click the **Create** button. The template opens.
5. Save the presentation as **Nature Portfolio *XXX*.pptx** (replace *XXX* with your initials).
6. Click the **Slide Show** button on the status bar to switch to Slide Show view and advance through the entire presentation. Notice the layouts, instructions, and content suggestions throughout.
7. On slide 1 in Normal view, select the title **CLASSIC PHOTO ALBUM** and type **LostArt Photos**.
8. On slide 1, click the **Click to add date and other details** placeholder and type **Nature Photography Portfolio**. Your screen should look similar to **Figure PPT 2–4**.

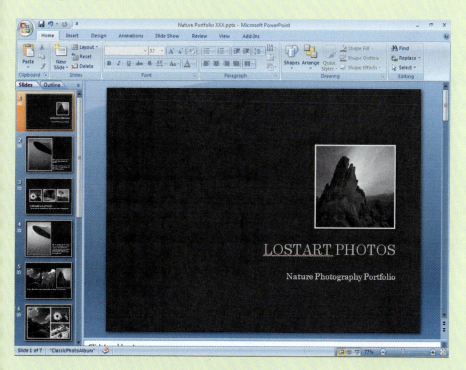

FIGURE PPT 2–4
Nature Portfolio *XXX*.pptx presentation

9. On slide 2, select the first paragraph of text that begins *This photo album contains* and type **Stock photos**.

10. Select the second paragraph of text that begins *To add your own pages* and type **On location photo shoots**.
11. On slide 3, select the **CHOOSE A LAYOUT** title and type **Flowers, Foliage, and Rocks**.
12. Select the second line that begins *...then click the placeholders* and type **All of nature is beautiful...**
13. On slide 5, select the text that begins *Picture Quick Styles* and type **For more information on purchasing stock photos or to request a quote for an on-location shoot, call 555-806-9876**.
14. Save the presentation and leave it open for use in the next Step-by-Step.

Formatting Text

> **VOCABULARY**
> **characters**
> **font**

Characters are individual letters, numbers, symbols, punctuation marks, and spaces. You can apply one or more formats to a single character or multiple characters. The character formats you can apply are font and font size; font style such as italic and bold; and font effects such as underline, color, and change case. The Font group is on the Home tab on the Ribbon, shown in **Figure PPT 2–5**, and contains buttons for formatting text. Later in this lesson you will learn to copy formats using the Format Painter button in the Clipboard group.

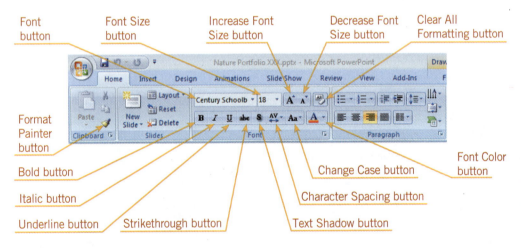

FIGURE PPT 2–5   Home tab

Using the Font dialog box, you can make multiple changes to characters. You access the Font dialog box using the dialog box launcher.

Changing Fonts and Font Sizes

A ***font*** is a design of a set of letters and numbers. Each set has a name. Below are some examples.

Times New Roman   Arial   **Impact**

LESSON 2 Formatting and Modifying Presentations

For presentations, it is important to choose simple fonts that are readable from a distance. The Font menu, which you access through the Font group on the Home tab on the Ribbon, displays each font's design. You can also access the Font menu on the Mini toolbar. By default, PowerPoint uses the Calibri 44 point font for titles, and Calibri 32 point for text for new blank presentations. You change to a different font by selecting text and choosing one of the fonts listed on the Font menu or in the Font dialog box. You also can choose to begin typing text with a new font by selecting the font at the insertion point.

Font sizes are measured in points. ***Point size*** refers to a measurement for the height of characters. A point is equal to approximately 1/72 inch. A 10-point font is approximately 10/72 inch high. The examples below show what different point sizes look like in the Times font. Font sizes must be large enough and the slide uncluttered enough for an audience to read the message easily.

> **VOCABULARY**
> point size
> font style
> **Format Painter**

18 Point   24 Point   36 Point

To change the font size for existing text, you first select the text and then choose a new size on the Font Size menu or in the Size list in the Font dialog box. You can change the size of text you are about to enter by choosing a new size at the insertion point location.

The Increase Font Size button increases font size one increment on the Font Size menu, which may be one point, two points, or eight points in the larger sizes, and the Decrease Font Size button decreases the size one increment.

Applying Font Styles and Effects

Font styles are variations in the shape or weight of a font's characters. Bold, italic, and underline are common font styles that you can access easily in the Font group.

Additional buttons are available to add effects to text. The Strikethrough button draws a line through the middle of text, the Text Shadow button adds a shadow behind text, and the Character Spacing button lets you adjust the space between characters. The Change Case button provides options for changing the capitalization of text, and the Font Color button lets you change the text color. You can add more than one effect to text, but make sure the text is still readable for the audience.

> **EXTRA FOR EXPERTS**
>
> You can use shortcut keys: Ctrl+B to apply bold, Ctrl+I to apply italic, and Ctrl+U to underline text.

Clearing Formatting

To remove formatting from selected text, you perform the same steps you took to apply the formatting, which effectively reverses the formatting. For example, if you want to remove bold formatting that you added to a word, you would click the Bold button again to remove the bold formatting from selected text. Or, use the Clear All Formatting button to remove all formatting from selected text. Reversing a font change does not work in the same way; if you want to restore a font you had previously used, you must select the text and use the Font button arrow to change the font back to the original.

Copying Formats Using the Format Painter

The ***Format Painter*** can save you time by allowing you to copy text that contains multiple formatting characteristics and then apply the same formatting to other parts of the presentation. When you click the Format Painter button, your mouse pointer changes to an I-beam with a paintbrush.

UNIT IV Microsoft PowerPoint

To copy formatting of a section of text, you first select the text or paragraph that contains the formatting you want to copy and then click the Format Painter button. The mouse pointer will change to an I-beam with a paintbrush "loaded" with the copied format. Next you can select the text to which you want to apply the formatting, or if you want to apply the formatting to a single word, you can click it.

Double-clicking the Format Painter button allows you to "paint" the copied formatting to more than one selection. When you finish painting formats, click the Format Painter button or press the Esc key to turn off the Format Painter.

Step-by-Step PPT 2.3

The Nature Portfolio XXX.pptx presentation from Step-by-Step PPT 2.2 should be open in the PowerPoint program window.

1. On slide 1, select the title, LOSTART PHOTOS.

2. On the Home tab, in the Font group, click the **Font** button arrow and click **Berlin Sans FB** from the menu, as shown in **Figure PPT 2–6**. If Berlin Sans FB is not available on your computer, select another font.

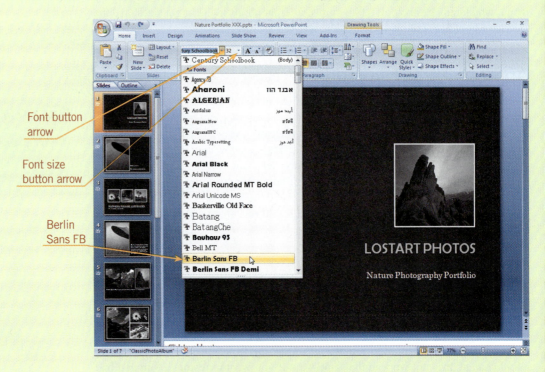

FIGURE PPT 2–6
Font menu

3. Click the **Font Size** button and click **40** to increase the font size.

4. Click the **Change Case** button Aa▾ and click **Capitalize Each Word** to change the case of text from all uppercase to capitalizing just the first letter of each word.

5. Select the **a** in *Lostart*. Click the **Change Case** button and click **UPPERCASE** to capitalize the letter.

6. Select the text **LostArt Photos**. Click the **Character Spacing** button ↔ and click **Loose**.

LESSON 2   Formatting and Modifying Presentations

7. With the title still selected, click the **Bold** button **B**. Click the **Bold** button again to remove the bold formatting.

8. Click the **Increase Font Size** button to increase the font size to 44 point.

9. Click the **Font Color** button arrow, and in the Theme Colors section, click **Black, Background 1**, as shown in **Figure PPT 2–7**.

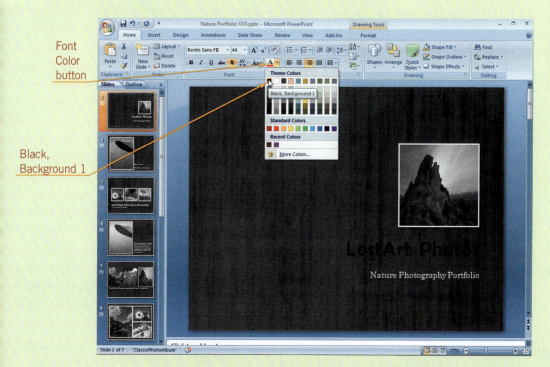

FIGURE PPT 2–7
Font Color button and palette

10. Click the **Clear All Formatting** button to remove all the applied formatting and return to the original font format.

11. Click the **Undo** button to restore formatting.

12. Select **LostArt Photos**. In the Clipboard group, click the **Format Painter** button to copy the formatting.

13. On slide 3, drag the paintbrush I-beam across FLOWERS, FOLIAGE, AND ROCKS and then release the mouse button to apply the copied formatting.

14. Save the presentation and leave it open for use in the next Step-by-Step.

Formatting Paragraphs

PowerPoint refers to a paragraph as any amount of text followed by a paragraph mark. Each design theme controls how paragraphs appear on a slide. You can, however, change the format of paragraphs by positioning your insertion point anywhere in the paragraph and then applying formatting. PowerPoint applies paragraph formats to the entire paragraph. You cannot apply paragraph formats to just a selection within a paragraph.

The Paragraph group on the Home tab, shown in **Figure PPT 2–8**, contains buttons for changing paragraph formatting. You can access additional commands in the Paragraph dialog box, which you can display by clicking the dialog box launcher.

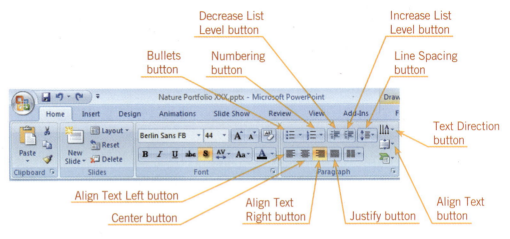

FIGURE PPT 2–8 Paragraph group on the Home tab

Aligning Text Horizontally and Vertically

Alignment is the position of text in relation to the edges of a placeholder on a slide. You can left-align, center, right-align, or justify text horizontally within a placeholder using the alignment buttons—Align Text Left, Center, Align Text Right, and Justify—in the Paragraph group on the Home tab.

The Align Text button arrow provides a menu of options for aligning text vertically within a placeholder. You can align text at the top, middle, or bottom of a placeholder or click More Options to specify other options such as Top Centered.

Setting Line Spacing

Line spacing determines the vertical distance between lines of text in a paragraph. The Line spacing button on the Home tab in the Paragraph group lets you choose a common line spacing option, such as 1.0 (single spacing) or 2.0 (double-spacing). You can also display the Paragraph dialog box, which contains options for creating custom line spacing and for adding spacing before or after a paragraph.

Changing Text Direction

If you want to display text rotated on its side or stacked vertically, use the Text Direction button arrow in the Paragraph group. The More Options command displays the Format Text Effects dialog box where several different options can be set in one place.

Formatting Lists

Bulleted lists are often used in presentations because they display text in a simple format that audiences can read quickly. Bulleted lists typically use short sentences, phrases, or keywords. The presenter can further discuss each bulleted item as needed. PowerPoint has several different bullet and numbering options. You can

> **VOCABULARY**
> alignment

> **EXTRA FOR EXPERTS**
> You can use shortcut keys: Ctrl+L to align text left, Ctrl+R to align text right, Ctrl+E to center text, and Ctrl+J to justify text.

LESSON 2 Formatting and Modifying Presentations

PPT 39

select an existing list and then click the Bullets button or the Numbering button in the Paragraph group to add or change bullets or numbers.

The Bullets and Numbering command displays the Bullets and Numbering dialog box where you can choose from a gallery of pictures or insert symbols to create custom bullets. You can also change the color and size of bullets or import your own picture to further customize the design.

PowerPoint automatically renumbers a numbered list when you insert, move, copy, or delete items. A new bullet is added on a blank line when you press Enter at the end of a bulleted item. You can use the Increase Indent and Decrease Indent buttons to promote or demote items to different outline levels.

> **EXTRA FOR EXPERTS**
>
> You should number a list when the items need to be in order, such as instructions, or if the number of items in the list is significant. Use bullets for a list if the items in the list do not require a specific order, such as a grocery list.

Step-by-Step PPT 2.4

The Nature Portfolio *XXX*.pptx presentation from Step-by-Step PPT 2.3 should be open in the PowerPoint program window.

1. On slide 4, select the text and click the **Align Text Right** button to right-align the text within the placeholder.
2. Click the **Center** button to center the text.
3. Click the **Line Spacing** button arrow and click **2.0** to double-space the lines of text.
4. With the placeholder text selected, type **It all depends on your perspective** to replace it.
5. Select the text and click the **Align Text** button, and then click **Top**, as shown in **Figure PPT 2–9** to align the text at the top of the placeholder.

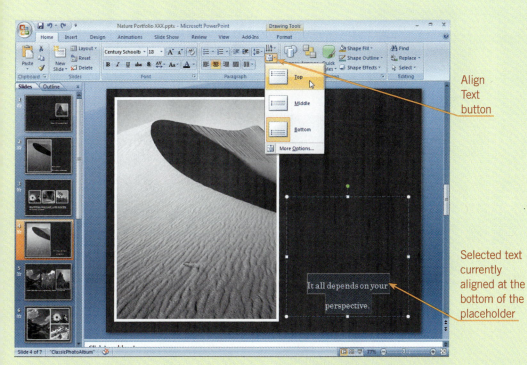

FIGURE PPT 2–9
Align Text button and menu

Align Text button

Selected text currently aligned at the bottom of the placeholder

6. Click the **Text Direction** button and click **Rotate all text 270°** to turn the text on its side, as shown in **Figure PPT 2–10**.

FIGURE PPT 2–10
Slide 4

7. On slide 2, select the two lines of text and click the **Increase List Level** button.

8. Click the **Bullets** button arrow and click the **Hollow Round Bullets** style, as shown in **Figure PPT 2–11**.

FIGURE PPT 2–11
Bullets button and gallery

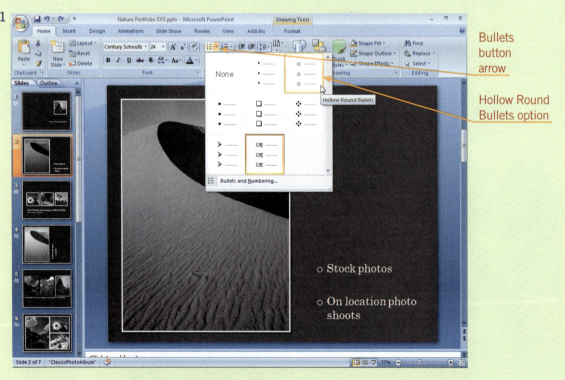

9. Save the presentation and switch to Slide Show view to view the presentation.

10. Close the presentation.

LESSON 2 Formatting and Modifying Presentations

Checking Spelling

PowerPoint automatically checks spelling as you type by comparing a document's language to PowerPoint's built-in dictionary. PowerPoint underlines words that might be misspelled with a wavy red line. You can right-click a word that has a wavy red line and see a shortcut menu with suggestions for corrections. If you don't want to use one of the suggested corrections, you can change the text manually. You should always spell check your presentations. Spelling and grammar mistakes are not only embarrassing, but they can also damage your credibility as a presenter.

You can also check the spelling in an entire presentation with a single action using the Spelling button in the Proofing group on the Review tab, as shown in **Figure PPT 2–12**. This approach is useful when you have finished editing a presentation, but you want to check it one more time to make sure you didn't miss any mistakes or introduce errors while editing.

FIGURE PPT 2–12   Review tab

When a possible error is detected, PowerPoint displays the Spelling dialog box to show you the error and suggest a correction. Use the Change button in the Spelling dialog box to correct an error, or use the Change All button to correct all instances of the same error. If the correct spelling does not appear in the Suggestions list, you can type the correct spelling in the Change to text box and then click the Change button.

The spelling checker will flag many proper nouns and other words as being incorrect. To ignore the word or phrase, or ignore all occurrences of the word or phrase, use the Ignore Once or Ignore All buttons as you spell check presentations.

The Spelling feature checks the entire presentation from the insertion point forward and then works from the beginning of the presentation to the insertion point.

Remember, the Spelling feature does not eliminate the need to proofread a presentation. If a word you misspelled is another English word (for example, you typed *there* instead of *their*), the spelling feature will not detect the error. Although it finds many common errors, the Spelling feature does not always understand the context of the text and might suggest inappropriate corrections. Examine suggestions carefully before you accept them.

> **EXTRA FOR EXPERTS**
>
> PowerPoint's main dictionary contains most common words, including country names, names of many U.S. cities, some company names, and many proper names. However, you probably use words that are not in PowerPoint's main dictionary. You can add those words to a custom dictionary so PowerPoint does not flag them each time you type them.

Step-by-Step PPT 2.5

1. Open the file **Step PPT 2-5.pptx** from the folder containing the data files for this lesson and save it as **Course Rules *XXX*.pptx** (replace *XXX* with your initials).

2. On slide 1, right-click the red underlined letters, *Couse*, to display the shortcut menu.

3. Click **Course**, which is the third option on the menu, as shown in **Figure PPT 2–13**.

FIGURE PPT 2–13
Correct misspelled words using the shortcut menu

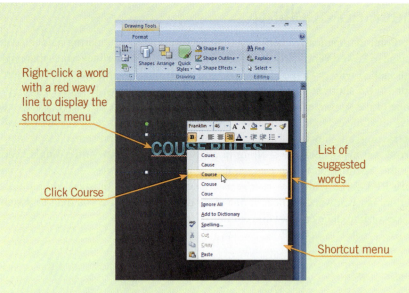

4. On the Review tab on the Ribbon, in the Proofing group, click the **Spelling** button to open the Spelling dialog box.

5. Click **Ignore** to ignore the suggestions for changing the name, as shown in **Figure PPT 2–14**.

FIGURE PPT 2–14
Spelling dialog box

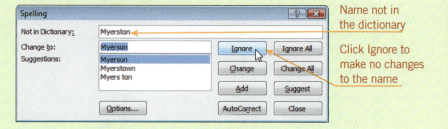

6. Click **Change** to accept the correct spelling of *Bring*.

7. Click **Change** to accept the correct spelling of *Know*.

8. Click **Change** to accept the correct spelling of *materials*.

9. The suggested correction for the next error is not the appropriate word. Click **posted** in the Suggestions list and click **Change**.

10. Click **OK** to respond to the prompt that the spelling check is complete.

11. Save the presentation and leave it open for use in the next Step-by-Step.

Finding and Replacing Text

The Find and Replace commands are two separate commands that are often used together to find and replace text. The Find and Replace commands are located in the Editing group on the Home tab on the Ribbon, as shown in **Figure PPT 2–15**.

LESSON 2 Formatting and Modifying Presentations

FIGURE PPT 2-15   Editing group on the Home tab

You can use the Find command alone to search for a specific word or phrase in a presentation. Enter the word or phrase you want to locate in the Find dialog box. You can designate that PowerPoint match case (find a word with the same uppercase and lowercase combination) and find whole words only (words like *work* but not compound words like *homework*) when searching for text. Click the Replace button when you want to find a word and then replace it with a new one.

Use the Find Next and Replace buttons to make just one replacement at a time. The Replace All button replaces all occurrences of a word without confirming each one. But be sure you want to replace every occurrence of the word. For instance, you can run into trouble using Replace All when changing a person's name, such as Jackson to Johnson. If a company name or city name in the document contains the name Jackson or Jacksonville, Replace All changes it to Johnson as well. Since PowerPoint also replaces partial words, you can also run into trouble when changing the word *class* to *course* because it would change the word *classic* to *courseic*.

> **EXTRA FOR EXPERTS**
>
> You can use the Replace Fonts command in the Replace menu to replace all occurrences of a font such as Arial with a new font, such as Calibri.

Step-by-Step PPT 2.6

The Course Rules *XXX*.pptx presentation from Step-by-Step PPT 2.5 should be open in the PowerPoint program window.

1. Display slide 1.
2. On the Home tab, in the Editing group, click the **Find** button to display the Find dialog box.
3. Type **Work** in the Find what box and click the **Match case** check box, as shown in **Figure PPT 2-16**, to search for the capitalized word.

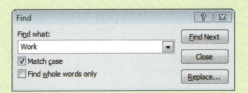

FIGURE PPT 2-16
Find dialog box

4. Click the **Find Next** button to start the search.
5. Click the **OK** button to respond to the message indicating that no search items were found.
6. Click the **Match case** check box to clear it.
7. Click the **Find Next** button. PowerPoint locates the word *work*. Click the **Replace** button. The Find dialog box changes to the Replace dialog box.
8. Type **assignments** in the Replace with box, as shown in **Figure PPT 2-17**, and click the **Replace** button to replace the word *work* with the word *assignments*.

FIGURE PPT 2–17
Replace dialog box

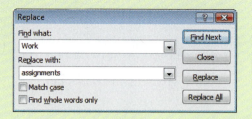

9. PowerPoint moves to the next occurrence and finds the word *coursework*. Click **Find Next** to move to the next search item without making changes.

10. Click the **OK** button to respond to the message indicating that no search items were found.

11. Click the **Find whole words** only check box to select it and click **Find Next** to make sure there are no more occurrences of the word *work*.

12. Click the **OK** button to respond to the message indicating that no search items were found.

13. Click the Replace dialog box **Close** button to end the search and close the dialog box.

14. Save the presentation and leave it open for use in the next Step-by-Step.

▶ **VOCABULARY**
themes

Applying Themes

PowerPoint provides so many different fonts, sizes, colors, font styles, and effects that it can be difficult to figure out which formatting options you should use together to create a professional-looking presentation. Unless you have an eye for design, it can be tricky to choose one font for titles, a coordinating font for content, and a background color and style that is attractive and readable. To make these decisions easier, PowerPoint includes built-in *themes*, which are sets of formatting choices that include colors, fonts, effects, and backgrounds that were predesigned to work well together. The themes are available in other Office programs as well, so you can apply the same theme to an Excel spreadsheet, a Word report, and a PowerPoint presentation, resulting in a professionally coordinated package of files.

Each presentation you create is associated with one of PowerPoint's presentation themes, which are accessed through the Themes gallery on the Design tab on the Ribbon. Even a new blank presentation is based on a theme. When you change the theme, you change the entire presentation's color scheme, fonts, and effects to the new design theme. PowerPoint provides several different built-in themes, or you can customize a theme's colors, fonts, and other effects using the buttons in the Themes group. See **Figure PPT 2–18**.

LESSON 2   Formatting and Modifying Presentations   PPT 45

FIGURE PPT 2–18   Design tab

Additional theme choices are available through the More Themes on Microsoft Office Online command, or use the Browse for Themes command to locate a presentation that contains a theme you want to apply to the current presentation. After you have customized a theme, you can use the Save Current Theme command to name and save it to the Document Themes folder.

> **EXTRA FOR EXPERTS**
>
> When customizing or creating a new theme, aim for high contrast (difference between light and dark) between the background color and the text color to provide maximum readability. For example, white text on a black background is much more readable than white text on a yellow background.

Step-by-Step PPT 2.7

The Course Rules *XXX*.pptx presentation from Step-by-Step PPT 2.6 should be open in the PowerPoint program window.

1. Display slide 1.
2. On the Design tab on the Ribbon, in the Themes group, click the **More** button to display the Themes gallery.
3. Point to several of the theme options to see a Live Preview of the choices available, then click the **Verve** option, as shown in **Figure PPT 2–19**.

FIGURE PPT 2-19
Themes gallery

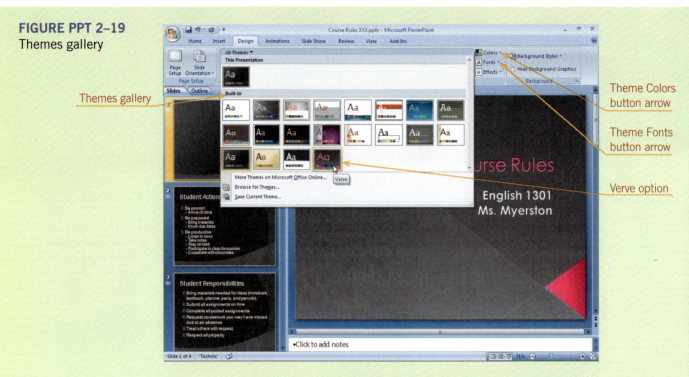

4. Click the **Theme Colors** button arrow and click **Origin**.
5. Click the **Theme Fonts** button arrow, scroll down, and then click **Solstice**.
6. Save the presentation and leave it open for use in the next Step-by-Step.

Customizing Slide Masters

▶ **VOCABULARY**
slide master
layout master

You already have learned that when you use a theme for a presentation, all the slides are set up with the formatting in that theme. Each theme has its own *slide master* and a set of layout masters. The slide master stores information about the theme (including fonts and background colors) and the layout (position and size of placeholders). When you make a change to the slide master, the change is made to the entire presentation. Slide masters provide a convenient way for you to further customize a presentation, especially one with many slides, with little effort. For example, if you have a 20-slide presentation and you want to change the color of all titles on all slides to match the blue of your company logo, you can open Slide Master view and change the color of the title on the slide master—an effect you cannot achieve by changing the theme colors. The change is applied to all titles in the presentation at once. The alternative would be to open all 20 slides and use the Font Color button to change the title colors one by one—a tedious way to accomplish the same result. In the same way, you can change the bullet styles used for the entire presentation or insert clip art on the slide master that will appear in the same position on every slide.

You can also alter the *layout masters*, which store information about the fonts, colors, effects and layout of each type of slide layout. If no changes are made to the layout masters, the layout masters follow the settings of the slide master and the applied theme. However, you can make changes to individual slide layouts and

LESSON 2 Formatting and Modifying Presentations

override the master slide settings if you want. For example, you have five title slides in your 20-slide presentation that introduce each of your five points. You decide that you want the titles on the title slides to appear in red instead of the blue you set earlier on the master slide. You could change the font color to red on the five title slides in the presentation, or you could make the change to the title slide layout master in Slide Master view. When you change the font color on the title slide layout master, the change will apply to all five title slides and any new title slides you might insert. The red color setting on the layout master overrides the blue font color setting on the slide master, but only for the title slide layouts.

In addition to changing formatting, you can also change the size and location of the placeholders on the layout masters or the slide master. You can add additional placeholders to the title slide layout master, for example to accommodate additional text.

In Slide Master view, PowerPoint displays the Slide Master tab on the Ribbon. Use the Close Master View button to return to Normal view.

> **EXTRA FOR EXPERTS**
>
> The Handout Master and Notes Master can be used to make universal changes to Handouts and Notes Pages for a presentation similar to the way you use the slide master. You can insert a graphic or text, add information to headers and footers, or move and resize placeholders so that each handout or notes page is formatted to your specifications.

Step-by-Step PPT 2.8

The Course Rules *XXX*.pptx presentation from Step-by-Step PPT 2.7 should be open in the PowerPoint program window.

1. Switch to Slide Show view and advance through the presentation. Notice the title font colors and alignments and the bullet styles used in the presentation.

2. On the View tab, in the Presentation Views group, click the **Slide Master View** button to change to Slide Master view.

3. Click the slide master, which is the top thumbnail in the left pane, as shown in **Figure PPT 2–20**.

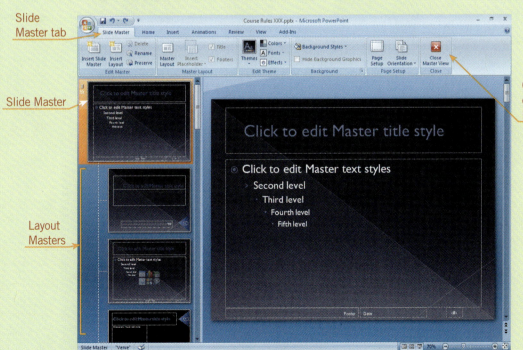

FIGURE PPT 2–20
Slide Master view

4. Select **Click to edit Master title style** at the top of the slide master.

5. On the Home tab, in the Font group, click the **Font Color** button arrow and click **Blue-Gray, Accent 1, Lighter 80%**, as shown in **Figure PPT 2–21**, to change the font color of all the titles in the presentation.

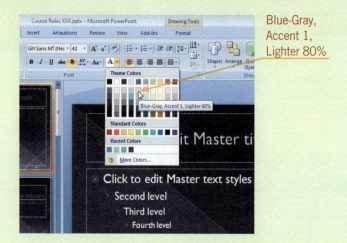

FIGURE PPT 2–21
Slide Master view

6. Select **Click to edit Master text styles** in the first bullet of the slide master.
7. On the Home tab, in the Paragraph group, click the **Bullets** button arrow and click the **Hollow Square Bullets** style.
8. Click the **Title Slide Layout Master**, the second thumbnail in the left pane.
9. Select **Click to edit Master title style**, as shown in **Figure PPT 2–22**.

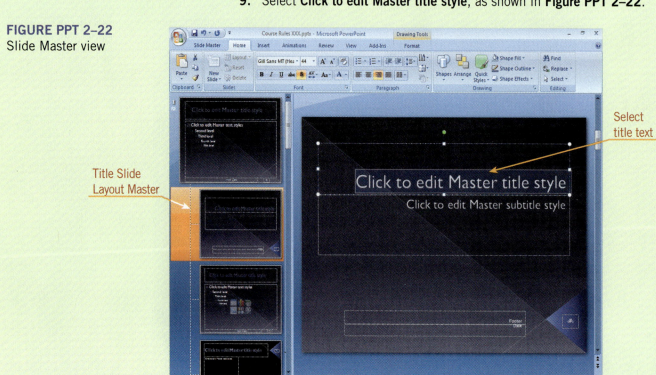

FIGURE PPT 2–22
Slide Master view

LESSON 2   Formatting and Modifying Presentations

10. On the Home tab, in the Font group, click the **Font Color** button arrow and click **White**, **Text 1** to change the text color to white.
11. In the Font group, click the **Bold** button  to change the text style to bold.
12. On the Slide Master tab, in the Close group, click the **Close Master View** button to return to Normal view.
13. Select slide 1 and then view the entire presentation. Notice that slides 2, 3, and 4 now have Hollow Square Bullets for first-level bulleted items, the title slide has a white, bolded title, and the remaining slides have gray titles.
14. Save and close the presentation.
15. Exit PowerPoint.

SUMMARY

In this lesson, you learned:

- How to create a new blank presentation using the New Presentation dialog box.
- Well-organized and attractive presentations can be quickly created with templates.
- How to apply character formats including fonts, font sizes, font styles, and font effects using the buttons in the Font group on the Home tab.
- Paragraph formatting, such as alignment and line spacing, can be changed using commands in the Paragraph group.
- How to use the Format Painter button to copy existing formats to other parts of a presentation.
- How spell checking works in PowerPoint.
- How to find a specific word in a presentation and replace it with a new word.
- Themes change the entire presentation's color scheme, fonts, and effects.
- Changes made to slide masters affect the entire presentation.

VOCABULARY REVIEW

Define the following terms:

alignment	Format Painter	template
characters	layout masters	themes
font	point size	
font styles	slide master	

REVIEW QUESTIONS

MULTIPLE CHOICE

Select the best response for the following statements.

1. _____ contain a group of slides with a layout, theme, background style, and suggestions for content that are standard for a particular type of presentation.
   - A. Slide masters
   - B. Templates
   - C. Themes
   - D. Lists

2. A _____ is a design of a set of letters and numbers.
   - A. font
   - B. font style
   - C. point size
   - D. template

3. _____ is the position of text in relation to the edge of the placeholder on a slide.
   - A. Alignment
   - B. Line spacing
   - C. Text direction
   - D. Point size

4. _____ are often used in presentations because they display text in a simple format that audiences can read quickly.
   - A. Bulleted lists
   - B. Layout masters
   - C. Slide masters
   - D. Theme Effects

5. The _____ button can rotate or stack text.
   - A. Align Text
   - B. Align Text Right
   - C. Text Direction
   - D. Increase Indent

6. The Spelling button is located on the _____ tab.
   - A. Home
   - B. Insert
   - C. Slide Show
   - D. Review

7. In the Find dialog box, clicking the _____ option will find the word *work* but not the word *homework*.
   - A. Match case
   - B. Replace
   - C. Find whole words only
   - D. Find what

8. The _____ button replaces all occurrences of a word at once without confirming each one.
   - A. Replace
   - B. Replace All
   - C. Find Next
   - D. Find what

9. _____ are sets of formatting choices that include colors, fonts, effects, and backgrounds that were predesigned to work well together.
   - A. Fonts
   - B. Slide masters
   - C. Templates
   - D. Themes

10. When you make a change to the _____, the change is made to the entire presentation.
    - A. layout master
    - B. list
    - C. slide master
    - D. paragraph

LESSON 2   Formatting and Modifying Presentations

FILL IN THE BLANK

Complete the following sentences by writing the correct word or words in the blanks provided.

1. To create a new, blank presentation, click the Office button on the Ribbon and then click _____.
2. _____ are individual letters, numbers, symbols, punctuation marks, and spaces.
3. Font sizes are measured in _____.
4. _____-clicking the Format Painter button allows you to "paint" the copied format to more than one selection.
5. The _____ button aligns text flush with the left margin and flush with the right margin.
6. _____-click a word that has a red wavy line to see a shortcut menu with suggestions for corrections.
7. Use the _____ command to search for a specific word or phrase in a presentation.
8. You can use the Theme _____ button to change the preestablished colors for a theme.
9. Each _____ has its own slide master and a set of layout masters.
10. The Slide Master View button is located on the _____ tab.

PROJECTS

PROJECT PPT 2-1

1. Start PowerPoint and create a new presentation using the **Introducing PowerPoint 2007** from the Installed Templates category in the New Presentation dialog box. Save it as **Introduction XXX.pptx** (replace *XXX* with your initials).
2. On slide 1, select the Introducing PowerPoint 2007 title and change the font to Bauhaus 93, or another font of your choice.
3. Change the color of the title to orange.
4. Copy the formatting on the title and apply it to the titles on slides 3, 7, 11, and 16.
5. On slide 2, in the left content placeholder, change the line spacing of the paragraph to 1.5 and then justify the paragraph.
6. Change the theme of the presentation to Trek.
7. Save the presentation and leave it open for use in the next project.

PROJECT PPT 2-2

The presentation **Introduction XXX.pptx** from Project PPT 2-1 should be open in the PowerPoint program window.

1. Save the document as **Introduction 2 XXX.pptx** (replace *XXX* with your initials).
2. Display slide 2. Copy the paragraph formatting in the left placeholder.
3. Switch to Slide Master view.
4. The layout master for the Two Content Layout should be displayed. Apply the copied format to the *Click to edit Master text styles* text in the left placeholder.
5. Close Slide Master view.
6. Switch to Slide Show view and advance through the entire presentation. Notice that the formatting was applied to all slides with the Two Content Layout.
7. Save and close the presentation.

ON YOUR OWN

Open the **Introduction 2 XXX.pptx** file. Change the look of all the title slides in the presentation. Change the placeholder layout, alignment, text color, font, and/or font size of the titles on the title slide layout master to apply the new style to all title slides. Save and close the presentation.

PROJECT PPT 2–3

1. Open the file **Project PPT 2-3.pptx** from the folder containing the data files for this lesson.
2. Save the document as **Fitness Challenge *XXX*.pptx** (replace *XXX* with your initials).
3. Find all the occurrences of the phrase *Health Challenge* and replace them with **Fitness Challenge**.
4. Spell check the document and correct any misspelled words.
5. Change the theme of the presentation to Module.
6. Change the theme colors to Flow.
7. On slide 1, bold *Company Fitness Challenge* and change the color to Turquoise, Accent 3.
8. Save and close the presentation.

ON YOUR OWN

Open the **Fitness Challenge *XXX*.pptx** file and create a custom bullet style for the first and second levels of bullets in the presentation. Apply the new style to the bullets on all slides.

PROJECT PPT 2–4

1. Open the file **Project PPT 2-4.pptx** from the folder containing the data files for this lesson. Save it as **Job Search *XXX*.pptx** (replace *XXX* with your initials).
2. Use the shortcut menu to correct the three misspelled words, indicated by red wavy lines, in the presentation.
3. Apply the Civic theme.
4. Change the Theme Fonts to Median.
5. On slide 1, change the *Job Search Strategies* title to 54 point and bold.
6. Increase the size of the subtitle, *Steps for Finding Employment*, to 20 point.
7. On slide 2, left-align the bulleted items.
8. On slide 3, change the case of the title, *Research*, to Capitalize Each Word.
9. Decrease the list level on the bulleted items.
10. On slide 4, change the line spacing of the bulleted list to 1.0.
11. On slide 5, change the vertical alignment of the text in the bulleted list to Top.
12. Save and close the presentation.

WEB PROJECT

PROJECT PPT 2–5

Explore the templates available in the Microsoft Office Online section of the New Presentation dialog box. This dialog box will acquire templates from the Microsoft Web site, so you must be connected to the Internet and have permission to download a presentation. Choose a favorite template to download (make sure to choose one provided by Microsoft), and modify it to your specifications.

 TEAMWORK PROJECT

PROJECT PPT 2–6

Use PowerPoint Help to find the article titled *Unconventional tips for eliminating the fear of public speaking*. With a partner, read the article and create a presentation that describes the three steps discussed in the article. Include information about how you think these steps can help a presenter communicate information to an audience.

LESSON 2 Formatting and Modifying Presentations

CRITICAL THINKING

ACTIVITY PPT 2-1

Open the Favorite Movies *XXX*.pptx presentation that you created in Step-by-Step PPT 2.1. Complete the presentation by adding slides and inserting content for about five of your favorite movies. (If you prefer, you may change the topic to another subject, such as favorite books, music, or hobbies.) Include the title, a brief description, and a statement describing the reasons why the movie is a favorite. Experiment with themes and background styles. Customize the slide master, and check the spelling. Be prepared to share your presentation with the class and describe the formatting and design options you incorporated.

ACTIVITY PPT 2-2

With your instructor's permission, use the More Themes on Microsoft Office Online link in the Themes gallery to access the Microsoft Web site and explore the additional themes available for download. What is the process for downloading themes? With permission, download a theme and apply it to a new blank presentation. Prepare two or three slides that describe what type of audience the theme might be appropriate for and why.

ACTIVITY PPT 2-3

Create a new theme by customizing one of the themes in the PowerPoint theme gallery. Name and save it. Prepare a brief presentation displaying your theme and explaining the fonts, colors, and other elements used in it. Include ideas for the types of presentations that would demonstrate the appropriate use of your theme.

ACTIVITY PPT 2-4

Open a new, blank presentation and apply a theme. Experiment with the commands in the Background group of the Design tab to answer the following questions. Use PowerPoint's Help system if necessary. What is a background style? What options are available? How do you apply background styles to individual slides? How do you apply background styles to all slides? What happens to the background style options when you change the theme? In what situations might you want to hide background graphics? Be prepared to demonstrate the use of background styles.

LESSON 3

Enhancing the Presentation

Estimated Time: 2.5 hours

■ OBJECTIVES

Upon completion of this lesson, you should be able to:

- Insert and modify illustrations.
- Create and modify tables.
- Insert text boxes.
- Insert headers and footers.
- Insert special effects.

■ DATA FILES

To complete this lesson, you will need these data files:

- Step PPT 3-1.pptx
- Project PPT 3-1.pptx
- Project PPT 3-2.pptx
- Project PPT 3-3.pptx
- Project PPT 3-4.pptx
- Activity PPT 3-1.pptx

■ VOCABULARY

action buttons
animations
cell
chart
clip art
drawing objects
footer
header
pictures
selection handles
SmartArt graphic
table
text box
transition
…

UNIT IV Microsoft PowerPoint

Introduction

Graphics are visual components that add impact to presentations and help explain the text. Pictures, clip art, shapes, SmartArt, and charts are all types of graphics that you can add to and customize in your PowerPoint presentations. Tables provide another way to illustrate, explain, or supplement text in a presentation. You can add text boxes to position text where there are no placeholders. Special effects such as transitions and animations make your slide show presentation truly professional. In this lesson, you will learn to insert and modify these graphic elements and insert special effects to complete your presentations.

Inserting and Modifying Illustrations

Pictures, clip art, shapes, SmartArt, and charts are types of illustrations you can add to your PowerPoint presentations. Many slide layouts contain content placeholders with buttons you can click to insert different types of graphics, as shown in **Figure PPT 3-1**. Inserting a graphic on a slide within content placeholders makes it easy to arrange your graphics and other elements on the slide. As you recall from Lesson 1, you can always change a slide's layout to accommodate the graphics and/or text that you want to include on the slide.

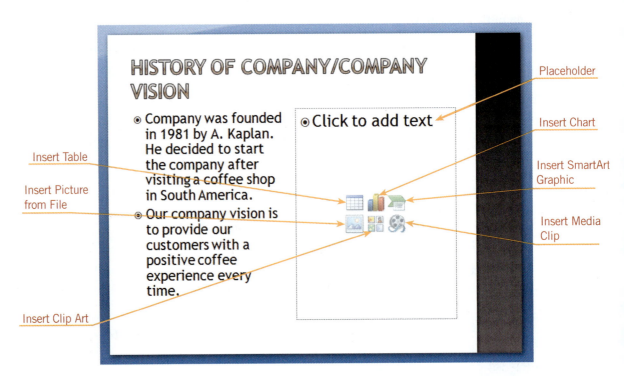

FIGURE PPT 3–1 Slide with placeholder for inserting graphics

You can also use buttons in the Illustrations group on the Insert tab on the Ribbon, shown in **Figure PPT 3-2**, to insert various types of graphic objects and position them anywhere on a slide.

LESSON 3 Enhancing the Presentation

FIGURE PPT 3–2 Insert tab

When you insert an illustration, you will be able to choose the graphic using a dialog box, task pane, or menu, depending on the type of illustration. After you insert an illustration, you have many options for modifying it, most of which are the same for each type of illustration.

Inserting and Modifying Pictures

The Insert Picture from File button can be used to insert *pictures,* or digital photographs or images, that are stored on your computer or network. You can insert pictures of various formats, including .tif, .gif, and .jpeg. The Insert Picture from File button opens the Insert Picture dialog box, which you can use to navigate to and insert a picture file from your computer or network.

Before you can modify or size a picture, clip art, or shape you must select it. To select a graphic, such as a picture or drawing, within a presentation and display the selection handles, click the graphic once. The small circles and squares at the sides and corners of the graphic are called *selection handles*. You drag these handles to change the graphic's size. When you want to resize a graphic proportionally, that is, to maintain the original ratio of height to width, you must display the sizing pointer and drag a corner handle. Some types of graphics require that you hold the Shift key while dragging a corner handle when sizing proportionally. If you want to distort a graphic horizontally or vertically, drag a middle handle. You can click the green rotate circle at the top of a graphic to rotate it on its central axis left or right to any position.

When a graphic is selected, you can copy, paste, and delete it the same way you would text using the Cut, Copy, and Paste commands. A copy of a graphic is the same size and contains the same formatting as the original graphic. When you paste a copy of a graphic, the new copy might appear on top of or next to the original. Simply drag it to the desired position.

After you insert a picture and any time the picture is selected, the Picture Tools Format contextual tab is displayed on the Ribbon. This tab contains commands for adjusting the picture, modifying the picture style, arranging the picture on the slide, and resizing the picture precisely.

> **VOCABULARY**
> pictures
>
> selection handles
>
> **EXTRA FOR EXPERTS**
>
> When sizing graphics, it can be helpful to display the vertical and horizontal rulers by clicking the Ruler check box in the Show/Hide group on the View tab.
>
> **EXTRA FOR EXPERTS**
>
> Large files can take longer to download and some might be rejected by e-mail servers. Including pictures in presentations increases file size, but you can use the Compress Pictures button to decrease a picture's file size by reducing the resolution, or the number of pixels in a picture.

Step-by-Step PPT 3.1

1. Start PowerPoint.
2. Open **Step PPT 3-1.pptx** from the folder containing the data files for this lesson and save the presentation as **Employee Orientation XXX**.pptx (replace *XXX* with your initials).
3. Display slide 3.
4. In the content placeholder, click the **Insert Picture from File** button to open the Insert Picture dialog box.
5. Navigate to the **Sample Pictures** folder and double-click to open it.
6. Click **Waterfall** (or another picture of your choice) to select the image and then click the **Insert** button. The picture is inserted on the slide, as shown in **Figure PPT 3-3**.

FIGURE PPT 3-3
Picture inserted into placeholder

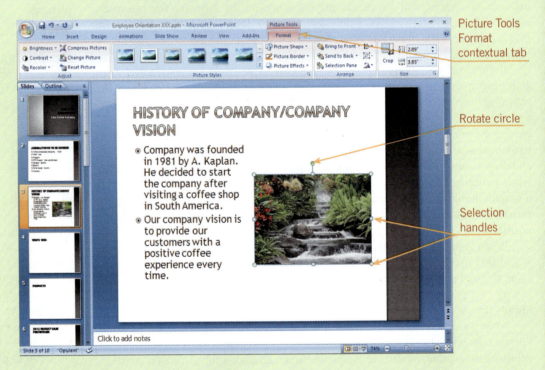

7. On the Picture Tools Format contextual tab, in the Adjust group, click the **Change Picture** button to display the Insert Picture dialog box.
8. Double-click **Forest** (or another picture of your choice) to insert the new picture.
9. In the Size group, click the **Crop** button to display the black cropping handles.
10. Drag the middle cropping handle on the right side to the left, as shown in **Figure PPT 3-4**, and release the mouse button to trim away the unwanted part of the picture.

LESSON 3 Enhancing the Presentation

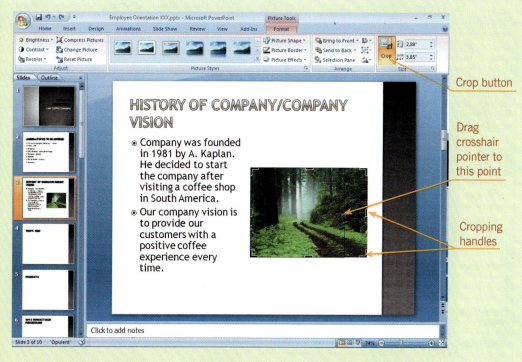

FIGURE PPT 3–4
Cropping a picture

11. In the Arrange group, click the **Rotate** button and click **Flip Horizontal** to flip the image.

12. In the Size group, click the **Shape Height** up arrow button until 3" is displayed in the box. Notice that the measurement in the Shape Width box changed to maintain the proportions.

13. In the Picture Styles group, click the **More** button to display the Picture Styles gallery. Point to several different options to see a live preview of some of the styles available, then click the **Rotated, White option**, shown in **Figure PPT 3-5**, to apply the style to the picture.

FIGURE PPT 3–5
Picture Styles gallery

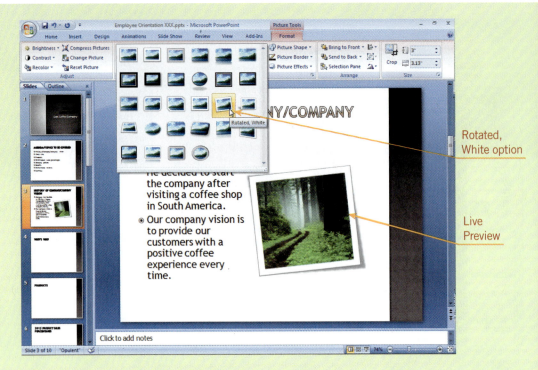

14. Save the presentation and leave it open for use in the next Step-by-Step.

Inserting and Modifying Clip Art

Clip art is artwork such as drawings or images that can be used in presentations. The Clip Art button in the Illustrations group displays the Clip Art task pane, shown in **Figure PPT 3–6**, which you can use to search for and insert clip art located on your computer, network, or on the Internet. The task pane contains a Search for text box where you can enter a keyword to find related clip art. The Search in menu lets you choose which collections to search, and the Results should be menu lets you choose the type of media file you are searching for, including clip art, pictures, sounds, and movies.

▶ **VOCABULARY**

clip art

⚠ **WARNING**

You can use the images, sounds, and movies Microsoft provides with PowerPoint or available for free on its Web site in any advertising, promotional and marketing materials, or product or service created with PowerPoint, as long as the material, product, or service is for noncommercial purposes. You may not sell any promotional and marketing materials or any products or services containing the images.

LESSON 3   Enhancing the Presentation

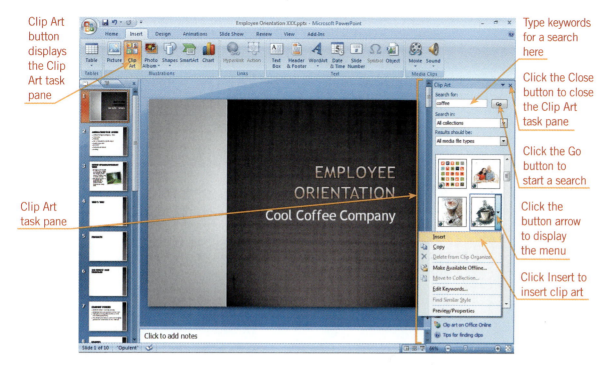

FIGURE PPT 3-6   Clip Art task pane

Point to a graphic in the Clip Art task pane and an arrow appears that displays a menu with the Insert command as well as other commands for copying and moving clip art and previewing clip art file properties. You can also insert clip art by clicking the image in the task pane. Contextual tabs let you modify clip art.

Step-by-Step PPT 3.2

The Employee Orientation *XXX*.pptx presentation from Step-by-Step PPT 3.1 should be open in the PowerPoint program window.

1. Display slide 1. Notice that there are no empty placeholders on the slide.

2. On the Insert tab, in the Illustrations group, click the **Clip Art** button to display the Clip Art task pane.

3. In the Search for box, type **coffee**. If necessary, click the **Search in** box arrow, and click the **Everywhere** check box to insert a check mark to search in All collections. Click the **Go** button to start the search.

4. In the Clip Art task pane, scroll down if necessary, and point to the picture of the coffee cup in the results pane (or choose a similar picture with a solid background), shown in **Figure PPT 3-7**. (The coffee cup clip art might appear in a different location in the Clip Art task pane.)

5. Click the button arrow on the right side of the image to display a menu.

6. Click **Insert** to insert the clip art on the slide.

7. Point to the upper-right corner handle. The pointer changes to a double-headed arrow. Click the **double-headed** arrow on the corner handle and drag it toward the center of the clip art to resize the image, as shown in **Figure PPT 3-7**.

FIGURE PPT 3–7
Resizing clip art

Drag resizing handle toward center of clip art to decrease the size

8. Click the image to display the four-sided move pointer and drag the clip art to the lower-left corner of the slide within the gray sidebar.

9. On the Picture Tools Format tab, in the Adjust group, click the **Recolor** button and click **Set Transparent Color** to change the pointer to the Set Transparent Color pointer.

10. Click the pointer anywhere in the white background of the clip art, as shown in **Figure PPT 3-8**. The white background becomes transparent, so the slide background shows through.

FIGURE PPT 3–8
Set Transparent Color

Click the Set Transparent Color pointer on the white background

11. Click outside the clip art to deselect it.
12. Click the **Close** button on the Clip Art task pane to close it.
13. Save the presentation and leave it open for use in the next Step-by-Step.

LESSON 3 Enhancing the Presentation

Inserting and Modifying Shapes

PowerPoint provides a set of common shapes that you can add to slides with one click and drag of the mouse. The Shapes button on the Insert tab on the Ribbon displays a menu containing lines, basic shapes, block arrows, flowchart elements, callouts, stars, banners, and action buttons that you can insert anywhere on your slides.

Action buttons contain graphic symbols such as arrows, a movie camera, and a sound speaker for commonly understood actions like going to next or previous slides or playing a movie or sound. When you insert an action button, PowerPoint displays the Action Settings dialog box so you can specify the action to occur when you click or mouse over the action button.

After inserting a shape, you can delete it using the Delete key while the shape is selected, or use the Undo button immediately after creating the shape.

Shapes, curves, and lines are considered *drawing objects*, which are created with PowerPoint and become part of your presentation, rather than being a separate file. After you insert a shape into a presentation, the Drawing Tools Format contextual tab is displayed on the Ribbon with commands for modifying drawing objects.

> **VOCABULARY**
> action buttons
> drawing objects

> **EXTRA FOR EXPERTS**
>
> Hold the Shift key when using rectangular or oval drawing shapes or tools to draw squares or circles. To create a straight line, hold the Shift key while using line tools.

> **EXTRA FOR EXPERTS**
>
> You might want to combine shapes to create a drawing object, such as several lines and shapes that combine to create a map. You can select multiple objects simultaneously by holding the Shift key while you click each of the objects. Use the Group command to combine them into one object, then you can move, format, and resize the grouped object.

Step-by-Step PPT 3.3

The Employee Orientation *XXX*.pptx presentation from Step-by-Step PPT 3.2 should be open in the PowerPoint program window.

1. Display slide 10.
2. On the Insert tab, in the Illustrations group, click the **Shapes** button to display the gallery.
3. In the Action Buttons category, click the **Action Button: Sound** icon, as shown in **Figure PPT 3-9**. The mouse pointer changes to a crosshair.

FIGURE PPT 3–9
Shapes button and menu

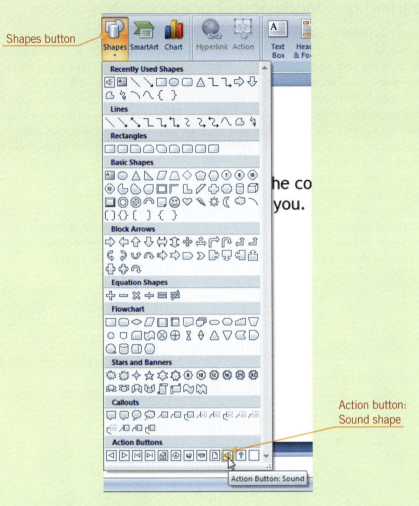

4. In the lower-right corner of the slide, drag down and to the right to draw the action button. The Action Settings dialog box opens when you finish drawing the shape.

5. In the Action Settings dialog box, click the **Mouse Over** tab, to specify actions that occur when the presenter holds the mouse pointer over the sound action button.

6. Click the **Play sound** check box.

7. Click the list box arrow and click **Applause**, as shown in **Figure PPT 3–10**.

LESSON 3 Enhancing the Presentation

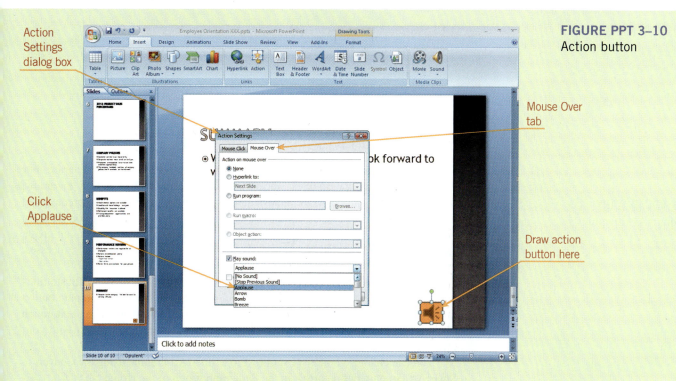

FIGURE PPT 3–10
Action button

8. Click the **OK** button to close the Action Settings dialog box.

9. On the Drawing Tools Format tab, in the Shape Styles group, click the **More** button to display the Shape Styles gallery. Point to several of the styles to preview some of the options available, then click the **Subtle Effect - Accent 5** option, as shown in **Figure PPT 3-11**.

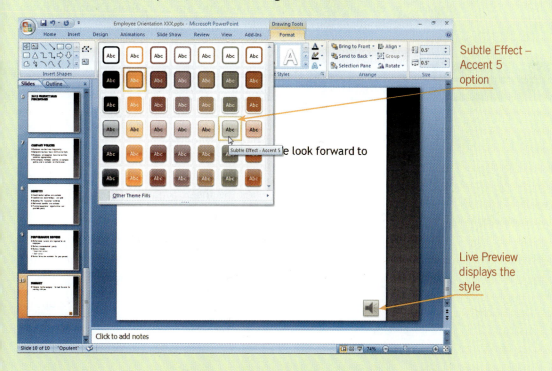

FIGURE PPT 3–11
Shape Styles gallery

10. Switch to Slide Show view and advance to slide 10, if necessary. Point to the action button you inserted to hear the sound.

11. Switch to Normal view.
12. Save the presentation and leave it open for use in the next Step-by-Step.

Inserting and Modifying SmartArt

Sometimes the best way to convey information is to use a chart or diagram. For example, an organization chart clearly shows a personnel reporting hierarchy, whereas a flow chart depicts a course of actions. A ***SmartArt graphic*** is a predesigned diagram made up of shapes containing text that illustrates a concept or idea. An organization chart is an example of one type of SmartArt graphic you can create easily in PowerPoint. Other types of SmartArt graphics include lists, processes, cycles, hierarchies, relationships, matrices, and pyramids.

You insert a diagram using the Insert SmartArt Graphic button in the Illustrations group on the Insert tab on the Ribbon, or by clicking the SmartArt Graphic button in a content placeholder. SmartArt graphics are inserted with placeholder text, much like the placeholders used in slides. You can replace the placeholder text with your own text.

You can change a bulleted list of text to a SmartArt graphic using the Convert to SmartArt Graphic button arrow in the Paragraph group of the Home tab.

After you insert a SmartArt graphic, the SmartArt Tools Design and Format contextual tabs are displayed on the Ribbon and provide access to a range of tools for customizing the graphic.

When you insert a SmartArt graphic, a text pane is also displayed to help simplify the process of entering text. You can click a [Text] placeholder beside a bullet in the Text pane to enter text in a shape. The Text pane can be hidden or displayed by clicking the Text Pane button on the SmartArt Tools Design tab in the Create Graphic group. You can also enter text directly into a shape.

> **VOCABULARY**
> **SmartArt graphic**

Step-by-Step PPT 3.4

The Employee Orientation *XXX*.pptx presentation from Step-by-Step PPT 3.3 should be open in the PowerPoint program window.

1. Display slide 4.
2. In the content placeholder, click the **Insert SmartArt Graphic** button to open the Choose a SmartArt Graphic dialog box.
3. Click the **Hierarchy** category and click the **Organization Chart** option, as shown in **Figure PPT 3-12**, and then click the **OK** button to insert the graphic into the slide. The SmartArt Tools Design tab is displayed and the text pane should be displayed. If it is not, click the **Text Pane** button in the Create Graphic group to display it.

LESSON 3   Enhancing the Presentation

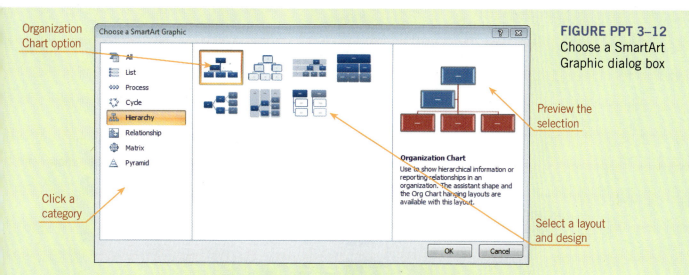

FIGURE PPT 3–12
Choose a SmartArt Graphic dialog box

4. In the text pane, type **A. Kaplan, CEO** beside the first-level bullet, as shown in **Figure PPT 3-13**. Notice that the text is entered in the shape, and the size automatically adjusts as you type.

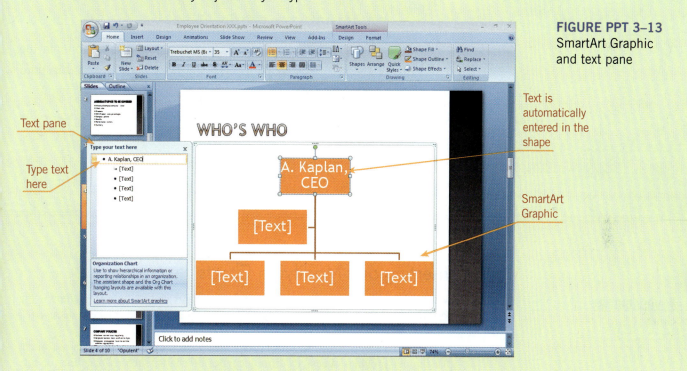

FIGURE PPT 3–13
SmartArt Graphic and text pane

5. Click the shape on the second row and press **Delete** to remove the shape from the graphic.

6. In the text pane, click the **[Text]** placeholder beside the second bullet and type **M. Jones, President of Operations**.

7. In the text pane, click the **[Text]** placeholder beside the third bullet and type **B. Petty, President of Procurement**.

8. In the SmartArt graphic, click the **[Text]** placeholder in the third shape and type **O. Donovan, President of Consumer Products**.

9. In the Create Graphic group, click the **Add Shape** button arrow and click **Add Shape After** to insert a new shape in the graphic. Type **K. Abii, CFO**.

10. In the Create Graphic group, click the **Text Pane** button to close the text pane.

11. In the Layouts group, click the **More** button to display the Layouts gallery and click the **Horizontal Hierarchy** layout, as shown in **Figure PPT 3-14**.

FIGURE PPT 3–14
Layouts gallery

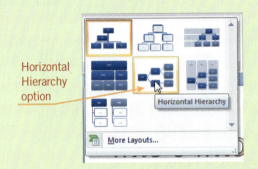

12. In the SmartArt Styles group, click the **Change Colors** button. In the Primary Theme Colors category, click the **Dark 2 Fill** option, the third option on the first row.

13. In the SmartArt Styles group, click the **More** button to display the SmartArt Styles gallery. In the Best Match for Document category, click the **Moderate Effect** option.

14. Save the presentation and leave it open for use in the next Step-by-Step.

Inserting and Modifying Charts

▶ **VOCABULARY**
chart

When you need to illustrate or compare data, such as budget figures, a ***chart*** is the best tool for the job. A chart is a graphical representation of data that can be inserted into PowerPoint.

The Chart button in the Illustrations group on the Insert tab or in a content placeholder provides access to different types of charts, such as bar, line, or pie. Using a chart in a PowerPoint presentation differs slightly from using other types of graphics because charts are composed of numerical data. The data that makes up the chart is stored in an Excel worksheet that is included in the PowerPoint file. (*Note*: When you initially create the chart, you enter data in the Excel worksheet; however, you do not need to be familiar with Excel to create a chart.)

As with other types of graphics, after you insert a chart on a slide, PowerPoint displays the Chart Tools Design, Layout, and Format contextual tab for customizing the chart.

LESSON 3   Enhancing the Presentation

Step-by-Step PPT 3.5

The Employee Orientation *XXX*.pptx presentation from Step-by-Step PPT 3.4 should be open in the PowerPoint program window.

1. Display slide 6.
2. In the content placeholder, click the **Insert Chart** button to display the Insert Chart dialog box.
3. If necessary, click the **Column** category and click the **100% Stacked Column** option, the third option in the first row.
4. Click the **OK** button. An Excel spreadsheet opens in a new window next to your presentation, as shown in **Figure PPT 3-15**, with sample data that you will replace.

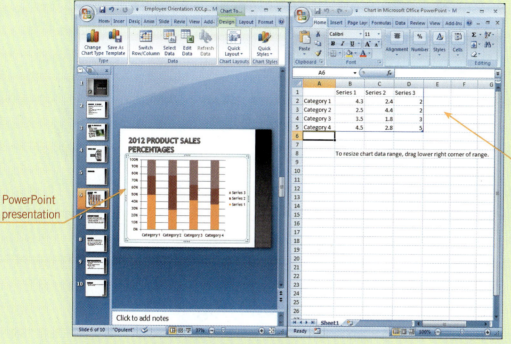

FIGURE PPT 3-15
Excel spreadsheet and PowerPoint presentation displayed side-by-side

5. Click in cell B1, which contains *Series 1*, and type **Drinks**. Press **Tab**.
6. In cell C1, type **Beans**. Press **Tab** to move to cell D1. Type **Other** and press **Tab**.
7. Enter the remaining data in the spreadsheet as shown below:

	Drinks	Beans	Other
Q1	50	40	10
Q2	55	30	15
Q3	60	25	15
Q4	65	25	10

8. Click the **Close** button of the Excel window to close the spreadsheet and view the chart in the slide.

9. On the Chart Tools Design tab, in the Chart Layouts group, click the **More** button to display the Layout gallery and click **Layout 4** to change the layout.

10. In the Chart Styles group, click the **More** button to display the Chart Styles gallery and click **Style 38**, as shown in **Figure PPT 3-16**.

FIGURE PPT 3-16
Chart Styles gallery

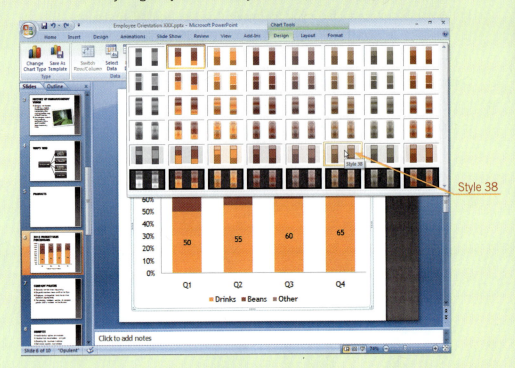

11. Save the presentation and leave it open for use in the next Step-by-Step.

Creating and Modifying Tables

A *table* is a grid of horizontal rows and vertical columns of numbers or text. Tables are useful for displaying or comparing data in a presentation. A *cell* is the intersection of a row and a column. You move from cell to cell from left to right and then down to the next row by pressing Tab. To move out of a table when you reach the last cell, press the down arrow key or click outside of the table.

PowerPoint offers three ways to create a table; these options are available whether you use the Table button in the Tables group on the Insert tab or in a content placeholder. You can use the Insert Table grid to drag across the number of rows and columns you want, the Insert Table dialog box to type in the number of columns and rows, or the Draw Table command to draw the rows and columns as you would with a pencil.

▶ **VOCABULARY**
table
cell

▶ **EXTRA FOR EXPERTS**

When you want to insert more than one row or column, select the number of rows before choosing the Insert Above or Insert Below command from the Table Tools Layout tab. PowerPoint inserts that many rows or columns.

LESSON 3   Enhancing the Presentation

You can apply various fonts, font styles, and font sizes to table text the same way you apply them to other text in a presentation. To modify the table design with an added row, you can press Tab in the last cell to create a new row and move the insertion point into it. To apply a style or other formatting to a table, you first need to select the table by clicking it.

When you insert a table, the contextual Table Tools Design and Layout tabs are displayed with options for modifying a table.

> **EXTRA FOR EXPERTS**
>
> You can use the Excel Spreadsheet command on the Table menu to insert a spreadsheet that you can use to display and calculate numerical data.

Step-by-Step PPT 3.6

The Employee Orientation *XXX*.pptx presentation from Step-by-Step PPT 3.5 should be open in the PowerPoint program window.

1. Display slide 5.
2. In the content placeholder, click the **Insert Table** button to display the Insert Table dialog box.
3. In the Number of columns box, type **3** and press **Tab**.
4. In the Number of rows box, type **3**.
5. Click the **OK** button to insert the blank table.
6. Type the following data in the table as shown, pressing **Tab** to move to the next cell and to the next row.

Coffee Drinks	Coffee Beans	Other
Cold Coffees	Signature Blends	Mugs
Hot Coffees	Decaf Blends	Brewing Equipment

7. Click to the left of the first row to select it.
8. On the Table Tools Layout tab, in the Alignment group, click the **Center** button to center the column headings.
9. Click in the bottom row of the table.
10. On the contextual Table Tools Layout tab, in the Rows & Columns group, click the **Insert Below** button to insert a new blank row at the bottom of the table.
11. Type the following data in the new row.

Herbal Teas	Seasonal Blends	Gift Baskets

12. On the contextual Table Tools Design tab, in the Table Styles group, click the **More** button to display the Table Styles gallery.
13. Scroll the gallery if necessary, and point to the **Dark Style 1 – Accent 4** option, the fifth option in the first row of the Dark category, then click to apply the style.
14. Save the presentation and leave it open for use in the next Step-by-Step.

PPT 72   UNIT IV   Microsoft PowerPoint

Inserting a Text Box

> **VOCABULARY**
> text box

A *text box* is a container for text—similar to a placeholder, but without the text prompts—that allows you to insert and position text anywhere on a slide. Text boxes can be especially useful for adding text to a slide outside of a placeholder, such as for a caption near a photo.

The Text Box button is located in the Text group on the Insert tab. Text boxes can be moved and resized; options are available for modifying borders, fills, and effects. You can apply custom formatting to text within a text box the same way you would any text.

Like a shape, a text box is considered a drawing object, so when you insert a text box, the Drawing Tools Format contextual tab is displayed on the Ribbon. This tab contains tools for modifying text boxes.

> **EXTRA FOR EXPERTS**
>
> You can insert text into a shape using a text box. Select the shape, click the Text Box button, and click inside the shape to add your text. Once you enter text in to a shape, the text attaches to the shape and moves with it.

Step-by-Step PPT 3.7

The Employee Orientation *XXX*.pptx presentation from Step-by-Step PPT 3.6 should be open in the PowerPoint program window.

1. Slide 5 should be displayed.
2. On the Insert tab, in the Text group, click the **Text Box** button.
3. Below the table, drag down and to the right to create a box similar to the one shown in **Figure PPT 3-17**.

FIGURE PPT 3–17
Drawing a text box

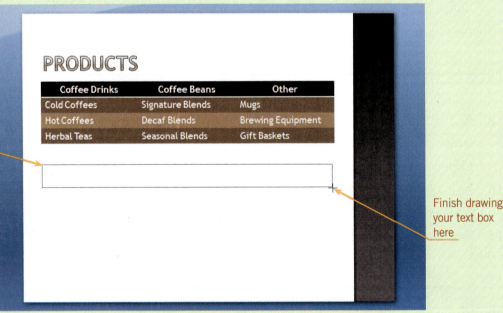

4. Release the mouse button. Notice that the text box borders change to dotted lines.
5. Type **You will learn more about each of these product categories during your individual and group training sessions**. Notice that the words wrap to the next line.

LESSON 3 Enhancing the Presentation

PPT 73

6. On the Drawing Tools Format tab, in the Shape Styles group, click the **More** button to display the Shape Styles gallery.

7. Point to several different options to see a preview of the available styles. Point to the **Colored Outline – Accent 4** option on the first row, and then click to apply the style.

8. Select the text inside the text box.

9. On the Home tab, in the Font group, click the **Italic** button *I* to italicize the text.

10. Click in blank space outside the text box to deselect it.

11. Save the presentation and leave it open for use in the next Step-by-Step.

Inserting Headers and Footers

A *header* is text that appears in the top margin of a slide, handout, or notes page. A *footer* refers to text that appears in the bottom margin. You can use headers and footers to include useful information that you would not include as text in the presentation, such as the title of a presentation, slide numbers, or the date.

To insert a footer on a slide, you use the Header & Footer button, located in the Text group on the Insert tab on the Ribbon. This button displays the Header and Footer dialog box where you can insert footers on slides and headers and footers on notes and handouts.

> **VOCABULARY**
> header
> footer

> **EXTRA FOR EXPERTS**
> You cannot add a header to a slide using the Header and Footer dialog box, but you can still add a header by inserting a text box in the top margin of the slide master and typing your text. In addition, if you want a header instead of a footer, you can drag the footer placeholder on the slide master to the top margin.

Step-by-Step PPT 3.8

The Employee Orientation *XXX*.pptx presentation from Step-by-Step PPT 3.7 should be open in the PowerPoint program window.

1. Display slide 2.

2. On the **Insert** tab on the Ribbon, in the Text group, click the **Header & Footer** button to open the Header and Footer dialog box.

3. Click the **Date and time** check box.

4. Click the **Update automatically** button, if necessary, and click the box arrow to choose a date format. Click the month, day, and year format (for example: September 28, 2012).

5. Click the **Slide number** check box.

6. Click the **Footer** check box. In the text box, type **Employee Orientation**.
7. Click the **Don't show on title slide** check box, as shown in **Figure PPT 3-18**, to prevent the footer from being displayed on the presentation's title slide.

FIGURE PPT 3-18
Header and Footer dialog box

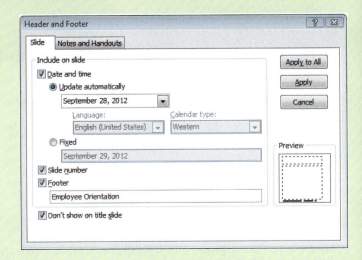

8. Click the **Apply to All** button to apply the settings to all slides and close the dialog box. Scroll through the presentation and notice the footer was applied to all slides except the title slide.
9. On the View tab, in the Presentation Views group, click the **Slide Master** button to display Slide Master view.
10. Click the slide master, the top slide in the left pane.
11. Select **Employee Orientation** in the footer.
12. On the Home tab, in the Paragraph group, click the **Align Text Left** button to change the alignment from right to left.
13. On the Slide Master tab, in the Close group, click the **Close Master View** button to close Slide Master view. Notice the alignment change was applied to the entire presentation.
14. Save the presentation and leave it open for use in the next Step-by-Step.

Inserting Special Effects

When you deliver a presentation on a computer, you can add special visual, sound, and animation effects to emphasize your points. When adding special effects, you must remember that moderation is very important. The content in your presentation should take center stage. Special effects should not draw attention to themselves.

The Animations tab on the Ribbon, shown in **Figure PPT 3-19**, contains options for previewing special effects, adding animations, and inserting transitions.

LESSON 3   Enhancing the Presentation

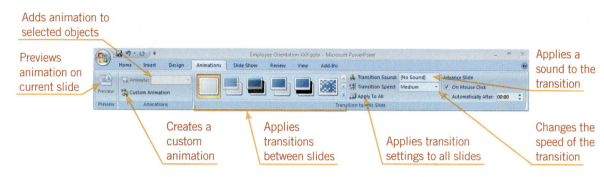

FIGURE PPT 3-19   Animations tab

After you insert an animation or transition effect, you will see an animation icon—a moving star—beside the thumbnail in Normal view and in Slide Sorter view indicating a transition or animation is in effect. Many templates have animations already applied. You can click the star icon to see a preview of the animation.

Inserting Transitions

A *transition* is an animated effect that controls how one slide is removed from the screen and the next one is presented. You can make your presentations more interesting by adding transitions. PowerPoint provides a variety of transitions that includes sound and varied speeds.

The Transitions gallery is located in the Transition to This Slide group of the Animations tab. It contains transitions in such categories as Fades and Dissolves, Wipes, Push and Cover, Stripes and Bars, and Random. Transition effects can apply to a single slide or multiple slides.

To remove a transition effect, select the slide or slides and click the No Transition style from the Transitions gallery.

Use the Preview button in the Preview group of the Animations tab to preview the effects applied to the current slide. Switch to Slide Show view to view the entire presentation, including all transitions.

> **VOCABULARY**
> transition

> **EXTRA FOR EXPERTS**
>
> In the Advance Slide section of the Transition to This Slide group, you can set slides to advance automatically after a certain amount of time instead of advancing them with a mouse click.

Step-by-Step PPT 3.9

The Employee Orientation *XXX*.pptx presentation from Step-by-Step PPT 3.8 should be open in the PowerPoint program window.

1. Display slide 1.
2. On the **Animations** tab on the Ribbon, in the Transition to This Slide group, click the **More** button to display the Transitions gallery.
3. Point to several of the transitions and see the Live Preview of each.
4. Click **Dissolve**, as shown in **Figure PPT 3-20**, to select it.

FIGURE PPT 3–20
Transitions gallery

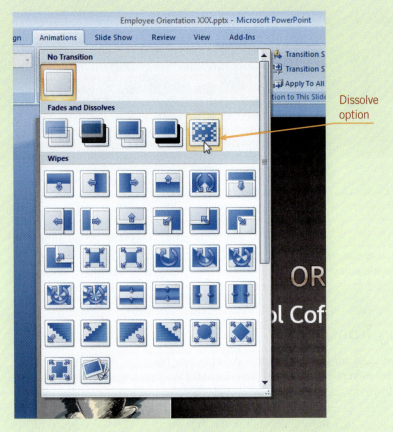

5. Click the **Transition Sound** button arrow and point to several of the sounds to hear live previews.
6. Click **Voltage** to select it.
7. Click the **Transition Speed** button arrow and then click **Fast**.
8. In the Preview group, click the **Preview** button to see and hear the transitions applied.
9. In the Transition to This Slide group, click the **Apply To All** button to apply the transition settings to all the slides in the presentation. Notice that all slides have the star animation icon beside the thumbnail in the Slide tab.
10. Switch to Slide Show view and view the presentation.
11. Save the presentation and leave it open for use in the next Step-by-Step.

Adding Animations

▶ **VOCABULARY**
animations

In addition to transitions, you can add a number of animation effects. *Animations* are visual or sound effects added to individual text, a picture, a chart, or other objects on a slide so you can control the flow of information and add interest to your presentation.

LESSON 3 Enhancing the Presentation

One common animation that you can include in a presentation is to have bulleted items appear one after the other rather than all at once. Titles or bulleted items can fly up from the bottom of the screen, box out from the center, or appear in other ways.

Animation options are located in the Animations group of the Animations tab. The Animate button arrow contains Fade, Wipe, and Fly In animations, or you can click the Custom Animation button to display the Custom Animation task pane on the right side of the screen. The task pane lets you further customize an animation by choosing an effect and then choosing start options, property or direction options, and speed effects. Click the Play button at the bottom of the task pane to preview an animation on the current slide. Click the Slide Show button to switch to Slide Show view and see the entire presentation with all the applied animations.

You can also preview your animation effects on the current slide with the Preview button in the Preview group of the Animations tab.

> **EXTRA FOR EXPERTS**
>
> Animations can begin with a mouse click, or you can use the Custom Animation task pane to plan the order of each animation and set them to run at the same time or sequentially.

Step-by-Step PPT 3.10

The Employee Orientation *XXX*.pptx presentation from Step-by-Step PPT 3.9 should be open in the PowerPoint program window.

1. Display slide 3 and select the picture.
2. On the Animations tab, in the Animations group, click the **Animate** button arrow and click **Fly In**. Notice that you get a preview of the animations applied to the current slide.
3. Select the placeholder containing the two bulleted paragraphs.
4. In the Animations group, click the **Animate** button arrow, and in the Fly In section, click **By 1st Level Paragraphs**. Notice that you get a preview of the applied animations.
5. In the Animations group, click the **Custom Animation** button to display the Custom Animation task pane.
6. Click the number **1** label on the picture in the slide to select the picture fly-in animation.
7. Click the **Change** button in the task pane. Point to **Entrance** and click **Box** from the submenu, as shown in **Figure PPT 3-21**.

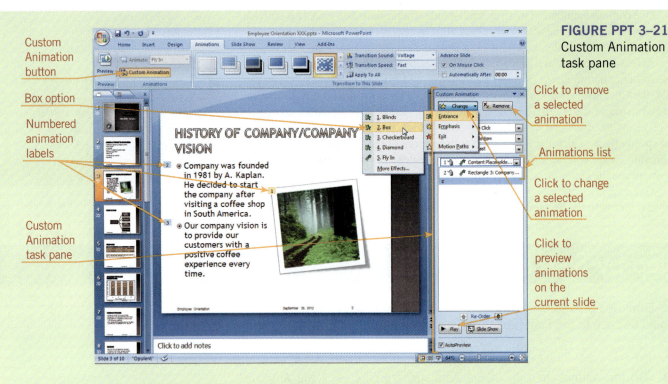

FIGURE PPT 3–21
Custom Animation task pane

8. Click the **Direction** button arrow and click **Out**.
9. Click the number **2** label beside the first paragraph of text to select the text fly-in animation.
10. Click the **Direction** button arrow and click **From Top**.
11. Click the **Play** button in the task pane to preview the animations on the current slide.
12. Click the **Close** box ✕ to close the Custom Animation task pane.
13. Save the presentation, run it from the beginning, and then close it.

SUMMARY

In this lesson, you learned:

- To insert and modify pictures, shapes, clip art, SmartArt, and charts to add visual impact to presentations.
- Text can be efficiently aligned and presented in rows and columns using tables.
- Text boxes can be used to insert text where there is no placeholder.
- Headers and footers may be used to display the title of a presentation, slide numbers, or the date.
- How to insert special effects such as transitions and animations to add interest to your presentation.

LESSON 3 Enhancing the Presentation

■ VOCABULARY REVIEW

Define the following terms:

action buttons	drawing objects	SmartArt graphic
animations	footer	table
cell	header	text box
chart	pictures	transition
clip art	selection handles	

■ REVIEW QUESTIONS

MULTIPLE CHOICE

Select the best response for the following statements.

1. The green circle at the top of a graphic is used to _____ a graphic.
   - A. insert
   - B. crop
   - C. resize
   - D. rotate

2. Small circles and squares at the sides and corners of a graphic are called _____.
   - A. SmartArt
   - B. pictures
   - C. selection handles
   - D. rotate circles

3. Enter a _____ to search for related clip art in the Clip Art task pane.
   - A. keyword
   - B. text box
   - C. picture
   - D. placeholder

4. _____ contain graphic symbols for commonly understood actions, such as going to next, previous, first, and last slides.
   - A. Charts
   - B. SmartArt graphics
   - C. Text boxes
   - D. Action buttons

5. An organization chart is an example of a _____.
   - A. table
   - B. transition
   - C. picture
   - D. SmartArt graphic

6. The data that makes up a chart is stored in a(n) _____.
   - A. table
   - B. Excel worksheet
   - C. text box
   - D. Word document

7. The _____ command combines cells so you can center a heading over an entire table.
   - A. Merge Cells
   - B. Properties
   - C. Insert Table
   - D. Group

8. A _____ is a container for text that is similar to a placeholder, but without the suggested text prompts.
   - A. chart
   - B. table
   - C. text box
   - D. transition

9. Slide numbers are usually displayed in the _____.
   A. footer
   B. Transitions gallery
   C. SmartArt graphic
   D. Animations tab

10. _____ are visual or sound effects added to individual text, a picture, a chart, or other objects so you can control the flow of information and add interest to your presentation.
    A. Transitions
    B. Animations
    C. Tables
    D. SmartArt graphics

FILL IN THE BLANK

Complete the following sentences by writing the correct word or words in the blanks provided.

1. _____ are digital photographs or images.
2. You can search for pictures, sounds, and movies in the _____ task pane.
3. SmartArt graphics are inserted with _____ text that you can replace with your own text.
4. Bar, line, and pie are types of _____.
5. A(n) _____ is a grid of horizontal rows and vertical columns of numbers or text.
6. A(n) _____ is the intersection of a row and a column.
7. Shapes and text boxes are considered _____ objects.
8. A(n) _____ is text that appears in the top margin of a slide.
9. The _____ button lets you view the animation or transition effects on the current slide.
10. A(n) _____ is an animated effect that controls how one slide is removed from the screen and the next one is presented.

■ PROJECTS

PROJECT PPT 3–1

1. Open the **Project PPT 3-1.pptx** presentation from the folder containing the data files for this lesson and save it as **Fitness Challenge2 XXX.pptx** (replace *XXX* with your initials).
2. Search for clip art with the keyword *treadmill* and insert the picture of a businessman on a treadmill with a green background (or another picture of your choice) on slide 1.
3. Position the clip art above the title on slide 1 and decrease the size proportionally by about 1/2".
4. On slide 5, insert a SmartArt graphic using the Continuous Block Process style.
5. Using the SmartArt Tools Design tab, change the SmartArt style to 3D Polished.
6. Enter and format text as shown in **Figure PPT 3-22**. (*Hint*: Enter text into the shapes of the graphic.)

FIGURE PPT 3–22
SmartArt graphic

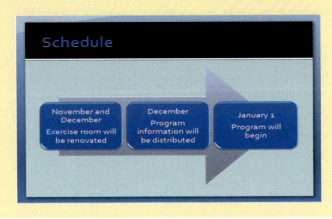

LESSON 3 Enhancing the Presentation

7. In the first shape, select *November* and *December* and change the Text Fill color to Turquoise, Accent 3 or another color of your choice.
8. Change the text color for *December* in the second shape and *January 1* in the third shape to Turquoise, Accent 3.
9. Change the layout to Continuous Arrow Process.
10. Insert the slide number and the words *Fitness Challenge* in a footer that does not display on the title slide.
11. Save and close the presentation.

ON YOUR OWN

Open the **Fitness Challenge2 XXX.pptx** presentation and add another SmartArt graphic of your choice using the bulleted list on slide 2. (*Hint*: Use the Convert to SmartArt Graphic command in the Paragraph group on the Home tab.)

PROJECT PPT 3–2

1. Open the **Project PPT 3-2.pptx** presentation from the folder containing the data files for this lesson and save it as **Tracking Graduates2** *XXX*.**pptx** (replace *XXX* with your initials).
2. Insert a text box below the clip art on the first slide. Type **Rams Alumni** and change the font to Arial Black 20 point.
3. Center the text in the text box and position it centered under the graphic.
4. On slide 5, insert a pie chart using the following data.

	Graduates
Attending Graduate School	36
Working	40
Searching for Work	14
Unable to locate	10

5. Change the chart layout to Layout 6.
6. Change the chart type to Pie in 3D.
7. Save and close the presentation.

PROJECT PPT 3–3

1. Open the **Project PPT 3-3.pptx** presentation from the folder containing the data files for this lesson and save it as **Course Rules2** *XXX*.**pptx** (replace *XXX* with your initials).
2. On slide 4, insert a table in the content placeholder using the following data:

Grading Scale	
A	90–100
B	80–89
C	70–79
D	65–69
F	0–64

3. Merge the two cells on the first row and center the title.
4. Resize the table. Change the height to 2.4" and the width to 2.5".
5. Apply the Themed Style 2 - Accent 1 table style.
6. Save and close the presentation.

ON YOUR OWN

Open **Course Rules2** *XXX*.**pptx**. Remove all the transitions applied to the presentation. Apply new transitions and add an animation to the chart. Save and close the presentation.

PROJECT PPT 3–4

1. Open the **Project PPT 3-4.pptx** presentation from the folder containing the data files for this lesson and save it as **Nature Portfolio2** *XXX***.pptx** (replace *XXX* with your initials).
2. Apply the Fade Through Black transition to all slides.
3. Apply the Camera transition sound to all slides.
4. Change the transition speed to medium on all slides.
5. On slide 1, select the photo and add a custom Blinds entrance effect using vertical direction.
6. Select the LostArt Photos placeholder and add a fly-in animation entrance effect.
7. View the entire presentation in Slide Show view.
8. Save and close the presentation.

ON YOUR OWN

Open **Nature Portfolio2** *XXX***.pptx**. Add a custom entrance effect for the text on slides 2, 3, 4, and 5. Save and close the presentation.

WEB PROJECT

PROJECT PPT 3–5

Create a five-slide presentation about your favorite state (or country). Use the Web to research information such as the date it became a state, the state nickname, state flower, bird, song, motto, and other interesting facts. Use the Clip art on Office Online link at the bottom of the Clip Art task pane to search Microsoft Office Online for clip art, pictures, or other media to include in your presentation. Include a footer and at least one chart, table, or SmartArt graphic. Apply transitions and animations where appropriate. Include an action button that links to a Web site about your state.

 TEAMWORK PROJECT

PROJECT PPT 3–6

With a partner, choose any presentation you have worked with in the PowerPoint unit or a presentation from the Internet and critique it. Divide responsibilities and rehearse your presentation. Deliver the slide show to the class as a team and point out elements you liked about the slide show as well as areas for improvement. Remember what you have learned about creating an effective presentation. Comment on the design as well as the use of graphics, transitions, and animations. Be prepared to answer questions from the audience.

 CRITICAL THINKING

ACTIVITY PPT 3–1

Open **Activity PPT 3-1.pptx** from the folder containing the data files for this lesson. Save it with a meaningful name. Insert graphics, transitions, and animations to make the presentation more interesting. Be prepared to deliver your presentation to the class, explaining the changes you made and why you think they improved the presentation.

ACTIVITY PPT 3–2

In this lesson, you learned how to insert a picture from a file in the Sample Pictures folder. Did you know you can also insert music in the same way? Open a blank presentation and find the Sound from File button and insert a sound from a file in the Sample Music folder and have it start either automatically or when clicked. Experiment with the Sound Tools Options contextual tab. What is looping? In what situations might it be useful to play music on a presentation? How do you remove a sound file from a presentation?

UNIT IV REVIEW
PowerPoint

REVIEW QUESTIONS

MULTIPLE CHOICE

Select the best response for the following statements.

1. A(n) _____ is a single image composed of text, graphics, or other content.
   - A. header
   - B. footer
   - C. slide
   - D. I-beam

2. Which feature automatically saves your presentation at regular intervals so that you can recover at least some of your work in case of a power outage or other unexpected shutdown?
   - A. Quick Access Toolbar
   - B. Print Preview
   - C. AutoRecover
   - D. word wrap

3. When you click the _____ button, the software prompts you to save your work if you made any changes since you last saved.
   - A. Margins
   - B. Save
   - C. Help
   - D. Close

4. The _____ button allows you to copy the formatting characteristics of text and then apply the same formatting to other parts of the document.
   - A. Paste
   - B. Copy
   - C. Redo
   - D. Format Painter

5. _____ is the vertical distance between lines of text in a paragraph.
   - A. Line spacing
   - B. Indentation
   - C. Alignment
   - D. Point size

6. _____ view displays thumbnail versions of all slides in a presentation.
   - A. Notes Page
   - B. Slide Sorter
   - C. Slide Show
   - D. Outline

PPT 83

UNIT IV REVIEW   Microsoft PowerPoint

7. _____ are sets of formatting choices that include colors, fonts, effects, and backgrounds that were predesigned to work well together.
   A. Paragraphs
   B. Templates
   C. Themes
   D. Placeholders

8. You can insert clip art using a _____.
   A. menu
   B. dialog box
   C. window
   D. task pane

9. A _____ allows you to insert and position text anywhere on a slide.
   A. text box
   B. theme
   C. template
   D. footer

10. Fades, dissolves, and wipes are types of _____.
    A. charts
    B. clip art
    C. transitions
    D. SmartArt

FILL IN THE BLANK

Complete the following sentences by writing the correct word or words in the blanks provided.

1. The _____ is the blinking vertical bar that signals where any text you type will appear.
2. The _____ button rearranges the placeholders on the slide, and the text adjusts to the new arrangement.
3. Click the _____ button to access the New command.
4. PowerPoint flags words that might be misspelled with a wavy _____ underline.
5. A(n) _____ is a sample presentation that provides a pattern or model that you can follow to create your own presentations.
6. You can use the _____ command to search for a specific word or phrase in a presentation.
7. Column and line are types of _____.
8. _____ are digital photographs or images.
9. Slide numbers are often displayed in the _____.
10. _____ are special action effects added to individual text (bullet points) or other objects such as images.

■ PROJECTS

PROJECT PPT 1

1. Create a new presentation using the **Contemporary Photo Album** from the Installed Templates category in the New Presentation dialog box. Save it as **Summer Album *XXX*.pptx** (replace *XXX* with your initials).
2. On slide 1, replace the title Contemporary Photo Album with **Summer Album**.
3. Replace the sideways placeholder text with **2012**.
4. Delete the flower photo and insert the **Garden** photo (or another photo of your choice) from the Sample Pictures folder.
5. Delete the photo on slide 2 and insert the **Dock** photo from the Sample Pictures folder (or another photo of your choice). Type **Dock** to replace the text in the placeholder.
6. On slide 3, delete the photos and change the slide layout to **2-Up Landscape with Captions**.

UNIT IV REVIEW   Microsoft PowerPoint

7. Insert the Humpback Whale photo (or another photo of your choice) from the Sample Pictures folder in the left placeholder, and type **Humpback Whale** in the placeholder below the picture.
8. Insert the Green Sea Turtle picture (or another photo of your choice) in the right placeholder and type **Green Sea Turtle** in the placeholder below it.
9. On slide 4, change the slide layout to Square with Caption.
10. Delete the photo and insert the Toco Toucan picture (or another photo of your choice) from the Sample Pictures folder. Type **Toucan** in the placeholder below it.
11. Delete slides 5 and 6.
12. Add the Metal Frame picture style to the pictures on slides 2, 3, and 4.
13. Add a camera transition sound to all the slides in the presentation.
14. View the presentation in Slide Show view, then save and it and leave it open.

PROJECT PPT 2

The presentation Summer Album *XXX*.pptx from Project 1 should be open in the PowerPoint program window.

1. Save the document as **Summer Album 2 *XXX*.pptx** (replace *XXX* with your initials).
2. On slide 1, change the size of the *2012* text to 80 points and the character spacing to Very Loose.
3. Change the theme to Origin.
4. Change the theme colors to Flow.
5. In Slide Master view, on the slide master, format the Master text styles (the first bulleted point on the slide master) to 40 point and bold; change the font color to Light Blue.
6. Insert a new slide with a blank layout after slide 4.
7. In the center of the slide, insert a text box and type the words **The End**.
8. Copy the text formatting from the word *Toucan* on slide 4 and apply it to the words *The End* on slide 5.
9. Center the text within the placeholder, and position the placeholder centered vertically and horizontally on the slide.
10. Preview the presentation before printing 6-slides-per-page handouts.
11. Save and close the presentation.

ON YOUR OWN

Open the **Summer Album 2 *XXX*.pptx** file. Add a new background style to each of the slides in the presentation. Save and close the presentation.

PROJECT PPT 3

1. Open the file **Project PPT 3.pptx** from the folder containing your data files for this lesson and save it as **Ways to Go Green *XXX*.pptx** (replace *XXX* with your initials).
2. Spell check the presentation and correct any misspellings.
3. Start at the beginning of the presentation and find the word *power* and replace it with the word *energy* when appropriate. (*Hint*: Replace two of the three occurrences.)
4. In Slide Sorter view, move slide 6 into the correct position before slide 4.
5. Switch to Normal view and insert a Title and Content layout slide after slide 8.
6. In the top placeholder, type **Bring your own reusable bags when shopping**.
7. Type **Eight** in the title placeholder at the bottom of the screen.
8. On slide 2, insert the following speaker note: **Mention cell phone chargers**.
9. Change the line spacing in the paragraph in the text placeholder to 1.0 and left-align the text.

10. Change the number format to bullets and add the following bulleted item:

    Plug computer and television equipment into power strips that you can turn off.
11. Change the font color of the word *Unplug* to white.
12. On slide 3, select the word *Two*. Copy the formatting and apply it to the word *One* on slide 2.
13. On slide 5, cut the speaker note and paste it in the text placeholder after the last sentence.
14. Save the presentation and leave it open for use in the next project.

PROJECT PPT 4

The Ways to Go Green *XXX*.pptx presentation from Project 3 should be open in the PowerPoint program window.

1. Save the presentation as **Ways to Go Green 2 *XXX*.pptx** (replace *XXX* with your initials).
2. On slide 8, insert the Basic Process SmartArt graphic.
3. Type ½ **teaspoon olive oil** in the first shape, ¼ **cup vinegar** in the second shape, and **Furniture polish** in the third shape.
4. Apply the Subtle Effect – Accent 5 shape style to the third shape.
5. On slide 9, insert a Clustered Column chart using the following data:

    Billions of Plastic Bags Consumed per Year

US	100
Australia	6.9
Ireland	1.2
Taiwan	20

6. Change the chart type to Clustered Cylinder and apply Layout 4 and chart style 31.
7. On slide 2, insert a table with the following data:

Appliance	Stand-by energy costs per year
TV	$10
VCR	$9
Computer in 'sleep' mode	$41

8. Apply the Themed Style 1-Accent 5 table style. (Adjust the size and/or position of the table to fit attractively on the page.)
9. On slide 7, resize the clip art to approximately 2 inches square and position it in the lower-right corner of the slide.
10. Apply the Fade animation to the clip art on slide 7 and the table on slide 2.
11. Apply the Fade One by One animation to the SmartArt graphic on slide 8.
12. Apply the Fade By Category animation to the chart on slide 9.
13. Apply the Fade Through Black, medium speed transition to all slides.
14. View the presentation in Slide Show view.
15. Save and close the presentation.

UNIT IV REVIEW   Microsoft PowerPoint   PPT 87

ON YOUR OWN

Open the **Ways to Go Green 2 *XXX*.pptx** file. Add a footer displaying the document title. Do not display it on the title page. Switch to Slide Master view and apply formatting options so that the footer is displayed attractively in the presentation. Save and close the presentation.

ON YOUR OWN

Open the **Ways to Go Green 2 *XXX*.pptx file**. Insert an appropriate piece of clip art in one of the slides that doesn't contain a graphic. Change its color, size, or style to be displayed attractively in the presentation. Save and close the presentation.

WEB PROJECT

Visit a job search Web site and conduct a search for jobs that require the use of Microsoft Office PowerPoint 2007. What job titles require experience with PowerPoint? What level of experience is required? What are the other job requirements? What are the salary ranges? Create a presentation that identifies five types of jobs that require experience with PowerPoint and answer these questions. Be prepared to deliver your presentation to the class.

TEAMWORK PROJECT

With a partner, research the admission requirements and procedures at your favorite college or university. Create a presentation that would instruct high school students on how to apply for admission. Also include some background information on the school, such as its location, date it was founded, and number of students enrolled. Use at least one chart, table, or SmartArt graphic in your presentation and be sure to include relevant clip art or pictures. Use transitions and animations. Collaborate on the content and design and be prepared to deliver the presentation to the class.

CRITICAL THINKING

ACTIVITY PPT 1

With your instructor's permission, use the More Themes on Microsoft Office Online link in the Themes gallery to access the Microsoft Web site and explore the additional themes available for download. What is the process for downloading themes? With permission, download a theme and apply it to a new blank presentation. Prepare two or three slides that describe what type of audience the theme might be appropriate for and why.

ACTIVITY PPT 2

Create a new presentation using the Quiz Show presentation from the Installed Templates category in the New Presentation dialog box. Analyze the presentation by viewing it in Slide Show view and identifying the transitions and animations applied. Replace three of the questions and answers with new ones related to PowerPoint or another Microsoft Office 2007 program. Add at least two new slides with the question format of your choice, and write a question and answer for each so that you have at least five questions in the presentation. Delete the unnecessary slides, and be prepared to deliver your presentation to the class.

PORTFOLIO CHECKLIST

_____	Lesson 1	Health Challenge *XXX*.pptx
		Office Space *XXX*.pptx
		Tracking Graduates *XXX*.pptx
_____	Lesson 2	Nature Portfolio *XXX*.pptx
		Job Search *XXX*.pptx
		Course Rules *XXX*.pptx
_____	Lesson 3	Employee Orientation *XXX*.pptx
		Fitness Challenge 2 *XXX*.pptx
_____	Unit Review	Ways to Go Green 2 *XXX*.pptx

UNIT V

MICROSOFT ACCESS

⏱ **Estimated Time for Unit:**
5 hours

LESSON 1   **2.5 HRS.**
Understanding Access Fundamentals

LESSON 2   **2.5 HRS.**
Creating Forms, Reports, and Queries

LESSON 1

Understanding Access Fundamentals

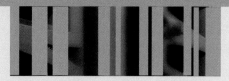

⏱ Estimated Time: 2.5 hours

■ OBJECTIVES

Upon completion of this lesson, you should be able to:

- Understand database concepts.
- Recognize the importance of planning and designing a database.
- Identify the elements of the Access program window.
- Start Access and create a new database.
- Create a table in Datasheet view.
- Open an existing database.
- Open tables and navigate records.
- Modify field properties.

■ DATA FILES

To complete this lesson, you will need these data files:

Camp Blue Zephyr.accdb

Contacts.accdb

Vehicle Records.accdb

Note: Because Access automatically saves a file as changes are made to it, you will not need to rename the data files in this lesson. The data files in this lesson have been given descriptive file names.

■ VOCABULARY

database

database management system (DBMS)

database object

datasheet

datasheet selector

data type

field

field name

field properties

field selector

field value

foreign key

key value

primary key

record

record selector

relational database

table

...

UNIT V Microsoft Access

VOCABULARY
database
database management system (DBMS)
table
record
field
datasheet
field name
field value

Introduction

Microsoft Access 2007 is the database program included in the Microsoft Office 2007 suite of software. A *database* is used to collect and organize information. Any type of list you create to collect information can be considered a database, even a simple list of phone numbers. When you collect more information than can be easily managed on paper, it is helpful to transfer it to a computerized *database management system (DBMS)* which is software designed to store, organize, and manage large amounts of data. This allows you to keep accurate records and retrieve records quickly.

Although all of the Office programs are designed to work alike using the same basic interface, there are some aspects of Access that are unique. In other Office programs, you can have more than one file open at a time. But in Access, you can only have one database open. You must close that database before opening another one. Another difference is that you do not need to use the Save command when you enter or edit information because Access automatically saves the data. You will also notice when you first open a database that the Access program window looks a little different than other Office programs you have used. One similarity to other Office programs is that the various tools for performing database tasks in Access are organized on the Ribbon tabs.

Using Access, you can create database files that are efficient, well-organized, and that can help you manage information effectively. Before you discover the power of Access to compile, track, report, and manage related information, you need to learn about the parts of a database and understand basic database concepts. In this lesson, you will learn the importance of planning and designing a database before creating one, as well as techniques for performing fundamental database skills using Access.

Understanding Database Concepts

Storing information in a database can be compared to using a filing cabinet to collect and organize information. Within the filing cabinet are folders that each contains a different group of related information. These folders are similar to tables in a database. *Tables* are the place in a database where all the data is stored. A database can contain many tables, just as a filing cabinet can contain many folders. Each table in a database stores data related to a different category, such as students or classes. Within a folder in filing cabinets are individual pieces of paper, which could correspond to the records in a database table. A *record* is all of the related information about a particular item in the table. For example, all the information about one specific student, such as the student's name, grade level, and phone number would be in one record. A category that stores a single characteristic of information in a table—like name, grade level, or phone number—is called a *field*.

By default, tables in a database are displayed in a format called a *datasheet*, which has columns and rows similar to a worksheet. Each field in a datasheet is displayed as a column and is identified by its *field name* at the top. Each piece of information in a field is called a *field value*. Each record in a datasheet is displayed as a row and contains the field values that belong to that particular item. **Figure AC 1–1** shows the parts of a datasheet.

LESSON 1 Understanding Access Fundamentals

FIGURE AC 1–1 Parts of a datasheet

Every table in a database will have a primary key. The ***primary key*** is the field that uniquely identifies each record. Each record in the database must have a ***key value***, shown in **Figure AC 1–1**, which is a value in the primary key field that makes the record unique. The key value cannot be left blank. By default, Access creates an ID field in every table that can serve as the primary key. Each time you enter a new record, Access assigns a unique number in the ID field as the key value. The primary key is important because it helps set up relationships between tables and tells Access how to associate the data with other tables in the database. When a primary key is included in another table, it is called a ***foreign key*** in the second table.

Access is considered a ***relational database*** because all of the data is stored in separate tables and then connected by establishing relationships between the tables. This is achieved by placing a common field in related tables. For example, you could include a Faculty ID field as the primary key in a Faculty table and also include a Faculty field in a Classes table to relate the two tables. Common fields are not required to have the same name. In Access, you can display the relationships between tables in a database to see how they are connected, as shown in **Figure AC 1–2**.

> **VOCABULARY**
> primary key
> key value
> foreign key
> relational database
> database object

> **EXTRA FOR EXPERTS**
> To create, edit, or delete table relationships, you can display the Relationship window by clicking the Relationships button in the Show/Hide group on the Database Tools tab.

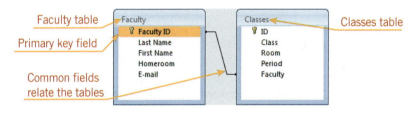

FIGURE AC 1–2 Related tables

There are many advantages to using an electronic filing system like a database, instead of a manual system like filing cabinets. There is more space to store records, and it is much easier to retrieve the records that you need. Plus, a database offers more flexibility in the ways you can work with the information. In addition to the tables that store the information, a database contains other objects that allow you to interact with the data. The common ***database objects*** are described in **Table AC 1–1**. In this lesson, you will focus on tables and in the next lesson you will learn more about forms, reports, and queries.

TABLE AC 1-1 Common database objects

OBJECT	ICON	DESCRIPTION
Table		Stores information related to a specific subject; made up of a collection of records and fields
Form		Can be used to enter, edit, maintain, and view records; similar in appearance to a paper form
Report		Summarizes and presents information from one or more tables in an easily readable format that can be printed
Query		Asks a question about the data stored in a database, and then searches for and retrieves specific database information in answer to the question; can also perform other tasks with the data such as adding, updating, or deleting

Planning and Designing a Database

Before you create a new database, it is essential to spend time planning it. You should decide what the purpose of the database is and what you want it to accomplish. You will also need to determine what types of information will be included, so it will be helpful if you can gather together all this information and organize it into categories. Each category will then become a table in the database. For example, if you are planning to create a database for a school administration office, you would need to include tables with information about students, faculty, and classes.

After you have decided what tables should be included in the database, you need to decide what information will be contained in each table. For example, a table of classes might include the name of the class, the days it meets, the times it meets, the room number, the teacher, and a class description. Each of these pieces of information would be a field in the table. When creating tables in a database, keep in mind how the information in each table might be linked together using common fields.

A great starting point when planning a database is to sketch it out on paper, being sure to identify the fields you want to include, and the types of data that each field will contain. This will help you determine the basic format of the database, figure out possible ways to organize the data, and determine how the different types of information are related. The more thorough and accurate you can be when designing the database, the fewer adjustments you will have to make later.

There are established standards and guidelines to help guide you in the process of creating a database. You can always use Access Help if you need assistance designing your database and structuring your tables correctly.

Exploring the Access Program Window

When you create or open an Access database, it is displayed in the Access program window, shown in **Figure AC 1–3**. You will notice that the Access program window is similar to the program windows in other Office programs in some ways, like the Ribbon and view buttons, but also has some differences.

LESSON 1 Understanding Access Fundamentals

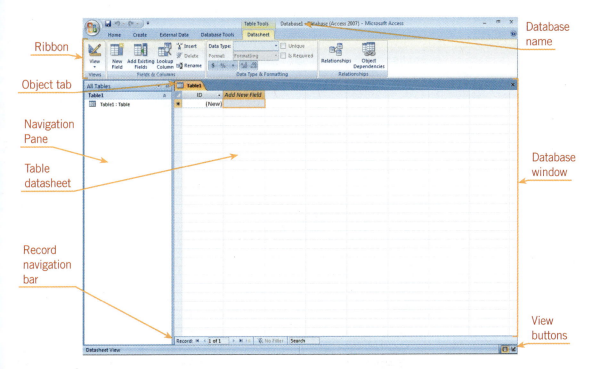

FIGURE AC 1–3 Access program window

The Navigation Pane on the left lists all of the objects in the database. When an object is open, it is displayed in the database window to the right of the Navigation Pane. In this lesson, you will be working in Datasheet view. The other views available depend on which type of database object you are working with, and each view allows you to perform different tasks related to the object. For example, if you display a table in Design view, you can make changes to the design of the table.

Starting Access and Creating a New Database

To begin using Access, you first need to start the program. You can do this by clicking the Start button on the Windows taskbar, and then clicking the program name on the All Programs menu, or by double-clicking an Access program icon on the desktop. When you start Access, the Getting Started with Microsoft Office Access window is displayed, as shown in **Figure AC 1–4**, where you have the option to create a new database using a template, create a new blank database, or open a recently used database. You can also access the resources on Microsoft Office Online from this window.

UNIT V Microsoft Access

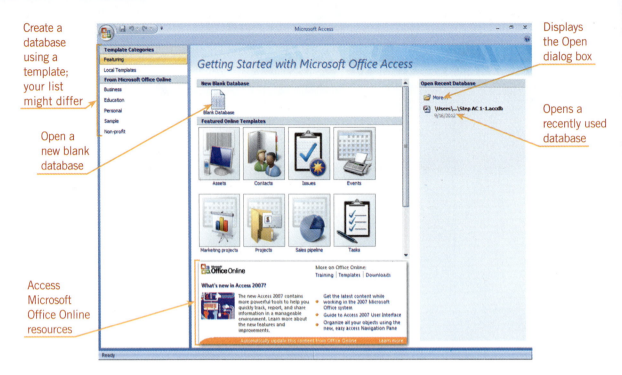

FIGURE AC 1–4 Getting Started with Microsoft Office Access window

> **EXTRA FOR EXPERTS**
>
> If you do not want to create a database from scratch, you can choose from one of the many templates available. Access templates are predesigned databases—such as a database for event management, inventory, or charitable contributions—that can save you time. You can access installed and online templates from the middle pane of the Getting Started with Microsoft Office Access window.

You can display the Getting Started with Microsoft Office Access window at any time by clicking the New command on the Office Button menu. To create a new blank database, you click the Blank Database icon in the center pane to display the Blank Database pane on the right. Access suggests a name for the new database in the File Name text box—you can accept it or replace it with your own file name. The location where the database will be saved is shown beneath the File Name text box. If you want to select a new location, you can click the folder icon next to the File Name text box to display the File New Database dialog box and browse for another location to store your database. When you click the Create button in the Blank Database pane, a new blank database is created.

Step-by-Step AC 1.1

1. Click the **Start** button on the Windows taskbar. The Start menu opens.
2. Point to **All Programs**. A list of programs and program folders opens.
3. Click the **Microsoft Office** program folder. A list of Microsoft Office programs opens.
4. Click **Microsoft Office Access 2007**. Access 2007 starts and the Getting Started with Microsoft Office Access window is displayed.

LESSON 1 Understanding Access Fundamentals

5. In the center pane, click the **Blank Database** icon to display the Blank Database pane on the right, as shown in **Figure AC 1–5**.

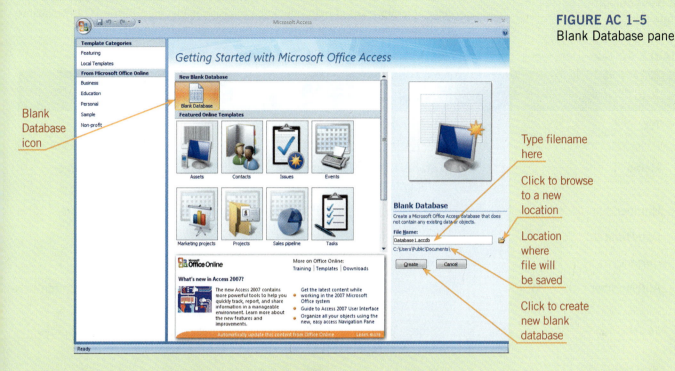

FIGURE AC 1–5
Blank Database pane

6. In the File Name text box, select the suggested name for the database and type **Oakville Hills School.accdb**.

7. Click the **Browse for a location to put your database** icon to open the File New Database dialog box, navigate to the location where you save your data files, and then click the **OK** button.

8. Click the **Create** button to create a new blank database. The database opens in the Access program window.

9. Leave the database open for use in the next Step-by-Step.

Creating a Table in Datasheet View

When you create a new database, a new table named Table1 is automatically created for you and displayed in Datasheet view, where you can then start to create fields for the table and enter data. You can also create a new, blank table in Datasheet view at any time by clicking the Table button in the Tables group on the Create tab.

Because every table needs a primary key, when you create a new table, Access creates a field named ID by default and sets it as the primary key. The ID field is also assigned the AutoNumber data type, which means Access will automatically enter a unique value each time you enter a record. You can choose to use the default ID field or change it to suit the design of your database. For example, you could change the primary key to a different field. Or, you could rename the ID field and change the data type so you can type your own values instead of letting Access automatically assign them. In that case, you would need to set the field property to make it required

> **EXTRA FOR EXPERTS**
>
> You can also use buttons in the Tables group on the Create tab to create a table in Design view, or to create a table using a table template with predefined fields. Another way to create a table is to import or link to external data by clicking a data source in the Import group on the External Data tab and then following the instructions in the dialog box that is displayed.

VOCABULARY
data type

for the field values to be unique. You will learn more about field properties later in this lesson.

In Datasheet view, the easiest way to create a field is to simply enter data in the Add New Field column in the table. Each field in a table has a ***data type*** that determines the types of field values you can enter in that field. **Table AC 1–2** explains the 10 different data types available in Access and their purpose.

TABLE AC 1–2 Data types

DATA TYPE	PURPOSE
Text	Stores text and/or numbers up to 255 characters; most common data type
Memo	Stores text and/or numbers up to 65,535 characters; used for larger amounts of text
Number	Stores numeric data that can be used in mathematical calculations
Date/Time	Stores dates and/or times
Currency	Stores monetary data displayed with dollar sign
AutoNumber	Unique value that Access assigns when you create a new record; often used as primary key field
Yes/No	Stores True/False, Yes/No, or On/Off values; used when only two values can be chosen
OLE Object	Stores objects from Office- and Windows-based programs
Hyperlink	Stores links such as Web addresses
Attachment	Stores any supported file type, such as images, documents, and charts

Access will automatically assign a data type based on the values that you enter in a field, but you can always change it by clicking the Data Type list arrow in the Data Type & Formatting group on the Table Tools Datasheet tab. You can also change the field name by clicking the Rename button in the Fields & Columns group on the Table Tools Datasheet tab and then typing a new field name. Other buttons you can use to create and modify fields are located in the Fields & Columns and Data Type & Formatting groups on the Datasheet tab on the Ribbon, shown in **Figure AC 1–6**.

FIGURE AC 1–6 Table Tools Datasheet tab

LESSON 1   Understanding Access Fundamentals

Entering Records

As you create a database, you will not only need to enter records into tables, but also keep the database up to date by editing and deleting data as well. Access tables are different from Excel worksheets because they exist just to hold the data. You do not format them or change the structure by inserting blank rows or columns. When you want to enter new data, you simply enter it in the last row or column. When you enter data in a new record or field, Access then automatically adds another new row or column after the one where you are typing.

To add a new record to a table, simply click a field in the (New) blank record, indicated by an asterisk in the box to the left of the row called the *record selector*, and type the information. Then press the Enter key or the Tab key to move to the next field and continue entering data until the record is complete. Access automatically saves the information as you enter it. If the column is not wide enough to display the data as you type, simply click the right border of the field name and drag to widen it.

▶ **VOCABULARY**
record selector

Step-by-Step AC 1.2

The Oakville Hills School.accdb database from Step-by-Step AC 1.1 should be open in the Access program window.

1. Click the field name of the default primary field, **ID**. On the Table Tools Datasheet Tab, in the Fields & Columns group, click **Rename** to select the field header name for editing.

2. Type **Student ID** and press **Enter** to rename the field.

3. On the Table Tools Datasheet Tab, in the Data Type & Formatting group, click the **Data Type** list arrow and then click **Number** to change the data type of the field.

4. On the Table Tools Datasheet Tab, in the Data Type & Formatting group, click the **Unique** check box to check this box, if necessary, to require values entered in this field to be unique.

5. Double-click the **Add New Field** field name, type **Last Name**, and then press **Enter** to create a new field. The insertion point moves to the field header for the next field in the database.

6. Type **First Name** and then press **Enter** to create a new field and select the next field header.

7. Type **Grade** and then press **Enter** to create a new field.

8. Click in the Student ID field of the (New) blank record and type **2618**.

9. Press **Tab** to enter the data and move to the next field in the record, the Last Name field. Notice that a pencil symbol is displayed in the record selector of the record you are creating and that the asterisk in the record selector, indicating a new record ready for data, moves to the next row when you begin to type, as shown in **Figure AC 1–7**.

FIGURE AC 1–7
Entering records

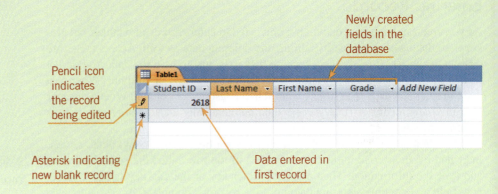

10. In the Last Name field of the first record, type **Ansman-Wolfe**, and then press **Tab** to enter the data. Because the data you entered in this field is all text, Access assigns the Text data type in the Data Type list box in the Data Type & Formatting Group on the Table Tools Datasheet tab.

11. Click the right border of the Last Name field header and drag to the right to widen the column to display all the data, as shown in **Figure AC 1–8**.

FIGURE AC 1–8
Widening a field in Datasheet view

12. Click in the First Name field of the first record, type **Pamela**, and then press **Tab** to enter the data.

13. Click in the Grade field of the first record, type **11**, and then press **Tab** to enter the data. Because the data you entered in this field is a number, Access assigns the Number data type to the field, as shown in the Data Type list box in the Data Type & Formatting Group on the Table Tools Datasheet tab.

14. Continue entering the rest of the data into the table, as shown in **Figure AC 1–9**.

FIGURE AC 1–9
Entering data in a table

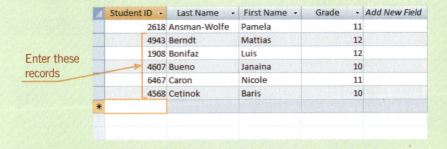

15. Leave the database open for use in the next Step-by-Step.

LESSON 1   Understanding Access Fundamentals

Saving and Closing a Table and Closing a Database

After you have created a table, you can save it by clicking the Save button on the Quick Access Toolbar to display the Save As dialog box, typing a table name, and clicking the OK button. Changes to data in the table are saved automatically as you enter it, but before you close the table any changes to the table design need to be saved by clicking the Save button on the Quick Access Toolbar.

Before closing a database, all database objects must be saved and closed. You can close a database object by clicking its Close button. If you have not saved an object in the database, you will be prompted to save it before closing. To close a database, you can click the Office Button and then click Close Database. The Getting Started with Microsoft Office Access window is then displayed again. To close Access, you click the Close button on the title bar.

Step-by-Step AC 1.3

The Oakville Hills School.accdb database from Step-by-Step AC 1.2 should be open in the Access program window.

1. Click the **Save** button on the Quick Access Toolbar to display the Save As dialog box.

2. Type **Students** in the Table Name box, and then click the **OK** button to save the table. Notice the new table name is now displayed on the object tab, as shown in **Figure AC 1–10**. Notice the records are rearranged so that the values in the Student ID field are in ascending numeric order.

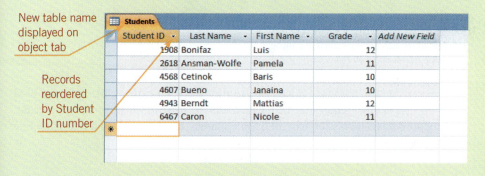

FIGURE AC 1–10
Saving a table

3. Click the **Close 'Students'** button to close the Students table.

4. Click the **Office** button and then click **Close Database**. The database closes and the Getting Started with Microsoft Office Access window is displayed.

5. Leave Access open for use in the next Step-by-Step.

Opening an Existing Database

When the Getting Started with Microsoft Office Access window is displayed, a list of recently opened databases is displayed in the Open Recent Database pane on the right. If an existing database that you want to use is not listed, you can click the More link to display the Open dialog box shown in **Figure AC 1–11**, and then locate and open the database file. You can also click the Open command on the Office Button menu, add an Open command to your Quick Access Toolbar, or use the keyboard shortcut Ctrl+O.

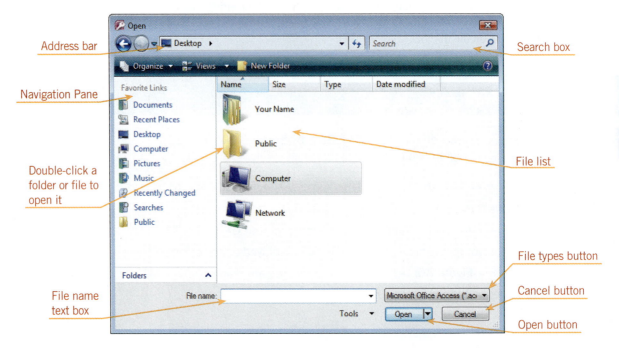

FIGURE AC 1–11   Open dialog box

EXTRA FOR EXPERTS

By default, the names of the most recent files you opened in Access will be listed in the Recent Documents list on the Office Button menu. You can click a file in the list to open it. You can customize the number of files displayed in the list using the Advanced section of the Access Options dialog box.

You can use the Open dialog box to find and open existing files on your hard drive, CD, or other removable media; on a network drive to which you are connected; on your organization's intranet; or on the Internet. Double-clicking a file in the File list will open the file.

The following are parts of the Open dialog box:

- The Navigation Pane displays favorite links to folders that contain databases. You can view a folder's contents or open the folder from the Navigation Pane.
- The Address bar at the top of the dialog box shows the folder path.
- The Search box allows you to find a file by name, file type, or location.
- The File type button lists other file types you can choose to open.
- The Open button opens the database and, because Access is designed so that multiple users can work on the same database, the Open button list arrow provides options for sharing access with others.
- The Cancel button closes the dialog box without opening a file.

LESSON 1 Understanding Access Fundamentals

When you open an existing database, a security warning is displayed in the Message Bar below the Ribbon, as shown in **Figure AC 1–12**, if Access does not recognize the source as being trustworthy. All the files provided for this book are safe to work with, so you can click the Options button to display the Microsoft Office Security Options dialog box and then choose to enable the content.

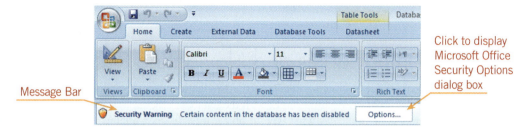

FIGURE AC 1–12 Message Bar warning when opening a database

Step-by-Step AC 1.4

1. Click the **Office** button on the Ribbon and then click **Open** to display the Open dialog box.

2. Navigate to the folder containing the data files for this lesson. Double-click the file named **Camp Blue Zephyr.accdb** in the File list. The database opens in the Access program window, as shown in **Figure AC 1–13**.

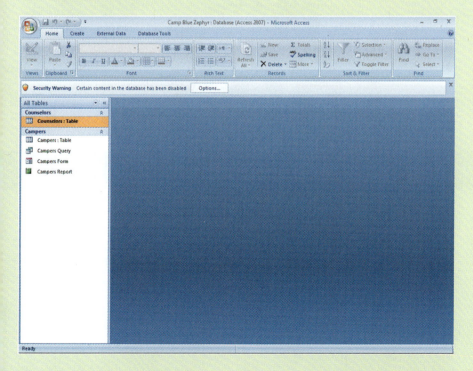

FIGURE AC 1–13
Opening an existing database

3. On the Message Bar, click the **Options** button to open the Microsoft Office Security Options dialog box.

4. Click the **Enable this content** option button and then click the **OK** button to remove the Message Bar warning and enable the content of the database.

5. Leave the database open for use in the next Step-by-Step.

Opening Tables and Navigating Records

When you open or create a database, the Navigation Pane is displayed on the left side of the program window and lists all the database objects. The icon to the left of the object name indicates what type of object it is. To open a table, or any database object, you can double-click it in the Navigation Pane. Multiple database objects can be open at the same time. You move between the open objects by clicking the tab with the object name at the top of the program window to display it.

In Datasheet view, you can navigate among the records in a table using the navigation buttons on the record navigation bar or using the keyboard. To use the navigation buttons, shown in **Figure AC 1–14**, click a button to move to the record you want—First, Previous, Next, Last, or New (blank). You can also type the number of the record in the Current Record text box and press the Enter key to move to a record, or you can type data in the Search text box to move to the next record in the table that matches the search data.

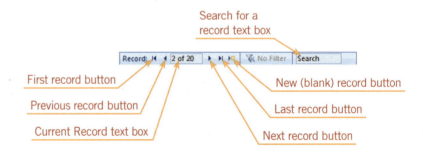

FIGURE AC 1–14 Record navigation bar

Step-by-Step AC 1.5

The Camp Blue Zephyr.accdb database from Step-by-Step AC 1.4 should be open in the Access program window.

1. In the Navigation Pane, double-click the **Counselors: Table** database object to open the table in the database window, as shown in **Figure AC 1–15**.

LESSON 1 Understanding Access Fundamentals

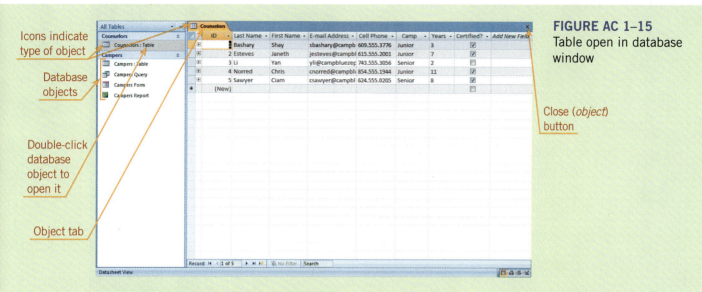

FIGURE AC 1–15
Table open in database window

2. In the Navigation Pane, double-click the **Campers: Table** database object to open the table. The first record is selected.

3. Click the **Next record** button ▶ at the bottom of the database window to move to record 2 in the Campers table, last name *Bolender*.

4. Click the **Last record** button ▶| to move to record 20 in the database, the record for *Uppal*.

5. Select the contents of the Current Record text box at the bottom of the database window, type **14**, and press **Enter** to move to record 14, last name *Netz*.

6. Click the **Counselors** object tab in the database window to display that table.

7. Click the **Close 'Counselors'** button ✕ to close the table. The Campers table is displayed in the database window.

8. Leave the database open for use in the next Step-by-Step.

Renaming and Deleting Tables

When you want to rename a table, you can right-click the table in the Navigation Pane to display the shortcut menu shown in **Figure AC 1–16**, and then click Rename on the shortcut menu. You can then type a new table name and press the Enter key to rename the table. You can only rename a table when it is closed.

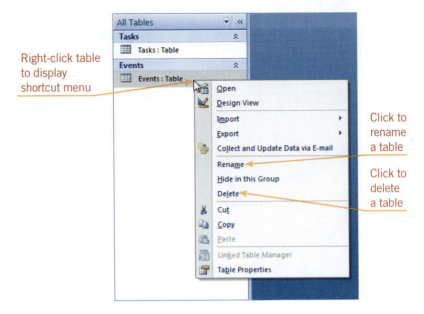

FIGURE AC 1-16 Table shortcut menu

If you need to delete a table, you can right-click the table in the Navigation Pane and click Delete on the shortcut menu, shown in **Figure AC 1-16**. You will be asked to confirm the deletion. Deleting a table is a permanent action and will affect any database objects that use the table as a source of data, so be sure you want to delete the table before proceeding.

Editing and Deleting Records

When you want to edit data in a record, select the contents in the field for that record and type new data to replace it. Or click in the field and use the Backspace or the Delete keys to make changes. If you make a mistake, you can always click the Undo button on the Quick Access Toolbar to undo the change. Or you can press the Esc key to prevent Access from accepting the changes you made. When you are editing data in a record, a pencil icon is displayed in the record selector.

To select all records in the database, you can click the ***datasheet selector*** box in the upper-left corner of the datasheet. If you want to select a single record, you can click the ***record selector*** box to the left of the row, as shown in **Figure AC 1-17**. The ***field selector*** is located at the top of column containing the field name, and you can click it to select an entire field.

▶ **VOCABULARY**
datasheet selector
record selector
field selector

FIGURE AC 1-17 Selecting records and fields

LESSON 1   Understanding Access Fundamentals

You can delete an entire record by selecting the record, and then pressing the Delete key. A message box is displayed asking you to confirm the deletion. Be sure you want to delete a record before you confirm the deletion. Deleting a record is a permanent action and cannot be undone.

Step-by-Step AC 1.6

The Camp Blue Zephyr.accdb database from Step-by-Step AC 1.5 should be open in the Access program window.

1. With the Campers table open in the database window, click the Home State field for record 4 (*Florida*).
2. Select the word **Florida** and then type **Georgia**. Notice the pencil icon in the record selector, indicating that the record is being edited, as shown in **Figure AC 1–18**.

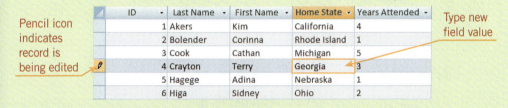

FIGURE AC 1–18
Editing a record

3. Press **Enter** to save changes to the data.
4. Click the record selector for record 2 to select it and press **Delete**. A message box is displayed, as shown in **Figure AC 1–19**, asking you to confirm you want to delete the selected record.

FIGURE AC 1–19
Deleting a record

5. Click the **Yes** button to confirm the deletion and delete the record.
6. Click the **Close 'Campers'** button ✕ to close the table.

FIGURE AC 1–20
Renaming a table

7. In the Navigation Pane, right-click the **Counselors: Table** object to display a shortcut menu.
8. Click **Rename** on the menu to select the object name and then type **Staff**, as shown in **Figure AC 1–20**.

9. Press **Enter** to rename the table.
10. Click the **Office** button and then click **Close Database**. The database closes and the Getting Started with Microsoft Office Access window is displayed.

Modifying Field Properties

After you have created the basic structure of a field by naming it and setting the data type, you still may need to make changes to the *field properties* that control the appearance and behavior of the field. You can rename a field, change the data type, and set other basic field properties using the Data Type & Formatting group commands in Datasheet view. The properties you can set for a field depend on its data type.

You might want to set the Format property of a field to determine how the data you enter will be formatted. For example, you could specify that numbers with decimals be formatted as percent, so that the number 0.63291 would be displayed as 63%. You can set the Unique field property when you want to require that the values in that field are unique for every record, as you did earlier in the lesson when you modified the default ID field when you created the Students table in the Oakville Hills School database. You can set the Required field property when you want to require that every record in the field contains a value.

To rearrange the order of fields in Datasheet view, you can select the field and drag it to a new position. If you decide you do not need a field, you can select the field and press the Delete key. This action is permanent, and any data in the field will also be deleted, so you will be asked to confirm the deletion before proceeding.

▶ **VOCABULARY**
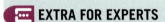
field properties

▶ **EXTRA FOR EXPERTS**
To access all of the available field properties, you need to work in Design view.

LESSON 1   Understanding Access Fundamentals

AC 21

Step-by-Step AC 1.7

The Getting Started with Microsoft Office Access window from Step-by-Step AC 1.6 should be open in the Access program window.

1. In the Open Recent Database pane on the right, shown in **Figure AC 1–21**, click the **Oakville Hills School.accdb** database that you created earlier in this lesson to open it. Enable the contents of the database.

FIGURE AC 1–21
Opening a recent database

2. In the Navigation Pane, double-click the **Students: Table** database object to open the table.
3. Click the **First Name** field selector to select the field.
4. Click the **First Name** field selector again, hold the mouse button to display a thick line to the left of the field, and then drag the First Name field to the left until the line is displayed between the Student ID field and the Last Name field, as shown in **Figure AC 1–22**.

FIGURE AC 1–22
Moving a field

5. Release the mouse button to move the field to its new location.
6. Click the **Last Name** field selector to select the field.

7. On the Datasheet tab on the Ribbon, in the Data Type & Formatting group, click the **Is Required** check box to select that option, requiring a value in that field, as shown in **Figure AC 1–23**.

FIGURE AC 1–23
Making a field required

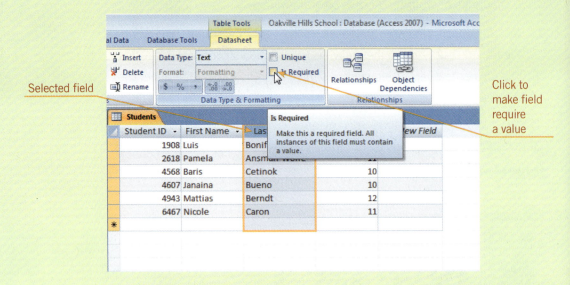

8. Double-click the **Add New Field** field name, type **Date Enrolled**, and press **Enter** to create a new field. Widen the column so the entire field name is visible.

9. In the Date Enrolled field of the first record, type **9/30/2012** and press **Enter** to enter the date.

10. Click the **Date Enrolled** field name to select the field. Notice that Access recognizes the data you entered in the field as a date and assigns the Date/Time data type on the Datasheet tab, in the Data Type & Formatting group, in the Data Type box.

11. On the Datasheet tab, in the Data Type & Formatting group, click the **Format list arrow** to display a list of formatting options for Date/Time fields, and then click **Medium Date**, as shown in **Figure AC 1–24**, to change the Date Enrolled field format.

FIGURE AC 1–24
Changing a field's data type

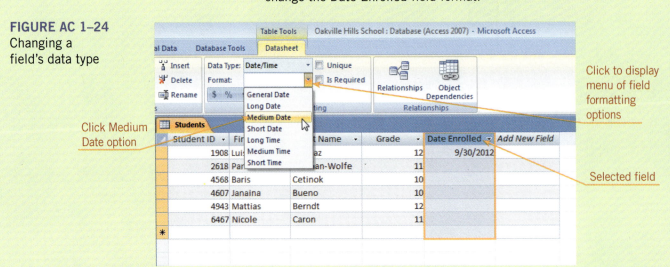

LESSON 1   Understanding Access Fundamentals

12. Save the changes you have made to the design of the Students table, and then close the table.
13. Close the database and close Access.

TECHNOLOGY CAREERS

Database administrators are responsible for planning and designing an organization's databases. This can require close coordination with the database users to ensure that the company's databases meet their needs. Database administrators also test and implement the database, making changes and updating it as necessary. In addition, they manage, maintain, and keep the database secure by performing tasks such as backing up, restoring, and encrypting the database with a password.

SUMMARY

In this lesson, you learned:

- Basic database concepts.
- The importance of planning and designing a database.
- To identify elements of the Access program window.
- The process for starting Access and creating a new database.
- How to create tables in Datasheet view.
- Methods for opening an existing database.
- To open tables, navigate records, and edit and delete records.
- Ways to modify field properties.

VOCABULARY REVIEW

Define the following terms:

database	field	key value
database management system (DBMS)	field name	primary key
database object	field properties	record
datasheet	field selector	record selector
datasheet selector	field value	relational database
data type	foreign key	table

REVIEW QUESTIONS

MULTIPLE CHOICE

Select the best response for the following statements.

1. Which database object stores and organizes all the data in the database?
   - A. table
   - B. query
   - C. form
   - D. record

2. Each _____ in a datasheet is displayed as a column.
   A. record
   B. field
   C. object
   D. table

3. Press _____ to navigate to the last field in the last record.
   A. Shift+Tab
   B. Ctrl+Home
   C. Ctrl+End
   D. none of the above

4. What is displayed after you close a database?
   A. Open dialog box
   B. Save dialog box
   C. Getting Started with Microsoft Office Access window
   D. Navigation Pane

5. By default, tables in a database are displayed in a format called a _____.
   A. form
   B. datasheet
   C. record
   D. report

6. The _____ is the field that uniquely identifies each record.
   A. field name
   B. foreign key
   C. key value
   D. primary key

7. The (New) row in a table in Datasheet view is indicated by a(n) _____.
   A. asterisk
   B. pencil icon
   C. key icon
   D. arrow

8. When you want to rename a table, you can right-click the table in the _____ to display the shortcut menu.
   A. design grid
   B. Open dialog box
   C. Navigation Pane
   D. Property Sheet pane

9. The _____ data type stores text and/or numbers up to 65,535 characters long.
   A. Text
   B. Memo
   C. Numbers
   D. Currency

10. To select a record, click the record selector box located _____.
    A. in the record navigation bar
    B. in the upper-left corner of the datasheet
    C. on the Datasheet tab on the Ribbon
    D. to the left of the row

FILL IN THE BLANK

Complete the following sentences by writing the correct word or words in the blanks provided.

1. When you open or create a database, the _____ is displayed on the left side of the screen and lists all the database objects.

2. When a primary key is included in another table, it is called a(n) _____ in the second table.

3. Access is considered a(n) _____ because all of the data is stored in separate tables and then connected by establishing relationships between the tables through common fields.

4. Each record in the database must have a(n) _____, which is a value in the primary key field that makes the record unique.

LESSON 1 Understanding Access Fundamentals

5. When you are editing data in a record, a(n) _____ icon is displayed in the record selector.

6. Each field in a table has a(n) _____ that characterizes the types of values contained in the field.

7. The _____ data type stores monetary data displayed with a dollar sign.

8. In the Blank Database pane, if you want to select a location for a new blank database other than the one shown below the File Name text box, you can click the _____ icon next to the File Name text box.

9. To close a database, you can click the _____ and then click Close Database.

10. When you _____ a table, record, or field, the action is permanent, so you will be asked to confirm before proceeding.

■ PROJECTS

PROJECT AC 1–1

1. Open the file **Contacts.accdb** from the folder containing the data files for this lesson.
2. Open the Business table.
3. Click the Job Title field of record 1 (*Human Resource Manager*) and edit it to read **Sales Manager**.
4. Widen the Company, E-mail Address, Address, and Web Site fields so all the data is visible.
5. Select the Country/Region field and delete it.
6. Save and close the Business table.
7. Rename the Personal table as **Friends**.
8. Leave the database open for use in the next project.

PROJECT AC 1–2

The Contacts.accdb database from Project AC 1–1 should be open in the Access program window.

1. Open the Friends table.
2. Rename the State/Province field as **State**.
3. Rename the ZIP/Postal Code field as **ZIP**.
4. Create a new field with a field name **Birthday**.
5. Navigate to the last field (*Birthday*) of the last record (*6*).
6. Enter **Sept 19** as the field value.
7. Make the Last Name field required.
8. Close the Friends table.
9. Close the database.

PROJECT AC 1–3

1. Open the file **Vehicle Records.accdb** from the folder containing the data files for this lesson.
2. Open the Vehicle table.
3. Enter the data shown below as a new record. (*Note*: Access will automatically add the number in the ID field.)

   Vehicle: **Nissan**

   Make: **Altima**

   Model: **2.5 S**

   Color: **Metallic Jade**

   Year Made: **2008**

   Date Purchased: **4/30/2008**

   Purchase Price: **$21,165**

   License Plate: **VLS-429**

4. Add a new field to the database named **Notes**.
5. Click the Notes field of the first record and type **7-yr warranty.**
6. Change the format of the Date Purchased field to **Medium Date**.
7. Make the Vehicle field required.
8. Close the Vehicle table.
9. Leave the database open for use in the next project.

ON YOUR OWN

Open the **Contacts.accdb** database and create another table named Family. Add at least five records with contact information for members of your family. Create fields and modify as needed to fit your data. Save the table and close the database.

PROJECT AC 1–4

The Vehicle Records.accdb database from Project AC 1–3 should be open in the Access program window.

1. On the Create tab, in the Tables group, click the Table button to create a new table.
2. Enter the following data as a new record and change the field names (and data types, if necessary) as you create the fields. Note that the ID field is created automatically.

   Vehicle (Text): **Jeep**
   Service Description (Memo): **oil change**
   Service Date (Date/Time): **6/12/2012**
   Mileage (Number): **58,034**
   Cost (Currency): **$36.95**
   Shop (Text): **Joe's Quick Change**
   Invoice # (Number): **102449**

3. Widen any fields as necessary to display the data.
4. Save the table as **Expenses** and close it.
5. Close the database.

ON YOUR OWN

Open the **Vehicle Records.accdb** database and open the Vehicle table. Create a field named **Online Info** with a **Hyperlink** data type. Search online to find the official Web site for each make of car in the table and enter the Web site address in the new Hyperlink field. Save the table and close the database.

ON YOUR OWN

Use Access Help to learn more about relating tables. Open the **Vehicle Records.accdb** database and make any changes necessary to relate the tables. Be prepared to explain to the class how you related them and demonstrate how to create a relationship between tables. Close the database.

 TEAMWORK PROJECT

PROJECT AC 1–5

Search for the demo in Access Help titled *Database design basics* and watch it. With a partner, plan a database that will contain information about all of the scholarships that are available locally to graduating seniors. Consider all of the data that might be stored and design the tables and fields accordingly. Compare your design with other teams. How were the plans similar or different? Incorporate all of the best ideas in the class into a single database plan.

WEB PROJECT

PROJECT AC 1–6

Visit a Web site with information about upcoming events in your area. Use the information you found to plan, design, and then create a new blank database that includes a table named Events. Create whatever fields you need to store the data and modify the table fields to suit your needs. Enter at least 10 records about events that you would be interested in attending.

 CRITICAL THINKING

ACTIVITY AC 1–1

You want to create a database about a collection you own (or would like to own). Deciding what type of information the database will contain and how it will be organized, then sketch a rough draft on paper, being sure to identify the fields and data types. Use Access to create the database using the skills you learned in this lesson. Compare the database to your original design. Did you need to make any adjustments? Enter at least 10 records in your database.

ACTIVITY AC 1–2

Search for the demo in Access Help titled *Up to speed with Access 2007* and watch it. What are some ways that Access 2007 is designed to help you work easier, faster, and more efficiently? Practice at least one new skill you have learned.

ACTIVITY AC 1–3

You want to create a database to help you manage your school assignments and projects. Use Access to create a new blank database and create a table within that database named Assignments. Spend some time deciding what type of information the Assignment table will contain and how it will be designed, then sketch a rough draft on paper, being sure to identify the fields and data types for each field if appropriate. Enter at least six class assignments as records in the table.

LESSON 2

Creating Queries, Forms, and Reports

Estimated Time: 2.5 hours

■ OBJECTIVES

Upon completion of this lesson, you should be able to:

- Create queries.
- Create and use forms.
- Modify the form's design.
- Create reports.
- Modify and print reports.
- Sort and filter records.

■ DATA FILES

To complete this lesson, you will need these data files:

- Caprock View Apartments.accdb
- CAV logo.jpg
- Contributions.accdb
- Math Department.accdb
- Math logo.jpg

■ VOCABULARY

AutoFormat
control
filter
form
Form Wizard
query
Query Wizard
record source
report
Report Wizard
run
select query
simple form
sort
...

AC 27

UNIT V Microsoft Access

Introduction

Once you have created a database with tables, you can work with the data in the database to create other database objects. In this lesson, you will learn about creating and using the other database objects—queries, forms, and reports—to manipulate, display, and present data in a database.

When you create a query, form, or report, it is based on an existing object in the database, called the *record source*. In this lesson, you will use a table as the record source.

Creating Queries

A *query* is a database object that is based upon a specific question you ask about the data in the database. Access displays the exact records that answer your question. For example, if you want to know which apartment unit would be available on a specific date, then you would create a query in which Access would locate the records in the database that meet that criteria. Queries are powerful tools that can extract data from one or more tables and can be saved to use again.

You can create several different types of queries using the Query Wizard, including a simple select query. A *select query* simply retrieves specific data out of a record source for you to use. For example, you might want to view all of the supporters who have donated to your organization. The *Query Wizard* is an Access tool that guides you through the process of creating a query. You can start the Query Wizard by clicking the Query Wizard button in the Other group on the Create tab. When you finish, the query is displayed in Datasheet view.

Because a database is continually being updated, if you want to see the query results again, you must run the query. When you *run* a query, you give instructions to display the records and fields you asked to see when you designed the query. To run a query at any time, double-click it in the Navigation Pane. The records that are displayed are based on the most current information in the database.

When you save a query, you are actually saving the design of the query, not the query results. You can save the query design the same way as other database objects—by clicking the Save button on the Quick Access Toolbar to display the Save As dialog box. When you click the Close Query button in the database window, if you have not already saved it, you will be prompted to save it before closing. If you create a query using the Query Wizard it is saved automatically when you complete the wizard.

You can display a query in different views. The most commonly used views are Datasheet view and Design view. You can use Datasheet view to see the results of a query, and Design view to create a query from scratch or modify the design of an existing query. To change views, click the View button arrow in the Views group on the Home tab to display a menu. You can also change views using the view buttons in the lower-right corner of the Access program window.

▶ **VOCABULARY**
record source
query
select query
Query Wizard
run

EXTRA FOR EXPERTS

If the queries you can create using the Query Wizard do not suit your needs, you can always create a query in Design view by clicking the Query Design button in the Other group on the Create tab. In Design view, you can create more advanced action queries that perform tasks on the data, such as adding, updating, or deleting.

Step-by-Step AC 2.1

1. Start Access.
2. Open **Caprock View Apartments.accdb** from the folder containing the data files for this lesson.
3. On the Message Bar, click the **Options** button to open the Microsoft Office Security Options dialog box.

LESSON 2 Creating Queries, Forms, and Reports

AC 29

4. Click the **Enable this content** option button, and then click **OK** to remove the Message Bar warning and enable the content of the database.

5. Double-click the **Units** table in the Navigation Pane to open it in the database window, as shown in **Figure AC 2–1**. Notice the table contains data about apartment units. Click the **Close 'Units'** button ✕ to close the table.

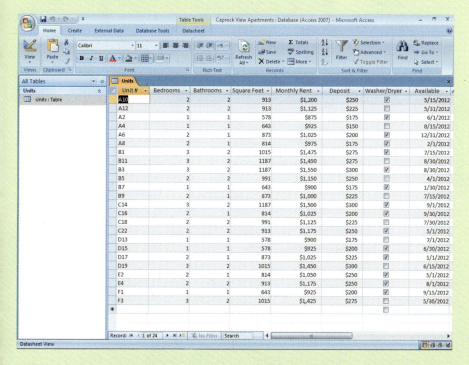

FIGURE AC 2–1
Units table to be used as a record source

6. If necessary, click the **Units** table in the Navigation Pane to select it. On the Create tab, in the Other group, click the **Query Wizard** button to open the New Query dialog box.

7. Make sure **Simple Query Wizard** is selected in the list, and then click the **OK** button to start the Query Wizard to create a simple select query.

8. In the first Simple Query Wizard dialog box, in the Available Fields list box, click **Unit #** to select it, and then click the **Add field** button [>] to move it to the Selected Fields list box.

9. Repeat Step 2 to move **Bedrooms**, **Bathrooms**, and **Available** to the Selected Fields list box. The Simple Query Wizard dialog box should look similar to **Figure AC 2–2**.

FIGURE AC 2–2
First Simple Query Wizard dialog box

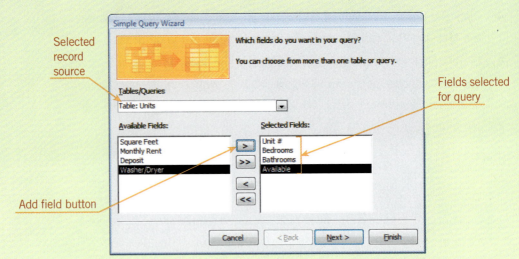

10. Click the **Next** button to move to the next Simple Query Wizard dialog box to specify the type of query results you want, detailed or summary.

11. Make sure the **Detail** option button is selected so that every field of every record will be shown, and then click the **Next** button to move to the next Simple Query Wizard dialog box in which you can specify a title for the query, and either preview the query or choose to make modifications to its design.

12. In the What title do you want for your query? text box, type **Unit Availability**. Make sure the **Open the query to view information** option button is selected, and then click the **Finish** button to create the query and display its results in Datasheet view, as shown in **Figure AC 2–3**.

FIGURE AC 2–3
Creating a query using the Query Wizard

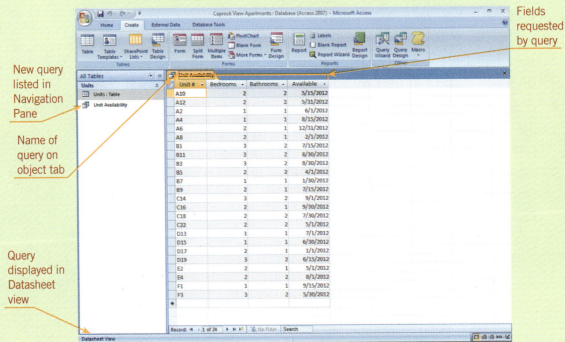

LESSON 2 Creating Queries, Forms, and Reports

13. Click the **Close 'Unit Availability'** button ✕ to close the query. There is no need to save the query as it was already saved when you created it using the Query Wizard.
14. Leave the database open for use in the next Step-by-Step.

Creating and Using Forms

An Access *form* is an object that you use to enter new records into the database, or to edit data in existing records. Although you can enter new records directly into a table datasheet, using a form is an easier way to view, enter, and edit records. Forms allow you to focus on one record at a time. Forms can also be used to control what types of information can be viewed, changed, or entered by certain users as they work with an established database. Often a database is used by multiple people, and forms can help prevent errors or unwanted changes to the database records or structure. For example, you can create a form that only includes certain fields or only allows certain tasks to be performed.

Access offers a variety of tools for creating different types of forms. You can design your own forms in Design view; use the Form Wizard, which is an Access tool that steps you through creating a form; or you can use the Form tool to create a simple form with a single mouse click. These options are all accessible from the Create tab on the Ribbon, in the Forms group.

▶ **VOCABULARY**
form
simple form

Creating a Simple Form Using the Form Tool

You can use the Form tool to create a *simple form* that includes all the fields from the selected record source. When you select the table in the Navigation Pane that you want to use as the record source for the form and then click the Form button in the Forms group on the Create tab, a simple form is created that includes all the fields from that table, as shown in **Figure AC 2–4**.

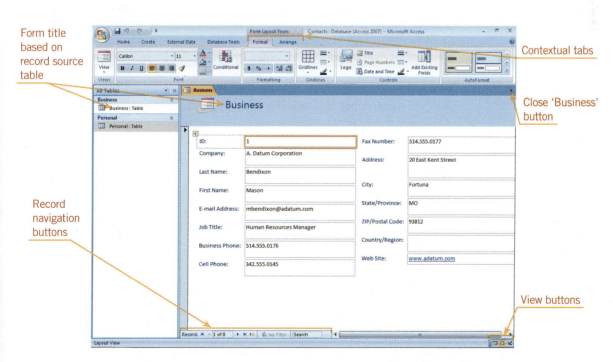

FIGURE AC 2–4 Simple form in Layout view

The form has a simple format and its title reflects the name of the record source table. Every field from the table is on the form, and the information from the first record is displayed.

When you create a simple form, it is initially displayed in Layout view. Layout view allows you to make modifications to the design of the form while the form displays data, allowing you to see the effect of your changes right away. You can make these types of design changes using the options on the Form Layout Tools Format and Arrange contextual tabs that are open on the Ribbon when a form is displayed in Layout view. The views available when working with form objects are summarized in **Table AC 2–1**. To change views, click the View button arrow in the Views group on the Form Layout Tools Format tab or on the Home tab.

TABLE AC 2-1 Views available for forms

VIEW NAME	ICON	DESCRIPTION
Form view		Allows you to view, enter, or edit data; you cannot alter the layout or design of the form in this view.
Layout view		Allows you to make design changes to the form while it is displaying data; useful for performing tasks that affect the visual appearance and usability of a form. Form Layout Tools contextual tabs are available in this view.
Design view		Gives a detailed view of the structure of the form; you cannot see the underlying data, but you have more control over the design of the form. Form Design Tools contextual tabs are available in this view.

You can use the form to enter new data into the table or edit existing records by switching to Form view. The navigation buttons at the bottom of the Access program window can be used to move among records in a form just as you used these navigation buttons to move between records in a table. Click a button to move to the record you want—First, Previous, Next, Last, or click the New (blank) button to create a new record. You can enter or edit data by typing or changing it in the boxes next to the field name. A pencil icon is displayed in the upper-left corner of the form when a record is being edited.

Saving Forms

Forms can be saved the same way as other database objects—by clicking the Save button on the Quick Access Toolbar to display the Save As dialog box. When you click a form's Close button, if you have not already saved it, you will be prompted to save it before closing.

LESSON 2 Creating Queries, Forms, and Reports

Step-by-Step AC 2.2

The Caprock View Apartments.accdb database from Step-by-Step AC 2.1 should be open in the Access program window.

1. Make sure the **Units** table is selected in the Navigation Pane. On the Create tab, in the Forms group, click the **Form** button to create a simple form based on the Units table, as shown in **Figure AC 2–5**.

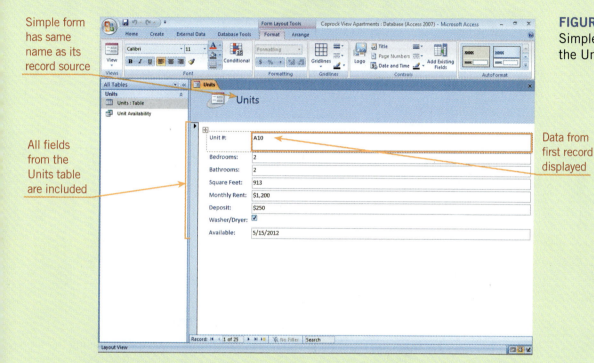

FIGURE AC 2–5
Simple form based on the Units table

Simple form has same name as its record source

All fields from the Units table are included

Data from first record displayed

2. Click the **Save** button on the Quick Access Toolbar to display the Save As dialog box.

3. Access displays **Units** in the Form Name box as the suggested name for the simple form. Click the **OK** button to save the form with the suggested name.

4. Click the **Next record** button at the bottom of the form window to display the next record, for Unit A12.

5. In the Views group on the Format tab, click the **View** button arrow and click **Form View** on the menu to switch to Form view so that you can enter a new record.

6. Click the **New (blank) record** button to create a new blank record.

7. Type the data in the new blank record, as shown in **Figure AC 2–6**. As you start entering data in the record, notice a pencil icon appears in the upper-left corner of the form, indicating the record is being edited. If you had more records to enter, you could press Enter after typing the last field value to display a new blank record.

FIGURE AC 2–6
New record to enter

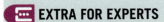

Pencil icon indicates record is being edited

8. Click the **Close 'Units'** button to close the form.
9. Open the Units table and notice that the data you entered using the form has been recorded and appears as the last record in the datasheet.
10. Close the Units table and leave the database open for use in the next Step-by-Step.

Using the Form Wizard

If you want to select which fields are included on a form and also choose the form layout and style, then you can use the ***Form Wizard***. The Form Wizard is an Access tool that guides you through the process of creating a form. You can start the Form Wizard by clicking the More Forms button in the Forms group on the Create tab.

Depending on the options that you choose, the resulting forms can vary. If the form is not what you expected, you can always modify it or just delete it and then start over. You can delete a form by right-clicking it in the Navigation Pane and clicking Delete on the shortcut menu.

▶ **VOCABULARY**
Form Wizard

EXTRA FOR EXPERTS

There are other tools that you can use to create different types of forms using the buttons in the Forms group on the Create tab. You can use Access Help to learn more about the purpose of these other types of forms.

LESSON 2 Creating Queries, Forms, and Reports

Step-by-Step AC 2.3

The Caprock View Apartments.accdb database from Step-by-Step AC 2.2 should be open in the Access program window.

1. If necessary, click the **Units** table in the Navigation Pane to select it.
2. On the Create tab, in the Forms group, click the **More Forms** button and then click **Form Wizard** to start the Form Wizard and display the first dialog box of the wizard. In this first dialog box, you select the data source to be used to create the form, and you select the fields to be included on the form.
3. If necessary, click **Unit #** in the Available Fields list box to select it, and then click the **Add field** button [>] to move it to the Selected Fields list box.
4. Repeat Step 3 to move **Monthly Rent** and **Deposit** to the Selected Fields list box. The Form Wizard dialog box should look similar to **Figure AC 2–7**.

FIGURE AC 2–7
Selecting fields in the Form Wizard

5. Click the **Next** button to move to the next Form Wizard dialog box, which provides layout options for the form.
6. Click the **Tabular** option button to select a form layout similar to a spreadsheet and display a sample of it in the Preview window.
7. Click the **Next** button to move to the next Form Wizard dialog box, which provides style options for the form.
8. Click the **Equity** option to select the form style and display this form style in the Preview window.
9. Click the **Next** button to move to the last Form Wizard dialog box in which you name the form and you decide what you want to do next: open the form or continue to work on it by modifying its design. Usually it is best to view the finished form before making design changes to it.

10. In the What title do you want for your form? text box, type **Unit Cost**.
11. Click the **Finish** button to create the form and display it in Form view in the database window, as shown in **Figure AC 2–8**.

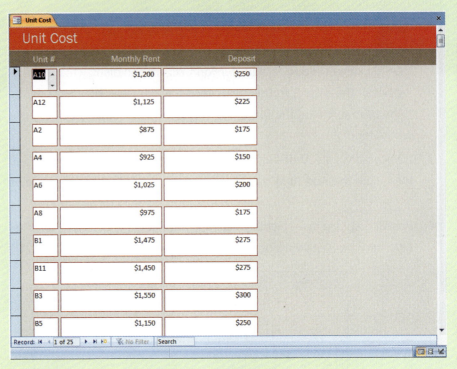

FIGURE AC 2–8
Form created using the Form Wizard

12. Click the **Close 'Unit Cost'** button ✕ to close the form.
13. Leave the database open for use in the next Step-by-Step.

Modifying the Form's Design

After you have created a form, you can modify it to fit your needs using Layout view or Design view. In this lesson, you will use Layout view. When the form is in Layout view, the Form Layout Tools Format and Arrange contextual tabs are displayed on the Ribbon so you can modify the layout of the form.

In the Controls group on the Format tab, you can add or modify the controls on the form. A *control* is any object on a form or report that you can change to modify or enhance the appearance of the form or report. Among the many control options, for example, you can insert a title, insert page numbers, add the date and time, or even insert a logo.

An easy way to change the appearance of a form is to use an AutoFormat. An *AutoFormat* is a predefined set of fonts, colors, and borders that Access provides to quickly give your form a professional and consistent look. AutoFormats are available in the AutoFormat group on the Form Layout Tools Format tab. You can click the More button to view the entire gallery of options or to access the AutoFormat Wizard. The AutoFormat Wizard allows you to customize or create an AutoFormat and also gives you the option to apply only specific formatting attributes to the form.

You can also modify a form by moving, adding, or deleting fields. To move a field, click the field name to select it, which is indicated by an orange border that appears around the field. Point to the selected field to display a four-headed arrow

▶ **VOCABULARY**
control
AutoFormat

LESSON 2 Creating Queries, Forms, and Reports

pointer, then click and drag the field to a new location on the form. To add a field, you click the Add Existing Fields button in the Controls group on the Form Layout Tools Format tab to display the Fields List pane, then you click the field and drag it to the form. To delete a field, click the field to select it, and then press the Delete key. If you decide you don't want to delete the field, just click the Undo button on the Quick Access toolbar to undo the deletion.

Step-by-Step AC 2.4

The Caprock View Apartments.accdb database from Step-by-Step AC 2.3 should be open in the Access program window.

1. Double-click the **Units** form in the Navigation Pane to open it.
2. On the Home tab, in the Views group, click the **View** button arrow and click **Layout View** on the menu to switch to Layout view and display the Form Layout Tools Format contextual tab.
3. On the Format tab, in the Controls group, click the **Title** button to select the title for editing and then type **Apartments**, as shown in **Figure AC 2–9**, and then press **Enter** to change the form title.

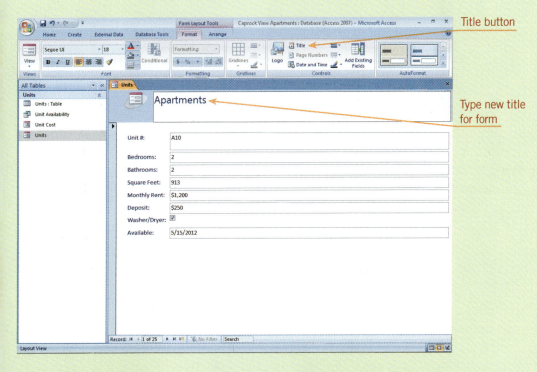

FIGURE AC 2–9
Changing the form title

4. On the Format tab, in the Controls group, click the **Logo** button to display the Insert Picture dialog box.
5. Navigate to the location where you store your data files for this lesson, select the **CAV logo.jpg** file, and then click the **OK** button to insert the logo onto the form.

6. Click the **Available** field name to select it, which is indicated by an orange border around the field name.

7. Point to the control to display a four-headed arrow pointer, click and drag the field up until the orange line is between the Unit # and Bedroom fields, as shown in **Figure AC 2–10**, then release the mouse button to place the field in the new location.

FIGURE AC 2–10
Moving a form field

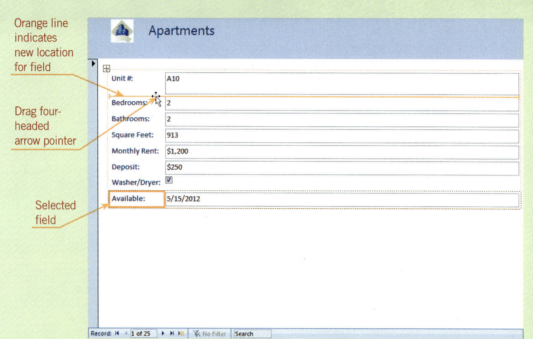

8. On the Format tab, in the AutoFormat group, click the **More** button to display the gallery, and then click **Paper**, as shown in **Figure AC 2–11**, to apply an AutoFormat.

LESSON 2 Creating Queries, Forms, and Reports

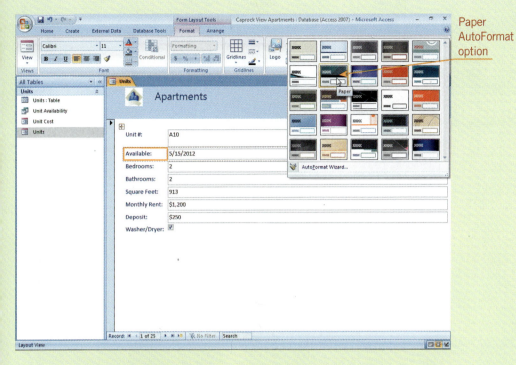

FIGURE AC 2-11
Applying an AutoFormat

9. Save and close the Units form, and then open the **Unit Cost** form and switch to Layout view.

10. Click the **Deposit** field name to select it and display it with an orange border, and then press **Delete** to delete the field from the form.

11. On the Form Layout Tools Format tab, in the Controls group, click the **Add Existing Fields** button to display the Field List pane on the right side of the database window.

12. Click the **Available** field in the Field List pane, drag it to the form until the orange line is displayed after the Monthly Rent field, as shown in **Figure AC 2-12**, then release the mouse button to add the field to the form.

FIGURE AC 2–12
Adding a field to a form

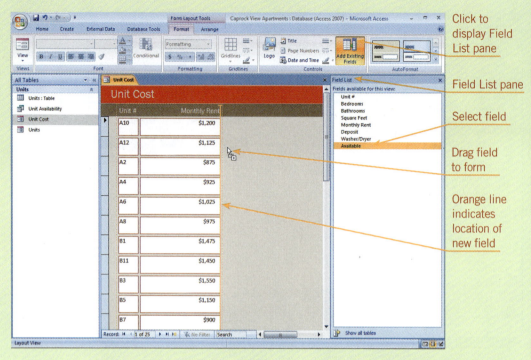

13. Click the **Close** button ☒ on the Field List pane to close it.
14. Save and close the Unit Cost form, and leave the database open for use in the next Step-by-Step.

▶ **VOCABULARY**

report

Creating Reports

Another type of database object is a report. A *report* is a formatted display or printout of the contents of one or more tables in a database. For example, you can use reports to create a formatted list of the records in a table. A report can also be generated from query results. When generated from a query, reports enable you to display a particular aspect of the data, such as how many items were sold last month or which cities had the most rainfall, or even to create mailing labels. After you have created a report, you can run it at any time by double-clicking it in the Navigation Pane to open it. Each time you run a report, it pulls the current data from the database, so it is always up to date. You can make adjustments to the design of a report so it presents the data you want to include in an attractive and readable format.

When you create a report, it is based on underlying data contained in a database object, just like a form. In this lesson, you will use a table as the record source. Access offers a variety of tools for creating different types of reports in the Reports group of the Create tab.

Using the Report Tool

You can use the Report tool to quickly create a simple report that includes all the fields from the underlying table. When you select the table in the Navigation Pane that you want to base the report on and then click the Report button in the Reports group on the Create tab, a report with a basic columnar format is displayed in Layout view, as shown in **Figure AC 2–13**.

LESSON 2 Creating Queries, Forms, and Reports

AC 41

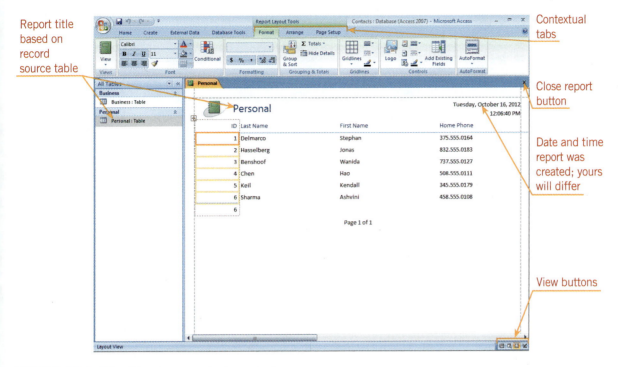

FIGURE AC 2-13 Simple report in Layout view

The report has a simple format and has the same title as the title of the record source table. Every field from the table is on the report, as well as the date and time the report was created. The Record Layout Tools Format, Arrange, and Page Setup contextual tabs are displayed providing tools you can use to modify the report.

You can display a report in different views. To change views, click the View button arrow in the Views group on the Home tab to display a menu. Layout view and Design view can be used to modify the report. Or, you can switch to Report view to view the report. You cannot make changes to the report in Report view. To see how a report will look when printed, you can display it in Print Preview.

Saving Reports

Reports can be saved the same way as other database objects—by clicking the Save button on the Quick Access Toolbar to display the Save As dialog box. When you click a report's Close button, if you have not saved it, you will be prompted to save it before closing.

Step-by-Step AC 2.5

The Caprock View Apartments.accdb database from Step-by-Step AC 2.4 should be open in the Access program window.

1. Click the **Units** table in the Navigation Pane to select it.
2. On the Create tab, in the Reports group, click the **Report** button to create a simple form based on the Units table, as shown in **Figure AC 2-14**.

FIGURE AC 2-14
Simple report based on Units table

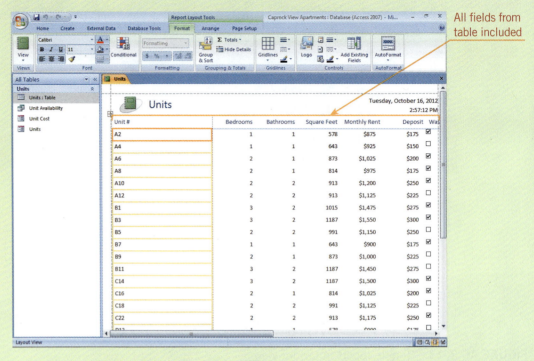

3. Click the **Save** button on the Quick Access Toolbar to display the Save As dialog box.

4. Type **All Units** in the Report Name text box and then click the **OK** button to save the report.

5. Click the **View** button arrow in the Views group on the Format tab, and then click **Report View** on the menu to display the report in Report view.

6. Click the **Close 'All Units'** button to close the report.

7. Leave the database open for use in the next Step-by-Step.

> **VOCABULARY**
> **Report Wizard**

Using the Report Wizard

If you want to select which fields are included on a report, how information is grouped or sorted, and also choose the report layout, orientation, and style, then you can use the **Report Wizard**. The Report Wizard is an Access tool that guides you through the process of creating a report. You start the Report Wizard by clicking the Report Wizard button in the Reports group on the Create tab.

Depending on the options that you choose, the resulting reports can vary. If the report is not what you expected, you can always modify it or just delete it and start over. You can delete a report by right-clicking it in the Navigation Pane and clicking Delete on the shortcut menu.

EXTRA FOR EXPERTS

If the tools you have learned in this lesson for creating reports do not suit your needs, you can always create a report from scratch using the Report Design button in the Reports group on the Create tab to create a new blank report in Design view, or by clicking the Blank Report button to build and customize a report in Layout view.

LESSON 2 Creating Queries, Forms, and Reports

Step-by-Step AC 2.6

The Caprock View Apartments.accdb database from Step-by-Step AC 2.5 should be open in the Access program window.

1. On the Create tab, in the Reports group, click the **Report Wizard** button to start the Report Wizard. In the first Report Wizard dialog box, you need to select the data source you want to use for generating the report, and you need to select the fields to be included in the report.

2. In the Available Fields list box, click **Unit #** to select it if necessary, and then click the **Add Field** button [>] to move it to the Selected Fields list box.

3. Repeat Step 2 to move **Bedrooms**, **Bathrooms**, **Monthly Rent**, and **Available** to the Selected Fields list box, as shown in **Figure AC 2–15**.

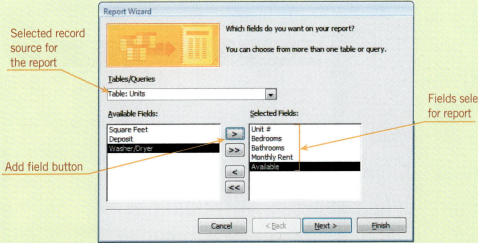

FIGURE AC 2–15
Selecting fields in the Report Wizard

4. Click the **Next** button to move to the next Report Wizard dialog box, which displays options for selecting grouping levels by choosing which field(s) to use to organize the data in the report.

5. Click **Monthly Rent** in the list box on the left, and then click the **Add field** button to organize the report information according to how much the monthly rent costs.

6. Click the **Next** button to move to the next Report Wizard dialog box, which displays options for sorting and summarizing detail records.

7. You do not want to sort the records or calculate summary values, so click the **Next** button to move to the next Report Wizard dialog box, which provides options for selecting various layouts for the report.

8. Click the **Outline** option button in the Layout section of the dialog box to have the report appear as an outline, as shown in the Preview in the dialog box.

9. Click the **Next** button to move to the next Report Wizard dialog box, which provides style options for the report.
10. Click **Foundry** in the Form AutoFormats list box, and then click the **Next** button to move to the next Report Wizard dialog box, in which you can specify a title for the report, and either preview the report or choose to make modifications to its design.
11. In the What title do you want for your report? text box, enter **Units By Price**.
12. Click the **Finish** button to create the report and display it in the Print Preview window, as shown in **Figure AC 2-16**.

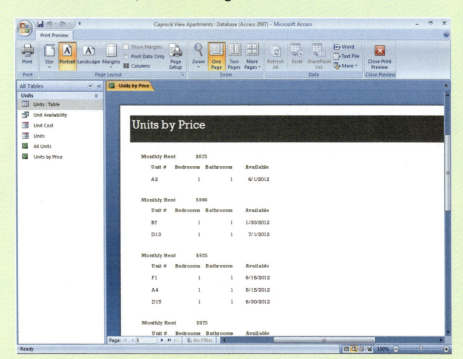

FIGURE AC 2-16
Completing a report using the Report Wizard

13. Click the **Close 'Units By Price'** button to close the report.
14. Leave the database open for use in the next Step-by-Step.

Modifying and Printing Reports

After you have created a report, you can modify it to fit your needs using Layout view. When the report is in Layout view, the Report Layout Tools Format and Arrange contextual tabs are displayed so you can modify the layout of the report. You can use Layout view to modify the format or appearance of a report while still viewing the underlying data. Just as you did with forms, you can easily change the appearance of a report by using an AutoFormat, available on the Report Layout Tools Format tab in the AutoFormat group.

You can also modify a report by moving, adding, or deleting fields. To move a field, click the field name to select it, as indicated by an orange border. Point to the field to display a four-headed arrow pointer, then click and drag the field to a new

LESSON 2 Creating Queries, Forms, and Reports

AC 45

location on the report. To add a field, you can click the Add Existing Fields button on the Report Layout Tools Format tab in the Controls group to display the Fields List pane, then click the field and drag it onto the report. To delete a field, click the field name to select it with an orange border, then press the Delete key. If you decide you don't want to delete the field, just click the Undo button on the Quick Access toolbar to undo the deletion. You can rename a field by double-clicking the field name, then editing the name or selecting the name and typing a new one.

After you are satisfied with the report, you can print it. Reports can be printed from any view or even while closed. Before printing a report, you should preview it in the Print Preview window to make sure it looks the way you want. The commands on the Print Preview tab can be used to make changes to page layout and setup or zoom to display the report differently. You can click the Close Print Preview button to close the Print Preview window.

Step-by-Step AC 2.7

The Caprock View Apartments.accdb database from Step-by-Step AC 2.6 should be open in the Access program window.

1. Double-click the **All Units** report in the Navigation Pane to open it.
2. On the Home tab, in the Views group, click the **View** button arrow and click **Layout View** on the menu to switch to Layout view and display the Report Layout Tools contextual tabs.
3. Click the **Unit #** field name to select it, and display it with an orange border.
4. On the Report Layout Tools Arrange tab, in the Position group, click the **Size to Fit** button to resize the field to fit the data.
5. Click the **Washer/Dryer** field name to select it and display it with an orange border and then press **Delete** to delete the field.
6. On the Report Layout Tools Format tab, in the AutoFormat group, click the **More** button to display the gallery and then click **Solstice**, as shown in **Figure AC 2–17**, to apply an AutoFormat.

FIGURE AC 2–17
Applying an AutoFormat to a report

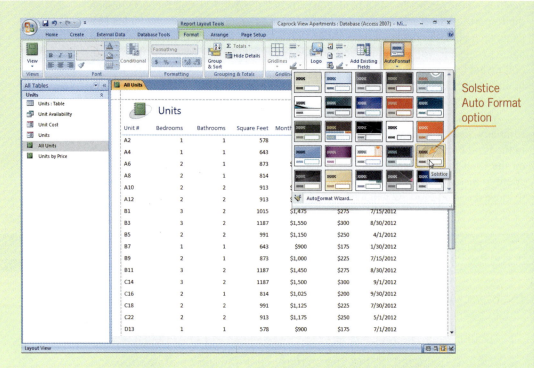

7. On the Format tab, in the Views group, click the **View** button arrow and click **Print Preview** on the menu to switch to Print Preview, as shown in **Figure AC 2–18**.

FIGURE AC 2–18
Viewing a report in Print Preview

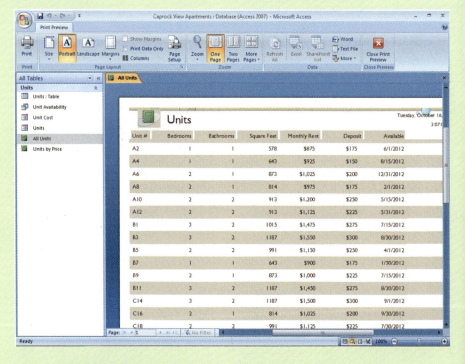

8. On the Print Preview tab, in the Zoom group, click the **Zoom** button to change the zoom level to see the entire report.

9. On the Print Preview tab, in the Print group, click the **Print** button to display the Print dialog box.

LESSON 2 Creating Queries, Forms, and Reports

10. Click the **OK** button to print the report. If you have been instructed not to print, click the **Cancel** button in the Print dialog box.
11. On the Print Preview tab, in the Close Preview group, click the **Close Print Preview** button to close Print Preview.
12. Save and close the All Units report.
13. Leave the database open for use in the next Step-by-Step.

Sorting and Filtering Records

Once you have created a database object—whether it is a table, query, form, or report—you can organize the data so that it is easier to work with and analyze by sorting or filtering the records. The commands to sort and filter data are located on the Home tab in the Sort & Filter group, as shown in **Figure AC 2–19**.

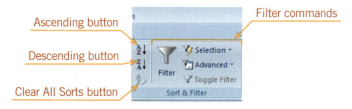

FIGURE AC 2–19 Sort & Filter group on Home tab

Sorting Data

When you *sort* data, Access rearranges selected data alphabetically, numerically, or chronologically. You can specify whether you want the lowest values displayed at the top (ascending order) or the highest values displayed at the top (descending order). When you choose ascending order, text is sorted from A to Z, numbers are sorted from 0 to 9, and dates are sorted from earliest to latest. Descending order sorts text from Z to A, numbers from 9 to 0, and dates from latest to earliest.

You can sort data in Form view of a form, in Layout view of a report, or in Datasheet view of a query or table. To sort by a field, you can select any field value in the column you want to sort by and then click the Ascending or Descending button in the Sort & Filter group on the Home tab. Access will rearrange the records to match the sort order you choose. To remove the sort, you can click the Clear All Sorts button in the Sort & Filter group on the Home tab.

> **VOCABULARY**
> sort
> filter

Using AutoFilter

A *filter* is helpful when you want to find and work with data that meets certain criteria or a specific set of conditions. For example, you might want to display only the records for employees in a certain department. The data in the database object you want to see will be visible and the rest is hidden until you remove the filter. A filter is different from a query because a filter temporarily displays certain records without changing the design of the database object, while a query is saved as a database object.

UNIT V Microsoft Access

If you need to specify complex conditions, you can click the Advanced button in the Sort & Filter group on the Home tab to display a menu with more advanced commands. But for most purposes, using AutoFilter is the quickest and easiest way to display the data you need. When you click a field header and then click the Filter button in the Sort & Filter group on the Home tab, an AutoFilter menu is displayed with options that are specific to the type of data in that field, as shown in **Figure AC 2–20**.

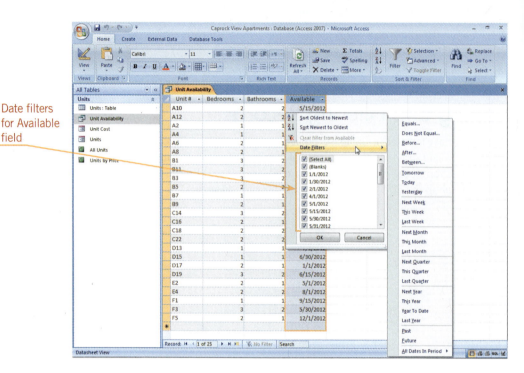

Date filters for Available field

FIGURE AC 2–20 AutoFilter commands

On the AutoFilter menu, you can choose to filter from a list of values by selecting or clearing the check boxes. You can also filter by common criteria using the options on the Text Filters submenu (or Date Filters or Number Filters, depending on the field's data type). To remove a filter, you click the Remove Filter button in the Sort & Filter group on the Home tab.

Step-by-Step AC 2.8

The Caprock View Apartments.accdb database from Step-by-Step AC 2.7 should be open in the Access program window.

1. Double-click the **All Units** report in the Navigation Pane to open it.
2. On the Home tab, in the Views group, click the **View** button arrow and click **Layout View** to display the report in Layout view.
3. Click the **Square Feet** field header to select this field.
4. On the Home tab, in the Sort & Filter group, click the **Descending** button to sort the records in descending order by square footage, as shown in **Figure AC 2–21**.

LESSON 2   Creating Queries, Forms, and Reports   AC 49

FIGURE AC 2–21
Sorting a report

Field sorted in descending order

Unit #	Bedrooms	Bathrooms	Square Feet	Monthly Rent	Deposit	Available
C14	3	2	1187	$1,500	$300	9/1/2012
B3	3	2	1187	$1,550	$300	8/30/2012
B11	3	2	1187	$1,450	$275	8/30/2012
B1	3	2	1015	$1,475	$275	7/15/2012
D19	3	2	1015	$1,450	$300	6/15/2012
F3	3	2	1015	$1,425	$275	5/30/2012
C18	2	2	991	$1,125	$225	7/30/2012
B5	2	2	991	$1,150	$250	4/1/2012
A10	2	2	913	$1,200	$250	5/15/2012
C22	2	2	913	$1,175	$250	5/1/2012
E4	2	2	913	$1,175	$250	8/1/2012
A12	2	2	913	$1,125	$225	5/31/2012
F5	2	1	873	$1,050	$225	12/1/2012
B9	2	1	873	$1,000	$225	7/15/2012
A6	2	1	873	$1,025	$200	12/31/2012
D17	2	1	873	$1,025	$225	1/1/2012

5. On the Home tab, in the Sort & Filter group, click the **Clear All Sorts** button to clear the sort.

6. Close the All Units report without saving the design changes.

7. Double-click the **Unit Cost** form in the Navigation Pane to open it, and then switch to Layout view.

8. Select the **Monthly Rent** field.

9. On the Home tab, in the Sort & Filter group, click the **Filter** button to display the AutoFilters for that field.

10. Point to **Number Filters** and then click **Less Than**, as shown in **Figure AC 2–22**, to open the Custom Filter dialog box.

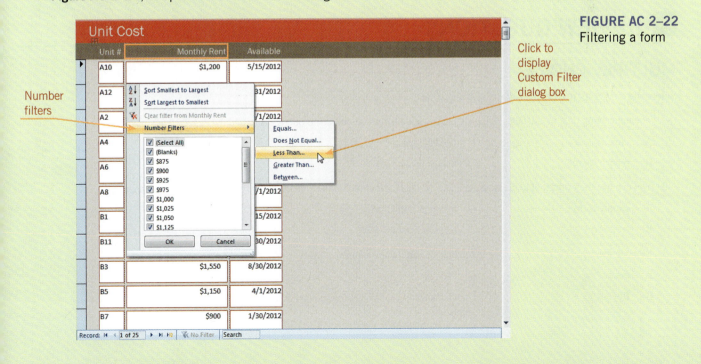

FIGURE AC 2–22
Filtering a form

Click to display Custom Filter dialog box

Number filters

11. If the Monthly rent is less than or equal to text box, type **1000** and then click the **OK** button to display only the records where the monthly rent is less than or equal to $1,000.

12. On the Home tab, in the Sort & Filter group, click the **Toggle Filter** button to remove the filter.

13. Close the Unit Cost form without saving the changes.

14. Close the database and close Access.

SUMMARY

In this lesson, you learned:

- The process of creating a query.
- Ways to create and use different forms.
- How to modify forms.
- Ways to create reports.
- How to modify and print reports.
- To sort and filter records.

■ VOCABULARY REVIEW

Define the following terms:

AutoFormat	query	run
control	Query Wizard	select query
filter	record source	simple form
form	report	sort
Form Wizard	Report Wizard	

■ REVIEW QUESTIONS

MULTIPLE CHOICE

Select the best response for the following statements.

1. The underlying data in a database that is used to create forms, records, and queries is called the _____.

   A. table source
   B. record source
   C. field source
   D. data source

2. You can use the Form tool to create a 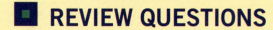 that includes all the fields from the selected record source.

   A. simple form
   B. split form
   C. multiple items form
   D. form in Design view

3. You can use _____ view to enter or edit data in a form.

   A. Form
   B. Layout
   C. Design
   D. Datasheet

LESSON 2 Creating Queries, Forms, and Reports

4. To select a table to use as the record source for a report, select it in the _____.
   A. Open dialog box
   B. Create tab
   C. Record Wizard
   D. Navigation Pane

5. You can print a report from _____ view.
   A. Report
   B. Print Preview
   C. Layout
   D. any of the above

6. A _____ is a database object that is based upon a specific question you ask about the data in the database.
   A. table
   B. query
   C. form
   D. report

7. When you use the Query Wizard to create a simple select query, it is initially displayed in _____ view.
   A. Datasheet
   B. Layout
   C. Design
   D. Query

8. When you click the Add Existing Fields button in the Controls group on the Form Layout Tools Format tab the _____ is displayed.
   A. Add Fields pane
   B. Add Fields dialog box
   C. Fields List pane
   D. Fields List dialog box

9. When you _____, Access rearranges selected data alphabetically, numerically, or chronologically.
   A. sort
   B. filter
   C. query
   D. save

10. To remove a filter, you can click the _____ button in the Sort & Filter group on the Home tab.
    A. Delete Filter
    B. Toggle Filter
    C. Remove Filter
    D. Clear Filter

FILL IN THE BLANK

Complete the following sentences by writing the correct word or words in the blanks provided.

1. When you use the Form tool to create a form that includes all fields from that table, it is displayed in _____ view.

2. To delete a field from a report in Layout view, click the field name to select it and display it with a(n) _____ border, then press the Delete key.

3. The _____ is an Access tool that guides you through the process of creating a form.

4. A(n) _____ is a database object used to present a summary of data in a table that is often printed out.

5. To see how a report will look when printed, you can display it in _____.

6. You can start the Report Wizard by clicking the Report Wizard button in the Reports group on the _____ tab.

7. A(n) _____ is a predefined set of fonts, colors, and borders that Access provides to quickly give your form or report a professional and consistent look.

8. A(n) _____ query retrieves specific data out of a record source for you to use.

9. _____ order sorts text from Z to A, numbers from 9 to 0, and dates from latest to earliest.

10. A(n) _____ _____ is any object on a form or report that you can change to modify or enhance the appearance of the form or report.

PROJECTS

PROJECT AC 2–1

1. Open the file **Contributions.accdb** from the folder containing the data files for this lesson and enable the database content.
2. Open the Donations table to view the data and then close it.
3. Create a simple form based on the Donations table.
4. Navigate through all the records.
5. Save the form as **Donations**.
6. View the form in Layout view.
7. Select the ID field and delete it from the form.
8. Move the Payment Method field so it appears between the Amount and Payment Date fields.
9. Switch to Form view. Create a new record with the following information:

   Contributor: **Consolidated Messenger**

   Amount: **$125**

   Payment Method: **cash**

   Payment Date: **12/16/2012**
10. Save and close the Donations form.
11. Open the Donations table and see that the new data was added.
12. Close the Donations table and leave the database open for use in the next project.

ON YOUR OWN

In the **Contributions.accdb** database, use the Form Wizard to create a form based on the Contributors table using all the fields except the ID field, with a Columnar layout, in Module style, and name it **Company Contributors**.

PROJECT AC 2–2

The **Contributions.accdb** database from Project AC 2-1 should be open in the Access program window.

1. Create a simple report based on the Donations table.
2. Save the report as **Donations**.
3. Use the Median AutoFormat to format the report.
4. Sort the Payment Date column in Descending order.
5. Clear the sort order.
6. Sort the Amount column in Ascending order.
7. Select the ID field and delete it.
8. Select the Payment Method field and size it to fit the data.
9. Switch to Print Preview view and print the report.
10. Close the Donations report. Leave the database open for use in the next project.

ON YOUR OWN

In the **Contributions.accdb** database, use the Report Wizard to create a report based on the Contributors table using the Company and Business Phone fields. Experiment with the options until you create a report that you like. Modify and format it as needed, and then print it.

PROJECT AC 2–3

The **Contributions.accdb** database from Project AC 2-2 should be open in the Access program window.

1. Create a simple query based on the Donations field that includes the Contributor, Amount, and Payment Date fields and title it **Donations Query**.
2. Filter the query to only show donations greater than or equal to $275.
3. Remove the filter.
4. Filter the query to only show donations made by the Graphic Design Institute.
5. Remove the filter.
6. Sort the query by the Amount field in Descending order.
7. Save and close the query.
8. Close the database.

PROJECT AC 2–4

1. Open the file **Math Department.accdb** from the folder containing the data files for this lesson and enable the content.
2. Select the Faculty table in the Navigation Pane.
3. Use the Form Wizard to create a form that includes all fields except the Faculty ID field. Give the form a Justified layout, with Technic style, and title it **Faculty**.
4. View the form in Form view. Navigate to the last record and change the Homeroom field value from 109 to 219.
5. Close the form.

LESSON 2 Creating Queries, Forms, and Reports

6. Use the Report Wizard to create a report based on the Classes table that includes the Period, Room, and Teacher fields, grouped by period, with Stepped layout, Origin style, and title it **Classes by Periods**.

7. Print the report and close it.

8. Create a simple form based on the Classes table.

9. Change the title of the form to **Math Classes**.

10. Switch to Layout view.

11. Insert the logo file **Math logo.jpg** from the location where you store your data files for this lesson.

12. Save the form as **Classes**.

13. Close the database.

TEAMWORK PROJECT

PROJECT AC 2–5

Open the **Caprock View Apartments.accdb** database that you worked with in this lesson. With a partner, take turns providing requirements for an apartment you might want to rent. For example, you might want to rent a two-bedroom apartment that has a washer and dryer. Or, you might want to rent something for less than $1,100 per month. Your partner can create a query to determine which apartments meet your requirements.

WEB PROJECT

PROJECT AC 2–6

Many businesses and organizations use databases to provide information online—for example, genealogy sites offer ancestral information and car dealerships show which cars are in stock. Search the Internet for other examples of how databases are used online. Visit the Web site of a local library that has an online database of available books. On a piece of paper, sketch a database table that would contain information about books the library has that you have read or want to check out. In Access, create the database table that you sketched and enter at least five records. Create a simple report based on the information and format it attractively.

CRITICAL THINKING

ACTIVITY AC 2–1

Open a database that you worked with in Access Lesson 1 and create a form that you can use to enter data into one of the tables. Which type of form did you create and why? View the form in Layout view and use the buttons on the Format Layout Tools Format and Arrange tabs to modify the design of the form to your liking.

ACTIVITY AC 2–2

Open a database that you worked with in Access Lesson 1 and create a report based on one of the tables. Which tool did you use to create the report and why? View the report in Layout view and use the buttons on the Report Layout Tools contextual tabs to modify the design of the form to your liking. Preview the report and then print it.

UNIT REVIEW

Access

REVIEW QUESTIONS

MULTIPLE CHOICE

Select the best response for the following statements.

1. All the information about one specific student in a table, such as the student's name, grade level, and phone number, would be stored in one _____.
   - A. field
   - B. record
   - C. datasheet
   - D. field value

2. Each field in a datasheet is displayed as a column and is identified by its _____ on the column header.
   - A. foreign key
   - B. primary key
   - C. field value
   - D. field name

3. Each record in the database must have a _____, which is the value in the primary key field that makes the record unique.
   - A. field value
   - B. key value
   - C. foreign key
   - D. record selector

4. Access is considered a _____ because all of the data is stored in separate tables and then connected by establishing relationships between the tables.
   - A. primary database
   - B. key database
   - C. relational database
   - D. table database

5. Which database object summarizes and presents information in an easily readable format suitable for printing?
   - A. table
   - B. query
   - C. form
   - D. report

6. The _____ on the left side of the Access program window lists all of the objects in the database.
   - A. Ribbon
   - B. Navigation Pane
   - C. Blank Database pane
   - D. Office Button menu

AC 55

7. When you create a simple form, it initially is displayed in _____ view.
   A. Form
   B. Layout
   C. Datasheet
   D. Design

8. You can start the Form Wizard by clicking the _____ button in the Forms group on the Create tab and then clicking Form Wizard.
   A. Form
   B. Blank Form
   C. More Forms
   D. Form Design

9. Each field in a table has a _____ that determines the types of field values you can enter in that field.
   A. key value
   B. field value
   C. data type
   D. field name

10. A _____ is any object on a form or report that you can change to modify or enhance the appearance of the form or report.
    A. key value
    B. filter
    C. record source
    D. control

FILL IN THE BLANK

Complete the following sentences by writing the correct word or words in the blanks provided.

1. The _____ is an Access tool that guides you through the process of creating a query.
2. You can display the Getting Started with Microsoft Office Access window at any time by clicking the _____ command on the Office Button menu.
3. When you create a new table, Access creates a field named _____ by default and sets it as the primary key.
4. An Access _____ is an object that you use to enter new records into the database, or to edit existing records.
5. You can use a form to enter new data into the table or edit existing records by switching to _____ view.
6. When you create a new table, Access creates a field by default, sets it as the primary key, and assigns it the _____ data type.
7. You can change the field name by clicking the _____ button in the Fields & Columns group on the Table Tools Datasheet tab and then typing a new field name.
8. After you have created a report, you can run it at any time by double-clicking it in the _____ to open it.
9. To see how a report will look when printed, you can display it in _____.
10. To remove a sort from a database object, you can click the _____ button in the Sort & Filter group on the Home tab.

■ PROJECTS

PROJECT AC 1

1. Start Access.
2. Open the file **Voting.accdb** from the folder containing the data files for this review and enable the database content.
3. Rename the Location table as **Polling Places**.
4. Open the Polling Places table.
5. Widen the fields so all data is visible.
6. Add a new field named **Early Voting** and assign a Yes/No data type.
7. Place check marks in the Early Voting field check boxes for records 2 and 5.
8. Edit the location in record 1 to read **Aurora City Hall**.
9. Create a field named **Notes** and assign it the Memo data type.

UNIT V Microsoft Access

10. In the Notes field of record 3, type **not wheelchair accessible**, and widen the column so the data is fully visible.
11. Save and close the Polling Places table.
12. Delete the table named Election Judges.
13. Close the database.

PROJECT AC 2

1. Create a new, blank database named **Swim Meets.accdb**.
2. Rename the default ID field as **Event ID** and change the data type to Text.
3. Add the following fields with corresponding data type:

    Event—Text data type

    Location—Text data type

    Event Date—Date data type

4. Enter the data into the table, as shown in **Figure AC 1**. Widen fields as necessary to fully display data.

Event ID	Event	Location	Event Date
MAC-S1	Time Trials	Massey Aquatic Center	9/30/2012
LRC-S2	Lorenzo Relays	Lorenzo Rec Center	10/15/2012
GSD-SD1	Early Bird Invitational	Greenville Swim Deck	10/25/2012
MAC-SD2	Northwest Invitational	Massey Aquatic Center	11/14/2012
FAC-SD3	Franklin Invitational	Franklin Athletic Complex	12/2/2012
GSD-SD4	Regional Championship	Greenville Swim Deck	1/9/2013
PMP-SD5	State Championship	Pierre Municipal Pool	1/17/2013

FIGURE AC 1 Swim Meet.accdb table

5. Save the table as **Events**.
6. In the Events table, move the Event Date field between the Event and Location fields.
7. Change the format of the Event Date field to Medium Date.
8. Make the Event field required.
9. Save and close the table.
10. Leave the database open for use in the next project.

PROJECT AC 3

The Swim Meets.accdb database from Project AC 2 should be open in the Access program window.

1. Create a simple form based on the Events table.
2. Save the form as **Events** and switch to Form view.
3. Use the form to create a new record with the following information:

    Event ID: **AWD-SD6**
    Event: **Award Ceremony**
    Location: **Massey Aquatic Center**
    Event Date: **January 30, 2013**

4. Switch to Layout view.
5. Change the title of the form to **Swimming and Diving**.
6. Apply the Flow AutoFormat to the form.
7. Insert a logo on the form using the **swim logo.jpg** file from the folder containing the data files for this review.

8. Save and close the form.
9. Create a simple report based on the Events table and save it as **Event Schedule**.
10. In the Event Schedule report, select the Event ID field and delete it.
11. Apply the Urban AutoFormat to the report.
12. Save the report, view it in Print Preview, and then print it.
13. Close the database.

PROJECT AC 4

1. Open the file **Film Festival.accdb** from the folder containing the data files for this review and enable the database content.
2. Create a query based on the Competition Shorts table that includes the Title, Director Last Name, and Director First Name fields. Title the query **Shorts Directors**.
3. Sort the query results by director last name in ascending order.
4. Save and close the query.
5. Use the Form Wizard to create a form based on the Competition Shorts table that includes the ID, Title, Minutes, and Seconds fields. Use the Columnar form and the Concourse style and title it **Short Times**.
6. Switch to Form view and navigate to record 5.
7. Capitalize the *i* in *is* and close the form.
8. Use the Report Wizard to create a report based on the Staff table that includes the Last Name and Title fields. Do not include any grouping or sort order. Use the Tabular layout and the Civic style and title it **Staff**.
9. Switch to Layout view and move the Title field before the Last Name field.
10. View the report in Print Preview and then print it.
11. Save the report and close it. Close the database.

ON YOUR OWN

Open the **Film Festival.accdb** database. Create a simple query, report, and form based on the Fundraisers table. Sort or filter the data and modify the format of each database object using the tools available on the contextual tabs. Close the database.

WEB PROJECT

You want to create a database that has information about your favorite restaurants. Plan the data that you want to include—such as restaurant name, location, phone number, type of food, or favorite dish—and sketch it out on paper. In Access, create a table that includes the fields you designed. Visit the Web sites for at least five restaurants in your city and gather the information you need. Enter at least five records into your table. Create a report based on the table, format it to suit the data, and then print it.

 ## TEAMWORK PROJECT

As a member of the school council, you have been asked to create a database of schoolwide activities for the school year. With a partner, discuss the tables you will need to create to contain this information, what fields will be used, and what data types will be assigned to each field. Sketch a rough draft on paper and then use Access to create the database. Create a form and use it to enter at least 20 records. What kind of database object would you create to find out all the activities going on next month? What are some practical ways your database could be used?

CRITICAL THINKING

ACTIVITY AC 1

Open the **Class Assignments.accdb** database from the folder containing the data files for this review. Open each of the tables and add at least two records to each. Use actual assignments or make them up. Create a report for each table, modify it to suit you, and then print each report.

ACTIVITY AC 2

Use Access Help to search for the demo titled *Meet the Navigation Pane* and watch it. Open the **Film Festival.accdb** database that you used in Project AC 4 and practice using the Navigation Pane to organize the objects in a database into categories and groups.

ACTIVITY AC 3

You want to create a database for all of your music CDs. Think about what kind of information the database will contain—for example, album, artist, year released, or genre of music. Spend some time deciding how it will be designed and sketch a rough draft on paper. After planning your database, use Access to create it. Create a simple form and use it to enter at least 10 records. Create a report that groups the records by some category—for example the most recent CDs or all CDs by one artist—and then print it.

PORTFOLIO CHECKLIST

_____	Lesson 1	Contacts.accdb
_____		Vehicle Records.accdb
_____	Lesson 2	Caprock View Apartments.accdb
_____		Math Department.accdb
_____	Unit Review	Voting.accdb
_____		Swim Meets.accdb

LESSON 1

**Estimated Time:
1.5 hours**

Understanding Publisher Fundamentals

■ OBJECTIVES

Upon completion of this lesson, you should be able to:

- Examine the Publisher program window.
- Start Publisher and choose a publication type.
- Enter and format text.
- Save a publication.
- Format the publication and change the template.
- Insert graphics.
- Preview and print a publication.
- Close a publication.

■ DATA FILES

You do not need data files to complete this lesson.

■ VOCABULARY

alignment
bullets
business information set
clip art
collate
cropping
desktop publishing software
font
font styles
Format Painter
I-beam
insertion point
landscape
pictures
placeholders
point size
portrait
publication
pull quote
scratch area
selection handles
Smart Tag button
story
template
text boxes
…

UNIT VI   Microsoft Publisher

Introduction

Microsoft Publisher 2007 is a desktop publishing program included in the Microsoft Office 2007 suite of software. ***Desktop publishing software*** is used to combine text and graphics to produce high-quality marketing and communications documents for print on a personal desktop printer or by a commercial printer.

Publisher offers a variety of publication templates and designs that you can combine and customize to create professional publications, or you can start from scratch with a blank page. In this lesson, you will learn to create publications using templates and customize them with predefined designs, text, and graphics. You will also learn how to save, print, and close publications.

Examining the Publisher Program Window

A Publisher file is called a publication. A ***publication*** is a document, such as a newsletter, brochure, business card, or greeting card that is created to market a product or communicate a message to an audience.

Unlike other Microsoft Office 2007 programs, Publisher does not organize commands within a Ribbon, but uses menus, toolbars, and task panes, as shown in **Figure PB 1–1**. Use this figure to become familiar with the parts of the Publisher program window.

> ▶ **VOCABULARY**
> desktop publishing software
> publication

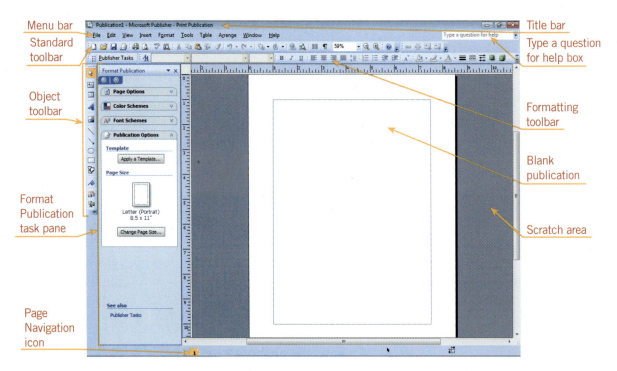

FIGURE PB 1–1   Publisher program window

The default file name of a new publication is Publication1; the filename is displayed at the top of the screen in the title bar, as shown in Figure PB 1–1. Below the title bar is the menu bar, which contains menus that list related commands. The Standard toolbar contains buttons for performing common tasks such as saving, printing, and zooming in or out of a page. The Formatting toolbar contains additional commands for changing the format of text or graphics, such as applying bold

LESSON 1 Understanding Publisher Fundamentals

to text, formatting text with bullets, and filling a shape with a color. The Object toolbar is positioned vertically on the left side of the screen with buttons for inserting various kinds of objects, such as text boxes, tables, shapes, pictures, and WordArt. The Format Publication task pane provides options for formatting the page, such as changing color schemes or font schemes. Publisher also displays horizontal and vertical rulers. The blank area around the publication is called the *scratch area*, which is a workspace that you can use to store or work with graphics or text boxes. Items on the scratch area are visible while you work on any page in your publication. For example, you can move a graphic from page 1 to the scratch area, continue working and then display page 5 and drag the graphic from the scratch area onto the page where you want it.

> **VOCABULARY**
> scratch area

Starting Publisher and Opening a Template

To begin using Publisher, you first need to open it by clicking the Start button on the Windows taskbar, and then clicking the program name on the All Programs menu, or by double-clicking a Publisher program icon on the desktop. Once Publisher is started, you can begin using it to create a new publication or open an existing publication. When you start Publisher, the Getting Started with Microsoft Office Publisher 2007 window opens, as shown in **Figure PB 1–2**.

> **EXTRA FOR EXPERTS**
> The arrow button at the right end of each toolbar allows you to access buttons that are not visible on the toolbar, and you can choose to customize toolbars with the commands you use often by adding or removing buttons.

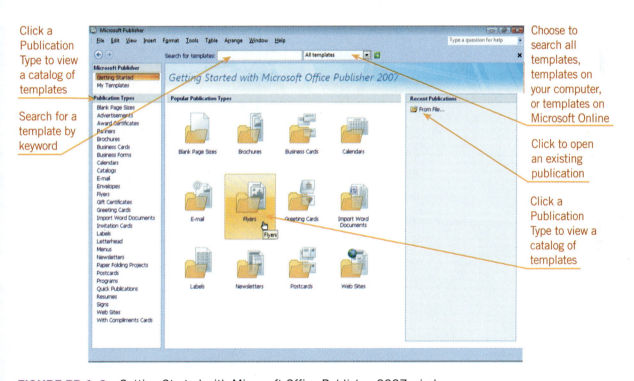

Click a Publication Type to view a catalog of templates

Search for a template by keyword

Choose to search all templates, templates on your computer, or templates on Microsoft Online

Click to open an existing publication

Click a Publication Type to view a catalog of templates

FIGURE PB 1–2 Getting Started with Microsoft Office Publisher 2007 window

You can choose a template for the type of publication you want to create from the Publication Types list in the left pane, or you can click a folder in the center pane to view the catalog of available templates within a category, such as brochures. Publisher also lists in the right pane publications that you have recently created. You can search Publisher's Help system by typing a question or keywords in the Type a question for help box.

UNIT VI Microsoft Publisher

One method of creating a well-designed publication quickly is to use a template. A *template* is a sample publication that provides a pattern or model that you can follow to create your own publication. Publisher includes templates for many common types of publications, including newsletters, brochures, greeting cards, flyers, and even Web sites.

Publisher's templates are organized in categories of publication types on the Getting Started screen. Additional templates are available for download from Microsoft Office Online. You can display these by clicking the View templates from Microsoft Office Online link within each publication catalog.

When you open a template, you are actually opening a copy of the template, so the original template is not altered as you customize the publication. A publication template contains a color scheme, font scheme, clip art or other graphics, text boxes, and placeholders for text. Add your own text in a template by clicking a placeholder and then typing. Name and save a new publication using the Save or Save As command.

You can create a new blank publication by clicking the Blank Page Sizes folder in the Publication Types category. A catalog of blank page sizes lets you select a size, or you can create a custom page size.

To open an existing publication, you can click the From File folder in the Recent Publications list where you can search for and then open Publisher files using the Open dialog box.

VOCABULARY
template

WARNING
To use a template from Microsoft Office Online, you must download it. The first time you download a template, Microsoft will verify that the software you are using is authentic. You cannot download templates without genuine Microsoft Office software.

Step-by-Step PB 1.1

1. Click the **Start** button on the Windows taskbar. The Start menu opens.
2. Click **All Programs**. A list of programs and program folders opens.
3. Click the **Microsoft Office** program folder. A list of Office programs opens.
4. Click **Microsoft Office Publisher 2007**. Publisher starts and the Getting Started with Microsoft Office Publisher 2007 window opens on the desktop.
5. In the Popular Publication Types area, click the **Flyers** folder to display a catalog of publication templates.
6. In the Informational section, click the **Bounce** option, as shown in **Figure PB 1–3**. Notice that a preview appears in the right pane, along with customizable design elements that you can change now or later.

LESSON 1   Understanding Publisher Fundamentals

FIGURE PB 1-3
Flyers template catalog

7. Click the **Create** button to open the template shown in **Figure PB 1-4**.

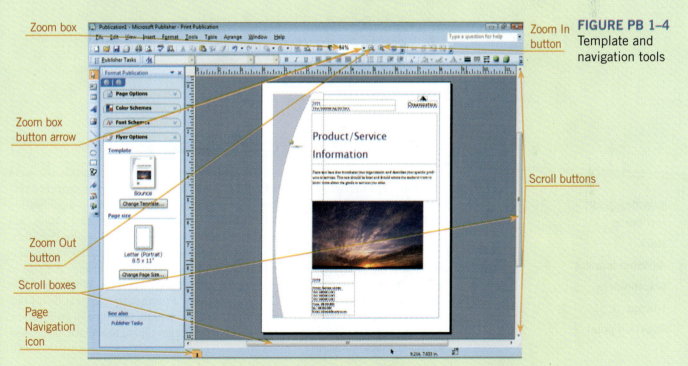

FIGURE PB 1-4
Template and navigation tools

8. Leave the publication open for use in the next Step-by-Step.

UNIT VI   Microsoft Publisher

Navigating the Publication

When working with a publication, it is important to know how to move from page to page and to zoom in and out. You navigate a publication in Publisher similar to the way you get around in other programs. Use the vertical and horizontal scroll boxes, shown in Figure PB 1–4, to display parts of a page. The Page Navigation icons at the bottom of the screen let you move from page to page. When you need to zoom in or out to work on a particular area of a publication, use the Zoom In or Zoom Out button on the Standard Toolbar or choose a zoom percentage by clicking the Zoom box button arrow. You can select an object and press the F9 key to zoom to 100%.

Step-by-Step PB 1.2

The publication from Step-by-Step PB 1.1 should be open in the Publisher program window.

1. On the Standard toolbar, click the **Zoom In** button.
2. Press the **F9** key to zoom to 100%.
3. Drag the vertical scroll box to the bottom.
4. Click the **Zoom** list button arrow 100% and click **200%**.
5. Click the **Zoom Out** button three times.
6. Click the **Zoom** list button arrow and click **Whole Page.**
7. Leave the publication open for use in the next Step-by-Step.

Entering and Formatting Text

Unlike Word, where you type on the page and the text flows from margin to margin and from page to page, a Publisher publication is made up of an arrangement of several different text boxes. *Text boxes* are containers for text. All text in a publication is stored within text boxes. All the text within a single text box is called a *story*, and you can select a story by pressing Ctrl+A. Text boxes are objects within Publisher, so you can click them once to select them. The small circles at the sides and corners of the text box are *selection handles*. You drag these handles to change the size of an object. A green rotate handle allows you to rotate the text box. When a text box is selected, you can add borders, fills, and effects. *Placeholders* are text boxes that contain suggestions for content that is standard for a particular type of publication. You can click the placeholder text to select it and begin typing to replace the content provided with your own.

> **VOCABULARY**
> text boxes
> story
> selection handles
> placeholders
> I-beam
> insertion point

Entering Text in a Text Box

To enter text in a text box, click the *I-beam* (the shape of the mouse pointer in a text box) anywhere in the text box. A blinking cursor, called an *insertion point*, indicates where your entry will appear. When you click placeholder text, all the text is selected and you can begin typing to replace the text. Click a blank space on publication to deselect.

LESSON 1   Understanding Publisher Fundamentals

After you enter text in a text box, you can easily edit, insert, delete, or copy text from one text box to another. Editing text in a text box is the same as editing text in Word or other Microsoft Office programs. You can select text within a text box by dragging or using keyboard combinations. To delete text in a text box, position the insertion point and press Backspace to delete characters to the left of the insertion point. Press Delete to delete characters to the right of the insertion point. When deleting more than a few characters, select the text to be deleted and press Delete.

You can delete a text box by selecting it and pressing the Delete key. To reverse, or undo, an action, use the Undo button on the Standard toolbar. If you perform an undo action but then decide against the undo, use the Redo button on the Standard toolbar to reverse the undo action.

You can draw a new text box using the Text Box tool on the Objects Toolbar. Click in the location where you want the text box and drag to draw the size text box that you want.

> **EXTRA FOR EXPERTS**
>
> You can connect, or link, two or more text boxes by selecting the first text box, clicking the Create Text Box Link button on the Connect Text Boxes toolbar, and then clicking the text box you want to link to with the pitcher pointer. The text would flow from one text box to the other as one story.

Creating a Business Information Set

A *business information set* is a group of data, such as name, address, and job title, that can be saved together as a set and used repeatedly to populate future publications. For example, you can create a business information set that includes a company logo, name, address, telephone number, and Web site address. You can create an unlimited number of business information sets to use in publications. You may have one for your organization and a different one for personal use. Business information sets can be edited, changed, and updated any time using the Business Information command on the Edit menu, or you can click a Smart Tag button to display a shortcut menu for editing, saving, or updating information. A *Smart Tag button* is a circle icon with an *i* in the center that appears when you point to or click on data that is part of a business information set. Nonprinting blue dots underline business information text in a publication.

> **VOCABULARY**
> **business information set**
> **Smart Tag button**

Step-by-Step PB 1.3

The publication from Step-by-Step PB 1.2 should be open in the Publisher program window.

1. Click the **Product/Service Information** placeholder text to select it, as shown in **Figure PB 1–5**.

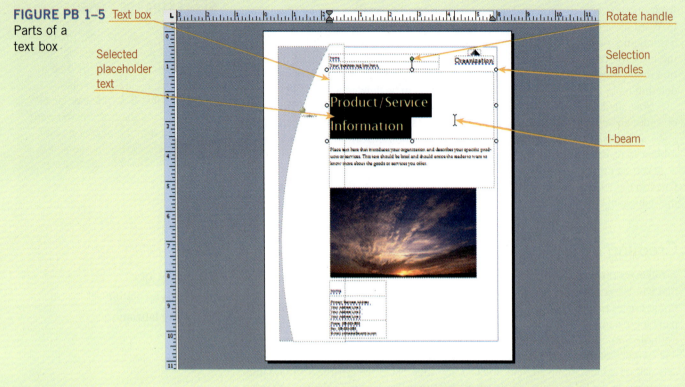

FIGURE PB 1–5 Parts of a text box

2. Type **Scuba Diving Lessons** as the title of the publication.
3. Press **F9** to zoom in so that you can read the text.
4. Click the placeholder text in the text box below the title that begins with *Place text here...* and type the following text:

   Whether you dream of swimming with colorful fish, brushing past a sea turtle, or investigating colorful coral, exploring the ocean is a very rewarding experience. Our goal is to train you to be a safe, confident diver. We offer a professional educational experience that will also be great fun. Contact us for a personal consultation.

5. Position the pointer over the word *home* in blue text below the picture at the bottom of the page until you see the Smart Tag button appear. (*Note:* If no one has set up a business information set on your computer before, the words *home*, *Microsoft*, or Business Name might be displayed as a placeholder. If a business information set has been created, the previously entered information will be displayed.)
6. Click the **Smart Tag** button to display the shortcut menu.
7. Click **Edit Business Information** to display the Create New Business Information Set dialog box. (Note: If a business information set already exists, click the **New** button to display the Create New Business Information Set dialog box.)
8. Type **Jacque Blue** in the Individual name box and press **Tab**.

LESSON 1 Understanding Publisher Fundamentals

9. Replace the placeholder data in the text boxes with the remaining business information, as shown in **Figure PB 1–6**.

FIGURE PB 1–6
Create New Business Information Set dialog box

10. Below the logo, click **Remove**. A message appears asking if you want to remove the logo. Click **Yes**.
11. Type **Azul Scuba Diving** in the Business Information set name box.
12. Click the **Save** button to save the business information set.
13. Click the **Update Publication** button to populate the publication. Notice that the publication now reflects the business set data.
14. Leave the publication open for use in the next Step-by-Step.

Changing Font Characteristics

A *font* is a design of a set of letters and numbers. Each set has a name, such as Arial or Times New Roman.

The Font menu on the formatting toolbar displays each font's design before you make a choice. You change to a different font by selecting text and choosing one of the fonts listed on the Font menu.

Font sizes are measured in points. *Point size* refers to a measurement for the height of characters. To change the font size for existing text, you first select the text and then choose a new size on the Font Size menu on the Formatting toolbar.

The Increase Font Size button increases font size one increment on the Font Size menu, which may be one point, two points, or eight points in the larger sizes, and the Decrease Font Size button decreases the size one increment.

Font styles are variations in the shape or weight of a font's characters. Bold, italic, and underline are common font styles that you can access easily on the Formatting toolbar. The Font Color button on the Formatting toolbar lets you change the text color.

> **VOCABULARY**
> font
> point size
> font styles

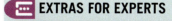 **EXTRAS FOR EXPERTS**

You can use shortcut keys: Ctrl+B to apply bold, Ctrl+I to apply italic, and Ctrl+U to underline text.

VOCABULARY
alignment
bullets
Format Painter

> **EXTRAS FOR EXPERTS**
>
> Another way to change fonts, font sizes, font styles, and font effects is to click the Format menu and choose Font to display the Font dialog box, where you can make several changes in one place.

> **EXTRAS FOR EXPERTS**
>
> You can use shortcut keys: Ctrl+L to align text left, Ctrl+R to align text right, Ctrl+E to center text, and Ctrl+J to justify text.

Aligning Text Horizontally

Alignment is the position of text in relation to the edges of a text box. You can left-align, center, right-align, or justify text horizontally within a text box using the alignment buttons—Align Text Left, Center, Align Text Right, and Justify—on the Formatting toolbar.

Setting Line Spacing

Line spacing determines the vertical distance between lines of text in a paragraph. The Line Spacing button on the Formatting toolbar displays the Paragraph dialog box, which contains options for creating custom line spacing and for adding spacing before or after a paragraph.

Formatting Lists

Bullets are small symbols that mark the beginning of a list item. You can select an existing list and then click the Bullets button or the Numbering button on the Formatting toolbar to add bullets or numbers. Use the Increase Indent Position and Decrease Indent Position buttons on the Formatting toolbar to move to a higher level or down to a lower level.

The Bullets and Numbering command on the Format menu displays the Bullets and Numbering dialog box where you can choose bullet characters and numbering formats.

Publisher automatically renumbers a numbered list when you insert, move, copy, or delete items. A new bullet is added on a blank line when you press Enter at the end of a bulleted item.

Copying Formats Using the Format Painter

The *Format Painter* can save you time and helps ensure consistency by allowing you to copy text that contains multiple formatting characteristics and then apply the same formatting to other parts of the publication. When you click the Format Painter button, your mouse pointer changes to an I-beam with a paintbrush.

To copy formatting of text, you first select the text or paragraph that contains the formatting you want to copy and then click the Format Painter button. The mouse pointer will change to an I-beam with a paintbrush "loaded" with the copied format. Next you click in the text box where you want to apply the formatting and the formatting is applied to the entire text box.

Step-by-Step PB 1.4

The publication from Step-by-Step PB 1.3 should be open in the Publisher program window.

1. Select **Scuba Diving Lessons**. Click the **Font** button arrow `Times New Roman`, scroll up, and click **Arial** to change the font.
2. Click the **Font Size** arrow `10`, scroll down, and click **48**.
3. Click the **Bold** button **B**.

LESSON 1   Understanding Publisher Fundamentals   PB 11

4. Click the **Center** button .

5. Leave the publication open for use in the next Step-by-Step.

Saving a Publication

The first time you save a publication, the options for saving include the Save button on the Standard Toolbar, or the Save and Save As commands on the File menu. Each of these methods displays the Save As dialog box, as shown in **Figure PB 1–7**.

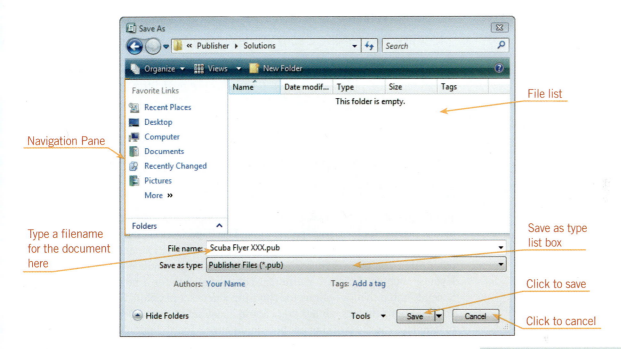

FIGURE PB 1–7   Save As dialog box

After you save a file the first time, the Save command saves your file with the previously specified name in the location you specified. The Save As command lets you make a copy of the file with a new name, location, or file type. The Save as type menu lets you save a publication in another format or as a template. To save a publication in a specific location, you use the Navigation Pane to navigate to the folder in which you want to save the publication. Once you have saved the file, you can use the Save button on the Standard Toolbar, the Save command on the File menu, or press Ctrl+S to save your changes.

Publisher's AutoRecover feature automatically saves your publication at regular intervals so that you can recover at least some of your work in case of a power outage or other unexpected shutdown. You can turn this feature on or off and change the setting to save more or less often by opening the Options dialog box from the Tools menu. On the Save tab, specify a number in the Save AutoRecover info every x minutes box. However, you should not rely on this automatic saving feature. Remember to save your work often.

> **EXTRAS FOR EXPERTS**
>
> Publisher files are saved with the extension .pub. If you want to save a publication as a template, choose the Publisher Template option from the Save as type list in the Save As dialog box. You can save a publication in the .pdf format after you download the necessary add-in. On the File menu, click Find add-ins for other formats to display a help page with a link to the Microsoft add-in web page.

> **EXTRA FOR EXPERTS**
>
> You can use Ctrl+S to save a file.

Step-by-Step PB 1.5

The publication from Step-by-Step PB 1.4 should be open in the Publisher program window.

1. Click the **File** menu and then click **Save As** to open the Save As dialog box.
2. Navigate to the location where you will save your files.
3. If necessary, select **Publication1.pub** in the File name text box and type **Scuba Flyer XXX.pub** (replace *XXX* with your initials) in the box to rename the file.
4. Click **Save** to save a copy of the publication with the new name in the specified location.
5. Leave the publication open for use in the next Step-by-Step.

Formatting the Publication and Changing the Template

The Format Publication task pane on the left side of the screen contains options for modifying the look of your publication. The Page Options tab provides suggested objects you can consider including in your publication. Depending on the type of publication you are working with, Page Options might include options for different layouts, such as choices for different column layouts for a newsletter. The Color Schemes tab provides options for choosing a new set of colors for your publication, and the Font Schemes tab lets you choose a new set of fonts. Depending on the type of template you are working on, you might have a fourth option tab for changing the design or page size of the template.

Within the options tab for the open publication is the Change Template button. This button opens the Change Template dialog box, which allows you to either create a new publication with the current data or transfer your current data to another template. If you change to a different type of template, the new template might not have placeholders for all of the data; for example, changing from a newsletter to a business card template will leave some of the newsletter content without an equivalent location in the new template. In this case, extra data is transferred to the Extra Content tab where you can add it to your publication, delete it, or save it to the Content library for use it in another publication.

WARNING

If you change templates without saving the file first, the original publication will be lost.

LESSON 1   Understanding Publisher Fundamentals

Step-by-Step PB 1.6

The Scuba Flyer *XXX*.pub publication from Step-by-Step PB 1.5 should be open in the Publisher program window.

1. In the Format Publication task pane, click the **Page Options** tab.
2. Scroll down to see all the suggested objects that can be included in your publication.
3. Click the **Color Schemes** tab.
4. Scroll down and point to the **Marine** option. Click the button arrow and click **Apply Scheme** to apply the new color scheme.
5. Click the **Font Schemes** tab.
6. Scroll down and point to the **Breve** option. Click the button arrow and click **Apply Scheme** to apply the new font scheme.
7. Click the **Flyer Options** tab.
8. Click the **Change Template** button, as shown in **Figure PB 1–8**, to display the Change Template dialog box.

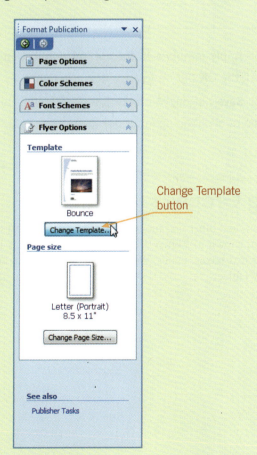

FIGURE PB 1–8
Format Publication task pane

9. Scroll down to the Classic Designs: Informational section and click **Waves,** as shown in **Figure PB 1–9**, and click **OK** to display the Change Template dialog box.

FIGURE PB 1–9
Change Template dialog box

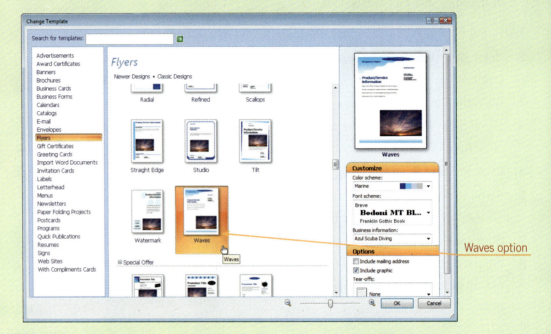

10. Click the **Apply template to the current publication** option button and then click the **OK** button to apply the new template.
11. Click the **Save** button on the Standard toolbar to save the changes. Leave the publication open for use in the next Step-by-Step.

Inserting Graphics

Pictures, clip art, and other graphic objects add visual interest to a publication. The Objects toolbar, shown in **Figure PB 1–10**, contains buttons for inserting graphic objects such as text boxes, tables, WordArt, pictures and clip art, lines, shapes, and Design Gallery Objects.

LESSON 1 Understanding Publisher Fundamentals

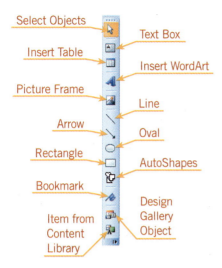

FIGURE PB 1–10 Object toolbar

When you click a button on the Objects toolbar, you will be able to choose the graphic object you want from a dialog box, task pane, or menu; the access method varies by object. You can modify the object after you insert it.

Inserting Design Gallery Objects

The Design Gallery contains predesigned objects that you can use in your publications. These include accent boxes, borders, coupons, mastheads, pull quotes, and logos. The size, shape, and content of these objects can be modified to fit your needs.

A *pull quote* is a quotation that is enlarged for emphasis. The Design Gallery contains many different pull quote designs. After you insert a pull quote or other Design Gallery Object, you can replace the placeholder text with your own.

> **EXTRA FOR EXPERTS**
>
> You can create a logo using the logo graphics in the Design Gallery and save it as a picture file. This allows you to use the graphic in other publications and include it in your business information set.
>
> ▶ **VOCABULARY**
> **pull quote**

Step-by-Step PB 1.7

The Scuba Flyer *XXX*.pub publication from Step-by-Step PB 1.6 should be open in the Publisher program window.

1. On the Objects toolbar, click the **Design Gallery Object** button to open the Design Gallery dialog box.
2. Click the **Pull Quotes** category in the left pane. The Waves option should be selected, as shown in **Figure PB 1–11**.

FIGURE PB 1–11
Design Gallery

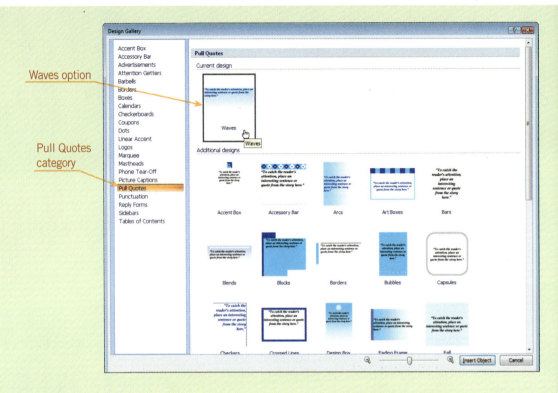

3. Click the **Insert Object** button to insert the pull quote.
4. Drag the pull quote into position above the picture, as shown in **Figure PB 1–12**.

FIGURE PB 1–12
Pull quote

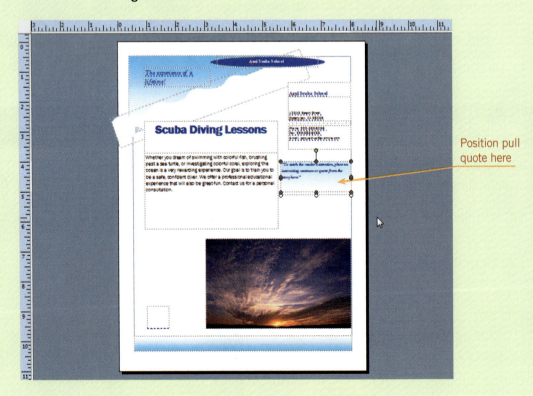

LESSON 1 Understanding Publisher Fundamentals

5. Zoom the publication to 100% or a readable size, click the placeholder text, and type **"The Azul Scuba School is great! The instructors are very knowledgeable and professional."**
6. Press **Enter** and type **Shelley Marc.**
7. Drag the upper-left resizing handle to the right, as shown in **Figure PB 1–13**, to resize the text box.

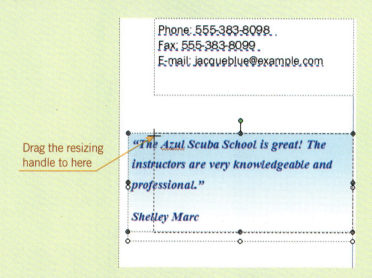

FIGURE PB 1–13
Resize a text box

8. Save and leave the publication open for use in the next Step-by-Step.

Inserting Pictures and Clip Art

The Picture Frame button on the Objects toolbar displays a menu that you can use to insert clip art, a picture from a file, an empty picture frame, or a picture from a camera or scanner. See **Figure PB 1–14**.

UNIT VI   Microsoft Publisher

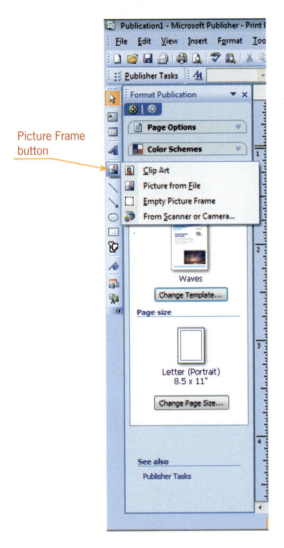

FIGURE PB 1-14   Picture Frame button and menu

▶ **VOCABULARY**

pictures

clip art

Pictures, or digital photographs or images, may be stored on your computer or network. The Insert Picture dialog box lets you navigate to and insert a picture file from your computer or network. You can insert pictures of various formats, including .tif, .gif, and .jpeg.

Clip art is artwork such as drawings or images. The Clip Art task pane lets you search for and insert clip art located on your computer, network, or on the Internet. The Search in menu lets you choose which collections to search, and the Results should be menu lets you choose the type of media file you are searching for, including clip art, pictures, sounds, and movies.

LESSON 1 Understanding Publisher Fundamentals

Before you can modify or resize a picture, clip art, or shape, you must select it. To select a graphic, such as a picture or drawing, within a publication and display the selection handles, click the graphic once. You drag these handles to change the graphic's size. When you want to resize a graphic proportionally, that is, to maintain the original ratio of height to width, you must display the sizing pointer and drag a corner handle. Some types of graphics require that you hold the Shift key while dragging a corner handle when sizing proportionally. If you want to distort a graphic horizontally or vertically, drag a middle handle.

You can click the green rotate circle at the top of a graphic to rotate it on its central axis left or right to any position.

When a graphic is selected, you can copy, paste, and delete it the same way you would with any text using the Cut, Copy, and Paste commands.

Any time the picture is selected, the Picture Toolbar is displayed. As shown in **Figure PB 1–15**, this toolbar contains commands for modifying the picture, such as adjusting the brightness, contrast, or color, and *cropping*, or removing, unwanted areas of a picture.

> **EXTRA FOR EXPERTS**
>
> Large files can take longer to download, and some may be rejected by e-mail servers. Including pictures in publications increases file size, but you can use the Compress Pictures button on the Picture Toolbar to decrease a picture's file size by reducing the resolution, or the number of pixels in a picture.

> **VOCABULARY**
> cropping

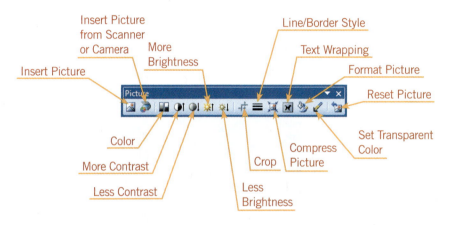

FIGURE PB 1–15 Picture toolbar

> **WARNING**
>
> You can use the images, sounds, and movies Microsoft provides with Publisher or for free on its Web site in any advertising, promotional and marketing materials, or product or service created with Publisher, as long as the material, product, or service is for noncommercial purposes. You may not sell any promotional and marketing materials or any products or services containing the images.

Step-by-Step PB 1.8

The Scuba Flyer *XXX*.pub publication from Step-by-Step PB 1.7 should be open in the Publisher program window.

1. Click the picture in the template to select it and click it again, if necessary, to display the Picture toolbar.

2. Zoom out, if necessary, and click the **Insert Picture** button on the toolbar to open the Insert Picture dialog box.

3. Navigate to the Sample Pictures folder and double-click the **Green Sea Turtle** picture to replace the one in the publication.

4. Click the **More Brightness** button on the Picture toolbar to increase the brightness of the picture.

5. Select the empty text box in the lower-left corner of the page and press **Delete**.

6. On the Objects toolbar, click the **Picture Frame** button and then click **Clip Art** from the menu to open the Clip Art task pane.

7. Type **scuba diving** in the Search box. If necessary, click the **Search in** box arrow, and click the **Everywhere** check box to insert a check mark to search in All collections. Click the **Results should be** box arrow and make sure the **All media types** check box contains a check mark. Click the **Go** button to start the search.

8. In the Clip Art task pane, scroll down if necessary, and click the picture of the **diver with the shark overhead**, as shown in **Figure PB 1–16,** to insert it.

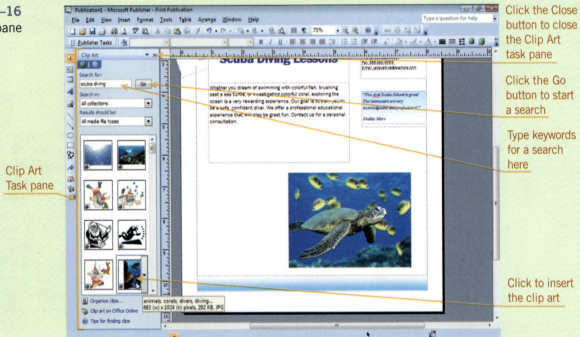

FIGURE PB 1–16
Clip Art task pane

9. Drag the picture to the left to position it in the lower corner of the page.

10. With the picture selected, click the **Crop** button on the Picture Toolbar.

11. Drag the upper-middle cropping handle down to just below the shark, as shown in **Figure PB 1–17,** to remove the unwanted portion of the picture.

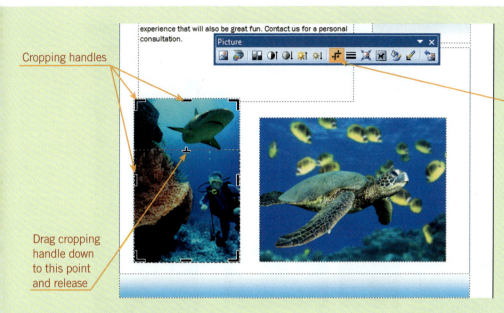

FIGURE PB 1–17
Cropping a picture

12. Click in a blank space to remove the cropping handles and then click the **Close** button ✖ on the Picture toolbar to close it.
13. Click the **Close** button ✖ on the Clip art task pane to close it.
14. Save and leave the publication open for use in the next Step-by-Step.

Previewing and Printing a Publication

Publications are usually printed either at a commercial printer or on a desktop printer. When printing your own publications, you can save time, ink, and paper by using Print Preview to review your choices.

Previewing Printouts

You can preview entire pages of a publication before printing by using the Print Preview command, available through the Standard toolbar or the File menu. In Print Preview mode, Publisher displays the current page and the toolbars and menu changes to the Print Preview toolbar. If you have not changed the default settings, your screen should look similar to the one in **Figure PB 1–18**. In Print Preview, the pointer changes from an arrow to a magnifying glass, which lets you zoom in on an area of a page by clicking the area you want to magnify. To return to the original magnification, click again. The tools on the Print Preview toolbar include the following:

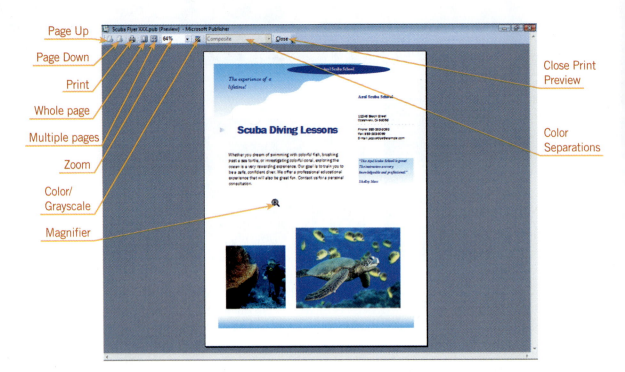

FIGURE PB 1–18 Print Preview

- Page Up and Page Down buttons let you view previous or next pages.
- The Print button displays the Print dialog box where you can set printing options.
- The Whole Page button displays the publication one page at a time.
- The Multiple Pages button lets you view up to six publication pages in the window at the same time.
- The Zoom box lets you type in a magnification percentage or click the button arrow to choose one from the menu.
- The Color/Grayscale button toggles between showing the publication in color or black and white.
- The Color Separations box allows you to view each color on the page separately. This feature is used for publications with commercial printing settings applied.
- The Close Print Preview button returns to the previous view.

Printing a Publication

Both the Print command on the File menu and the Print button on the Print Preview toolbar display the Print dialog box, as shown in **Figure PB 1–19**. The settings in the Print dialog box will differ according to the printer you are using, but some options are common to all printers, including the following:

- The Printer name area, where you select a printer from the list of available printers
- The Printing options area, where you can specify the number of pages to print per sheet

LESSON 1 Understanding Publisher Fundamentals

- The Paper area, where you can specify the size and source of the paper
- The Orientation area, where you can specify *portrait* (vertical page setup) or *landscape* (horizontal page setup) orientation
- The Page range area, where you specify whether to print all pages, the current page, or specified pages of a publication
- The Copies area, where you indicate quantity of copies to print, two-sided printing options, and whether to *collate* the pages, which prints them in order

> **VOCABULARY**
> portrait
> landscape
> collate

> **EXTRA FOR EXPERTS**
> You can use the Print button on the Standard toolbar to print to the default printer without opening the Print dialog box.

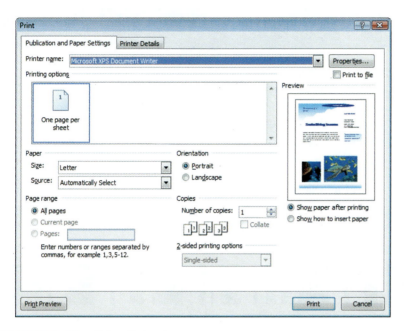

FIGURE PB 1–19 Print dialog box

> **WARNING**
> If you have been instructed not to print, click the Cancel button in the Print dialog box.

Step-by-Step PB 1.9

The Scuba Flyer *XXX*.pub publication from Step-by-Step PB 1.8 should be open in the Publisher program window.

1. Click the **Print Preview** button on the Standard toolbar.
2. Point to the scuba diver picture on the page, and click the **Magnifier** pointer to zoom in.
3. Click the **Color/Grayscale** button to display the page in gray scale.
4. Click the **Color/Grayscale** button again to display the page in color.
5. Click the **Magnifier** point again to return to the previous magnification.
6. Click the **Print** button to display the Print dialog box.
7. Click the **Print** button to print the publication.
8. Save the publication and leave it open for use in the next Step-by-Step.

Closing a Publication

When you are finished with a publication, you can remove it from your screen using the Close command. To close a publication without closing Publisher, choose the Close command on the File menu. When you only have one publication open, you can click the Close button on the title bar or choose the Exit command on the File menu to close the publication and exit Publisher at the same time. The program prompts you to save your work if you made any changes since you last saved the file.

Step-by-Step PB 1.10

The Scuba Flyer *XXX*.pub publication from Step-by-Step PB 1.9 should be open in the Publisher program window.

1. Click the **File** menu and click **Close**. The publication closes and the Getting Started with Microsoft Office Publisher 2007 window is displayed.
2. Click the **Close** button  on the program title bar to exit the program.

TECHNOLOGY CAREERS

Graphic Designer

A graphic designer is often involved in planning, designing, creating, and maintaining a client's Web site. Projects can range from a single Web page to complex sites that include e-commerce capabilities and other advanced interactive features. When creating a Web site, a graphic designer incorporates design principles, typography, graphics manipulation, and technology using publishing software such as Microsoft Publisher to create a positive user experience.

SUMMARY

In this lesson, you learned:

- Publisher does not organize commands within a Ribbon, but uses menus, toolbars, and task panes.
- To start Publisher and open a design template.
- That it is often necessary to use zoom in and zoom out commands to work with a publication.
- To enter and format text within text boxes.
- The Format Publication task pane contains options for modifying the look of a publication and changing the template.
- To insert Design Gallery objects, clip art, and pictures.
- To use the Save As command to save a publication for the first time.
- To preview publications before printing.
- When you close a publication, Publisher prompts you to save your work if you made any changes since you last saved.

LESSON 1 Understanding Publisher Fundamentals

VOCABULARY REVIEW

Define the following terms:

alignment	Format Painter	publication
bullets	I-beam	pull quote
business information set	insertion point	scratch area
clip art	landscape	selection handles
collate	pictures	Smart Tag button
cropping	placeholders	story
desktop publishing software	point size	template
font	portrait	text boxes
font styles		

REVIEW QUESTIONS

MULTIPLE CHOICE

Select the best response for the following statements.

1. The _____ toolbar is positioned vertically on the left side of the screen with buttons for inserting text boxes, tables, shapes, and pictures.

    A. Standard   C. Object
    B. Formatting   D. Picture

2. The blank area around the publication is called the _____.

    A. placeholder   C. desktop
    B. text box   D. scratch area

3. All text in a publication is stored within _____.

    A. text boxes   C. placeholders
    B. I-beams   D. selection handles

4. A _____ appears when you point to business information text.

    A. rotate handle   C. magnifier pointer
    B. Smart Tag button D. bullet

5. Arial and Times New Roman are examples of _____.

    A. fonts   C. bullets
    B. font styles   D. objects

6. The _____ command is used to apply a new template design.

    A. Font Schemes   C. Design Gallery
    B. Color Schemes   D. Change Template

7. To resize a graphic proportionally, drag a _____ handle.

    A. corner   C. green
    B. middle   D. square

8. When you click the Format Painter button, your mouse pointer changes to a(n) _____.
   A. magnifying glass
   B. double-sided arrow
   C. crosshair
   D. I-beam with a paintbrush

9. The _____ button removes unwanted parts of a picture.
   A. Compress Pictures
   B. Crop
   C. Undo
   D. More Brightness

10. When you have one publication open, you can click the _____ to close the publication and exit Publisher at the same time.
    A. Print button
    B. Close command on the File menu
    C. Close button on the title bar
    D. Exit button on the title bar

FILL IN THE BLANK

Complete the following sentences by writing the correct word or words in the blanks provided.

1. A Publisher file is called a(n) _____.

2. The _____ toolbar contains buttons for performing common tasks such as saving, printing, and zooming in or out of a page.

3. One method of creating a well-designed publication quickly is to use a(n) _____.

4. _____ is the position of text in relation to the edges of a text box.

5. The _____ key is used to zoom an object to 100%.

6. The green _____ circle is located at the top of a graphic or text box.

7. You can search for clip art, pictures, sounds, and movies in the _____ task pane.

8. To remove a text box, select it and press the _____ key.

9. The Print command is on the _____ menu.

10. When you _____ a publication, the program prompts you to save your work if you made any changes since you last saved.

■ PROJECTS

PROJECT PB 1–1

1. Start Publisher and create a new award certificate using the Employee of the Month template and save it as **Employee Award XXX.pub** (replace *XXX* with your initials).

2. Create a new business information set (remove the logo if necessary) using the following data:
   Eli Parker
   Head Chef
   Eli's Catering
   9876 Main St.
   Kansas City, MO 64188
   Phone: 555-816-9876
   Tagline or motto: We cater to you!
   Business Information set name: Eli's Catering

3. Update the publication with the new business information set.

4. Change the Color Scheme to Concourse.

5. Change the Font Scheme to Archival.

6. Change the font size of the Employee of the Month text to 26 and apply bold.

7. Change the Name of Recipient placeholder text with Mac Wilmon and change the font color to Accent 2.

8. Change the Month and Year placeholder text with June 2012.

9. Save the publication and leave it open for use in the next project.

LESSON 1   Understanding Publisher Fundamentals

PROJECT PB 1–2

1. The **Employee Award XXX.pub** publication from Project PB 1–1 should be open in the Publisher program window.
2. Save the publication with the filename **Employee Award 2 XXX.pub** (replace *XXX* with your initials).
3. Open the Design Gallery and display the Logos category.
4. Select the **Suspended Rectangle**, and in the Options section under Graphic, click **None** and insert the object.
5. Replace the Organization text with **Eli's Catering**.
6. Position the logo in the lower-right corner of the certificate, below the second Date text box.
7. Delete the empty text box in the lower-left corner under the second Signature text box.
8. Change the font size of the first Signature text to 10 point and italics.
9. Use the Format Painter button to copy the format and apply it to the second Signature text and both of the Date text.
10. Save and close the publication.

ON YOUR OWN

Open Employee Award 2 *XXX*.pub. Insert an appropriate piece of clip art and position it anywhere on the publication.

PROJECT PB 1–3

1. Create business cards using the business information for Eli's Catering using the Color Band business card template and save it as **Business Cards XXX.pub**.
2. Change the Color Scheme to Concourse and the Font Scheme to Archival.
3. Delete the empty text box in the lower-left corner.
4. Apply bold to *Eli's Catering*.
5. Change the template to the Arrows design by applying it to the current publication.
6. Use the Text Box button to draw a new text box on the scratch area to the right of the business card. The new text box should be approximately 1" x 1".
7. Type the following list of items, using Georgia 6 point and pressing Enter after each item:
   Meetings
   Events
   Weddings
8. Add bullets to the list and change the line spacing to 0 before and after paragraphs and 0.96 sp between lines.
9. Drag the text box from the scratch area onto the business card below Eli's Catering.
10. Search the clip art task pane for clip art related to the keyword catering.
11. Insert the clip art of the cartoon waiter character with a blue suit and red tie.
12. Resize the clip art and position it as shown in **Figure PB 1–20**. (If necessary, adjust the position of the bulleted list text box as shown.)

FIGURE PB 1–20   Business card

13. View the publication in Print Preview before printing one page.
14. Save and close the publication.

PROJECT PB 1-4

1. Create a current monthly calendar using the Photo Album template and save it as **Calendar *XXX*.pub**.
2. Replace the photo with the Tree picture from the Sample Pictures folder.
3. Change the Color Scheme to Black and White.
4. Change the Font Scheme to Online.
5. Change the picture color to Grayscale.
6. Save and close the publication.

ON YOUR OWN

Open Calendar *XXX*.pub. Change the template to a new calendar template of your choice and create a new publication. Save it with a new name. Apply new fonts, colors, clip art, or pictures of your choice.

WEB PROJECT

PROJECT PB 1-5

Use the View templates from Microsoft Office Online link within the Greeting Cards or Invitation Cards catalog to download a template of your choice. Create a greeting card or invitation using your own information. Change the Color Scheme and/or Font Scheme. Add graphics and text boxes as necessary.

 TEAMWORK PROJECT

PROJECT PB 1-6

With a partner, create an advertisement publication type for the Azul Scuba School that is consistent in design with the flyer you created in this lesson. Work together to create the design and to write any necessary text for the advertisement. Be prepared to present your advertisement to the class.

 CRITICAL THINKING

ACTIVITY PB 1-1

On the Getting Started with Microsoft Office Publisher 2007 screen, open the Scuba Flyer *XXX*.pub file from the Recent Publications pane. Change the template to a Gift Certificate, insert the green sea turtle picture from the Extra Content tab, and delete the text box that contains the pull quote. Save the publication with a new name, print multiple copies per sheet, and close it. Do not save the data in the Extra Content tab.

ACTIVITY PB 1-2

Choose a letterhead template to use for personal stationery for yourself. Create a new business information set with your information. Insert objects, pictures, and/or clip art of your choice. Apply the Font Scheme and Color Scheme of your choice. Print one copy. Save the publication.

LESSON 1

Understanding Integration Fundamentals

Estimated Time:
1.5 hours

■ OBJECTIVES

Upon completion of this lesson, you should be able to:

- Explain methods for sharing information between Office programs.
- Create a PowerPoint presentation from a Word outline.
- Create a mail merge document.
- Link an Excel table in a Word document.
- Embed an Excel table in a PowerPoint presentation.
- Import Excel data into Access.
- Export data from an Access query to Word.

■ DATA FILES

To complete this lesson, you will need these data files:

Step INT 1-1.docx
Step INT 1-1.xlsx
Step INT 1-3.pptx
Step INT 1-4.docx
Step INT 1-5.docx
Honors Band.accdb
Step INT 1-6.xlsx

Project INT 1-1.docx
Project INT 1-2.docx
Bank Customers.accdb
Project INT 1-3.docx
Project INT 1-3.xlsx
Project INT 1-4.xlsx
Project INT 1-5.xlsx

■ VOCABULARY

destination file
destination program
embed
export
import
integration
link
mail merge
merge fields
object
object linking and embedding (OLE)
source file
source program
...

1

UNIT VII Integration Basics

> **VOCABULARY**
> integration
> object
> source program
> source file
> destination program
> destination file
> object linking and embedding (OLE)
> link
> embed

Introduction

Office programs are designed to let you easily share information between programs through integration. *Integration* is the process of using information in a file created in one program and incorporating it into a file created in another program. When you integrate information between programs, the information being shared is referred to as an *object*. The program used to create the object is called the *source program*, and the originating file is called the *source file*. The *destination program* is the program used to create the *destination file* in which the object is inserted. For instance, you can insert an Excel chart into a PowerPoint slide, create a presentation from a Word outline, or create a table in Access using data from an Excel worksheet.

In this lesson, you will learn more about how to share information between programs by linking, embedding, importing, and exporting information.

Methods for Sharing Information Between Office Programs

There are a variety of ways to share information between files created in the different Office programs. Each integration method provides unique options for working with the shared information.

You are already familiar with using the Office Clipboard to copy and paste data within a document, worksheet, or presentation. You can also use the Office Clipboard to copy and paste between two files created in different Office programs. This method is best when you need to share information between programs once and you do not need to work with the two programs together again, and the commands and tools in the program into which the information has been copied are sufficient for any changes you might need to make to it.

Object linking and embedding (OLE) is an integration technology in Office that allows you to share information between Office programs. OLE is used to make content that is created in the source program available and fully editable in the destination program. You will learn more about OLE and using the Paste Special command in the Office programs to embed and link data later in this lesson.

Importing and exporting data is an integration method in which you convert information from the source program into a format supported by the destination program, so it can be fully manipulated in the destination program. Importing refers to converting data from a source program's format to the format of the destination program, while working in the destination program. Exporting refers to converting data from a source program's format to the format of the destination program while working in the source program. Office includes specialized importing and exporting tools, such as Mail Merge, that you will work with later in this lesson.

Linking and Embedding

OLE allows you to either link or embed an object in a destination file. The main difference between linking and embedding has to do with where the information is stored and edited. When you *link* an object, the object remains in the source file and you place a link to the object in the destination file. The object is updated in the destination file when changes are made in the source file. When you *embed* an object, you place a copy of the object in the destination file that is no longer connected to the original object in the source file. In this way, embedding is similar to copying and pasting an object. However, the difference between simply pasting an object and embedding it is that the embedded object can be edited using the source program's commands and features.

LESSON 1   Understanding Integration Fundamentals

Linking an Excel Table in a Word Document

Linking data is useful when the information in a file needs to continually be kept up to date using data that is maintained separately. Linking is also a good choice if file size and efficient use of disk storage space is important, because the source file is not resaved in the destination file. It may take longer, however, for Office to open files with links.

To link objects between files created in different programs, you must have access to both programs when working with the destination file, and the source and destination files must be stored on the same computer or network. A destination file cannot display linked data without being able to access the source file.

When linking between two Office programs, you should have both programs open and save any open documents before you begin linking. You also should check your computer's clock to be sure it is set with the correct time and date because links use the date of the source file for the most recent information.

To link an Excel object such as a table to a Word document, you need to have both the destination Word document and the source Excel worksheet open at the same time. Then you can copy the Excel table, switch to Word, and use the Paste Special command to insert the table as a linked object.

Step-by-Step INT 1.1

1. Start Word, and then open the **Step INT 1-1.docx** file from the folder containing the data files for this lesson.

2. Save the document as **Fundraiser Letter XXX.docx** (replace *XXX* with your initials).

3. Start Excel and then open the **Step INT 1-1.xlsx** workbook from the folder containing the data files for this lesson.

4. Save the workbook as **Band Fundraiser XXX.xlsx** (replace *XXX* with your initials).

5. Select the table in range **A1:D6** in the Band Fundraiser *XXX*.xlxs workbook.

6. On the Home tab, in the Clipboard group, click the **Copy** button to copy the table object.

7. Switch to the Fundraiser Letter *XXX*.xls document in Word and place the insertion point in the blank line after the last line of the letter and before *Sincerely*.

8. On the Home tab, in the Clipboard group, click the **Paste** button arrow and then click **Paste Special** to display the Paste Special dialog box.

9. Click the **Paste link** option button, and then click **Microsoft Office Excel Worksheet Object** in the As list box, as shown in **Figure INT 1–1**.

FIGURE INT 1-1
Linking using the Paste Special dialog box

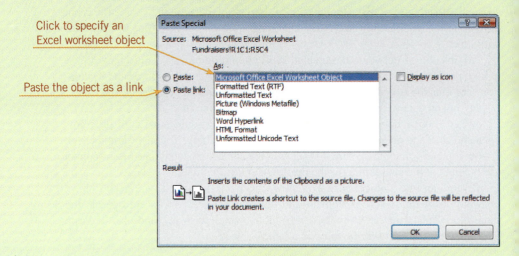

10. Click the **OK** button to paste the Excel table as a linked object in the document. Your document window should look similar to **Figure INT 1–2**.

FIGURE INT 1-2
Inserting a linked object

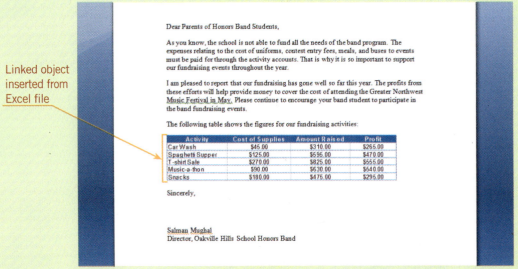

11. Save the Fundraiser Letter *XXX*.docx document, close it, and exit Word.
12. Leave the Band Fundraiser *XXX*.xlsx workbook open in the Excel program window for use in the next Step-by-Step.

Updating and Breaking Links

If the destination file containing a linked object is open when you make a change to the original object in the source file, the object in the destination file is changed at the same time. If the destination file containing the linked object is not open when you make changes to the object in the source file, the next time you open the destination file, you will see a message indicating the file is linked to source data and asking if you want to update the data.

LESSON 1 Understanding Integration Fundamentals

If you decide you no longer want an object linked between the source and destination files, you can break the link between the source file and the destination file; the object in the destination file will become just a static copy of the original object. To view or edit links in the destination file, you can click the Office Button, point to Prepare, and then click Edit Links to Files, as shown in **Figure INT 1–3**, to display the Links dialog box.

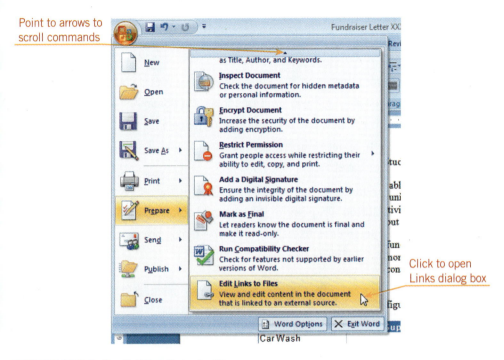

FIGURE INT 1–3 Editing links to files

To break a link, you can select the link in the Links dialog box, and then click the Break Link button. When you rename or move a source file, you must redirect the link so the destination file looks for the correct filename and the correct location of the file to update the link. You can redirect the link using the Change Source button in the Links dialog box. To lock a link, temporarily preventing it from being updated, you can use the Locked option in the Links dialog box.

> **EXTRA FOR EXPERTS**
>
> If you have many links in a document and it is taking too long to update each time you open the document, if you want to control when the links are updated, or if you only want to update certain links, you can select the Manual update option button in the Links dialog box to update links manually.

Step-by-Step INT 1.2

The Band Fundraiser XXX.xlsx workbook from Step-by-Step INT 1.1 should be open in the Excel program window.

1. Click cell **A6**.
2. Edit the content of the cell to replace *Snacks* with **Concession Stand** and press **Enter**.
3. Start Word and open the Fundraiser Letter *XXX*.docx file. A message is displayed asking if you want to update the document with data from the linked file. Click the **Yes** button and notice that the linked Excel table has been updated to reflect the change you just made to the source object in Excel.
4. In the Fundraiser Letter *XXX*.docx file in the Word window, click the **Office Button** , point to **Prepare**, and scroll down if necessary to click **Edit Links to Files** to display the Links dialog box with the link selected, as shown in **Figure INT 1–4**.

FIGURE INT 1–4
Links dialog box

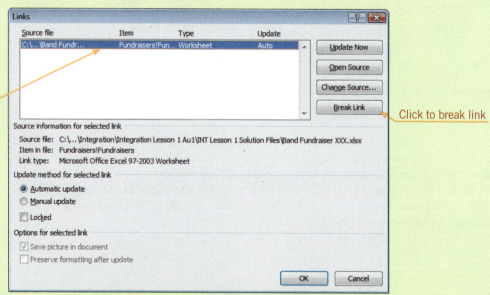

5. Click the **Break Link** button to break the link and then click the **Yes** button to confirm the action. The link is broken and the Excel table becomes just a table in the Word document, without any connection to the source program.
6. Save and close the Fundraiser Letter *XXX*.docx document and exit Word.
7. Save the Band Fundraiser *XXX*.xlsx workbook and leave it open for use in the next Step-by-Step.

LESSON 1   Understanding Integration Fundamentals

Embedding an Excel Table in a PowerPoint Presentation

When you embed an object from a source file into a destination file, you are copying and pasting the object itself, and also a connection to the source program. This allows you to work with the embedded object to format or edit it using the source program's commands and features, while within the destination file. You simply double-click the embedded object in the destination file, to open the object's source program and make your changes—without leaving the destination file. When you click outside the object to deselect it, the source program is closed, and you return to the object in the destination program. Embedding is useful when the object you are integrating requires tools and features not normally supported by the destination program.

Because the source file is duplicated in the destination file and increases the size of the file, use embedding if the size of the file is not important.

Step-by-Step INT 1.3

The Band Fundraiser *XXX*.xlsx workbook from Step-by-Step INT 1.2 should be open in the Excel program window.

1. Select the table in range **A1:D6**.
2. On the Home tab, in the Clipboard group, click the **Copy** button to copy the table.
3. Start PowerPoint and open the **Step INT 1-3.pptx** presentation from the folder containing the data files for this lesson and save the presentation as **Band Trip Presentation *XXX*.pptx** (replace *XXX* with your initials).
4. On the Home tab, in the Slides group, click the **New Slide** button arrow to display the menu, and click **Title Only** to insert a new slide.
5. Click the **Click to add title** placeholder, type **Fundraisers**, and then click a blank area of the slide.
6. On the Home tab, in the Clipboard group, click the **Paste** button arrow and click **Paste Special** to display the Paste Special dialog box, shown in **Figure INT 1–5**.

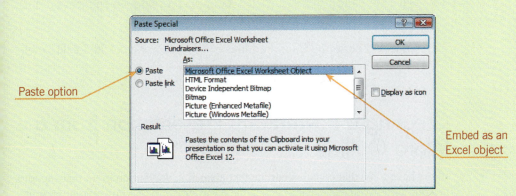

FIGURE INT 1–5
Embedding using the Paste Special dialog box

UNIT VII   Integration Basics

7. Make sure the Paste option button is selected, and that Microsoft Office Excel Worksheet Object is selected in the As list box, and then click the **OK** button to close the dialog box and paste the Excel table as an embedded object on the slide.

8. Drag a corner of the object to make it larger, and then drag the object to center it on the slide, if necessary.

9. Double-click the embedded table to display Excel's commands and features for editing. Your slide should look similar to **Figure INT 1–6**.

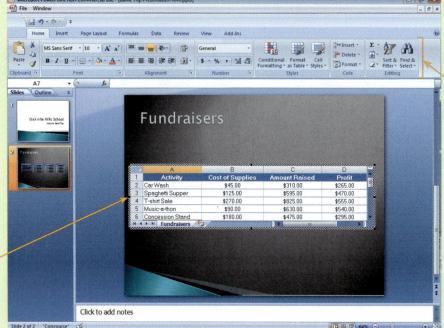

FIGURE INT 1–6
Slide with embedded Excel table selected for editing

Excel commands and features on the Ribbon in PowerPoint

Table selected for editing and displayed in Excel program window

10. Double-click cell **A4** of the embedded table, select **T-shirt**, type **Sweatshirt**, and press **Enter** to edit the text.

11. Click the slide outside the table to close Excel's commands and features.

12. Save the Band Trip Presentation *XXX*.pptx presentation and leave it open for use in the next Step-by-Step.

13. Save and close the Band Fundraiser *XXX*.xlsx workbook and exit Excel.

Creating a PowerPoint Presentation from a Word Outline

If you have a file that contains outline text created in another program that supports heading styles, you can use it to create the basic structure of a PowerPoint presentation. For example, you may have an existing report in Word that you want to present.

LESSON 1 Understanding Integration Fundamentals

When you use an outline from Word, PowerPoint converts the heading levels in the outline into titles and bulleted lists on slides. Although you may have to make some minor adjustments, this is a quick way to convert text from a word-processing program into a slide presentation.

To use an existing outline, you start PowerPoint and on the Home tab in the Slides group, click the New Slide button arrow, and then click Slides from Outline to display the Insert Outline dialog box. When you select the file that contains the outline and click Insert, the slides are created based on the outline text.

Step-by-Step INT 1.4

The Band Trip Presentation *XXX*.pptx presentation from Step-by-Step INT 1.3 should be open in the PowerPoint program window.

1. Start Word and open the **Step INT 1-4.docx** file from the folder containing the data files for this lesson. Notice the document is displayed in Outline view. This will be the text that will be converted to slides.

2. Save the document as **Band Trip Outline *XXX*.docx** (replace *XXX* with your initials).

3. Close the document and exit Word.

4. In PowerPoint, select **slide 1** in the Slides tab in the left pane.

5. On the Home tab, in the Slides group, click the **New Slide** button arrow, and then click **Slides from Outline** from the menu to display the Insert Outline dialog box.

6. Navigate to the folder containing the data files for this lesson, select the **Band Trip Outline *XXX*.docx** file, and then click **Insert** to create slides based on the outline text, as shown in **Figure INT 1–7**.

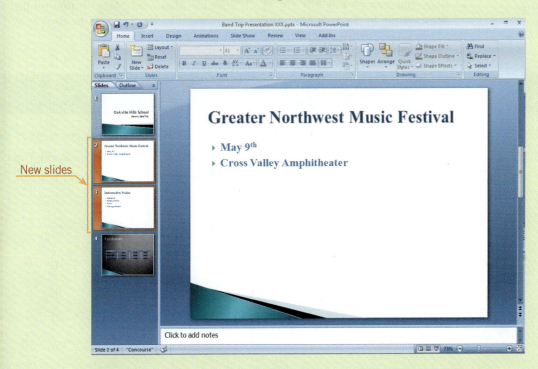

FIGURE INT 1–7
Creating slides from a Word outline

7. Display slide 1 and on the View tab, in the Presentation Views group, click the **Slide Show** button to view the presentation as a slide show. Advance through all the slides and exit the slide show.
8. Save and close the Band Trip Presentation *XXX*.pptx presentation and exit PowerPoint.

Creating a Mail Merge Document

If you have a lot of form letters, cards, e-mail messages, or envelopes to send, you can simplify the process by using the information in an Access table or Excel worksheet as a data source and creating a mail merge operation using the Microsoft Word Mail Merge Wizard. A *mail merge* is used to create a set of documents that are identical except for custom or personalized information in specific areas. For example, you could create a set of form letters with the same message, but personalized for each client using name and address information from the data source.

Each mail merge follows the same process:

1. Set up the main document that contains the static information.
2. Connect to the data source that contains the variable information.
3. Select the list of recipients.
4. Add placeholders—called *merge fields*—to the main document that indicate where the information from the data source will go.
5. Preview the documents.
6. Complete the merge.

You can set up the mail merge yourself, or use the Mail Merge Wizard, which leads you through this process, by clicking the Start Mail Merge button on the Mailings tab in the Start Mail Merge group and then clicking Step by Step Mail Merge Wizard to open the Mail Merge Wizard task pane.

> **VOCABULARY**
> mail merge
> merge fields

> **EXTRA FOR EXPERTS**
> You can also start the Microsoft Mail Merge Wizard from Access by selecting in the Navigation Pane the table or query you want to use as the mail merge data source. Then on the External Data tab, in the Export group, click the More button, and then click Merge it with Microsoft Office Word.

Step-by-Step INT 1.5

1. Start Word and open the **Step INT 1-5.docx** file from the folder containing the data files for this lesson and save the document as **Band Trip Letter Main *XXX*.docx** (replace *XXX* with your initials). You will use this document as the main document for the mail merge.

LESSON 1 Understanding Integration Fundamentals

2. On the Mailings tab, in the Start Mail Merge group, click the **Start Mail Merge** button, and then click **Step by Step Mail Merge Wizard** to display the Mail Merge Wizard task pane, Step 1 of 6. The Letters option button should be selected in the Select Document Type section, as shown in **Figure INT 1–8**.

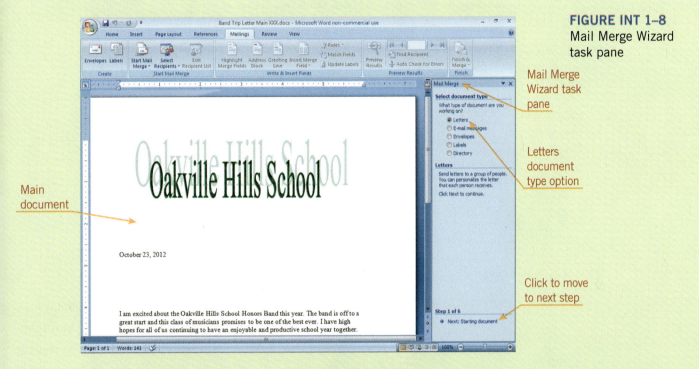

FIGURE INT 1–8
Mail Merge Wizard task pane

3. In the Mail Merge Wizard task pane, click **Next: Starting document** to move to Step 2 of the Mail Merge Wizard.

4. Make sure the **Use the current document** option button is selected in the Select Starting Document section. Click **Next: Select recipients** to move to Step 3 of the Mail Merge Wizard.

5. Make sure the **Use an existing list** option button is selected in the Select recipients section, and in the Use an existing list section, click **Browse** to display the Select Data Source dialog box.

6. Navigate to the folder containing the data files for this lesson, select the **Honors Band.accdb** database file, and then click the **Open** button.

UNIT VII   Integration Basics

7. Click the **Band Members** table in the Select Table dialog box, and then click the **OK** button to display the Mail Merge Recipients dialog box, shown in **Figure INT 1–9**.

FIGURE INT 1–9
Mail Merge Recipients dialog box

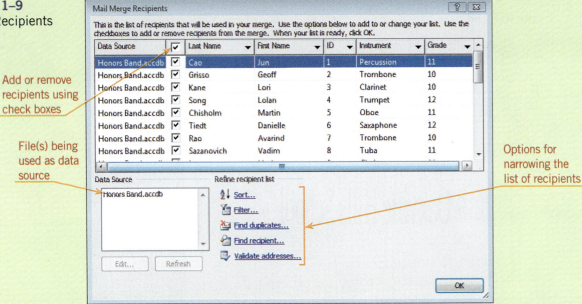

Add or remove recipients using check boxes

File(s) being used as data source

Options for narrowing the list of recipients

8. Click the **OK** button to use the list of recipients in the list without making any changes and close the Mail Merge Recipients dialog box. In the Mail Merge Wizard task pane, click **Next: Write your letter** to move to Step 4 of the Mail Merge Wizard.

9. In the document window, place the insertion point in the blank line above the first paragraph. In the Mail Merge Wizard task pane, click **Greeting line** to display the Insert Greeting Line dialog box, shown in **Figure INT 1–10**.

FIGURE INT 1–10
Insert Greeting Line dialog box

Format options

Options for invalid recipient names

Preview of greeting line

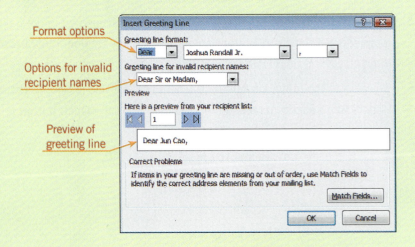

LESSON 1 Understanding Integration Fundamentals

10. Click the **OK** button to insert the <<GreetingLine>> merge field in the document. In the Mail Merge Wizard task pane, click **Next: Preview your letters** to move to Step 5 of the Mail Merge Wizard and preview one of the letters in the document window, the one for Jun Cao.

11. In the Preview your letters section of the Mail Merge Wizard task pane, click the **Next Record** button to preview the letter for the second recipient. Continue clicking the **Next Record** button until you get to Recipient 23, Belinda Newman, and notice how the name in the greeting line changes each time.

12. In the Mail Merge Wizard task pane, click **Next: Complete the merge** to move to Step 6 of the Mail Merge Wizard. In the Merge section, click **Print** to display the Merge to Printer dialog box.

13. Click the **Current record** option and then click the **OK** button to display the Print dialog box and click the **OK** button to print the first letter.

14. In the Mail Merge Wizard task pane, click **Edit individual letters** to display the Merge to New Document dialog box.

15. Click the **All** option button and then click the **OK** button to merge all 23 letters to a new document. Scroll through the document to see that each letter is on a separate page. Save the document as **Band Trip Letter Merge *XXX*.docx** (replace *XXX* with your initials) and close it.

16. Save and close the main document, Band Trip Letter Main *XXX*.docx. If you open the main document again in the future, you will get a message asking if you want to maintain the connection to the external data source.

Importing and Exporting Data

You can also share information between programs by importing or exporting. When you *import* information, you transfer source data into a destination file, changing the source data's format or characteristics in such a way that it can be viewed, edited, or otherwise manipulated using the destination program. For example, you could import the data in an Access table into Excel so you could perform calculations on it in a worksheet. Similarly, when you *export* information, you transfer data from the source file to a destination file in a format that can be used by the destination program. For example, you could export the data in an Access query to a Word document to use in a report. Importing and exporting are one-time operations—there is no connection established between the data in the two programs, and the data in the source file is not altered.

> **VOCABULARY**
> import
>
> export

> **EXTRA FOR EXPERTS**
>
> When you are finished importing or exporting data in Access, you can save the steps of the process so that they can easily be repeated again in the future without using the wizard.

UNIT VII Integration Basics

Importing Excel Data into an Access Table

When you import from Excel into Access, a copy of the data is brought into Access and stored in a new or existing table. To import data, you can use the Import Wizard in the destination program to guide you through the process and make decisions such as whether to change data types or add headers. In Access, on the External Data tab, in the Import group, you can click the Excel button to start importing data. The Excel workbook, the source file, should be closed before you begin importing data from it. Formulas will not be imported from Excel to Access, only the results of the formulas.

Step-by-Step INT 1.6

1. Start Excel, open the **Step INT 1-6.xlxs** workbook from the folder containing the data files for this lesson, view the data, and then close the file and exit Excel.

2. Start Access and open the **Honors Band.accdb** database from the folder containing the data files for this lesson. Click the **Options** button on the Message Bar, click the **Enable this content** option button, and then click the **OK** button to enable the database content.

3. On the External Data tab, in the Import group, click the **Excel** button to display the Get External Data – Excel Spreadsheet dialog box, shown in **Figure INT 1–11**.

FIGURE INT 1–11
Get External Data–
Excel Speadsheet
dialog box

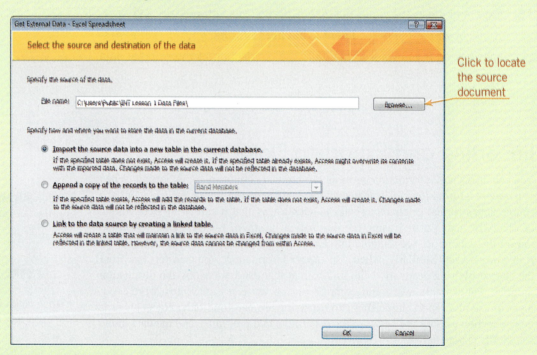

Click to locate the source document

4. Click the **Browse** button to display the File Open dialog box.

LESSON 1   Understanding Integration Fundamentals

5. Navigate to the folder containing the data files for this lesson, click the **Step INT 1-6.xlsx** file, click the **Open** button to return to the Get External Data – Excel Spreadsheet dialog box, and display this file as the data source in the File name text box.

6. Click the **OK** button to open the Import Spreadsheet Wizard, shown in **Figure INT 1–12**. The first step in the wizard requires you to specify the worksheet or range containing the data to be imported.

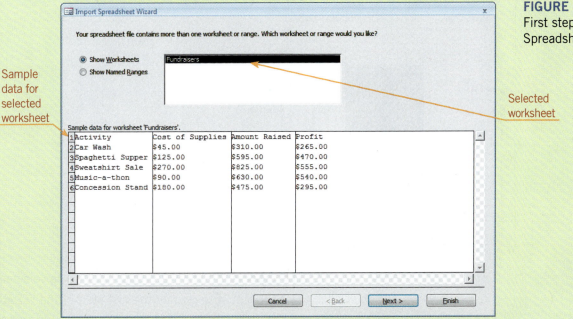

FIGURE INT 1–12
First step in the Import Spreadsheet Wizard

Sample data for selected worksheet

Selected worksheet

7. Make sure the Fundraisers worksheet is selected in the list box, and then click the **Next** button to display the next step in the wizard, where you specify what should be used for field names in the table.

8. To use column headings as field names, make sure the **First Row Contains Column Headings** check box is selected, and then click the **Next** button to display the next step in the wizard to specify information about the fields to be imported; for example, the Activity field has a Text data type.

9. Click the **Cost of Supplies** field and notice that the data type is already set at *Currency*, as shown in **Figure INT 1-13**. Click the **Next** button to display the next step in the wizard, where you specify the primary key for the table.

FIGURE INT 1-13
Fields to be imported

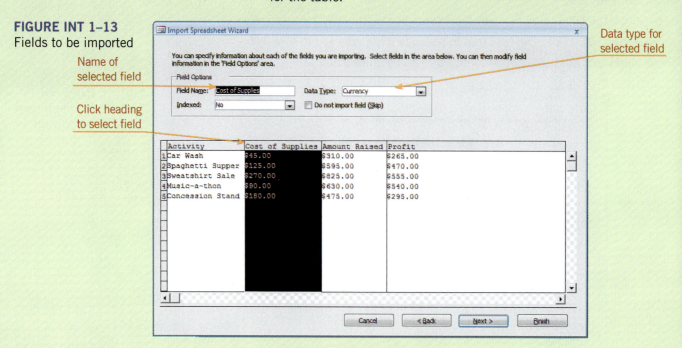

10. Make sure the **Let Access add primary key** option button is selected, and then click the **Next** button to display the last step in the wizard, where you can name the table. In this case, Fundraisers is displayed in the Import to Table text box.

11. Click the **Finish** button to accept the name Fundraisers and display the Get External Data – Excel Spreadsheet dialog box.

12. Click the **Close** button to close the dialog box and create the table without saving the import steps.

13. Double-click the **Fundraisers** table in the Navigation Pane to display the table in the database window, as shown in **Figure INT 1–14**.

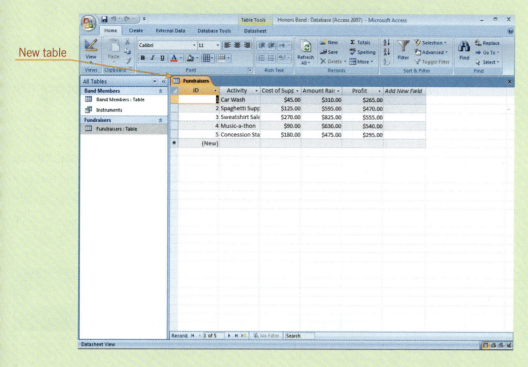

FIGURE INT 1–14
Importing data to a new table

14. Close the Fundraisers table and leave the Honors Band.accdb database open for use in the next Step-by-Step.

Exporting an Access Query to Word

You can export a table, query, form, or report from Access to a variety of Office programs, including an Excel worksheet, another Access database, a Word document, or a text file. No matter what program you are exporting the Access object to, the process is similar.

For example, to export data from an Access query to a Word document, you select the query in the Navigation Pane in Access and then on the External Data tab, in the Export group, click the Export to RTF file button to use the Export Wizard. When you export from Access to Word, the data is always displayed in a new document. You do not have the option of adding the data to an existing document.

UNIT VII Integration Basics

Step-by-Step INT 1.7

The Honors Band.accdb database from Step-by-Step INT 1.6 should be open in the Access program window.

1. Select the **Instruments** query in the Navigation Pane.
2. On the External Data tab, in the Export group, click the **Export to RTF file** button to display the Export – RTF File dialog box.
3. Click the **Browse** button to display the File Save dialog box.
4. Navigate to the folder that contains the data files for this lesson. Notice the file name, *Instruments.rtf*, already appears in the File name text box and that Rich Text Format is already listed as the format type, as shown in **Figure INT 1–15**. Click the **Save** button to return to the Export – RTF File dialog box.

FIGURE INT 1–15
File Save dialog box

File name and format type are already selected

5. Click the **Open the destination file after the export operation is complete** check box to select this option.

LESSON 1 Understanding Integration Fundamentals

6. Click the **OK** button to export the query data and display it as a table in a new Word document, as shown in **Figure INT 1–16**. Notice the Table Tools contextual tab appears on the Ribbon in Word.

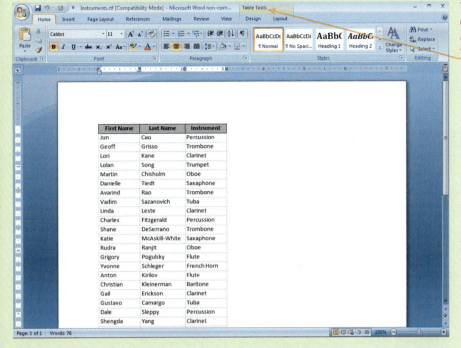

FIGURE INT 1–16
Access query exported as a table to a Word document

7. Close the Instruments.rtf document and exit Word.
8. In Access, click the **Close** button in the Export – RTF File dialog box to close it without saving the export steps.
9. Close the database and exit Access.

SUMMARY

In this lesson, you learned:

- The methods for sharing information between Office programs.
- To link an Excel table in a Word document.
- How to embed an Excel table in a PowerPoint presentation.
- How to create a PowerPoint presentation from a Word outline.
- The process for creating a mail merge document.
- The steps to import Excel data into Access.
- The steps to export data from an Access query to Word.

UNIT VII Integration Basics

■ VOCABULARY REVIEW

Define the following terms:

destination file

destination program

embed

export

import

integration

link

mail merge

merge fields

object

object linking and embedding (OLE)

source file

source program

■ REVIEW QUESTIONS

MULTIPLE CHOICE

Select the best response for the following statements.

1. Which of the following is an example of integration?
    A. inserting an Excel chart into a PowerPoint slide
    B. creating a presentation from a Word outline
    C. creating an Access table using Excel data
    D. all of the above

2. You can set up a mail merge yourself, or use the Mail Merge _____ which leads you through the process.
    A. dialog box   C. wizard
    B. group   D. tab

3. In a mail merge, the _____ contains the static information.
    A. main document   C. placeholder
    B. data source   D. list of recipients

4. When you _____ an object, the object remains in the source document and you place a connection to the object in the destination document.
    A. link   C. import
    B. embed   D. export

5. When you _____ an object, you place a copy of the object in the destination document that it is no longer connected to the source document, but is a separate object.
    A. link   C. import
    B. embed   D. export

6. You can use the _____ command to insert a range as a linked object.
    A. Insert   C. Paste
    B. Link   D. Paste Special

7. If the destination document with a linked object is open when you make a change in the source document, changes are made in the destination document _____.
    A. at the same time   C. the next time you open the file
    B. when you close the file   D. when you click the Update button

LESSON 1   Understanding Intergration Fundamentals   21

8. When you _____ information, you transfer data into a destination file in a format that allows it to be used in the destination program.
   A. link
   B. embed
   C. import
   D. export

9. When you _____ information, you transfer data from a source file to a destination file in a format that can be used by the destination program.
   A. link
   B. embed
   C. import
   D. export

10. In Access, on the _____ tab, in the Import group, you can click the Excel button to start importing data.
    A. Home
    B. Create
    C. External Data
    D. Database Tools

FILL IN THE BLANK

Complete the following sentences by writing the correct word or words in the blanks provided.

1. _____ is taking a file or object from one program and incorporating it into a file in another program.

2. When you integrate information between programs, the _____ is the program used to create the original information.

3. When you integrate information between programs, the _____ is the program used to create the destination file.

4. To import an outline into PowerPoint, on the Home tab in the Slides group, click the _____ button arrow, and then click Slides from Outline to display the Insert Outline dialog box.

5. A(n) _____ is used to create a set of documents that are identical except for custom or personalized information in specific areas.

6. When you integrate information between two files, a(n) _____ is shared information.

7. You can break the link between the source document and the destination document in the _____ dialog box.

8. _____ are placeholders in the main document of a mail merge that indicate where the information from the data source will go.

9. A destination file cannot display linked data without being able to access the _____.

10. To export data from an Access query to a Word document, first select the query in the _____.

■ PROJECTS

PROJECT INT 1–1

1. Start Word and open **Project INT 1-1.docx** from the folder containing the data files for this lesson.
2. Save the document as **Card Safety XXX.docx** (replace *XXX* with your initials).
3. View the outline text, close the document, and exit Word.
4. Start PowerPoint and open a new, blank presentation.
5. On Slide 1, type **ATM/Debit Card Safety** as the title and **Tips for Secure Transactions** as the subtitle.
6. Use the **Card Safety XXX.docx** file to create slides based on the outlined text.
7. Apply the Foundry theme to the presentation.
8. Save the presentation as **Security Tips XXX.pptx** (replace *XXX* with your initials).
9. View the presentation as a slideshow.
10. Close the presentation and exit PowerPoint.

PROJECT INT 1–2

1. Start Word and open **Project INT 1-2.docx** from the folder containing the data files for this lesson.
2. Save the document as **Overdraft Service Main XXX.docx** (replace *XXX* with your initials) to use as the main document for the mail merge.
3. Start the Mail Merge Wizard and select Letters as the document type.

4. Move to the next step in the Mail Merge Wizard task pane where Use the current document should be selected as the starting document.

5. Move to the next step of the Mail Merge Wizard task pane and browse to select the **Bank Customers.accdb** database file as the data source.

6. In the Mail Merge Recipients dialog box, use the list of recipients in the list without making any changes.

7. Move to the next step of the Mail Merge Wizard task pane and insert a <<GreetingLine>> merge field in the document between the date and the first paragraph.

8. Move to the next step to preview your letters. Preview each of the 20 letters.

9. Move to the last step in the Mail Merge Wizard task pane to complete the merge. Merge the letters to the printer and then print the first letter.

10. Merge all the records to a new document. Scroll through the document to see that each letter is on a separate page, save it as **Overdraft Service Merge *XXX*.docx**, and close it.

11. Save and close the Overdraft Service Main *XXX*.docx document. Leave Word open for the next project.

ON YOUR OWN

Open the **Overdraft Service Main *XXX*.docx**, and add an address merge field to the document that will insert the customer's address between the date and the greeting line. Preview the letters, then merge the letters and print the first letter. Save the merged document as **Overdraft Service Merge2 *XXX*.docx** (replace *XXX* with your initials) and close the document. Save and close the main document.

PROJECT INT 1-3

1. In Word, open **Project INT 1-3.docx** from the folder containing the data files for this lesson.

2. Save the document as **Best Sellers *XXX*.docx** (replace *XXX* with your initials).

3. Start Excel and open **Project INT 1-3.xlsx** from the folder containing the data files for this lesson.

4. Save the workbook as **Sweet Time Best *XXX*.xlsx** (replace *XXX* with your initials).

5. Select the table in the range A1:G7 and copy it.

6. Switch to Word and place the insertion point below the *Best Sellers* subtitle and then paste the Excel table as a linked object.

7. Save the Best Sellers *XXX*.docx document and close it.

8. In the Excel worksheet, enter **Blends** in cell G5, **Organic** in cell G6, and **Herbal** in cell G7.

9. Open the Best Sellers *XXX*.docx linked document and choose to update the data. Notice that the data has been updated with the change you just made in Excel.

10. Open the Links dialog box and break the link.

11. Save and close the Best Sellers *XXX*.docx document and exit Word.

12. Save the Sweet Time Best *XXX*.xlsx workbook and close it.

PROJECT INT 1-4

1. Open the **Project INT 1-4.xlsx** file from the folder containing the data files for this lesson.

2. Select the table in the range B3:C9 and copy the information.

3. Open PowerPoint and open the **Security Tips *XXX*.pptx** presentation that you created in Project INT 1-1.

4. Insert a new Title Only slide at the end of the presentation.

5. Type **Contact Information** as the title.

6. Embed the copied range onto the slide.

7. Increase the font size of the pasted information, resize the embedded object if necessary, and place it attractively on the slide.

8. Save and close the Security Tips *XXX*.pptx presentation and exit PowerPoint.

9. Close the Project INT 1-4.xlsx workbook without saving it and exit Excel.

PROJECT INT 1-5

1. Start Access, open **Bank Customers.accdb** from the folder containing the data files for this lesson, and enable the database content.

2. Display the Get External Data – Excel Spreadsheet dialog box.

3. Display the File Open dialog box, select the **Project INT 1-5.xlsx** file from the folder containing the data files for this lesson, and return to the Get External Data – Excel Spreadsheet dialog box.

4. Choose to import the source data into a new table in the current database and then open the Import Spreadsheet Wizard.

5. Choose to use column headings from the first row as field names in the table.

6. Move to the next step in the wizard, and do not change any information about the fields you are importing.

7. Move to the next step in the wizard, and if necessary, select the option for Access to define a primary key.

LESSON 1   Understanding Intergration Fundamentals

8. Move to the last step of the wizard, name the table **New Customers**, then finish the wizard and return to the Get External Data – Excel Spreadsheet dialog box.

9. Close the dialog box without saving the import steps.

10. Open the New Customers table in the database window.

11. Close the New Customers table and leave the database open for the next project.

PROJECT INT 1–6

The **Bank Customers.accdb** database from Project INT 1-5 should be open in the Access program window.

1. Select the New Customers table in the Navigation Pane.
2. Display the Export – RTF File dialog box.
3. Display the File Save dialog box, select the folder that contains the data files for this lesson, and return to the Export – RTF File dialog box.
4. Select the Open the destination file after the export operation is complete check box.
5. Export the table data with the default name and display it in a new Word document named **New Customers.rtf**.
6. Close the New Customers.rtf document and exit Word.
7. In Access, close the Export – RTF File dialog box without saving the export steps.
8. Close the Bank Customers.accdb database and exit Access.

WEB PROJECT

PROJECT INT 1–7

Search the Web for information about a place you would like to visit. To create a presentation about your findings, in Word, create an outline that lists pertinent information about this place, such as weather, things to do, and places to eat. Include enough headings and bullet points for at least three slides. Create a presentation by importing the outline into PowerPoint. Enhance the presentation however you like and run your presentation for the class.

 ## TEAMWORK PROJECT

PROJECT INT 1–8

With a partner, create a mail merge letter that gives information about an upcoming event at school, a class assignment, or a new school policy. Work together to create the main document in Word and to create a data source in Access that contains information about your recipients. Try to include more than one merge field placeholder in the main document. Merge the information and print the letters.

■ CRITICAL THINKING

ACTIVITY INT 1–1

In this lesson, you have learned just a few of the ways to integrate Office programs. There are other ways you can share information using different combinations of programs. For example, you can import a plain Word document into Publisher to work with it in a desktop publishing program. In Word, write a short thank-you note to someone and save the document. Open Publisher and choose one of the greeting card Thank You templates. Use the Text File command on the Insert menu to import your thank-you note into Publisher. Format the publication, then save, preview, and print it. Use Publisher Help if you need assistance.

ACTIVITY INT 1–2

Search for the Excel Help article titled *Top 10 reasons to use Access with Excel*. Choose one of the reasons and read about it. Click the link(s) to more information to find out more. Select one of the demos at the end of the article that you are interested in and watch it. As an extra challenge, try putting the information you just learned into practice using Excel and Access together.

APPENDIX A

Understanding Windows Vista Fundamentals

⏱ Estimated Time: 1 hour

■ OBJECTIVES

Upon completion of this lesson, you should be able to:

- Start Windows Vista.
- Identify parts of the Windows Vista desktop.
- Customize the desktop.
- Manage files and folders.
- Get help.
- Shut down Windows Vista.

■ DATA FILES

You do not need data files to complete this appendix.

■ VOCABULARY

Control Panel
desktop
folder
gadgets
icon
notification area
operating system
password
personal folder
Quick Launch toolbar
Recycle Bin
screen saver
taskbar
user account
user name
wallpaper
Windows Sidebar
...

APPENDIX A Understanding Windows Vista Fundamentals

Introduction

Microsoft Windows Vista is an operating system that can help enhance your experience using Microsoft Office 2007. An ***operating system*** is the program that manages and controls the basic operations of your computer. In this appendix, you will become familiar with the parts of the Vista desktop, customize your Vista environment, manage files and folders, and learn how to get help.

Starting Windows Vista

If Windows Vista is already installed, it will start automatically when you turn on the computer. The first screen you will see is the Welcome screen, which you will use to log on to Windows. The Welcome screen displays all of the user accounts on the computer. A ***user account*** is a collection of information about a specific person who is a regular user of the computer—including unique settings and preferences, and which files and programs that user can access. If you are the only one using the computer, there may be only one user account. If there are multiple users, each person can have a separate account so that you can all share the same computer while maintaining individual settings and files. Each user account on the computer has a ***user name*** that identifies it. For security purposes, you may also have a password associated with your user account. A ***password*** is a secret set of characters that a user types to log on to a computer or account. On the Welcome screen, you can choose which user account you want to access and then type the password, if necessary.

There are different versions of Vista, so not all features may be available, and your screens may look different than those in this appendix.

Identifying Parts of the Windows Vista Desktop

The basic Windows Vista desktop is shown in **Figure VIS–1**. The ***desktop*** is the main area of the screen that is displayed when you turn the computer on and log on to Windows with your user name and password. Use this figure to become familiar with the parts of the Windows Vista desktop.

> **VOCABULARY**
> **operating system**
> **user account**
> **user name**
> **password**
> **desktop**

APPENDIX A Understanding Windows Vista Fundamentals

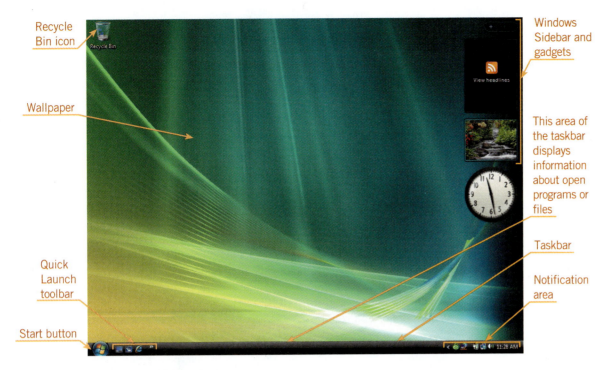

FIGURE VIS–1 Windows Vista desktop

Your desktop includes *icons*—small pictures that represent programs, folders, files, and other objects, such as the Recycle Bin. The *Recycle Bin* contains the files and folders you have deleted. The *Windows Sidebar* is a transparent panel on the side of the desktop that has mini-programs and tools, called *gadgets*, that can help make your computer time more enjoyable and more productive.

The *taskbar* is displayed at the bottom of the desktop. This horizontal bar contains the Start button to open the Start menu; the *Quick Launch toolbar* with shortcuts to frequently used programs; a section showing which files or folders you have open and allowing you to switch between them; and a *notification area* with the time and icons that provide information about programs and computer settings.

You can point to an icon or object on the desktop to see a ScreenTip with its description. When you are working in a maximized program window, the desktop is not visible, but you can always display it without closing the program window you are working in by clicking the Show desktop icon on the Quick Launch toolbar.

There are many ways to control what you see on the desktop, so yours may not look exactly the same as the figures in this appendix. For example, you can choose to remove the Quick Launch toolbar from the taskbar or hide the Recycle Bin.

> **VOCABULARY**
> icon
> Recycle Bin
> Windows Sidebar
> gadgets
> taskbar
> Quick Launch toolbar
> notification area

Step-by-Step VIS 1

1. Turn on your computer and the monitor, if necessary, to start Windows Vista.

2. On the Welcome screen, click your **user name** and type your **password**, if prompted, to display the desktop. If a Welcome Center dialog box opens, click the **Close** button to close it.

3. Point to the **Recycle Bin** to display a ScreenTip with its description.
4. Leave the computer on with the Windows Vista desktop displayed for the next Step-by-Step.

Customizing Vista

You can customize many aspects of your Windows Vista environment by modifying properties and settings or personalizing aspects of the desktop's appearance and sounds. Many of these options can be accessed in the Appearance and Personalization window in the Control Panel, shown in **Figure VIS–2**. The *Control Panel* is used to change the settings for Windows, including how it looks and works. The Control Panel can be displayed by clicking the Start button, clicking Control Panel, and then clicking Appearance and Personalization. There are many ways to change how you work using Windows Vista—if it isn't covered in this appendix, you can explore the various options on your own.

> **VOCABULARY**
> **Control Panel**

> **EXTRA FOR EXPERTS**
> Windows Aero is an advanced appearance setting only available in some versions of Windows Vista (Windows Vista Business, Windows Vista Enterprise, Windows Vista Home Premium, and Windows Vista Ultimate). It features a distinctive semi-transparent visual style, and offers useful effects such as Windows Flip 3D to quickly scan through windows, and windows previews to identify buttons on the taskbar by displaying thumbnails.

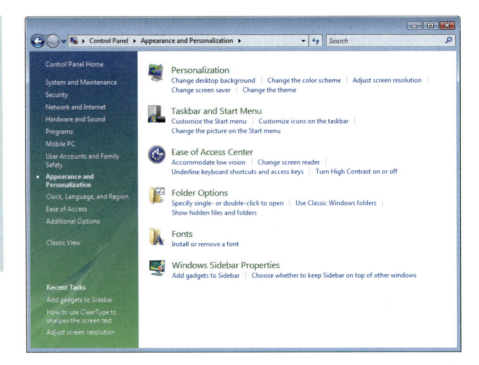

FIGURE VIS–2 Control Panel Appearance and Personalization options

Customizing the Taskbar and the Start Menu

As stated earlier, the taskbar displays the Start button, the Quick Launch toolbar, and a notification area containing icons that provide information about programs and your connection status to a network or the Internet. For example, you can click the time on the far right of the taskbar to view or change the time and date settings. The middle section of the taskbar displays a button for each open program or file and can be used to help organize or move between the open windows.

APPENDIX A   Understanding Windows Vista Fundamentals

You can customize the taskbar by right-clicking it and clicking Properties to display the Taskbar tab of the Taskbar and Start Menu Properties dialog box, shown in **Figure VIS–3**. For more information on customizing the taskbar, you can click the *How do I customize the taskbar?* link at the bottom of the dialog box. Other tabs in the dialog box provide other customization options.

To add a program to the Quick Launch toolbar so that you can open it easily, just click the program icon on the Start menu or desktop and drag it to the Quick Launch toolbar. To remove the shortcut, right-click the program icon on the Quick Launch toolbar and click Delete on the shortcut menu.

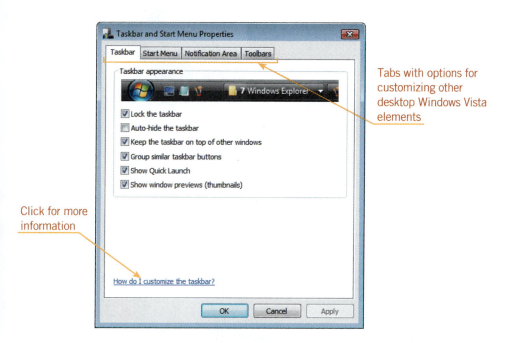

FIGURE VIS–3   Taskbar and Start Menu Properties dialog box

Clicking the Start button on the taskbar opens the Start menu. The Start menu is used for many common tasks, such as starting programs, accessing common folders, searching for files, getting help, switching to a different user account, or turning off the computer. The Start menu is divided into two panes. The left pane shows recently used programs. You can create a shortcut on the Start menu to a program you use regularly by right-clicking a program icon on the Start menu or desktop and then clicking Pin to Start Menu on the shortcut menu. Pinned icons are displayed above the bar in the left pane. To unpin an icon from the Start menu, you can click it and then click Unpin from Start Menu. The right pane of the Start menu displays links to the parts of Windows that you are likely to use frequently, such as your personal folders, a list of files you've opened recently, and the Control Panel.

Each user account has a picture associated with it, and this picture appears on the top of the right pane of the Start menu and on the Welcome screen when you start Vista. If you want to change the picture associated with your user account, click the picture at the top of the right pane of the Start menu to display the User Accounts window, click Change your picture, and then choose a new picture.

EXTRA FOR EXPERTS

You can customize other Start menu settings—such as the size of the icons or the number of recent programs displayed—in the Customize Start Menu dialog box. You open the Customize Start menu dialog box by right-clicking the Start button, clicking Properties to display the Start Menu tab of the Taskbar and Start Menu Properties dialog box, then clicking the Customize button.

APPENDIX A   Understanding Windows Vista Fundamentals

Step-by-Step VIS 2

1. Click the **Start** button on the taskbar. The Start menu opens, as shown in **Figure VIS–4**.

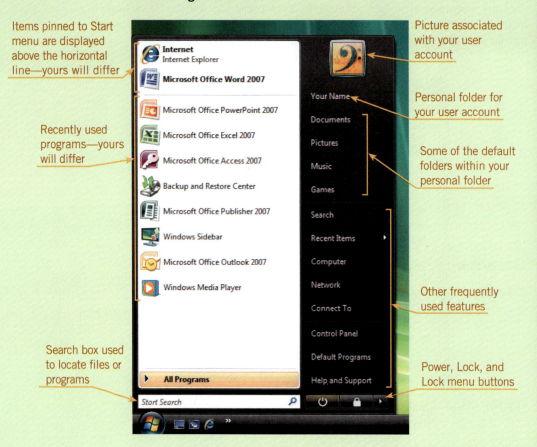

FIGURE VIS–4 Start Menu

- Items pinned to Start menu are displayed above the horizontal line—yours will differ
- Recently used programs—yours will differ
- Search box used to locate files or programs
- Picture associated with your user account
- Personal folder for your user account
- Some of the default folders within your personal folder
- Other frequently used features
- Power, Lock, and Lock menu buttons

2. In the left pane, right-click a program you use frequently and then click **Pin to Start Menu** on the shortcut menu to move it to above the bar in the left pane; this program icon will now always be displayed on the Start menu.

3. Right-click the program icon that you just pinned above the bar in the left pane of the Start menu and then click **Unpin from Start Menu** on the shortcut menu to remove the icon.

4. Click a blank area of the desktop to close the Start menu.

5. Click the time in the notification area of the taskbar to display the time and date settings, as shown in **Figure VIS–5**.

APPENDIX A Understanding Windows Vista Fundamentals

FIGURE VIS–5
Time and date settings

6. Right-click a blank area of the taskbar and click **Properties** on the shortcut menu to display the Taskbar tab of the Taskbar and Start Menu Properties dialog box.

7. Click the **Auto-hide the taskbar** check box to place a checkmark in it, and then click the **OK** button to close the dialog box and hide the taskbar.

8. Point to the bottom of the desktop to display the taskbar, right-click a blank area of the taskbar, and click **Properties** to display the Taskbar tab of the Taskbar and Start Menu Properties dialog box.

9. Click the **Auto-hide the taskbar** check box to remove the checkmark in it, and then click the **OK** button to close the dialog box and display the taskbar again.

10. Leave the computer on with the Windows Vista desktop displayed for the next Step-by-Step.

Personalizing Appearance and Sound

You can change various aspects of the desktop's appearance and sounds for your computer using the Personalization window in the Control Panel. For example, you can change the background picture on your desktop, called *wallpaper*, or choose a different *screen saver*, which is the moving picture or pattern that is displayed on the screen when the computer has been inactive for a certain amount of time. You can also pick which sounds are emitted for different actions, apply another theme, or adjust the display settings. You can display these options by clicking the Start button, Control Panel, Appearance and Personalization, and then Personalization. A shortcut to accessing these options is to right-click a blank area of the desktop and then to click Personalize.

▶ **VOCABULARY**
wallpaper
screen saver

Managing the Windows Sidebar

The Windows Sidebar is useful for keeping the information you need easily available without cluttering your workspace. For example, by adding or customizing gadgets you can use these mini-programs to display updated weather, view a calendar, use

APPENDIX A Understanding Windows Vista Fundamentals

sticky note reminders, or track the news. If the Sidebar is not displayed, you can open it by clicking the Start button, pointing to All Programs, clicking Accessories, and then clicking Windows Sidebar. You can customize the Sidebar by right-clicking a blank area on the Sidebar and then clicking Properties to display the Windows Sidebar Properties dialog box.

To add a gadget, you can click the Add Gadgets button at the top of the Sidebar, shown in **Figure VIS–6**, to display the gadget gallery. You can download a gadget by clicking the Get more gadgets online link in the gadget gallery. When you point to a gadget, a Close button is displayed that you can click to remove it from the Sidebar. If the gadget has settings that can be changed, an Options button is also displayed that you can use to customize it. Other controls may be displayed for a particular gadget. For example, when you point to the Slideshow gadget, the Previous, Pause, Next, and View buttons are displayed.

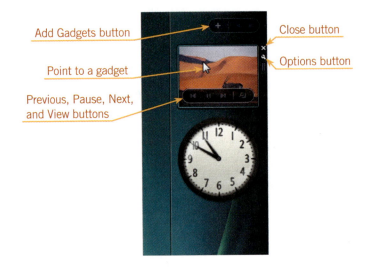

FIGURE VIS–6 Windows Sidebar

Step-by-Step VIS 3

1. Right-click a blank area of the desktop and then click **Personalize** on the shortcut menu to display the Personalization window.

2. Click **Desktop Background** to display the Desktop Background window, shown in **Figure VIS–7**.

APPENDIX A   Understanding Windows Vista Fundamentals

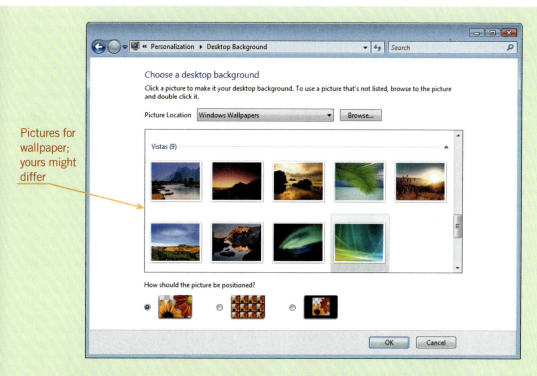

FIGURE VIS–7
Desktop Background window

Pictures for wallpaper; yours might differ

3. Scroll through the pictures available for use as a desktop background, and then click the **Cancel** button to close the dialog box without changing the desktop background.

4. In the Personalization window, click **Screen Saver** to display the Screen Saver Setting dialog box, shown in **Figure VIS–8**.

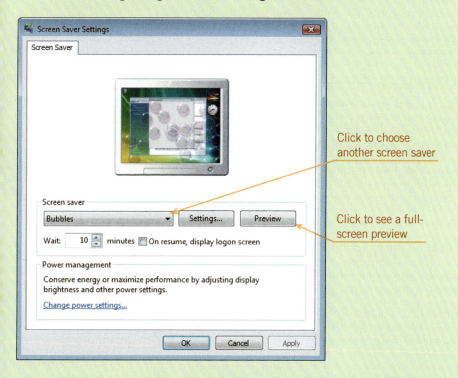

FIGURE VIS–8
Screen Saver Settings dialog box

Click to choose another screen saver

Click to see a full-screen preview

5. Click the **Screen saver** button arrow, click **Bubbles**, and then click the **Preview** button to see a full-screen preview of the screen saver.

APPENDIX A   Understanding Windows Vista Fundamentals

6. Move the mouse or press a key to return to the dialog box and then click the **Cancel** button to close the dialog box without changing the screen saver.
7. Click the **Close** button to close the Personalization window.
8. If the Windows Sidebar is not already displayed, click the **Start** button , point to **All Programs**, click **Accessories**, and then click **Windows Sidebar**.
9. At the top of the Windows Sidebar, click the **Add Gadget** button to display the gadget gallery, shown in **Figure VIS–9**.

FIGURE VIS–9
Gadget gallery

Click a gadget icon

Click to view and download gadgets from Microsoft

10. Click the **Show Details** button, and then click the **Notes** gadget icon and read the description of this gadget at the bottom of the gadget gallery.
11. Click the **Close** button on the gadget gallery to close it.
12. Leave the computer on with the Windows Vista desktop displayed for the next Step-by-Step.

Managing Files and Folders

In the lessons for individual Office programs, you learn to open, close, and save files. At times, you may need to move, rename, or delete a file as well. To manage your files, you also need to know how to use folders. A ***folder*** is a container for storing and organizing files and can also contain subfolders. Each user account has a ***personal folder***, labeled with your user name that stores your frequently used folders

▶ **VOCABULARY**
folder

personal folder

APPENDIX A Understanding Windows Vista Fundamentals

in one convenient location. Within your personal folder, Windows Vista provides default folders that you can use as a starting point for organizing your files—such as Documents, Downloads, Music, and Pictures—or you can create your own.

Some of these common folders are located on the Start menu in the top section of the right pane, or you can click the Start button and then click your user name at the top of the Start menu's right pane to display a folder window showing the contents of the personal folder for your user account, as shown in **Figure VIS–10**. Use this figure and **Table VIS–1** to become familiar with the parts of a folder window. Folder windows in Windows Vista are designed so that you can navigate to other folders without closing the current folder window.

> **EXTRA FOR EXPERTS**
>
> If you want to share files with other users on the same computer or through a network, you can store them in the Public folder. Be sure you want to share the files you put there, because you cannot restrict access to the Public folder.

FIGURE VIS–10   Folder window

TABLE VIS–1   Elements of a folder window

ELEMENT	USED TO
Navigation Pane	Access common folders; quickly navigate to any folder on the computer
Address bar	Display your current location; navigate to another folder
Back and Forward buttons	Return to the previously viewed folder in either direction
Search box	Look for a file or folder in the current folder that contains the search word or phrase
Toolbar	Perform common tasks related to the folder that is displayed
Details pane	View information about the file such as the author, size, or date created
Files and folders list	Display the files and folders located in the current folder
Column headings	Change how the files are organized by sorting, grouping, or stacking

APPENDIX A   Understanding Windows Vista Fundamentals

Changing Views

You might want to see different kinds of information about the files in a folder, or prefer the icons be a different size. You can change how files are displayed in the folder window by clicking the Views button arrow on the toolbar and then dragging the slider to another view, as shown in **Figure VIS–11**.

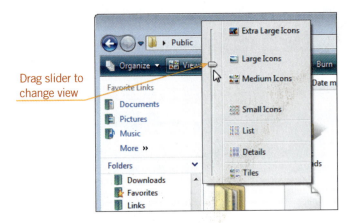

FIGURE VIS–11   Views menu

Create, Rename, and Delete Files and Folders

You can manage your files and folders by clicking the Organize button on the toolbar in the folder window. On the menu that is displayed, you can create a new folder by clicking New Folder, rename a selected file or folder by clicking Rename and typing a new name, and delete a selected file or folder by clicking Delete.

Deleting unneeded files or folders saves space and reduces clutter on your computer. When you delete a file or folder, a message will be displayed asking you to confirm the deletion, and then the file or folder will be temporarily stored in the Recycle Bin. This allows you to retrieve a file or folder if you deleted it accidentally. The Recycle Bin is similar to a trash can—you can throw something away, but it is not permanently gone. However, occasionally you should free up space by emptying the Recycle Bin. This will permanently delete all the files and folders that were temporarily stored there.

> **EXTRA FOR EXPERTS**
>
> You can return a file or folder that you deleted to its original location by double-clicking the Recycle Bin icon to open it, clicking an item, and then clicking Restore this item on the toolbar. You can empty the Recycle Bin by opening it and then clicking Empty the Recycle Bin on the toolbar.

Copying and Moving Files and Folders

If you want to change where files and folders are stored on your computer or copy them to a different location, the easiest way is to use the drag-and-drop method. Click the file or folder you want to move or copy, drag it to another location, and drop it. If the folders are located on the same hard drive, the item will be moved so that you don't have multiple copies. If the folders are located on different hard drives, such as a network or CD, the item will be copied so that you don't lose the original.

> **EXTRA FOR EXPERTS**
>
> If you want to copy or move a file to a folder that is not visible in the folder window, you can open another folder window, and then use the same method to drag and drop the file between folder windows.

APPENDIX A   Understanding Windows Vista Fundamentals

Step-by-Step VIS 4

1. Click the **Start** button on the taskbar and then click your *user name* in the top of the right pane to display the folder window displaying the contents of the personal folder belonging to your user account.

2. Click the **Downloads** folder to select it and notice the folder information displayed in the Details pane.

3. On the toolbar, click the **Organize** button to display the menu, as shown in **Figure VIS–12**.

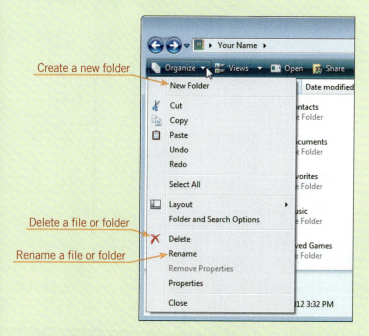

FIGURE VIS–12
Organize menu

4. Click the **New Folder** button to create a new folder and then type **Receipts** and press **Enter** to name the new folder.

5. With the new folder selected, click the **Organize** button on the toolbar and then click **Rename** to select the folder name.

6. Type **Invoices** and then press **Enter** to rename the folder.

7. On the toolbar, click the **Views** button arrow to display the menu, and notice what the current setting is, and then drag the slider up to the **Extra Large Icons** setting to change the view. Notice the size of the icons in the folder window changes as you drag the slider.

8. On the toolbar, click the **Views** button arrow and move the slider to reset the view to its previous setting.

9. Select the **Invoices** folder you created. Be sure the Documents folder is visible within the folder window.

10. Drag the Invoices folder to the Documents folder, as shown in **Figure VIS 13**, and drop it in its new location.

FIGURE VIS-13
Moving a folder

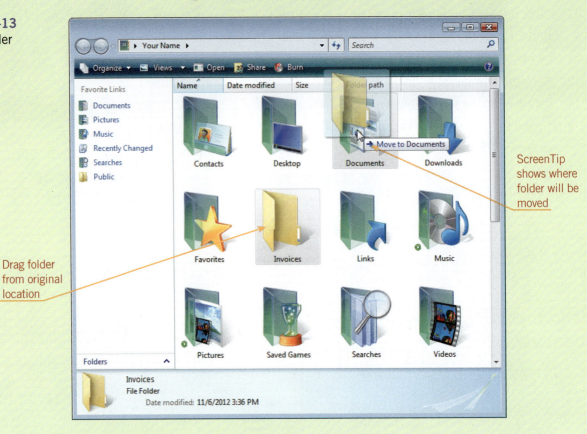

11. Double-click the **Documents** folder to open it and select the **Invoices** folder you moved there.
12. Click the **Organize** button on the toolbar and then click **Delete**. Click the **Yes** button to confirm the deletion and delete the folder.
13. Click the **Close** button on the folder window to close it.
14. Leave the computer on with the Windows Vista desktop displayed for the next Step-by-Step.

Getting Help

If you need more information about Windows features, the Windows Help and Support system, shown in **Figure VIS-14**, can answer questions, troubleshoot problems, and give instructions. You can access it by clicking the Start button and then clicking Help and Support.

APPENDIX A Understanding Windows Vista Fundamentals

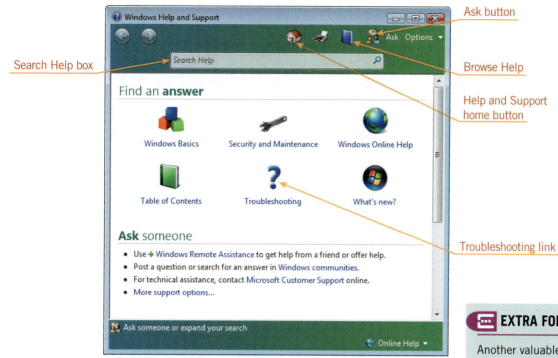

FIGURE VIS–14 Windows Help and Support

You can type a word or phrase in the Search box, browse the topics by clicking the Browse Help button, or get customer support options for your computer by clicking the Ask button. In the Find an answer section, you can click a help category. For example, you can troubleshoot specific types of Windows problems by clicking the Troubleshooting link. Because there are many different types of help you can access, it is a good idea to explore Windows Help to familiarize yourself with the various options.

> **EXTRA FOR EXPERTS**
>
> Another valuable help resource is the Knowledge Base, a large online database of articles from users and other sources provided by Microsoft to help with specific problems and computer errors. You can access it by clicking the Ask button on the toolbar of the Windows Help and Support window and then clicking the Knowledge Base link.

Step-by-Step VIS 5

1. Click the **Start** button, then click **Help and Support** to display the Windows Help and Support window.
2. Click the **Browse Help** button on the toolbar to display a list of help categories.
3. In the Search Help box, type **Windows desktop** and press **Enter** to display a list of results.
4. In the list of results, click the **What's new with the Windows desktop?** link and then read the article.
5. Click the **Help and Support home** button on the toolbar to return to the home page.
6. In the Find an answer section, click the **Troubleshooting** link to display the Troubleshooting in Windows window, as shown in **Figure VIS–15**.

FIGURE VIS–15
Troubleshooting in Windows

7. Scroll down to the Your computer section at the end, click the **Ways to improve your computer's performance** link, and read about the tasks that can help improve your computer's performance.

8. Click the **Ask** button on the toolbar to display the Get customer support or other types of help window. Notice the link to the online Knowledge Base.

9. Click the **Close** button to close Windows Help and Support.

10. Leave the computer on with the Windows Vista desktop displayed for the next Step-by-Step.

Shutting Down Windows Vista

When you are finished working on the computer, you can close your Windows Vista session and shut down the computer by clicking the Start button and then clicking the arrow next to the Lock button to display the menu shown in **Figure VIS–16**, and then clicking Shut Down.

APPENDIX A   Understanding Windows Vista Fundamentals

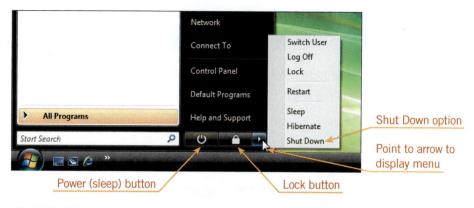

FIGURE VIS-16   Lock button menu

The Lock menu also provides other options which are described in **Table VIS-2**.

TABLE VIS-2   Lock menu options

OPTION	DESCRIPTION
Switch User	Changes users on a computer without closing programs and files first
Log Off	Closes all the open programs, but does not turn the computer off
Lock	Displays the Welcome screen to prevent other people from accessing or viewing your work; useful when you will be away from the computer for short periods of time in a public place; can also be accessed by clicking the Start button and then clicking the Lock button
Restart	Shuts the computer down and then starts it back up
Sleep	Power-saving mode that saves all files and programs to computer memory and allows you to quickly resume working; can also be accessed by clicking the Start button and then clicking the Power (sleep) button
Hibernate	Power-saving mode that saves all files and programs to the computer hard disk and then turns off the computer
Shut Down	Closes all programs and files and turns off the computer; best option if you won't be using your computer for several days or longer

Not all computers are the same, so some of these options may not be available or they may operate differently. For example, the Sleep option may not be supported by your computer or your system administrator may have turned the Hibernate option off. On most computers, you can resume working by pressing the power button, but you may be able to press a key or use the mouse button to wake the computer. If you have questions about your computer, check the documentation or the manufacturer's Web site.

Step-by-Step VIS 6

1. Click the **Start** button  and point to the arrow next to the Lock button ▶ to display the menu.
2. Click **Shut Down** to close Windows Vista and turn off the computer.

SUMMARY

In this appendix, you learned:

- How to start Windows Vista.
- The parts of the Windows Vista desktop.
- Ways to customize Vista.
- Methods for managing files and folders.
- The ways for getting Windows help.
- How to shut down Windows Vista.

Estimated Time:
1 hour

APPENDIX B

Understanding Outlook Fundamentals

■ OBJECTIVES

Upon completion of this appendix, you should be able to:

- Start Outlook and view the folders.
- Send and receive e-mail.
- Enter contacts.
- Create and manage tasks.
- Enter appointments in the Calendar.
- Preview and print Outlook items.
- Exit Outlook.

■ DATA FILES

You do not need data files to complete this appendix.

■ VOCABULARY

appointment
contact
Date Navigator
e-mail
event
forward
mail server
personal information manager software
task
To-Do List
…

APPENDIX B Understanding Outlook Fundamentals

Introduction

Microsoft Outlook 2007 is the e-mail and personal information manager (PIM) program included in the Microsoft Office 2007 suite of software. **Personal information manager software** is software that helps you communicate and organize business and personal information. Using Outlook, you can send and receive e-mail, add contacts to your address book, manage tasks, and enter appointments and reminders in the calendar.

Starting Outlook and Changing Views

You open Outlook by clicking the Start button on the Windows taskbar, and then clicking the program name on the All Programs menu, or by double-clicking an Outlook program icon on the desktop. Once Outlook is started, you can begin using it to organize your tasks and information.

Outlook has different screens for its various functions. You access the e-mail, task, contact, and calendar functions of the software through the appropriate buttons in the Navigation pane. In these areas of Outlook, you will see toolbars and menus for accessing commands. When you create, edit, and format e-mail messages, contacts, tasks, or appointments, the familiar Ribbon is displayed. The Outlook Today screen, shown in **Figure OL-1**, displays a Standard toolbar, Web toolbar, and Menu bar at the top of the screen and the Navigation pane on the left. This screen gives you a summary of your schedule for the day. Almost every part of the Outlook screen can be rearranged, hidden, or customized to your specifications, so your screen may look different.

> **VOCABULARY**
> personal information manager software

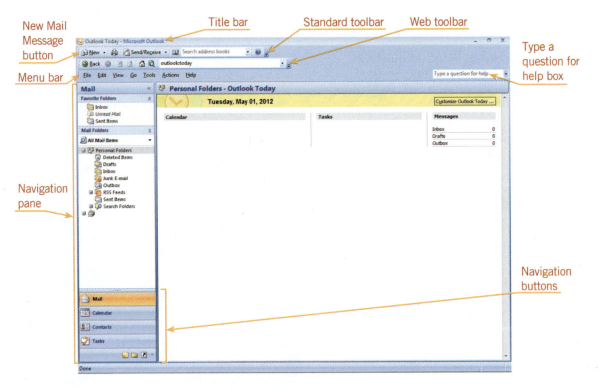

FIGURE OL-1 Outlook Today screen

APPENDIX B   Understanding Outlook Fundamentals

The Navigation pane contains buttons you can use to access the different features of Outlook:

- Mail—Displays the folders, message lists, and toolbars necessary for sending and receiving e-mail
- Calendar—Contains a planner you can use to organize appointments, meetings, holidays, and events
- Contacts—Contains names, addresses, e-mail addresses, and other information about people you contact regularly
- Tasks—Lets you create action lists

Step-by-Step OL 1

1. Click the **Start** button on the Windows taskbar. The Start menu opens.
2. Click **All Programs**. A list of programs and program folders opens.
3. Click the **Microsoft Office** program folder. A list of Office programs opens.
4. Click **Microsoft Office Outlook 2007**. Outlook starts and the Outlook 2007 Mail window opens on the desktop. (*Note*: If you get a message that Outlook is not your default mail program, check with your instructor about whether you should set Outlook as the default mail program on your system.)
5. In the Navigation pane, click the **Calendar** button to display the calendar in Daily view.
6. In the Navigation pane, click the **Contacts** button to display Contacts.
7. In the Navigation pane, click the **Tasks** button to display the To-Do List.
8. In the Navigation pane, click the **Mail** button to display the Mail screen.
9. Leave the Outlook window open for use in the next Step-by-Step.

Sending and Receiving E-Mail

When you click the Mail button in the Navigation pane, the Mail screen is displayed. The Mail Folders list, located in the Navigation pane, contains folders you can use to organize your Outlook e-mail messages. When you click a Mail folder, the contents are displayed in the center pane.

Your list might include different categories of folders. The folders you need to become familiar with include the following:

- Deleted Items—Contains messages you have deleted
- Drafts—Contains drafts of messages you have saved but have not yet sent
- Inbox—Contains all the e-mail messages you have received
- Junk E-mail—Contains the e-mail messages that you received that were considered spam or junk

> **EXTRA FOR EXPERTS**
>
> You can create new folders in which to file your e-mail messages. In addition, you can create a wide variety of rules that will send e-mail from a particular person or of a particular type to a specific folder as soon as it arrives in your Inbox.

APPENDIX B Understanding Outlook Fundamentals

- Outbox—Contains the e-mail messages that you have written but that the computer has not yet sent
- Sent Items—Contains a copy of the messages you have sent

VOCABULARY
e-mail

Creating a New E-Mail Message

Mail is probably the most used feature of Outlook. *E-mail*, short for electronic mail, is a way to send and receive messages over the Internet or another network. Sending e-mail is as simple as entering an e-mail address, a subject, and a message and clicking the Send button. You open a blank e-mail message by clicking the New Mail Message button on the Standard toolbar. The Untitled – Message dialog box opens, as shown in **Figure OL-2**. Notice that the dialog box contains a Ribbon similar to the one you've used in other Office 2007 programs, with tabs, groups, and commands for creating an e-mail message.

EXTRA FOR EXPERTS

It's a good idea to check your spelling before sending a message. Use the Spelling button in the Proofing group of the Message tab to check spelling and grammar, use the thesaurus, or look up a word in the dictionary.

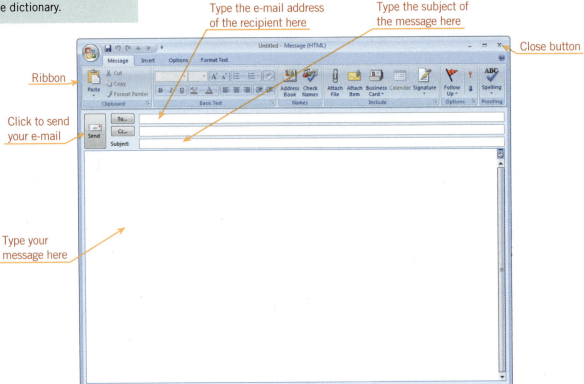

FIGURE OL-2 Untitled – Message dialog box

WARNING

To send and receive e-mail, your computer and Outlook software must be configured to communicate with an Internet Service Provider (ISP) and an e-mail account must be established. If your computer is set up to handle e-mail, you can easily send and receive e-mail using Outlook. If you need help setting up an e-mail account, choose an option from the Help menu.

If you want to use formatting options such as bullets, alignment, or colored text in your message, you can do so as long as your mail format is set to the default HTML format. Other formats might not provide these options. You can select the text you want to format and use the buttons on the Ribbon to apply the formatting of your choice.

Many people like to include a signature with their e-mail messages. A signature is text and or graphics, such as a picture, that is added automatically to the end of a message. You can use the Signature button in the Include group of the Message tab to create one signature or as many as you like.

APPENDIX B Understanding Outlook Fundamentals

Step-by-Step OL 2

The Mail Screen should be displayed from Step-by-Step OL 1.

1. In the Navigation pane, click the **Inbox** folder, if necessary, to display the Inbox in the center pane.
2. On the Standard toolbar, click the **New Mail Message** button to display the Untitled – Message dialog box.
3. In the To box, type your own e-mail address.
4. In the Subject box, type **Outlook**.
5. In the message area, type **Mail is probably the most popular feature of Outlook**.
6. Select the word **Mail**. In the Message tab, in the Basic Text group, click the **Bold** button .
7. Select the entire sentence. In the Basic Text group, click the **Font Color** button to apply the color Red.
8. Click the **Send** button to remove the message from the screen.
9. Leave Outlook open for use in the next Step-by-Step.

Receiving and Replying to E-Mail

In **Figure OL-3**, there is a bold number 1 in parentheses (**1**) beside Inbox in the Mail Folders list. This number indicates that there is one unread message in the Inbox. As you see, one message is shown in the Inbox pane, which displays the message's sender, subject, and the date it was sent. The Reading pane to the right of the Inbox displays a preview of the message. You can turn on or off the Reading Pane or move it using the Reading Pane command on the View menu. The To-Do List may be displayed in the right pane.

When you reply to or forward an e-mail message, Outlook includes the original message at the bottom of the screen. You can use the Options command on the Tools menu to change this setting.

> **EXTRA FOR EXPERTS**
>
> To attach a file to an e-mail message, click the Attach File button on the Ribbon. The Insert File dialog box appears where you can locate your file and then click the Insert button. The filename will appear beside the word *Attached:* below the Subject.

APPENDIX B   Understanding Outlook Fundamentals

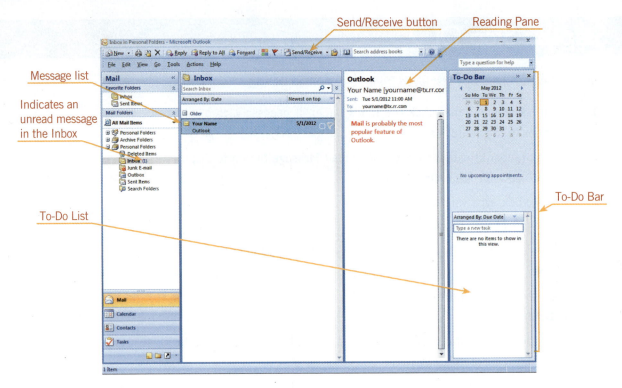

FIGURE OL-3   Inbox

You double-click a message to open it in a new window. The Message tab on the Ribbon within the message dialog box has buttons for working with an e-mail message. In the Respond group, the Reply button lets you reply to the sender of the message you received. Reply to All sends a message to all the addresses on a message. The *Forward* button sends the message to someone else. The Ribbon also contains buttons for moving the message to a folder, deleting it, or flagging it for follow-up.

By default, Outlook is configured to send a message as soon as you click the Send button. If you are not connected to the Internet, the message will be stored in the Outbox folder until you are connected again. Outlook is set to automatically perform a send/receive action every 10 minutes, meaning Outlook will send any messages in the Outbox folder and retrieve messages from the *mail server*, a computer at your Internet service provider (ISP) that transfers messages from one computer to another. You can change these settings using the Options dialog box on the Tools menu. You can also click the Send/Receive button on the Standard toolbar to prompt Outlook to perform a send/receive action at any time.

▶ VOCABULARY
forward

mail server

📑 EXTRA FOR EXPERTS

You can sort messages in the Inbox quickly by clicking an Arrange By column heading and choosing an option from the menu. For example, you can display all messages from Microsoft by clicking a message from Microsoft and then clicking the Arrange By column heading and clicking From on the menu.

APPENDIX B   Understanding Outlook Fundamentals

Step-by-Step OL 3

The Mail screen should be displayed from Step-by-Step OL 2.

1. On the Standard toolbar, click the **Send/Receive** button, if necessary, to prompt Outlook to retrieve messages.
2. In the message list, double-click the **Outlook** message to open the e-mail message in a new window.
3. On the Message tab, in the Respond group, click the **Reply** button to open a reply e-mail with RE: Outlook as the subject.
4. Type **It is important to reply to e-mails in a timely manner and to keep your messages brief**.
5. Click the **Send** button.
6. Click the **Close** button X on the Outlook message.

Entering Contacts

Because the Address Book stores all contact information within Outlook, the Address Book is Outlook's second-most popular feature. A *contact* is the information you have about one person, such as their name, title, address, telephone and fax numbers, and e-mail address. All contacts are stored in the Address Book. Adding contacts to the Address Book makes it easy for you to access that information when you want to e-mail, call, fax, or write to a contact. In fact, after you enter contacts, you can click the To button in a new e-mail message to easily access your contacts list and click the contact to whom you want to send the e-mail, so you don't have to type in the address.

When you click the Contacts button in the Navigation Pane, the Contacts are displayed in the center pane, as shown in **Figure OL-4**. By choosing Current View from the View menu and clicking an option on the submenu, you can view contacts several ways, including as Business Cards, Address Cards, by Category, or by Company.

> **VOCABULARY**
> contact

APPENDIX B   Understanding Outlook Fundamentals

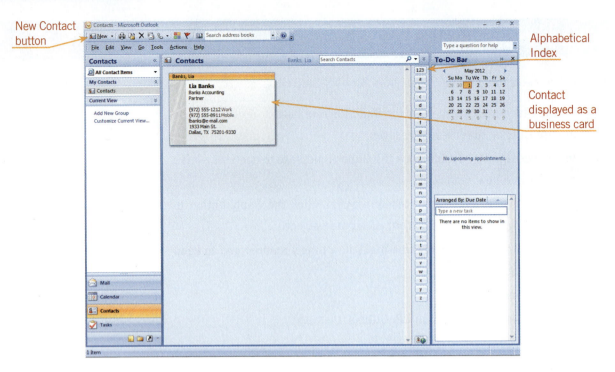

FIGURE OL-4 Contacts

You can use the toolbar buttons to create a new contact; flag a contact for follow-up; open, print, and delete contacts; categorize contacts; and find contacts. Click a letter in the alphabetical index on the right side of the center pane to display contacts by the first letter of the last name.

You can add new contacts easily using the New Contact button on the Standard toolbar. Just type the contact information into the Untitled – Contact dialog box and save it when you are finished.

Enter as much or as little information about a contact as you want. If you have only a person's name and e-mail address, just enter those. You can always double-click to open and edit the contact to add other information.

The Save & Close button saves the contact information and closes the dialog box. If you want to enter another contact, click the Save & New button instead, to close the current dialog box and open a new blank one. You can assign the contact a category with the Categorize button. For example, you might want to categorize all work-related contacts with a green color and friends with blue, so that you can distinguish them easily. Click the Delete button to remove a contact from your Address Book.

EXTRA FOR EXPERTS

You can create contacts quickly from e-mail messages. Just right-click the name or e-mail address in the From area of the e-mail message and click Add to Outlook Contacts. The name and e-mail address will be added to the Contact dialog box for you, and you can add more information or save and close it.

EXTRA FOR EXPERTS

You can create a distribution list using the New button arrow that includes the addresses of a group of people and then send the same e-mail message to the entire group.

APPENDIX B Understanding Outlook Fundamentals

OL 9

Step-by-Step OL 4

The Mail Screen should be displayed from Step-by-Step OL 3.

1. In the Navigation pane, click the **Contacts** navigation button to display the Contacts list.
2. Click the **New Contact** button to display the Untitled – Contact dialog box.
3. Enter the data for the contact, as shown in **Figure OL 5**. (Don't worry about adding underlines, parentheses, or other formatting; Outlook will add it for you.)

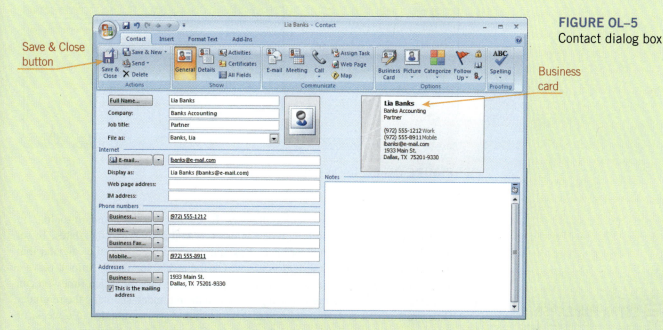

FIGURE OL-5
Contact dialog box

4. Click the **Save & Close** button to save the contact and close the dialog box. Lia Banks' contact information now appears in the Contacts list displayed as a business card.
5. Leave Outlook open for use in the next Step-by-Step.

Creating and Managing Tasks

A *task* is a job or duty that you must complete. Outlook's *To-Do List* is similar to a handwritten to-do list that displays all your tasks. However, in Outlook you can set reminders and due dates so that Outlook can help you stay on top of your work. A task that repeats on a regular basis, such as creating a weekly report each Friday, can be set to recur every week in your task list.

The To-Do List, shown in **Figure OL 6**, displays all your tasks and lets you arrange them in different ways, such as by due date, start date, or category. Icons beside a task in the To-Do List let you know at a glance the priority, follow-up, whether a reminder is set, and category. The Current View section of the Navigation pane has more options for displaying tasks, such as displaying only overdue tasks or completed tasks.

> **VOCABULARY**
> task
> To-Do List

APPENDIX B   Understanding Outlook Fundamentals

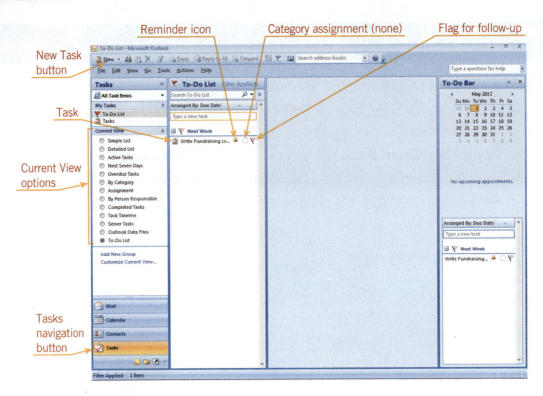

FIGURE OL-6   To-Do List

> **EXTRA FOR EXPERTS**
>
> After you create a task, you can assign it to someone else using the Assign Task button in the Manage Task group of the Task tab. That person will receive the task by e-mail and then he or she has the choice of accepting, declining, or assigning the task to someone else.

Create a new task by clicking the New Task button on the Standard toolbar. In the Untitled – Task dialog box, type a subject as well as start and due dates. To set a reminder, click the Reminder check box and choose a date from the calendar that appears when you click the button arrow. On the task's due date, Outlook plays a sound and displays a notification reminding you of the task, at which time you can respond by opening the item to change or delete the reminder, snoozing the reminder (like pressing the snooze button on an alarm clock) for five minutes to a week, or dismissing the reminder. You can also click the Complete check box to mark the item as completed and dismiss the reminder.

To help you rank the importance of tasks, you can prioritize them by assigning each one a high, normal, or low priority. After you save a task, it appears in the To-Do List and in the To-Do Bar. When you finish a task, you can open the task and adjust the % Complete box to 100%, or you can right-click the flag in the To-Do List and click Mark Complete on the shortcut menu. If a task becomes past due, it appears red in the To-Do List.

APPENDIX B Understanding Outlook Fundamentals

Step-by-Step OL 5

The Contacts screen should be displayed from Step-by-Step OL 4.

1. In the Navigation pane, click the **Tasks** button to display the To-Do List.
2. Click the **New Task** button on the Standard toolbar to display the Untitled – Task dialog box.
3. Type **Write Fundraising Letter** in the Subject box.
4. Click the **Due date** button arrow to display a calendar, and click the day that is one week from today.
5. Click the **Reminder** check box and the date button arrow beside it to display the calendar. Click tomorrow's date to set a reminder that will play a sound and display a Reminder dialog box tomorrow.
6. Click the **Priority** button arrow, and click **High** to specify that the task is in the high priority category. Your screen should look similar to **Figure OL-7**.

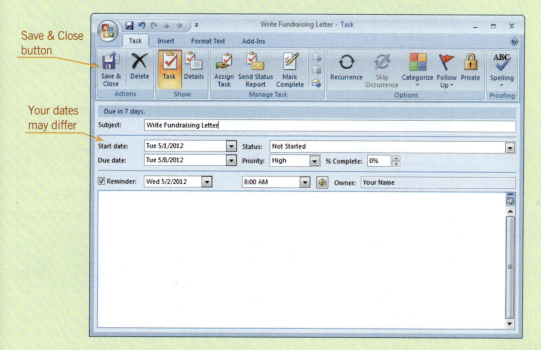

FIGURE OL–7
Task dialog box

7. On the Task tab, in the Actions group, click the **Save & Close** button to save the task and close the dialog box.
8. Notice that the task you created appears in the To-Do List and in the To-Do bar.
9. Leave Outlook open for use in the next Step-by-Step.

APPENDIX B Understanding Outlook Fundamentals

Entering Appointments and Events in the Calendar

The Outlook Calendar can help you keep track of appointments, meetings, events, and holidays in your schedule, just as you can on a paper calendar. But as you've learned with tasks, the Outlook Calendar can do more, such as schedule recurring appointments or events such as a birthday. You can enter the birthday information once and set Outlook to display that event every year on the same day. You can set up a reminder to notify you a few days in advance.

There are various ways to view the Outlook Calendar, shown in **Figure OL-8**. Click a date on the *Date Navigator*, which is the small monthly calendar at the top of the Navigation pane, then use the buttons at the top of the window to display the calendar by Day, Week, and Month.

VOCABULARY
Date Navigator
appointment
event

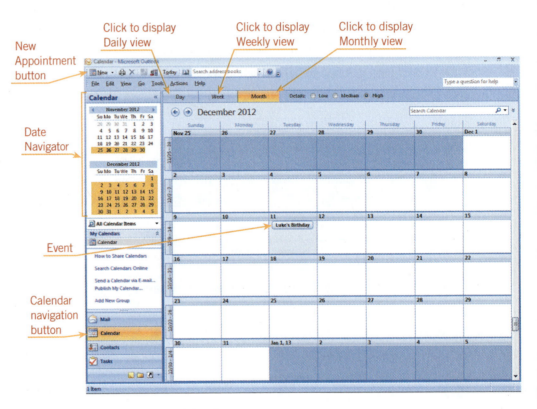

FIGURE OL-8 Calendar

EXTRA FOR EXPERTS

Instead of requiring you to enter each holiday in the calendar, Outlook has compiled the major holidays for various countries/regions and religions into groups. To add the holiday group of your choice, choose the Options command from the Tools menu and click the Calendar Options button to display the Calendar Options dialog box.

To enter a new appointment or an all-day event, you click the New Appointment button on the Standard toolbar. An *appointment*, such as a dentist's appointment, has a beginning and ending time and occupies that amount of time on your calendar. An *event*, such as a birthday, lasts all day and is displayed on your calendar as a banner but does not occupy all the time in your schedule. You might have a friend's birthday entered in your calendar, but you can still schedule a dentist's appointment in your calendar for an hour on that day.

You can also schedule a meeting by clicking the button arrow on the New menu and then clicking Meeting Request. Outlook will send e-mail invitations to the attendees that you specify. Recipients using Outlook will have the option of accepting or declining the meeting request or proposing a new meeting time. If a recipient accepts the meeting request, a meeting entry will be added to his or her Outlook calendar.

APPENDIX B Understanding Outlook Fundamentals

When scheduling a recurring event, such as a class, use the Recurrence button to specify the recurrence pattern. Reminders can be set in increments of minutes, hours, or days. For a meeting, you might want to set a reminder for 30 minutes in advance; for a birthday, you might want to be reminded a few days before the event.

You can double-click an event or appointment in the calendar to open it and edit it. If it is a recurring event, you might see a message asking if you want to edit the entire series of events or just this one occurrence.

Step-by-Step OL 6

The To-Do List should be displayed from Step-by-Step OL 5.

1. In the Navigation pane, click the **Calendar** button to display the Calendar.
2. In the Date Navigator, click tomorrow's date to display the daily view.
3. Click the **Week** button at the top of the window to display the weekly view.
4. Click the **Month** button to display the monthly view.
5. On the Standard toolbar, click the **New Appointment** button to display the Untitled – Appointment dialog box.
6. Type **Luke's Birthday** in the Subject box.
7. Click the button arrow at the end of the Start time box. Use the arrows to move to **December** of the current or coming year. Click day **11** on the calendar. You do not need to set the time in the hour boxes.
8. Click the **All day event** check box. Notice the End time is changed automatically to match the start time and the hour boxes are dimmed. Your screen should look similar to **Figure OL-9**.

FIGURE OL–9
Event dialog box

APPENDIX B   Understanding Outlook Fundamentals

9. On the Event tab, in the Options group, click the **Recurrence** button to display the Appointment Recurrence dialog box.

10. In the Recurrence pattern area, click the **Yearly** button, as shown in **Figure OL 10**, and then click **OK** to set Luke's birthday as a yearly event.

FIGURE OL–10
Appointment Recurrence dialog box

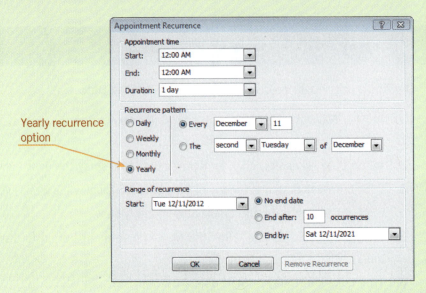

11. On the Recurring Event tab, in the Actions group, click the **Save & Close** button to save the event and close the dialog box.

12. In the Calendar, click the arrows in the Date Navigator to go to the month of December to see the event on the calendar.

13. Leave Outlook open for use in the next Step-by-Step.

Previewing and Printing Outlook Items

You can print individual calendars, e-mail messages, contacts, and tasks. Both the Print command on the File menu and the Print button on the toolbar display the Print dialog box.

The settings and options in the Print dialog box will differ according to the printer you are using and the item you are printing, but include choosing a print style, or layout, and a print range.

The Preview button displays what the item will look like when printed.

Step-by-Step OL 7

The Calendar should be displayed from Step-by-Step OL 6.

1. Click the **File** menu and click **Print** to display the Print dialog box.

2. If necessary, click **Monthly Style** in the Print style area.

APPENDIX B Understanding Outlook Fundamentals

3. In the Print range area, click the **Start** button arrow, navigate to December in the calendar, and click **December 1**.
4. In the Print range area, click the **End** button arrow and click **December 31**.
5. Click the **Preview** button to see a preview of the page.
6. Click the **Print** button to return to the Print dialog box, and click **OK** to print the page and close the preview. (*Note*: If you have been instructed not to print, click the Close button on the Preview toolbar.)
7. Leave Outlook open for use in the next Step-by-Step.

Exiting Outlook

When you are working at your computer, you may find that you leave Outlook open most of the day and check your e-mail periodically along with updating tasks and adding appointments. When you are finished working in Outlook, you can remove it from your screen using the Exit command on the File menu or by clicking the Close button on the title bar.

Step-by-Step OL 8

The Calendar should be displayed from Step-by-Step OL 7.

1. Click the **File** menu and click **Exit** to quit the program.

COMPUTER ETHICS

E-mail has many advantages—it is easy to compose and can be rapidly sent. But some advantages can tempt misuse, including being able to send the same message to many people at once. Sending unsolicited bulk e-mail is called spamming. Spamming generates unwanted junk e-mail, wastes time as people sort through it, and violates basic e-mail ethics. Outlook has a Junk Mail Filter you can use to identify and manage junk mail.

SUMMARY

In this appendix, you learned:

- Personal information manager software helps you organize and communicate information.
- The Navigation pane buttons let you access the mail, calendar, contacts, and task features of Outlook.
- Sending e-mail requires entering an e-mail address, a subject, and a message and clicking the Send button.
- The Reading Pane lets you view a message without opening it in a new window.
- Adding contacts to the Outlook Address Book makes it easy for you to access that information when you want to e-mail, call, fax, or write to a contact.
- The Outlook To-Do List lets you set reminders and due dates so that Outlook can help you accomplish those tasks.
- The Outlook Calendar can help you schedule appointments, meetings, holidays, and other important events.
- You can preview and print calendars, e-mail messages, contacts, and tasks using the Print command on the File menu.

GLOSSARY

A

absolute reference In Excel, a permanent reference to a cell, which does not change in relation to the location of the formula.

action buttons Graphic symbols within PowerPoint that cause an action to occur when you click or mouse over the button.

active cell The currently selected cell in an Excel worksheet.

alignment The position of text in relation to the margins in a document or the edges of a text box, cell, or placeholder.

animations Visual or audio effects used to control the flow of information and add interest to a PowerPoint presentation.

appointment An entry in the Outlook Calendar that has a beginning and end time.

argument The values or cell references on which an Excel function is to be performed.

arithmetic operator The element of a formula that performs basic mathematical operations to produce numeric results in an Excel formula.

Auto Fill A feature in Excel that automatically fills in adjacent worksheet cells with data in any direction.

AutoFormat A predefined set of fonts, colors, and borders for formatting documents, spreadsheets, presentations, and publications.

B

badge A small label with a number or letter that appears on each command on the Ribbon when you activate KeyTips.

borders Lines or repeated artwork that outline a page or slide.

building blocks Predesigned, reusable document parts.

bullets Small symbols that mark the beginning of a list item.

business information set A group of data in Publisher, such as name, address, and job title, that can be saved together as a set and used again to populate a future publication.

C

cell The rectangle where a column and row intersect in an Excel worksheet or Word table.

cell reference The column letter followed by the row number that identifies a worksheet cell, such as B5.

cell style A defined combination of cell formatting characteristics in Excel, such as number, alignment, font, border, and fill.

characters Individual letters, numbers, symbols, punctuation marks, and spaces.

chart area The complete Excel chart and all its elements.

chart A graphical representation of data.

chart sheet A separate worksheet in an Excel workbook that contains a chart.

clip art Predefined set of artwork such as drawings or images that comes with Microsoft Office programs.

Clipboard An area of memory in Windows that temporarily stores up to 24 cut or copied selections.

collate To print the pages in a document or file in a specific order.

column The cells that display vertically in an Excel worksheet or other table. In Excel, cells are labeled from left to right beginning with A through Z, then AA through AZ, and so on.

columns A way to format text where it flows from the bottom of one vertical section to the top of the next.

conditional formatting A feature in Excel that changes the appearance of cells that meet specific conditions.

constant A number entered directly into an Excel formula that does not change.

contact In Outlook, the set of information you have about one person.

contextual tabs The tabs on the Ribbon that appear only when you have selected a specific object or you are completing a specific task, and provide commands that relate to the selected object or the task that you are performing.

Control Panel A Windows Vista tool providing options for selecting and changing the settings for Windows, including how it looks and works.

copy To duplicate a selection so you can paste it into another location.

cover page The first page of a Word document, which provides introductory information about the document such as the title, author, and date.

crop To remove unwanted parts of a picture or object.

cut To remove a selection from a location in a file.

D

data marker A dot, a bar, or a symbol used to represent one number from the worksheet in a chart.

data series A series of related values from an Excel worksheet graphically represented by a distinct data marker in the plot area of a chart.

data source A range of cells in an Excel worksheet that contain the data for a chart.

data type The kind of values (such as text or number) contained in a field in an Access database.

database A tool used to collect and organize information.

database management system (DBMS) A program designed to store, organize, and manage large amounts of data.

datasheet In Access, a table with columns and rows similar to a spreadsheet.

datasheet selector The box in the upper-left corner of the datasheet that selects all the records in an Access table.

Date Navigator A small monthly calendar in Outlook from which you can choose a date to view.

desktop In Windows Vista, the main area of the computer screen.

desktop publishing software The software used to combine text and graphics to produce high quality marketing and communications documents for print on an in-house printer or by a commercial printer.

destination file The file into which data is transferred when integrating between Office programs.

destination program The program used to create the destination file, which is the file to which the information is added when integrating information between files.

dialog box launcher A small arrow in the lower-right corner of a group on the Ribbon that you click to open a dialog box or task pane with more options.

document Written information that can be typed, then printed on paper or distributed electronically.

drag To click and hold the mouse button over an object and then move the mouse, bringing the selected object with it.

drag-and-drop To use the mouse to move or copy a selection by dragging a selection and dropping it in a new location.

drawing objects Shapes, curves, and lines that become part of a document, worksheet, or presentation, rather than being a separate file.

drop cap A large initial capital letter or a large first word used to add visual interest to text.

E

e-mail Short for electronic mail; a way to send and receive messages over the Internet or another network.

embed To place a copy of an object that can be modified using the tools from the source file while working on the object in the destination file.

embedded chart A chart that is saved as part of the Excel worksheet in which the data source resides.

GLOSSARY

event An entry in the Outlook Calendar that lasts all day, or 24 hours.

export To transfer data from a file created in one program in a format that can be used by another program.

F

field A category that stores a single characteristic of information in an Access database table.

field name Identifies a field in an Access database.

field properties Characteristics that control the appearance and behavior of a field in an Access database.

field selector The box located at the top of column in an Access database table that contains the field name and can be clicked to select an entire field.

field value A piece of information stored in a field in a database table.

fill A background color or pattern in a worksheet cell.

fill handle A little black square in the bottom-right corner of the selected cell in an Excel worksheet; it is used to fill a range cells with data based on contents of the selected cells.

filter To display data that meets certain criteria or a specific set of conditions in an Excel worksheet or an Access datasheet.

first-line indent Indenting only the first line of a paragraph in a document.

floating picture A picture that can be positioned so that text can wrap around and flow in front of or behind it.

folder A container for storing and organizing files.

font The design of a set of letters and numbers.

font styles Variations in the shape or weight of a font's characters.

footer Text or graphics that appears in the bottom margin of each page in a document or presentation.

form A database object that provides a way to enter, edit, and delete data from tables.

Form Wizard A tool in Access that walks you through the process of creating a form.

Format Painter A tool that copies multiple formatting characteristics and then applies the same formatting to other parts of the presentation, document, or worksheet.

Formatting toolbar A toolbar containing additional commands for changing the format of text or graphics, such as applying bold to text, formatting text with bullets, and filling a shape with a color.

formula A set of instructions used to perform calculations on values in an Excel worksheet.

formula bar Located next to the Name box in the Excel program window and displays the contents of the active cell.

forward To send a message to a different e-mail address in Outlook.

freeze panes To lock specified rows or columns into place in the Excel worksheet window.

function A built-in shortcut for entering formulas in Excel.

G

gadgets Mini programs and tools located in the Windows Sidebar on the Windows Vista desktop.

gallery A set of options on the Ribbon that shows you a sample end result.

gridlines Lines extending from the vertical or horizontal axes across the plot area of a chart.

groups A logical organization of commands on a Ribbon tab.

H

hanging indent Indenting all the lines from the left except the first one in a Word document.

header Text or graphics that appears in the top margin of each page in a document.

horizontal axis A line on a chart used for showing categories, also called X-axis.

I

I-beam The shape of the mouse pointer when it is positioned in a text area.

icon A small picture that represents a program, folder, file, or other objects and can appear on the desktop, the Ribbon, a menu, the taskbar, etc.

import To transfer data into a file from another location.

indent The spaces between text and the margin.

inline object An object that moves with the text around it.

insertion point   A blinking vertical bar that indicates where any newly typed text will appear.

integration   The process of taking a file or object created in one program and incorporating it into a file created in another program.

interface   A uniform set of commands and elements that create an environment and means for interacting with a computer program.

K

key value   The value in the primary key field that makes the record unique in a database.

KeyTip   A label that appears on commands on the Ribbon when you press the ALT key and allows you to use the keyboard instead of the mouse to execute the command.

L

landscape   A horizontal page orientation.

launch   To start a program.

layout   The arrangement of text and other objects on a PowerPoint slide.

layout masters   Master slides that store information about the fonts, colors, effects, and layout of each type of slide layout.

leaders   Dotted, dashed, or solid lines used to fill the empty space before a tab stop.

legend   A list that identifies the patterns or colors of the data series or categories in a chart.

line spacing   The amount of vertical space taken up by each line of text in a paragraph.

link   In the integration technique of object linking and embedding (OLE), the connection between an object in the source file and an object in the destination file.

list   A series of related words, numbers, or phrases, with each item in the list starting with a bullet or number.

Live Preview   An Office 2007 feature that applies the editing or formatting change to your document as you point to a gallery option.

M

mail merge   The creation of a set of Word documents that are identical except for custom or personalized information in specific areas; the personalized information is integrated into the Word document from another data source such as a Word table or Excel spreadsheet.

mail server   A computer at an Internet Service Provider (ISP) that transfers messages from one computer to another.

margins   The white space that borders the text on the edges of a page.

menu bar   Located at the top of the program window, and contains menus that list related commands.

merge fields   Placeholders in the main document of a mail merge that indicate where the information from the data source will go.

Microsoft Office 2007   A group of computer programs that provide different tools for completing certain tasks.

Mini toolbar   A small toolbar of common formatting commands that becomes available when you select text.

mixed reference   A cell reference in Excel that contains either an absolute row or an absolute column reference.

N

Name box   In Excel, a box located below the Ribbon that displays the cell reference of the active cell.

Negative indent   An indent that extends into the left margin.

Notes pane   An area in the PowerPoint program window in which you can type speaker notes for the active presentation.

notification area   The section of the Windows taskbar that provides information about programs and computer settings.

O

object   In object linking and embedding (OLE), the information from the source file that is displayed in the destination file.

object linking and embedding (OLE)   An integration technology in Office that allows you to share information between Office programs.

GLOSSARY

Object toolbar In Publisher, the toolbar located vertically on the left side of the screen with buttons for inserting various kinds of objects.

Office Button In all Office 2007 programs, the button that provides access to common commands, such as New, Open, Save, Save As, and Print.

operating system The program that manages and controls the basic operations of a computer.

operator A sign or symbol that indicates what calculation is to be performed in a formula in Excel.

order of operation A specific sequence used to calculate the value of a formula in Excel.

orphan A single line that appears at the bottom of a page in a document.

Outline tab In PowerPoint, a tab that displays the title and text of each slide in a presentation in outline form.

P

page break A command that ends a page and starts a new one in a Word document.

paragraph Any amount of text or other items followed by a paragraph mark.

password A secret set of characters that a user types to log on to a computer or account.

paste To insert copied or moved contents to another location.

personal folder A location on the computer labeled with the user name that stores frequently used folders for that account.

personal information manager software Software that helps you communicate and organize business and personal information.

pictures Digital photographs or images.

placeholder Within an Office program, a text box that appears in a specific location in a file and that indicates the type of text to be placed in the box.

plot area The area in the chart where the values from the data series are displayed graphically.

point size A measurement for the height of characters.

portrait Vertical page orientation.

presentation A collection of slides that communicate ideas, facts, suggestions, or other information to an audience.

presentation software Software that lets you prepare a series of slides that are referred to collectively as a presentation.

primary key A field that uniquely identifies each record in an Access table.

publication A document that is created to market a product or communicate a message to an audience.

pull quote In Word or Publisher, an enlarged quotation that is placed on the page for emphasis.

Q

query A database object that allows you to answer specific questions about the data in a database or perform an action on the data.

Query Wizard A tool in Access that guides you through the process of creating a query.

Quick Access Toolbar A toolbar located on the program window's title bar; it can be customized with commands used most frequently.

Quick Launch toolbar The section of the Windows taskbar with icons you can use to quickly open programs.

Quick Parts In Word, a type of building block made up of an image and/or text that you can create, save, and reuse.

R

range A group of select adjacent cells.

record All of the related information about a particular item in an Access table.

record selector The box to the left of a row that selects a single record in an Access table.

record source The underlying data in a database used to create forms, records, and queries.

Recycle Bin A storage location on the computer for the files and folders you have deleted.

relational database Information stored in separate tables that is connected by establishing connections between the tables through common fields.

relative reference The reference to a cell that changes in relation to the location of the formula in the worksheet.

report A database object used to present a summary of data in a table.

Report Wizard A tool in Access that guides you through the process of creating a report.

Ribbon A collection of commands organized by tabs and groups that appears at the top of the program window.

row The cells that display horizontally and are numbered consecutively down the left side of the worksheet.

run To give a query or a report instructions to display certain records and fields that meet criteria you specify.

S

scratch area In Publisher, a workspace that you can use for storing or working with graphics or text boxes.

screen saver A moving picture or pattern that is displayed on the screen when the computer has been inactive for a certain amount of time.

ScreenTip A box that appears when you rest the mouse pointer on a button and that displays the name of the button and a description of its function.

select To highlight text, a cell, or a range of cells.

select query A query in Access that retrieves specific data out of a record source for you to use.

selection handles Small circles at the sides and corners of a text box or graphic used to resize the object.

sheet See *worksheet*.

sheet tab Displays the name of each sheet in the workbook.

simple form Displays data from one record at a time in an Access table.

slide A single image in a PowerPoint presentation made up of text, graphics, or other content.

slide master The first slide in a hierarchy of master slides in a presentation and controls the fonts, font size, font color, background color, and special effects.

Slide pane In PowerPoint, an area of the screen that displays the slide selected in the Slide tab or Outline.

Slide tab In PowerPoint, a tab that displays thumbnails of the slides in a presentation.

Smart Tag button Displays a shortcut menu for editing, saving, or updating business information sets in Publisher.

SmartArt graphic A predesigned diagram made up of shapes that contains text and illustrates a concept or idea.

sort To rearrange selected data alphabetically, numerically, or chronologically.

source file The file containing the original information when transferring data between programs.

source program In integration, the program used to create the source file.

spreadsheet software A program used to electronically calculate, analyze, and visually represent numerical data.

Standard toolbar A toolbar containing buttons for performing common tasks such as saving, printing, and zooming in or out of a page.

story All the text within a single text box or linked text boxes.

style A reusable set of character or paragraph formats stored with a name.

suite A combination of Office programs packaged together.

syntax A set of established rules that specifies how a function must be entered in Excel.

T

table A grid of horizontal rows and vertical columns of numbers, text, or graphics. In Access, a database object that stores information related to a specific subject; made up of a collection of records and fields.

tabs Category of commands on the Ribbon that relate to a particular activity. Also, stops used to align text in a Word document.

task A job or duty that you must complete and can be tracked in Outlook.

GLOSSARY

taskbar   A horizontal strip at the bottom of the Windows Vista desktop containing the Start button, Quick Launch toolbar, and notification area.

template   A sample file included with an Office program that provides a pattern or model for a new document, worksheet, presentation, or publication.

text box   A container that allows you to position text or graphics.

themes   Sets of formatting choices that include colors, fonts, and effects that were predesigned to work well together in a Word document, PowerPoint presentation, or Excel worksheet.

thumbnails   Miniature pictures of slides in a presentation.

title   In Excel, descriptive name that identifies the chart, or the chart's axes.

To-Do List   A list that displays all your tasks in Outlook.

transition   An animated effect that controls how one slide is removed from the screen and the next one appears in a presentation.

U

user account   A collection of information that contains unique settings and preferences and tells Windows which files and programs on a computer a specific user may access.

user name   A word or phrase that identifies a person's account on the computer.

V

vertical axis   The line on chart used for plotting values, also called Y-axis.

W

wallpaper   The background picture on the computer desktop.

watermark   Text or a graphic that appears behind text in a document.

widow   A single line that appears at the top of a page.

Windows Sidebar   Transparent panel on the side of the Windows Vista desktop containing gadgets.

word processing software   A program that lets you insert and manipulate text and graphics electronically to create all kinds of professional-looking documents.

word wrap   A feature that automatically continues text to the next line within a paragraph when you enter new text.

WordArt   A drawing tool that turns words into a graphic image.

workbook   An Excel file that consists of a worksheet or a collection of related worksheets.

workbook window   An area of the Excel program window where the active sheet is displayed.

worksheet   In Excel, a grid with columns and rows where you enter and summarize data.

INDEX

A

absolute cell references, **EX 71–72**
Access 2007
  described, GS 4
  exporting queries to Word, INT 17–19
  importing Excel data into table, INT 14–17
  introduction to, AC 4–6
  program window, AC 6–7
action buttons, inserting, using, **PPT 63–66**
Action Settings dialog box, PPT 64–65
active cells
  changing, EX 8
  described, **EX 5**
Add Views dialog box, EX 24
adding
  See also inserting
  animations, PPT 77–80
  cell borders, EX 41
  commands to Quick Access Toolbar, GS 9
  contacts to Address Book, OL 7–9
  cover pages, WD 92–93
  fields to forms, AC 36–40
  gadgets to Windows Sidebar, VIS 8, VIS 10
  headers and footers, WD 82–86
  line spacing, WD 43–44
  page backgrounds, borders, WD 76–79
  page borders, WD 78–79
  programs to Quick Launch toolbar, VIS 5
  records to tables, AC 11–13
  report fields, AC 44–45
  text boxes, WD 113–115
  text to documents, WD 13
  transitions to slides, PPT 76–77
  WordArt, WD 115–117
  words to dictionary, PPT 41
  worksheets, EX 19–20
addition operator (+), EX 68
Address Book, Outlook, OL 7–9
aligning
  text, WD 41–43
  worksheet cells, EX 43
alignment of text, **PB 10**, **PPT 38**
Alt key, and KeyTips, GS 12
animations
  described, **PPT 77**
  using in presentations, PPT 75–76
Animations tab, Ribbon, PPT 75–76
antonyms, WD 56–57
appointments, entering in Calendar, **OL 12–14**
area charts, EX 88
arguments
  entering, EX 76–78
  in functions, **EX 75**
arithmetic operators
  See also specific operator
  types (table), **EX 68**
art
  clip. *See* clip art
  WordArt, inserting, WD 115–117
assigning tasks, OL 10
asterisk (*)
  database fields, AC 11
  multiplication operator, EX 68
attaching files to e-mail, OL 5
auditing formulas, EX 79–81
Auto Fill, copying formulas using, **EX 73–74**
AutoComplete, Formula, EX 68
AutoFilter, using, AC 47–48
AutoFit button, using on tables, WD 122–123
AutoFormat, using, AC 36, AC 39, AC 44–47
AutoRecover feature
  described, PB 11, PPT 19
  turning on, off, EX 10, WD 15
AutoSum command, EX 75–76, EX 78
Average function, EX 76, EX 78
axes in charts, **EX 89**, EX 96–99

B

backgrounds
  adding page, WD 76–79
  wallpaper, changing, VIS 8–9
badges (KeyTips), **GS 12**
bar charts, EX 88
blank pages, inserting, WD 89–92
bold
  shortcut key for, WD 33
  using in worksheets, EX 39–40
Bookmark button, WD 8
borders
  adding to pages, **WD 78–79**
  of cell references, EX 69
  worksheet cell, EX 41
Borders and Shading dialog box, WD 79
Borders menu, EX 41–42
breaking
  links, INT 4–6
  pages, WD 88–89
browsing. *See* searching
building blocks, inserting, WD 118–120

INDEX

Building Blocks Organizer command, WD 118
bullets
  described, **PB 10**, **PPT 15**
  styles, PPT 39
Bullets button, gallery, PPT 40
bulleted lists, PPT 15
  See also bullets
  changing to SmartArt graphic, PPT 66
  creating, WD 74
  formatting, PPT 38–39
business, customizing documents for company use, EX 62
business information sets, creating, **PB 7–9**
buttons
  See also specific button
  using on menus, GS 7–8

C

calendar, using Outlook's, OL 12–14
careers
  computer support, WD 25
  technical writers, WD 59
caret (^), exponentiation operator, EX 68
case
  changing, WD 33
  inserting drop caps, WD 117–118
cell references
  described, **EX 5**
  entering, EX 69
  in formulas, EX 68
  using relative, absolute, and mixed, EX 71–74
cell styles, applying, EX 49–51
cells
  alignment of data in, EX 14, EX 43
  applying number formats, EX 45–47
  applying styles, EX 49–51
  editing contents, EX 16–17
  fill colors, EX 41–42
  formatting, EX 37–47
  selecting, EX 11–13
  table, **PPT 71**, **WD 120**
  worksheet, **EX 5**

centering text, WD 42
Change Template dialog box, PB 14
changing
  See also modifying
  cell alignment, EX 43
  chart design, EX 92
  desktop wallpaper, VIS 7
  document orientation, WD 19–22
  document themes, WD 69–72
  document views, WD 16–17
  file and folder views, VIS 12
  font characteristics, PB 9
  fonts, font sizes, WD 33, PPT 34–35
  form titles, AC 37
  form views, AC 32
  Office program options, GS 13–16
  page backgrounds, borders, colors, WD 76–79
  page formatting, WD 18–22
  slide layout, PPT 13–15
  templates, PB 12–13
  text direction, PPT 38
  user account pictures on Start Menu, VIS 5–6
  workbook views, EX 21–24
  worksheet rows, columns, EX 53–56
characters
  described, **PPT 34**
  formatting, **WD 32–36**
chart area, **EX 89**
chart sheets, **EX 92**
Chart Styles gallery (fig), WD 113
Chart Tools contextual tabs, PPT 69
Chart Tools Design tab, EX 92
Chart Tools Format tab, EX 98
Chart Tools Layout tab, EX 96–97
charts
  creating, EX 89–91
  formatting elements of, EX 98–101
  inserting, modifying, **PPT 68–71**, **WD 110–113**
  modifying, EX 92–98
  organization, WD 108
  types and uses, **EX 88–89**
clearing
  cell data, EX 16–17
  cell formats, EX 43–45

print area of worksheet, EX 28
  tabs, WD 38
  text formatting, PPT 35, WD 36–37
clip art
  See also graphics, illustrations
  described, **PB 18**
  inserting, modifying, **PPT 60–62**, **WD 104–107**
  inserting in publications, PB 17–21
  using in worksheets, **EX 102**
Clip Art task pane, PB 20, PPT 60–62, WD 105–107
Clipboard
  copying and pasting between programs, INT 2
  described, using, EX 59
  editing text using, WD 48–50
  opening, GS 7
closing
  documents, WD 24–25
  forms, AC 32, AC 34
  Mini toolbar, GS 11
  Office programs, GS 20
  Outlook, OL 15
  presentations, PPT 23
  publications, PB 23
  tables, databases, AC 13
  Windows Vista sessions, VIS 16–18
  workbooks, EX 30
clustered bar charts, EX 91
collate pages, **PPT 22**
collating pages, **PB 23**, **WD 23**
colors
  See also styles, themes
  changing fill, EX 41–42
  changing page, WD 77
  changing sheet tab, EX 19
  changing text, PB 9
  filling cells with, EX 37–38
  filling shapes with, WD 116–117
  font, PPT 37, EX 39–40
  setting transparency, PPT 62
  theme, WD 69–71
column charts, EX 88
columns
  changing, WD 92
  creating text, **WD 80–82**

INDEX

and freeze panes, EX 22–24
inserting, PPT 71
modifying in tables, WD 122–124
working with, EX 53–56
worksheet, **EX 4–5**
Columns dialog box, WD 82
combining shapes, PPT 63, WD 103
commands
  See also specific command
  accessing on Ribbon, GS 7
  Excel keyboard, EX 59–60
  Mini toolbar, GS 11–12
comparison operators
  types (table), EX 70
  using, **EX 70–71**
compressing pictures, PB 19, PPT 57, WD 100, WD 102
computer support careers, WD 25
computers
  See also specific component, feature
  lock menu options, VIS 16–17
  use policies, GS 20
conditional formatting, using, EX 51–53
Connection Status menu, GS 17
constants in formulas, **EX 68**
contacts
  entering in Outlook, **OL 7–9**
  previewing, printing, OL 14–15
content placeholders. *See* placeholders
contextual tabs
  Chart Tools, PPT 69
  on Ribbon, **GS 7**, GS 11–12
Control Panel, **VIS 4**
controls on forms, reports, **AC 36**
converting
  See also exporting, importing
  text to tables, tables to text, WD 122
  Word outlines into presentations, INT 8–10
copying
  with Clipboard, **EX 59**
  files, folders, VIS 12–14
  formats with Format Painter, PB 10, PPT 35–37
  formulas using Auto Fill, EX 73–74
  graphics, PPT 57
  and moving data, EX 59–60, PPT 17–18

slides, PPT 13
text, WD 48–50
text formatting, WD 36–37
worksheet formatting, EX 41
worksheets within workbooks, EX 20–21
copyright issues
  images from the Web, WD 124
  Microsoft objects, downloads, PPT 60
corporate trainers, PPT 24
COUNT function, EX 75, EX 76
counting words, WD 58–59
cover pages, adding, **WD 92–93**
creating
  business information sets, PB 7–9
  charts, EX 89–91
  conditional formatting rules, EX 51
  database objects, AC 28
  databases in Datasheet view, AC 9–13
  e-mail contacts, OL 8–9
  e-mail messages, OL 4–5
  files, folders, VIS 12–14
  forms, AC 31–36
  indents, WD 45–48
  lists, WD 74
  logos, PB 15
  Mail Merge documents, INT 10–13
  new databases, AC 7–8
  new documents, WD 4, WD 30–32
  new documents from templates, WD 66–69
  new folders, VIS 12
  presentations, PPT 30–34
  presentations from Word outline, INT 8–10
  publications from templates, PB 3–5
  pull quotes, PB 15–16
  queries, AC 28–31
  Quick Parts, WD 118–120
  reports, AC 40–44
  tables, PPT 71–72, WD 120–124
  tasks, OL 10–11
  text columns, WD 80–82
  workbooks, EX 36–37
cropping pictures, **PB 19**, PB 21, PPT 58, WD 101–102
crosshair mouse pointer, WD 103–104

Ctrl key, and drag-and-drop editing, WD 49
current date, adding to worksheets, EX 25
cursor. *See* insertion point
curves, inserting and modifying, PPT 63
customizing
  See also personalizing
  animations, PPT 78
  charts, PPT 69–70, EX 92, WD 111
  document margins, WD 21
  files, folders, VIS 10–11
  Office programs, GS 13–16
  Quick Access Toolbar, GS 9–11
  Recent Documents list, AC 14
  reports, AC 42
  slide masters, PPT 46–49
  templates for company use, EX 62
  themes, PPT 45
  toolbars, PB 3
  Vista environment, VIS 4–10
  Windows Vista, VIS 4–7
cutting
  and pasting, **EX 59**
  text, WD 48–50

D

data
  aligning, EX 14, EX 43
  clearing cell, EX 16–17
  copying with Auto Fill, EX 73–74
  dragging and dropping, PPT 17–18
  entering in databases, AC 10–13
  entering in worksheets, EX 13–16
  finding and replacing, EX 56–58
  importing, exporting, INT 13
  importing Excel, into Access table, INT 14–17
  sorting, AC 47
data markers in charts, **EX 89**
data series in charts, **EX 89**
data source for charts, EX 89
data types
  available in Access, **AC 10**
  changing field's, AC 22
  described, EX 14

INDEX

database administrators, AC 23
database management system (DBMS), **AC 4**
database objects
  closing, AC 13
  creating and using, AC 28
  described, **AC 5–6**
databases
  concepts, AC 4–6
  creating in Datasheet view, AC 9–13
  creating new, AC 7–8
  creating queries, AC 28–31
  described, **AC 4**
  editing, deleting records, AC 18–20
  opening existing, AC 14–16
  opening tables, navigating records, AC 16–18
  relational, **AC 5**
  saving, closing, AC 13
datasheet described, **AC 4–5**
datasheet selector, **AC 18**
Datasheet view
  creating databases in, AC 9–13
  viewing queries in, AC 28
DATE function, EX 75
Date Navigator, **OL 12–14**
dates
  adding current, to worksheets, EX 25
  automatically updating, PPT 74
  in placeholder text, WD 93
  time and date settings, VIS 6–7
DBMS (database management system), **AC 4**
deleting
  See also removing
  cell data, EX 16–17
  cells, rows, columns, EX 53
  contacts from Address Book, OL 8
  database fields, AC 20
  database records, tables, AC 18–20
  database tables, AC 17–18
  fields from forms, AC 37
  files, folders, VIS 12
  forms, AC 34
  report fields, AC 44–45
  shapes, WD 103
  slides, PPT 13–14

text, WD 48
text boxes, PB 7
text in placeholders, PPT 16
worksheets, EX 20
delivering presentations with views, PPT 9–12
deselecting slides, PPT 12
Design Gallery objects, inserting, PB 15–17
Design tab, PPT 44–45
Design view
  accessing field properties, AC 20
  creating databases in, AC 9
  creating forms in, AC 32
  creating queries in, AC 28
designing
  charts, EX 89–98
designing, *continued*
  databases, AC 6
  modifying forms, AC 36–40
  queries, AC 28
  reports from scratch, AC 42
desktop, Windows Vista
  components, VIS 2–4
  described, GS 5
desktop publishing software, **PB 2**
destination files, and integration, **INT 2**
diagrams, inserting, PPT 66
dialog box launcher, **GS 7**
dialog boxes, using, GS 7–8
dictionary, using, PPT 41, WD 54–56
displaying
  Control Panel, VIS 4
  formulas, values, EX 79–81
  galleries, GS 7
  gridlines on charts, EX 96–98
  Help window, GS 17
  KeyTips, GS 12
  New Document dialog box, WD 67
  Open dialog box, WD 5
  queries in different views, AC 28
  ruler, PPT 57, WD 16, WD 23
  ScreenTips, GS 18
  text formatting marks, WD 41–43
distribution lists, creating e-mail, OL 8
division operator (/), EX 68
.doc files, WD 14

documents
  See also pages
  adding cover pages, WD 92–93
  adding headers, footers, WD 82–86
  changing page formatting, WD 18–22
  changing themes, WD 69–72
  changing views, WD 16–17
  closing, WD 24–25
  creating from templates, WD 66–69
  creating Mail Merge, INT 10–13
  creating new, WD 30–32
  customizing for company use, EX 62
  described, **WD 4**
  e-mail. *See* e-mail
  linking Excel table in, INT 3–4
  navigating, WD 6–9
  opening existing, WD 4–6
  previewing, printing, WD 22–24
  printing, WD 22–24
  proofing, WD 53–54
  saving, WD 14–15
  selecting entire, WD 9–12
  styles. *See* styles
.docx files, WD 14
.dotm files, WD 67
dotted lines (Page Breaks), WD 88
.dotx (template) files, WD 67
Draft view, WD 16–17
drag-and-drop
  See also dragging
  copying and moving data using, **EX 59–60**, PPT 17–18
  editing, **WD 49–50**
dragging
  See also drag-and-drop
  Auto Fill options, EX 73–74
  described, **WD 7**
  to select text, WD 10
  worksheets to copy or move, EX 20–21
drawing
  shapes, WD 102–104
  text boxes, PB 7
drawing objects
  creating, WD 103
  inserting in worksheets, **EX 102**
  using in presentations, **PPT 63–66**

INDEX

Drawing Tools Format contextual tab, WD 103
drop caps, inserting, **WD 117–118**

E

editing
  cell contents, EX 16–17
  database records, AC 18–20
  documents in Print Preview mode, WD 22–23
  drop-and-drag, WD 49–50
  forms, AC 36–40
  formulas, EX 79–82
  headers and footers, WD 84–86
  links to files, INT 5
  masters with views, PPT 11–12
  text, WD 30, WD 48–50
  text on slides, PPT 15–16
  WordArt, WD 115–117
Editing group, Home tab, PPT 43, WD 52
effects
  See also specific effect
  applying font, PPT 35, WD 33–36
  theme, EX 47, WD 69
e-mail
  described, **OL 4**
  entering contacts, OL 7–9
  handling junk, OL 15
  opening attachments in Word, WD 16
  previewing, printing, OL 14–15
  replying to, OL 5–7
  sending, receiving, OL 3–5
embedded charts, **EX 92**
embedding
  described, **INT 2**
  Excel tables in presentations, INT 7–8
entering
  formulas in worksheets, EX 68–71
  text on slides, PPT 15–18
equal sign (=) in formulas, EX 68
equal to (=) operator, EX 70
Error Checking dialog box, EX 80
errors
  See also mistakes
  Excel's handling of formula, EX 79–81

ethics in technology
  computer use policies, GS 20
  and e-mail, OL 15
  software piracy, WD 94
events, entering in Calendar, **OL 12–14**
Excel 2007
  See also workbooks, worksheets
  described, GS 4
  introduction to, EX 4–7
  keyboard commands, EX 59–60
  using worksheets with presentations, PPT 69–70
  and Word charts, WD 110
  .xlsx and .xls files, EX 10
Export Wizard, INT 17
exporting
  Access queries to Word, INT 17–19
  described, **INT 13**
  and integration, INT 2
Extensible Markup Language. *See* XML

F

Fade animations, PPT 78
field names, **AC 4–5**
field properties, modifying, **AC 20–23**
field selector, **AC 18**
field values, **AC 4–5**
fields
  database, **AC 4–5**
  making required, AC 22
  merge, INT 10
  modifying on forms, AC 36–40
File Save dialog box, INT 18
files
  creating, renaming, deleting, VIS 12
  finding, opening, WD 5
  managing, VIS 10–14
  sharing, VIS 11
  source and destination, INT 2
Fill Color menu, EX 41–42
fill effects, WD 69, WD 116–117
fill handles, **EX 73–74**
filling a series, EX 73
fills
  changing colors, EX 41–42
  formatting cells using, **EX 37–38**

filtering
  data using AutoFilter, AC 47–48
  forms, AC 49–50
  records, AC 47
filters described, **AC 47**
Find & Select button, EX 56–58
Find and Replace dialog box, WD 8–9, WD 53
Find dialog box, PPT 43
finding
  and replacing data, EX 56–58
  and replacing text, PPT 42–44, WD 52–53
first line indents, **WD 45–48**
flagging contacts, OL 8
floating pictures, **WD 100–101**
Fly In animations, PPT 78
flyers, creating, PB 4–5
folders
  creating, renaming, deleting, VIS 12
  creating for e-mail, OL 3–4
  and folder windows, **VIS 10–12**
Font button, menu, WD 34–35
Font Color button, palette, PPT 37
Font dialog box, WD 35
Font group, Home tab, EX 38–39, WD 32
font styles, EX 39, **PB 9**, **PPT 35**
fonts
  changing, sizing, **WD 33**
  changing characteristics, **PB 9**
  commands on Ribbon, GS 7
  formatting worksheet, EX 38–40
  modifying in tables, PPT 71
  replacing, PPT 43
  themes. *See* themes
  using in presentations, **PPT 34–35**
footers
  adding to documents, **WD 82–86**
  adding to worksheets, **EX 25**
  inserting on slides, **PPT 74–75**
foreign keys, **AC 5**
foreign languages, editing and proofing, WD 54
form letters, INT 10
Form view, AC 32
Form Wizard, using, AC 31, **AC 34–36**
Format As Table dialog box, EX 50

INDEX

Format Painter
  copying formats using, PB 10
  formatting cells using, EX 37, EX 41
  formatting presentation text using, **PPT 35–37**
  formatting text with, WD 36–37
Format Publication task pane, PB 12–13
formats, conditional (table), EX 51
formatting
  applying number, EX 45–47
  changing page, WD 18–22
  characters, fonts, WD 32–36
  chart elements, EX 98–101
  clearing cell, EX 43–45
  conditional, EX 51–53
  copying with Format Painter, WD 36–37
  e-mail, OL 4–5
  paragraphs, PPT 37–40, WD 40–48
  publications, PB 12–14
  text, WD 30
  text columns, WD 80–82
  text in presentations, PPT 34–37
  text shortcuts, PB 9
  worksheet cells, EX 37–47
Formatting toolbar, **PB 2–3**
forms
  creating, **AC 31–34**
  creating with Form Wizard, AC 34–36
  customizing for company use, EX 62
  described, AC 6
  modifying design of, AC 36–40
  sorting data in, AC 47
Formula AutoComplete feature, EX 68
formula bar
  described, **EX 5**
  reviewing formulas in, EX 69
formulas
  See also specific formula
  copying with Auto Fill, EX 73–74
  entering in worksheets, **EX 68–71**
  order of operations, EX 70
  reviewing and editing, EX 79–82
  switching cell references in, EX 72
forwarding e-mail, **OL 6**
Freeze Panes command, EX 22, EX 25
freezing panes, **EX 22–24**
Full Screen Reading view, WD 16–17
Function Arguments dialog box, EX 77

Function Library group, Formulas tab, EX 76
functions
  See also specific function
  using, **EX 75**

G

Gadget Gallery, VIS 10
gadgets
  adding to Windows Sidebar, VIS 8, VIS 10
  described, **VIS 3**
galleries
  See also specific gallery
  Quick Styles, WD 72
  Ribbon tabs, **GS 7**
  using Live Preview, GS 7–9
Go To command
  navigating worksheets with, EX 9
  using, WD 8–9
grammar, checking document's, WD 54–55
graphic designers, PB 24
graphics
  See also art, illustrations, images, pictures
  charts. *See* charts
  described, WD 99
  highlighting, WD 9
  inserting in publications, PB 14–21
  modifying, PPT 57–59
  selecting using keyboard, WD 12–13
  sizing, WD 100
  SmartArt. *See* SmartArt graphics
  using with presentations, PPT 56
greater than (>) operator, EX 70
greater than or equal to (>=) operator, EX 70
gridlines
  chart, **EX 89**, EX 96–98
  showing, hiding, printing, EX 28
groups, command, on tabs, GS 7

H

Handout Master, PPT 47
hanging indents, **WD 45–48**

Header and Footer dialog box, PPT 74–75
headers
  adding to documents, **WD 82–85**
  adding to worksheets, **EX 25**
  inserting on slides, **PPT 74–75**
height, adjusting columns, row, EX 53–56
help
  getting Office, GS 17–19
  ScreenTips, **GS 18–19**

help, *continued*
  Windows Help and Support system, VIS 14–16
help-desk personnel, WD 25
hiding
  KeyTips, GS 12
  nonprinting symbols, WD 41, WD 43
  program windows, EX 23
hierarchies, PPT 66–68
highlighting
  searched-for words, WD 52
  text, graphics, WD 9
holidays, in Outlook Calendar, OL 12–14
horizontal alignment of text, PPT 38
horizontal axis (x) in charts, EX 89
HTML format, e-mail, OL 4

I

I-beam
  mouse pointer, **WD 7**
  and placeholder text, **PB 6, PPT 15–16**
icons
  desktop, **VIS 3**
  pinning, VIS 4–6
illustrations
  See also graphics, images, pictures
  cropping, WD 101–102
  inserting, modifying, EX 101–104, WD 100–102
  inserting charts, WD 110–113
  using in presentations, PPT 56–60
Illustrations group, Insert tab, PPT 56–57, WD 100

INDEX

images
See also graphics, illustrations, pictures
copyright restrictions on, WD 105, WD 124
thumbnails, PPT 4
Import Spreadsheet Wizard, INT 15–16
Import Wizard, INT 14
importing
described, **INT 13**
Excel data into Access table, INT 14–17
and integration, INT 2
Inbox, Outlook, OL 5–6
indents, setting, **WD 45–48**
inline objects, **WD 100**
Insert Chart dialog box, EX 90
Insert tab, Ribbon, EX 88
Insert Table dialog box (fig.), WD 121
inserting
See also adding
attachments to e-mail, OL 5
bookmarks, WD 8
cells, rows, columns, EX 53
charts, PPT 68–71, WD 110–113
clip art, PPT 60–61, WD 104–107
functions, EX 76–78
illustrations, WD 100–102
illustrations in charts, EX 101–104
illustrations in presentations, PPT 56–60
lines between text columns, WD 80
linked objects, INT 4
objects, WD 113–120
page numbers, WD 83, WD 86–87
pages, WD 88–92
Quick Parts, WD 118–120
shapes, PPT 63–66, WD 102–105
slides into presentations, PPT 13–15
SmartArt, PPT 66–68, WD 107–110
special effects into presentations, PPT 75–76
tables, PPT 71–72, WD 120–122
text boxes, PPT 73–74
watermarks, WD 76–77
worksheets in workbooks, EX 19–20

insertion point
described, **WD 6**
keyboard shortcuts for moving (table), WD 8
and placeholder text, **PB 6**, **PPT 15–16**
integrate, Office programs, **GS 4–5**
integration
See also specific programs
across Office programs, **INT 2**
creating mail merge document, INT 10–13
creating presentations from Word outlines, INT 8–10
editing across Office programs, WD 48
embedding, INT 7–8
importing and exporting data, INT 13–19
linking, INT 3–6
Intense Quote style, GS 8
interface described, **GS 4**
ISPs (Internet Service Providers), and Internet service, OL 4
italic
shortcut key for, WD 33
using in worksheets, EX 39–40

J

jobs. *See* technology careers
junk e-mail, OL 15
justifying text, WD 42

K

Keep On Top button, help window, GS 19
keyboard
Excel commands, EX 59–60
navigating worksheets with, EX 8
selecting text using, WD 12–13
keyboard shortcuts
See also specific operation
moving insertion point (table), WD 8
using, GS 18
KeyTips, using, **GS 12**

L

landscape orientation
changing document to, **WD 19–22**
described, **PB 23**
languages, editing and proofing non-English, WD 54
launching programs, **GS 4–5**
layout
changing slide, PPT 13–15
chart options, EX 92
presentation, **PPT 7**
layout masters, using, PPT 46–49
Layout view
creating forms in, AC 32
creating reports in, AC 40–41
Layouts gallery, WD 109
leaders, setting type of, **WD 38–40**
legends, chart, **EX 89**
less than (<) operator, EX 70
less than or equal to (<=) operator, EX 70
letters, creating from templates, WD 67–68
line charts, EX 88–89
line effects, WD 69
line spacing, setting, PB 10, PPT 38, WD 43–44
lines
creating straight, PPT 63
inserting between text columns, WD 80
linking
data to databases, AC 9
and embedding objects, INT 2
Excel table in Word document, INT 3–4
text boxes, PB 7
links
described, **INT 2**
editing, WD 49
updating, breaking, INT 4–6
Links dialog box, INT 6
lists
bulleted. *See* bulleted lists
formatting, PB 10, PPT 38–39
numbered and bulleted, WD 74

INDEX

sorting, WD 74–76
working with, WD 73
Live Preview
  described, **GS 7–9**
  previewing themes using, EX 49–50
lock menu options, VIS 16–17
locking links, INT 5
logos, creating, PB 15
LOWER function, EX 75

M

magnifying. *See* zooming
mail. *See* e-mail
mail merge
  creating document, INT 10–13
  described, **INT 10**
Mail Merge Wizard, INT 10–13
mail servers, **OL 6**
managing
  files, folders, VIS 10–14
  Windows Sidebar, VIS 7–10
  worksheets, EX 19–21
maps, creating, PPT 63
margins
  setting custom, WD 21
  setting document, **WD 18–19**
  setting text indents, WD 45–48
masters
  customizing, PPT 46–49
  editing slide, with views, **PPT 11–12**
Max function, EX 76
maximizing windows, GS 14–16
meetings, managing, OL 12–14
menu bar, Publisher, **PB 2**
menus
  See also specific menu
  opening Office Button, GS 15
  using shortcut, GS 11–12
Merge & Center menu, EX 43–44
merge fields, **INT 10**
Microsoft Knowledge Base, VIS 15
Microsoft Office 2007. *See* Office 2007
Microsoft Office Online
  copyright restrictions on downloads, PPT 60

obtaining presentation templates from, PPT 31
obtaining templates from, PB 4, WD 66
obtaining themes from, EX 47, WD 70
Min function, EX 76
Mini toolbar, using, **GS 11–12**
minimizing windows, GS 14–16
minus sign (-), subtraction operator, EX 68
mistakes
  Excel's handling of formula errors, EX 79–81
  undoing, EX 18, WD 50–51
mixed cell references, **EX 71–73**
modifying
  See also changing
  charts, EX 92–98, PPT 68–71, WD 110–113
  clip art, PPT 60–62, WD 104–107
  database field properties, AC 20–23
  forms' design, AC 36–40
  illustrations, WD 100–102
  illustrations in charts, EX 101–104
  illustrations in presentations, PPT 56–60
  objects, WD 113–120
  reports, AC 44–47
  shapes, PPT 63–66, WD 102–105
  slides, PPT 12–18
  SmartArt, PPT 66–68, WD 108–110
  tables, PPT 71–72, WD 122–124
  text boxes, PPT 73–74
  WordArt, WD 115–117
mouse
  crosshair pointer, WD 103–104
  navigating documents using, WD 6–7
  selecting text using, WD 9–10
  selecting worksheet cells using, EX 12–13
moving
  charts, EX 92–95
  data, EX 59–60
  database fields, AC 21
  dragging and dropping, PPT 17–18
  files, folders, VIS 12–14
  form fields, AC 38
  report fields, AC 44

text boxes, WD 114
worksheets within workbooks, EX 20–21
multiplication operator (*), EX 68

N

Name box, **EX 5**
names, database field, AC 4
naming
  databases, AC 8–9
  files, WD 5
  worksheets, EX 19
navigating
  database records, AC 16–17
  databases, AC 7
  presentations, PPT 7–8
  publications, PB 5–6
  Word documents, WD 6–9
  worksheets, EX 7–10
Navigation Pane
  Open dialog box, EX 5–6, WD 5
  Outlook, OL 2–3
negative indents, **WD 45–48**
New command, WD 66
New Document dialog box, WD 30, WD 66–67
New Presentation dialog box, PPT 30–31
New Workbook dialog box, EX 36–37
nonprinting symbols, displaying, WD 41
Normal template, WD 67
not equal to (<>) operator, EX 70
Notes Master, PPT 47
Notes Page view, PPT 10
Notes pane, **PPT 4**
notification area on desktop, **VIS 3**
Number format menu, EX 45–46
number formats, worksheet cell, EX 45–47
Number group, Home tab, EX 45–46
numbered lists
  creating, PB 10, WD 74
  using, PPT 39
Numbering button, menu, WD 75

INDEX

numbers, adding page, EX 25, WD 83, WD 86–87
numeric data, entering, EX 14–16

O

object linking and embedding. *See* OLE
Object toolbar, **PB 3**
objects
  database, **AC 5–6**
  described, **INT 2**
  drawing. *See* drawing objects
  graphics. *See* graphics
  inserting, modifying, WD 113–120
  inserting Design Object, PB 15–17
  linking and embedding, INT 2
  selection handles on, PPT 57
  updating, breaking links, INT 4–6
Office 2007
  See also specific programs
  closing programs, GS 20
  common window elements, using, GS 5–13
  contextual tools, accessing, GS 11–12
  copyright restrictions on images, sounds, movies, WD 105
  customizing programs, GS 13–16
  editing across programs, WD 48
  getting help, GS 17–19
  integration. *See* integration
  introduction to, **GS 4**
  programs (table), GS 4
Office Button
  Recent Documents list, EX 5
  using, GS 9, GS 15
Office Online button, GS 17
OLE (object linking and embedding), **INT 2**
online Microsoft Office. *See* Microsoft Office Online
Open command, EX 5
Open dialog box, AC 14, EX 5–6, PPT 5–6, WD 5
opening
  database tables, AC 16–17
  existing database, AC 14–16
  existing document, WD 4–6
  existing publications, PB 4–5

  existing workbook, EX 5–6
  Mini toolbar, GS 11–12
  Outlook, OL 2
  presentations, PPT 5
  templates, PB 3–5
operating systems
  See also Windows Vista
  described, **VIS 2**
operators
  See also specific operator
  in formulas, **EX 68**
OR function, EX 75
order of operations in formulas, EX 70
organization charts, EX 102–104, PPT 66–68, WD 108
orientation, changing document, WD 19–22
orphans, avoiding, WD 88–89, WD 91
Outbox, Outlook, OL 6
outdents, setting, WD 45
Outline tab
  described, **PPT 4**
  entering text on slides, PPT 15–16
  Normal view, PPT 9
Outline view, WD 16–17
outlines
  creating presentations from Word, INT 8–10
  presentations displayed as, PPT 9
Outlook 2007
  See also e-mail
  creating, managing tasks, OL 9–11
  described, GS 4
  previewing, printing items, OL 14–15
  starting, changing views, OL 2–3
  using Outlook Calendar, OL 12–14
Outlook Today screen, OL 2–3

P

page formatting, changing, WD 18–22
Page Layout tab (fig.), WD 18
Page Layout view, EX 22, EX 25
page numbers
  adding, WD 83, WD 86–87
  adding to worksheets, EX 25
Page Setup group, WD 18–19, WD 89

pages
  See also documents
  adding backgrounds, borders, WD 76–79
  adding cover, WD 92–93
  collating, PPT 22
  inserting, breaking, WD 88–92
  inserting numbers, WD 83, WD 86–87
  printing, WD 23–24
panes, freezing and unfreezing, EX 22–24
paper sizes, choosing, WD 18–19
Paragraph dialog box, WD 44, WD 46
Paragraph group, Home tab, PPT 38
paragraphs
  formatting, PPT 37–40, **WD 40–48**
  selecting, WD 10–11
parentheses (()) in formulas, EX 78
passwords described, **VIS 2**
Paste Hyperlink command, WD 49
Paste Special command, WD 49
Paste Special dialog box
  embedding using, INT 7–8
  linking using, INT 4
pasting
  from Clipboard, **EX 59**
  text, WD 48–50
.pdf files, saving publications as, PB 11
percent sign (%), percent operator, EX 68
personal folders, **VIS 10**
personal information manager software, **OL 2**
personalizing
  See also customizing
  Vista appearance and sound, VIS 7
Picture Frame button, menu, PB 17–18
Picture toolbar, PB 19
Picture Tools Format contextual tab, WD 100–101
pictures
  compressing, PB 19, PPT 57, WD 100, WD 102
  cropping, PB 19
  described, **PB 18**
  floating, WD 100–101
  inserting in documents, **WD 100–102**
  inserting in publications, PB 17–21

INDEX

inserting in worksheets, **EX 102–104**
inserting into presentations, **PPT 57–60**
selection handles on, PPT 57
on Start Menu user accounts, VIS 5–6
thumbnails, PPT 4
pie charts, EX 88
pinning icons, customizing desktop, VIS 5–6
placeholder text
  for cover pages, WD 92–93
  deleting, PPT 16
  and SmartArt, EX 102–103
  on templates, WD 67
placeholders
  See also placeholder text
  header and footer, EX 25
  in slides, **PPT 15–16**
  text box, **PB 6**
plot area, **EX 89**
plus sign (+)
  addition operator, EX 68
  copied selection, PPT 17
PMT function, EX 75
point size, **EX 38**, **PB 9**, **PPT 35**, **WD 33**
policies, computer use, GS 20
portrait orientation, **PB 23**, **WD 19–22**
positioning
  toolbars, GS 9
  using ruler, WD 16
pound sign (#)
  and cell formatting, EX 45
  series in worksheet cell (#####), EX 80
PowerPoint 2007
  See also presentations
  described, GS 4
  introduction to, PPT 4
  .pptx and .ppt files, PPT 19
  program window, PPT 4
  starting, opening presentations, PPT 4–5
  views, PPT 8–12
.ppt files, PPT 19
.pptx files, PPT 19, PPT 31
presentation software, **PPT 4**

presentations
  See also slides
  applying themes, PPT 44–46
  closing, PPT 23
  creating, PPT 30–34
  creating from Word outline. *See* integration
  described, **PPT 4**
  embedding Excel table in, INT 7–8
  formatting text in, PPT 34–37
  inserting slides, PPT 13–15
  inserting special effects, PPT 75–76
  navigating, PPT 7–8
  opening existing, PPT 5–6
  previewing, printing, PPT 20–24
  saving, PPT 18–20
  spell checking, PPT 41–42
  templates, PPT 31–34
  using clip art in, PPT 60–62
  using illustrations in, PPT 56–60
  viewing, PPT 8–9
previewing
  documents for printing, WD 22–24
  e-mail, OL 5
  Outlook items, OL 14–15
  presentation printouts, PPT 20–23
  publications, PB 21–22
  reports, AC 46–47
  slide effects, PPT 76
  worksheets for printing, EX 28–30
primary keys
  default, AC 9
  described, **AC 5**
Print Area button, EX 25, EX 27
Print dialog box, PB 23, WD 23–24
Print Layout view, WD 16
Print Preview mode, WD 22–23
Print Preview tab, PPT 20–21
Print Preview window, AC 46–47, EX 28–29, PB 21–22
printers, changing options, WD 23–24
printing
  areas of worksheets, EX 25–28
  documents, WD 22–24
  Outlook items, OL 14–15
  presentation notes, PPT 10

  presentations, PPT 21–24
  publications, PB 21–23
  reports, AC 45–46
  workbooks, worksheets, EX 25–30
printouts, previewing and printing, PPT 20–23
prioritizing tasks, OL 10–11
program windows
  Access, AC 6–7
  described, GS 5–6
  Excel, EX 4–5
  PowerPoint, PPT 4
  Publisher, PB 2–3
  resizing, GS 14–16
  tiling, hiding, EX 23
  Word, WD 4
programs
  adding to Quick Launch toolbar, VIS 5
  closing Office, GS 20
  customizing Office, GS 13–16
  customizing options, GS 13–16
  integration. *See* integration
  launching, GS 4
  starting Office, GS 4–5
  suites, GS 4
proofing documents, WD 53–54
properties
  See also specific property
  database field, AC 20–23
.pub files, PB 11
Public folder, sharing files on, VIS 11
publications
  described, **PB 2**
  entering, formatting text, PB 6–11
  formatting, PB 12–14
  inserting graphics in, PB 14–21
  navigating, PB 5–6
  previewing, printing, PB 21–23
  saving, PB 11–12
Publisher 2007
  See also publications
  described, GS 4
  Help system, PB 3
  introduction to, PB 2
  program window, PB 2–3
pull quotes, using, **PB 15–16**

INDEX

Q

queries
  creating, **AC 28–31**
  database, AC 6
  exporting to Word, INT 17–19
  vs. filters, AC 47
  sorting data for, AC 47
Query Wizard, using, **AC 28–31**
Quick Access Toolbar
  See also specific commands
  keyboard shortcut to, WD 5
  Undo and Repeat buttons, WD 50
  using, customizing, GS 9–11
Quick Launch toolbar, **VIS 3**
Quick Parts, creating and inserting, **WD 118–120**
Quick Print command, EX 29, PPT 21, WD 23
Quick Styles, applying, WD 72–73
Quick Tables, WD 120

R

ranges
  applying styles, colors, EX 48–50
  printing, EX 25
  using AutoSum command with, EX 75–76
  of worksheet cells, **EX 11–13**
Reading Highlight button, WD 52
rearranging field order, AC 20
receiving e-mail, OL 3–5
Record navigation bar, AC 16–17
record selector, AC 18
record sources for queries, **AC 28**
records
  database, **AC 4–5**
  editing, deleting, AC 18–20
  entering, AC 11–13
  navigating, AC 16–17
  sorting, filtering, AC 47
recovering work after shutdown, WD 15
Recycle Bin
  described, **VIS 3**
  retrieving deleted files from, VIS 12
redirecting links, INT 5

Redo button, EX 18, WD 50
relational databases, **AC 5**
relationships in relational databases, AC 5
relative references, **EX 71–72**
Remove Content Control command, WD 93
removing
  See also deleting
  cell borders, EX 41
  filters, AC 48
  links, INT 4–6
  shapes, PPT 67
  shortcuts from Quick Launch toolbar, VIS 5
renaming
  See also naming
  database tables, AC 17–18, AC 20
  files, folders, VIS 12–14
  worksheets, EX 19
Replace dialog box, PPT 44
replacing
  data, EX 56–58
  fonts, PPT 43
  text, PPT 42–44, WD 52–53
replying to e-mail, OL 5–7
Report tool, using, AC 40–41
Report Wizard, using, **AC 42–44**
reports
  creating, **AC 40–44**
  database, AC 6
  modifying, AC 44–47
  printing, AC 45–46
Research pane, WD 56
resizing
  See also sizing
  charts, EX 92–93
  clip art, WD 107
  program windows, GS 14–16
  SmartArt, WD 110
  table columns, AC 11
  table contents with AutoFit, WD 122–123
  text boxes, PB 16
resizing handles on charts, EX 94–95
Restore Down/Maximize button, GS 14, GS 16

restoring deleted files, items, VIS 12
reversing actions, EX 18, WD 50–51
reviewing formulas, EX 79–82
RFT files, exporting to, INT 17–18
Ribbon
  See also specific tool, command
  accessing with KeyTips, GS 12
  adding commands to Quick Access Toolbar from, GS 9
  changing styles from, GS 8–9
  Help system, GS 17
  using, **GS 6–7**
rotating graphics, PPT 59
rows
  and freeze panes, EX 22–24
  inserting, PPT 71
  working with, EX 53–56
  worksheet, **EX 5**
ruler
  displaying, PPT 57, WD 16, WD 23
  setting tabs using, WD 38–39
running queries, **AC 28**

S

Save As command
  described, WD 5
  saving files as .doc, WD 14
Save As dialog box, EX 10, PB 11, PPT 19, WD 14–15
saving
  database data, AC 11
  documents, WD 14–15
  documents as templates, WD 67
  export, import processes, INT 13
  forms, AC 32
  presentations, PPT 18–20, PPT 23
  presentations as templates, PPT 31
  publications, PB 11–12
  publications as templates, PB 11
  queries, AC 28, AC 31
  Quick Parts, WD 119
  reports, AC 41–42
  styles, WD 72
  tables, databases, AC 13
  workbooks, EX 10–11
scatter charts, EX 88

INDEX

scheduling meetings, events, OL 12–14
schemes, color and font, PB 12
scratch area described, **PB 3**
screen savers, choosing, **VIS 7**, VIS 9–10
ScreenTips
  described, using, VIS 3, **GS 18–19**
  and worksheet navigation, EX 7–8
scroll bars, using, WD 7
scroll wheels, using, WD 7
searching
  for document themes, WD 70
  Help topics, VIS 15–16
  and highlighting words, WD 52–53
  for installed templates, WD 66
section breaks
  inserting, WD 89
  and page size, orientation, WD 19
select queries, **AC 28**
selecting
  chart elements, EX 96–97
  database records, AC 18
  graphics, PPT 57
  slides, PPT 12
  toolbars, **WD 9–13**
  using keyboard, WD 12–13
  worksheet cells, **EX 11–13**
selection handles
  on pictures, objects, **PPT 57**, **WD 100**
  on text boxes, **PB 6**
sending e-mail, OL 3–7
series
  filling, EX 73
  of pound signs (#####), EX 80
servers, mail, **OL 6**
setting
  AutoRecover feature, PB 11
  line spacing, PB 10, WD 43–44
  margins, WD 18–19
  and resetting themes, WD 69–72
  tabs, WD 38–39
  text indents, WD 45–48
  worksheet print area, EX 25–28
shadow effects, WD 104–105
Shape Fill button, color palette, WD 117
shapes
  inserting, modifying, WD 102–105

  inserting text into, PPT 73–74
  shortcut key for, WD 100
  using in presentations, PPT 62–66
Shapes button, menu, PPT 63–64
Shapes Styles gallery, PPT 65
sheet tabs
  changing colors, EX 19
  described, **EX 4**
sheets
  See also worksheets
  described, **EX 4**
shortcut keys
  See also specific operation
  text formatting, PB 9, PPT 38
shortcut menus, using, GS 11–12
shortcuts, adding, removing from Quick Launch toolbar, VIS 5–7
shortcuts, keyboard
  See also specific action
  described, GS 18
Show/Hide (¶) button
  displaying nonprinting symbols, WD 89
  using, WD 41–43
shutting down Vista, VIS 16–18
signatures, adding to e-mail, OL 4
simple forms, creating, **AC 31–34**
sizing
  See also resizing
  cells, rows, columns, EX 53–56
  charts, EX 92–95, EX 98
  compressing pictures, WD 100
  fonts, PPT 34–35, WD 33
  graphics, PPT 57
  WordArt, WD 115–117
  worksheet fonts, EX 38
slash (/), division operator, EX 68
Slide Master view, PPT 47–49
slide masters
  See also masters
  described, using, PPT 46–49
Slide pane described, **PPT 4**
Slide Show view, PPT 11
Slide Sorter view, PPT 9–10
slides
  See also presentations
  and content placeholders, PPT 56

  described, using, **PPT 6–7**
  embedding Excel table in, INT 7–8
  entering text on, PPT 15–18
  inserting headers, footers, PPT 74–75
  inserting into presentations, PPT 13–15
  inserting transitions, PPT 76–77
  modifying, PPT 12–18
  navigating, PPT 7–8
  setting to advance automatically, PPT 76
  using placeholders, PPT 15–16
Slides tab, **PPT 4**
Smart Tag buttons in business information sets, PB 7–8
SmartArt graphics
  inserting, modifying, **PPT 66–68**, **WD 107–110**
  using in worksheets, **EX 102–104**
software
  DBMS (database management system), **AC 4**
  desktop publishing, **PB 2**
  personal information manager, **OL 2**
  presentation, **PPT 4**
  spreadsheet, **EX 4**
  word-processing, **WD 4**
Sort Text dialog box, WD 74
sorting
  data, **AC 47**
  lists, **WD 74–76**
  records, AC 47
  reports, AC 48–49
source files, and integration, **INT 2**
source programs, and integration, **INT 2**
spacing, setting line, PB 10, PPT 38, WD 43–44
spamming, OL 15
special effects
  See also specific effect
  inserting into presentations, PPT 75–76
spell checking
  documents, WD 54–55
  e-mail, OL 4
  presentations, PPT 41–42
  workbooks, EX 61–62

INDEX

Spelling and Grammar dialog box, WD 54–55
splitting worksheets into panes, EX 23
spreadsheet software
  See also Excel 2007
  described, **EX 4**
spreadsheets, inserting, PPT 71
SQRT function, EX 75
Standard toolbar, **PB 2**
Start Menu, customizing, VIS 4–5
starting
  Access, AC 7–8
  animations, PPT 77
  Excel, EX 5–6
  Office programs, GS 4–5
  Outlook, OL 2
  PowerPoint, PPT 5
  Publisher, PB 3
  Query Wizard, AC 28
  Windows Vista, VIS 2
  Word, WD 4–6
statistical functions, EX 76
story (text boxes), **PB 6**
styles
  applying font, WD 33–36
  changing from Ribbon, GS 8–9
  chart, EX 93–94
  font, PB 9, EX 39
  Quick Styles, applying, **WD 72–73**
  table, WD 123
  tables and cells, EX 48–51
subtraction operator (-), EX 68
suite, Office, **GS 4**
SUM function, EX 75, EX 76
support, Windows Help and Support, VIS 14–16
symbols, displaying or hiding text formatting, WD 41–43
synonyms, replacing words with, WD 56–57
syntax of functions, **EX 75**

T

Table Styles gallery, EX 47, PPT 72, WD 123
Table Tools Datasheet tab, AC 10
Table Tools Layout tab, PPT 72
tables
  See also worksheets
  adding records to, AC 11–13
  converting to text, WD 122
  creating, modifying, **PPT 71–72, WD 120–124**
  database, **AC 4–6**
  deleting, AC 18
  Excel, embedding in presentations, INT 7–8
  Excel, linking in Word document, INT 3–4
  exporting queries to Word as, INT 17–19
  importing Excel data into Access, INT 14–17
  opening, AC 16–17
  renaming, deleting, AC 17–18
  saving, closing, AC 13
  working with styles, EX 48–50
tabs
  contextual, **GS 7**
  setting stops, WD 38–39
Tabs dialog box, WD 39
task panes, using, GS 7–8
taskbar
  customizing, VIS 4–5
  described, **VIS 3**
Taskbar and Start Menu Properties dialog box, VIS 4–5
tasks
  creating, managing, OL 9–11
  described, **OL 9**
technology careers
  computer support, WD 25
  corporate trainers, PPT 24
  database administrators, AC 23
  graphic designers, PB 24
  technical writers, WD 59
templates
  changing, PB 12–14
  creating databases from, AC 8
  creating new documents using, **WD 66–69**
  creating presentations from, **PPT 31–34**
  creating workbooks from, EX 36
  customizing, EX 62
  described, **PB 4**
templates, *continued*
  opening Publisher, PB 3–5
  placeholder text. *See* placeholder text
  saving presentation as, PPT 19
  saving publications as, PB 11
text
  adding to templates, PPT 31
  aligning, PB 10, WD 41–43
  aligning, changing direction, PPT 38
  changing in charts, EX 96–97
  colors, and readability, PPT 45
  converting to tables, WD 122
  copying formatting with Format Painter, PPT 35–37
  creating columns, WD 80–82
  data, entering, EX 14–16
  editing, WD 48–50
  entering, formatting in publications, PB 6–11
  entering in documents, WD 13–14
  entering into SmartArt graphic, WD 108
  entering on slides, PPT 15–18
  finding and replacing, PPT 42–44, WD 52–53
  formatting and editing, WD 30–37
  formatting in presentations, PPT 34–37
  formatting shortcuts, PB 9
  inserting into shapes, PPT 66–68
  inserting to shapes, PPT 73–74
  line spacing, WD 43–44
  selecting, WD 9–13
  using drop caps, WD 117–118
  using with SmartArt, PPT 66–68
  WordArt effects, WD 115–117
Text Box tool, PB 7
text boxes
  entering text in, **PB 6–7**
  inserting, **PPT 73–74, WD 113–115**
  linking, PB 7
  resizing, PB 16
Text group, Insert tab, WD 113–114
text panes, SmartArt, PPT 66
Text Wrapping button, WD 101

INDEX

themes
  applying to presentations, **PPT 44–46**
  applying workbook, **EX 47–51**
  changing document, **WD 69–72**
Themes group on Page Layout tab, WD 69–72
Thesaurus, using, WD 56–57
thumbnails described, **PPT 4**
tiling program windows, EX 23
time and date settings, VIS 6–7
titles
  changing form, AC 37
  chart, **EX 89**
To-Do List, Outlook, **OL 9–10**
toolbars. *See specific toolbar*
tools, Print Preview, WD 23
transitions, adding slide, **PPT 76–77**

U

underlining
  shortcut key for, WD 33
  spelling and grammar mistakes, WD 54
  in worksheets, EX 39–40
Undo button, EX 18, WD 50–51
undoing actions, EX 18, WD 50–51
unfreezing panes, EX 22–24
updating
  of charts, EX 90
  links, INT 4–6
user accounts
  described, **VIS 2**
  on Start Menu, VIS 5–6
user names, **VIS 2**

V

values
  error (table), EX 80
  field, **AC 4–5**
  filtering data by, AC 48
  key, **AC 5**
vertical alignment of text, PPT 38
vertical axis (y) in charts, EX 89

viewing
  links, INT 5
  presentations, PPT 8–9
views
  See also specific view
  changing document, WD 16–17
  changing Outlook, OL 2–3
  changing workbook, EX 21–24
  file and folder, VIS 12
  form, AC 32
  PowerPoint, PPT 8–12
  query, AC 28
Vista. *See* Windows Vista

W

wallpaper, changing, **VIS 7**, VIS 8–9
warnings upon opening databases, AC 15
Watermark button, menu, WD 78
watermarks, using, **WD 76–77**
Web images, and copyright issues, WD 124
Web Layout view, WD 16–17
widows, avoiding, WD 88–89, WD 91
width, adjusting column or row, EX 53–56
windows
  common Office elements, GS 5–13
  folder, VIS 10–11
  program. *See* program windows
Windows Aero, VIS 4
Windows Help and Support system, using, VIS 14–16
Windows Sidebar, managing, VIS 7–10
Windows Vista
  customizing, VIS 4–7
  desktop, GS 5, VIS 2–4
  obtaining help, VIS 14–16
  shutting down, VIS 16–18
  starting, VIS 2
Wipe animations, PPT 78
wizards. *See specific wizard*
Word 2007
  customizing program settings, GS 13–16
  described, GS 4

.docx and .doc files, WD 14
  exporting Access queries to, INT 17–19
  getting help, GS 18–19
  integration. *See* integration
  program window, WD 4
  using commands, dialog boxes, GS 7–8
Word Count command, WD 58–59
word wrap
  described, **WD 13**
  in text boxes, WD 114
  Text Wrapping button, WD 101
WordArt
  inserting, modifying, **WD 115–117**
  using in charts, **EX 98–99**, EX 101
WordArt Style gallery, EX 101
word-processing software, **WD 4**

words
  counting, WD 58–59
  looking up in dictionary, WD 56
workbook window, **EX 4**
workbooks
  applying themes, EX 47–51
  changing views, EX 21–24
  closing, EX 30
  creating new, EX 36–37
  described, **EX 4**
  inserting worksheets into, EX 19–20
  opening existing, EX 5–6
  printing, EX 25–30
  saving, EX 10–11
worksheets, EX 79–82
  adding headers, footers, EX 25
  cell references. *See* cell references
  checking spelling, EX 61–62
  copying and moving data, EX 59–60
  described, **EX 4**
  entering data in, EX 13–16
  formatting cells, EX 37–47
  formatting fonts, EX 38–40
  inserting charts into, EX 90–91
  inserting into workbooks, deleting, EX 19–20
  linking Excel table in Word document, INT 3–4

INDEX

managing, EX 19–21
moving, copying within workbooks, EX 20–21
naming, renaming, EX 19
navigating, EX 7–10
printing, EX 29–30
selecting cells, ranges, EX 11–13
showing, hiding, printing gridlines, EX 28
using formulas. *See* formulas
using functions. *See* functions
using illustrations in, EX 101–104

X

XLM (Extensible Markup Language), EX 10
.xls format, saving files in, EX 10
.xlsx files, EX 6–7, EX 10

Z

Zoom controls, using, GS 14–16
Zoom dialog box (fig.), GS 16
zooming
 and previewing documents, WD 22
 on publications, PB 6